Marc Amstutz / Pascal Pichonr
Franz Werro (eds.)

European Private Law
Selected directives

Marc Amstutz / Pascal Pichonnaz /
Thomas Probst / Franz Werro
(eds.)

European Private Law
Selected directives

Stämpfli Publishers Ltd. Berne · 2011

eleven
international publishing

Marc Amstutz / Pascal Pichonnaz / Thomas Probst / Franz Werro (eds.)
European Private Law: Selected directives
Berne, Stämpfli, 2011

Bibliographic information published by the Deutsche Nationalbibliothek
The Deutsche Nationalbibliothek lists this publication in the Deutsche Nationalbibliografie; detailed bibliographic data are available on the Internet at http://dnb.d-nb.de.

Produced by
Stämpfli Publications Ltd., Berne
Printed in Switzerland

ISBN 978-3-7272-1491-2 (Stämpfli)
ISBN 978-94-90947-12-5 (eleven)

Foreword

This book contains a selection of European directives in the field of private law, primarily in the law of contract and tort. All texts are presented in their updated version. This publication is also available in German and in French.

This book gives easy access to an important part of European legislation. It helps students and practitioners gain a better understanding of the role this legislation plays in the current shaping of national private law in the European Union and in its partner countries.

We would like to thank Ms Cindy Felley, MLaw and assistant at Fribourg School of Law, for her help in formatting these directives. We thank also the publisher, Staempfli edition, for its support of this project.

Fribourg, January 2011 The editors

Table of contents

CONTRACTS

1. Council Directive 85/577/EEC of 20 December 1985 to protect the consumer in respect of contracts negotiated away from business premises

(OJ L 372 , 31/12/1985 p. 31 – 33)

THE COUNCIL OF THE EUROPEAN COMMUNITIES,

Having regard to the Treaty establishing the European Economic Community, and in particular Article 100 thereof, Having regard to the proposal from the Commission[1] , Having regard to the opinion of the European Parliament[2], Having regard to the opinion of the Economic and Social Committee[3], Whereas it is a common form of commercial practice in the Member States for the conclusion of a contract or a unilateral engagement between a trader and consumer to be made away from the business premises of the trader, and whereas such contracts and engagements are the subject of legislation which differs from one Member State to another; Whereas any disparity between such legislation may directly affect the functioning of the common market; whereas it is therefore necessary to approximate laws in this field; Whereas the preliminary programme of the European Economic Community for a consumer protection and information policy[4] provides inter alia, under paragraphs 24 and 25, that appropriate measures be taken to protect consumers against unfair commercial practices in respect of doorstep selling; whereas the second programme of the European Economic Community for a consumer protection and information policy[5] confirmed that the action and priorities defined in the preliminary programme would be pursued; Whereas the special feature of contracts concluded away from the business premises of the trader is that as a rule it is the trader who initiates the contract negotiations, for which the consumer is unprepared or which he does not except; whereas the consumer is often unable to compare the quality and price of the offer with other offers; whereas this surprise element generally exists not only in contracts made at the doorstep but also in other forms of contract concluded by the trader away from his business premises; Whereas the consumer should be given a right of cancellation over a period of at least seven days in order to enable him to assess the obligations arising under the contract; Whereas appropriate measures should be taken to ensure that the consumer is informed in writing of this period for reflection; Whereas the freedom of Member States to maintain or introduce a total or partial prohibition on the conclusion of contracts away from business premises, inasmuch as they consider this to be in the interest of consumers, must not be affected;

---

1 OJ No C 22, 29. 1. 1977, p. 6; OJ No C 127, 1. 6. 1978, p. 6.

2 OJ No C 241, 10. 10. 1977, p. 26.

3 OJ No C 180, 18. 7. 1977, p. 39.

4 OJ No C 92, 25. 4. 1975, p. 2.

5 OJ No C 133, 3. 6. 1981, p. 1.

HAS ADOPTED THIS DIRECTIVE:

Article 1

1. This Directive shall apply to contracts under which a trader supplies goods or services to a consumer and which are concluded:- during an excursion organized by the trader away from his business premises, or-during a visit by a trader

(i) to the consumer's home or to that of another consumer;

(ii) to the consumer's place of work; where the visit does not take place at the express request of the consumer.

2. This Directive shall also apply to contracts for the supply of goods or services other than those concerning which the consumer requested the visit of the trader, provided that when he requested the visit the consumer did not know, or could not reasonably have known, that the supply of those other goods or services formed part of the trader's commercial or professional activities.
3. This Directive shall also apply to contracts in respect of which an offer was made by the consumer under conditions similar to those described in paragraph 1 or paragraph 2 although the consumer was not bound by that offer before its acceptance by the trader.
4. This Directive shall also apply to offers made contractually by the consumer under conditions similar to those described in paragraph 1 or paragraph 2 where the consumer is bound by his offer.

Article 2

For the purposes of this Directive: 'consumer' means a natural person who, in transactions covered by this Directive, is acting for purposes which can be regarded as outside his trade or profession; 'trader' means a natural or legal person who, for the transaction in question, acts in his commercial or professional capacity, and anyone acting in the name or on behalf of a trader.

Article 3

1. The Member States may decide that this Directive shall apply only to contracts for which the payment to be made by the consumer exceeds a specified amount. This amount may not exceed 60 ECU. The Council, acting on a proposal from the Commission, shall examine and, if necessary, revise this amount for the first time no later than four years after notification of the Directive and thereafter every two years, taking into account economic and monetary developments in the Community.
2. This Directive shall not apply to:
   a) contracts for the construction, sale and rental of immovable property or contracts concerning other rights relating to immovable property.Contracts for the supply of goods and for their incorporation in immovable property or contracts for repairing immovable property shall fall within the scope of this Directive;

b) contracts for the supply of foodstuffs or beverages or other goods intended for current consumption in the household and supplied by regular roundsmen;
c) contracts for the supply of goods or services, provided that all three of the following conditions are met:
   (i) the contract is concluded on the basis of a trader's catalogue which the consumer has a proper opportunity of reading in the absence of the trader's representative,
   (ii) there is intended to be continuity of contact between the trader's representative and the consumer in relation to that or any subsequent transaction,
   (iii)both the catalogue and the contract clearly inform the consumer of his right to return goods to the supplier within a period of not less than seven days of receipt or otherwise to cancel the contract within that period without obligation of any kind other than to take reasonable care of the goods;
d) insurance contracts;
e) contracts for securities.

3. By way of derogation from Article 1 (2), Member States may refrain from applying this Directive to contracts for the supply of goods or services having a direct connection with the goods or services concerning which the consumer requested the visit of the trader.

Article 4

In the case of transactions within the scope of Article 1, traders shall be required to give consumers written notice of their right of cancellation within the period laid down in Article 5, together with the name and address of a person against whom that right may be exercised. Such notice shall be dated and shall state particulars enabling the contract to be identified. It shall be given to the consumer:

a) in the case of Article 1 (1), at the time of conclusion of the contract;
b) in the case of Article 1 (2), not later than the time of conclusion of the contract;
c) in the case of Article 1 (3) and 1 (4), when the offer is made by the consumer.

Member States shall ensure that their national legislation lays down appropriate consumer protection measures in cases where the information referred to in this Article is not supplied.

Article 5

1. The consumer shall have the right to renounce the effects of his undertaking by sending notice within a period of not less than seven days from receipt by the consumer of the notice referred to in Article 4, in accordance with the procedure laid down by national law. It shall be sufficient if the notice is dispatched before the end of such period.
2. The giving of the notice shall have the effect of releasing the consumer from any obligations under the cancelled contract.

Article 6

The consumer may not waive the rights conferred on him by this Directive.

Article 7

If the consumer exercises his right of renunciation, the legal effects of such renunciation shall be governed by national laws, particularly regarding the reimbursement of payments for goods or services provided and the return of goods received.

Article 8

This Directive shall not prevent Member States from adopting or maintaining more favourable provisions to protect consumers in the field which it covers.

Article 9

1. Member States shall take the measures necessary to comply with this Directive within 24 months of its notification[1] (1). They shall forthwith inform the Commission thereof. 2. Member States shall ensure that the texts of the main provisions of national law which they adopt in the field covered by this Directive are communicated to the Commission.

Article 10

This Directive is addressed to the Member States.

Done at Brussels,

20 December 1985.

For the Council The President R. KRIEPS

[1] This Directive was notified to the Member States on 23 December 1985.

2. Council Directive 90/314/EEC of 13 June 1990 on package travel, package holidays and package tours

(OJ L 158, 23/06/1990 p. 59 - 64)

THE COUNCIL OF THE EUROPEAN COMMUNITIES,

Having regard to the Treaty establishing the European Economic Community, and in particular Article 100a thereof,

Having regard to the proposal from the Commission[1],

In cooperation with the European Parliament[2],

Having regard to the opinion of the Economic and Social Committee[3],

Whereas one of the main objectives of the Community is to complete the internal market, of which the tourist sector is an essential part;

Whereas the national laws of Member States concerning package travel, package holidays and package tours, hereinafter referred to as 'packages', show many disparities and national practices in this field are markedly different, which gives rise to obstacles to the freedom to provide services in respect of packages and distortions of competition amongst operators established in different Member States;

Whereas the establishment of common rules on packages will contribute to the elimination of these obstacles and thereby to the achievement of a common market in services, thus enabling operators established in one Member State to offer their services in other Member States and Community consumers to benefit from comparable conditions when buying a package in any Member State;

Whereas paragraph 36 (b) of the Annex to the Council resolution of 19 May 1981 on a second programme of the European Economic Community for a consumer protection and information policy[4] invites the Commission to study, inter alia, tourism and, if appropriate, to put forward suitable proposals, with due regard for their significance for consumer protection and the effects of differences in Member States' legislation on the proper functioning of the common market;

Whereas in the resolution on a Community policy on tourism on 10 April 1984[5] the Council welcomed the Commission's initiative in drawing attention to the importance of tourism and took note of the Commission's initial guidelines for a Community policy on tourism;

Whereas the Commission communication to the Council entitled 'A New Impetus for Consumer Protection Policy', which was approved by resolution of the Council

---

1 OJ No C 96, 12. 4. 1988, p. 5.

2 OJ No C 69, 20. 3. 1989, p. 102 and OJ No C 149, 18. 6. 1990.

3 OJ No C 102, 24. 4. 1989, p. 27.

4 OJ No C 165, 23. 6. 1981, p. 24.

5 OJ No C 115, 30. 4. 1984, p. 1.

on 6 May 1986[1], lists in paragraph 37, among the measures proposed by the Commission, the harmonization of legislation on packages;

Whereas tourism plays an increasingly important role in the economies of the Member States; whereas the package system is a fundamental part of tourism; whereas the package travel industry in Member States would be stimulated to greater growth and productivity if at least a minimum of common rules were adopted in order to give it a Community dimension; whereas this would not only produce benefits for Community citizens buying packages organized on the basis of those rules, but would attract tourists from outside the Community seeking the advantages of guaranteed standards in packages;

Whereas disparities in the rules protecting consumers in different Member States are a disincentive to consumers in one Member State from buying packages in another Member State;

Whereas this disincentive is particularly effective in deterring consumers from buying packages outside their own Member State, and more effective than it would be in relation to the acquisition of other services, having regard to the special nature of the services supplied in a package which generally involve the expenditure of substantial amounts of money in advance and the supply of the services in a State other than that in which the consumer is resident;

Whereas the consumer should have the benefit of the protection introduced by this Directive irrespective of whether he is a direct contracting party, a transferee or a member of a group on whose behalf another person has concluded a contract in respect of a package;

Whereas the organizer of the package and/or the retailer of it should be under obligation to ensure that in descriptive matter relating to packages which they respectively

organize and sell, the information which is given is not misleading and brochures made available to consumers contain information which is comprehensible and accurate;

Whereas the consumer needs to have a record of the terms of contract applicable to the package; whereas this can conveniently be achieved by requiring that all the terms of the contract be stated in writing of such other documentary form as shall be comprehensible and accessible to him, and that he be given a copy thereof;

Whereas the consumer should be at liberty in certain circumstances to transfer to a willing third person a booking made by him for a package;

Whereas the price established under the contract should not in principle be subject to revision except where the possibility of upward or downward revision is expressly provided for in the contract; whereas that possibility should nonetheless be subject to certain conditions;

Whereas the consumer should in certain circumstances be free to withdraw before departure from a package travel contract;

---

1 OJ No C 118, 7. 3. 1986, p. 28.

Whereas there should be a clear definition of the rights available to the the consumer in circumstances where the organizer of the package cancels it before the agreed date of departure;

Whereas if, after the consumer has departed, there occurs a significant failure of performance of the services for which he has contracted or the organizer perceives that he will be unable to procure a significant part of the services to be provided; the organizer should have certain obligations towards the consumer;

Whereas the organizer and/or retailer party to the contract should be liable to the consumer for the proper performance of the obligations arising from the contract; whereas, moreover, the organizer and/or retailer should be liable for the damage resulting for the consumer from failure to perform or improper performance of the contract unless the defects in the performance of the contract are attributable neither to any fault of theirs nor to that of another supplier of services;

Whereas in cases where the organizer and/or retailer is liable for failure to perform or improper performance of the services involved in the package, such liability should be limited in accordance with the international conventions governing such services, in particular the Warsaw Convention of 1929 in International Carriage by Air, the Berne Convention of 1961 on Carriage by Rail, the Athens Convention of 1974 on Carriage by Sea and the Paris Convention of 1962 on the Liability of Hotel-keepers; whereas, moreover, with regard to damage other than personal injury, it should be possible for liability also to be limited under the package contract provided, however, that such limits are not unreasonable;

Whereas certain arrangements should be made for the information of consumers and the handling of complaints;

Whereas both the consumer and the package travel industry would benefit if organizers and/or retailers were placed under an obligation to provide sufficient evidence of security in the event of insolvency;

Whereas Member States should be at liberty to adopt, or retain, more stringent provisions relating to package travel for the purpose of protecting the consumer,

HAS ADOPTED THIS DIRECTIVE:

Article 1

The purpose of this Directive is to approximate the laws, regulations and administrative provisions of the Member States relating to packages sold or offered for sale in the territory of the Community.

Article 2

For the purposes of this Directive:

1. 'package' means the pre-arranged combination of not fewer than two of the following when sold or offered for sale at an inclusive price and when the service covers a period of more than twenty-four hours or includes overnight accommodation:
   (a) transport;

(b) accommodation;
(c) other tourist services not ancillary to transport or accommodation and accounting for a significant proportion of the package.

The separate billing of various components of the same package shall not absolve the organizer or retailer from the obligations under this Directive;

2. 'organizer' means the person who, other than ocasionally, organizes packages and sells or offers them for sale, whether directly or through a retailer;
3. 'retailer' means the person who sells or offers for sale the package put together by the organizer;
4. 'consumer' means the person who takes or agrees to take the package ('the principal contractor'), or any person on whose behalf the principal contractor agrees to purchase the package ('the other beneficiaries') or any person to whom the principal contractor or any of the other beneficiaries transfers the package ('the transferee');
5. 'contract' means the agreement linking the consumer to the organizer and/or the retailer.

Article 3

1. Any descriptive matter concerning a package and supplied by the organizer or the retailer to the consumer, the price of the package and any other conditions applying to the contract must not contain any misleading information. 2. When a brochure is made available to the consumer, it shall indicate in a legible, comprehensible and accurate manner both the price and adequate information concerning:
   (a) the destination and the means, characteristics and categories of transport used;
   (b) the type of accommodation, its location, category or degree of comfort and its main features, its approval and tourist classification under the rules of the host Member State concerned;
   (c) the meal plan;
   (d) the itinerary;
   (e) general information on passport and visa requirements for nationals of the Member State or States concerned and health formalities required for the journey and the stay;
   (f) either the monetary amount or the percentage of the price which is to be paid on account, and the timetable for payment of the balance;
   (g) whether a minimum number of persons is required for the package to take place and, if so, the deadline for informing the consumer in the event of cancellation.

   The particulars contained in the brochure are binding on the organizer or retailer, unless:

- changes in such particulars have been clearly communicated to the consumer before conclusion of the contract, in which case the brochure shall expressly state so,
- changes are made later following an agreement between the parties to the contract.

Article 4

1. (a) The organizer and/or the retailer shall provide the consumer, in writing or any other appropriate form, before the contract is concluded, with general information on passport and visa requirements applicable to nationals of the Member State or States concerned and in particular on the periods for obtaining them, as well as with information on the health formalities required for the journey and the stay;
   (b) The organizer and/or retailer shall also provide the consumer, in writing or any other appropriate form, with the following information in good time before the start of the journey:
      (i) the times and places of intermediate stops and transport connections as well as details of the place to be occupied by the traveller, e.g. cabin or berth on ship, sleeper compartment on train;
      (ii) the name, address and telephone number of the organizer's and/or retailer's local representative or, failing that, of local agencies on whose assistance a consumer in difficulty could call.
      Where no such representatives or agencies exist, the consumer must in any case be provided with an emergency telephone number or any other information that will enable him to contract the organizer and/or the retailer;
      (iii) in the case of journeys or stays abroad by minors, information enabling direct contact to be established with the child or the person responsible at the child's place of stay;
      (iv) information on the optional conclusion of an insurance policy to cover the cost of cancellation by the consumer or the cost of assistance, including repatriation, in the event of accident or illness.
2. Member States shall ensure that in relation to the contract the following principles apply:
   (a) depending on the particular package, the contract shall contain at least the elements listed in the Annex;
   (b) all the terms of the contract are set out in writing or such other form as is comprehensible and accessible to the consumer and must be communicated to him before the conclusion of the contract; the consumer is given a copy of these terms;
   (c) the provision under (b) shall not preclude the belated conclusion of last-minute reservations or contracts.
3. Where the consumer is prevented from proceeding with the package, he may transfer his booking, having first given the organizer or the retailer reasonable

notice of his intention before departure, to a person who satisfies all the conditions applicable to the package. The transferor of the package and the transferee shall be jointly and severally liable to the organizer or retailer party to the contract for payment of the balance due and for any additional costs arising from such transfer.

4. (a) The prices laid down in the contract shall not be subject to revision unless the contract expressly provides for the possibility of upward or downward revision and states precisely how the revised price is to be calculated, and solely to allow for variations in:
   - transportation costs, including the cost of fuel,
   - dues, taxes or fees chargeable for certain services, such as landing taxes or embarkation or disembarkation fees at ports and airports,
   - the exchange rates applied to the particular package.

   (b) During the twenty days prior to the departure date stipulated, the price stated in the contract shall not be increased.

5. If the organizer finds that before the departure he is constrained to alter significantly any of the essential terms, such as the price, he shall notify the consumer as quickly as possible in order to enable him to take appropriate decisions and in particular:
   - either to withdraw from the contract without penalty,
   - or to accept a rider to the contract specifying the alterations made and their impact on the price.

   The consumer shall inform the organizer or the retailer of his decision as soon as possible.

6. If the consumer withdraws from the contract pursuant to paragraph 5, or if, for whatever cause, other than the fault of the consumer, the organizer cancels the package before the agreed date of departure, the consumer shall be entitled:

   (a) either to take a substitute package of equivalent or higher quality where the organizer and/or retailer is able to offer him such a substitute. If the replacement package offered is of lower quality, the organizer shall refund the difference in price to the consumer;

   (b) or to be repaid as soon as possible all sums paid by him under the contract. In such a case, he shall be entitled, if appropriate, to be compensated by either the organizer or the retailer, whichever the relevant Member State's law requires, for non-performance of the contract, except where:

      (i) cancellation is on the grounds that the number of persons enrolled for the package is less than the minimum number required and the consumer is informed of the cancellation, in writing, within the period indicated in the package description; or

      (ii) cancellation, excluding overbooking, is for reasons of force majeure, i.e. unusual and unforeseeable circumstances beyond the control of the party by whom it is pleaded, the consequences of which could not have been avoided even if all due care had been exercised.

7. Where, after departure, a significant proportion of the services contracted for is not provided or the organizer perceives that he will be unable to procure a significant proportion of the services to be provided, the organizer shall make suitable alternative arrangements, at no extra cost to the consumer, for the continuation of the packag, and where appropriate compensate the consumer for the difference between the services offered and those supplied.

   If it is impossible to make such arrangements or these are not accepted by the consumer for good reasons, the organizer shall, where appropriate, provide the consumer, at no extra cost, with equivalent transport back to the place of departure, or to another return-point to which the consumer has agreed and shall, where appropriate, compensate the consumer.

Article 5

1. Member States shall take the necessary steps to ensure that the organizer and/or retailer party to the contract is liable to the consumer for the proper performance of the obligations arising from the contract, irrespective of whether such obligations are to be performed by that organizer and/or retailer or by other suppliers of services without prejudice to the right of the organizer and/or retailer to pursue those other suppliers of services.
2. With regard to the damage resulting for the consumer from the failure to perform or the improper performance of the contract, Member States shall take the necessary steps to ensure that the organizer and/or retailer is/are liable unless such failure to perform or improper performance is attributable neither to any fault of theirs nor to that of another supplier of services, because:
   - the failures which occur in the performance of the contract are attributable to the consumer,
   - such failures are attributable to a third party unconnected with the provision of the services contracted for, and are unforeseeable or unavoidable,
   - such failures are due to a case of force majeure such as that defined in Article 4 (6), second subparagraph (ii), or to an event which the organizer and/or retailer or the supplier of services, even with all due care, could not foresee or forestall.

   In the cases referred to in the second and third indents, the organizer and/or retailer party to the contract shall be required to give prompt assistance to a consumer in difficulty.

   In the matter of damages arising from the non-performance or improper performance of the services involved in the package, the Member States may allow compensation to be limited in accordance with the international conventions governing such services.

   In the matter of damage other than personal injury resulting from the non-performance or improper performance of the services involved in the package, the Member States may allow compensation to be limited under the contract. Such limitation shall not be unreasonable.

3. Without prejudice to the fourth subparagraph of paragraph 2, there may be no exclusion by means of a contractual clause from the provisions of paragraphs 1 and 2.
4. The consumer must communicate any failure in the performance of a contract which he perceives on the spot to the supplier of the services concerned and to the organizer and/or retailer in writing or any other appropriate form at the earliest opportunity.

   This obligation must be stated clearly and explicily in the contract.

Article 6

In cases of complaint, the organizer and/or retailer or his local representative, if there is one, must make prompt efforts to find appropriate solutions.

Article 7

The organizer and/or retailer party to the contract shall provide sufficient evidence of security for the refund of money paid over and for the repatriation of the consumer in the event of insolvency.

Article 8

Member States may adopt or return more stringent provisions in the field covered by this Directive to protect the consumer.

Article 9

1. Member States shall bring into force the measures necessary to comply with this Directive before 31 December 1992. They shall forthwith inform the Commission thereof.
2. Member States shall communicate to the Commission the texts of the main provisions of national law which they adopt in the field governed by this Directive. The Commission shall inform the other Member States thereof.

Article 10

This Directive is addressed to the Member States.

Done at Luxembourg, 13 June 1990.

For the Council

The President

D. J. O'MALLEY

ANNEX

Elements to be included in the contract if relevant to the particular package;

(a) the travel destination(s) and, where periods of stay are involved, the relevant periods, with dates;

(b) the means, characteristics and categories of transport to be used, the dates, times and points of departure and return;

(c) where the package includes accommodation, its location, its tourist category or degree of comfort, its main features, its compliance with the rules of the host Member State concerned and the meal plan;

(d) whether a minimum number of persons is required for the package to take place and, if so, the deadline for informing the consumer in the event of cancellation;

(e) the itinerary;

(f) visits, excursions or other services which are included in the total price agreed for the package;

(g) the name and address of the organizer, the retailer and, where appropriate, the insurer;

(h) the price of the package, an indication of the possibility of price revisions under Article 4 (4) and an indication of any dues, taxes or fees chargeable for certain services (landing, embarkation or disembarkation fees at ports and airports, tourist taxes) where such costs are not included in the package;

(i) the payment schedule and method of payment;

(j) special requirements which the consumer has communicated to the organizer or retailer when making the booking, and which both have accepted;

(k) periods within which the consumer must make any complaint concerning failure to perform or improper performance of the contract.

3. Council Directive 93/13/EEC of 5 April 1993 on unfair terms in consumer contracts

(OJ L 095 , 21/04/1993 p. 29 – 34)

THE COUNCIL OF THE EUROPEAN COMMUNITIES,

Having regard to the Treaty establishing the European Economic Community, and in particular Article 100 A thereof,

Having regard to the proposal from the Commission[1],

In cooperation with the European Parliament[2],

Having regard to the opinion of the Economic and Social Committee[3],

Whereas it is necessary to adopt measures with the aim of progressively establishing the internal market before 31 December 1992; whereas the internal market comprises an area without internal frontiers in which goods, persons, services and capital move freely;

Whereas the laws of Member States relating to the terms of contract between the seller of goods or supplier of services, on the one hand, and the consumer of them, on the other hand, show many disparities, with the result that the national markets for the sale of goods and services to consumers differ from each other and that distortions of competition may arise amongst the sellers and suppliers, notably when they sell and supply in other Member States;

Whereas, in particular, the laws of Member States relating to unfair terms in consumer contracts show marked divergences;

Whereas it is the responsibility of the Member States to ensure that contracts concluded with consumers do not contain unfair terms;

Whereas, generally speaking, consumers do not know the rules of law which, in Member States other than their own, govern contracts for the sale of goods or services; whereas this lack of awareness may deter them from direct transactions for the purchase of goods or services in another Member State;

Whereas, in order to facilitate the establishment of the internal market and to safeguard the citizen in his role as consumer when acquiring goods and services under contracts which are governed by the laws of Member States other than his own, it is essential to remove unfair terms from those contracts;

Whereas sellers of goods and suppliers of services will thereby be helped in their task of selling goods and supplying services, both at home and throughout the internal market; whereas competition will thus be stimulated, so contributing to increased choice for Community citizens as consumers;

---

1 OJ No C 73, 24. 3. 1992, p. 7.

2 OJ No C 326, 16. 12. 1991, p. 108 and OJ No C 21, 25. 1. 1993.

3 OJ No C 159, 17. 6. 1991, p. 34.

Whereas the two Community programmes for a consumer protection and information policy[1] underlined the importance of safeguarding consumers in the matter of unfair terms of contract; whereas this protection ought to be provided by laws and regulations which are either harmonized at Community level or adopted directly at that level;

Whereas in accordance with the principle laid down under the heading 'Protection of the economic interests of the consumers', as stated in those programmes: 'acquirers of goods and services should be protected against the abuse of power by the seller or supplier, in particular against one-sided standard contracts and the unfair exclusion of essential rights in contracts';

Whereas more effective protection of the consumer can be achieved by adopting uniform rules of law in the matter of unfair terms; whereas those rules should apply to all contracts concluded between sellers or suppliers and consumers; whereas as a result inter alia contracts relating to employment, contracts relating to succession rights, contracts relating to rights under family law and contracts relating to the incorporation and organization of companies or partnership agreements must be excluded from this Directive;

Whereas the consumer must receive equal protection under contracts concluded by word of mouth and written contracts regardless, in the latter case, of whether the terms of the contract are contained in one or more documents;

Whereas, however, as they now stand, national laws allow only partial harmonization to be envisaged; whereas, in particular, only contractual terms which have not been individually negotiated are covered by this Directive; whereas Member States should have the option, with due regard for the Treaty, to afford consumers a higher level of protection through national provisions that are more stringent than those of this Directive;

Whereas the statutory or regulatory provisions of the Member States which directly or indirectly determine the terms of consumer contracts are presumed not to contain unfair terms; whereas, therefore, it does not appear to be necessary to subject the terms which reflect mandatory statutory or regulatory provisions and the principles or provisions of international conventions to which the Member States or the Community are party; whereas in that respect the wording 'mandatory statutory or regulatory provisions' in Article 1 (2) also covers rules which, according to the law, shall apply between the contracting parties provided that no other arrangements have been established;

Whereas Member States must however ensure that unfair terms are not included, particularly because this Directive also applies to trades, business or professions of a public nature;

Whereas it is necessary to fix in a general way the criteria for assessing the unfair character of contract terms;

[1] OJ No C 92, 25. 4. 1975, p. 1 and OJ No C 133, 3. 6. 1981, p. 1.

Whereas the assessment, according to the general criteria chosen, of the unfair character of terms, in particular in sale or supply activities of a public nature providing collective services which take account of solidarity among users, must be supplemented by a means of making an overall evaluation of the different interests involved; whereas this constitutes the requirement of good faith; whereas, in making an assessment of good faith, particular regard shall be had to the strength of the bargaining positions of the parties, whether the consumer had an inducement to agree to the term and whether the goods or services were sold or supplied to the special order of the consumer; whereas the requirement of good faith may be satisfied by the seller or supplier where he deals fairly and equitably with the other party whose legitimate interests he has to take into account;

Whereas, for the purposes of this Directive, the annexed list of terms can be of indicative value only and, because of the cause of the minimal character of the Directive, the scope of these terms may be the subject of amplification or more restrictive editing by the Member States in their national laws;

Whereas the nature of goods or services should have an influence on assessing the unfairness of contractual terms;

Whereas, for the purposes of this Directive, assessment of unfair character shall not be made of terms which describe the main subject matter of the contract nor the quality/price ratio of the goods or services supplied; whereas the main subject matter of the contract and the price/quality ratio may nevertheless be taken into account in assessing the fairness of other terms; whereas it follows, inter alia, that in insurance contracts, the terms which clearly define or circumscribe the insured risk and the insurer's liability shall not be subject to such assessment since these restrictions are taken into account in calculating the premium paid by the consumer;

Whereas contracts should be drafted in plain, intelligible language, the consumer should actually be given an opportunity to examine all the terms and, if in doubt, the interpretation most favourable to the consumer should prevail;

Whereas Member States should ensure that unfair terms are not used in contracts concluded with consumers by a seller or supplier and that if, nevertheless, such terms are so used, they will not bind the consumer, and the contract will continue to bind the parties upon those terms if it is capable of continuing in existence without the unfair provisions;

Whereas there is a risk that, in certain cases, the consumer may be deprived of protection under this Directive by designating the law of a non-Member country as the law applicable to the contract; whereas provisions should therefore be included in this Directive designed to avert this risk;

Whereas persons or organizations, if regarded under the law of a Member State as having a legitimate interest in the matter, must have facilities for initiating proceedings concerning terms of contract drawn up for general use in contracts concluded with consumers, and in particular unfair terms, either before a court or before an administrative authority competent to decide upon complaints or to initiate appropriate legal proceedings; whereas this possibility does not, however, entail prior verification of the general conditions obtaining in individual economic sectors;

Whereas the courts or administrative authorities of the Member States must have at their disposal adequate and effective means of preventing the continued application of unfair terms in consumer contracts,

HAS ADOPTED THIS DIRECTIVE:

Article 1

1. The purpose of this Directive is to approximate the laws, regulations and administrative provisions of the Member States relating to unfair terms in contracts concluded between a seller or supplier and a consumer.
2. The contractual terms which reflect mandatory statutory or regulatory provisions and the provisions or principles of international conventions to which the Member States or the Community are party, particularly in the transport area, shall not be subject to the provisions of this Directive.

Article 2

For the purposes of this Directive:

(a) 'unfair terms' means the contractual terms defined in Article 3;

(b) 'consumer' means any natural person who, in contracts covered by this Directive, is acting for purposes which are outside his trade, business or profession;

(c) 'seller or supplier' means any natural or legal person who, in contracts covered by this Directive, is acting for purposes relating to his trade, business or profession, whether publicly owned or privately owned.

Article 3

1. A contractual term which has not been individually negotiated shall be regarded as unfair if, contrary to the requirement of good faith, it causes a significant imbalance in the parties' rights and obligations arising under the contract, to the detriment of the consumer.
2. A term shall always be regarded as not individually negotiated where it has been drafted in advance and the consumer has therefore not been able to influence the substance of the term, particularly in the context of a pre-formulated standard contract.

   The fact that certain aspects of a term or one specific term have been individually negotiated shall not exclude the application of this Article to the rest of a contract if an overall assessment of the contract indicates that it is nevertheless a pre-formulated standard contract.

   Where any seller or supplier claims that a standard term has been individually negotiated, the burden of proof in this respect shall be incumbent on him.

3. The Annex shall contain an indicative and non-exhaustive list of the terms which may be regarded as unfair.

Article 4

1. Without prejudice to Article 7, the unfairness of a contractual term shall be assessed, taking into account the nature of the goods or services for which the contract was concluded and by referring, at the time of conclusion of the contract, to all the circumstances attending the conclusion of the contract and to all the other terms of the contract or of another contract on which it is dependent.
2. Assessment of the unfair nature of the terms shall relate neither to the definition of the main subject matter of the contract nor to the adequacy of the price and remuneration, on the one hand, as against the services or goods supplies in exchange, on the other, in so far as these terms are in plain intelligible language.

Article 5

In the case of contracts where all or certain terms offered to the consumer are in writing, these terms must always be drafted in plain, intelligible language. Where there is doubt about the meaning of a term, the interpretation most favourable to the consumer shall prevail. This rule on interpretation shall not apply in the context of the procedures laid down in Article 7 (2).

Article 6

1. Member States shall lay down that unfair terms used in a contract concluded with a consumer by a seller or supplier shall, as provided for under their national law, not be binding on the consumer and that the contract shall continue to bind the parties upon those terms if it is capable of continuing in existence without the unfair terms.
2. Member States shall take the necessary measures to ensure that the consumer does not lose the protection granted by this Directive by virtue of the choice of the law of a non-Member country as the law applicable to the contract if the latter has a close connection with the territory of the Member States.

Article 7

1. Member States shall ensure that, in the interests of consumers and of competitors, adequate and effective means exist to prevent the continued use of unfair terms in contracts concluded with consumers by sellers or suppliers.
2. The means referred to in paragraph 1 shall include provisions whereby persons or organizations, having a legitimate interest under national law in protecting consumers, may take action according to the national law concerned before the courts or before competent administrative bodies for a decision as to whether contractual terms drawn up for general use are unfair, so that they can apply appropriate and effective means to prevent the continued use of such terms.
3. With due regard for national laws, the legal remedies referred to in paragraph 2 may be directed separately or jointly against a number of sellers or suppliers

from the same economic sector or their associations which use or recommend the use of the same general contractual terms or similar terms.

Article 8

Member States may adopt or retain the most stringent provisions compatible with the Treaty in the area covered by this Directive, to ensure a maximum degree of protection for the consumer.

Article 9

The Commission shall present a report to the European Parliament and to the Council concerning the application of this Directive five years at the latest after the date in Article 10 (1).

Article 10

1. Member States shall bring into force the laws, regulations and administrative provisions necessary to comply with this Directive no later than 31 December 1994. They shall forthwith inform the Commission thereof.

   These provisions shall be applicable to all contracts concluded after 31 December 1994.
2. When Member States adopt these measures, they shall contain a reference to this Directive or shall be accompanied by such reference on the occasion of their official publication. The methods of making such a reference shall be laid down by the Member States.
3. Member States shall communicate the main provisions of national law which they adopt in the field covered by this Directive to the Commission.

Article 11

This Directive is addressed to the Member States.

Done at Luxembourg, 5 April 1993.

For the Council

The President

N. HELVEG PETERSEN

ANNEX

TERMS REFERRED TO IN ARTICLE 3 (3)

1. Terms which have the object or effect of:
   (a) excluding or limiting the legal liability of a seller or supplier in the event of the death of a consumer or personal injury to the latter resulting from an act or omission of that seller or supplier;
   (b) inappropriately excluding or limiting the legal rights of the consumer vis-à-vis the seller or supplier or another party in the event of total or partial non-performance or inadequate performance by the seller or supplier of any of the contractual obligations, including the option of offsetting a debt owed to the seller or supplier against any claim which the consumer may have against him;
   (c) making an agreement binding on the consumer whereas provision of services by the seller or supplier is subject to a condition whose realization depends on his own will alone;
   (d) permitting the seller or supplier to retain sums paid by the consumer where the latter decides not to conclude or perform the contract, without providing for the consumer to receive compensation of an equivalent amount from the seller or supplier where the latter is the party cancelling the contract;
   (e) requiring any consumer who fails to fulfil his obligation to pay a disproportionately high sum in compensation;
   (f) authorizing the seller or supplier to dissolve the contract on a discretionary basis where the same facility is not granted to the consumer, or permitting the seller or supplier to retain the sums paid for services not yet supplied by him where it is the seller or supplier himself who dissolves the contract;
   (g) enabling the seller or supplier to terminate a contract of indeterminate duration without reasonable notice except where there are serious grounds for doing so;
   (h) automatically extending a contract of fixed duration where the consumer does not indicate otherwise, when the deadline fixed for the consumer to express this desire not to extend the contract is unreasonably early;
   (i) irrevocably binding the consumer to terms with which he had no real opportunity of becoming acquainted before the conclusion of the contract;
   (j) enabling the seller or supplier to alter the terms of the contract unilaterally without a valid reason which is specified in the contract;
   (k) enabling the seller or supplier to alter unilaterally without a valid reason any characteristics of the product or service to be provided;
   (l) providing for the price of goods to be determined at the time of delivery or allowing a seller of goods or supplier of services to increase their price without in both cases giving the consumer the corresponding right to cancel the contract if the final price is too high in relation to the price agreed when the contract was concluded;

(m) giving the seller or supplier the right to determine whether the goods or services supplied are in conformity with the contract, or giving him the exclusive right to interpret any term of the contract;
(n) limiting the seller's or supplier's obligation to respect commitments undertaken by his agents or making his commitments subject to compliance with a particular formality;
(o) obliging the consumer to fulfil all his obligations where the seller or supplier does not perform his;
(p) giving the seller or supplier the possibility of transferring his rights and obligations under the contract, where this may serve to reduce the guarantees for the consumer, without the latter's agreement;
(q) excluding or hindering the consumer's right to take legal action or exercise any other legal remedy, particularly by requiring the consumer to take disputes exclusively to arbitration not covered by legal provisions, unduly restricting the evidence available to him or imposing on him a burden of proof which, according to the applicable law, should lie with another party to the contract.

2. Scope of subparagraphs (g), (j) and (l)

(a) Subparagraph (g) is without hindrance to terms by which a supplier of financial services reserves the right to terminate unilaterally a contract of indeterminate duration without notice where there is a valid reason, provided that the supplier is required to inform the other contracting party or parties thereof immediately.
(b) Subparagraph (j) is without hindrance to terms under which a supplier of financial services reserves the right to alter the rate of interest payable by the consumer or due to the latter, or the amount of other charges for financial services without notice where there is a valid reason, provided that the supplier is required to inform the other contracting party or parties thereof at the earliest opportunity and that the latter are free to dissolve the contract immediately.
Subparagraph (j) is also without hindrance to terms under which a seller or supplier reserves the right to alter unilaterally the conditions of a contract of indeterminate duration, provided that he is required to inform the consumer with reasonable notice and that the consumer is free to dissolve the contract.
(c) Subparagraphs (g), (j) and (l) do not apply to:
- transactions in transferable securities, financial instruments and other products or services where the price is linked to fluctuations in a stock exchange quotation or index or a financial market rate that the seller or supplier does not control;
- contracts for the purchase or sale of foreign currency, traveller's cheques or international money orders denominated in foreign currency;
(d) Subparagraph (l) is without hindrance to price-indexation clauses, where lawful, provided that the method by which prices vary is explicitly described.

4. Directive 97/7/EC of the European Parliament and of the Council of 20 May 1997 on the protection of consumers in respect of distance contracts - Statement by the Council and the Parliament re Article 6 (1) - Statement by the Commission re Article 3 (1), first indent

(OJ L 144 , 04/06/1997 p. 19 – 27)

THE EUROPEAN PARLIAMENT AND THE COUNCIL OF THE EUROPEAN UNION,

Having regard to the Treaty establishing the European Community, and in particular Article 100a thereof,

Having regard to the proposal from the Commission[1],

Having regard to the opinion of the Economic and Social Committee[2],

Acting in accordance with the procedure laid down in Article 189b of the Treaty[3], in the light of the joint text approved by the Conciliation Committee on 27 November 1996,

(1) Whereas, in connection with the attainment of the aims of the internal market, measures must be taken for the gradual consolidation of that market;

(2) Whereas the free movement of goods and services affects not only the business sector but also private individuals; whereas it means that consumers should be able to have access to the goods and services of another Member State on the same terms as the population of that State;

(3) Whereas, for consumers, cross-border distance selling could be one of the main tangible results of the completion of the internal market, as noted, inter alia, in the communication from the Commission to the Council entitled 'Towards a single market in distribution`; whereas it is essential to the smooth operation of the internal market for consumers to be able to have dealings with a business outside their country, even if it has a subsidiary in the consumer's country of residence;

(4) Whereas the introduction of new technologies is increasing the number of ways for consumers to obtain information about offers anywhere in the Community and to place orders; whereas some Member States have already taken different or diverging measures to protect consumers in respect of distance selling, which has had a detrimental effect on competition between businesses in the internal market; whereas it is therefore necessary to introduce at Community level a minimum set of common rules in this area;

---

1 OJ No C 156, 23. 6. 1992, p. 14 and OJ No C 308, 15. 11. 1993, p. 18.

2 OJ No C 19, 25. 1. 1993, p. 111.

3 Opinion of the European Parliament of 26 May 1993 (OJ No C 176, 28. 6. 1993, p. 95), Council common position of 29 June 1995 (OJ No C 288, 30. 10. 1995, p. 1) and Decision of the European Parliament of 13 December 1995 (OJ No C 17, 22. 1. 1996, p. 51). Decision of the European Parliament of 16 January 1997 and Council Decision of 20 January 1997.

(5) Whereas paragraphs 18 and 19 of the Annex to the Council resolution of 14 April 1975 on a preliminary programme of the European Economic Community for a consumer protection and information policy[1] point to the need to protect the purchasers of goods or services from demands for payment for unsolicited goods and from high-pressure selling methods;

(6) Whereas paragraph 33 of the communication from the Commission to the Council entitled 'A new impetus for consumer protection policy`, which was approved by the Council resolution of 23 June 1986[2], states that the Commission will submit proposals regarding the use of new information technologies enabling consumers to place orders with suppliers from their homes;

(7) Whereas the Council resolution of 9 November 1989 on future priorities for relaunching consumer protection policy[3] calls upon the Commission to give priority to the areas referred to in the Annex to that resolution; whereas that Annex refers to new technologies involving teleshopping; whereas the Commission has responded to that resolution by adopting a three-year action plan for consumer protection policy in the European Economic Community (1990-1992); whereas that plan provides for the adoption of a Directive;

(8) Whereas the languages used for distance contracts are a matter for the Member States;

(9) Whereas contracts negotiated at a distance involve the use of one or more means of distance communication; whereas the various means of communication are used as part of an organized distance sales or service-provision scheme not involving the simultaneous presence of the supplier and the consumer; whereas the constant development of those means of communication does not allow an exhaustive list to be compiled but does require principles to be defined which are valid even for those which are not as yet in widespread use;

(10) Whereas the same transaction comprising successive operations or a series of separate operations over a period of time may give rise to different legal descriptions depending on the law of the Member States; whereas the provisions of this Directive cannot be applied differently according to the law of the Member States, subject to their recourse to Article 14; whereas, to that end, there is therefore reason to consider that there must at least be compliance with the provisions of this Directive at the time of the first of a series of successive operations or the first of a series of separate operations over a period of time which may be considered as forming a whole, whether that operation or series of operations are the subject of a single contract or successive, separate contracts;

(11) Whereas the use of means of distance communication must not lead to a reduction in the information provided to the consumer; whereas the information that is required to be sent to the consumer should therefore be determined,

---

1 OJ No C 92, 25. 4. 1975, p. 1.

2 OJ No C 167, 5. 7. 1986, p. 1.

3 OJ No C 294, 22. 11. 1989, p. 1.

whatever the means of communication used; whereas the information supplied must also comply with the other relevant Community rules, in particular those in Council Directive 84/450/EEC of 10 September 1984 relating to the approximation of the laws, regulations and administrative provisions of the Member States concerning misleading advertising[1]; whereas, if exceptions are made to the obligation to provide information, it is up to the consumer, on a discretionary basis, to request certain basic information such as the identity of the supplier, the main characteristics of the goods or services and their price;

(12) Whereas in the case of communication by telephone it is appropriate that the consumer receive enough information at the beginning of the conversation to decide whether or not to continue;

(13) Whereas information disseminated by certain electronic technologies is often ephemeral in nature insofar as it is not received on a permanent medium; whereas the consumer must therefore receive written notice in good time of the information necessary for proper performance of the contract;

(14) Whereas the consumer is not able actually to see the product or ascertain the nature of the service provided before concluding the contract; whereas provision should be made, unless otherwise specified in this Directive, for a right of withdrawal from the contract; whereas, if this right is to be more than formal, the costs, if any, borne by the consumer when exercising the right of withdrawal must be limited to the direct costs for returning the goods; whereas this right of withdrawal shall be without prejudice to the consumer's rights under national laws, with particular regard to the receipt of damaged products and services or of products and services not corresponding to the description given in the offer of such products or services; whereas it is for the Member States to determine the other conditions and arrangements following exercise of the right of withdrawal;

(15) Whereas it is also necessary to prescribe a time limit for performance of the contract if this is not specified at the time of ordering;

(16) Whereas the promotional technique involving the dispatch of a product or the provision of a service to the consumer in return for payment without a prior request from, or the explicit agreement of, the consumer cannot be permitted, unless a substitute product or service is involved;

(17) Whereas the principles set out in Articles 8 and 10 of the European Convention for the Protection of Human Rights and Fundamental Freedoms of 4 November 1950 apply; whereas the consumer's right to privacy, particularly as regards freedom from certain particularly intrusive means of communication, should be recognized; whereas specific limits on the use of such means should therefore be stipulated; whereas Member States should take appropriate measures to protect effectively those consumers, who do not wish to be contacted through certain means of communication, against such contacts,

[1] OJ No L 250, 19. 9. 1984, p. 17

without prejudice to the particular safeguards available to the consumer under Community legislation concerning the protection of personal data and privacy;

(18) Whereas it is important for the minimum binding rules contained in this Directive to be supplemented where appropriate by voluntary arrangements among the traders concerned, in line with Commission recommendation 92/295/EEC of 7 April 1992 on codes of practice for the protection of consumers in respect of contracts negotiated at a distance[1];

(19) Whereas in the interest of optimum consumer protection it is important for consumers to be satisfactorily informed of the provisions of this Directive and of codes of practice that may exist in this field;

(20) Whereas non-compliance with this Directive may harm not only consumers but also competitors; whereas provisions may therefore be laid down enabling public bodies or their representatives, or consumer organizations which, under national legislation, have a legitimate interest in consumer protection, or professional organizations which have a legitimate interest in taking action, to monitor the application thereof;

(21) Whereas it is important, with a view to consumer protection, to address the question of cross-border complaints as soon as this is feasible; whereas the Commission published on 14 February 1996 a plan of action on consumer access to justice and the settlement of consumer disputes in the internal market; whereas that plan of action includes specific initiatives to promote out-of-court procedures; whereas objective criteria (Annex II) are suggested to ensure the reliability of those procedures and provision is made for the use of standardized claims forms (Annex III);

(22) Whereas in the use of new technologies the consumer is not in control of the means of communication used; whereas it is therefore necessary to provide that the burden of proof may be on the supplier;

(23) Whereas there is a risk that, in certain cases, the consumer may be deprived of protection under this Directive through the designation of the law of a non-member country as the law applicable to the contract; whereas provisions should therefore be included in this Directive to avert that risk;

(24) Whereas a Member State may ban, in the general interest, the marketing on its territory of certain goods and services through distance contracts; whereas that ban must comply with Community rules; whereas there is already provision for such bans, notably with regard to medicinal products, under Council Directive 89/552/EEC of 3 October 1989 on the coordination of certain provisions laid down by law, regulation or administrative action in Member States concerning the pursuit of television broadcasting activities[2] and Council Directive

1 OJ No L 156, 10. 6. 1992, p. 21.

2 OJ No L 298, 17. 10. 1989, p. 23.

92/28/EEC of 31 March 1992 on the advertising of medicinal products for human use[1],

HAVE ADOPTED THIS DIRECTIVE:

Article 1 Object

The object of this Directive is to approximate the laws, regulations and administrative provisions of the Member States concerning distance contracts between consumers and suppliers.

Article 2 Definitions

For the purposes of this Directive:

(1) 'distance contract` means any contract concerning goods or services concluded between a supplier and a consumer under an organized distance sales or service-provision scheme run by the supplier, who, for the purpose of the contract, makes exclusive use of one or more means of distance communication up to and including the moment at which the contract is concluded;

(2) 'consumer` means any natural person who, in contracts covered by this Directive, is acting for purposes which are outside his trade, business or profession;

(3) 'supplier` means any natural or legal person who, in contracts covered by this Directive, is acting in his commercial or professional capacity;

(4) 'means of distance communication` means any means which, without the simultaneous physical presence of the supplier and the consumer, may be used for the conclusion of a contract between those parties. An indicative list of the means covered by this Directive is contained in Annex I;

(5) 'operator of a means of communication` means any public or private natural or legal person whose trade, business or profession involves making one or more means of distance communication available to suppliers.

Article 3 Exemptions

1. This Directive shall not apply to contracts:
   - relating to financial services, a non-exhaustive list of which is given in Annex II,
   - concluded by means of automatic vending machines or automated commercial premises,
   - concluded with telecommunications operators through the use of public payphones,
   - concluded for the construction and sale of immovable property or relating to other immovable property rights, except for rental,
   - concluded at an auction.
2. Articles 4, 5, 6 and 7 (1) shall not apply:

[1] OJ No L 113, 30. 4. 1992, p. 13.

- to contracts for the supply of foodstuffs, beverages or other goods intended for everyday consumption supplied to the home of the consumer, to his residence or to his workplace by regular roundsmen,
- to contracts for the provision of accommodation, transport, catering or leisure services, where the supplier undertakes, when the contract is concluded, to provide these services on a specific date or within a specific period; exceptionally, in the case of outdoor leisure events, the supplier can reserve the right not to apply Article 7 (2) in specific circumstances.

Article 4 Prior information

1. In good time prior to the conclusion of any distance contract, the consumer shall be provided with the following information:
   (a) the identity of the supplier and, in the case of contracts requiring payment in advance, his address;
   (b) the main characteristics of the goods or services;
   (c) the price of the goods or services including all taxes;
   (d) delivery costs, where appropriate;
   (e) the arrangements for payment, delivery or performance;
   (f) the existence of a right of withdrawal, except in the cases referred to in Article 6 (3);
   (g) the cost of using the means of distance communication, where it is calculated other than at the basic rate;
   (h) the period for which the offer or the price remains valid;
   (i) where appropriate, the minimum duration of the contract in the case of contracts for the supply of products or services to be performed permanently or recurrently.
2. The information referred to in paragraph 1, the commercial purpose of which must be made clear, shall be provided in a clear and comprehensible manner in any way appropriate to the means of distance communication used, with due regard, in particular, to the principles of good faith in commercial transactions, and the principles governing the protection of those who are unable, pursuant to the legislation of the Member States, to give their consent, such as minors.
3. Moreover, in the case of telephone communications, the identity of the supplier and the commercial purpose of the call shall be made explicitly clear at the beginning of any conversation with the consumer.

Article 5 Written confirmation of information

1. The consumer must receive written confirmation or confirmation in another durable medium available and accessible to him of the information referred to in Article 4 (1) (a) to (f), in good time during the performance of the contract, and at the latest at the time of delivery where goods not for delivery to third parties are concerned, unless the information has already been given to the consumer prior to conclusion of the contract in writing or on another durable medium available and accessible to him.

In any event the following must be provided:

- written information on the conditions and procedures for exercising the right of withdrawal, within the meaning of Article 6, including the cases referred to in the first indent of Article 6 (3),
- the geographical address of the place of business of the supplier to which the consumer may address any complaints,
- information on after-sales services and guarantees which exist,
- the conclusion for cancelling the contract, where it is of unspecified duration or a duration exceeding one year.

2. Paragraph 1 shall not apply to services which are performed through the use of a means of distance communication, where they are supplied on only one occasion and are invoiced by the operator of the means of distance communication. Nevertheless, the consumer must in all cases be able to obtain the geographical address of the place of business of the supplier to which he may address any complaints.

Article 6 Right of withdrawal

1. For any distance contract the consumer shall have a period of at least seven working days in which to withdraw from the contract without penalty and without giving any reason. The only charge that may be made to the consumer because of the exercise of his right of withdrawal is the direct cost of returning the goods.

   The period for exercise of this right shall begin:

   - in the case of goods, from the day of receipt by the consumer where the obligations laid down in Article 5 have been fulfilled,
   - in the case of services, from the day of conclusion of the contract or from the day on which the obligations laid down in Article 5 were fulfilled if they are fulfilled after conclusion of the contract, provided that this period does not exceed the three-month period referred to in the following subparagraph.

     If the supplier has failed to fulfil the obligations laid down in Article 5, the period shall be three months. The period shall begin:

   - in the case of goods, from the day of receipt by the consumer,
   - in the case of services, from the day of conclusion of the contract.

If the information referred to in Article 5 is supplied within this three-month period, the seven working day period referred to in the first subparagraph shall begin as from that moment.

2. Where the right of withdrawal has been exercised by the consumer pursuant to this Article, the supplier shall be obliged to reimburse the sums paid by the consumer free of charge. The only charge that may be made to the consumer because of the exercise of his right of withdrawal is the direct cost of returning the goods. Such reimbursement must be carried out as soon as possible and in any case within 30 days.

3. Unless the parties have agreed otherwise, the consumer may not exercise the right of withdrawal provided for in paragraph 1 in respect of contracts:
   - for the provision of services if performance has begun, with the consumer's agreement, before the end of the seven working day period referred to in paragraph 1,
   - for the supply of goods or services the price of which is dependent on fluctuations in the financial market which cannot be controlled by the supplier,
   - for the supply of goods made to the consumer's specifications or clearly personalized or which, by reason of their nature, cannot be returned or are liable to deteriorate or expire rapidly,
   - for the supply of audio or video recordings or computer software which were unsealed by the consumer,
   - for the supply of newspapers, periodicals and magazines,
   - for gaming and lottery services.
4. The Member States shall make provision in their legislation to ensure that:
   - if the price of goods or services is fully or partly covered by credit granted by the supplier, or
   - if that price is fully or partly covered by credit granted to the consumer by a third party on the basis of an agreement between the third party and the supplier, the credit agreement shall be cancelled, without any penalty, if the consumer exercises his right to withdraw from the contract in accordance with paragraph 1.

   Member States shall determine the detailed rules for cancellation of the credit agreement.

Article 7 Performance

1. Unless the parties have agreed otherwise, the supplier must execute the order within a maximum of 30 days from the day following that on which the consumer forwarded his order to the supplier.
2. Where a supplier fails to perform his side of the contract on the grounds that the goods or services ordered are unavailable, the consumer must be informed of this situation and must be able to obtain a refund of any sums he has paid as soon as possible and in any case within 30 days.
3. Nevertheless, Member States may lay down that the supplier may provide the consumer with goods or services of equivalent quality and price provided that this possibility was provided for prior to the conclusion of the contract or in the contract. The consumer shall be informed of this possibility in a clear and comprehensible manner. The cost of returning the goods following exercise of the right of withdrawal shall, in this case, be borne by the supplier, and the consumer must be informed of this. In such cases the supply of goods or services may not be deemed to constitute inertia selling within the meaning of Article 9.

Article 8 Payment by card

Member States shall ensure that appropriate measures exist to allow a consumer:

- to request cancellation of a payment where fraudulent use has been made of his payment card in connection with distance contracts covered by this Directive,
- in the event of fraudulent use, to be recredited with the sums paid or have them returned.

Article 9 Inertia selling

Member States shall take the measures necessary to:

- prohibit the supply of goods or services to a consumer without their being ordered by the consumer beforehand, where such supply involves a demand for payment,
- exempt the consumer from the provision of any consideration in cases of unsolicited supply, the absence of a response not constituting consent.

Article 10 Restrictions on the use of certain means of distance communication

1. Use by a supplier of the following means requires the prior consent of the consumer:
   - automated calling system without human intervention (automatic calling machine),
   - facsimile machine (fax).
2. Member States shall ensure that means of distance communication, other than those referred to in paragraph 1, which allow individual communications may be used only where there is no clear objection from the consumer.

Article 11 Judicial or administrative redress

1. Member States shall ensure that adequate and effective means exist to ensure compliance with this Directive in the interests of consumers.
2. The means referred to in paragraph 1 shall include provisions whereby one or more of the following bodies, as determined by national law, may take action under national law before the courts or before the competent administrative bodies to ensure that the national provisions for the implementation of this Directive are applied:
   (a) public bodies or their representatives;
   (b) consumer organizations having a legitimate interest in protecting consumers;
   (c) professional organizations having a legitimate interest in acting.
3. (a) Member States may stipulate that the burden of proof concerning the existence of prior information, written confirmation, compliance with time-limits or consumer consent can be placed on the supplier.
   (b) Member States shall take the measures needed to ensure that suppliers and operators of means of communication, where they are able to do so, cease practices which do not comply with measures adopted pursuant to this Directive.

4. Member States may provide for voluntary supervision by self-regulatory bodies of compliance with the provisions of this Directive and recourse to such bodies for the settlement of disputes to be added to the means which Member States must provided to ensure compliance with the provisions of this Directive.

Article 12 Binding nature

1. The consumer may not waive the rights conferred on him by the transposition of this Directive into national law.
2. Member States shall take the measures needed to ensure that the consumer does not lose the protection granted by this Directive by virtue of the choice of the law of a non-member country as the law applicable to the contract if the latter has close connection with the territory of one or more Member States.

Article 13 Community rules

1. The provisions of this Directive shall apply insofar as there are no particular provisions in rules of Community law governing certain types of distance contracts in their entirety.
2. Where specific Community rules contain provisions governing only certain aspects of the supply of goods or provision of services, those provisions, rather than the provisions of this Directive, shall apply to these specific aspects of the distance contracts.

Article 14 Minimal clause

Member States may introduce or maintain, in the area covered by this Directive, more stringent provisions compatible with the Treaty, to ensure a higher level of consumer protection. Such provisions shall, where appropriate, include a ban, in the general interest, on the marketing of certain goods or services, particularly medicinal products, within their territory by means of distance contracts, with due regard for the Treaty.

Article 15 Implementation

1. Member States shall bring into force the laws, regulations and administrative provisions necessary to comply with this Directive no later than three years after it enters into force. They shall forthwith inform the Commission thereof.
2. When Member States adopt the measures referred to in paragraph 1, these shall contain a reference to this Directive or shall be accompanied by such reference on the occasion of their official publication. The procedure for such reference shall be laid down by Member States.
3. Member States shall communicate to the Commission the text of the provisions of national law which they adopt in the field governed by this Directive.
4. No later than four years after the entry into force of this Directive the Commission shall submit a report to the European Parliament and the Council on the implementation of this Directive, accompanied if appropriate by a proposal for the revision thereof.

Article 16 Consumer information

Member States shall take appropriate measures to inform the consumer of the national law transposing this Directive and shall encourage, where appropriate, professional organizations to inform consumers of their codes of practice.

Article 17 Complaints systems

The Commission shall study the feasibility of establishing effective means to deal with consumers' complaints in respect of distance selling. Within two years after the entry into force of this Directive the Commission shall submit a report to the European Parliament and the Council on the results of the studies, accompanied if appropriate by proposals.

Article 18

This Directive shall enter into force on the day of its publication in the Official Journal of the European Communities.

Article 19

This Directive is addressed to the Member States.

Done at Brussels, 20 May 1997.

For the European Parliament

The President

J.M. GIL-ROBLES

For the Council

The President

J. VAN AARTSEN

ANNEX I

Means of communication covered by Article 2 (4)

- Unaddressed printed matter
- Addressed printed matter
- Standard letter
- Press advertising with order form
- Catalogue
- Telephone with human intervention
- Telephone without human intervention (automatic calling machine, audiotext)
- Radio
- Videophone (telephone with screen)
- Videotex (microcomputer and television screen) with keyboard or touch screen
- Electronic mail
- Facsimile machine (fax)
- Television (teleshopping).

ANNEX II

Financial services within the meaning of Article 3 (1)

- Investment services
- Insurance and reinsurance operations
- Banking services
- Operations relating to dealings in futures or options.

Such services include in particular:

- investment services referred to in the Annex to Directive 93/22/EEC[1]; services of collective investment undertakings,
- services covered by the activities subject to mutual recognition referred to in the Annex to Directive 89/646/EEC[2];
- operations covered by the insurance and reinsurance activities referred to in:
- Article 1 of Directive 73/239/EEC[3],
- the Annex to Directive 79/267/EEC[4],
- Directive 64/225/EEC[5],
- Directives 92/49/EEC[1] and 92/96/EEC[2].

1 OJ No L 141, 11. 6. 1993, p. 27.

2 OJ No L 386, 30. 12. 1989, p. 1. Directive as amended by Directive 92/30/EEC (OJ No L 110, 28. 4. 1992, p. 52).

3 OJ No L 228, 16. 8. 1973, p. 3. Directive as last amended by Directive 92/49/EEC (OJ No L 228, 11. 8. 1992, p.1.

4 OJ No L 63, 13. 3. 1979, p. 1. Directive as last amended by Directive 90/619/EEC (OJ No L 330, 29. 11. 1990, p. 50.

5 OJ No 56, 4. 4. 1964, p. 878/64. Directive as amended by the 1973 Act of Accession.

Statement by the Council and the Parliament re Article 6 (1)

The Council and the Parliament note that the Commission will examine the possibility and desirability of harmonizing the method of calculating the cooling-off period under existing consumer-protection legislation, notably Directive 85/577/EEC of 20 December 1985 on the protection of consumers in respect of contracts negotiated away from commercial establishments ('door-to-door sales`)[3].

Statement by the Commission re Article 3 (1), first indent

The Commission recognizes the importance of protecting consumers in respect of distance contracts concerning financial services and has published a Green Paper entitled 'Financial services: meeting consumers' expectations`. In the light of reactions to the Green Paper the Commission will examine ways of incorporating consumer protection into the policy on financial services and the possible legislative implications and, if need be, will submit appropriate proposals.

---

1 OJ No L 228, 11. 8. 1992, p. 1.
2 OJ No L 360, 9. 12. 1992, p. 1.
3 OJ No L 372, 31. 12. 1985, p. 31.

5. Directive 98/6/EC of the European Parliament and of the Council of 16 February 1998 on consumer protection in the indication of the prices of products offered to consumers

(OJ L 080 , 18/03/1998 p. 27 – 31)

THE EUROPEAN PARLIAMENT AND THE COUNCIL OF THE EUROPEAN UNION,

Having regard to the Treaty establishing the European Community, and in particular Article 129a(2) thereof,

Having regard to the proposal from the Commission[1],

Having regard to the opinion of the Economic and Social Committee[2],

Acting in accordance with the procedure laid down in Article 189b of the Treaty[3], in the light of the joint text approved by the Conciliation Committee on 9 December 1997,

(1) Whereas transparent operation of the market and correct information is of benefit to consumer protection and healthy competition between enterprises and products;

(2) Whereas consumers must be guaranteed a high level of protection; whereas the Community should contribute thereto by specific action which supports and supplements the policy pursued by the Member States regarding precise, transparent and unambiguous information for consumers on the prices of products offered to them;

(3) Whereas the Council Resolution of 14 April 1975 on a preliminary programme of the European Economic Community for a consumer protection and information policy[4] and the Council Resolution of 19 May 1981 on a second programme of the European Economic Community for a consumer protection and information policy[5] provide for the establishment of common principles for indicating prices;

1 OJ C 260, 5. 10. 1995, p. 5 and OJ C 249, 27. 8. 1996, p. 2.

2 OJ C 82, 19. 3. 1996, p. 32.

3 Opinion of the European Parliament of 18 April 1996 (OJ C 141, 13. 5. 1996, p. 191). Council Common Position of 27 September 1996 (OJ C 333, 7. 11. 1996, p. 7) and Decision of the European Parliament of 18 February 1997 (OJ C 85, 17. 3. 1997, p. 26). Decision of the European Parliament of 16 December 1997 and Decision of the Council of 18 December 1997.

4 OJ C 92, 25. 4. 1975, p. 1.

5 OJ C 133, 3. 6. 1981, p. 1.

(4) Whereas these principles have been established by Directive 79/581/EEC concerning the indication of prices of certain foodstuffs[1] and Directive 88/314/EEC concerning the indication of prices of non-food products[2];

(5) Whereas the link between indication of the unit price of products and their pre-packaging in pre-established quantities or capacities corresponding to the values of the ranges adopted at Community level has proved overly complex to apply; whereas it is thus necessary to abandon this link in favour of a new simplified mechanism and in the interest of the consumer, without prejudice to the rules governing packaging standardisation;

(6) Whereas the obligation to indicate the selling price and the unit price contributes substantially to improving consumer information, as this is the easiest way to enable consumers to evaluate and compare the price of products in an optimum manner and hence to make informed choices on the basis of simple comparisons;

(7) Whereas, therefore, there should be a general obligation to indicate both the selling price and the unit price for all products except for products sold in bulk, where the selling price cannot be determined until the consumer indicates how much of the product is required;

(8) Whereas it is necessary to take into account the fact that certain products are customarily sold in quantities different from one kilogramme, one litre, one metre, one square metre or one cubic metre; whereas it is thus appropriate to allow Member States to authorise that the unit price refer to a different single unit of quantity, taking into account the nature of the product and the quantities in which it is customarily sold in the Member State concerned;

(9) Whereas the obligation to indicate the unit price may entail an excessive burden for certain small retail businesses under certain circumstances; whereas Member States should therefore be allowed to refrain from applying this obligation during an appropriate transitional period;

(10) Whereas Member States should also remain free to waive the obligation to indicate the unit price in the case of products for which such price indication would not be useful or would be liable to cause confusion for instance when indication of the quantity is not relevant for price comparison purposes, or when different products are marketed in the same packaging;

(11) Whereas in the case of non-food products, Member States, with a view to facilitating application of the mechanism implemented, are free to draw up a list of products or categories of products for which the obligation to indicate the unit price remains applicable;

(12) Whereas Community-level rules can ensure homogenous and transparent information that will benefit all consumers in the context of the internal market;

[1] OJ L 158, 26. 6. 1979, p. 19. Directive as last amended by Directive 95/58/EC (OJ L 299, 12. 12. 1995, p. 11).

[2] OJ L 142, 9. 6. 1988, p. 19. Directive as last amended by Directive 95/58/EC (OJ L 299, 12. 12. 1995, p. 11).

whereas the new, simplified approach is both necessary and sufficient to achieve this objective;

(13) Whereas Member States must make sure that the system is effective; whereas the transparency of the system should also be maintained when the euro is introduced; whereas, to that end, the maximum number of prices to be indicated should be limited;

(14) Whereas particular attention should be paid to small retail businesses; whereas, to this end, the Commission should, in its report on the application of this Directive to be presented no later than three years after the date referred to in Article 11(1), take particular account of the experience gleaned in the application of the Directive by small retail businesses, inter alia, regarding technological developments and the introduction of the single currency; whereas this report, having regard to the transitional period referred to in Article 6, should be accompanied by a proposal,

HAVE ADOPTED THIS DIRECTIVE:

Article 1

The purpose of this Directive is to stipulate indication of the selling price and the price per unit of measurement of products offered by traders to consumers in order to improve consumer information and to facilitate comparison of prices.

Article 2

For the purposes of this Directive:

(a) selling price shall mean the final price for a unit of the product, or a given quantity of the product, including VAT and all other taxes;

(b) unit price shall mean the final price, including VAT and all other taxes, for one kilogramme, one litre, one metre, one square metre or one cubic metre of the product or a different single unit of quantity which is widely and customarily used in the Member State concerned in the marketing of specific products;

(c) products sold in bulk shall mean products which are not pre-packaged and are measured in the presence of the consumer;

(d) trader shall mean any natural or legal person who sells or offers for sale products which fall within his commercial or professional activity;

(e) consumer shall mean any natural person who buys a product for purposes that do not fall within the sphere of his commercial or professional activity.

Article 3

1. The selling price and the unit price shall be indicated for all products referred to in Article 1, the indication of the unit price being subject to the provisions of Article 5. The unit price need not be indicated if it is identical to the sales price.
2. Member States may decide not to apply paragraph 1 to:
   - products supplied in the course of the provision of a service,

- sales by auction and sales of works of art and antiques.

3. For products sold in bulk, only the unit price must be indicated.
4. Any advertisement which mentions the selling price of products referred to in Article 1 shall also indicate the unit price subject to Article 5.

Article 4

1. The selling price and the unit price must be unambiguous, easily identifiable and clearly legible. Member States may provide that the maximum number of prices to be indicated be limited.
2. The unit price shall refer to a quantity declared in accordance with national and Community provisions.

   Where national or Community provisions require the indication of the net weight and the net drained weight for certain pre-packed products, it shall be sufficient to indicate the unit price of the net drained weight.

Article 5

1. Member States may waive the obligation to indicate the unit price of products for which such indication would not be useful because of the products' nature or purpose or would be liable to create confusion.
2. With a view to implementing paragraph 1, Member States may, in the case of non-food products, establish a list of the products or product categories to which the obligation to indicate the unit price shall remain applicable.

Article 6

If the obligation to indicate the unit price were to constitute an excessive burden for certain small retail businesses because of the number of products on sale, the sales area, the nature of the place of sale, specific conditions of sale where the product is not directly accessible for the consumer or certain forms of business, such as certain types of itinerant trade, Member States may, for a transitional period following the date referred to in Article 11 (1), provide that the obligation to indicate the unit price of products other than those sold in bulk, which are sold in the said businesses, shall not apply, subject to Article 12.

Article 7

Member States shall provide appropriate measures to inform all persons concerned of the national law transposing this Directive.

Article 8

Member States shall lay down penalties for infringements of national provisions adopted in application of this Directive, and shall take all necessary measures to ensure that these are enforced. These penalties must be effective, proportionate and dissuasive.

Article 9

1. The transition period of nine years referred to in Article 1 of Directive 95/58/EC of the European Parliament and of the Council of 29 November 1995 amending Directive 79/581/EEC on consumer protection in the indication of the prices of foodstuffs and Directive 88/314/EEC on consumer protection in the indication of the prices of non-food products[1] shall be extended until the date referred to in Article 11(1) of this Directive.
2. Directives 79/581/EEC and 88/314/EEC shall be repealed with effect from the date referred to in Article 11 (1) of this Directive.

Article 10

This Directive shall not prevent Member States from adopting or maintaining provisions which are more favourable as regards consumer information and comparison of prices, without prejudice to their obligations under the Treaty.

Article 11

1. Member States shall bring into force the laws, regulations and administrative provisions necessary to comply with this Directive not later than 18 March 2000. They shall forthwith inform the Commission thereof. The provisions adopted shall be applicable as of that date.

   When Member States adopt these measures, they shall contain a reference to this Directive or shall be accompanied by such reference at the time of their official publication. The methods of making such reference shall be laid down by Member States.
2. Member States shall communicate to the Commission the text of the provisions of national law which they adopt in the field governed by this Directive.
3. Member States shall communicate the provisions governing the penalties provided for in Article 8, and any later amendments thereto.

Article 12

The Commission shall, not later than three years after the date referred to in Article 11(1), submit to the European Parliament and the Council a comprehensive report on the application of this Directive, in particular on the application of Article 6, accompanied by a proposal.

The European Parliament and the Council shall, on this basis, re-examine the provisions of Article 6 and shall act, in accordance with the Treaty, within three years of the presentation by the Commission of the proposal referred to in the first paragraph.

Article 13

This Directive shall enter into force on the day of its publication in the Official Journal of the European Communities.

---

[1] OJ L 299, 12. 12. 1995, p. 11.

Article 14

This Directive is addressed to the Member States.

Done at Brussels, 16 February 1998.

For the European Parliament

The President

J. M. GIL-ROBLES

For the Council

The President

J. CUNNINGHAM

Commission Declaration

Article 2(b):

The Commission takes the view that the expression 'for one kilogramme, one litre, one metre, one square metre or cubic metre of the product or a different single unit of quantity` in Article 2(b) also applies to products sold by individual item or singly.

Commission Declaration

Article 12, first paragraph:

The Commission considers that Article 12, first paragraph, of the Directive cannot be construed as calling into question its right of initiative.

6. Council Directive 98/59/EC of 20 July 1998 on the approximation of the laws of the Member States relating to collective redundancies

(OJ L 225 , 12/08/1998 p. 16 – 21)

THE COUNCIL OF THE EUROPEAN UNION,

Having regard to the Treaty establishing the European Community, and in particular Article 100 thereof,

Having regard to the proposal from the Commission,

Having regard to the opinion of the European Parliament[1],

Having regard to the opinion of the Economic and Social Committee[2],

(1) Whereas for reasons of clarity and rationality Council Directive 75/129/EEC of 17 February 1975 on the approximation of the laws of the Member States relating to collective redundancies[3] should be consolidated;

(2) Whereas it is important that greater protection should be afforded to workers in the event of collective redundancies while taking into account the need for balanced economic and social development within the Community;

(3) Whereas, despite increasing convergence, differences still remain between the provisions in force in the Member States concerning the practical arrangements and procedures for such redundancies and the measures designed to alleviate the consequences of redundancy for workers;

(4) Whereas these differences can have a direct effect on the functioning of the internal market;

(5) Whereas the Council resolution of 21 January 1974 concerning a social action programme[4] made provision for a directive on the approximation of Member States' legislation on collective redundancies;

(6) Whereas the Community Charter of the fundamental social rights of workers, adopted at the European Council meeting held in Strasbourg on 9 December 1989 by the Heads of State or Government of 11 Member States, states, inter alia, in point 7, first paragraph, first sentence, and second paragraph; in point 17, first paragraph; and in point 18, third indent:

7. The completion of the internal market must lead to an improvement in the living and working conditions of workers in the European Community (. . .).

The improvement must cover, where necessary, the development of certain aspects of employment regulations such as procedures for collective redundancies and those regarding bankruptcies.

(. . .)

1 OJ C 210, 6. 7. 1998.

2 OJ C 158, 26. 5. 1997, p. 11.

3 OJ L 48, 22. 2. 1975, p. 29. Directive as amended by Directive 92/56/EEC (OJ L 245, 26. 8. 1992, p. 3).

4 OJ C 13, 12. 2. 1974, p. 1.

17. Information, consultation and participation for workers must be developed along appropriate lines, taking account of the practices in force in the various Member States.

(. . .)

18. Such information, consultation and participation must be implemented in due time, particularly in the following cases:

(- . . .)

(- . . .)

- in cases of collective redundancy procedures;(- . . .)`;

(7) Whereas this approximation must therefore be promoted while the improvement is being maintained within the meaning of Article 117 of the Treaty;

(8) Whereas, in order to calculate the number of redundancies provided for in the definition of collective redundancies within the meaning of this Directive, other forms of termination of employment contracts on the initiative of the employer should be equated to redundancies, provided that there are at least five redundancies;

(9) Whereas it should be stipulated that this Directive applies in principle also to collective redundancies resulting where the establishment's activities are terminated as a result of a judicial decision;

(10) Whereas the Member States should be given the option of stipulating that workers' representatives may call on experts on grounds of the technical complexity of the matters which are likely to be the subject of the informing and consulting;

(11) Whereas it is necessary to ensure that employers' obligations as regards information, consultation and notification apply independently of whether the decision on collective redundancies emanates from the employer or from an undertaking which controls that employer;

(12) Whereas Member States should ensure that workers' representatives and/or workers have at their disposal administrative and/or judicial procedures in order to ensure that the obligations laid down in this Directive are fulfilled;

(13) Whereas this Directive must not affect the obligations of the Member States concerning the deadlines for transposition of the Directives set out in Annex I, Part B,

HAS ADOPTED THIS DIRECTIVE:

Section I : **Definitions and scope**

Article 1

1. For the purposes of this Directive:

   (a) 'collective redundancies` means dismissals effected by an employer for one or more reasons not related to the individual workers concerned where, according to the choice of the Member States, the number of redundancies is:

(i) either, over a period of 30 days:

- at least 10 in establishments normally employing more than 20 and less than 100 workers,
- at least 10 % of the number of workers in establishments normally employing at least 100 but less than 300 workers,
- at least 30 in establishments normally employing 300 workers or more,

(ii) or, over a period of 90 days, at least 20, whatever the number of workers normally employed in the establishments in question;

(b) 'workers' representatives` means the workers' representatives provided for by the laws or practices of the Member States.

For the purpose of calculating the number of redundancies provided for in the first subparagraph of point (a), terminations of an employment contract which occur on the employer's initiative for one or more reasons not related to the individual workers concerned shall be assimilated to redundancies, provided that there are at least five redundancies.

2. This Directive shall not apply to:

(a) collective redundancies effected under contracts of employment concluded for limited periods of time or for specific tasks except where such redundancies take place prior to the date of expiry or the completion of such contracts;

(b) workers employed by public administrative bodies or by establishments governed by public law (or, in Member States where this concept is unknown, by equivalent bodies);

(c) the crews of seagoing vessels.

Section II : **Information and consultation**

Article 2

1. Where an employer is contemplating collective redundancies, he shall begin consultations with the workers' representatives in good time with a view to reaching an agreement.

2. These consultations shall, at least, cover ways and means of avoiding collective redundancies or reducing the number of workers affected, and of mitigating the consequences by recourse to accompanying social measures aimed, inter alia, at aid for redeploying or retraining workers made redundant.

   Member States may provide that the workers' representatives may call on the services of experts in accordance with national legislation and/or practice.

3. To enable workers' representatives to make constructive proposals, the employers shall in good time during the course of the consultations:

(a) supply them with all relevant information and

(b) in any event notify them in writing of:

(i) the reasons for the projected redundancies;
(ii) the number and categories of workers to be made redundant;
(iii) the number and categories of workers normally employed;
(iv) the period over which the projected redundancies are to be effected;
(v) the criteria proposed for the selection of the workers to be made redundant in so far as national legislation and/or practice confers the power therefor upon the employer;
(vi) the method for calculating any redundancy payments other than those arising out of national legislation and/or practice.

The employer shall forward to the competent public authority a copy of, at least, the elements of the written communication which are provided for in the first subparagraph, point (b), subpoints (i) to (v).

4. The obligations laid down in paragraphs 1, 2 and 3 shall apply irrespective of whether the decision regarding collective redundancies is being taken by the employer or by an undertaking controlling the employer.

   In considering alleged breaches of the information, consultation and notification requirements laid down by this Directive, account shall not be taken of any defence on the part of the employer on the ground that the necessary information has not been provided to the employer by the undertaking which took the decision leading to collective redundancies.

Section III : **Procedure for collective redundances**

Article 3

1. Employers shall notify the competent public authority in writing of any projected collective redundancies.

   However, Member States may provide that in the case of planned collective redundancies arising from termination of the establishment's activities as a result of a judicial decision, the employer shall be obliged to notify the competent public authority in writing only if the latter so requests.

   This notification shall contain all relevant information concerning the projected collective redundancies and the consultations with workers' representatives provided for in Article 2, and particularly the reasons for the redundancies, the number of workers to be made redundant, the number of workers normally employed and the period over which the redundancies are to be effected.

2. Employers shall forward to the workers' representatives a copy of the notification provided for in paragraph 1.

   The workers' representatives may send any comments they may have to the competent public authority.

Article 4

1. Projected collective redundancies notified to the competent public authority shall take effect not earlier than 30 days after the notification referred to in

Article 3(1) without prejudice to any provisions governing individual rights with regard to notice of dismissal.

Member States may grant the competent public authority the power to reduce the period provided for in the preceding subparagraph.

2. The period provided for in paragraph 1 shall be used by the competent public authority to seek solutions to the problems raised by the projected collective redundancies.
3. Where the initial period provided for in paragraph 1 is shorter than 60 days, Member States may grant the competent public authority the power to extend the initial period to 60 days following notification where the problems raised by the projected collective redundancies are not likely to be solved within the initial period.

   Member States may grant the competent public authority wider powers of extension.

   The employer must be informed of the extension and the grounds for it before expiry of the initial period provided for in paragraph 1.
4. Member States need not apply this Article to collective redundancies arising from termination of the establishment's activities where this is the result of a judicial decision.

Section IV : **Final provisions**

Article 5

This Directive shall not affect the right of Member States to apply or to introduce laws, regulations or administrative provisions which are more favourable to workers or to promote or to allow the application of collective agreements more favourable to workers.

Article 6

Member States shall ensure that judicial and/or administrative procedures for the enforcement of obligations under this Directive are available to the workers' representatives and/or workers.

Article 7

Member States shall forward to the Commission the text of any fundamental provisions of national law already adopted or being adopted in the area governed by this Directive.

Article 8

1. The Directives listed in Annex I, Part A, are hereby repealed without prejudice to the obligations of the Member States concerning the deadlines for transposition of the said Directive set out in Annex I, Part B.
2. References to the repealed Directives shall be construed as references to this Directive and shall be read in accordance with the correlation table in Annex II.

Article 9

This Directive shall enter into force on the 20th day following its publication in the Official Journal of the European Communities.

Article 10

This Directive is addressed to the Member States.

Done at Brussels, 20 July 1998.

For the Council

The President

W. MOLTERER

ANNEX I

PART A

Repealed Directives (referred to by Article 8)
Council Directive 75/129/EEC and its following amendment:
Council Directive 92/56/EEC.

PART B

Deadlines for transposition into national law (referred to by Article 8)

Directive	Deadline for transposition
75/129/CEE (OJ L 48 du 22. 2. 1975, p. 29)	19 February 1977
92/56/CEE (JO L 245 du 26. 8. 1992, p. 3)	24 June1994

ANNEX II

Directive 75/129/CEE	This Directive
Article 1er, first subparagraph, point(a), first indent, point 1	Article 1er1(1), first subparagraph, point (a)(i), first indent
Article 1(1), first subparagraph, point (a), first indent, point 2	Article 1(1), first subparagraph, point (a)(i), second indent
Article 1(1), first subparagraph, point(a), first indent, point 3	Article 1(1), first subparagraph, point (a)(i), third indent
Article 1(1), first subparagraph, point (a), second indent	Article 1(1), first subparagraph, point (a)(ii)
Article 1(1), first subparagraph, point (b)	Article 1(1), first subparagraph, point (b)
Article 1(1), second subparagraph	Article 1(1), second subparagraph
Article 1(1), second subparagraph	Article 1(1), second subparagraph
Article 1(2)	Article 1(2)
Article 2	

	Article 2
Article 3	Article 3
Article 4	Article 4
Article 5	Article 5
Article 5a	Article 6
Article 6 (1)	-
Article 6 (2)	Article 7
Article 7	-
-	Article 8
-	Article 9
-	Article 10
-	Annexe I
-	Annexe II

7. Directive 1999/44/EC of the European Parliament and of the Council of 25 May 1999 on certain aspects of the sale of consumer goods and associated guarantees

(OJ L 171 , 07/07/1999 p. 12 – 16)

THE EUROPEAN PARLIAMENT AND THE COUNCIL OF THE EUROPEAN UNION,

Having regard to the Treaty establishing the European Community, and in particular Article 95 thereof,

Having regard to the proposal from the Commission[1],

Having regard to the opinion of the Economic and Social Committee[2],

Acting in accordance with the procedure laid down in Article 251 of the Treaty in the light of the joint text approved by the Conciliation Committee on 18 May 1999[3],

(1) Whereas Article 153(1) and (3) of the Treaty provides that the Community should contribute to the achievement of a high level of consumer protection by the measures it adopts pursuant to Article 95 thereof;

(2) Whereas the internal market comprises an area without internal frontiers in which the free movement of goods, persons, services and capital is guaranteed; whereas free movement of goods concerns not only transactions by persons acting in the course of a business but also transactions by private individuals; whereas it implies that consumers resident in one Member State should be free to purchase goods in the territory of another Member State on the basis of a uniform minimum set of fair rules governing the sale of consumer goods;

(3) Whereas the laws of the Member States concerning the sale of consumer goods are somewhat disparate, with the result that national consumer goods markets differ from one another and that competition between sellers may be distorted;

(4) Whereas consumers who are keen to benefit from the large market by purchasing goods in Member States other than their State of residence play a fundamental role in the completion of the internal market; whereas the artificial reconstruction of frontiers and the compartmentalisation of markets should be prevented; whereas the opportunities available to consumers have been greatly broadened by new communication technologies which allow ready access to distribution systems in other Member States or in third countries; whereas, in the absence of minimum harmonisation of the rules governing the sale of consumer

1 OJ C 307, 16.10.1996, p. 8 and OJ C 148, 14.5.1998, p. 12.

2 OJ C 66, 3.3.1997, p. 5.

3 Opinion of the European Parliament of 10 March 1998 (OJ C 104, 6.4.1998, p. 30), Council Common Position of 24 September 1998 (OJ C 333, 30.10.1998, p. 46) and Decision of the European Parliament of 17 December 1998. (OJ C 98, 9.4.1999, p. 226). Decision of the European Parliament of 5 May 1999. Council Decision of 17 May 1999.

goods, the development of the sale of goods through the medium of new distance communication technologies risks being impeded;

(5) Whereas the creation of a common set of minimum rules of consumer law, valid no matter where goods are purchased within the Community, will strengthen consumer confidence and enable consumers to make the most of the internal market;

(6) Whereas the main difficulties encountered by consumers and the main source of disputes with sellers concern the non-conformity of goods with the contract; whereas it is therefore appropriate to approximate national legislation governing the sale of consumer goods in this respect, without however impinging on provisions and principles of national law relating to contractual and non-contractual liability;

(7) Whereas the goods must, above all, conform with the contractual specifications; whereas the principle of conformity with the contract may be considered as common to the different national legal traditions; whereas in certain national legal traditions it may not be possible to rely solely on this principle to ensure a minimum level of protection for the consumer; whereas under such legal traditions, in particular, additional national provisions may be useful to ensure that the consumer is protected in cases where the parties have agreed no specific contractual terms or where the parties have concluded contractual terms or agreements which directly or indirectly waive or restrict the rights of the consumer and which, to the extent that these rights result from this Directive, are not binding on the consumer;

(8) Whereas, in order to facilitate the application of the principle of conformity with the contract, it is useful to introduce a rebuttable presumption of conformity with the contract covering the most common situations; whereas that presumption does not restrict the principle of freedom of contract; whereas, furthermore, in the absence of specific contractual terms, as well as where the minimum protection clause is applied, the elements mentioned in this presumption may be used to determine the lack of conformity of the goods with the contract; whereas the quality and performance which consumers can reasonably expect will depend inter alia on whether the goods are new or second-hand; whereas the elements mentioned in the presumption are cumulative; whereas, if the circumstances of the case render any particular element manifestly inappropriate, the remaining elements of the presumption nevertheless still apply;

(9) Whereas the seller should be directly liable to the consumer for the conformity of the goods with the contract; whereas this is the traditional solution enshrined in the legal orders of the Member States; whereas nevertheless the seller should be free, as provided for by national law, to pursue remedies against the producer, a previous seller in the same chain of contracts or any other intermediary, unless he has renounced that entitlement; whereas this Directive does not affect the principle of freedom of contract between the seller, the producer, a previous

seller or any other intermediary; whereas the rules governing against whom and how the seller may pursue such remedies are to be determined by national law;

(10) Whereas, in the case of non-conformity of the goods with the contract, consumers should be entitled to have the goods restored to conformity with the contract free of charge, choosing either repair or replacement, or, failing this, to have the price reduced or the contract rescinded;

(11) Whereas the consumer in the first place may require the seller to repair the goods or to replace them unless those remedies are impossible or disproportionate; whereas whether a remedy is disproportionate should be determined objectively; whereas a remedy would be disproportionate if it imposed, in comparison with the other remedy, unreasonable costs; whereas, in order to determine whether the costs are unreasonable, the costs of one remedy should be significantly higher than the costs of the other remedy;

(12) Whereas in cases of a lack of conformity, the seller may always offer the consumer, by way of settlement, any available remedy; whereas it is for the consumer to decide whether to accept or reject this proposal;

(13) Whereas, in order to enable consumers to take advantage of the internal market and to buy consumer goods in another Member State, it should be recommended that, in the interests of consumers, the producers of consumer goods that are marketed in several Member States attach to the product a list with at least one contact address in every Member State where the product is marketed;

(14) Whereas the references to the time of delivery do not imply that Member States have to change their rules on the passing of the risk;

(15) Whereas Member States may provide that any reimbursement to the consumer may be reduced to take account of the use the consumer has had of the goods since they were delivered to him; whereas the detailed arrangements whereby rescission of the contract is effected may be laid down in national law;

(16) Whereas the specific nature of second-hand goods makes it generally impossible to replace them; whereas therefore the consumer's right of replacement is generally not available for these goods; whereas for such goods, Member States may enable the parties to agree a shortened period of liability;

(17) Whereas it is appropriate to limit in time the period during which the seller is liable for any lack of conformity which exists at the time of delivery of the goods; whereas Member States may also provide for a limitation on the period during which consumers can exercise their rights, provided such a period does not expire within two years from the time of delivery; whereas where, under national legislation, the time when a limitation period starts is not the time of delivery of the goods, the total duration of the limitation period provided for by national law may not be shorter than two years from the time of delivery;

(18) Whereas Member States may provide for suspension or interruption of the period during which any lack of conformity must become apparent and of the limitation period, where applicable and in accordance with their national law, in

the event of repair, replacement or negotiations between seller and consumer with a view to an amicable settlement;

(19) Whereas Member States should be allowed to set a period within which the consumer must inform the seller of any lack of conformity; whereas Member States may ensure a higher level of protection for the consumer by not introducing such an obligation; whereas in any case consumers throughout the Community should have at least two months in which to inform the seller that a lack of conformity exists;

(20) Whereas Member States should guard against such a period placing at a disadvantage consumers shopping across borders; whereas all Member States should inform the Commission of their use of this provision; whereas the Commission should monitor the effect of the varied application of this provision on consumers and on the internal market; whereas information on the use made of this provision by a Member State should be available to the other Member States and to consumers and consumer organisations throughout the Community; whereas a summary of the situation in all Member States should therefore be published in the Official Journal of the European Communities;

(21) Whereas, for certain categories of goods, it is current practice for sellers and producers to offer guarantees on goods against any defect which becomes apparent within a certain period; whereas this practice can stimulate competition; whereas, while such guarantees are legitimate marketing tools, they should not mislead the consumer; whereas, to ensure that consumers are not misled, guarantees should contain certain information, including a statement that the guarantee does not affect the consumer's legal rights;

(22) Whereas the parties may not, by common consent, restrict or waive the rights granted to consumers, since otherwise the legal protection afforded would be thwarted; whereas this principle should apply also to clauses which imply that the consumer was aware of any lack of conformity of the consumer goods existing at the time the contract was concluded; whereas the protection granted to consumers under this Directive should not be reduced on the grounds that the law of a non-member State has been chosen as being applicable to the contract;

(23) Whereas legislation and case-law in this area in the various Member States show that there is growing concern to ensure a high level of consumer protection; whereas, in the light of this trend and the experience acquired in implementing this Directive, it may be necessary to envisage more far-reaching harmonisation, notably by providing for the producer's direct liability for defects for which he is responsible;

(24) Whereas Member States should be allowed to adopt or maintain in force more stringent provisions in the field covered by this Directive to ensure an even higher level of consumer protection;

(25) Whereas, according to the Commission recommendation of 30 March 1998 on the principles applicable to the bodies responsible for out-of-court settlement of

consumer disputes[1], Member States can create bodies that ensure impartial and efficient handling of complaints in a national and cross-border context and which consumers can use as mediators;

(26) Whereas it is appropriate, in order to protect the collective interests of consumers, to add this Directive to the list of Directives contained in the Annex to Directive 98/27/EC of the European Parliament and of the Council of 19 May 1998 on injunctions for the protection of consumers' interests[2],

HAVE ADOPTED THIS DIRECTIVE:

Article 1 Scope and definitions

1. The purpose of this Directive is the approximation of the laws, regulations and administrative provisions of the Member States on certain aspects of the sale of consumer goods and associated guarantees in order to ensure a uniform minimum level of consumer protection in the context of the internal market.
2. For the purposes of this Directive:
   (a) consumer: shall mean any natural person who, in the contracts covered by this Directive, is acting for purposes which are not related to his trade, business or profession;
   (b) consumer goods: shall mean any tangible movable item, with the exception of:
      - goods sold by way of execution or otherwise by authority of law,
      - water and gas where they are not put up for sale in a limited volume or set quantity,
      - electricity;
   (c) seller: shall mean any natural or legal person who, under a contract, sells consumer goods in the course of his trade, business or profession;
   (d) producer: shall mean the manufacturer of consumer goods, the importer of consumer goods into the territory of the Community or any person purporting to be a producer by placing his name, trade mark or other distinctive sign on the consumer goods;
   (e) guarantee: shall mean any undertaking by a seller or producer to the consumer, given without extra charge, to reimburse the price paid or to replace, repair or handle consumer goods in any way if they do not meet the specifications set out in the guarantee statement or in the relevant advertising;
   (f) repair: shall mean, in the event of lack of conformity, bringing consumer goods into conformity with the contract of sale.
3. Member States may provide that the expression "consumer goods" does not cover second-hand goods sold at public auction where consumers have the opportunity of attending the sale in person.

1 OJ L 115, 17.4.1998, p. 31.
2 OJ L 166, 11.6.1998, p. 51.

4. Contracts for the supply of consumer goods to be manufactured or produced shall also be deemed contracts of sale for the purpose of this Directive.

Article 2 Conformity with the contract

1. The seller must deliver goods to the consumer which are in conformity with the contract of sale.
2. Consumer goods are presumed to be in conformity with the contract if they:
   (a) comply with the description given by the seller and possess the qualities of the goods which the seller has held out to the consumer as a sample or model;
   (b) are fit for any particular purpose for which the consumer requires them and which he made known to the seller at the time of conclusion of the contract and which the seller has accepted;
   (c) are fit for the purposes for which goods of the same type are normally used;
   (d) show the quality and performance which are normal in goods of the same type and which the consumer can reasonably expect, given the nature of the goods and taking into account any public statements on the specific characteristics of the goods made about them by the seller, the producer or his representative, particularly in advertising or on labelling.
3. There shall be deemed not to be a lack of conformity for the purposes of this Article if, at the time the contract was concluded, the consumer was aware, or could not reasonably be unaware of, the lack of conformity, or if the lack of conformity has its origin in materials supplied by the consumer.
4. The seller shall not be bound by public statements, as referred to in paragraph 2(d) if he:
   - shows that he was not, and could not reasonably have been, aware of the statement in question,
   - shows that by the time of conclusion of the contract the statement had been corrected, or
   - shows that the decision to buy the consumer goods could not have been influenced by the statement.
5. Any lack of conformity resulting from incorrect installation of the consumer goods shall be deemed to be equivalent to lack of conformity of the goods if installation forms part of the contract of sale of the goods and the goods were installed by the seller or under his responsibility. This shall apply equally if the product, intended to be installed by the consumer, is installed by the consumer and the incorrect installation is due to a shortcoming in the installation instructions.

Article 3 Rights of the consumer

1. The seller shall be liable to the consumer for any lack of conformity which exists at the time the goods were delivered.

2. In the case of a lack of conformity, the consumer shall be entitled to have the goods brought into conformity free of charge by repair or replacement, in accordance with paragraph 3, or to have an appropriate reduction made in the price or the contract rescinded with regard to those goods, in accordance with paragraphs 5 and 6.
3. In the first place, the consumer may require the seller to repair the goods or he may require the seller to replace them, in either case free of charge, unless this is impossible or disproportionate.

   A remedy shall be deemed to be disproportionate if it imposes costs on the seller which, in comparison with the alternative remedy, are unreasonable, taking into account:

   - the value the goods would have if there were no lack of conformity,
   - the significance of the lack of conformity, and
   - whether the alternative remedy could be completed without significant inconvenience to the consumer.

   Any repair or replacement shall be completed within a reasonable time and without any significant inconvenience to the consumer, taking account of the nature of the goods and the purpose for which the consumer required the goods.
4. The terms "free of charge" in paragraphs 2 and 3 refer to the necessary costs incurred to bring the goods into conformity, particularly the cost of postage, labour and materials.
5. The consumer may require an appropriate reduction of the price or have the contract rescinded:
   - if the consumer is entitled to neither repair nor replacement, or
   - if the seller has not completed the remedy within a reasonable time, or
   - if the seller has not completed the remedy without significant inconvenience to the consumer.
6. The consumer is not entitled to have the contract rescinded if the lack of conformity is minor.

Article 4 Right of redress

Where the final seller is liable to the consumer because of a lack of conformity resulting from an act or omission by the producer, a previous seller in the same chain of contracts or any other intermediary, the final seller shall be entitled to pursue remedies against the person or persons liable in the contractual chain. the person or persons liable against whom the final seller may pursue remedies, together with the relevant actions and conditions of exercise, shall be determined by national law.

Article 5 Time limits

1. The seller shall be held liable under Article 3 where the lack of conformity becomes apparent within two years as from delivery of the goods. If, under national legislation, the rights laid down in Article 3(2) are subject to a limitation

period, that period shall not expire within a period of two years from the time of delivery.

2. Member States may provide that, in order to benefit from his rights, the consumer must inform the seller of the lack of conformity within a period of two months from the date on which he detected such lack of conformity.

   Member States shall inform the Commission of their use of this paragraph. The Commission shall monitor the effect of the existence of this option for the Member States on consumers and on the internal market.

   Not later than 7 January 2003, the Commission shall prepare a report on the use made by Member States of this paragraph. This report shall be published in the Official Journal of the European Communities.

3. Unless proved otherwise, any lack of conformity which becomes apparent within six months of delivery of the goods shall be presumed to have existed at the time of delivery unless this presumption is incompatible with the nature of the goods or the nature of the lack of conformity.

Article 6 Guarantees

1. A guarantee shall be legally binding on the offerer under the conditions laid down in the guarantee statement and the associated advertising.
2. The guarantee shall:
   - state that the consumer has legal rights under applicable national legislation governing the sale of consumer goods and make clear that those rights are not affected by the guarantee,
   - set out in plain intelligible language the contents of the guarantee and the essential particulars necessary for making claims under the guarantee, notably the duration and territorial scope of the guarantee as well as the name and address of the guarantor.
3. On request by the consumer, the guarantee shall be made available in writing or feature in another durable medium available and accessible to him.
4. Within its own territory, the Member State in which the consumer goods are marketed may, in accordance with the rules of the Treaty, provide that the guarantee be drafted in one or more languages which it shall determine from among the official languages of the Community.
5. Should a guarantee infringe the requirements of paragraphs 2, 3 or 4, the validity of this guarantee shall in no way be affected, and the consumer can still rely on the guarantee and require that it be honoured.

Article 7 Binding nature

1. Any contractual terms or agreements concluded with the seller before the lack of conformity is brought to the seller's attention which directly or indirectly waive or restrict the rights resulting from this Directive shall, as provided for by national law, not be binding on the consumer.

Member States may provide that, in the case of second-hand goods, the seller and consumer may agree contractual terms or agreements which have a shorter time period for the liability of the seller than that set down in Article 5(1). Such period may not be less than one year.

2. Member States shall take the necessary measures to ensure that consumers are not deprived of the protection afforded by this Directive as a result of opting for the law of a non-member State as the law applicable to the contract where the contract has a close connection with the territory of the Member States.

Article 8 National law and minimum protection

1. The rights resulting from this Directive shall be exercised without prejudice to other rights which the consumer may invoke under the national rules governing contractual or non-contractual liability.
2. Member States may adopt or maintain in force more stringent provisions, compatible with the Treaty in the field covered by this Directive, to ensure a higher level of consumer protection.

Article 9

Member States shall take appropriate measures to inform the consumer of the national law transposing this Directive and shall encourage, where appropriate, professional organisations to inform consumers of their rights.

Article 10

The Annex to Directive 98/27/EC shall be completed as follows: "10. Directive 1999/44/EC of the European Parliament and of the Council of 25 May 1999 on certain aspects of the sale of consumer goods and associated guarantees (OJ L 171, 7.7.1999, p. 12).".

Article 11 Transposition

1. Member States shall bring into force the laws, regulations and administrative provisions necessary to comply with this Directive not later than 1 January 2002. They shall forthwith inform the Commission thereof.

   When Member States adopt these measures, they shall contain a reference to this Directive, or shall be accompanied by such reference at the time of their official publication. The procedure for such reference shall be adopted by Member States.
2. Member States shall communicate to the Commission the provisions of national law which they adopt in the field covered by this Directive.

Article 12 Review

The Commission shall, not later than 7 July 2006, review the application of this Directive and submit to the European Parliament and the Council a report. The report shall examine, inter alia, the case for introducing the producer's direct liability and, if appropriate, shall be accompanied by proposals.

Article 13 Entry into force

This Directive shall enter into force on the day of its publication in the Official Journal of the European Communities.

Article 14

This Directive is addressed to the Member States.

Done at Brussels, 25 May 1999.

For the European Parliament

The President

J. M. GIL-ROBLES

For the Council

The President

H. EICHEL

8. Directive 1999/93/EC of the European Parliament and of the Council of 13 December 1999 on a Community framework for electronic signatures

(OJ L 013 , 19/01/2000 p. 12 – 20)

THE EUROPEAN PARLIAMENT AND THE COUNCIL OF THE EUROPEAN UNION,

Having regard to the Treaty establishing the European Community, and in particular Articles 47(2), 55 and 95 thereof,

Having regard to the proposal from the Commission[1],

Having regard to the opinion of the Economic and Social Committee[2],

Having regard to the opinion of the Committee of the Regions[3],

Acting in accordance with the procedure laid down in Article 251 of the Treaty[4],

Whereas:

(1) On 16 April 1997 the Commission presented to the European Parliament, the Council, the Economic and Social Committee and the Committee of the Regions a Communication on a European Initiative in Electronic Commerce;

(2) On 8 October 1997 the Commission presented to the European Parliament, the Council, the Economic and Social Committee and the Committee of the Regions a Communication on ensuring security and trust in electronic communication - towards a European framework for digital signatures and encryption;

(3) On 1 December 1997 the Council invited the Commission to submit as soon as possible a proposal for a Directive of the European Parliament and of the Council on digital signatures;

(4) Electronic communication and commerce necessitate " electronic signatures" and related services allowing data authentication; divergent rules with respect to legal recognition of electronic signatures and the accreditation of certification-service providers in the Member States may create a significant barrier to the use of electronic communications and electronic commerce; on the other hand, a clear Community framework regarding the conditions applying to electronic signatures will strengthen confidence in, and general acceptance of, the new technologies; legislation in the Member States should not hinder the free movement of goods and services in the internal market;

(5) The interoperability of electronic-signature products should be promoted; in accordance with Article 14 of the Treaty, the internal market comprises an area without internal frontiers in which the free movement of goods is ensured;

---

1 OJ C 325, 23.10.1998, p. 5.

2 OJ C 40, 15.2.1999, p. 29.

3 OJ C 93, 6.4.1999, p. 33.

4 Opinion of the European Parliament of 13 January 1999 (OJ C 104, 14.4.1999, p. 49), Council Common Position of 28 June 1999 (OJ C 243, 27.8.1999, p. 33) and Decision of the European Parliament of 27 October 1999 (not yet published in the Official Journal). Council Decision of 30 November 1999.

essential requirements specific to electronic-signature products must be met in order to ensure free movement within the internal market and to build trust in electronic signatures, without prejudice to Council Regulation (EC) No 3381/94 of 19 December 1994 setting up a Community regime for the control of exports of dual-use goods[1] and Council Decision 94/942/CFSP of 19 December 1994 on the joint action adopted by the Council concerning the control of exports of dual-use goods[2];

(6) This Directive does not harmonise the provision of services with respect to the confidentiality of information where they are covered by national provisions concerned with public policy or public security;

(7) The internal market ensures the free movement of persons, as a result of which citizens and residents of the European Union increasingly need to deal with authorities in Member States other than the one in which they reside; the availability of electronic communication could be of great service in this respect;

(8) Rapid technological development and the global character of the Internet necessitate an approach which is open to various technologies and services capable of authenticating data electronically;

(9) Electronic signatures will be used in a large variety of circumstances and applications, resulting in a wide range of new services and products related to or using electronic signatures; the definition of such products and services should not be limited to the issuance and management of certificates, but should also encompass any other service and product using, or ancillary to, electronic signatures, such as registration services, time-stamping services, directory services, computing services or consultancy services related to electronic signatures;

(10) The internal market enables certification-service-providers to develop their cross-border activities with a view to increasing their competitiveness, and thus to offer consumers and businesses new opportunities to exchange information and trade electronically in a secure way, regardless of frontiers; in order to stimulate the Community-wide provision of certification services over open networks, certification-service-providers should be free to provide their services without prior authorisation; prior authorisation means not only any permission whereby the certification-service-provider concerned has to obtain a decision by national authorities before being allowed to provide its certification services, but also any other measures having the same effect;

(11) Voluntary accreditation schemes aiming at an enhanced level of service-provision may offer certification-service-providers the appropriate framework for developing further their services towards the levels of trust, security and quality demanded by the evolving market; such schemes should encourage the development of best practice among certification-service-providers; certification-

---

1 OJ L 367, 31.12.1994, p. 1. Regulation as amended by Regulation (EC) No 837/95 (OJ L 90, 21.4.1995, p. 1).

2 OJ L 367, 31.12.1994, p. 8. Decision as last amended by Decision 99/193/CFSP (OJ L 73, 19.3.1999, p. 1).

service-providers should be left free to adhere to and benefit from such accreditation schemes;

(12) Certification services can be offered either by a public entity or a legal or natural person, when it is established in accordance with the national law; whereas Member States should not prohibit certification-service-providers from operating outside voluntary accreditation schemes; it should be ensured that such accreditation schemes do not reduce competition for certification services;

(13) Member States may decide how they ensure the supervision of compliance with the provisions laid down in this Directive; this Directive does not preclude the establishment of private-sector-based supervision systems; this Directive does not oblige certification-service-providers to apply to be supervised under any applicable accreditation scheme;

(14) It is important to strike a balance between consumer and business needs;

(15) Annex III covers requirements for secure signature-creation devices to ensure the functionality of advanced electronic signatures; it does not cover the entire system environment in which such devices operate; the functioning of the internal market requires the Commission and the Member States to act swiftly to enable the bodies charged with the conformity assessment of secure signature devices with Annex III to be designated; in order to meet market needs conformity assessment must be timely and efficient;

(16) This Directive contributes to the use and legal recognition of electronic signatures within the Community; a regulatory framework is not needed for electronic signatures exclusively used within systems, which are based on voluntary agreements under private law between a specified number of participants; the freedom of parties to agree among themselves the terms and conditions under which they accept electronically signed data should be respected to the extent allowed by national law; the legal effectiveness of electronic signatures used in such systems and their admissibility as evidence in legal proceedings should be recognised;

(17) This Directive does not seek to harmonise national rules concerning contract law, particularly the formation and performance of contracts, or other formalities of a non-contractual nature concerning signatures; for this reason the provisions concerning the legal effect of electronic signatures should be without prejudice to requirements regarding form laid down in national law with regard to the conclusion of contracts or the rules determining where a contract is concluded;

(18) The storage and copying of signature-creation data could cause a threat to the legal validity of electronic signatures;

(19) Electronic signatures will be used in the public sector within national and Community administrations and in communications between such administrations and with citizens and economic operators, for example in the public procurement, taxation, social security, health and justice systems;

(20) Harmonised criteria relating to the legal effects of electronic signatures will preserve a coherent legal framework across the Community; national law lays

down different requirements for the legal validity of hand-written signatures; whereas certificates can be used to confirm the identity of a person signing electronically; advanced electronic signatures based on qualified certificates aim at a higher level of security; advanced electronic signatures which are based on a qualified certificate and which are created by a secure-signature-creation device can be regarded as legally equivalent to hand-written signatures only if the requirements for hand-written signatures are fulfilled;

(21) In order to contribute to the general acceptance of electronic authentication methods it has to be ensured that electronic signatures can be used as evidence in legal proceedings in all Member States; the legal recognition of electronic signatures should be based upon objective criteria and not be linked to authorisation of the certification-service-provider involved; national law governs the legal spheres in which electronic documents and electronic signatures may be used; this Directive is without prejudice to the power of a national court to make a ruling regarding conformity with the requirements of this Directive and does not affect national rules regarding the unfettered judicial consideration of evidence;

(22) Certification-service-providers providing certification-services to the public are subject to national rules regarding liability;

(23) The development of international electronic commerce requires cross-border arrangements involving third countries; in order to ensure interoperability at a global level, agreements on multilateral rules with third countries on mutual recognition of certification services could be beneficial;

(24) In order to increase user confidence in electronic communication and electronic commerce, certification-service-providers must observe data protection legislation and individual privacy;

(25) Provisions on the use of pseudonyms in certificates should not prevent Member States from requiring identification of persons pursuant to Community or national law;

(26) The measures necessary for the implementation of this Directive are to be adopted in accordance with Council Decision 1999/468/EC of 28 June 1999 laying down the procedures for the exercise of implementing powers conferred on the Commission[1];

(27) Two years after its implementation the Commission will carry out a review of this Directive so as, inter alia, to ensure that the advance of technology or changes in the legal environment have not created barriers to achieving the aims stated in this Directive; it should examine the implications of associated technical areas and submit a report to the European Parliament and the Council on this subject;

(28) In accordance with the principles of subsidiarity and proportionality as set out in Article 5 of the Treaty, the objective of creating a harmonised legal

---

[1] OJ L 184, 17.7.1999, p. 23.

framework for the provision of electronic signatures and related services cannot be sufficiently achieved by the Member States and can therefore be better achieved by the Community; this Directive does not go beyond what is necessary to achieve that objective,

HAVE ADOPTED THIS DIRECTIVE:

Article 1 Scope

The purpose of this Directive is to facilitate the use of electronic signatures and to contribute to their legal recognition. It establishes a legal framework for electronic signatures and certain certification-services in order to ensure the proper functioning of the internal market.

It does not cover aspects related to the conclusion and validity of contracts or other legal obligations where there are requirements as regards form prescribed by national or Community law nor does it affect rules and limits, contained in national or Community law, governing the use of documents.

Article 2 Definitions

For the purpose of this Directive:

1. "electronic signature" means data in electronic form which are attached to or logically associated with other electronic data and which serve as a method of authentication;
2. "advanced electronic signature" means an electronic signature which meets the following requirements:
   (a) it is uniquely linked to the signatory;
   (b) it is capable of identifying the signatory;
   (c) it is created using means that the signatory can maintain under his sole control; and
   (d) it is linked to the data to which it relates in such a manner that any subsequent change of the data is detectable;
3. "signatory" means a person who holds a signature-creation device and acts either on his own behalf or on behalf of the natural or legal person or entity he represents;
4. "signature-creation data" means unique data, such as codes or private cryptographic keys, which are used by the signatory to create an electronic signature;
5. "signature-creation device" means configured software or hardware used to implement the signature-creation data;
6. "secure-signature-creation device" means a signature-creation device which meets the requirements laid down in Annex III;
7. "signature-verification-data" means data, such as codes or public cryptographic keys, which are used for the purpose of verifying an electronic signature;

8. "signature-verification device" means configured software or hardware used to implement the signature-verification-data;
9. "certificate" means an electronic attestation which links signature-verification data to a person and confirms the identity of that person;
10. "qualified certificate" means a certificate which meets the requirements laid down in Annex I and is provided by a certification-service-provider who fulfils the requirements laid down in Annex II;
11. "certification-service-provider" means an entity or a legal or natural person who issues certificates or provides other services related to electronic signatures;
12. "electronic-signature product" means hardware or software, or relevant components thereof, which are intended to be used by a certification-service-provider for the provision of electronic-signature services or are intended to be used for the creation or verification of electronic signatures;
13. "voluntary accreditation" means any permission, setting out rights and obligations specific to the provision of certification services, to be granted upon request by the certification-service-provider concerned, by the public or private body charged with the elaboration of, and supervision of compliance with, such rights and obligations, where the certification-service-provider is not entitled to exercise the rights stemming from the permission until it has received the decision by the body.

Article 3 Market access

1. Member States shall not make the provision of certification services subject to prior authorisation.
2. Without prejudice to the provisions of paragraph 1, Member States may introduce or maintain voluntary accreditation schemes aiming at enhanced levels of certification-service provision. All conditions related to such schemes must be objective, transparent, proportionate and non-discriminatory. Member States may not limit the number of accredited certification-service-providers for reasons which fall within the scope of this Directive.
3. Each Member State shall ensure the establishment of an appropriate system that allows for supervision of certification-service-providers which are established on its territory and issue qualified certificates to the public.
4. The conformity of secure signature-creation-devices with the requirements laid down in Annex III shall be determined by appropriate public or private bodies designated by Member States. The Commission shall establish criteria for Member States to determine whether a body should be so designated. That measure, designed to amend non-essential elements of this Directive by supplementing it, shall be adopted in accordance with the regulatory procedure with scrutiny referred to in Article 9(3).

A determination of conformity with the requirements laid down in Annex III made by the bodies referred to in the first subparagraph shall be recognised by all Member States.

5. The Commission may, in accordance with the procedure laid down in Article 9 (2), establish and publish reference numbers of generally recognised standards for electronic-signature products in the Official Journal of the European Communities. Member States shall presume that there is compliance with the requirements laid down in Annex II, point (f), and Annex III when an electronic signature product meets those standards.
6. Member States and the Commission shall work together to promote the development and use of signature-verification devices in the light of the recommendations for secure signature-verification laid down in Annex IV and in the interests of the consumer.
7. Member States may make the use of electronic signatures in the public sector subject to possible additional requirements. Such requirements shall be objective, transparent, proportionate and non-discriminatory and shall relate only to the specific characteristics of the application concerned. Such requirements may not constitute an obstacle to cross-border services for citizens.

Article 4 Internal market principles

1. Each Member State shall apply the national provisions which it adopts pursuant to this Directive to certification-service-providers established on its territory and to the services which they provide. Member States may not restrict the provision of certification-services originating in another Member State in the fields covered by this Directive.
2. Member States shall ensure that electronic-signature products which comply with this Directive are permitted to circulate freely in the internal market.

Article 5 Legal effects of electronic signatures

1. Member States shall ensure that advanced electronic signatures which are based on a qualified certificate and which are created by a secure-signature-creation device:
   (a) satisfy the legal requirements of a signature in relation to data in electronic form in the same manner as a handwritten signature satisfies those requirements in relation to paper-based data; and
   (b) are admissible as evidence in legal proceedings.
2. Member States shall ensure that an electronic signature is not denied legal effectiveness and admissibility as evidence in legal proceedings solely on the grounds that it is:
   - in electronic form, or
   - not based upon a qualified certificate, or
   - not based upon a qualified certificate issued by an accredited certification-service provider, or
   - not created by a secure signature-creation device.

Article 6 Liability

1. As a minimum, Member States shall ensure that by issuing a certificate as a qualified certificate to the public or by guaranteeing such a certificate to the public a certification-service-provider is liable for damage caused to any entity or legal or natural person who reasonably relies on that certificate:
   (a) as regards the accuracy at the time of issuance of all information contained in the qualified certificate and as regards the fact that the certificate contains all the details prescribed for a qualified certificate;
   (b) for assurance that at the time of the issuance of the certificate, the signatory identified in the qualified certificate held the signature-creation data corresponding to the signature-verification data given or identified in the certificate;
   (c) for assurance that the signature-creation data and the signature-verification data can be used in a complementary manner in cases where the certification-service-provider generates them both;

   unless the certification-service-provider proves that he has not acted negligently.
2. As a minimum Member States shall ensure that a certification-service-provider who has issued a certificate as a qualified certificate to the public is liable for damage caused to any entity or legal or natural person who reasonably relies on the certificate for failure to register revocation of the certificate unless the certification-service-provider proves that he has not acted negligently.
3. Member States shall ensure that a certification-service-provider may indicate in a qualified certificate limitations on the use of that certificate. provided that the limitations are recognisable to third parties. The certification-service-provider shall not be liable for damage arising from use of a qualified certificate which exceeds the limitations placed on it.
4. Member States shall ensure that a certification-service-provider may indicate in the qualified certificate a limit on the value of transactions for which the certificate can be used, provided that the limit is recognisable to third parties.

   The certification-service-provider shall not be liable for damage resulting from this maximum limit being exceeded.
5. The provisions of paragraphs 1 to 4 shall be without prejudice to Council Directive 93/13/EEC of 5 April 1993 on unfair terms in consumer contracts[1].

Article 7 International aspects

1. Member States shall ensure that certificates which are issued as qualified certificates to the public by a certification-service-provider established in a third country are recognised as legally equivalent to certificates issued by a certification-service-provider established within the Community if:

[1] OJ L 95, 21.4.1993, p. 29.

(a) the certification-service-provider fulfils the requirements laid down in this Directive and has been accredited under a voluntary accreditation scheme established in a Member State; or
(b) a certification-service-provider established within the Community which fulfils the requirements laid down in this Directive guarantees the certificate; or
(c) the certificate or the certification-service-provider is recognised under a bilateral or multilateral agreement between the Community and third countries or international organisations.

2. In order to facilitate cross-border certification services with third countries and legal recognition of advanced electronic signatures originating in third countries, the Commission shall make proposals, where appropriate, to achieve the effective implementation of standards and international agreements applicable to certification services. In particular, and where necessary, it shall submit proposals to the Council for appropriate mandates for the negotiation of bilateral and multilateral agreements with third countries and international organisations. The Council shall decide by qualified majority.
3. Whenever the Commission is informed of any difficulties encountered by Community undertakings with respect to market access in third countries, it may, if necessary, submit proposals to the Council for an appropriate mandate for the negotiation of comparable rights for Community undertakings in these third countries. The Council shall decide by qualified majority.

   Measures taken pursuant to this paragraph shall be without prejudice to the obligations of the Community and of the Member States under relevant international agreements.

Article 8 Data protection

1. Member States shall ensure that certification-service-providers and national bodies responsible for accreditation or supervision comply with the requirements laid down in Directive 95/46/EC of the European Parliament and of the Council of 24 October 1995 on tile protection of individuals with regard to the processing of personal data and on the free movement of such data[1].
2. Member States shall ensure that a certification-service-provider which issues certificates to the public may collect personal data only directly from the data subject, or after the explicit consent of the data subject, and only insofar as it is necessary for the purposes of issuing and maintaining the certificate. The data may not be collected or processed for any other purposes without the explicit consent of the data subject.
3. Without prejudice to the legal effect given to pseudonyms under national law, Member States shall not prevent certification service providers from indicating in the certificate a pseudonym instead of the signatory's name.

[1] OJ L 281, 23.11.1995, p. 31.

Article 9 Committee procedure

1. The Commission shall be assisted by the Electronic-Signature Committee.
2. Where reference is made to this paragraph, Articles 4 and 7 of Decision 1999/468/EC shall apply, having regard to the provisions of Article 8 thereof.

   The period provided for in Article 4(3) of Decision 1999/468/EC shall be set at three months.
3. Where reference is made to this paragraph, Article 5a(1) to (4) and Article 7 of Decision 1999/468/EC shall apply, having regard to the provisions of Article 8 thereof.

Article 10 Tasks of the committee

The committee shall clarify the requirements laid down in the Annexes of this Directive, the criteria referred to in Article 3(4) and the generally recognised standards for electronic signature products established and published pursuant to Article 3(5), in accordance with the procedure laid down in Article 9(2).

Article 11 Notification

1. Member States shall notify to the Commission and the other Member States the following:
   (a) information on national voluntary accreditation schemes, including any additional requirements pursuant to Article 3(7);
   (b) the names and addresses of the national bodies responsible for accreditation and supervision as well as of the bodies referred to in Article 3(4);
   (c) the names and addresses of all accredited national certification service providers.
2. Any information supplied under paragraph 1 and changes in respect of that information shall be notified by the Member States as soon as possible.

Article 12 Review

1. The Commission shall review the operation of this Directive and report thereon to the European Parliament and to the Council by 19 July 2003 at the latest.
2. The review shall inter alia assess whether the scope of this Directive should be modified, taking account of technological, market and legal developments. The report shall in particular include an assessment, on the basis of experience gained, of aspects of harmonisation. The report shall be accompanied, where appropriate, by legislative proposals.

Article 13 Implementation

1. Member States shall bring into force the laws, regulations and administrative provisions necessary to comply with this Directive before 19 July 2001. They shall forthwith inform the Commission thereof.

   When Member States adopt these measures, they shall contain a reference to this Directive or shall be accompanied by such a reference on the occasion of their official publication. The methods of making such reference shall be laid down by the Member States.

2. Member States shall communicate to the Commission the text of the main provisions of domestic law which they adopt in the field governed by this Directive.

Article 14 Entry into force

This Directive shall enter into force on the day of its publication in the Official Journal of the European Communities

Article 15 Addressees

This Directive is addressed to the Member States.

Done at Brussels, 13 December 1999.

For the European Parliament

The President

N. FONTAINE

For the Council

The President

S. HASSI

ANNEX I

Requirements for qualified certificates

Qualified certificates must contain:

(a) an indication that the certificate is issued as a qualified certificate;

(b) the identification of the certification-service-provider and the State in which it is established;

(c) the name of the signatory or a pseudonym, which shall be identified as such;

(d) provision for a specific attribute of the signatory to be included if relevant, depending on the purpose for which the certificate is intended;

(e) signature-verification data which correspond to signature-creation data under the control of the signatory;

(f) an indication of the beginning and end of the period of validity of the certificate;

(g) the identity code of the certificate;

(h) the advanced electronic signature of the certification-service-provider issuing it;

(i) limitations on the scope of use of the certificate, if applicable; and

(j) limits on the value of transactions for which the certificate can be used, if applicable.

ANNEX II

Requirements for certification-service-providers issuing qualified certificates

Certification-service-providers must:

(a) demonstrate the reliability necessary for providing certification services;

(b) ensure the operation of a prompt and secure directory and a secure and immediate revocation service;

(c) ensure that the date and time when a certificate is issued or revoked can be determined precisely;

(d) verify, by appropriate means in accordance with national law, the identity and, if applicable, any specific attributes of the person to which a qualified certificate is issued;

(e) employ personnel who possess the expert knowledge, experience, and qualifications necessary for the services provided, in particular competence at managerial level, expertise in electronic signature techology and familiarity with proper security procedures; they must also apply administrative and management procedures which are adequate and correspond to recognised standards;

(f) use trustworthy systems and products which are protected against modification and ensure the technical and cryptographic security of the process supported by them;

(g) take measures against forgery of certificates, and, in cases where the certification-service-provider generates signature-creation data, guarantee confidentiality during the process of generating such data;

(h) maintain sufficient financial resources to operate in conformity with the requirements laid down in the Directive, in particular to bear the risk of liability for damages, for example, by obtaining appropriate insurance;

(i) record all relevant information concerning a qualified certificate for an appropriate period of time, in particular for the purpose of providing evidence of certification for the purposes of legal proceedings. Such recording may be done electronically;

(j) not store or copy signature-creation data of the person to whom the certification-service-provider provided key management services;

(k) before entering into a contractual relationship with a person seeking a certificate to support his electronic signature inform that person by a durable means of communication of the precise terms and conditions regarding the use of the certificate, including any limitations on its use, the existence of a voluntary accreditation scheme and procedures for complaints and dispute settlement. Such information, which may be transmitted electronically, must be in writing and in redily understandable language. Relevant parts of this information must also be made available on request to third-parties relying on the certificate;

(l) use trustworthy systems to store certificates in a verifiable form so that:
   - only authorised persons can make entries and changes,
   - information can be checked for authenticity,
   - certificates are publicly available for retrieval in only those cases for which the certificate-holder's consent has been obtained, and
   - any technical changes compromising these security requirements are apparent to the operator.

ANNEX III

Requirements for secure signature-creation devices

1. Secure signature-creation devices must, by appropriate technical and procedural means, ensure at the least that:
   (a) the signature-creation-data used for signature generation can practically occur only once, and that their secrecy is reasonably assured;
   (b) the signature-creation-data used for signature generation cannot, with reasonable assurance, be derived and the signature is protected against forgery using currently available technology;
   (c) the signature-creation-data used for signature generation can be reliably protected by the legitimate signatory against the use of others.

2. Secure signature-creation devices must not alter the data to be signed or prevent such data from being presented to the signatory prior to the signature process.

ANNEX IV

Recommendations for secure signature verification

During the signature-verification process it should be ensured with reasonable certainty that:

(a) the data used for verifying the signature correspond to the data displayed to the verifier;

(b) the signature is reliably verified and the result of that verification is correctly displayed;

(c) the verifier can, as necessary, reliably establish the contents of the signed data;

(d) the authenticity and validity of the certificate required at the time of signature verification are reliably verified;

(e) the result of verification and the signatory's identity are correctly displayed;

(f) the use of a pseudonym is clearly indicated; and

(g) any security-relevant changes can be detected.

9. Directive 2000/31/EC of the European Parliament and of the Council of 8 June 2000 on certain legal aspects of information society services, in particular electronic commerce, in the Internal Market ('Directive on electronic commerce')

(OJ L 178 , 17/07/2000 P.01 – 16)

THE EUROPEAN PARLIAMENT AND THE COUNCIL OF THE EUROPEAN UNION,

Having regard to the Treaty establishing the European Community, and in particular Articles 47(2), 55 and 95 thereof,

Having regard to the proposal from the Commission[1],

Having regard to the opinion of the Economic and Social Committee[2],

Acting in accordance with the procedure laid down in Article 251 of the Treaty[3],

Whereas:

(1) The European Union is seeking to forge ever closer links between the States and peoples of Europe, to ensure economic and social progress; in accordance with Article 14(2) of the Treaty, the internal market comprises an area without internal frontiers in which the free movements of goods, services and the freedom of establishment are ensured; the development of information society services within the area without internal frontiers is vital to eliminating the barriers which divide the European peoples.

(2) The development of electronic commerce within the information society offers significant employment opportunities in the Community, particularly in small and medium-sized enterprises, and will stimulate economic growth and investment in innovation by European companies, and can also enhance the competitiveness of European industry, provided that everyone has access to the Internet.

(3) Community law and the characteristics of the Community legal order are a vital asset to enable European citizens and operators to take full advantage, without consideration of borders, of the opportunities afforded by electronic commerce; this Directive therefore has the purpose of ensuring a high level of Community legal integration in order to establish a real area without internal borders for information society services.

(4) It is important to ensure that electronic commerce could fully benefit from the internal market and therefore that, as with Council Directive 89/552/EEC of 3 October 1989 on the coordination of certain provisions laid down by law,

---

1 OJ C 30, 5.2.1999, p. 4.

2 OJ C 169, 16.6.1999, p. 36.

3 Opinion of the European Parliament of 6 May 1999 (OJ C 279, 1.10.1999, p. 389), Council common position of 28 February 2000 (OJ C 128, 8.5.2000, p. 32) and Decision of the European Parliament of 4 May 2000 (not yet published in the Official Journal).

regulation or administrative action in Member States concerning the pursuit of television broadcasting activities[1], a high level of Community integration is achieved.

(5) The development of information society services within the Community is hampered by a number of legal obstacles to the proper functioning of the internal market which make less attractive the exercise of the freedom of establishment and the freedom to provide services; these obstacles arise from divergences in legislation and from the legal uncertainty as to which national rules apply to such services; in the absence of coordination and adjustment of legislation in the relevant areas, obstacles might be justified in the light of the case-law of the Court of Justice of the European Communities; legal uncertainty exists with regard to the extent to which Member States may control services originating from another Member State.

(6) In the light of Community objectives, of Articles 43 and 49 of the Treaty and of secondary Community law, these obstacles should be eliminated by coordinating certain national laws and by clarifying certain legal concepts at Community level to the extent necessary for the proper functioning of the internal market; by dealing only with certain specific matters which give rise to problems for the internal market, this Directive is fully consistent with the need to respect the principle of subsidiarity as set out in Article 5 of the Treaty.

(7) In order to ensure legal certainty and consumer confidence, this Directive must lay down a clear and general framework to cover certain legal aspects of electronic commerce in the internal market.

(8) The objective of this Directive is to create a legal framework to ensure the free movement of information society services between Member States and not to harmonise the field of criminal law as such.

(9) The free movement of information society services can in many cases be a specific reflection in Community law of a more general principle, namely freedom of expression as enshrined in Article 10(1) of the Convention for the Protection of Human Rights and Fundamental Freedoms, which has been ratified by all the Member States; for this reason, directives covering the supply of information society services must ensure that this activity may be engaged in freely in the light of that Article, subject only to the restrictions laid down in paragraph 2 of that Article and in Article 46(1) of the Treaty; this Directive is not intended to affect national fundamental rules and principles relating to freedom of expression.

(10) In accordance with the principle of proportionality, the measures provided for in this Directive are strictly limited to the minimum needed to achieve the objective of the proper functioning of the internal market; where action at Community level is necessary, and in order to guarantee an area which is truly without internal frontiers as far as electronic commerce is concerned, the

[1] OJ L 298, 17.10.1989, p. 23. Directive as amended by Directive 97/36/EC of the European Parliament and of the Council (OJ L 202, 30.7.1997, p. 60).

Directive must ensure a high level of protection of objectives of general interest, in particular the protection of minors and human dignity, consumer protection and the protection of public health; according to Article 152 of the Treaty, the protection of public health is an essential component of other Community policies.

(11) This Directive is without prejudice to the level of protection for, in particular, public health and consumer interests, as established by Community acts; amongst others, Council Directive 93/13/EEC of 5 April 1993 on unfair terms in consumer contracts[1] and Directive 97/7/EC of the European Parliament and of the Council of 20 May 1997 on the protection of consumers in respect of distance contracts[2] form a vital element for protecting consumers in contractual matters; those Directives also apply in their entirety to information society services; that same Community acquis, which is fully applicable to information society services, also embraces in particular Council Directive 84/450/EEC of 10 September 1984 concerning misleading and comparative advertising[3], Council Directive 87/102/EEC of 22 December 1986 for the approximation of the laws, regulations and administrative provisions of the Member States concerning consumer credit[4], Council Directive 93/22/EEC of 10 May 1993 on investment services in the securities field[5], Council Directive 90/314/EEC of 13 June 1990 on package travel, package holidays and package tours[6], Directive 98/6/EC of the European Parliament and of the Council of 16 February 1998 on consumer production in the indication of prices of products offered to consumers[7], Council Directive 92/59/EEC of 29 June 1992 on general product safety[8], Directive 94/47/EC of the European Parliament and of the Council of 26 October 1994 on the protection of purchasers in respect of certain aspects on contracts relating to the purchase of the right to use immovable properties on a timeshare basis[9], Directive 98/27/EC of the European Parliament and of the Council of 19 May 1998 on injunctions for the protection of consumers' interests[10], Council Directive 85/374/EEC of 25 July 1985 on the approximation of the laws, regulations and administrative provisions concerning liability for defective products[11], Directive 1999/44/EC of the European Parliament and of the Council of 25 May 1999 on certain aspects of the sale of consumer goods

1 OJ L 95, 21.4.1993, p. 29.
2 OJ L 144, 4.6.1999, p. 19.
3 OJ L 250, 19.9.1984, p. 17. Directive as amended by Directive 97/55/EC of the European Parliament and of the Council (OJ L 290, 23.10.1997, p. 18).
4 OJ L 42, 12.2.1987, p. 48. Directive as last amended by Directive 98/7/EC of the European Parliament and of the Council (OJ L 101, 1.4.1998, p. 17).
5 OJ L 141, 11.6.1993, p. 27. Directive as last amended by Directive 97/9/EC of the European Parliament and of the Council (OJ L 84, 26.3.1997, p. 22).
6 OJ L 158, 23.6.1990, p. 59
7 OJ L 80, 18.3.1998, p. 27.
8 OJ L 228, 11.8.1992, p. 24.
9 OJ L 280, 29.10.1994, p. 83.
10 OJ L 166, 11.6.1998, p. 51. Directive as amended by Directive 1999/44/EC (OJ L 171, 7.7.1999, p. 12).
11 OJ L 210, 7.8.1985, p. 29. Directive as amended by Directive 1999/34/EC (OJ L 141, 4.6.1999, p. 20).

and associated guarantees[1], the future Directive of the European Parliament and of the Council concerning the distance marketing of consumer financial services and Council Directive 92/28/EEC of 31 March 1992 on the advertising of medicinal products[2]; this Directive should be without prejudice to Directive 98/43/EC of the European Parliament and of the Council of 6 July 1998 on the approximation of the laws, regulations and administrative provisions of the Member States relating to the advertising and sponsorship of tobacco products[3] adopted within the framework of the internal market, or to directives on the protection of public health; this Directive complements information requirements established by the abovementioned Directives and in particular Directive 97/7/EC.

(12) It is necessary to exclude certain activities from the scope of this Directive, on the grounds that the freedom to provide services in these fields cannot, at this stage, be guaranteed under the Treaty or existing secondary legislation; excluding these activities does not preclude any instruments which might prove necessary for the proper functioning of the internal market; taxation, particularly value added tax imposed on a large number of the services covered by this Directive, must be excluded form the scope of this Directive.

(13) This Directive does not aim to establish rules on fiscal obligations nor does it pre-empt the drawing up of Community instruments concerning fiscal aspects of electronic commerce.

(14) The protection of individuals with regard to the processing of personal data is solely governed by Directive 95/46/EC of the European Parliament and of the Council of 24 October 1995 on the protection of individuals with regard to the processing of personal data and on the free movement of such data[4] and Directive 97/66/EC of the European Parliament and of the Council of 15 December 1997 concerning the processing of personal data and the protection of privacy in the telecommunications sector[5] which are fully applicable to information society services; these Directives already establish a Community legal framework in the field of personal data and therefore it is not necessary to cover this issue in this Directive in order to ensure the smooth functioning of the internal market, in particular the free movement of personal data between Member States; the implementation and application of this Directive should be made in full compliance with the principles relating to the protection of personal data, in particular as regards unsolicited commercial communication and the liability of intermediaries; this Directive cannot prevent the anonymous use of open networks such as the Internet.

(15) The confidentiality of communications is guaranteed by Article 5 Directive 97/66/EC; in accordance with that Directive, Member States must prohibit any

[1] OJ L 171, 7.7.1999, p. 12.
[2] OJ L 113, 30.4.1992, p. 13.
[3] OJ L 213, 30.7.1998, p. 9.
[4] OJ L 281, 23.11.1995, p. 31.
[5] OJ L 24, 30.1.1998, p. 1.

kind of interception or surveillance of such communications by others than the senders and receivers, except when legally authorised.

(16) The exclusion of gambling activities from the scope of application of this Directive covers only games of chance, lotteries and betting transactions, which involve wagering a stake with monetary value; this does not cover promotional competitions or games where the purpose is to encourage the sale of goods or services and where payments, if they arise, serve only to acquire the promoted goods or services.

(17) The definition of information society services already exists in Community law in Directive 98/34/EC of the European Parliament and of the Council of 22 June 1998 laying down a procedure for the provision of information in the field of technical standards and regulations and of rules on information society services[1] and in Directive 98/84/EC of the European Parliament and of the Council of 20 November 1998 on the legal protection of services based on, or consisting of, conditional access[2]; this definition covers any service normally provided for remuneration, at a distance, by means of electronic equipment for the processing (including digital compression) and storage of data, and at the individual request of a recipient of a service; those services referred to in the indicative list in Annex V to Directive 98/34/EC which do not imply data processing and storage are not covered by this definition.

(18) Information society services span a wide range of economic activities which take place on-line; these activities can, in particular, consist of selling goods on-line; activities such as the delivery of goods as such or the provision of services off-line are not covered; information society services are not solely restricted to services giving rise to on-line contracting but also, in so far as they represent an economic activity, extend to services which are not remunerated by those who receive them, such as those offering on-line information or commercial communications, or those providing tools allowing for search, access and retrieval of data; information society services also include services consisting of the transmission of information via a communication network, in providing access to a communication network or in hosting information provided by a recipient of the service; television broadcasting within the meaning of Directive EEC/89/552 and radio broadcasting are not information society services because they are not provided at individual request; by contrast, services which are transmitted point to point, such as video-on-demand or the provision of commercial communications by electronic mail are information society services; the use of electronic mail or equivalent individual communications for instance by natural persons acting outside their trade, business or profession including their use for the conclusion of contracts between such persons is not an information society service; the contractual relationship between an employee and his employer is not an information society service; activities which by their very nature cannot be carried out at a distance and by electronic means, such as

1 OJ L 204, 21.7.1998, p. 37. Directive as amended by Directive 98/48/EC (OJ L 217, 5.8.1998, p. 18).
2 OJ L 320, 28.11.1998, p. 54.

the statutory auditing of company accounts or medical advice requiring the physical examination of a patient are not information society services.

(19) The place at which a service provider is established should be determined in conformity with the case-law of the Court of Justice according to which the concept of establishment involves the actual pursuit of an economic activity through a fixed establishment for an indefinite period; this requirement is also fulfilled where a company is constituted for a given period; the place of establishment of a company providing services via an Internet website is not the place at which the technology supporting its website is located or the place at which its website is accessible but the place where it pursues its economic activity; in cases where a provider has several places of establishment it is important to determine from which place of establishment the service concerned is provided; in cases where it is difficult to determine from which of several places of establishment a given service is provided, this is the place where the provider has the centre of his activities relating to this particular service.

(20) The definition of "recipient of a service" covers all types of usage of information society services, both by persons who provide information on open networks such as the Internet and by persons who seek information on the Internet for private or professional reasons.

(21) The scope of the coordinated field is without prejudice to future Community harmonisation relating to information society services and to future legislation adopted at national level in accordance with Community law; the coordinated field covers only requirements relating to on-line activities such as on-line information, on-line advertising, on-line shopping, on-line contracting and does not concern Member States' legal requirements relating to goods such as safety standards, labelling obligations, or liability for goods, or Member States' requirements relating to the delivery or the transport of goods, including the distribution of medicinal products; the coordinated field does not cover the exercise of rights of pre-emption by public authorities concerning certain goods such as works of art.

(22) Information society services should be supervised at the source of the activity, in order to ensure an effective protection of public interest objectives; to that end, it is necessary to ensure that the competent authority provides such protection not only for the citizens of its own country but for all Community citizens; in order to improve mutual trust between Member States, it is essential to state clearly this responsibility on the part of the Member State where the services originate; moreover, in order to effectively guarantee freedom to provide services and legal certainty for suppliers and recipients of services, such information society services should in principle be subject to the law of the Member State in which the service provider is established.

(23) This Directive neither aims to establish additional rules on private international law relating to conflicts of law nor does it deal with the jurisdiction of Courts; provisions of the applicable law designated by rules of private

international law must not restrict the freedom to provide information society services as established in this Directive.

(24) In the context of this Directive, notwithstanding the rule on the control at source of information society services, it is legitimate under the conditions established in this Directive for Member States to take measures to restrict the free movement of information society services.

(25) National courts, including civil courts, dealing with private law disputes can take measures to derogate from the freedom to provide information society services in conformity with conditions established in this Directive.

(26) Member States, in conformity with conditions established in this Directive, may apply their national rules on criminal law and criminal proceedings with a view to taking all investigative and other measures necessary for the detection and prosecution of criminal offences, without there being a need to notify such measures to the Commission.

(27) This Directive, together with the future Directive of the European Parliament and of the Council concerning the distance marketing of consumer financial services, contributes to the creating of a legal framework for the on-line provision of financial services; this Directive does not pre-empt future initiatives in the area of financial services in particular with regard to the harmonisation of rules of conduct in this field; the possibility for Member States, established in this Directive, under certain circumstances of restricting the freedom to provide information society services in order to protect consumers also covers measures in the area of financial services in particular measures aiming at protecting investors.

(28) The Member States' obligation not to subject access to the activity of an information society service provider to prior authorisation does not concern postal services covered by Directive 97/67/EC of the European Parliament and of the Council of 15 December 1997 on common rules for the development of the internal market of Community postal services and the improvement of quality of service[1] consisting of the physical delivery of a printed electronic mail message and does not affect voluntary accreditation systems, in particular for providers of electronic signature certification service.

(29) Commercial communications are essential for the financing of information society services and for developing a wide variety of new, charge-free services; in the interests of consumer protection and fair trading, commercial communications, including discounts, promotional offers and promotional competitions or games, must meet a number of transparency requirements; these requirements are without prejudice to Directive 97/7/EC; this Directive should not affect existing Directives on commercial communications, in particular Directive 98/43/EC.

(30) The sending of unsolicited commercial communications by electronic mail may be undesirable for consumers and information society service providers and

[1] OJ L 15, 21.1.1998, p. 14.

may disrupt the smooth functioning of interactive networks; the question of consent by recipient of certain forms of unsolicited commercial communications is not addressed by this Directive, but has already been addressed, in particular, by Directive 97/7/EC and by Directive 97/66/EC; in Member States which authorise unsolicited commercial communications by electronic mail, the setting up of appropriate industry filtering initiatives should be encouraged and facilitated; in addition it is necessary that in any event unsolicited commercial communities are clearly identifiable as such in order to improve transparency and to facilitate the functioning of such industry initiatives; unsolicited commercial communications by electronic mail should not result in additional communication costs for the recipient.

(31) Member States which allow the sending of unsolicited commercial communications by electronic mail without prior consent of the recipient by service providers established in their territory have to ensure that the service providers consult regularly and respect the opt-out registers in which natural persons not wishing to receive such commercial communications can register themselves.

(32) In order to remove barriers to the development of cross-border services within the Community which members of the regulated professions might offer on the Internet, it is necessary that compliance be guaranteed at Community level with professional rules aiming, in particular, to protect consumers or public health; codes of conduct at Community level would be the best means of determining the rules on professional ethics applicable to commercial communication; the drawing-up or, where appropriate, the adaptation of such rules should be encouraged without prejudice to the autonomy of professional bodies and associations.

(33) This Directive complements Community law and national law relating to regulated professions maintaining a coherent set of applicable rules in this field.

(34) Each Member State is to amend its legislation containing requirements, and in particular requirements as to form, which are likely to curb the use of contracts by electronic means; the examination of the legislation requiring such adjustment should be systematic and should cover all the necessary stages and acts of the contractual process, including the filing of the contract; the result of this amendment should be to make contracts concluded electronically workable; the legal effect of electronic signatures is dealt with by Directive 1999/93/EC of the European Parliament and of the Council of 13 December 1999 on a Community framework for electronic signatures[1]; the acknowledgement of receipt by a service provider may take the form of the on-line provision of the service paid for.

(35) This Directive does not affect Member States' possibility of maintaining or establishing general or specific legal requirements for contracts which can be

[1] OJ L 13, 19.1.2000, p. 12.

fulfilled by electronic means, in particular requirements concerning secure electronic signatures.

(36) Member States may maintain restrictions for the use of electronic contracts with regard to contracts requiring by law the involvement of courts, public authorities, or professions exercising public authority; this possibility also covers contracts which require the involvement of courts, public authorities, or professions exercising public authority in order to have an effect with regard to third parties as well as contracts requiring by law certification or attestation by a notary.

(37) Member States' obligation to remove obstacles to the use of electronic contracts concerns only obstacles resulting from legal requirements and not practical obstacles resulting from the impossibility of using electronic means in certain cases.

(38) Member States' obligation to remove obstacles to the use of electronic contracts is to be implemented in conformity with legal requirements for contracts enshrined in Community law.

(39) The exceptions to the provisions concerning the contracts concluded exclusively by electronic mail or by equivalent individual communications provided for by this Directive, in relation to information to be provided and the placing of orders, should not enable, as a result, the by-passing of those provisions by providers of information society services.

(40) Both existing and emerging disparities in Member States' legislation and case-law concerning liability of service providers acting as intermediaries prevent the smooth functioning of the internal market, in particular by impairing the development of cross-border services and producing distortions of competition; service providers have a duty to act, under certain circumstances, with a view to preventing or stopping illegal activities; this Directive should constitute the appropriate basis for the development of rapid and reliable procedures for removing and disabling access to illegal information; such mechanisms could be developed on the basis of voluntary agreements between all parties concerned and should be encouraged by Member States; it is in the interest of all parties involved in the provision of information society services to adopt and implement such procedures; the provisions of this Directive relating to liability should not preclude the development and effective operation, by the different interested parties, of technical systems of protection and identification and of technical surveillance instruments made possible by digital technology within the limits laid down by Directives 95/46/EC and 97/66/EC.

(41) This Directive strikes a balance between the different interests at stake and establishes principles upon which industry agreements and standards can be based.

(42) The exemptions from liability established in this Directive cover only cases where the activity of the information society service provider is limited to the technical process of operating and giving access to a communication network

over which information made available by third parties is transmitted or temporarily stored, for the sole purpose of making the transmission more efficient; this activity is of a mere technical, automatic and passive nature, which implies that the information society service provider has neither knowledge of nor control over the information which is transmitted or stored.

(43) A service provider can benefit from the exemptions for "mere conduit" and for "caching" when he is in no way involved with the information transmitted; this requires among other things that he does not modify the information that he transmits; this requirement does not cover manipulations of a technical nature which take place in the course of the transmission as they do not alter the integrity of the information contained in the transmission.

(44) A service provider who deliberately collaborates with one of the recipients of his service in order to undertake illegal acts goes beyond the activities of "mere conduit" or "caching" and as a result cannot benefit from the liability exemptions established for these activities.

(45) The limitations of the liability of intermediary service providers established in this Directive do not affect the possibility of injunctions of different kinds; such injunctions can in particular consist of orders by courts or administrative authorities requiring the termination or prevention of any infringement, including the removal of illegal information or the disabling of access to it.

(46) In order to benefit from a limitation of liability, the provider of an information society service, consisting of the storage of information, upon obtaining actual knowledge or awareness of illegal activities has to act expeditiously to remove or to disable access to the information concerned; the removal or disabling of access has to be undertaken in the observance of the principle of freedom of expression and of procedures established for this purpose at national level; this Directive does not affect Member States' possibility of establishing specific requirements which must be fulfilled expeditiously prior to the removal or disabling of information.

(47) Member States are prevented from imposing a monitoring obligation on service providers only with respect to obligations of a general nature; this does not concern monitoring obligations in a specific case and, in particular, does not affect orders by national authorities in accordance with national legislation.

(48) This Directive does not affect the possibility for Member States of requiring service providers, who host information provided by recipients of their service, to apply duties of care, which can reasonably be expected from them and which are specified by national law, in order to detect and prevent certain types of illegal activities.

(49) Member States and the Commission are to encourage the drawing-up of codes of conduct; this is not to impair the voluntary nature of such codes and the possibility for interested parties of deciding freely whether to adhere to such codes.

(50) It is important that the proposed directive on the harmonisation of certain aspects of copyright and related rights in the information society and this Directive come into force within a similar time scale with a view to establishing a clear framework of rules relevant to the issue of liability of intermediaries for copyright and relating rights infringements at Community level.

(51) Each Member State should be required, where necessary, to amend any legislation which is liable to hamper the use of schemes for the out-of-court settlement of disputes through electronic channels; the result of this amendment must be to make the functioning of such schemes genuinely and effectively possible in law and in practice, even across borders.

(52) The effective exercise of the freedoms of the internal market makes it necessary to guarantee victims effective access to means of settling disputes; damage which may arise in connection with information society services is characterised both by its rapidity and by its geographical extent; in view of this specific character and the need to ensure that national authorities do not endanger the mutual confidence which they should have in one another, this Directive requests Member States to ensure that appropriate court actions are available; Member States should examine the need to provide access to judicial procedures by appropriate electronic means.

(53) Directive 98/27/EC, which is applicable to information society services, provides a mechanism relating to actions for an injunction aimed at the protection of the collective interests of consumers; this mechanism will contribute to the free movement of information society services by ensuring a high level of consumer protection.

(54) The sanctions provided for under this Directive are without prejudice to any other sanction or remedy provided under national law; Member States are not obliged to provide criminal sanctions for infringement of national provisions adopted pursuant to this Directive.

(55) This Directive does not affect the law applicable to contractual obligations relating to consumer contracts; accordingly, this Directive cannot have the result of depriving the consumer of the protection afforded to him by the mandatory rules relating to contractual obligations of the law of the Member State in which he has his habitual residence.

(56) As regards the derogation contained in this Directive regarding contractual obligations concerning contracts concluded by consumers, those obligations should be interpreted as including information on the essential elements of the content of the contract, including consumer rights, which have a determining influence on the decision to contract.

(57) The Court of Justice has consistently held that a Member State retains the right to take measures against a service provider that is established in another Member State but directs all or most of his activity to the territory of the first Member State if the choice of establishment was made with a view to evading

the legislation that would have applied to the provider had he been established on the territory of the first Member State.

(58) This Directive should not apply to services supplied by service providers established in a third country; in view of the global dimension of electronic commerce, it is, however, appropriate to ensure that the Community rules are consistent with international rules; this Directive is without prejudice to the results of discussions within international organisations (amongst others WTO, OECD, Uncitral) on legal issues.

(59) Despite the global nature of electronic communications, coordination of national regulatory measures at European Union level is necessary in order to avoid fragmentation of the internal market, and for the establishment of an appropriate European regulatory framework; such coordination should also contribute to the establishment of a common and strong negotiating position in international forums.

(60) In order to allow the unhampered development of electronic commerce, the legal framework must be clear and simple, predictable and consistent with the rules applicable at international level so that it does not adversely affect the competitiveness of European industry or impede innovation in that sector.

(61) If the market is actually to operate by electronic means in the context of globalisation, the European Union and the major non-European areas need to consult each other with a view to making laws and procedures compatible.

(62) Cooperation with third countries should be strengthened in the area of electronic commerce, in particular with applicant countries, the developing countries and the European Union's other trading partners.

(63) The adoption of this Directive will not prevent the Member States from taking into account the various social, societal and cultural implications which are inherent in the advent of the information society; in particular it should not hinder measures which Member States might adopt in conformity with Community law to achieve social, cultural and democratic goals taking into account their linguistic diversity, national and regional specificities as well as their cultural heritage, and to ensure and maintain public access to the widest possible range of information society services; in any case, the development of the information society is to ensure that Community citizens can have access to the cultural European heritage provided in the digital environment.

(64) Electronic communication offers the Member States an excellent means of providing public services in the cultural, educational and linguistic fields.

(65) The Council, in its resolution of 19 January 1999 on the consumer dimension of the information society[1], stressed that the protection of consumers deserved special attention in this field; the Commission will examine the degree to which existing consumer protection rules provide insufficient protection in the context of the information society and will identify, where necessary, the deficiencies of

[1] OJ C 23, 28.1.1999, p. 1.

this legislation and those issues which could require additional measures; if need be, the Commission should make specific additional proposals to resolve such deficiencies that will thereby have been identified,

HAVE ADOPTED THIS DIRECTIVE:

CHAPTER I : GENERAL PROVISIONS

Article 1 Objective and scope

1. This Directive seeks to contribute to the proper functioning of the internal market by ensuring the free movement of information society services between the Member States.
2. This Directive approximates, to the extent necessary for the achievement of the objective set out in paragraph 1, certain national provisions on information society services relating to the internal market, the establishment of service providers, commercial communications, electronic contracts, the liability of intermediaries, codes of conduct, out-of-court dispute settlements, court actions and cooperation between Member States.
3. This Directive complements Community law applicable to information society services without prejudice to the level of protection for, in particular, public health and consumer interests, as established by Community acts and national legislation implementing them in so far as this does not restrict the freedom to provide information society services.
4. This Directive does not establish additional rules on private international law nor does it deal with the jurisdiction of Courts.
5. This Directive shall not apply to:
   (a) the field of taxation;
   (b) questions relating to information society services covered by Directives 95/46/EC and 97/66/EC;
   (c) questions relating to agreements or practices governed by cartel law;
   (d) the following activities of information society services:
      - the activities of notaries or equivalent professions to the extent that they involve a direct and specific connection with the exercise of public authority,
      - the representation of a client and defence of his interests before the courts,
      - gambling activities which involve wagering a stake with monetary value in games of chance, including lotteries and betting transactions.
6. This Directive does not affect measures taken at Community or national level, in the respect of Community law, in order to promote cultural and linguistic diversity and to ensure the defence of pluralism.

Article 2 Definitions

For the purpose of this Directive, the following terms shall bear the following meanings:

(a) "information society services": services within the meaning of Article 1(2) of Directive 98/34/EC as amended by Directive 98/48/EC;
(b) "service provider": any natural or legal person providing an information society service;
(c) "established service provider": a service provider who effectively pursues an economic activity using a fixed establishment for an indefinite period. The presence and use of the technical means and technologies required to provide the service do not, in themselves, constitute an establishment of the provider;
(d) "recipient of the service": any natural or legal person who, for professional ends or otherwise, uses an information society service, in particular for the purposes of seeking information or making it accessible;
(e) "consumer": any natural person who is acting for purposes which are outside his or her trade, business or profession;
(f) "commercial communication": any form of communication designed to promote, directly or indirectly, the goods, services or image of a company, organisation or person pursuing a commercial, industrial or craft activity or exercising a regulated profession. The following do not in themselves constitute commercial communications:
  - information allowing direct access to the activity of the company, organisation or person, in particular a domain name or an electronic-mail address,
  - communications relating to the goods, services or image of the company, organisation or person compiled in an independent manner, particularly when this is without financial consideration;
(g) "regulated profession": any profession within the meaning of either Article 1(d) of Council Directive 89/48/EEC of 21 December 1988 on a general system for the recognition of higher-education diplomas awarded on completion of professional education and training of at least three-years' duration[1] or of Article 1(f) of Council Directive 92/51/EEC of 18 June 1992 on a second general system for the recognition of professional education and training to supplement Directive 89/48/EEC[2];
(h) "coordinated field": requirements laid down in Member States' legal systems applicable to information society service providers or information society services, regardless of whether they are of a general nature or specifically designed for them.
  (i) The coordinated field concerns requirements with which the service provider has to comply in respect of:
    - the taking up of the activity of an information society service, such as requirements concerning qualifications, authorisation or notification,
    - the pursuit of the activity of an information society service, such as requirements concerning the behaviour of the service provider,

[1] OJ L 19, 24.1.1989, p. 16.

[2] OJ L 209, 24.7.1992, p. 25. Directive as last amended by Commission Directive 97/38/EC (OJ L 184, 12.7.1997, p. 31).

requirements regarding the quality or content of the service including those applicable to advertising and contracts, or requirements concerning the liability of the service provider;

(ii) The coordinated field does not cover requirements such as:

- requirements applicable to goods as such,
- requirements applicable to the delivery of goods,
- requirements applicable to services not provided by electronic means.

Article 3 Internal market

1. Each Member State shall ensure that the information society services provided by a service provider established on its territory comply with the national provisions applicable in the Member State in question which fall within the coordinated field.
2. Member States may not, for reasons falling within the coordinated field, restrict the freedom to provide information society services from another Member State.
3. Paragraphs 1 and 2 shall not apply to the fields referred to in the Annex.
4. Member States may take measures to derogate from paragraph 2 in respect of a given information society service if the following conditions are fulfilled:

   (a) the measures shall be:

   (i) necessary for one of the following reasons:

   - public policy, in particular the prevention, investigation, detection and prosecution of criminal offences, including the protection of minors and the fight against any incitement to hatred on grounds of race, sex, religion or nationality, and violations of human dignity concerning individual persons,
   - the protection of public health,
   - public security, including the safeguarding of national security and defence,
   - the protection of consumers, including investors;

   (ii) taken against a given information society service which prejudices the objectives referred to in point (i) or which presents a serious and grave risk of prejudice to those objectives;

   (iii) proportionate to those objectives;

   (b) before taking the measures in question and without prejudice to court proceedings, including preliminary proceedings and acts carried out in the framework of a criminal investigation, the Member State has:

   - asked the Member State referred to in paragraph 1 to take measures and the latter did not take such measures, or they were inadequate,
   - notified the Commission and the Member State referred to in paragraph 1 of its intention to take such measures.

5. Member States may, in the case of urgency, derogate from the conditions stipulated in paragraph 4(b). Where this is the case, the measures shall be notified in the shortest possible time to the Commission and to the Member

State referred to in paragraph 1, indicating the reasons for which the Member State considers that there is urgency.

6. Without prejudice to the Member State's possibility of proceeding with the measures in question, the Commission shall examine the compatibility of the notified measures with Community law in the shortest possible time; where it comes to the conclusion that the measure is incompatible with Community law, the Commission shall ask the Member State in question to refrain from taking any proposed measures or urgently to put an end to the measures in question.

CHAPTER II : PRINCIPLES

Section 1: **Establishment and information requirements**

Article 4 Principle excluding prior authorisation

1. Member States shall ensure that the taking up and pursuit of the activity of an information society service provider may not be made subject to prior authorisation or any other requirement having equivalent effect.
2. Paragraph 1 shall be without prejudice to authorisation schemes which are not specifically and exclusively targeted at information society services, or which are covered by Directive 97/13/EC of the European Parliament and of the Council of 10 April 1997 on a common framework for general authorisations and individual licences in the field of telecommunications services[1].

Article 5 General information to be provided

1. In addition to other information requirements established by Community law, Member States shall ensure that the service provider shall render easily, directly and permanently accessible to the recipients of the service and competent authorities, at least the following information:
   (a) the name of the service provider;
   (b) the geographic address at which the service provider is established;
   (c) the details of the service provider, including his electronic mail address, which allow him to be contacted rapidly and communicated with in a direct and effective manner;
   (d) where the service provider is registered in a trade or similar public register, the trade register in which the service provider is entered and his registration number, or equivalent means of identification in that register;
   (e) where the activity is subject to an authorisation scheme, the particulars of the relevant supervisory authority;
   (f) as concerns the regulated professions:
      - any professional body or similar institution with which the service provider is registered,
      - the professional title and the Member State where it has been granted,

[1] OJ L 117, 7.5.1997, p. 15.

- a reference to the applicable professional rules in the Member State of establishment and the means to access them;

(g) where the service provider undertakes an activity that is subject to VAT, the identification number referred to in Article 22(1) of the sixth Council Directive 77/388/EEC of 17 May 1977 on the harmonisation of the laws of the Member States relating to turnover taxes - Common system of value added tax: uniform basis of assessment[1].

2. In addition to other information requirements established by Community law, Member States shall at least ensure that, where information society services refer to prices, these are to be indicated clearly and unambiguously and, in particular, must indicate whether they are inclusive of tax and delivery costs.

Section 2: **Commercial communications**

Article 6 Information to be provided

In addition to other information requirements established by Community law, Member States shall ensure that commercial communications which are part of, or constitute, an information society service comply at least with the following conditions:

(a) the commercial communication shall be clearly identifiable as such;
(b) the natural or legal person on whose behalf the commercial communication is made shall be clearly identifiable;
(c) promotional offers, such as discounts, premiums and gifts, where permitted in the Member State where the service provider is established, shall be clearly identifiable as such, and the conditions which are to be met to qualify for them shall be easily accessible and be presented clearly and unambiguously;
(d) promotional competitions or games, where permitted in the Member State where the service provider is established, shall be clearly identifiable as such, and the conditions for participation shall be easily accessible and be presented clearly and unambiguously.

Article 7 Unsolicited commercial communication

1. In addition to other requirements established by Community law, Member States which permit unsolicited commercial communication by electronic mail shall ensure that such commercial communication by a service provider established in their territory shall be identifiable clearly and unambiguously as such as soon as it is received by the recipient.

2. Without prejudice to Directive 97/7/EC and Directive 97/66/EC, Member States shall take measures to ensure that service providers undertaking unsolicited commercial communications by electronic mail consult regularly and respect the opt-out registers in which natural persons not wishing to receive such commercial communications can register themselves.

---

[1] OJ L 145, 13.6.1977, p. 1. Directive as last amended by Directive 1999/85/EC (OJ L 277, 28.10.1999, p. 34).

Article 8 Regulated professions

1. Member States shall ensure that the use of commercial communications which are part of, or constitute, an information society service provided by a member of a regulated profession is permitted subject to compliance with the professional rules regarding, in particular, the independence, dignity and honour of the profession, professional secrecy and fairness towards clients and other members of the profession.
2. Without prejudice to the autonomy of professional bodies and associations, Member States and the Commission shall encourage professional associations and bodies to establish codes of conduct at Community level in order to determine the types of information that can be given for the purposes of commercial communication in conformity with the rules referred to in paragraph 1
3. When drawing up proposals for Community initiatives which may become necessary to ensure the proper functioning of the Internal Market with regard to the information referred to in paragraph 2, the Commission shall take due account of codes of conduct applicable at Community level and shall act in close cooperation with the relevant professional associations and bodies.
4. This Directive shall apply in addition to Community Directives concerning access to, and the exercise of, activities of the regulated professions.

Section 3: **Contracts concluded by electronic means**

Article 9 Treatment of contracts

1. Member States shall ensure that their legal system allows contracts to be concluded by electronic means. Member States shall in particular ensure that the legal requirements applicable to the contractual process neither create obstacles for the use of electronic contracts nor result in such contracts being deprived of legal effectiveness and validity on account of their having been made by electronic means.
2. Member States may lay down that paragraph 1 shall not apply to all or certain contracts falling into one of the following categories:
   (a) contracts that create or transfer rights in real estate, except for rental rights;
   (b) contracts requiring by law the involvement of courts, public authorities or professions exercising public authority;
   (c) contracts of suretyship granted and on collateral securities furnished by persons acting for purposes outside their trade, business or profession;
   (d) contracts governed by family law or by the law of succession.
3. Member States shall indicate to the Commission the categories referred to in paragraph 2 to which they do not apply paragraph 1. Member States shall submit to the Commission every five years a report on the application of paragraph 2 explaining the reasons why they consider it necessary to maintain the category referred to in paragraph 2(b) to which they do not apply paragraph 1.

Article 10 Information to be provided

1. In addition to other information requirements established by Community law, Member States shall ensure, except when otherwise agreed by parties who are not consumers, that at least the following information is given by the service provider clearly, comprehensibly and unambiguously and prior to the order being placed by the recipient of the service:
   (a) the different technical steps to follow to conclude the contract;
   (b) whether or not the concluded contract will be filed by the service provider and whether it will be accessible;
   (c) the technical means for identifying and correcting input errors prior to the placing of the order;
   (d) the languages offered for the conclusion of the contract.
2. Member States shall ensure that, except when otherwise agreed by parties who are not consumers, the service provider indicates any relevant codes of conduct to which he subscribes and information on how those codes can be consulted electronically.
3. Contract terms and general conditions provided to the recipient must be made available in a way that allows him to store and reproduce them.
4. Paragraphs 1 and 2 shall not apply to contracts concluded exclusively by exchange of electronic mail or by equivalent individual communications.

Article 11 Placing of the order

1. Member States shall ensure, except when otherwise agreed by parties who are not consumers, that in cases where the recipient of the service places his order through technological means, the following principles apply:
   - the service provider has to acknowledge the receipt of the recipient's order without undue delay and by electronic means,
   - the order and the acknowledgement of receipt are deemed to be received when the parties to whom they are addressed are able to access them.
2. Member States shall ensure that, except when otherwise agreed by parties who are not consumers, the service provider makes available to the recipient of the service appropriate, effective and accessible technical means allowing him to identify and correct input errors, prior to the placing of the order.
3. Paragraph 1, first indent, and paragraph 2 shall not apply to contracts concluded exclusively by exchange of electronic mail or by equivalent individual communications.

Section 4: **Liability of intermediary service providers**

Article 12 "Mere conduit"

1. Where an information society service is provided that consists of the transmission in a communication network of information provided by a recipient of the service, or the provision of access to a communication network, Member

States shall ensure that the service provider is not liable for the information transmitted, on condition that the provider:

(a) does not initiate the transmission;
(b) does not select the receiver of the transmission; and
(c) does not select or modify the information contained in the transmission.

2. The acts of transmission and of provision of access referred to in paragraph 1 include the automatic, intermediate and transient storage of the information transmitted in so far as this takes place for the sole purpose of carrying out the transmission in the communication network, and provided that the information is not stored for any period longer than is reasonably necessary for the transmission.
3. This Article shall not affect the possibility for a court or administrative authority, in accordance with Member States' legal systems, of requiring the service provider to terminate or prevent an infringement.

Article 13 "Caching"

1. Where an information society service is provided that consists of the transmission in a communication network of information provided by a recipient of the service, Member States shall ensure that the service provider is not liable for the automatic, intermediate and temporary storage of that information, performed for the sole purpose of making more efficient the information's onward transmission to other recipients of the service upon their request, on condition that:

(a) the provider does not modify the information;
(b) the provider complies with conditions on access to the information;
(c) the provider complies with rules regarding the updating of the information, specified in a manner widely recognised and used by industry;
(d) the provider does not interfere with the lawful use of technology, widely recognised and used by industry, to obtain data on the use of the information; and
(e) the provider acts expeditiously to remove or to disable access to the information it has stored upon obtaining actual knowledge of the fact that the information at the initial source of the transmission has been removed from the network, or access to it has been disabled, or that a court or an administrative authority has ordered such removal or disablement.

2. This Article shall not affect the possibility for a court or administrative authority, in accordance with Member States' legal systems, of requiring the service provider to terminate or prevent an infringement.

Article 14 Hosting

1. Where an information society service is provided that consists of the storage of information provided by a recipient of the service, Member States shall ensure that the service provider is not liable for the information stored at the request of a recipient of the service, on condition that:

(a) the provider does not have actual knowledge of illegal activity or information and, as regards claims for damages, is not aware of facts or circumstances from which the illegal activity or information is apparent; or
(b) the provider, upon obtaining such knowledge or awareness, acts expeditiously to remove or to disable access to the information.

2. Paragraph 1 shall not apply when the recipient of the service is acting under the authority or the control of the provider.
3. This Article shall not affect the possibility for a court or administrative authority, in accordance with Member States' legal systems, of requiring the service provider to terminate or prevent an infringement, nor does it affect the possibility for Member States of establishing procedures governing the removal or disabling of access to information.

Article 15 No general obligation to monitor

1. Member States shall not impose a general obligation on providers, when providing the services covered by Articles 12, 13 and 14, to monitor the information which they transmit or store, nor a general obligation actively to seek facts or circumstances indicating illegal activity.
2. Member States may establish obligations for information society service providers promptly to inform the competent public authorities of alleged illegal activities undertaken or information provided by recipients of their service or obligations to communicate to the competent authorities, at their request, information enabling the identification of recipients of their service with whom they have storage agreements.

CHAPTER III : IMPLEMENTATION

Article 16 Codes of conduct

1. Member States and the Commission shall encourage:
   (a) the drawing up of codes of conduct at Community level, by trade, professional and consumer associations or organisations, designed to contribute to the proper implementation of Articles 5 to 15;
   (b) the voluntary transmission of draft codes of conduct at national or Community level to the Commission;
   (c) the accessibility of these codes of conduct in the Community languages by electronic means;
   (d) the communication to the Member States and the Commission, by trade, professional and consumer associations or organisations, of their assessment of the application of their codes of conduct and their impact upon practices, habits or customs relating to electronic commerce;
   (e) the drawing up of codes of conduct regarding the protection of minors and human dignity.
2. Member States and the Commission shall encourage the involvement of associations or organisations representing consumers in the drafting and

implementation of codes of conduct affecting their interests and drawn up in accordance with paragraph 1(a). Where appropriate, to take account of their specific needs, associations representing the visually impaired and disabled should be consulted.

Article 17 Out-of-court dispute settlement

1. Member States shall ensure that, in the event of disagreement between an information society service provider and the recipient of the service, their legislation does not hamper the use of out-of-court schemes, available under national law, for dispute settlement, including appropriate electronic means.
2. Member States shall encourage bodies responsible for the out-of-court settlement of, in particular, consumer disputes to operate in a way which provides adequate procedural guarantees for the parties concerned.
3. Member States shall encourage bodies responsible for out-of-court dispute settlement to inform the Commission of the significant decisions they take regarding information society services and to transmit any other information on the practices, usages or customs relating to electronic commerce.

Article 18 Court actions

1. Member States shall ensure that court actions available under national law concerning information society services' activities allow for the rapid adoption of measures, including interim measures, designed to terminate any alleged infringement and to prevent any further impairment of the interests involved.
2. The Annex to Directive 98/27/EC shall be supplemented as follows:

   "11. Directive 2000/31/EC of the European Parliament and of the Council of 8 June 2000 on certain legal aspects on information society services, in particular electronic commerce, in the internal market (Directive on electronic commerce) (OJ L 178, 17.7.2000, p. 1)."

Article 19 Cooperation

1. Member States shall have adequate means of supervision and investigation necessary to implement this Directive effectively and shall ensure that service providers supply them with the requisite information.
2. Member States shall cooperate with other Member States; they shall, to that end, appoint one or several contact points, whose details they shall communicate to the other Member States and to the Commission.
3. Member States shall, as quickly as possible, and in conformity with national law, provide the assistance and information requested by other Member States or by the Commission, including by appropriate electronic means.
4. Member States shall establish contact points which shall be accessible at least by electronic means and from which recipients and service providers may:
   (a) obtain general information on contractual rights and obligations as well as on the complaint and redress mechanisms available in the event of disputes, including practical aspects involved in the use of such mechanisms;

(b) obtain the details of authorities, associations or organisations from which they may obtain further information or practical assistance.

5. Member States shall encourage the communication to the Commission of any significant administrative or judicial decisions taken in their territory regarding disputes relating to information society services and practices, usages and customs relating to electronic commerce. The Commission shall communicate these decisions to the other Member States.

Article 20 Sanctions

Member States shall determine the sanctions applicable to infringements of national provisions adopted pursuant to this Directive and shall take all measures necessary to ensure that they are enforced. The sanctions they provide for shall be effective, proportionate and dissuasive.

CHAPTER IV : FINAL PROVISIONS

Article 21 Re-examination

1. Before 17 July 2003, and thereafter every two years, the Commission shall submit to the European Parliament, the Council and the Economic and Social Committee a report on the application of this Directive, accompanied, where necessary, by proposals for adapting it to legal, technical and economic developments in the field of information society services, in particular with respect to crime prevention, the protection of minors, consumer protection and to the proper functioning of the internal market.
2. In examining the need for an adaptation of this Directive, the report shall in particular analyse the need for proposals concerning the liability of providers of hyperlinks and location tool services, "notice and take down" procedures and the attribution of liability following the taking down of content. The report shall also analyse the need for additional conditions for the exemption from liability, provided for in Articles 12 and 13, in the light of technical developments, and the possibility of applying the internal market principles to unsolicited commercial communications by electronic mail.

Article 22 Transposition

1. Member States shall bring into force the laws, regulations and administrative provisions necessary to comply with this Directive before 17 January 2002. They shall forthwith inform the Commission thereof.
2. When Member States adopt the measures referred to in paragraph 1, these shall contain a reference to this Directive or shall be accompanied by such reference at the time of their official publication. The methods of making such reference shall be laid down by Member States.

Article 23 Entry into force

This Directive shall enter into force on the day of its publication in the Official Journal of the European Communities.

Article 24 Addressees

This Directive is addressed to the Member States.

Done at Luxemburg, 8 June 2000.

For the European Parliament

The President

N. Fontaine

For the Council

The President

G. d'Oliveira Martins

ANNEX

DEROGATIONS FROM ARTICLE 3

As provided for in Article 3(3), Article 3(1) and (2) do not apply to:

- copyright, neighbouring rights, rights referred to in Directive 87/54/EEC[1] and Directive 96/9/EC[2] as well as industrial property rights,
- the emission of electronic money by institutions in respect of which Member States have applied one of the derogations provided for in Article 8(1) of Directive 2000/46/EC[3],
- Article 44(2) of Directive 85/611/EEC[4],
- Article 30 and Title IV of Directive 92/49/EEC[5], Title IV of Directive 92/96/EEC[6], Articles 7 and 8 of Directive 88/357/EEC[7] and Article 4 of Directive 90/619/EEC[8],
- the freedom of the parties to choose the law applicable to their contract,
- contractual obligations concerning consumer contacts,
- formal validity of contracts creating or transferring rights in real estate where such contracts are subject to mandatory formal requirements of the law of the Member State where the real estate is situated,
- the permissibility of unsolicited commercial communications by electronic mail.

1 OJ L 24, 27.1.1987, p. 36.
2 OJ L 77, 27.3.1996, p. 20.
3 Not yet published in the Official Journal.
4 OJ L 375, 31.12.1985, p. 3. Directive as last amended by Directive 95/26/EC (OJ L 168, 18.7.1995, p. 7).
5 OJ L 228, 11.8.1992, p. 1. Directive as last amended by Directive 95/26/EC.
6 OJ L 360, 9.12.1992, p. 2. Directive as last amended by Directive 95/26/EC.
7 OJ L 172, 4.7.1988, p. 1. Directive as last amended by Directive 92/49/EC.
8 OJ L 330, 29.11.1990, p. 50. Directive as last amended by Directive 92/96/EC.

10.Council Directive 2000/78/EC of 27 November 2000 establishing a general framework for equal treatment in employment and occupation

(OJ L 303, 02/12/2000 p. 16 – 22)

THE COUNCIL OF THE EUROPEAN UNION,

Having regard to the Treaty establishing the European Community, and in particular Article 13 thereof,

Having regard to the proposal from the Commission[1],

Having regard to the Opinion of the European Parliament[2],

Having regard to the Opinion of the Economic and Social Committee[3],

Having regard to the Opinion of the Committee of the Regions[4],

Whereas:

(1) In accordance with Article 6 of the Treaty on European Union, the European Union is founded on the principles of liberty, democracy, respect for human rights and fundamental freedoms, and the rule of law, principles which are common to all Member States and it respects fundamental rights, as guaranteed by the European Convention for the Protection of Human Rights and Fundamental Freedoms and as they result from the constitutional traditions common to the Member States, as general principles of Community law.

(2) The principle of equal treatment between women and men is well established by an important body of Community law, in particular in Council Directive 76/207/EEC of 9 February 1976 on the implementation of the principle of equal treatment for men and women as regards access to employment, vocational training and promotion, and working conditions[5].

(3) In implementing the principle of equal treatment, the Community should, in accordance with Article 3(2) of the EC Treaty, aim to eliminate inequalities, and to promote equality between men and women, especially since women are often the victims of multiple discrimination.

(4) The right of all persons to equality before the law and protection against discrimination constitutes a universal right recognised by the Universal Declaration of Human Rights, the United Nations Convention on the Elimination of All Forms of Discrimination against Women, United Nations Covenants on Civil and Political Rights and on Economic, Social and Cultural Rights and by the European Convention for the Protection of Human Rights and Fundamental Freedoms, to which all Member States are signatories. Convention No 111 of the

[1] OJ C 177 E, 27.6.2000, p. 42.

[2] Opinion delivered on 12 October 2000 (not yet published in the Official Journal).

[3] OJ C 204, 18.7.2000, p. 82.

[4] OJ C 226, 8.8.2000, p. 1.

[5] OJ L 39, 14.2.1976, p. 40.

International Labour Organisation (ILO) prohibits discrimination in the field of employment and occupation.

(5) It is important to respect such fundamental rights and freedoms. This Directive does not prejudice freedom of association, including the right to establish unions with others and to join unions to defend one's interests.

(6) The Community Charter of the Fundamental Social Rights of Workers recognises the importance of combating every form of discrimination, including the need to take appropriate action for the social and economic integration of elderly and disabled people.

(7) The EC Treaty includes among its objectives the promotion of coordination between employment policies of the Member States. To this end, a new employment chapter was incorporated in the EC Treaty as a means of developing a coordinated European strategy for employment to promote a skilled, trained and adaptable workforce.

(8) The Employment Guidelines for 2000 agreed by the European Council at Helsinki on 10 and 11 December 1999 stress the need to foster a labour market favourable to social integration by formulating a coherent set of policies aimed at combating discrimination against groups such as persons with disability. They also emphasise the need to pay particular attention to supporting older workers, in order to increase their participation in the labour force.

(9) Employment and occupation are key elements in guaranteeing equal opportunities for all and contribute strongly to the full participation of citizens in economic, cultural and social life and to realising their potential.

(10) On 29 June 2000 the Council adopted Directive 2000/43/EC[1] implementing the principle of equal treatment between persons irrespective of racial or ethnic origin. That Directive already provides protection against such discrimination in the field of employment and occupation.

(11) Discrimination based on religion or belief, disability, age or sexual orientation may undermine the achievement of the objectives of the EC Treaty, in particular the attainment of a high level of employment and social protection, raising the standard of living and the quality of life, economic and social cohesion and solidarity, and the free movement of persons.

(12) To this end, any direct or indirect discrimination based on religion or belief, disability, age or sexual orientation as regards the areas covered by this Directive should be prohibited throughout the Community. This prohibition of discrimination should also apply to nationals of third countries but does not cover differences of treatment based on nationality and is without prejudice to provisions governing the entry and residence of third-country nationals and their access to employment and occupation.

(13) This Directive does not apply to social security and social protection schemes whose benefits are not treated as income within the meaning given to that term

[1] OJ L 180, 19.7.2000, p. 22.

for the purpose of applying Article 141 of the EC Treaty, nor to any kind of payment by the State aimed at providing access to employment or maintaining employment.

(14) This Directive shall be without prejudice to national provisions laying down retirement ages.

(15) The appreciation of the facts from which it may be inferred that there has been direct or indirect discrimination is a matter for national judicial or other competent bodies, in accordance with rules of national law or practice. Such rules may provide, in particular, for indirect discrimination to be established by any means including on the basis of statistical evidence.

(16) The provision of measures to accommodate the needs of disabled people at the workplace plays an important role in combating discrimination on grounds of disability.

(17) This Directive does not require the recruitment, promotion, maintenance in employment or training of an individual who is not competent, capable and available to perform the essential functions of the post concerned or to undergo the relevant training, without prejudice to the obligation to provide reasonable accommodation for people with disabilities.

(18) This Directive does not require, in particular, the armed forces and the police, prison or emergency services to recruit or maintain in employment persons who do not have the required capacity to carry out the range of functions that they may be called upon to perform with regard to the legitimate objective of preserving the operational capacity of those services.

(19) Moreover, in order that the Member States may continue to safeguard the combat effectiveness of their armed forces, they may choose not to apply the provisions of this Directive concerning disability and age to all or part of their armed forces. The Member States which make that choice must define the scope of that derogation.

(20) Appropriate measures should be provided, i.e. effective and practical measures to adapt the workplace to the disability, for example adapting premises and equipment, patterns of working time, the distribution of tasks or the provision of training or integration resources.

(21) To determine whether the measures in question give rise to a disproportionate burden, account should be taken in particular of the financial and other costs entailed, the scale and financial resources of the organisation or undertaking and the possibility of obtaining public funding or any other assistance.

(22) This Directive is without prejudice to national laws on marital status and the benefits dependent thereon.

(23) In very limited circumstances, a difference of treatment may be justified where a characteristic related to religion or belief, disability, age or sexual orientation constitutes a genuine and determining occupational requirement, when the objective is legitimate and the requirement is proportionate. Such circumstances

should be included in the information provided by the Member States to the Commission.

(24) The European Union in its Declaration No 11 on the status of churches and non-confessional organisations, annexed to the Final Act of the Amsterdam Treaty, has explicitly recognised that it respects and does not prejudice the status under national law of churches and religious associations or communities in the Member States and that it equally respects the status of philosophical and non-confessional organisations. With this in view, Member States may maintain or lay down specific provisions on genuine, legitimate and justified occupational requirements which might be required for carrying out an occupational activity.

(25) The prohibition of age discrimination is an essential part of meeting the aims set out in the Employment Guidelines and encouraging diversity in the workforce. However, differences in treatment in connection with age may be justified under certain circumstances and therefore require specific provisions which may vary in accordance with the situation in Member States. It is therefore essential to distinguish between differences in treatment which are justified, in particular by legitimate employment policy, labour market and vocational training objectives, and discrimination which must be prohibited.

(26) The prohibition of discrimination should be without prejudice to the maintenance or adoption of measures intended to prevent or compensate for disadvantages suffered by a group of persons of a particular religion or belief, disability, age or sexual orientation, and such measures may permit organisations of persons of a particular religion or belief, disability, age or sexual orientation where their main object is the promotion of the special needs of those persons.

(27) In its Recommendation 86/379/EEC of 24 July 1986 on the employment of disabled people in the Community[1], the Council established a guideline framework setting out examples of positive action to promote the employment and training of disabled people, and in its Resolution of 17 June 1999 on equal employment opportunities for people with disabilities[2], affirmed the importance of giving specific attention inter alia to recruitment, retention, training and lifelong learning with regard to disabled persons.

(28) This Directive lays down minimum requirements, thus giving the Member States the option of introducing or maintaining more favourable provisions. The implementation of this Directive should not serve to justify any regression in relation to the situation which already prevails in each Member State.

(29) Persons who have been subject to discrimination based on religion or belief, disability, age or sexual orientation should have adequate means of legal protection. To provide a more effective level of protection, associations or legal entities should also be empowered to engage in proceedings, as the Member States so determine, either on behalf or in support of any victim, without

[1] OJ L 225, 12.8.1986, p. 43.
[2] OJ C 186, 2.7.1999, p. 3.

prejudice to national rules of procedure concerning representation and defence before the courts.

(30) The effective implementation of the principle of equality requires adequate judicial protection against victimisation.

(31) The rules on the burden of proof must be adapted when there is a prima facie case of discrimination and, for the principle of equal treatment to be applied effectively, the burden of proof must shift back to the respondent when evidence of such discrimination is brought. However, it is not for the respondent to prove that the plaintiff adheres to a particular religion or belief, has a particular disability, is of a particular age or has a particular sexual orientation.

(32) Member States need not apply the rules on the burden of proof to proceedings in which it is for the court or other competent body to investigate the facts of the case. The procedures thus referred to are those in which the plaintiff is not required to prove the facts, which it is for the court or competent body to investigate.

(33) Member States should promote dialogue between the social partners and, within the framework of national practice, with non-governmental organisations to address different forms of discrimination at the workplace and to combat them.

(34) The need to promote peace and reconciliation between the major communities in Northern Ireland necessitates the incorporation of particular provisions into this Directive.

(35) Member States should provide for effective, proportionate and dissuasive sanctions in case of breaches of the obligations under this Directive.

(36) Member States may entrust the social partners, at their joint request, with the implementation of this Directive, as regards the provisions concerning collective agreements, provided they take any necessary steps to ensure that they are at all times able to guarantee the results required by this Directive.

(37) In accordance with the principle of subsidiarity set out in Article 5 of the EC Treaty, the objective of this Directive, namely the creation within the Community of a level playing-field as regards equality in employment and occupation, cannot be sufficiently achieved by the Member States and can therefore, by reason of the scale and impact of the action, be better achieved at Community level. In accordance with the principle of proportionality, as set out in that Article, this Directive does not go beyond what is necessary in order to achieve that objective,

HAS ADOPTED THIS DIRECTIVE:

CHAPTER I : GENERAL PROVISIONS

Article 1 Purpose

The purpose of this Directive is to lay down a general framework for combating discrimination on the grounds of religion or belief, disability, age or sexual orientation as regards employment and occupation, with a view to putting into effect in the Member States the principle of equal treatment.

Article 2 Concept of discrimination

1. For the purposes of this Directive, the "principle of equal treatment" shall mean that there shall be no direct or indirect discrimination whatsoever on any of the grounds referred to in Article 1.
2. For the purposes of paragraph 1:
   (a) direct discrimination shall be taken to occur where one person is treated less favourably than another is, has been or would be treated in a comparable situation, on any of the grounds referred to in Article 1;
   (b) indirect discrimination shall be taken to occur where an apparently neutral provision, criterion or practice would put persons having a particular religion or belief, a particular disability, a particular age, or a particular sexual orientation at a particular disadvantage compared with other persons unless:
      (i) that provision, criterion or practice is objectively justified by a legitimate aim and the means of achieving that aim are appropriate and necessary, or
      (ii) as regards persons with a particular disability, the employer or any person or organisation to whom this Directive applies, is obliged, under national legislation, to take appropriate measures in line with the principles contained in Article 5 in order to eliminate disadvantages entailed by such provision, criterion or practice.
3. Harassment shall be deemed to be a form of discrimination within the meaning of paragraph 1, when unwanted conduct related to any of the grounds referred to in Article 1 takes place with the purpose or effect of violating the dignity of a person and of creating an intimidating, hostile, degrading, humiliating or offensive environment. In this context, the concept of harassment may be defined in accordance with the national laws and practice of the Member States.
4. An instruction to discriminate against persons on any of the grounds referred to in Article 1 shall be deemed to be discrimination within the meaning of paragraph 1.
5. This Directive shall be without prejudice to measures laid down by national law which, in a democratic society, are necessary for public security, for the maintenance of public order and the prevention of criminal offences, for the protection of health and for the protection of the rights and freedoms of others.

Article 3 Scope

1. Within the limits of the areas of competence conferred on the Community, this Directive shall apply to all persons, as regards both the public and private sectors, including public bodies, in relation to:
   (a) conditions for access to employment, to self-employment or to occupation, including selection criteria and recruitment conditions, whatever the branch

of activity and at all levels of the professional hierarchy, including promotion;

(b) access to all types and to all levels of vocational guidance, vocational training, advanced vocational training and retraining, including practical work experience;

(c) employment and working conditions, including dismissals and pay;

(d) membership of, and involvement in, an organisation of workers or employers, or any organisation whose members carry on a particular profession, including the benefits provided for by such organisations.

2. This Directive does not cover differences of treatment based on nationality and is without prejudice to provisions and conditions relating to the entry into and residence of third-country nationals and stateless persons in the territory of Member States, and to any treatment which arises from the legal status of the third-country nationals and stateless persons concerned.

3. This Directive does not apply to payments of any kind made by state schemes or similar, including state social security or social protection schemes.

4. Member States may provide that this Directive, in so far as it relates to discrimination on the grounds of disability and age, shall not apply to the armed forces.

Article 4 Occupational requirements

1. Notwithstanding Article 2(1) and (2), Member States may provide that a difference of treatment which is based on a characteristic related to any of the grounds referred to in Article 1 shall not constitute discrimination where, by reason of the nature of the particular occupational activities concerned or of the context in which they are carried out, such a characteristic constitutes a genuine and determining occupational requirement, provided that the objective is legitimate and the requirement is proportionate.

2. Member States may maintain national legislation in force at the date of adoption of this Directive or provide for future legislation incorporating national practices existing at the date of adoption of this Directive pursuant to which, in the case of occupational activities within churches and other public or private organisations the ethos of which is based on religion or belief, a difference of treatment based on a person's religion or belief shall not constitute discrimination where, by reason of the nature of these activities or of the context in which they are carried out, a person's religion or belief constitute a genuine, legitimate and justified occupational requirement, having regard to the organisation's ethos. This difference of treatment shall be implemented taking account of Member States' constitutional provisions and principles, as well as the general principles of Community law, and should not justify discrimination on another ground.

   Provided that its provisions are otherwise complied with, this Directive shall thus not prejudice the right of churches and other public or private organisations, the ethos of which is based on religion or belief, acting in conformity with national constitutions and laws, to require individuals working for them to act in good faith and with loyalty to the organisation's ethos.

Article 5 Reasonable accommodation for disabled persons

In order to guarantee compliance with the principle of equal treatment in relation to persons with disabilities, reasonable accommodation shall be provided. This means that employers shall take appropriate measures, where needed in a particular case, to enable a person with a disability to have access to, participate in, or advance in employment, or to undergo training, unless such measures would impose a disproportionate burden on the employer. This burden shall not be disproportionate when it is sufficiently remedied by measures existing within the framework of the disability policy of the Member State concerned.

Article 6 Justification of differences of treatment on grounds of age

1. Notwithstanding Article 2(2), Member States may provide that differences of treatment on grounds of age shall not constitute discrimination, if, within the context of national law, they are objectively and reasonably justified by a legitimate aim, including legitimate employment policy, labour market and vocational training objectives, and if the means of achieving that aim are appropriate and necessary.

   Such differences of treatment may include, among others:

   (a) the setting of special conditions on access to employment and vocational training, employment and occupation, including dismissal and remuneration conditions, for young people, older workers and persons with caring responsibilities in order to promote their vocational integration or ensure their protection;

   (b) the fixing of minimum conditions of age, professional experience or seniority in service for access to employment or to certain advantages linked to employment;

   (c) the fixing of a maximum age for recruitment which is based on the training requirements of the post in question or the need for a reasonable period of employment before retirement.

2. Notwithstanding Article 2(2), Member States may provide that the fixing for occupational social security schemes of ages for admission or entitlement to retirement or invalidity benefits, including the fixing under those schemes of different ages for employees or groups or categories of employees, and the use, in the context of such schemes, of age criteria in actuarial calculations, does not constitute discrimination on the grounds of age, provided this does not result in discrimination on the grounds of sex.

Article 7 Positive action

1. With a view to ensuring full equality in practice, the principle of equal treatment shall not prevent any Member State from maintaining or adopting specific

measures to prevent or compensate for disadvantages linked to any of the grounds referred to in Article 1.

2. With regard to disabled persons, the principle of equal treatment shall be without prejudice to the right of Member States to maintain or adopt provisions on the protection of health and safety at work or to measures aimed at creating or maintaining provisions or facilities for safeguarding or promoting their integration into the working environment.

Article 8 Minimum requirements

1. Member States may introduce or maintain provisions which are more favourable to the protection of the principle of equal treatment than those laid down in this Directive.
2. The implementation of this Directive shall under no circumstances constitute grounds for a reduction in the level of protection against discrimination already afforded by Member States in the fields covered by this Directive.

CHAPTER II : REMEDIES AND ENFORCEMENT

Article 9 Defence of rights

1. Member States shall ensure that judicial and/or administrative procedures, including where they deem it appropriate conciliation procedures, for the enforcement of obligations under this Directive are available to all persons who consider themselves wronged by failure to apply the principle of equal treatment to them, even after the relationship in which the discrimination is alleged to have occurred has ended.
2. Member States shall ensure that associations, organisations or other legal entities which have, in accordance with the criteria laid down by their national law, a legitimate interest in ensuring that the provisions of this Directive are complied with, may engage, either on behalf or in support of the complainant, with his or her approval, in any judicial and/or administrative procedure provided for the enforcement of obligations under this Directive.
3. Paragraphs 1 and 2 are without prejudice to national rules relating to time limits for bringing actions as regards the principle of equality of treatment.

Article 10 Burden of proof

1. Member States shall take such measures as are necessary, in accordance with their national judicial systems, to ensure that, when persons who consider themselves wronged because the principle of equal treatment has not been applied to them establish, before a court or other competent authority, facts from which it may be presumed that there has been direct or indirect discrimination, it shall be for the respondent to prove that there has been no breach of the principle of equal treatment.
2. Paragraph 1 shall not prevent Member States from introducing rules of evidence which are more favourable to plaintiffs.

3. Paragraph 1 shall not apply to criminal procedures.
4. Paragraphs 1, 2 and 3 shall also apply to any legal proceedings commenced in accordance with Article 9(2).
5. Member States need not apply paragraph 1 to proceedings in which it is for the court or competent body to investigate the facts of the case.

Article 11 Victimisation

Member States shall introduce into their national legal systems such measures as are necessary to protect employees against dismissal or other adverse treatment by the employer as a reaction to a complaint within the undertaking or to any legal proceedings aimed at enforcing compliance with the principle of equal treatment.

Article 12 Dissemination of information

Member States shall take care that the provisions adopted pursuant to this Directive, together with the relevant provisions already in force in this field, are brought to the attention of the persons concerned by all appropriate means, for example at the workplace, throughout their territory.

Article 13 Social dialogue

1. Member States shall, in accordance with their national traditions and practice, take adequate measures to promote dialogue between the social partners with a view to fostering equal treatment, including through the monitoring of workplace practices, collective agreements, codes of conduct and through research or exchange of experiences and good practices.
2. Where consistent with their national traditions and practice, Member States shall encourage the social partners, without prejudice to their autonomy, to conclude at the appropriate level agreements laying down anti-discrimination rules in the fields referred to in Article 3 which fall within the scope of collective bargaining. These agreements shall respect the minimum requirements laid down by this Directive and by the relevant national implementing measures.

Article 14 Dialogue with non-governmental organisations

Member States shall encourage dialogue with appropriate non-governmental organisations which have, in accordance with their national law and practice, a legitimate interest in contributing to the fight against discrimination on any of the grounds referred to in Article 1 with a view to promoting the principle of equal treatment.

CHAPTER III : PARTICULAR PROVISIONS

Article 15 Northern Ireland

1. In order to tackle the under-representation of one of the major religious communities in the police service of Northern Ireland, differences in treatment regarding recruitment into that service, including its support staff, shall not

constitute discrimination insofar as those differences in treatment are expressly authorised by national legislation.

2. In order to maintain a balance of opportunity in employment for teachers in Northern Ireland while furthering the reconciliation of historical divisions between the major religious communities there, the provisions on religion or belief in this Directive shall not apply to the recruitment of teachers in schools in Northern Ireland in so far as this is expressly authorised by national legislation.

CHAPTER IV : FINAL PROVISIONS

Article 16 Compliance

Member States shall take the necessary measures to ensure that:

(a) any laws, regulations and administrative provisions contrary to the principle of equal treatment are abolished;

(b) any provisions contrary to the principle of equal treatment which are included in contracts or collective agreements, internal rules of undertakings or rules governing the independent occupations and professions and workers' and employers' organisations are, or may be, declared null and void or are amended.

Article 17 Sanctions

Member States shall lay down the rules on sanctions applicable to infringements of the national provisions adopted pursuant to this Directive and shall take all measures necessary to ensure that they are applied. The sanctions, which may comprise the payment of compensation to the victim, must be effective, proportionate and dissuasive. Member States shall notify those provisions to the Commission by 2 December 2003 at the latest and shall notify it without delay of any subsequent amendment affecting them.

Article 18 Implementation

Member States shall adopt the laws, regulations and administrative provisions necessary to comply with this Directive by 2 December 2003 at the latest or may entrust the social partners, at their joint request, with the implementation of this Directive as regards provisions concerning collective agreements. In such cases, Member States shall ensure that, no later than 2 December 2003, the social partners introduce the necessary measures by agreement, the Member States concerned being required to take any necessary measures to enable them at any time to be in a position to guarantee the results imposed by this Directive. They shall forthwith inform the Commission thereof.

In order to take account of particular conditions, Member States may, if necessary, have an additional period of 3 years from 2 December 2003, that is to say a total of 6 years, to implement the provisions of this Directive on age and disability discrimination. In that event they shall inform the Commission forthwith. Any Member State which chooses to use this additional period shall report annually to the Commission on the steps it is taking to tackle age and disability discrimination and on the progress it is making towards implementation. The Commission shall report annually to the Council.

When Member States adopt these measures, they shall contain a reference to this Directive or be accompanied by such reference on the occasion of their official publication. The methods of making such reference shall be laid down by Member States.

Article 19 Report

1. Member States shall communicate to the Commission, by 2 December 2005 at the latest and every five years thereafter, all the information necessary for the Commission to draw up a report to the European Parliament and the Council on the application of this Directive.
2. The Commission's report shall take into account, as appropriate, the viewpoints of the social partners and relevant non-governmental organisations. In accordance with the principle of gender mainstreaming, this report shall, inter alia, provide an assessment of the impact of the measures taken on women and men. In the light of the information received, this report shall include, if necessary, proposals to revise and update this Directive.

Article 20 Entry into force

This Directive shall enter into force on the day of its publication in the Official Journal of the European Communities.

Article 21 Addressees

This Directive is addressed to the Member States.

Done at Brussels, 27 November 2000.

For the Council

The President

É. Guigou

11. Council Directive 2001/23/EC of 12 March 2001 on the approximation of the laws of the Member States relating to the safeguarding of employees' rights in the event of transfers of undertakings, businesses or parts of undertakings or businesses

(OJ L 082 , 22/03/2001 p. 16 -20)

THE COUNCIL OF THE EUROPEAN UNION,

Having regard to the Treaty establishing the European Community, and in particular Article 94 thereof,

Having regard to the proposal from the Commission,

Having regard to the opinion of the European Parliament[1],

Having regard to the opinion of the Economic and Social Committee[2],

Whereas:

(1) Council Directive 77/187/EEC of 14 February 1977 on the approximation of the laws of the Member States relating to the safeguarding of employees' rights in the event of transfers of undertakings, businesses or parts of undertakings or businesses[3] has been substantially amended[4]. In the interests of clarity and rationality, it should therefore be codified.

(2) Economic trends are bringing in their wake, at both national and Community level, changes in the structure of undertakings, through transfers of undertakings, businesses or parts of undertakings or businesses to other employers as a result of legal transfers or mergers.

(3) It is necessary to provide for the protection of employees in the event of a change of employer, in particular, to ensure that their rights are safeguarded.

(4) Differences still remain in the Member States as regards the extent of the protection of employees in this respect and these differences should be reduced.

(5) The Community Charter of the Fundamental Social Rights of Workers adopted on 9 December 1989 ("Social Charter") states, in points 7, 17 and 18 in particular that: "The completion of the internal market must lead to an improvement in the living and working conditions of workers in the European Community. The improvement must cover, where necessary, the development of certain aspects of employment regulations such as procedures for collective redundancies and those regarding bankruptcies. Information, consultation and participation for workers must be developed along appropriate lines, taking account of the practice in force in the various Member States. Such information, consultation and participation must be implemented in due time, particularly in

[1] Opinion delivered on 25 October 2000 (not yet published in the Official Journal).

[2] OJ C 367, 20.12.2000, p. 21

[3] OJ L 61, 5.3.1977, p. 26.

[4] See Annex I, Part A.

connection with restructuring operations in undertakings or in cases of mergers having an impact on the employment of workers".

(6) In 1977 the Council adopted Directive 77/187/EEC to promote the harmonisation of the relevant national laws ensuring the safeguarding of the rights of employees and requiring transferors and transferees to inform and consult employees' representatives in good time.

(7) That Directive was subsequently amended in the light of the impact of the internal market, the legislative tendencies of the Member States with regard to the rescue of undertakings in economic difficulties, the case-law of the Court of Justice of the European Communities, Council Directive 75/129/EEC of 17 February 1975 on the approximation of the laws of the Member States relating to collective redundancies[1] and the legislation already in force in most Member States.

(8) Considerations of legal security and transparency required that the legal concept of transfer be clarified in the light of the case-law of the Court of Justice. Such clarification has not altered the scope of Directive 77/187/EEC as interpreted by the Court of Justice.

(9) The Social Charter recognises the importance of the fight against all forms of discrimination, especially based on sex, colour, race, opinion and creed.

(10) This Directive should be without prejudice to the time limits set out in Annex I Part B within which the Member States are to comply with Directive 77/187/EEC, and the act amending it,

HAS ADOPTED THIS DIRECTIVE:

CHAPTER I : SCOPE AND DEFINITIONS

Article 1

1. (a) This Directive shall apply to any transfer of an undertaking, business, or part of an undertaking or business to another employer as a result of a legal transfer or merger.
   (b) Subject to subparagraph (a) and the following provisions of this Article, there is a transfer within the meaning of this Directive where there is a transfer of an economic entity which retains its identity, meaning an organised grouping of resources which has the objective of pursuing an economic activity, whether or not that activity is central or ancillary.
   (c) This Directive shall apply to public and private undertakings engaged in economic activities whether or not they are operating for gain. An administrative reorganisation of public administrative authorities, or the transfer of administrative functions between public administrative authorities, is not a transfer within the meaning of this Directive.

[1] OJ L 48, 22.2.1975, p. 29. Directive replaced by Directive 98/59/EC (OJ L 225, 12.8.1998, p. 16).

2. This Directive shall apply where and in so far as the undertaking, business or part of the undertaking or business to be transferred is situated within the territorial scope of the Treaty.
3. This Directive shall not apply to seagoing vessels.

Article 2

1. For the purposes of this Directive:
(a) "transferor" shall mean any natural or legal person who, by reason of a transfer within the meaning of Article 1(1), ceases to be the employer in respect of the undertaking, business or part of the undertaking or business;
(b) "transferee" shall mean any natural or legal person who, by reason of a transfer within the meaning of Article 1(1), becomes the employer in respect of the undertaking, business or part of the undertaking or business;
(c) "representatives of employees" and related expressions shall mean the representatives of the employees provided for by the laws or practices of the Member States;
(d) "employee" shall mean any person who, in the Member State concerned, is protected as an employee under national employment law.
2. This Directive shall be without prejudice to national law as regards the definition of contract of employment or employment relationship.

However, Member States shall not exclude from the scope of this Directive contracts of employment or employment relationships solely because:
(a) of the number of working hours performed or to be performed,
(b) they are employment relationships governed by a fixed-duration contract of employment within the meaning of Article 1(1) of Council Directive 91/383/EEC of 25 June 1991 supplementing the measures to encourage improvements in the safety and health at work of workers with a fixed-duration employment relationship or a tempory employment relationship[1], or
(c) they are temporary employment relationships within the meaning of Article 1(2) of Directive 91/383/EEC, and the undertaking, business or part of the undertaking or business transferred is, or is part of, the temporary employment business which is the employer.

CHAPTER II : SAFEGUARDING OF EMPLOYEES' RIGHTS

Article 3

1. The transferor's rights and obligations arising from a contract of employment or from an employment relationship existing on the date of a transfer shall, by reason of such transfer, be transferred to the transferee.

Member States may provide that, after the date of transfer, the transferor and the transferee shall be jointly and severally liable in respect of obligations which

[1] OJ L 206, 29.7.1991, p. 19.

arose before the date of transfer from a contract of employment or an employment relationship existing on the date of the transfer.

2. Member States may adopt appropriate measures to ensure that the transferor notifies the transferee of all the rights and obligations which will be transferred to the transferee under this Article, so far as those rights and obligations are or ought to have been known to the transferor at the time of the transfer. A failure by the transferor to notify the transferee of any such right or obligation shall not affect the transfer of that right or obligation and the rights of any employees against the transferee and/or transferor in respect of that right or obligation.
3. Following the transfer, the transferee shall continue to observe the terms and conditions agreed in any collective agreement on the same terms applicable to the transferor under that agreement, until the date of termination or expiry of the collective agreement or the entry into force or application of another collective agreement.

   Member States may limit the period for observing such terms and conditions with the proviso that it shall not be less than one year.
4. (a) Unless Member States provide otherwise, paragraphs 1 and 3 shall not apply in relation to employees' rights to old-age, invalidity or survivors' benefits under supplementary company or intercompany pension schemes outside the statutory social security schemes in Member States.

   (b) Even where they do not provide in accordance with subparagraph (a) that paragraphs 1 and 3 apply in relation to such rights, Member States shall adopt the measures necessary to protect the interests of employees and of persons no longer employed in the transferor's business at the time of the transfer in respect of rights conferring on them immediate or prospective entitlement to old age benefits, including survivors' benefits, under supplementary schemes referred to in subparagraph (a).

Article 4

1. The transfer of the undertaking, business or part of the undertaking or business shall not in itself constitute grounds for dismissal by the transferor or the transferee. This provision shall not stand in the way of dismissals that may take place for economic, technical or organisational reasons entailing changes in the workforce.

   Member States may provide that the first subparagraph shall not apply to certain specific categories of employees who are not covered by the laws or practice of the Member States in respect of protection against dismissal.
2. If the contract of employment or the employment relationship is terminated because the transfer involves a substantial change in working conditions to the detriment of the employee, the employer shall be regarded as having been responsible for termination of the contract of employment or of the employment relationship.

Article 5

1. Unless Member States provide otherwise, Articles 3 and 4 shall not apply to any transfer of an undertaking, business or part of an undertaking or business where the transferor is the subject of bankruptcy proceedings or any analogous insolvency proceedings which have been instituted with a view to the liquidation of the assets of the transferor and are under the supervision of a competent public authority (which may be an insolvency practioner authorised by a competent public authority).
2. Where Articles 3 and 4 apply to a transfer during insolvency proceedings which have been opened in relation to a transferor (whether or not those proceedings have been instituted with a view to the liquidation of the assets of the transferor) and provided that such proceedings are under the supervision of a competent public authority (which may be an insolvency practioner determined by national law) a Member State may provide that:
   (a) notwithstanding Article 3(1), the transferor's debts arising from any contracts of employment or employment relationships and payable before the transfer or before the opening of the insolvency proceedings shall not be transferred to the transferee, provided that such proceedings give rise, under the law of that Member State, to protection at least equivalent to that provided for in situations covered by Council Directive 80/987/EEC of 20 October 1980 on the approximation of the laws of the Member States relating to the protection of employees in the event of the insolvency of their employer[1], and, or alternatively, that,
   (b) the transferee, transferor or person or persons exercising the transferor's functions, on the one hand, and the representatives of the employees on the other hand may agree alterations, in so far as current law or practice permits, to the employees' terms and conditions of employment designed to safeguard employment opportunities by ensuring the survival of the undertaking, business or part of the undertaking or business.
3. A Member State may apply paragraph 20(b) to any transfers where the transferor is in a situation of serious economic crisis, as defined by national law, provided that the situation is declared by a competent public authority and open to judicial supervision, on condition that such provisions already existed in national law on 17 July 1998.

   The Commission shall present a report on the effects of this provision before 17 July 2003 and shall submit any appropriate proposals to the Council.
4. Member States shall take appropriate measures with a view to preventing misuse of insolvency proceedings in such a way as to deprive employees of the rights provided for in this Directive.

[1] OJ L 283, 20.10.1980, p. 23. Directive as last amended by the 1994 Act of Accession.

Article 6

1. If the undertaking, business or part of an undertaking or business preserves its autonomy, the status and function of the representatives or of the representation of the employees affected by the transfer shall be preserved on the same terms and subject to the same conditions as existed before the date of the transfer by virtue of law, regulation, administrative provision or agreement, provided that the conditions necessary for the constitution of the employee's representation are fulfilled.

   The first subparagraph shall not supply if, under the laws, regulations, administrative provisions or practice in the Member States, or by agreement with the representatives of the employees, the conditions necessary for the reappointment of the representatives of the employees or for the reconstitution of the representation of the employees are fulfilled.

   Where the transferor is the subject of bankruptcy proceedings or any analogous insolvency proceedings which have been instituted with a view to the liquidation of the assets of the transferor and are under the supervision of a competent public authority (which may be an insolvency practitioner authorised by a competent public authority), Member States may take the necessary measures to ensure that the transferred employees are properly represented until the new election or designation of representatives of the employees.

   If the undertaking, business or part of an undertaking or business does not preserve its autonomy, the Member States shall take the necessary measures to ensure that the employees transferred who were represented before the transfer continue to be properly represented during the period necessary for the reconstitution or reappointment of the representation of employees in accordance with national law or practice.
2. If the term of office of the representatives of the employees affected by the transfer expires as a result of the transfer, the representatives shall continue to enjoy the protection provided by the laws, regulations, administrative provisions or practice of the Member States.

CHAPTER III : INFORMATION AND CONSULTATION

Article 7

1. The transferor and transferee shall be required to inform the representatives of their respective employees affected by the transfer of the following:
   - the date or proposed date of the transfer,
   - the reasons for the transfer,
   - the legal, economic and social implications of the transfer for the employees,
   - any measures envisaged in relation to the employees.

   The transferor must give such information to the representatives of his employees in good time, before the transfer is carried out.

The transferee must give such information to the representatives of his employees in good time, and in any event before his employees are directly affected by the transfer as regards their conditions of work and employment.

2. Where the transferor or the transferee envisages measures in relation to his employees, he shall consult the representatives of this employees in good time on such measures with a view to reaching an agreement.
3. Member States whose laws, regulations or administrative provisions provide that represenatives of the employees may have recourse to an arbitration board to obtain a decision on the measures to be taken in relation to employees may limit the obligations laid down in paragraphs 1 and 2 to cases where the transfer carried out gives rise to a change in the business likely to entail serious disadvantages for a considerable number of the employees.

   The information and consultations shall cover at least the measures envisaged in relation to the employees.

   The information must be provided and consultations take place in good time before the change in the business as referred to in the first subparagraph is effected.
4. The obligations laid down in this Article shall apply irrespective of whether the decision resulting in the transfer is taken by the employer or an undertaking controlling the employer.

   In considering alleged breaches of the information and consultation requirements laid down by this Directive, the argument that such a breach occurred because the information was not provided by an undertaking controlling the employer shall not be accepted as an excuse.
5. Member States may limit the obligations laid down in paragraphs 1, 2 and 3 to undertakings or businesses which, in terms of the number of employees, meet the conditions for the election or nomination of a collegiate body representing the employees.
6. Member States shall provide that, where there are no representatives of the employees in an undertaking or business through no fault of their own, the employees concerned must be informed in advance of:
   - the date or proposed date of the transfer,
   - the reason for the transfer,
   - the legal, economic and social implications of the transfer for the employees,
   - any measures envisaged in relation to the employees.

CHAPTER IV: FINAL PROVISIONS

Article 8

This Directive shall not affect the right of Member States to apply or introduce laws, regulations or administrative provisions which are more favourable to employees or to promote or permit collective agreements or agreements between social partners more favourable to employees.

Article 9

Member States shall introduce into their national legal systems such measures as are necessary to enable all employees and representatives of employees who consider themselves wronged by failure to comply with the obligations arising from this Directive to pursue their claims by judicial process after possible recourse to other competent authorities.

Article 10

The Commission shall submit to the Council an analysis of the effect of the provisions of this Directive before 17 July 2006. It shall propose any amendment which may seem necessary.

Article 11

Member States shall communicate to the Commission the texts of the laws, regulations and administrative provisions which they adopt in the field covered by this Directive.

Article 12

Directive 77/187/EEC, as amended by the Directive referred to in Annex I, Part A, is repealed, without prejudice to the obligations of the Member States concerning the time limits for implementation set out in Annex I, Part B.

References to the repealed Directive shall be construed as references to this Directive and shall be read in accordance with the correlation table in Annex II.

Article 13

This Directive shall enter into force on the 20th day following its publication in the Official Journal of the European Communities.

Article 14

This Directive is addressed to the Member States.

Done at Brussels, 12 March 2001.

For the Council

The President

B. Ringholm

ANNEX I

PART A

Repealed Directive and its amending Directive
(referred to in Article 12)

Council Directive 77/187/EEC (OJ L 61, 5.3.1977, p. 26)
Council Directive 98/50/EC (OJ L 201, 17.7.1998, p. 88)

PART B

Deadlines for transposition into national law
(referred to in Article 12)

Directive	Deadlines for transposition
77/187/EEC 98/50/EC	16 February 1979 17 July 2001

ANNEX II

CORRELATION TABLE

Directive 77/187/EEC	This Directive
Article 1	Article 1
Article 2	Article 2
Article 3	Article 3
Article 4	Article 4
Article 4a	Article 5
Article 5	Article 6
Article 6	Article 7
Article 7	Article 8
Article 7a	Article 9
Article 7b	Article 10
Article 8	Article 11
-	Article 13
-	Article 14
-	ANNEX I
-	ANNEX II

12. Directive 2002/47/EC of the European Parliament and of the Council of 6 June 2002 on financial collateral arrangements

(OJ L 168 , 27/06/2002 p. 43 – 50)

Having regard to the Treaty establishing the European Community, and in particular Article 95 thereof,

Having regard to the proposal from the Commission[1],

Having regard to the opinion of the European Central Bank[2],

Having regard to the opinion of the Economic and Social Committee[3],

Acting in accordance with the procedure laid down in Article 251 of the Treaty[4],

Whereas:

(1) Directive 98/26/EC of the European Parliament and of the Council of 19 May 1998 on settlement finality in payment and securities settlement systems[5] constituted a milestone in establishing a sound legal framework for payment and securities settlement systems. Implementation of that Directive has demonstrated the importance of limiting systemic risk inherent in such systems stemming from the different influence of several jurisdictions, and the benefits of common rules in relation to collateral constituted to such systems.

(2) In its communication of 11 May 1999 to the European Parliament and to the Council on financial services: implementing the framework for financial markets: action plan, the Commission undertook, after consultation with market experts and national authorities, to work on further proposals for legislative action on collateral urging further progress in the field of collateral, beyond Directive 98/26/EC.

(3) A Community regime should be created for the provision of securities and cash as collateral under both security interest and title transfer structures including repurchase agreements (repos). This will contribute to the integration and cost-efficiency of the financial market as well as to the stability of the financial system in the Community, thereby supporting the freedom to provide services and the free movement of capital in the single market in financial services. This Directive focuses on bilateral financial collateral arrangements.

(4) This Directive is adopted in a European legal context which consists in particular of the said Directive 98/26/EC as well as Directive 2001/24/EC of the European Parliament and of the Council of 4 April 2001 on the reorganisation

1 OJ C 180 E, 26.6.2001, p. 312.

2 OJ C 196, 12.7.2001, p. 10.

3 OJ C 48, 21.2.2002, p. 1.

4 Opinion of the European Parliament of 13 December 2001 (not yet published in the Official Journal), Council Common Position of 5 March 2002 (not yet published in the Official Journal) and Decision of the European Parliament of 15 May 2002.

5 OJ L 166, 11.6.1998, p. 45.

and winding up of credit institutions[1], Directive 2001/17/EC of the European Parliament and of the Council of 19 March 2001 on the reorganisation and winding-up of insurance undertakings[2] and Council Regulation (EC) No 1346/2000 of 29 May 2000 on insolvency proceedings[3]. This Directive is in line with the general pattern of these previous legal acts and is not opposed to it. Indeed, this Directive complements these existing legal acts by dealing with further issues and going beyond them in connection with particular matters already dealt with by these legal acts.

(5) In order to improve the legal certainty of financial collateral arrangements, Member States should ensure that certain provisions of insolvency law do not apply to such arrangements, in particular, those that would inhibit the effective realisation of financial collateral or cast doubt on the validity of current techniques such as bilateral close-out netting, the provision of additional collateral in the form of top-up collateral and substitution of collateral.

(6) This Directive does not address rights which any person may have in respect of assets provided as financial collateral, and which arise otherwise than under the terms of the financial collateral arrangement and otherwise than on the basis of any legal provision or rule of law arising by reason of the commencement or continuation of winding-up proceedings or reorganisation measures, such as restitution arising from mistake, error or lack of capacity.

(7) The principle in Directive 98/26/EC, whereby the law applicable to book entry securities provided as collateral is the law of the jurisdiction where the relevant register, account or centralised deposit system is located, should be extended in order to create legal certainty regarding the use of such securities held in a cross-border context and used as financial collateral under the scope of this Directive.

(8) The lex rei sitae rule, according to which the applicable law for determining whether a financial collateral arrangement is properly perfected and therefore good against third parties is the law of the country where the financial collateral is located, is currently recognised by all Member States. Without affecting the application of this Directive to directly-held securities, the location of book entry securities provided as financial collateral and held through one or more intermediaries should be determined. If the collateral taker has a valid and effective collateral arrangement according to the governing law of the country in which the relevant account is maintained, then the validity against any competing title or interest and the enforceability of the collateral should be governed solely by the law of that country, thus preventing legal uncertainty as a result of other unforeseen legislation.

(9) In order to limit the administrative burdens for parties using financial collateral under the scope of this Directive, the only perfection requirement which national law may impose in respect of financial collateral should be that the financial

[1] OJ L 125, 5.5.2001, p. 15.
[2] OJ L 110, 20.4.2001, p. 28.
[3] OJ L 160, 30.6.2000, p. 1.

collateral is delivered, transferred, held, registered or otherwise designated so as to be in the possession or under the control of the collateral taker or of a person acting on the collateral taker's behalf while not excluding collateral techniques where the collateral provider is allowed to substitute collateral or to withdraw excess collateral.

(10) For the same reasons, the creation, validity, perfection, enforceability or admissibility in evidence of a financial collateral arrangement, or the provision of financial collateral under a financial collateral arrangement, should not be made dependent on the performance of any formal act such as the execution of any document in a specific form or in a particular manner, the making of any filing with an official or public body or registration in a public register, advertisement in a newspaper or journal, in an official register or publication or in any other matter, notification to a public officer or the provision of evidence in a particular form as to the date of execution of a document or instrument, the amount of the relevant financial obligations or any other matter. This Directive must however provide a balance between market efficiency and the safety of the parties to the arrangement and third parties, thereby avoiding inter alia the risk of fraud. This balance should be achieved through the scope of this Directive covering only those financial collateral arrangements which provide for some form of dispossession, i.e. the provision of the financial collateral, and where the provision of the financial collateral can be evidenced in writing or in a durable medium, ensuring thereby the traceability of that collateral. For the purpose of this Directive, acts required under the law of a Member State as conditions for transferring or creating a security interest on financial instruments, other than book entry securities, such as endorsement in the case of instruments to order, or recording on the issuer's register in the case of registered instruments, should not be considered as formal acts.

(11) Moreover, this Directive should protect only financial collateral arrangements which can be evidenced. Such evidence can be given in writing or in any other legally enforceable manner provided by the law which is applicable to the financial collateral arrangement.

(12) The simplification of the use of financial collateral through the limitation of administrative burdens promotes the efficiency of the cross-border operations of the European Central Bank and the national central banks of Member States participating in the economic and monetary union, necessary for the implementation of the common monetary policy. Furthermore, the provision of limited protection of financial collateral arrangements from some rules of insolvency law in addition supports the wider aspect of the common monetary policy, where the participants in the money market balance the overall amount of liquidity in the market among themselves, by cross-border transactions backed by collateral.

(13) This Directive seeks to protect the validity of financial collateral arrangements which are based upon the transfer of the full ownership of the financial collateral, such as by eliminating the so-called re-characterisation of such

financial collateral arrangements (including repurchase agreements) as security interests.

(14) The enforceability of bilateral close-out netting should be protected, not only as an enforcement mechanism for title transfer financial collateral arrangements including repurchase agreements but more widely, where close-out netting forms part of a financial collateral arrangement. Sound risk management practices commonly used in the financial market should be protected by enabling participants to manage and reduce their credit exposures arising from all kinds of financial transactions on a net basis, where the credit exposure is calculated by combining the estimated current exposures under all outstanding transactions with a counterparty, setting off reciprocal items to produce a single aggregated amount that is compared with the current value of the collateral.

(15) This Directive should be without prejudice to any restrictions or requirements under national law on bringing into account claims, on obligations to set-off, or on netting, for example relating to their reciprocity or the fact that they have been concluded prior to when the collateral taker knew or ought to have known of the commencement (or of any mandatory legal act leading to the commencement) of winding-up proceedings or reorganisation measures in respect of the collateral provider.

(16) The sound market practice favoured by regulators whereby participants in the financial market use top-up financial collateral arrangements to manage and limit their credit risk to each other by mark-to-market calculations of the current market value of the credit exposure and the value of the financial collateral and accordingly ask for top-up financial collateral or return the surplus of financial collateral should be protected against certain automatic avoidance rules. The same applies to the possibility of substituting for assets provided as financial collateral other assets of the same value. The intention is merely that the provision of top-up or substitution financial collateral cannot be questioned on the sole basis that the relevant financial obligations existed before that financial collateral was provided, or that the financial collateral was provided during a prescribed period. However, this does not prejudice the possibility of questioning under national law the financial collateral arrangement and the provision of financial collateral as part of the initial provision, top-up or substitution of financial collateral, for example where this has been intentionally done to the detriment of the other creditors (this covers inter alia actions based on fraud or similar avoidance rules which may apply in a prescribed period).

(17) This Directive provides for rapid and non-formalistic enforcement procedures in order to safeguard financial stability and limit contagion effects in case of a default of a party to a financial collateral arrangement. However, this Directive balances the latter objectives with the protection of the collateral provider and third parties by explicitly confirming the possibility for Member States to keep or introduce in their national legislation an a posteriori control which the Courts can exercise in relation to the realisation or valuation of financial collateral and the calculation of the relevant financial obligations. Such control should allow

for the judicial authorities to verify that the realisation or valuation has been conducted in a commercially reasonable manner.

(18) It should be possible to provide cash as collateral under both title transfer and secured structures respectively protected by the recognition of netting or by the pledge of cash collateral. Cash refers only to money which is represented by a credit to an account, or similar claims on repayment of money (such as money market deposits), thus explicitly excluding banknotes.

(19) This Directive provides for a right of use in case of security financial collateral arrangements, which increases liquidity in the financial market stemming from such reuse of "pledged" securities. This reuse however should be without prejudice to national legislation about separation of assets and unfair treatment of creditors.

(20) This Directive does not prejudice the operation and effect of the contractual terms of financial instruments provided as financial collateral, such as rights and obligations and other conditions contained in the terms of issue and any other rights and obligations and other conditions which apply between the issuers and holders of such instruments.

(21) This Act complies with the fundamental rights and follows the principles laid down in particular in the Charter of Fundamental Rights of the European Union.

(22) Since the objective of the proposed action, namely to create a minimum regime relating to the use of financial collateral, cannot be sufficiently achieved by the Member States and can therefore, by reason of the scale and effects of the action, be better achieved at Community level, the Community may adopt measures, in accordance with the principle of subsidiarity as set out in Article 5 of the Treaty. In accordance with the principle of proportionality, as set out in that Article, this Directive does not go beyond what is necessary in order to achieve that objective,

HAVE ADOPTED THIS DIRECTIVE:

Article 1 Subject matter and scope

1. This Directive lays down a Community regime applicable to financial collateral arrangements which satisfy the requirements set out in paragraphs 2 and 5 and to financial collateral in accordance with the conditions set out in paragraphs 4 and 5.
2. The collateral taker and the collateral provider must each belong to one of the following categories:
   (a) a public authority (excluding publicly guaranteed undertakings unless they fall under points (b) to (e)) including:
      (i) public sector bodies of Member States charged with or intervening in the management of public debt, and
      (ii) public sector bodies of Member States authorised to hold accounts for customers;

(b) a central bank, the European Central Bank, the Bank for International Settlements, a multilateral development bank as defined in Article 1(19) of Directive 2000/12/EC of the European Parliament and of the Council of 20 March 2000 relating to the taking up and pursuit of the business of credit institutions[1], the International Monetary Fund and the European Investment Bank;

(c) a financial institution subject to prudential supervision including:

(i) a credit institution as defined in Article 1(1) of Directive 2000/12/EC, including the institutions listed in Article 2(3) of that Directive;

(ii) an investment firm as defined in Article 1(2) of Council Directive 93/22/EEC of 10 May 1993 on investment services in the securities field[2];

(iii) a financial institution as defined in Article 1(5) of Directive 2000/12/EC;

(iv) an insurance undertaking as defined in Article 1(a) of Council Directive 92/49/EEC of 18 June 1992 on the coordination of laws, regulations and administrative provisions relating to direct insurance other than life assurance[3] and a life assurance undertaking as defined in Article 1(a) of Council Directive 92/96/EEC of 10 November 1992 on the coordination of laws, regulations and administrative provisions relating to direct life assurance[4];

(v) an undertaking for collective investment in transferable securities (UCITS) as defined in Article 1(2) of Council Directive 85/611/EEC of 20 December 1985 on the coordination of laws, regulations and administrative provisions relating to undertakings for collective investment in transferable securities (UCITS)[5];

(vi) a management company as defined in Article 1a(2) of Directive 85/611/EEC;

(d) a central counterparty, settlement agent or clearing house, as defined respectively in Article 2(c), (d) and (e) of Directive 98/26/EC, including similar institutions regulated under national law acting in the futures, options and derivatives markets to the extent not covered by that Directive, and a person, other than a natural person, who acts in a trust or representative capacity on behalf of any one or more persons that includes any bondholders or holders of other forms of securitised debt or any institution as defined in points (a) to (d);

---

1 OJ L 126, 26.5.2000, p. 1. Directive as amended by Directive 2000/28/EC (OJ L 275, 27.10.2000, p. 37).

2 OJ L 141, 11.6.1993, p. 27. Directive as last amended by Directive 2000/64/EC of the European Parliament and of the Council (OJ L 290, 17.11.2000, p. 27).

3 OJ L 228, 11.8.1992, p. 1. Directive as last amended by Directive 2000/64/EC of the European Parliament and of the Council.

4 OJ L 360, 9.12.1992, p. 1. Directive as last amended by Directive 2000/64/EC of the European Parliament and of the Council

5 OJ L 375, 31.12.1985, p. 3. Directive as last amended by Directive 2001/108/EC of the European Parliament and of the Council. (OJ L 41, 13.2.2002, p. 35).

(e) a person other than a natural person, including unincorporated firms and partnerships, provided that the other party is an institution as defined in points (a) to (d).

3. Member States may exclude from the scope of this Directive financial collateral arrangements where one of the parties is a person mentioned in paragraph 2(e).

   If they make use of this option Member States shall inform the Commission which shall inform the other Member States thereof.

4. (a) The financial collateral to be provided must consist of cash or financial instruments.

   (b) Member States may exclude from the scope of this Directive financial collateral consisting of the collateral provider's own shares, shares in affiliated undertakings within the meaning of seventh Council Directive 83/349/EEC of 13 June 1983 on consolidated accounts[1], and shares in undertakings whose exclusive purpose is to own means of production that are essential for the collateral provider's business or to own real property.

5. This Directive applies to financial collateral once it has been provided and if that provision can be evidenced in writing.

   The evidencing of the provision of financial collateral must allow for the identification of the financial collateral to which it applies. For this purpose, it is sufficient to prove that the book entry securities collateral has been credited to, or forms a credit in, the relevant account and that the cash collateral has been credited to, or forms a credit in, a designated account.

   This Directive applies to financial collateral arrangements if that arrangement can be evidenced in writing or in a legally equivalent manner.

Article 2 Definitions

1. For the purpose of this Directive:

   (a) "financial collateral arrangement" means a title transfer financial collateral arrangement or a security financial collateral arrangement whether or not these are covered by a master agreement or general terms and conditions;

   (b) "title transfer financial collateral arrangement" means an arrangement, including repurchase agreements, under which a collateral provider transfers full ownership of financial collateral to a collateral taker for the purpose of securing or otherwise covering the performance of relevant financial obligations;

   (c) "security financial collateral arrangement" means an arrangement under which a collateral provider provides financial collateral by way of security in favour of, or to, a collateral taker, and where the full ownership of the financial collateral remains with the collateral provider when the security right is established;

[1] OJ L 193, 18.7.1983, p. 1. Directive as last amended by Directive 2001/65/EC of the European Parliament and of the Council (OJ L 283, 27.10.2001, p. 28).

(d) "cash" means money credited to an account in any currency, or similar claims for the repayment of money, such as money market deposits;

(e) "financial instruments" means shares in companies and other securities equivalent to shares in companies and bonds and other forms of debt instruments if these are negotiable on the capital market, and any other securities which are normally dealt in and which give the right to acquire any such shares, bonds or other securities by subscription, purchase or exchange or which give rise to a cash settlement (excluding instruments of payment), including units in collective investment undertakings, money market instruments and claims relating to or rights in or in respect of any of the foregoing;

(f) "relevant financial obligations" means the obligations which are secured by a financial collateral arrangement and which give a right to cash settlement and/or delivery of financial instruments.

Relevant financial obligations may consist of or include:

(i) present or future, actual or contingent or prospective obligations (including such obligations arising under a master agreement or similar arrangement);

(ii) obligations owed to the collateral taker by a person other than the collateral provider; or

(iii) obligations of a specified class or kind arising from time to time;

(g) "book entry securities collateral" means financial collateral provided under a financial collateral arrangement which consists of financial instruments, title to which is evidenced by entries in a register or account maintained by or on behalf of an intermediary;

(h) "relevant account" means in relation to book entry securities collateral which is subject to a financial collateral arrangement, the register or account - which may be maintained by the collateral taker - in which the entries are made by which that book entry securities collateral is provided to the collateral taker;

(i) "equivalent collateral":

(i) in relation to cash, means a payment of the same amount and in the same currency;

(ii) in relation to financial instruments, means financial instruments of the same issuer or debtor, forming part of the same issue or class and of the same nominal amount, currency and description or, where a financial collateral arrangement provides for the transfer of other assets following the occurrence of any event relating to or affecting any financial instruments provided as financial collateral, those other assets;

(j) "winding-up proceedings" means collective proceedings involving realisation of the assets and distribution of the proceeds among the creditors, shareholders or members as appropriate, which involve any intervention by administrative or judicial authorities, including where the collective proceedings are terminated by a composition or other analogous measure, whether or not they are founded on insolvency or are voluntary or compulsory;

(k) "reorganisation measures" means measures which involve any intervention by administrative or judicial authorities which are intended to preserve or restore the financial situation and which affect pre-existing rights of third parties, including but not limited to measures involving a suspension of payments, suspension of enforcement measures or reduction of claims;

(l) "enforcement event" means an event of default or any similar event as agreed between the parties on the occurrence of which, under the terms of a financial collateral arrangement or by operation of law, the collateral taker is entitled to realise or appropriate financial collateral or a close-out netting provision comes into effect;

(m) "right of use" means the right of the collateral taker to use and dispose of financial collateral provided under a security financial collateral arrangement as the owner of it in accordance with the terms of the security financial collateral arrangement;

(n) "close-out netting provision" means a provision of a financial collateral arrangement, or of an arrangement of which a financial collateral arrangement forms part, or, in the absence of any such provision, any statutory rule by which, on the occurrence of an enforcement event, whether through the operation of netting or set-off or otherwise:

(i) the obligations of the parties are accelerated so as to be immediately due and expressed as an obligation to pay an amount representing their estimated current value, or are terminated and replaced by an obligation to pay such an amount; and/or

(ii) an account is taken of what is due from each party to the other in respect of such obligations, and a net sum equal to the balance of the account is payable by the party from whom the larger amount is due to the other party.

2. References in this Directive to financial collateral being "provided", or to the "provision" of financial collateral, are to the financial collateral being delivered, transferred, held, registered or otherwise designated so as to be in the possession or under the control of the collateral taker or of a person acting on the collateral taker's behalf. Any right of substitution or to withdraw excess financial collateral in favour of the collateral provider shall not prejudice the financial collateral having been provided to the collateral taker as mentioned in this Directive.

3. References in this Directive to "writing" include recording by electronic means and any other durable medium.

Article 3 Formal requirements

1. Member States shall not require that the creation, validity, perfection, enforceability or admissibility in evidence of a financial collateral arrangement

or the provision of financial collateral under a financial collateral arrangement be dependent on the performance of any formal act.

2. Paragraph 1 is without prejudice to the application of this Directive to financial collateral only once it has been provided and if that provision can be evidenced in writing and where the financial collateral arrangement can be evidenced in writing or in a legally equivalent manner.

Article 4 Enforcement of financial collateral arrangements

1. Member States shall ensure that on the occurrence of an enforcement event, the collateral taker shall be able to realise in the following manners, any financial collateral provided under, and subject to the terms agreed in, a security financial collateral arrangement:
   (a) financial instruments by sale or appropriation and by setting off their value against, or applying their value in discharge of, the relevant financial obligations;
   (b) cash by setting off the amount against or applying it in discharge of the relevant financial obligations.
2. Appropriation is possible only if:
   (a) this has been agreed by the parties in the security financial collateral arrangement; and
   (b) the parties have agreed in the security financial collateral arrangement on the valuation of the financial instruments.
3. Member States which do not allow appropriation on 27 June 2002 are not obliged to recognise it.

   If they make use of this option, Member States shall inform the Commission which in turn shall inform the other Member States thereof.
4. The manners of realising the financial collateral referred to in paragraph 1 shall, subject to the terms agreed in the security financial collateral arrangement, be without any requirement to the effect that:
   (a) prior notice of the intention to realise must have been given;
   (b) the terms of the realisation be approved by any court, public officer or other person;
   (c) the realisation be conducted by public auction or in any other prescribed manner; or
   (d) any additional time period must have elapsed.
5. Member States shall ensure that a financial collateral arrangement can take effect in accordance with its terms notwithstanding the commencement or continuation of winding-up proceedings or reorganisation measures in respect of the collateral provider or collateral taker.
6. This Article and Articles 5, 6 and 7 shall be without prejudice to any requirements under national law to the effect that the realisation or valuation of financial collateral and the calculation of the relevant financial obligations must be conducted in a commercially reasonable manner.

Article 5 Right of use of financial collateral under security financial collateral arrangements

1. If and to the extent that the terms of a security financial collateral arrangement so provide, Member States shall ensure that the collateral taker is entitled to exercise a right of use in relation to financial collateral provided under the security financial collateral arrangement.
2. Where a collateral taker exercises a right of use, he thereby incurs an obligation to transfer equivalent collateral to replace the original financial collateral at the latest on the due date for the performance of the relevant financial obligations covered by the security financial collateral arrangement.

   Alternatively, the collateral taker shall, on the due date for the performance of the relevant financial obligations, either transfer equivalent collateral, or, if and to the extent that the terms of a security financial collateral arrangement so provide, set off the value of the equivalent collateral against or apply it in discharge of the relevant financial obligations.
3. The equivalent collateral transferred in discharge of an obligation as described in paragraph 2, first subparagraph, shall be subject to the same security financial collateral agreement to which the original financial collateral was subject and shall be treated as having been provided under the security financial collateral arrangement at the same time as the original financial collateral was first provided.
4. Member States shall ensure that the use of financial collateral by the collateral taker according to this Article does not render invalid or unenforceable the rights of the collateral taker under the security financial collateral arrangement in relation to the financial collateral transferred by the collateral taker in discharge of an obligation as described in paragraph 2, first subparagraph.
5. If an enforcement event occurs while an obligation as described in paragraph 2 first subparagraph remains outstanding, the obligation may be the subject of a close-out netting provision.

Article 6 Recognition of title transfer financial collateral arrangements

1. Member States shall ensure that a title transfer financial collateral arrangement can take effect in accordance with its terms.
2. If an enforcement event occurs while any obligation of the collateral taker to transfer equivalent collateral under a title transfer financial collateral arrangement remains outstanding, the obligation may be the subject of a close-out netting provision.

Article 7 Recognition of close-out netting provisions

1. Member States shall ensure that a close-out netting provision can take effect in accordance with its terms:

(a) notwithstanding the commencement or continuation of winding-up proceedings or reorganisation measures in respect of the collateral provider and/or the collateral taker; and/or

(b) notwithstanding any purported assignment, judicial or other attachment or other disposition of or in respect of such rights.

2. Member States shall ensure that the operation of a close-out netting provision may not be subject to any of the requirements that are mentioned in Article 4(4), unless otherwise agreed by the parties.

Article 8 Certain insolvency provisions disapplied

1. Member States shall ensure that a financial collateral arrangement, as well as the provision of financial collateral under such arrangement, may not be declared invalid or void or be reversed on the sole basis that the financial collateral arrangement has come into existence, or the financial collateral has been provided:

   (a) on the day of the commencement of winding-up proceedings or reorganisation measures, but prior to the order or decree making that commencement; or

   (b) in a prescribed period prior to, and defined by reference to, the commencement of such proceedings or measures or by reference to the making of any order or decree or the taking of any other action or occurrence of any other event in the course of such proceedings or measures.

2. Member States shall ensure that where a financial collateral arrangement or a relevant financial obligation has come into existence, or financial collateral has been provided on the day of, but after the moment of the commencement of, winding-up proceedings or reorganisation measures, it shall be legally enforceable and binding on third parties if the collateral taker can prove that he was not aware, nor should have been aware, of the commencement of such proceedings or measures.

3. Where a financial collateral arrangement contains:

   (a) an obligation to provide financial collateral or additional financial collateral in order to take account of changes in the value of the financial collateral or in the amount of the relevant financial obligations, or

   (b) a right to withdraw financial collateral on providing, by way of substitution or exchange, financial collateral of substantially the same value,

   Member States shall ensure that the provision of financial collateral, additional financial collateral or substitute or replacement financial collateral under such an obligation or right shall not be treated as invalid or reversed or declared void on the sole basis that:

   (i) such provision was made on the day of the commencement of winding-up proceedings or reorganisation measures, but prior to the order or decree making that commencement or in a prescribed period prior to, and defined by reference to, the commencement of winding-up proceedings or reorganisation measures or by reference to the making of any order or decree or the taking of any other action or occurrence of any other event in the course of such proceedings or measures; and/or

(ii) the relevant financial obligations were incurred prior to the date of the provision of the financial collateral, additional financial collateral or substitute or replacement financial collateral.

4. Without prejudice to paragraphs 1, 2 and 3, this Directive leaves unaffected the general rules of national insolvency law in relation to the voidance of transactions entered into during the prescribed period referred to in paragraph 1(b) and in paragraph 3(i).

Article 9 Conflict of laws

1. Any question with respect to any of the matters specified in paragraph 2 arising in relation to book entry securities collateral shall be governed by the law of the country in which the relevant account is maintained. The reference to the law of a country is a reference to its domestic law, disregarding any rule under which, in deciding the relevant question, reference should be made to the law of another country.
2. The matters referred to in paragraph 1 are:
   (a) the legal nature and proprietary effects of book entry securities collateral;
   (b) the requirements for perfecting a financial collateral arrangement relating to book entry securities collateral and the provision of book entry securities collateral under such an arrangement, and more generally the completion of the steps necessary to render such an arrangement and provision effective against third parties;
   (c) whether a person's title to or interest in such book entry securities collateral is overridden by or subordinated to a competing title or interest, or a good faith acquisition has occurred;
   (d) the steps required for the realisation of book entry securities collateral following the occurrence of an enforcement event.

Article 10 Report by the Commission

Not later than 27 December 2006, the Commission shall present a report to the European Parliament and the Council on the application of this Directive, in particular on the application of Article 1(3), Article 4(3) and Article 5, accompanied where appropriate by proposals for its revision.

Article 11 Implementation

Member States shall bring into force the laws, regulations and administrative provisions necessary to comply with this Directive by 27 December 2003 at the latest. They shall forthwith inform the Commission thereof.

When Member States adopt those provisions, they shall contain a reference to this Directive or be accompanied by such reference on the occasion of their official publication. Member States shall determine how such reference is to be made.

Article 12 Entry into force

This Directive shall enter into force on the day of its publication in the Official Journal of the European Communities.

Article 13 Addressees

This Directive is addressed to the Member States.

Done at Brussels, 6 June 2002.

For the European Parliament

The President

P. Cox

For the Council

The President

A. M. Birulés Y Bertrán

13. Directive 2002/65/EC of the European Parliament and of the Council of 23 September 2002 concerning the distance marketing of consumer financial services and amending Council Directive 90/619/EEC and Directives 97/7/EC and 98/27/EC

(OJ L 271 , 09/10/2002 p. 16 – 24)

THE EUROPEAN PARLIAMENT AND THE COUNCIL OF THE EUROPEAN UNION,

Having regard to the Treaty establishing the European Community, and in particular Article 47(2), Article 55 and Article 95 thereof,

Having regard to the proposal from the Commission[1],

Having regard to the opinion of the Economic and Social Committee[2],

Acting in accordance with the procedure laid down in Article 251 of the Treaty[3],

Whereas:

(1) It is important, in the context of achieving the aims of the single market, to adopt measures designed to consolidate progressively this market and those measures must contribute to attaining a high level of consumer protection, in accordance with Articles 95 and 153 of the Treaty.

(2) Both for consumers and suppliers of financial services, the distance marketing of financial services will constitute one of the main tangible results of the completion of the internal market.

(3) Within the framework of the internal market, it is in the interest of consumers to have access without discrimination to the widest possible range of financial services available in the Community so that they can choose those that are best suited to their needs. In order to safeguard freedom of choice, which is an essential consumer right, a high degree of consumer protection is required in order to enhance consumer confidence in distance selling.

(4) It is essential to the smooth operation of the internal market for consumers to be able to negotiate and conclude contracts with a supplier established in other Member States, regardless of whether the supplier is also established in the Member State in which the consumer resides.

(5) Because of their intangible nature, financial services are particularly suited to distance selling and the establishment of a legal framework governing the distance marketing of financial services should increase consumer confidence in

---

1 OJ C 385, 11.12.1998, p. 10 and OJ C 177 E, 27.6.2000, p. 21.

2 OJ C 169, 16.6.1999, p. 43.

3 Opinion of the European Parliament of 5 May 1999 (OJ C 279, 1.10.1999, p. 207), Council Common Position of 19 December 2001 (OJ C 58 E, 5.3.2002, p. 32) and Decision of the European Parliament of 14 May 2002 (not yet published in the Official Journal). Council Decision of 26 June 2002 (not yet published in the Official Journal).

the use of new techniques for the distance marketing of financial services, such as electronic commerce.

(6) This Directive should be applied in conformity with the Treaty and with secondary law, including Directive 2000/31/EC[1] on electronic commerce, the latter being applicable solely to the transactions which it covers.

(7) This Directive aims to achieve the objectives set forth above without prejudice to Community or national law governing freedom to provide services or, where applicable, host Member State control and/or authorisation or supervision systems in the Member States where this is compatible with Community legislation.

(8) Moreover, this Directive, and in particular its provisions relating to information about any contractual clause on law applicable to the contract and/or on the competent court does not affect the applicability to the distance marketing of consumer financial services of Council Regulation (EC) No 44/2001 of 22 December 2000 on jurisdiction and the recognition and enforcement of judgements in civil and commercial matters[2] or of the 1980 Rome Convention on the law applicable to contractual obligations.

(9) The achievement of the objectives of the Financial Services Action Plan requires a higher level of consumer protection in certain areas. This implies a greater convergence, in particular, in non harmonised collective investment funds, rules of conduct applicable to investment services and consumer credits. Pending the achievement of the above convergence, a high level of consumer protection should be maintained.

(10) Directive 97/7/EC of the European Parliament and of the Council of 20 May 1997 on the protection of consumers in respect of distance contracts[3], lays down the main rules applicable to distance contracts for goods or services concluded between a supplier and a consumer. However, that Directive does not cover financial services.

(11) In the context of the analysis conducted by the Commission with a view to ascertaining the need for specific measures in the field of financial services, the Commission invited all the interested parties to transmit their comments, notably in connection with the preparation of its Green Paper entitled "Financial Services - Meeting Consumers' Expectations". The consultations in this context showed that there is a need to strengthen consumer protection in this area. The Commission therefore decided to present a specific proposal concerning the distance marketing of financial services.

(12) The adoption by the Member States of conflicting or different consumer protection rules governing the distance marketing of consumer financial services could impede the functioning of the internal market and competition between firms in the market. It is therefore necessary to enact common rules at

1 OJ L 178, 17.7.2000, p. 1.
2 OJ L 12, 16.1.2001, p. 1.
3 OJ L 144, 4.6.1997, p. 19.

Community level in this area, consistent with no reduction in overall consumer protection in the Member States.

(13) A high level of consumer protection should be guaranteed by this Directive, with a view to ensuring the free movement of financial services. Member States should not be able to adopt provisions other than those laid down in this Directive in the fields it harmonises, unless otherwise specifically indicated in it.

(14) This Directive covers all financial services liable to be provided at a distance. However, certain financial services are governed by specific provisions of Community legislation which continue to apply to those financial services. However, principles governing the distance marketing of such services should be laid down.

(15) Contracts negotiated at a distance involve the use of means of distance communication which are used as part of a distance sales or service-provision scheme not involving the simultaneous presence of the supplier and the consumer. The constant development of those means of communication requires principles to be defined that are valid even for those means which are not yet in widespread use. Therefore, distance contracts are those the offer, negotiation and conclusion of which are carried out at a distance.

(16) A single contract involving successive operations or separate operations of the same nature performed over time may be subject to different legal treatment in the different Member States, but it is important that this Directive be applied in the same way in all the Member States. To that end, it is appropriate that this Directive should be considered to apply to the first of a series of successive operations or separate operations of the same nature performed over time which may be considered as forming a whole, irrespective of whether that operation or series of operations is the subject of a single contract or several successive contracts.

(17) An "initial service agreement" may be considered to be for example the opening of a bank account, acquiring a credit card, concluding a portfolio management contract, and "operations" may be considered to be for example the deposit or withdrawal of funds to or from the bank account, payment by credit card, transactions made within the framework of a portfolio management contract. Adding new elements to an initial service agreement, such as a possibility to use an electronic payment instrument together with one's existing bank account, does not constitute an "operation" but an additional contract to which this Directive applies. The subscription to new units of the same collective investment fund is considered to be one of "successive operations of the same nature".

(18) By covering a service-provision scheme organised by the financial services provider, this Directive aims to exclude from its scope services provided on a strictly occasional basis and outside a commercial structure dedicated to the conclusion of distance contracts.

(19) The supplier is the person providing services at a distance. This Directive should however also apply when one of the marketing stages involves an intermediary. Having regard to the nature and degree of that involvement, the pertinent provisions of this Directive should apply to such an intermediary, irrespective of his or her legal status.

(20) Durable mediums include in particular floppy discs, CD-ROMs, DVDs and the hard drive of the consumer's computer on which the electronic mail is stored, but they do not include Internet websites unless they fulfil the criteria contained in the definition of a durable medium.

(21) The use of means of distance communications should not lead to an unwarranted restriction on the information provided to the client. In the interests of transparency this Directive lays down the requirements needed to ensure that an appropriate level of information is provided to the consumer both before and after conclusion of the contract. The consumer should receive, before conclusion of the contract, the prior information needed so as to properly appraise the financial service offered to him and hence make a well-informed choice. The supplier should specify how long his offer applies as it stands.

(22) Information items listed in this Directive cover information of a general nature applicable to all kinds of financial services. Other information requirements concerning a given financial service, such as the coverage of an insurance policy, are not solely specified in this Directive. This kind of information should be provided in accordance, where applicable, with relevant Community legislation or national legislation in conformity with Community law.

(23) With a view to optimum protection of the consumer, it is important that the consumer is adequately informed of the provisions of this Directive and of any codes of conduct existing in this area and that he has a right of withdrawal.

(24) When the right of withdrawal does not apply because the consumer has expressly requested the performance of a contract, the supplier should inform the consumer of this fact.

(25) Consumers should be protected against unsolicited services. Consumers should be exempt from any obligation in the case of unsolicited services, the absence of a reply not being construed as signifying consent on their part. However, this rule should be without prejudice to the tacit renewal of contracts validly concluded between the parties whenever the law of the Member States permits such tacit renewal.

(26) Member States should take appropriate measures to protect effectively consumers who do not wish to be contacted through certain means of communication or at certain times. This Directive should be without prejudice to the particular safeguards available to consumers under Community legislation concerning the protection of personal data and privacy.

(27) With a view to protecting consumers, there is a need for suitable and effective complaint and redress procedures in the Member States with a view to settling

potential disputes between suppliers and consumers, by using, where appropriate, existing procedures.

(28) Member States should encourage public or private bodies established with a view to settling disputes out of court to cooperate in resolving cross-border disputes. Such cooperation could in particular entail allowing consumers to submit to extra-judicial bodies in the Member State of their residence complaints concerning suppliers established in other Member States. The establishment of FIN-NET offers increased assistance to consumers when using cross-border services.

(29) This Directive is without prejudice to extension by Member States, in accordance with Community law, of the protection provided by this Directive to non-profit organisations and persons making use of financial services in order to become entrepreneurs.

(30) This Directive should also cover cases where the national legislation includes the concept of a consumer making a binding contractual statement.

(31) The provisions in this Directive on the supplier's choice of language should be without prejudice to provisions of national legislation, adopted in conformity with Community law governing the choice of language.

(32) The Community and the Member States have entered into commitments in the context of the General Agreement on Trade in Services (GATS) concerning the possibility for consumers to purchase banking and investment services abroad. The GATS entitles Member States to adopt measures for prudential reasons, including measures to protect investors, depositors, policy-holders and persons to whom a financial service is owed by the supplier of the financial service. Such measures should not impose restrictions going beyond what is required to ensure the protection of consumers.

(33) In view of the adoption of this Directive, the scope of Directive 97/7/EC and Directive 98/27/EC of the European Parliament and of the Council of 19 May 1998 on injunctions for the protection of consumers' interests[1] and the scope of the cancellation period in Council Directive 90/619/EEC of 8 November 1990 on the coordination of laws, regulations and administrative provisions relating to direct life assurance, laying down provisions to facilitate the effective exercise of freedom to provide services[2] should be adapted.

(34) Since the objectives of this Directive, namely the establishment of common rules on the distance marketing of consumer financial services cannot be sufficiently achieved by the Member States and can therefore be better achieved at Community level, the Community may adopt measures, in accordance with the principles of subsidiarity as set out in Article 5 of the Treaty. In accordance

[1] OJ L 166, 11.6.1998, p. 51. Directive as last amended by Directive 2000/31/EC (OJ L 178, 17.7.2001, p. 1).

[2] OJ L 330, 29.11.1990, p. 50. Directive as last amended by Directive 92/96/EEC (OJ L 360, 9.12.1992, p. 1).

with the principle of proportionality, as set out in that Article, this Directive does not go beyond what is necessary to achieve that objective,

HAVE ADOPTED THIS DIRECTIVE:

Article 1 Object and scope

1. The object of this Directive is to approximate the laws, regulations and administrative provisions of the Member States concerning the distance marketing of consumer financial services.
2. In the case of contracts for financial services comprising an initial service agreement followed by successive operations or a series of separate operations of the same nature performed over time, the provisions of this Directive shall apply only to the initial agreement.

   In case there is no initial service agreement but the successive operations or the separate operations of the same nature performed over time are performed between the same contractual parties, Articles 3 and 4 apply only when the first operation is performed. Where, however, no operation of the same nature is performed for more than one year, the next operation will be deemed to be the first in a new series of operations and, accordingly, Articles 3 and 4 shall apply.

Article 2 Definitions

For the purposes of this Directive:

(a) "distance contract" means any contract concerning financial services concluded between a supplier and a consumer under an organised distance sales or service-provision scheme run by the supplier, who, for the purpose of that contract, makes exclusive use of one or more means of distance communication up to and including the time at which the contract is concluded;

(b) "financial service" means any service of a banking, credit, insurance, personal pension, investment or payment nature;

(c) "supplier" means any natural or legal person, public or private, who, acting in his commercial or professional capacity, is the contractual provider of services subject to distance contracts;

(d) "consumer" means any natural person who, in distance contracts covered by this Directive, is acting for purposes which are outside his trade, business or profession;

(e) "means of distance communication" refers to any means which, without the simultaneous physical presence of the supplier and the consumer, may be used for the distance marketing of a service between those parties;

(f) "durable medium" means any instrument which enables the consumer to store information addressed personally to him in a way accessible for future reference for a period of time adequate for the purposes of the information and which allows the unchanged reproduction of the information stored;

(g) "operator or supplier of a means of distance communication" means any public or private, natural or legal person whose trade, business or profession involves making one or more means of distance communication available to suppliers.

Article 3 Information to the consumer prior to the conclusion of the distance contract

1. In good time before the consumer is bound by any distance contract or offer, he shall be provided with the following information concerning:

(1) the supplier

(a) the identity and the main business of the supplier, the geographical address at which the supplier is established and any other geographical address relevant for the customer's relations with the supplier;

(b) the identity of the representative of the supplier established in the consumer's Member State of residence and the geographical address relevant for the customer's relations with the representative, if such a representative exists;

(c) when the consumer's dealings are with any professional other than the supplier, the identity of this professional, the capacity in which he is acting vis-à-vis the consumer, and the geographical address relevant for the customer's relations with this professional;

(d) where the supplier is registered in a trade or similar public register, the trade register in which the supplier is entered and his registration number or an equivalent means of identification in that register;

(e) where the supplier's activity is subject to an authorisation scheme, the particulars of the relevant supervisory authority;

(2) the financial service

(a) a description of the main characteristics of the financial service;

(b) the total price to be paid by the consumer to the supplier for the financial service, including all related fees, charges and expenses, and all taxes paid via the supplier or, when an exact price cannot be indicated, the basis for the calculation of the price enabling the consumer to verify it;

(c) where relevant notice indicating that the financial service is related to instruments involving special risks related to their specific features or the operations to be executed or whose price depends on fluctuations in the financial markets outside the supplier's control and that historical performances are no indicators for future performances;

(d) notice of the possibility that other taxes and/or costs may exist that are not paid via the supplier or imposed by him;

(e) any limitations of the period for which the information provided is valid;

(f) the arrangements for payment and for performance;

(g) any specific additional cost for the consumer of using the means of distance communication, if such additional cost is charged;

(3) the distance contract

(a) the existence or absence of a right of withdrawal in accordance with Article 6 and, where the right of withdrawal exists, its duration and the conditions for exercising it, including information on the amount which the consumer may be required to pay on the basis of Article 7(1), as well as the consequences of non-exercise of that right;

(b) the minimum duration of the distance contract in the case of financial services to be performed permanently or recurrently;

(c) information on any rights the parties may have to terminate the contract early or unilaterally by virtue of the terms of the distance contract, including any penalties imposed by the contract in such cases;

(d) practical instructions for exercising the right of withdrawal indicating, inter alia, the address to which the notification of a withdrawal should be sent;

(e) the Member State or States whose laws are taken by the supplier as a basis for the establishment of relations with the consumer prior to the conclusion of the distance contract;

(f) any contractual clause on law applicable to the distance contract and/or on competent court;

(g) in which language, or languages, the contractual terms and conditions, and the prior information referred to in this Article are supplied, and furthermore in which language, or languages, the supplier, with the agreement of the consumer, undertakes to communicate during the duration of this distance contract;

(4) redress

(a) whether or not there is an out-of-court complaint and redress mechanism for the consumer that is party to the distance contract and, if so, the methods for having access to it;

(b) the existence of guarantee funds or other compensation arrangements, not covered by Directive 94/19/EC of the European Parliament and of the Council of 30 May 1994 on deposit guarantee schemes[1] and Directive 97/9/EC of the European Parliament and of the Council of 3 March 1997 on investor compensation schemes[2].

2. The information referred to in paragraph 1, the commercial purpose of which must be made clear, shall be provided in a clear and comprehensible manner in any way appropriate to the means of distance communication used, with due regard, in particular, to the principles of good faith in commercial transactions, and the principles governing the protection of those who are unable, pursuant to the legislation of the Member States, to give their consent, such as minors.

3. In the case of voice telephony communications

---

1 OJ L 135, 31.5.1994, p. 5.

2 OJ L 84, 26.3.1997, p. 22.

(a) the identity of the supplier and the commercial purpose of the call initiated by the supplier shall be made explicitly clear at the beginning of any conversation with the consumer;

(b) subject to the explicit consent of the consumer only the following information needs to be given:

- the identity of the person in contact with the consumer and his link with the supplier,
- a description of the main characteristics of the financial service,
- the total price to be paid by the consumer to the supplier for the financial service including all taxes paid via the supplier or, when an exact price cannot be indicated, the basis for the calculation of the price enabling the consumer to verify it,
- notice of the possibility that other taxes and/or costs may exist that are not paid via the supplier or imposed by him,
- the existence or absence of a right of withdrawal in accordance with Article 6 and, where the right of withdrawal exists, its duration and the conditions for exercising it, including information on the amount which the consumer may be required to pay on the basis of Article 7(1).

The supplier shall inform the consumer that other information is available on request and of what nature this information is. In any case the supplier shall provide the full information when he fulfils his obligations under Article 5.

4. Information on contractual obligations, to be communicated to the consumer during the pre-contractual phase, shall be in conformity with the contractual obligations which would result from the law presumed to be applicable to the distance contract if the latter were concluded.

Article 4 Additional information requirements

1. Where there are provisions in the Community legislation governing financial services which contain prior information requirements additional to those listed in Article 3(1), these requirements shall continue to apply.
2. Pending further harmonisation, Member States may maintain or introduce more stringent provisions on prior information requirements when the provisions are in conformity with Community law.
3. Member States shall communicate to the Commission national provisions on prior information requirements under paragraphs 1 and 2 of this Article when these requirements are additional to those listed in Article 3(1). The Commission shall take account of the communicated national provisions when drawing up the report referred to in Article 20(2).
4. The Commission shall, with a view to creating a high level of transparency by all appropriate means, ensure that information, on the national provisions communicated to it, is made available to consumers and suppliers.

5. Where Directive 2007/64/EC of the European Parliament and of the Council of 13 November 2007 on payment services in the internal market (1) is also applicable, the information provisions under Article 3 (1) of this Directive, with the exception of paragraphs (2)(c) to (g), (3) (a), (d) and (e), and (4)(b), shall be replaced with Articles 36, 37, 41 and 42 of that Directive.

Article 5 Communication of the contractual terms and conditions and of the prior information

1. The supplier shall communicate to the consumer all the contractual terms and conditions and the information referred to in Article 3(1) and Article 4 on paper or on another durable medium available and accessible to the consumer in good time before the consumer is bound by any distance contract or offer.
2. The supplier shall fulfil his obligation under paragraph 1 immediately after the conclusion of the contract, if the contract has been concluded at the consumer's request using a means of distance communication which does not enable providing the contractual terms and conditions and the information in conformity with paragraph 1.
3. At any time during the contractual relationship the consumer is entitled, at his request, to receive the contractual terms and conditions on paper. In addition, the consumer is entitled to change the means of distance communication used, unless this is incompatible with the contract concluded or the nature of the financial service provided.

Article 6 Right of withdrawal

1. The Member States shall ensure that the consumer shall have a period of 14 calendar days to withdraw from the contract without penalty and without giving any reason. However, this period shall be extended to 30 calendar days in distance contracts relating to life insurance covered by Directive 90/619/EEC and personal pension operations.

   The period for withdrawal shall begin:

   - either from the day of the conclusion of the distance contract, except in respect of the said life assurance, where the time limit will begin from the time when the consumer is informed that the distance contract has been concluded, or
   - from the day on which the consumer receives the contractual terms and conditions and the information in accordance with Article 5(1) or (2), if that is later than the date referred to in the first indent.

     Member States, in addition to the right of withdrawal, may provide that the enforceability of contracts relating to investment services is suspended for the same period provided for in this paragraph.
2. The right of withdrawal shall not apply to:

(a) financial services whose price depends on fluctuations in the financial market outside the suppliers control, which may occur during the withdrawal period, such as services related to:
   - foreign exchange,
   - money market instruments,
   - transferable securities,
   - units in collective investment undertakings,
   - financial-futures contracts, including equivalent cash-settled instruments,
   - forward interest-rate agreements (FRAs),
   - interest-rate, currency and equity swaps,
   - options to acquire or dispose of any instruments referred to in this point including equivalent cash-settled instruments. This category includes in particular options on currency and on interest rates;

(b) travel and baggage insurance policies or similar short-term insurance policies of less than one month's duration;

(c) contracts whose performance has been fully completed by both parties at the consumer's express request before the consumer exercises his right of withdrawal.

3. Member States may provide that the right of withdrawal shall not apply to:

   (a) any credit intended primarily for the purpose of acquiring or retaining property rights in land or in an existing or projected building, or for the purpose of renovating or improving a building, or

   (b) any credit secured either by mortgage on immovable property or by a right related to immovable property, or

   (c) declarations by consumers using the services of an official, provided that the official confirms that the consumer is guaranteed the rights under Article 5(1).

   This paragraph shall be without prejudice to the right to a reflection time to the benefit of the consumers that are resident in those Member States where it exists, at the time of the adoption of this Directive.

4. Member States making use of the possibility set out in paragraph 3 shall communicate it to the Commission.

5. The Commission shall make available the information communicated by Member States to the European Parliament and the Council and shall ensure that it is also available to consumers and suppliers who request it.

6. If the consumer exercises his right of withdrawal he shall, before the expiry of the relevant deadline, notify this following the practical instructions given to him in accordance with Article 3(1)(3)(d) by means which can be proved in accordance with national law. The deadline shall be deemed to have been observed if the notification, if it is on paper or on another durable medium available and accessible to the recipient, is dispatched before the deadline expires.

7. This Article does not apply to credit agreements cancelled under the conditions of Article 6(4) of Directive 97/7/EC or Article 7 of Directive 94/47/EC of the European Parliament and of the Council of 26 October 1994 on the protection of purchasers in respect of certain aspects of contracts relating to the purchase of the right to use immovable properties on a timeshare basis[1].

   If to a distance contract of a given financial service another distance contract has been attached concerning services provided by the supplier or by a third party on the basis of an agreement between the third party and the supplier, this additional distance contract shall be cancelled, without any penalty, if the consumer exercises his right of withdrawal as provided for in Article 6(1).
8. The provisions of this Article are without prejudice to the Member States' laws and regulations governing the cancellation or termination or non-enforceability of a distance contract or the right of a consumer to fulfil his contractual obligations before the time fixed in the distance contract. This applies irrespective of the conditions for and the legal effects of the winding-up of the contract.

Article 7 Payment of the service provided before withdrawal

1. When the consumer exercises his right of withdrawal under Article 6(1) he may only be required to pay, without any undue delay, for the service actually provided by the supplier in accordance with the contract. The performance of the contract may only begin after the consumer has given his approval. The amount payable shall not:
   - exceed an amount which is in proportion to the extent of the service already provided in comparison with the full coverage of the contract,
   - in any case be such that it could be construed as a penalty.
2. Member States may provide that the consumer cannot be required to pay any amount when withdrawing from an insurance contract.
3. The supplier may not require the consumer to pay any amount on the basis of paragraph 1 unless he can prove that the consumer was duly informed about the amount payable, in conformity with Article 3(1)(3)(a). However, in no case may he require such payment if he has commenced the performance of the contract before the expiry of the withdrawal period provided for in Article 6(1) without the consumer's prior request.
4. The supplier shall, without any undue delay and no later than within 30 calendar days, return to the consumer any sums he has received from him in accordance with the distance contract, except for the amount referred to in paragraph 1. This period shall begin from the day on which the supplier receives the notification of withdrawal.

[1] OJ L 280, 29.10.1994, p. 83.

5. The consumer shall return to the supplier any sums and/or property he has received from the supplier without any undue delay and no later than within 30 calendar days. This period shall begin from the day on which the consumer dispatches the notification of withdrawal.

Article 8 (Abrogated)[1]

Article 9 Unsolicited services

Given the prohibition of inertia selling practices laid down in Directive 2005/29/EC of 11 May 2005 of the European Parliament and of the Council concerning unfair business-to-consumer commercial practices in the internal market[2] and without prejudice to the provisions of Member States' legislation on the tacit renewal of distance contracts, when such rules permit tacit renewal, Member States shall take measures to exempt the consumer from any obligation in the event of unsolicited supplies, the absence of a reply not constituting consent.

Article 10 Unsolicited communications

1. The use by a supplier of the following distance communication techniques shall require the consumer's prior consent:
   (a) automated calling systems without human intervention (automatic calling machines);
   (b) fax machines.
2. Member States shall ensure that means of distance communication other than those referred to in paragraph 1, when they allow individual communications:
   (a) shall not be authorised unless the consent of the consumers concerned has been obtained, or
   (b) may only be used if the consumer has not expressed his manifest objection.
3. The measures referred to in paragraphs 1 and 2 shall not entail costs for consumers.

Article 11 Sanctions

Member States shall provide for appropriate sanctions in the event of the supplier's failure to comply with national provisions adopted pursuant to this Directive.

They may provide for this purpose in particular that the consumer may cancel the contract at any time, free of charge and without penalty.

These sanctions must be effective, proportional and dissuasive.

Article 12 Imperative nature of this Directive's provisions

1. Consumers may not waive the rights conferred on them by this Directive.

---

[1] OJ L 319 1, 05.12.2007 p. 34
[2] OJ L 149, 11.6.2005 p. 22.

2. Member States shall take the measures needed to ensure that the consumer does not lose the protection granted by this Directive by virtue of the choice of the law of a non-member country as the law applicable to the contract, if this contract has a close link with the territory of one or more Member States.

Article 13 Judicial and administrative redress

1. Member States shall ensure that adequate and effective means exist to ensure compliance with this Directive in the interests of consumers.
2. The means referred to in paragraph 1 shall include provisions whereby one or more of the following bodies, as determined by national law, may take action in accordance with national law before the courts or competent administrative bodies to ensure that the national provisions for the implementation of this Directive are applied:
   (a) public bodies or their representatives;
   (b) consumer organisations having a legitimate interest in protecting consumers;
   (c) professional organisations having a legitimate interest in acting.
3. Member States shall take the measures necessary to ensure that operators and suppliers of means of distance communication put an end to practices that have been declared to be contrary to this Directive, on the basis of a judicial decision, an administrative decision or a decision issued by a supervisory authority notified to them, where those operators or suppliers are in a position to do so.

Article 14 Out-of-court redress

1. Member States shall promote the setting up or development of adequate and effective out-of-court complaints and redress procedures for the settlement of consumer disputes concerning financial services provided at distance.
2. Member States shall, in particular, encourage the bodies responsible for out-of-court settlement of disputes to cooperate in the resolution of cross-border disputes concerning financial services provided at distance.

Article 15 Burden of proof

Without prejudice to Article 7(3), Member States may stipulate that the burden of proof in respect of the supplier's obligations to inform the consumer and the consumer's consent to conclusion of the contract and, where appropriate, its performance, can be placed on the supplier.

Any contractual term or condition providing that the burden of proof of the respect by the supplier of all or part of the obligations incumbent on him pursuant to this Directive should lie with the consumer shall be an unfair term within the meaning of Council Directive 93/13/EEC of 5 April 1993 on unfair terms in consumer contracts[1].

---

[1] OJ L 95, 21.4.1993, p. 29.

Article 16 Transitional measures

Member States may impose national rules which are in conformity with this Directive on suppliers established in a Member State which has not yet transposed this Directive and whose law has no obligations corresponding to those provided for in this Directive.

Article 17 Directive 90/619/EC

In Article 15(1) of Directive 90/619/EEC the first subparagraph shall be replaced by the following: "1. Each Member State shall prescribe that a policyholder who concludes an individual life-assurance contract shall have a period of 30 calendar days, from the time when he was informed that the contract had been concluded, within which to cancel the contract."

Article 18 Directive 97/7/EC

Directive 97/7/EC is hereby amended as follows:

1. the first indent of Article 3(1) shall be replaced by the following: "- relating to any financial service to which Directive 2002/65/EC of the European Parliament and of the Council of 23 September 2002 concerning the distance marketing of consumer financial services and amending Council Directive 90/619/EEC and Directives 97/7/EC and 98/27/EC[1] applies,";
2. Annex II shall be deleted.

Article 19 Directive 98/27/EC

The following point shall be added to the Annex of Directive 98/27/EC: "11. Directive 2002/65/EC of the European Parliament and of the Council of 23 September 2002 concerning the distance marketing of consumer financial services and amending Council Directive 90/619/EEC and Directives 97/7/EC and 98/27/EC[2]."

Article 20 Review

1. Following the implementation of this Directive, the Commission shall examine the functioning of the internal market in financial services in respect of the marketing of those services. It should seek to analyse and detail the difficulties that are, or might be faced by both consumers and suppliers, in particular arising from differences between national provisions regarding information and right of withdrawal.
2. Not later than 9 April 2006 the Commission shall report to the European Parliament and the Council on the problems facing both consumers and suppliers seeking to buy and sell financial services, and shall submit, where appropriate, proposals to amend and/or further harmonise the information and

[1] OJ L 271, 9.10.2002, p. 16.

[2] OJ L 271, 9.10.2002, p. 16.

right of withdrawal provisions in Community legislation concerning financial services and/or those covered in Article 3.

Article 21 Transposition

1. Member States shall bring into force the laws, regulations and administrative provisions necessary to comply with this Directive not later than 9 October 2004. They shall forthwith inform the Commission thereof.

   When Member States adopt these measures, they shall contain a reference to this Directive or shall be accompanied by such a reference on the occasion of their official publication. The methods of making such reference shall be laid down by Member States.

2. Member States shall communicate to the Commission the text of the main provisions of national law which they adopt in the field governed by this Directive together with a table showing how the provisions of this Directive correspond to the national provisions adopted.

Article 22 Entry into force

This Directive shall enter into force on the day of its publication in the Official Journal of the European Communities.

Article 23 Addressees

This Directive is addressed to the Member States.

Done at Brussels, 23 September 2002.

For the European Parliament

The President

P. Cox

For the Council

The President

M. Fischer Boel

14. Directive 2006/54/EC of the European Parliament and of the Council of 5 July 2006 on the implementation of the principle of equal opportunities and equal treatment of men and women in matters of employment and occupation (recast)

(OJ L 204 , 26/07/2006 p. 23 -36)

THE EUROPEAN PARLIAMENT AND THE COUNCIL OF THE EUROPEAN UNION,

Having regard to the Treaty establishing the European Community, and in particular Article 141(3) thereof,

Having regard to the proposal from the Commission,

Having regard to the opinion of the European Economic and Social Committee[1],

Acting in accordance with the procedure laid down in Article 251 of the Treaty [2],

Whereas:

(1) Council Directive 76/207/EEC of 9 February 1976 on the implementation of the principle of equal treatment for men and women as regards access to employment, vocational training and promotion, and working conditions[3] and Council Directive 86/378/EEC of 24 July 1986 on the implementation of the principle of equal treatment for men and women in occupational social security schemes[4] have been significantly amended[5]. Council Directive 75/117/EEC of 10 February 1975 on the approximation of the laws of the Member States relating to the application of the principle of equal pay for men and women[6] and Council Directive 97/80/EC of 15 December 1997 on the burden of proof in cases of discrimination based on sex[7] also contain provisions which have as their purpose the implementation of the principle of equal treatment between men and women. Now that new amendments are being made to the said Directives, it is desirable, for reasons of clarity, that the provisions in question should be recast by bringing together in a single text the main provisions existing in this field as well as certain developments arising out of the case-law of the Court of Justice of the European Communities (hereinafter referred to as the Court of Justice).

(2) Equality between men and women is a fundamental principle of Community law under Article 2 and Article 3(2) of the Treaty and the case-law of the Court

1 OJ C 157, 28.6.2005, p. 83.

2 Opinion of the European Parliament of 6 July 2005 (not yet published in the Official Journal), Council Common Position of 10 March 2006(OJ C 126 E, 30.5.2006, p. 33) and Position of the European Parliament of 1 June 2006 (not yet published in the Official Journal).

3 OJ L 39, 14.2.1976, p. 40. Directive as amended by Directive 2002/73/EC of the European Parliament and of the Council (OJ L 269, 5.10.2002, p. 15).

4 OJ L 225, 12.8.1986, p. 40. Directive as amended by Directive 96/97/EC (OJ L 46, 17.2.1997, p. 20).

5 See Annex I Part A.

6 OJ L 45, 19.2.1975, p. 19.

7 OJ L 14, 20.1.1998, p. 6. Directive as amended by Directive 98/52/EC (OJ L 205, 22.7.1998, p. 66).

of Justice. Those Treaty provisions proclaim equality between men and women as a "task" and an "aim" of the Community and impose a positive obligation to promote it in all its activities.

(3) The Court of Justice has held that the scope of the principle of equal treatment for men and women cannot be confined to the prohibition of discrimination based on the fact that a person is of one or other sex. In view of its purpose and the nature of the rights which it seeks to safeguard, it also applies to discrimination arising from the gender reassignment of a person.

(4) Article 141(3) of the Treaty now provides a specific legal basis for the adoption of Community measures to ensure the application of the principle of equal opportunities and equal treatment in matters of employment and occupation, including the principle of equal pay for equal work or work of equal value.

(5) Articles 21 and 23 of the Charter of Fundamental Rights of the European Union also prohibit any discrimination on grounds of sex and enshrine the right to equal treatment between men and women in all areas, including employment, work and pay.

(6) Harassment and sexual harassment are contrary to the principle of equal treatment between men and women and constitute discrimination on grounds of sex for the purposes of this Directive. These forms of discrimination occur not only in the workplace, but also in the context of access to employment, vocational training and promotion. They should therefore be prohibited and should be subject to effective, proportionate and dissuasive penalties.

(7) In this context, employers and those responsible for vocational training should be encouraged to take measures to combat all forms of discrimination on grounds of sex and, in particular, to take preventive measures against harassment and sexual harassment in the workplace and in access to employment, vocational training and promotion, in accordance with national law and practice.

(8) The principle of equal pay for equal work or work of equal value as laid down by Article 141 of the Treaty and consistently upheld in the case-law of the Court of Justice constitutes an important aspect of the principle of equal treatment between men and women and an essential and indispensable part of the acquis communautaire, including the case-law of the Court concerning sex discrimination. It is therefore appropriate to make further provision for its implementation.

(9) In accordance with settled case-law of the Court of Justice, in order to assess whether workers are performing the same work or work of equal value, it should be determined whether, having regard to a range of factors including the nature of the work and training and working conditions, those workers may be considered to be in a comparable situation.

(10) The Court of Justice has established that, in certain circumstances, the principle of equal pay is not limited to situations in which men and women work for the same employer.

(11) The Member States, in collaboration with the social partners, should continue to address the problem of the continuing gender-based wage differentials and marked gender segregation on the labour market by means such as flexible working time arrangements which enable both men and women to combine family and work commitments more successfully. This could also include appropriate parental leave arrangements which could be taken up by either parent as well as the provision of accessible and affordable child-care facilities and care for dependent persons.

(12) Specific measures should be adopted to ensure the implementation of the principle of equal treatment in occupational social security schemes and to define its scope more clearly.

(13) In its judgment of 17 May 1990 in Case C-262/88[1], the Court of Justice determined that all forms of occupational pension constitute an element of pay within the meaning of Article 141 of the Treaty.

(14) Although the concept of pay within the meaning of Article 141 of the Treaty does not encompass social security benefits, it is now clearly established that a pension scheme for public servants falls within the scope of the principle of equal pay if the benefits payable under the scheme are paid to the worker by reason of his/her employment relationship with the public employer, notwithstanding the fact that such scheme forms part of a general statutory scheme. According to the judgments of the Court of Justice in Cases C-7/93[2] and C-351/00[3], that condition will be satisfied if the pension scheme concerns a particular category of workers and its benefits are directly related to the period of service and calculated by reference to the public servant's final salary. For reasons of clarity, it is therefore appropriate to make specific provision to that effect.

(15) The Court of Justice has confirmed that whilst the contributions of male and female workers to a defined-benefit pension scheme are covered by Article 141 of the Treaty, any inequality in employers' contributions paid under funded defined-benefit schemes which is due to the use of actuarial factors differing according to sex is not to be assessed in the light of that same provision.

(16) By way of example, in the case of funded defined - benefit schemes, certain elements, such as conversion into a capital sum of part of a periodic pension, transfer of pension rights, a reversionary pension payable to a dependant in return for the surrender of part of a pension or a reduced pension where the worker opts to take earlier retirement, may be unequal where the inequality of the amounts results from the effects of the use of actuarial factors differing according to sex at the time when the scheme's funding is implemented.

(17) It is well established that benefits payable under occupational social security schemes are not to be considered as remuneration insofar as they are attributable

[1] C-262/88: Barber v Guardian Royal Exchange Assurance Group (1990 ECR I - 1889).

[2] C-7/93: Bestuur van het Algemeen Burgerlijk Pensioenfonds v G. A. Beune (1994 ECR I - 4471).

[3] C-351/00: Pirkko Niemi (2002 ECR I-7007).

to periods of employment prior to 17 May 1990, except in the case of workers or those claiming under them who initiated legal proceedings or brought an equivalent claim under the applicable national law before that date. It is therefore necessary to limit the implementation of the principle of equal treatment accordingly.

(18) The Court of Justice has consistently held that the Barber Protocol[1] does not affect the right to join an occupational pension scheme and that the limitation of the effects in time of the judgment in Case C-262/88 does not apply to the right to join an occupational pension scheme. The Court of Justice also ruled that the national rules relating to time limits for bringing actions under national law may be relied on against workers who assert their right to join an occupational pension scheme, provided that they are not less favourable for that type of action than for similar actions of a domestic nature and that they do not render the exercise of rights conferred by Community law impossible in practice. The Court of Justice has also pointed out that the fact that a worker can claim retroactively to join an occupational pension scheme does not allow the worker to avoid paying the contributions relating to the period of membership concerned.

(19) Ensuring equal access to employment and the vocational training leading thereto is fundamental to the application of the principle of equal treatment of men and women in matters of employment and occupation. Any exception to this principle should therefore be limited to those occupational activities which necessitate the employment of a person of a particular sex by reason of their nature or the context in which they are carried out, provided that the objective sought is legitimate and complies with the principle of proportionality.

(20) This Directive does not prejudice freedom of association, including the right to establish unions with others and to join unions to defend one's interests. Measures within the meaning of Article 141(4) of the Treaty may include membership or the continuation of the activity of organisations or unions whose main objective is the promotion, in practice, of the principle of equal treatment between men and women.

(21) The prohibition of discrimination should be without prejudice to the maintenance or adoption of measures intended to prevent or compensate for disadvantages suffered by a group of persons of one sex. Such measures permit organisations of persons of one sex where their main object is the promotion of the special needs of those persons and the promotion of equality between men and women.

(22) In accordance with Article 141(4) of the Treaty, with a view to ensuring full equality in practice between men and women in working life, the principle of equal treatment does not prevent Member States from maintaining or adopting measures providing for specific advantages in order to make it easier for the under-represented sex to pursue a vocational activity or to prevent or

[1] Protocol 17 concerning Article 141 of the Treaty establishing the European Community (1992).

compensate for disadvantages in professional careers. Given the current situation and bearing in mind Declaration No 28 to the Amsterdam Treaty, Member States should, in the first instance, aim at improving the situation of women in working life.

(23) It is clear from the case-law of the Court of Justice that unfavourable treatment of a woman related to pregnancy or maternity constitutes direct discrimination on grounds of sex. Such treatment should therefore be expressly covered by this Directive.

(24) The Court of Justice has consistently recognised the legitimacy, as regards the principle of equal treatment, of protecting a woman's biological condition during pregnancy and maternity and of introducing maternity protection measures as a means to achieve substantive equality. This Directive should therefore be without prejudice to Council Directive 92/85/EEC of 19 October 1992 on the introduction of measures to encourage improvements in the safety and health at work of pregnant workers and workers who have recently given birth or are breastfeeding[1]. This Directive should further be without prejudice to Council Directive 96/34/EC of 3 June 1996 on the framework agreement on parental leave concluded by UNICE, CEEP and the ETUC[2].

(25) For reasons of clarity, it is also appropriate to make express provision for the protection of the employment rights of women on maternity leave and in particular their right to return to the same or an equivalent post, to suffer no detriment in their terms and conditions as a result of taking such leave and to benefit from any improvement in working conditions to which they would have been entitled during their absence.

(26) In the Resolution of the Council and of the Ministers for Employment and Social Policy, meeting within the Council, of 29 June 2000 on the balanced participation of women and men in family and working life[3], Member States were encouraged to consider examining the scope for their respective legal systems to grant working men an individual and non - transferable right to paternity leave, while maintaining their rights relating to employment.

(27) Similar considerations apply to the granting by Member States to men and women of an individual and non-transferable right to leave subsequent to the adoption of a child. It is for the Member States to determine whether or not to grant such a right to paternity and/or adoption leave and also to determine any conditions, other than dismissal and return to work, which are outside the scope of this Directive.

(28) The effective implementation of the principle of equal treatment requires appropriate procedures to be put in place by the Member States.

---

1 OJ L 348, 28.11.1992, p. 1.

2 OJ L 145, 19.6.1996, p. 4. Directive as amended by Directive 97/75/EC (OJ L 10, 16.1.1998, p. 24).

3 OJ C 218, 31.7.2000, p. 5.

(29) The provision of adequate judicial or administrative procedures for the enforcement of the obligations imposed by this Directive is essential to the effective implementation of the principle of equal treatment.

(30) The adoption of rules on the burden of proof plays a significant role in ensuring that the principle of equal treatment can be effectively enforced. As the Court of Justice has held, provision should therefore be made to ensure that the burden of proof shifts to the respondent when there is a prima facie case of discrimination, except in relation to proceedings in which it is for the court or other competent national body to investigate the facts. It is however necessary to clarify that the appreciation of the facts from which it may be presumed that there has been direct or indirect discrimination remains a matter for the relevant national body in accordance with national law or practice. Further, it is for the Member States to introduce, at any appropriate stage of the proceedings, rules of evidence which are more favourable to plaintiffs.

(31) With a view to further improving the level of protection offered by this Directive, associations, organisations and other legal entities should also be empowered to engage in proceedings, as the Member States so determine, either on behalf or in support of a complainant, without prejudice to national rules of procedure concerning representation and defence.

(32) Having regard to the fundamental nature of the right to effective legal protection, it is appropriate to ensure that workers continue to enjoy such protection even after the relationship giving rise to an alleged breach of the principle of equal treatment has ended. An employee defending or giving evidence on behalf of a person protected under this Directive should be entitled to the same protection.

(33) It has been clearly established by the Court of Justice that in order to be effective, the principle of equal treatment implies that the compensation awarded for any breach must be adequate in relation to the damage sustained. It is therefore appropriate to exclude the fixing of any prior upper limit for such compensation, except where the employer can prove that the only damage suffered by an applicant as a result of discrimination within the meaning of this Directive was the refusal to take his/her job application into consideration.

(34) In order to enhance the effective implementation of the principle of equal treatment, Member States should promote dialogue between the social partners and, within the framework of national practice, with non-governmental organisations.

(35) Member States should provide for effective, proportionate and dissuasive penalties for breaches of the obligations under this Directive.

(36) Since the objectives of this Directive cannot be sufficiently achieved by the Member States and can therefore be better achieved at Community level, the Community may adopt measures in accordance with the principle of subsidiarity as set out in Article 5 of the Treaty. In accordance with the principle of

proportionality, as set out in that Article, this Directive does not go beyond what is necessary in order to achieve those objectives.

(37) For the sake of a better understanding of the different treatment of men and women in matters of employment and occupation, comparable statistics disaggregated by sex should continue to be developed, analysed and made available at the appropriate levels.

(38) Equal treatment of men and women in matters of employment and occupation cannot be restricted to legislative measures. Instead, the European Union and the Member States should continue to promote the raising of public awareness of wage discrimination and the changing of public attitudes, involving all parties concerned at public and private level to the greatest possible extent. The dialogue between the social partners could play an important role in this process.

(39) The obligation to transpose this Directive into national law should be confined to those provisions which represent a substantive change as compared with the earlier Directives. The obligation to transpose the provisions which are substantially unchanged arises under the earlier Directives.

(40) This Directive should be without prejudice to the obligations of the Member States relating to the time limits for transposition into national law and application of the Directives set out in Annex I, Part B.

(41) In accordance with paragraph 34 of the Interinstitutional agreement on better law - making[1], Member States are encouraged to draw up, for themselves and in the interest of the Community, their own tables, which will, as far as possible, illustrate the correlation between this Directive and the transposition measures and to make them public,

HAVE ADOPTED THIS DIRECTIVE:

TITLE I : GENERAL PROVISIONS

Article 1 Purpose

The purpose of this Directive is to ensure the implementation of the principle of equal opportunities and equal treatment of men and women in matters of employment and occupation.

To that end, it contains provisions to implement the principle of equal treatment in relation to:

(a) access to employment, including promotion, and to vocational training;
(b) working conditions, including pay;
(c) occupational social security schemes.

It also contains provisions to ensure that such implementation is made more effective by the establishment of appropriate procedures.

---

1 OJ C 321, 31.12.2003, p. 1.

Article 2 Definitions

1. For the purposes of this Directive, the following definitions shall apply:

(a) "direct discrimination": where one person is treated less favourably on grounds of sex than another is, has been or would be treated in a comparable situation;

(b) "indirect discrimination": where an apparently neutral provision, criterion or practice would put persons of one sex at a particular disadvantage compared with persons of the other sex, unless that provision, criterion or practice is objectively justified by a legitimate aim, and the means of achieving that aim are appropriate and necessary;

(c) "harassment": where unwanted conduct related to the sex of a person occurs with the purpose or effect of violating the dignity of a person, and of creating an intimidating, hostile, degrading, humiliating or offensive environment;

(d) "sexual harassment": where any form of unwanted verbal, non-verbal or physical conduct of a sexual nature occurs, with the purpose or effect of violating the dignity of a person, in particular when creating an intimidating, hostile, degrading, humiliating or offensive environment;

(e) "pay": the ordinary basic or minimum wage or salary and any other consideration, whether in cash or in kind, which the worker receives directly or indirectly, in respect of his/her employment from his/her employer;

(f) "occupational social security schemes": schemes not governed by Council Directive 79/7/EEC of 19 December 1978 on the progressive implementation of the principle of equal treatment for men and women in matters of social security[1] whose purpose is to provide workers, whether employees or self-employed, in an undertaking or group of undertakings, area of economic activity, occupational sector or group of sectors with benefits intended to supplement the benefits provided by statutory social security schemes or to replace them, whether membership of such schemes is compulsory or optional.

2. For the purposes of this Directive, discrimination includes:

   (a) harassment and sexual harassment, as well as any less favourable treatment based on a person's rejection of or submission to such conduct;
   (b) instruction to discriminate against persons on grounds of sex;
   (c) any less favourable treatment of a woman related to pregnancy or maternity leave within the meaning of Directive 92/85/EEC.

Article 3 Positive action

Member States may maintain or adopt measures within the meaning of Article 141(4) of the Treaty with a view to ensuring full equality in practice between men and women in working life.

---

[1] OJ L 6, 10.1.1979, p. 24.

TITLE II : SPECIFIC PROVISIONS

CHAPTER 1 : EQUAL PAY

Article 4 Prohibition of discrimination

For the same work or for work to which equal value is attributed, direct and indirect discrimination on grounds of sex with regard to all aspects and conditions of remuneration shall be eliminated.

In particular, where a job classification system is used for determining pay, it shall be based on the same criteria for both men and women and so drawn up as to exclude any discrimination on grounds of sex.

CHAPTER 2 : EQUAL TREATMENT IN OCCUPATIONAL SOCIAL SECURITY SCHEMES

Article 5 Prohibition of discrimination

Without prejudice to Article 4, there shall be no direct or indirect discrimination on grounds of sex in occupational social security schemes, in particular as regards:

(a) the scope of such schemes and the conditions of access to them;
(b) the obligation to contribute and the calculation of contributions;
(c) the calculation of benefits, including supplementary benefits due in respect of a spouse or dependants, and the conditions governing the duration and retention of entitlement to benefits.

Article 6 Personal scope

This Chapter shall apply to members of the working population, including self-employed persons, persons whose activity is interrupted by illness, maternity, accident or involuntary unemployment and persons seeking employment and to retired and disabled workers, and to those claiming under them, in accordance with national law and/or practice.

Article 7 Material scope

1. This Chapter applies to:

(a) occupational social security schemes which provide protection against the following risks:
  (i) sickness,
  (ii) invalidity,
  (iii) old age, including early retirement,
  (iv) industrial accidents and occupational diseases,
  (v) unemployment;
(b) occupational social security schemes which provide for other social benefits, in cash or in kind, and in particular survivors' benefits and family allowances, if such benefits constitute a consideration paid by the employer to the worker by reason of the latter's employment.

2. This Chapter also applies to pension schemes for a particular category of worker such as that of public servants if the benefits payable under the scheme are paid by reason of the employment relationship with the public employer. The fact that such a scheme forms part of a general statutory scheme shall be without prejudice in that respect.

Article 8 Exclusions from the material scope

1. This Chapter does not apply to:
   (a) individual contracts for self-employed persons;
   (b) single-member schemes for self-employed persons;
   (c) insurance contracts to which the employer is not a party, in the case of workers;
   (d) optional provisions of occupational social security schemes offered to participants individually to guarantee them:
      (i) either additional benefits,
      (ii) or a choice of date on which the normal benefits for self-employed persons will start, or a choice between several benefits;
   (e) occupational social security schemes in so far as benefits are financed by contributions paid by workers on a voluntary basis.
2. This Chapter does not preclude an employer granting to persons who have already reached the retirement age for the purposes of granting a pension by virtue of an occupational social security scheme, but who have not yet reached the retirement age for the purposes of granting a statutory retirement pension, a pension supplement, the aim of which is to make equal or more nearly equal the overall amount of benefit paid to these persons in relation to the amount paid to persons of the other sex in the same situation who have already reached the statutory retirement age, until the persons benefiting from the supplement reach the statutory retirement age.

Article 9 Examples of discrimination

1. Provisions contrary to the principle of equal treatment shall include those based on sex, either directly or indirectly, for:
   (a) determining the persons who may participate in an occupational social security scheme;
   (b) fixing the compulsory or optional nature of participation in an occupational social security scheme;
   (c) laying down different rules as regards the age of entry into the scheme or the minimum period of employment or membership of the scheme required to obtain the benefits thereof;
   (d) laying down different rules, except as provided for in points (h) and (j), for the reimbursement of contributions when a worker leaves a scheme without having fulfilled the conditions guaranteeing a deferred right to long-term benefits;

(e) setting different conditions for the granting of benefits or restricting such benefits to workers of one or other of the sexes;
(f) fixing different retirement ages;
(g) suspending the retention or acquisition of rights during periods of maternity leave or leave for family reasons which are granted by law or agreement and are paid by the employer;
(h) setting different levels of benefit, except in so far as may be necessary to take account of actuarial calculation factors which differ according to sex in the case of defined-contribution schemes; in the case of funded defined-benefit schemes, certain elements may be unequal where the inequality of the amounts results from the effects of the use of actuarial factors differing according to sex at the time when the scheme's funding is implemented;
(i) setting different levels for workers' contributions;
(j) setting different levels for employers' contributions, except:
   (i) in the case of defined-contribution schemes if the aim is to equalise the amount of the final benefits or to make them more nearly equal for both sexes,
   (ii) in the case of funded defined-benefit schemes where the employer's contributions are intended to ensure the adequacy of the funds necessary to cover the cost of the benefits defined;
(k) laying down different standards or standards applicable only to workers of a specified sex, except as provided for in points (h) and (j), as regards the guarantee or retention of entitlement to deferred benefits when a worker leaves a scheme.

2. Where the granting of benefits within the scope of this Chapter is left to the discretion of the scheme's management bodies, the latter shall comply with the principle of equal treatment.

Article 10 Implementation as regards self-employed persons

1. Member States shall take the necessary steps to ensure that the provisions of occupational social security schemes for self-employed persons contrary to the principle of equal treatment are revised with effect from 1 January 1993 at the latest or for Member States whose accession took place after that date, at the date that Directive 86/378/EEC became applicable in their territory.
2. This Chapter shall not preclude rights and obligations relating to a period of membership of an occupational social security scheme for self-employed persons prior to revision of that scheme from remaining subject to the provisions of the scheme in force during that period.

Article 11 Possibility of deferral as regards self-employed persons

As regards occupational social security schemes for self-employed persons, Member States may defer compulsory application of the principle of equal treatment with regard to:

(a) determination of pensionable age for the granting of old-age or retirement pensions, and the possible implications for other benefits:
    (i) either until the date on which such equality is achieved in statutory schemes,
    (ii) or, at the latest, until such equality is prescribed by a directive;
(b) survivors' pensions until Community law establishes the principle of equal treatment in statutory social security schemes in that regard;
(c) the application of Article 9(1)(i) in relation to the use of actuarial calculation factors, until 1 January 1999 or for Member States whose accession took place after that date until the date that Directive 86/378/EEC became applicable in their territory.

Article 12 Retroactive effect

1. Any measure implementing this Chapter, as regards workers, shall cover all benefits under occupational social security schemes derived from periods of employment subsequent to 17 May 1990 and shall apply retroactively to that date, without prejudice to workers or those claiming under them who have, before that date, initiated legal proceedings or raised an equivalent claim under national law. In that event, the implementation measures shall apply retroactively to 8 April 1976 and shall cover all the benefits derived from periods of employment after that date. For Member States which acceded to the Community after 8 April 1976, and before 17 May 1990, that date shall be replaced by the date on which Article 141 of the Treaty became applicable in their territory.
2. The second sentence of paragraph 1 shall not prevent national rules relating to time limits for bringing actions under national law from being relied on against workers or those claiming under them who initiated legal proceedings or raised an equivalent claim under national law before 17 May 1990, provided that they are not less favourable for that type of action than for similar actions of a domestic nature and that they do not render the exercise of rights conferred by Community law impossible in practice.
3. For Member States whose accession took place after 17 May 1990 and which were on 1 January 1994 Contracting Parties to the Agreement on the European Economic Area, the date of 17 May 1990 in the first sentence of paragraph 1 shall be replaced by 1 January 1994.
4. For other Member States whose accession took place after 17 May 1990, the date of 17 May 1990 in paragraphs 1 and 2 shall be replaced by the date on which Article 141 of the Treaty became applicable in their territory.

Article 13 Flexible pensionable age

Where men and women may claim a flexible pensionable age under the same conditions, this shall not be deemed to be incompatible with this Chapter.

CHAPTER 3 : EQUAL TREATMENT AS REGARDS ACCESS TO EMPLOYMENT, VOCATIONAL TRAINING AND PROMOTION AND WORKING CONDITIONS

Article 14 Prohibition of discrimination

1. There shall be no direct or indirect discrimination on grounds of sex in the public or private sectors, including public bodies, in relation to:
   (a) conditions for access to employment, to self-employment or to occupation, including selection criteria and recruitment conditions, whatever the branch of activity and at all levels of the professional hierarchy, including promotion;
   (b) access to all types and to all levels of vocational guidance, vocational training, advanced vocational training and retraining, including practical work experience;
   (c) employment and working conditions, including dismissals, as well as pay as provided for in Article 141 of the Treaty;
   (d) membership of, and involvement in, an organisation of workers or employers, or any organisation whose members carry on a particular profession, including the benefits provided for by such organisations.
2. Member States may provide, as regards access to employment including the training leading thereto, that a difference of treatment which is based on a characteristic related to sex shall not constitute discrimination where, by reason of the nature of the particular occupational activities concerned or of the context in which they are carried out, such a characteristic constitutes a genuine and determining occupational requirement, provided that its objective is legitimate and the requirement is proportionate.

Article 15 Return from maternity leave

A woman on maternity leave shall be entitled, after the end of her period of maternity leave, to return to her job or to an equivalent post on terms and conditions which are no less favourable to her and to benefit from any improvement in working conditions to which she would have been entitled during her absence.

Article 16 Paternity and adoption leave

This Directive is without prejudice to the right of Member States to recognise distinct rights to paternity and/or adoption leave. Those Member States which recognise such rights shall take the necessary measures to protect working men and women against dismissal due to exercising those rights and ensure that, at the end of such leave, they are entitled to return to their jobs or to equivalent posts on terms and conditions which are no less favourable to them, and to benefit from any improvement in working conditions to which they would have been entitled during their absence.

TITLE III : HORIZONTAL PROVISIONS

CHAPTER 1 : REMEDIES AND ENFORCEMENT

Section 1 : **Remedies**

Article 17 Defence of rights

1. Member States shall ensure that, after possible recourse to other competent authorities including where they deem it appropriate conciliation procedures, judicial procedures for the enforcement of obligations under this Directive are available to all persons who consider themselves wronged by failure to apply the principle of equal treatment to them, even after the relationship in which the discrimination is alleged to have occurred has ended.
2. Member States shall ensure that associations, organisations or other legal entities which have, in accordance with the criteria laid down by their national law, a legitimate interest in ensuring that the provisions of this Directive are complied with, may engage, either on behalf or in support of the complainant, with his/her approval, in any judicial and/or administrative procedure provided for the enforcement of obligations under this Directive.
3. Paragraphs 1 and 2 are without prejudice to national rules relating to time limits for bringing actions as regards the principle of equal treatment.

Article 18 Compensation or reparation

Member States shall introduce into their national legal systems such measures as are necessary to ensure real and effective compensation or reparation as the Member States so determine for the loss and damage sustained by a person injured as a result of discrimination on grounds of sex, in a way which is dissuasive and proportionate to the damage suffered. Such compensation or reparation may not be restricted by the fixing of a prior upper limit, except in cases where the employer can prove that the only damage suffered by an applicant as a result of discrimination within the meaning of this Directive is the refusal to take his/her job application into consideration.

Section 2 : **Burden of proof**

Article 19 Burden of proof

1. Member States shall take such measures as are necessary, in accordance with their national judicial systems, to ensure that, when persons who consider themselves wronged because the principle of equal treatment has not been applied to them establish, before a court or other competent authority, facts from which it may be presumed that there has been direct or indirect discrimination, it shall be for the respondent to prove that there has been no breach of the principle of equal treatment.
2. Paragraph 1 shall not prevent Member States from introducing rules of evidence which are more favourable to plaintiffs.

3. Member States need not apply paragraph 1 to proceedings in which it is for the court or competent body to investigate the facts of the case.
4. Paragraphs 1, 2 and 3 shall also apply to:
   (a) the situations covered by Article 141 of the Treaty and, insofar as discrimination based on sex is concerned, by Directives 92/85/EEC and 96/34/EC;
   (b) any civil or administrative procedure concerning the public or private sector which provides for means of redress under national law pursuant to the measures referred to in (a) with the exception of out-of-court procedures of a voluntary nature or provided for in national law.
5. This Article shall not apply to criminal procedures, unless otherwise provided by the Member States.

CHAPTER 2 : PROMOTION OF EQUAL TREATMENT — DIALOGUE

Article 20 Equality bodies

1. Member States shall designate and make the necessary arrangements for a body or bodies for the promotion, analysis, monitoring and support of equal treatment of all persons without discrimination on grounds of sex. These bodies may form part of agencies with responsibility at national level for the defence of human rights or the safeguard of individuals' rights.
2. Member States shall ensure that the competences of these bodies include:
   (a) without prejudice to the right of victims and of associations, organisations or other legal entities referred to in Article 17(2), providing independent assistance to victims of discrimination in pursuing their complaints about discrimination;
   (b) conducting independent surveys concerning discrimination;
   (c) publishing independent reports and making recommendations on any issue relating to such discrimination;
   (d) at the appropriate level exchanging available information with corresponding European bodies such as any future European Institute for Gender Equality.

Article 21 Social dialogue

1. Member States shall, in accordance with national traditions and practice, take adequate measures to promote social dialogue between the social partners with a view to fostering equal treatment, including, for example, through the monitoring of practices in the workplace, in access to employment, vocational training and promotion, as well as through the monitoring of collective agreements, codes of conduct, research or exchange of experience and good practice.
2. Where consistent with national traditions and practice, Member States shall encourage the social partners, without prejudice to their autonomy, to promote equality between men and women, and flexible working arrangements, with the

aim of facilitating the reconciliation of work and private life, and to conclude, at the appropriate level, agreements laying down anti-discrimination rules in the fields referred to in Article 1 which fall within the scope of collective bargaining. These agreements shall respect the provisions of this Directive and the relevant national implementing measures.

3. Member States shall, in accordance with national law, collective agreements or practice, encourage employers to promote equal treatment for men and women in a planned and systematic way in the workplace, in access to employment, vocational training and promotion.
4. To this end, employers shall be encouraged to provide at appropriate regular intervals employees and/or their representatives with appropriate information on equal treatment for men and women in the undertaking.

   Such information may include an overview of the proportions of men and women at different levels of the organisation; their pay and pay differentials; and possible measures to improve the situation in cooperation with employees' representatives.

Article 22 Dialogue with non - governmental organisations

Member States shall encourage dialogue with appropriate non-governmental organisations which have, in accordance with their national law and practice, a legitimate interest in contributing to the fight against discrimination on grounds of sex with a view to promoting the principle of equal treatment.

CHAPTER 3 : GENERAL HORIZONTAL PROVISIONS

Article 23 Compliance

Member States shall take all necessary measures to ensure that:

(a) any laws, regulations and administrative provisions contrary to the principle of equal treatment are abolished;
(b) provisions contrary to the principle of equal treatment in individual or collective contracts or agreements, internal rules of undertakings or rules governing the independent occupations and professions and workers' and employers' organisations or any other arrangements shall be, or may be, declared null and void or are amended;
(c) occupational social security schemes containing such provisions may not be approved or extended by administrative measures.

Article 24 Victimisation

Member States shall introduce into their national legal systems such measures as are necessary to protect employees, including those who are employees' representatives provided for by national laws and/or practices, against dismissal or other adverse treatment by the employer as a reaction to a complaint within the undertaking or to any legal proceedings aimed at enforcing compliance with the principle of equal treatment.

Article 25 Penalties

Member States shall lay down the rules on penalties applicable to infringements of the national provisions adopted pursuant to this Directive, and shall take all measures necessary to ensure that they are applied. The penalties, which may comprise the payment of compensation to the victim, must be effective, proportionate and dissuasive. The Member States shall notify those provisions to the Commission by 5 October 2005 at the latest and shall notify it without delay of any subsequent amendment affecting them.

Article 26 Prevention of discrimination

Member States shall encourage, in accordance with national law, collective agreements or practice, employers and those responsible for access to vocational training to take effective measures to prevent all forms of discrimination on grounds of sex, in particular harassment and sexual harassment in the workplace, in access to employment, vocational training and promotion.

Article 27 Minimum requirements

1. Member States may introduce or maintain provisions which are more favourable to the protection of the principle of equal treatment than those laid down in this Directive.
2. Implementation of this Directive shall under no circumstances be sufficient grounds for a reduction in the level of protection of workers in the areas to which it applies, without prejudice to the Member States' right to respond to changes in the situation by introducing laws, regulations and administrative provisions which differ from those in force on the notification of this Directive, provided that the provisions of this Directive are complied with.

Article 28 Relationship to Community and national provisions

1. This Directive shall be without prejudice to provisions concerning the protection of women, particularly as regards pregnancy and maternity.
2. This Directive shall be without prejudice to the provisions of Directive 96/34/EC and Directive 92/85/EEC.

Article 29 Gender mainstreaming

Member States shall actively take into account the objective of equality between men and women when formulating and implementing laws, regulations, administrative provisions, policies and activities in the areas referred to in this Directive.

Article 30 Dissemination of information

Member States shall ensure that measures taken pursuant to this Directive, together with the provisions already in force, are brought to the attention of all the persons concerned by all suitable means and, where appropriate, at the workplace.

TITLE IV : FINAL PROVISIONS

Article 31 Reports

1. By 15 February 2011, the Member States shall communicate to the Commission all the information necessary for the Commission to draw up a report to the European Parliament and the Council on the application of this Directive.
2. Without prejudice to paragraph 1, Member States shall communicate to the Commission, every four years, the texts of any measures adopted pursuant to Article 141(4) of the Treaty, as well as reports on these measures and their implementation. On the basis of that information, the Commission will adopt and publish every four years a report establishing a comparative assessment of any measures in the light of Declaration No 28 annexed to the Final Act of the Treaty of Amsterdam.
3. Member States shall assess the occupational activities referred to in Article 14(2), in order to decide, in the light of social developments, whether there is justification for maintaining the exclusions concerned. They shall notify the Commission of the results of this assessment periodically, but at least every 8 years.

Article 32 Review

By 15 February 2011 at the latest, the Commission shall review the operation of this Directive and if appropriate, propose any amendments it deems necessary.

Article 33 Implementation

Member States shall bring into force the laws, regulations and administrative provisions necessary to comply with this Directive by 15 August 2008 at the latest or shall ensure, by that date, that management and labour introduce the requisite provisions by way of agreement. Member States may, if necessary to take account of particular difficulties, have up to one additional year to comply with this Directive. Member States shall take all necessary steps to be able to guarantee the results imposed by this Directive. They shall forthwith communicate to the Commission the texts of those measures.

When Member States adopt these measures, they shall contain a reference to this Directive or be accompanied by such reference on the occasion of their official publication. They shall also include a statement that references in existing laws, regulations and administrative provisions to the Directives repealed by this Directive shall be construed as references to this Directive. Member States shall determine how such reference is to be made and how that statement is to be formulated.

The obligation to transpose this Directive into national law shall be confined to those provisions which represent a substantive change as compared with the earlier Directives. The obligation to transpose the provisions which are substantially unchanged arises under the earlier Directives.

Member States shall communicate to the Commission the text of the main provisions of national law which they adopt in the field covered by this Directive.

Article 34 Repeal

1. With effect from 15 August 2009 Directives 75/117/EEC, 76/207/EEC, 86/378/EEC and 97/80/EC shall be repealed without prejudice to the obligations of the Member States relating to the time-limits for transposition into national law and application of the Directives set out in Annex I, Part B.
2. References made to the repealed Directives shall be construed as being made to this Directive and should be read in accordance with the correlation table in Annex II.

Article 35 Entry into force

This Directive shall enter into force on the 20th day following its publication in the Official Journal of the European Union.

Article 36 Addressees

This Directive is addressed to the Member States.

Done at Strasbourg, 5 July 2006.

For the European Parliament

The President

J. Borrell Fontelles

For the Council

The President

P. Lehtomäki

ANNEX I

PART A

Repealed Directives with their successive amendments

Council Directive 75/117/EEC	OJ L 45, 19.2.1975, p. 19
Council Directive 76/207/EEC	OJ L 39, 14.2.1976, p. 40
Directive 2002/73/EC of the European Parliament and of the Council	OJ L 269, 5.10.2002, p. 15
Council Directive 86/378/EEC	OJ L 225, 12.8.1986, p. 40
Council Directive 96/97/EC	OJ L 46, 17.2.1997, p. 20
Council Directive 97/80/EC	OJ L 14, 20.1.1998, p. 6
Council Directive 98/52/EC	OJ L 205, 22.7.1998, p. 66

PART B

List of time limits for transposition into national law and application dates (referred to in Article 34(1))

Directive	Time-limit for transposition	Date of application
Directive 75/117/EEC	19.2.1976	
Directive 76/207/EEC	14.8.1978	
Directive 86/378/EEC	1.1.1993	
Directive 96/97/EC	1.7.1997	17.5.1990 in relation to workers, except for those workers or those claiming under them who had before that date initiated legal proceedings or raised an equivalent claim under national law. Article 8 of Directive 86/378/EEC — 1.1.1993 at the latest. Article 6(1)(i), first indent of Directive 86/378/EEC – 1.1.1999 at the latest
Directive 97/80/EC	1.1.2001	As regards the United Kingdom of Great Britain and Northern Ireland 22.7.2001

Directive 98/52/EC	22.7.2001	
Directive 2002/73/EC	5.10.2005	

ANNEX II

Correlation table

Directive 75/117/EEC	Directive 76/207/EEC	Directive 86/378/EEC	Directive 97/80/EC	This Directive
	Article 1(1)	Article 1	Article 1	Article 1
	Article 1(2)			
	Article 2(2), first indent			Article 2(1), (a)
	Article 2(2), second indent		Article 2(2)	Article 2(1), (b)
	Article 2(2), third and fourth indents			Article 2(1), (c) and (d)
				Article 2(1), (e)
		Article 2(1)		Article 2(1), (f)
	Article 2(3) and (4) and Article 2(7) third subparagraph			Article 2(2)
	Article 2(8)			Article 3
Article 1				Article 4
		Article 5(1)		Article 5
		Article 3		Article 6
		Article 4		Article 7(1)
				Article 7(2)
		Article 2(2)		Article 8(1)
		Article 2(3)		Article 8(2)
		Article 6		Article 9
		Article 8		Article 10

Directive 75/117/EEC	Directive 76/207/EEC	Directive 86/378/EEC	Directive 97/80/EC	This Directive
		Article 9		Article 11
		(Article 2 of Directive 96/97/EC)		Article 12
		Article 9a		Article 13
	Articles 2(1) and 3(1)		Article 2(1)	Article 14(1)
	Article 2(6)			Article 14(2)
	Article 2(7), second subparagraph			Article 15
	Article 2(7), fourth subparagraph, second and third sentence			Article 16
Article 2	Article 6(1)	Article 10		Article 17(1)
	Article 6(3)			Article 17(2)
	Article 6(4)			Article 17(3)
	Article 6(2)			Article 18
			Articles 3 and 4	Article 19
	Article 8a			Article 20
	Article 8b			Article 8b
	Article 8c			Article 22
Articles 3 and 6	Articles 3 and 6			Article 23(a)
Article 4	Article 3(2)(b)	Article 7(a)		Article 23(b)
		Article 7(b)		Article 23(c)
Article 5	Article 7	Article 11		Article 24
Article 6				
	Article 8d			Article 25
Article 2(5)				Article 26
	Article 8e(1)		Article 4(2)	Article 27(1)
	Article 8e(2)		Article 6	Article 27(2)

Directive 75/117/EEC	Directive 76/207/EEC	Directive 86/378/EEC	Directive 97/80/EC	This Directive
	Article 2(7) first subparagraph	Article 5(2)		Article 28(1)
	Article 2(7) fourth subparagraph first sentence			Article 28(2)
	Article 1(1a)			Article 29
Article 7	Article 8		Article 5	Article 30
Article 9	Article 10	Article 12(2)	Article 7, fourth subparagraph	Article 31(1) and (2)
	Article 9(2)			Article 31(3)
				Article 32
Article 8	Article 9(1), first subparagraph and 9(2) and (3)	Article 12(1)	Article 7, first, second and third subparagraphs	Article 33
	Article 9(1), second subparagraph			
				Article 34
				Article 35
				Article 36
		Annex		

15. Directive 2006/114/EC of the European Parliament and of the Council of 12 December 2006 concerning misleading and comparative advertising (codified version) (Text with EEA relevance)

(OJ L 376 , 27/12/2006 P.21 -27)

THE EUROPEAN PARLIAMENT AND THE COUNCIL OF THE EUROPEAN UNION,

Having regard to the Treaty establishing the European Community, and in particular Article 95 thereof,

Having regard to the proposal from the Commission,

Having regard to the opinion of the European Economic and Social Committee[1],

Acting in accordance with the procedure laid down in Article 251 of the Treaty[2],

Whereas:

(1) Council Directive 84/450/EEC of 10 September 1984 concerning misleading and comparative advertising[3] has been substantially amended several times[4]. In the interests of clarity and rationality the said Directive should be codified.

(2) The laws against misleading advertising in force in the Member States differ widely. Since advertising reaches beyond the frontiers of individual Member States, it has a direct effect on the smooth functioning of the internal market.

(3) Misleading and unlawful comparative advertising can lead to distortion of competition within the internal market.

(4) Advertising, whether or not it induces a contract, affects the economic welfare of consumers and traders.

(5) The differences between the laws of the Member States on advertising which misleads business hinder the execution of advertising campaigns beyond national boundaries and thus affect the free circulation of goods and provision of services.

(6) The completion of the internal market means a wide range of choice. Given that consumers and traders can and must make the best possible use of the internal market, and that advertising is a very important means of creating genuine outlets for all goods and services throughout the Community, the basic provisions governing the form and content of comparative advertising should be uniform and the conditions of the use of comparative advertising in the Member States should be harmonised. If these conditions are met, this will help

---

1 Opinion of 26 October 2006 (not yet published in the Official Journal).

2 Opinion of the European Parliament of 12 October 2006 (not yet published in the Official Journal) and Council Decision of 30 November 2006.

3 OJ L 250, 19.9.1984, p. 17. Directive as last amended by Directive 2005/29/EC of the European Parliament and of the Council (OJ L 149, 11.6.2005, p. 22).

4 See Annex I, Part A.

demonstrate objectively the merits of the various comparable products. Comparative advertising can also stimulate competition between suppliers of goods and services to the consumer's advantage.

(7) Minimum and objective criteria for determining whether advertising is misleading should be established.

(8) Comparative advertising, when it compares material, relevant, verifiable and representative features and is not misleading, may be a legitimate means of informing consumers of their advantage. It is desirable to provide a broad concept of comparative advertising to cover all modes of comparative advertising.

(9) Conditions of permitted comparative advertising, as far as the comparison is concerned, should be established in order to determine which practices relating to comparative advertising may distort competition, be detrimental to competitors and have an adverse effect on consumer choice. Such conditions of permitted advertising should include criteria of objective comparison of the features of goods and services.

(10) The international conventions on copyright as well as the national provisions on contractual and non-contractual liability should apply when the results of comparative tests carried out by third parties are referred to or reproduced in comparative advertising.

(11) The conditions of comparative advertising should be cumulative and respected in their entirety. In accordance with the Treaty, the choice of forms and methods for the implementation of these conditions should be left to the Member States, insofar as those forms and methods are not already determined by this Directive.

(12) These conditions should include, in particular, consideration of the provisions resulting from Council Regulation (EC) No 510/2006 of 20 March 2006 on the protection of geographical indications and designations of origin for agricultural products and foodstuffs[1], and in particular Article 13 thereof, and of the other Community provisions adopted in the agricultural sphere.

(13) Article 5 of First Council Directive 89/104/EEC of 21 December 1988 to approximate the laws of the Member States relating to trade marks[2] confers exclusive rights on the proprietor of a registered trade mark, including the right to prevent all third parties from using, in the course of trade, any sign which is identical to, or similar to, the trade mark in relation to identical goods or services or even, where appropriate, other goods.

(14) It may, however, be indispensable, in order to make comparative advertising effective, to identify the goods or services of a competitor, making reference to a trade mark or trade name of which the latter is the proprietor.

(15) Such use of another's trade mark, trade name or other distinguishing marks does not breach this exclusive right in cases where it complies with the

---

1 OJ L 40, 11.2.1989, p. 1. Directive as amended by Decision 92/10/EEC (OJ L 6, 11.1.1992, p. 35).

2 OJ L 40, 11.2.1989, p. 1. Directive as amended by Decision 92/10/EEC (OJ L 6, 11.1.1992, p. 35).

conditions laid down by this Directive, the intended target being solely to distinguish between them and thus to highlight differences objectively.

(16) Persons or organisations regarded under national law as having a legitimate interest in the matter should have facilities for initiating proceedings against misleading and unlawful comparative advertising, either before a court or before an administrative authority which is competent to decide upon complaints or to initiate appropriate legal proceedings.

(17) The courts or administrative authorities should have powers enabling them to order or obtain the cessation of misleading and unlawful comparative advertising. In certain cases it may be desirable to prohibit misleading and unlawful comparative advertising even before it is published. However, this in no way implies that Member States are under an obligation to introduce rules requiring the systematic prior vetting of advertising.

(18) The voluntary control exercised by self-regulatory bodies to eliminate misleading or unlawful comparative advertising may avoid recourse to administrative or judicial action and ought therefore to be encouraged.

(19) While it is for national law to determine the burden of proof, it is appropriate to enable courts and administrative authorities to require traders to produce evidence as to the accuracy of factual claims they have made.

(20) Regulating comparative advertising is necessary for the smooth functioning of the internal market. Action at Community level is therefore required. The adoption of a Directive is the appropriate instrument because it lays down uniform general principles while allowing the Member States to choose the form and appropriate method by which to attain these objectives. It is in accordance with the principle of subsidiarity.

(21) This Directive should be without prejudice to the obligations of the Member States relating to the time-limits for transposition into national law and application of the Directives as set out in Part B of Annex I,

HAVE ADOPTED THIS DIRECTIVE:

Article 1

The purpose of this Directive is to protect traders against misleading advertising and the unfair consequences thereof and to lay down the conditions under which comparative advertising is permitted.

Article 2

For the purposes of this Directive:

(a) "advertising" means the making of a representation in any form in connection with a trade, business, craft or profession in order to promote the supply of goods or services, including immovable property, rights and obligations;

(b) "misleading advertising" means any advertising which in any way, including its presentation, deceives or is likely to deceive the persons to whom it is addressed or whom it reaches and which, by reason of its deceptive nature, is likely to affect their economic behaviour or which, for those reasons, injures or is likely to injure a competitor;

(c) "comparative advertising" means any advertising which explicitly or by implication identifies a competitor or goods or services offered by a competitor;

(d) "trader" means any natural or legal person who is acting for purposes relating to his trade, craft, business or profession and anyone acting in the name of or on behalf of a trader;

(e) "code owner" means any entity, including a trader or group of traders, which is responsible for the formulation and revision of a code of conduct and/or for monitoring compliance with the code by those who have undertaken to be bound by it.

Article 3

In determining whether advertising is misleading, account shall be taken of all its features, and in particular of any information it contains concerning:

(a) the characteristics of goods or services, such as their availability, nature, execution, composition, method and date of manufacture or provision, fitness for purpose, uses, quantity, specification, geographical or commercial origin or the results to be expected from their use, or the results and material features of tests or checks carried out on the goods or services;

(b) the price or the manner in which the price is calculated, and the conditions on which the goods are supplied or the services provided;

(c) the nature, attributes and rights of the advertiser, such as his identity and assets, his qualifications and ownership of industrial, commercial or intellectual property rights or his awards and distinctions.

Article 4

Comparative advertising shall, as far as the comparison is concerned, be permitted when the following conditions are met:

(a) it is not misleading within the meaning of Articles 2(b), 3 and 8(1) of this Directive or Articles 6 and 7 of Directive 2005/29/EC of the European Parliament and of the Council of 11 May 2005 concerning unfair business-to-consumer commercial practices in the internal market ("Unfair Commercial Practices Directive")[1];

(b) it compares goods or services meeting the same needs or intended for the same purpose;

(c) it objectively compares one or more material, relevant, verifiable and representative features of those goods and services, which may include price;

[1] OJ L 149, 11.6.2005, p. 22.

(d) it does not discredit or denigrate the trade marks, trade names, other distinguishing marks, goods, services, activities or circumstances of a competitor;

(e) for products with designation of origin, it relates in each case to products with the same designation;

(f) it does not take unfair advantage of the reputation of a trade mark, trade name or other distinguishing marks of a competitor or of the designation of origin of competing products;

(g) it does not present goods or services as imitations or replicas of goods or services bearing a protected trade mark or trade name;

(h) it does not create confusion among traders, between the advertiser and a competitor or between the advertiser's trade marks, trade names, other distinguishing marks, goods or services and those of a competitor.

Article 5

1. Member States shall ensure that adequate and effective means exist to combat misleading advertising and enforce compliance with the provisions on comparative advertising in the interests of traders and competitors.

   Such means shall include legal provisions under which persons or organisations regarded under national law as having a legitimate interest in combating misleading advertising or regulating comparative advertising may:

   (a) take legal action against such advertising;

   or

   (b) bring such advertising before an administrative authority competent either to decide on complaints or to initiate appropriate legal proceedings.

2. It shall be for each Member State to decide which of the facilities referred to in the second subparagraph of paragraph 1 shall be available and whether to enable the courts or administrative authorities to require prior recourse to other established means of dealing with complaints, including those referred to in Article 6.

   It shall be for each Member State to decide:

   (a) whether these legal facilities may be directed separately or jointly against a number of traders from the same economic sector;

   and

   (b) whether these legal facilities may be directed against a code owner where the relevant code promotes non-compliance with legal requirements.

3. Under the provisions referred to in paragraphs 1 and 2, Member States shall confer upon the courts or administrative authorities powers enabling them, in cases where they deem such measures to be necessary taking into account all the interests involved and in particular the public interest:

(a) to order the cessation of, or to institute appropriate legal proceedings for an order for the cessation of, misleading advertising or unlawful comparative advertising;

or

(b) if the misleading advertising or unlawful comparative advertising has not yet been published but publication is imminent, to order the prohibition of, or to institute appropriate legal proceedings for an order for the prohibition of, such publication.

The first subparagraph shall apply even where there is no proof of actual loss or damage or of intention or negligence on the part of the advertiser.

Member States shall make provision for the measures referred to in the first subparagraph to be taken under an accelerated procedure either with interim effect or with definitive effect, at the Member States' discretion.

4. Member States may confer upon the courts or administrative authorities powers enabling them, with a view to eliminating the continuing effects of misleading advertising or unlawful comparative advertising, the cessation of which has been ordered by a final decision:
   (a) to require publication of that decision in full or in part and in such form as they deem adequate;
   (b) to require in addition the publication of a corrective statement.

5. The administrative authorities referred to in point (b) of the second subparagraph of paragraph 1 must:
   (a) be composed so as not to cast doubt on their impartiality;
   (b) have adequate powers, where they decide on complaints, to monitor and enforce the observance of their decisions effectively;
   (c) normally give reasons for their decisions.

6. Where the powers referred to in paragraphs 3 and 4 are exercised exclusively by an administrative authority, reasons for its decisions shall always be given. In this case, provision must be made for procedures whereby improper or unreasonable exercise of its powers by the administrative authority or improper or unreasonable failure to exercise the said powers can be the subject of judicial review.

Article 6

This Directive does not exclude the voluntary control, which Member States may encourage, of misleading or comparative advertising by self-regulatory bodies and recourse to such bodies by the persons or organisations referred to in the second subparagraph of Article 5(1) on condition that proceedings before such bodies are additional to the court or administrative proceedings referred to in that Article.

Article 7

Member States shall confer upon the courts or administrative authorities powers enabling them in the civil or administrative proceedings referred to in Article 5:

(a) to require the advertiser to furnish evidence as to the accuracy of factual claims in advertising if, taking into account the legitimate interest of the advertiser and any other party to the proceedings, such a requirement appears appropriate on the basis of the circumstances of the particular case and in the case of comparative advertising to require the advertiser to furnish such evidence in a short period of time;

and

(b) to consider factual claims as inaccurate if the evidence demanded in accordance with point (a) is not furnished or is deemed insufficient by the court or administrative authority.

Article 8

1. This Directive shall not preclude Member States from retaining or adopting provisions with a view to ensuring more extensive protection, with regard to misleading advertising, for traders and competitors.

   The first subparagraph shall not apply to comparative advertising as far as the comparison is concerned.
2. The provisions of this Directive shall apply without prejudice to Community provisions on advertising for specific products and/or services or to restrictions or prohibitions on advertising in particular media.
3. The provisions of this Directive concerning comparative advertising shall not oblige Member States which, in compliance with the provisions of the Treaty, maintain or introduce advertising bans regarding certain goods or services, whether imposed directly or by a body or organisation responsible, under the law of the Member States, for regulating the exercise of a commercial, industrial, craft or professional activity, to permit comparative advertising regarding those goods or services. Where these bans are limited to particular media, this Directive shall apply to the media not covered by these bans.
4. Nothing in this Directive shall prevent Member States, in compliance with the provisions of the Treaty, from maintaining or introducing bans or limitations on the use of comparisons in the advertising of professional services, whether imposed directly or by a body or organisation responsible, under the law of the Member States, for regulating the exercise of a professional activity.

Article 9

Member States shall communicate to the Commission the text of the main provisions of national law which they adopt in the field covered by this Directive.

Article 10

Directive 84/450/EEC is hereby repealed, without prejudice to the obligations of the Member States relating to the time-limits for transposition into national law and application of the Directives, as set out in Part B of Annex I.

References made to the repealed Directive shall be construed as being made to this Directive and should be read in accordance with the correlation table set out in Annex II.

Article 11

This Directive shall enter into force on 12 December 2007.

Article 12

This Directive is addressed to the Member States.

Done at Strasbourg, 12 December 2006.

For the European Parliament

The President

J. Borrell Fontelles

For the Council

The President

M. Pekkarinen

ANNEX I

PART A

Repealed Directive with its successive amendments

Council Directive 84/450/EEC (OJ L 250, 19.9.1984, p. 17)	
Directive 97/55/EC of the European Parliament and of the Council (OJ L 290, 23.10.1997, p. 18)	
Directive 2005/29/EC of the European Parliament and of the Council (OJ L 149, 11.6.2005, p. 22)	only Article 14

PART B

List of time-limits for transposition into national law and application (referred to in Article 10)

Directive	Time-limit for transposition	Date of application
84/450/EEC	1 October 1986	
97/55/EC	23 April 2000	
2005/29/EC	12 June 2007	12 December 2007

ANNEX II
CORRELATION TABLE

Directive 84/450/EEC	This Directive
Article 1	Article 1
Article 2, introductory words	Article 2, introductory words
Article 2, point 1	Article 2(a)
Article 2, point 2	Article 2(b)
Article 2, point 2a	Article 2(c)
Article 2, point 3	Article 2(d)
Article 2, point 4	Article 2(e)
Article 3	Article 3
Article 3a(1)	Article 4
Article 4(1), first subparagraph, first sentence	Article 5(1), first subparagraph
Article 4(1), first subparagraph, second sentence	Article 5(1), second subparagraph
Article 4(1), second subparagraph	Article 5(2), first subparagraph
Article 4(1), third subparagraph	Article 5(2), second subparagraph
Article 4(2), first subparagraph, introductory words	Article 5(3), first subparagraph, introductory words
Article 4(2), first subparagraph, first indent	Article 5(3), first subparagraph, point (a)
Article 4(2), first subparagraph, second indent	Article 5(3), first subparagraph, point (b)
Article 4(2), first subparagraph, final words	Article 5(3), second subparagraph
Article 4(2), second subparagraph, introductory words	Article 5(3), third subparagraph
Article 4(2), second subparagraph, first indent	Article 5(3), third subparagraph
Article 4(2), second subparagraph, second indent	Article 5(3), third subparagraph
Article 4(2), second subparagraph, final words	Article 5(3), third subparagraph
Article 4(2), third subparagraph, introductory words	Article 5(4), introductory words
Article 4(2), third subparagraph, first indent	Article 5(4), point (a)
Article 4(2), third subparagraph, second indent	Article 5(4), point (b)
Article 4(3), first subparagraph	Article 5(5)

Article 4(3), second subparagraph	Article 5(6)
Article 5	Article 6
Article 6	Article 7
Article 7(1)	Article 8(1), first subparagraph
Article 7(2)	Article 8(1), second subparagraph
Article 7(3)	Article 8(2)
Article 7(4)	Article 8(3
Article 7(5)	Article 8(4)
Article 8, first subparagraph	
Article 8, second subparagraph	Article 9
	Article 10 |
	Article 11
Article 9	Article 12
	Annex I

16. Directive 2007/64/EC of the European Parliament and of the Council of 13 November 2007 on payment services in the internal market amending Directives 97/7/EC, 2002/65/EC, 2005/60/EC and 2006/48/EC and repealing Directive 97/5/EC Text with EEA relevance

(OJ L 319 , 05/12/2007 p. 0001 – 0036)

THE EUROPEAN PARLIAMENT AND THE COUNCIL OF THE EUROPEAN UNION,

Having regard to the Treaty establishing the European Community, and in particular the first and third sentences of Article 47(2) and Article 95 thereof,

Having regard to the proposal from the Commission,

Having consulted the European Economic and Social Committee,

Having regard to the opinion of the European Central Bank[1],

Acting in accordance with the procedure laid down in Article 251 of the Treaty[2],

Whereas:

(1) It is essential for the establishment of the internal market that all internal frontiers in the Community be dismantled so as to enable the free movement of goods, persons, services and capital. The proper operation of the single market in payment services is therefore vital. At present, however, the lack of harmonisation in this area hinders the operation of that market.

(2) Currently, the payment services markets of the Member States are organised separately, along national lines and the legal framework for payment services is fragmented into 27 national legal systems.

(3) Several Community acts have already been adopted in this area, namely Directive 97/5/EC of the European Parliament and of the Council of 27 January 1997 on cross-border credit transfers[3] and Regulation (EC) No 2560/2001 of the European Parliament and of the Council of 19 December 2001 on cross-border payments in euro[4], but these have not sufficiently remedied this situation any more than have Commission Recommendation 87/598/EEC of 8 December 1987 on a European Code of Conduct relating to electronic payment (relations between financial institutions, traders and service establishments, and consumers)[5], Commission Recommendation 88/590/EEC of 17 November 1988 concerning payment systems, and in particular the relationship between cardholder and card issuer[6], or Commission Recommendation 97/489/EC of 30

[1] OJ C 109, 9.5.2006, p. 10.

[2] Opinion of the European Parliament of 24 April 2007 (not yet published in the Official Journal) and Council Decision of 15 October 2007.

[3] OJ L 43, 14.2.1997, p. 25.

[4] OJ L 344, 28.12.2001, p. 13.

[5] OJ L 365, 24.12.1987, p. 72.

[6] OJ L 317, 24.11.1988, p. 55.

July 1997 concerning transactions by electronic payment instruments and in particular the relationship between issuer and holder[1]. These measures continue to be insufficient. The co-existence of national provisions and an incomplete Community framework gives rise to confusion and a lack of legal certainty.

(4) It is vital, therefore, to establish at Community level a modern and coherent legal framework for payment services, whether or not the services are compatible with the system resulting from the financial sector initiative for a single euro payments area, which is neutral so as to ensure a level playing field for all payment systems, in order to maintain consumer choice, which should mean a considerable step forward in terms of consumer cost, safety and efficiency, as compared with the present national systems.

(5) That legal framework should ensure the coordination of national provisions on prudential requirements, the access of new payment service providers to the market, information requirements, and the respective rights and obligations of payment services users and providers. Within that framework, the provisions of Regulation (EC) No 2560/2001, which created a single market for euro payments as far as prices are concerned, should be maintained. The provisions of Directive 97/5/EC and the recommendations made in Recommendations 87/598/EEC, 88/590/EEC and 97/489/EC should be integrated in a single act with binding force.

(6) However, it is not appropriate for that legal framework to be fully comprehensive. Its application should be confined to payment service providers whose main activity consists in the provision of payment services to payment service users. Nor is it appropriate for it to apply to services where the transfer of funds from the payer to the payee or their transport is executed solely in bank notes and coins or where the transfer is based on a paper cheque, paper-based bill of exchange, promissory note or other instrument, paper-based vouchers or cards drawn upon a payment service provider or other party with a view to placing funds at the disposal of the payee. Furthermore, a differentiation should be made in the case of means offered by telecommunication, information technology or network operators to facilitate purchasing of digital goods or services, such as ring tones, music or digital newspapers, besides traditional voice services and their distribution to digital devices. The content of these goods or services may be produced either by a third party or by the operator, who may add intrinsic value to them in the form of access, distribution or search facilities. In the latter case, where the goods or services are distributed by one of those operators, or, for technical reasons, by a third party, and where they can be used only through digital devices, such as mobile phones or computers, that legal framework should not apply as the activity of the operator goes beyond a mere payment transaction. However, it is appropriate for that legal framework to apply to cases where the operator acts only as an intermediary who simply arranges for payment to be made to a third-party supplier.

[1] OJ L 317, 24.11.1988, p. 55.

(7) Money remittance is a simple payment service that is usually based on cash provided by a payer to a payment service provider, which remits the corresponding amount, for example via communication network, to a payee or to another payment service provider acting on behalf of the payee. In some Member States supermarkets, merchants and other retailers provide to the public a corresponding service enabling the payment of utility and other regular household bills. Those bill-paying services should be treated as money remittance as defined in this Directive, unless the competent authorities consider the activity to fall under another payment service listed in the Annex.

(8) It is necessary to specify the categories of payment service providers which may legitimately provide payment services throughout the Community, namely, credit institutions which take deposits from users that can be used to fund payment transactions and which should continue to be subject to the prudential requirements under Directive 2006/48/EC of the European Parliament and of the Council of 14 June 2006 relating to the taking up and pursuit of the business of credit institutions[1], electronic money institutions which issue electronic money that can be used to fund payment transactions and which should continue to be subject to the prudential requirements under Directive 2000/46/EC of the European Parliament and of the Council of 18 September 2000 on the taking-up, pursuit and prudential supervision of the business of electronic money institutions[2], and post office giro institutions which are so entitled under national law.

(9) This Directive should lay down rules on the execution of payment transactions where the funds are electronic money, as defined in Article 1(3)(b) of Directive 2000/46/EC. This Directive should, however, neither regulate issuance of electronic money nor amend the prudential regulation of electronic money institutions as provided for in Directive 2000/46/EC. Therefore, payment institutions should not be allowed to issue electronic money.

(10) However, in order to remove legal barriers to market entry, it is necessary to establish a single licence for all providers of payment services which are not connected to taking deposits or issuing electronic money. It is appropriate, therefore, to introduce a new category of payment service providers, "payment institutions", by providing for the authorisation, subject to a set of strict and comprehensive conditions, of legal persons outside the existing categories to provide payment services throughout the Community. Thus, the same conditions would apply Community-wide to such services.

(11) The conditions for granting and maintaining authorisation as payment institutions should include prudential requirements proportionate to the operational and financial risks faced by such bodies in the course of their business. In this connection, there is a need for a sound regime of initial capital

[1] OJ L 177, 30.6.2006, p. 1. Directive as amended by Commission Directive 2007/44/EC (OJ L 247, 21.9.2007, p. 1).

[2] OJ L 275, 27.10.2000, p. 39.

combined with ongoing capital which could be elaborated in a more sophisticated way in due course depending on the needs of the market. Due to the range of variety in the payments services area, this Directive should allow various methods combined with a certain range of supervisory discretion to ensure that the same risks are treated the same way for all payment service providers. The requirements for the payment institutions should reflect the fact that payment institutions engage in more specialised and limited activities, thus generating risks that are narrower and easier to monitor and control than those that arise across the broader spectrum of activities of credit institutions. In particular, payment institutions should be prohibited from accepting deposits from users and permitted to use funds received from users only for rendering payment services. Provision should be made for client funds to be kept separate from the payment institution's funds for other business activities. Payment institutions should also be made subject to effective anti-money laundering and anti-terrorist financing requirements.

(12) Payment institutions should draw up their annual and consolidated accounts in accordance with Council Directive 78/660/EEC of 25 July 1978 on the annual accounts of certain types of companies[1] and, where applicable, Council Directive 83/349/EEC of 13 June 1983 on consolidated accounts[2] and Council Directive 86/635/EEC of 8 December 1986 on the annual accounts and consolidated accounts of banks and other financial institutions[3]. The annual accounts and consolidated accounts should be audited, unless the payment institution is exempted from this obligation under Directive 78/660/EEC and, where applicable, Directives 83/349/EEC and 86/635/EEC.

(13) This Directive should regulate the granting of credit by payment institutions, i.e. the granting of credit lines and the issuance of credit cards, only where it is closely linked to payment services. Only if credit is granted in order to facilitate payment services and such credit is of a short-term nature and is granted for a period not exceeding twelve months, including on a revolving basis, is it appropriate to allow payment institutions to grant such credit with regard to their cross-border activities, on condition that it is refinanced using mainly the payment institution's own funds, as well as other funds from the capital markets, but not the funds held on behalf of clients for payment services. The above should be without prejudice to Council Directive 87/102/EEC of 22 December 1986 for the approximation of the laws, regulations and administrative provisions of the Member States concerning consumer credit[4] or other relevant Community or national legislation regarding conditions for granting credit to consumers not harmonised by this Directive.

---

[1] OJ L 222, 14.8.1978, p. 11. Directive as last amended by Directive 2006/46/EC of the European Parliament and of the Council (OJ L 224, 16.8.2006, p. 1).

[2] OJ L 193, 18.7.1983, p. 1. Directive as last amended by Directive 2006/99/EC (OJ L 363, 20.12.2006, p. 137).

[3] OJ L 372, 31.12.1986, p. 1. Directive as last amended by Directive 2006/46/EC.

[4] OJ L 42, 12.2.1987, p. 48. Directive as last amended by Directive 98/7/EC of the European Parliament and of the Council (OJ L 101, 1.4.1998, p. 17).

(14) It is necessary for the Member States to designate the authorities responsible for granting authorisations to payment institutions, carrying out controls and deciding on the withdrawal of those authorisations. In order to ensure equality of treatment, Member States should apply to payment institutions no requirements other than those provided for in this Directive. However, all decisions made by the competent authorities should be contestable before the courts. In addition, the tasks of the competent authorities should be without prejudice to the oversight of payment systems, which, in line with the fourth indent of Article 105(2) of the Treaty, is a task to be carried out by the European System of Central Banks.

(15) Given the desirability of registering the identity and whereabouts of all persons providing remittance services and of according them all a measure of acceptance, irrespective of whether they are able to meet the full range of conditions for authorisation as payment institutions, so that none are forced into the black economy and bring all persons providing remittance service within the ambit of certain minimum legal and regulatory requirements, it is appropriate and in line with the rationale of Special Recommendation VI of the Financial Action Task Force on Money Laundering to provide a mechanism whereby payment service providers unable to meet all those conditions may nevertheless be treated as payment institutions. For those purposes, Member States should enter such persons in the register of payment institutions while not applying all or part of the conditions for authorisation. However, it is essential to make the possibility of waiver subject to strict requirements relating to the volume of payment transactions. Payment institutions benefiting from a waiver should have neither the right of establishment nor the freedom to provide services, nor should they indirectly exercise those rights when being a member of a payment system.

(16) It is essential for any payment service provider to be able to access the services of technical infrastructures of payment systems. Such access should, however, be subject to appropriate requirements in order to ensure integrity and stability of those systems. Each payment service provider applying for a participation in a payment system should furnish proof to the participants of the payment system that its internal arrangements are sufficiently robust against all kinds of risk. These payment systems typically include e.g. the four-party card schemes as well as major systems processing credit transfers and direct debits. In order to ensure equality of treatment throughout the Community as between the different categories of authorised payment service providers, according to the terms of their licence, it is necessary to clarify the rules concerning access to the provision of payment services and access to payment systems. Provision should be made for the non-discriminatory treatment of authorised payment institutions and credit institutions so that any payment service provider competing in the internal market is able to use the services of the technical infrastructures of these payment systems under the same conditions. It is appropriate to provide for different treatment for authorised payment service providers and for those

benefiting from a waiver under this Directive as well as from the waiver under the Article 8 of the Directive 2000/46/EC, due to the differences in their prudential framework. In any case differences in price conditions should be allowed only when this is motivated by differences in costs induced by the payment service providers. This should be without prejudice to Member States' right to limit access to systemically important systems in accordance with Directive 98/26/EC of the European Parliament and of the Council of 19 May 1998 on settlement finality in payment and securities settlement systems[1] and without prejudice to the competence of the European Central Bank and the European System of Central Banks (ESCB), as laid down in Article 105(2) of the Treaty and Article 3(1) and Article 22 of the Statute of the ESCB, concerning access to payment systems.

(17) The provisions of the access to payment systems should not apply to systems set up and operated by a single payment service provider. Those payment systems can operate either in direct competition to payment systems, or, more typically, in a market niche not adequately covered by payment systems. They typically cover three-party schemes, such as three party card schemes, payment services offered by telecommunication providers or money remittance services where the scheme operator is the payment service provider to both the payer and payee as well as internal systems of banking groups. In order to stimulate the competition that can be provided by such payment systems to established mainstream payment systems, it should in principle not be appropriate to grant third parties access to these payment systems. Nevertheless, such systems should always be subject to Community and national competition rules which may require that access be granted to the schemes in order to maintain effective competition in payments markets.

(18) A set of rules should be established in order to ensure transparency of conditions and information requirements for payment services.

(19) This Directive should apply neither to payment transactions made in cash since a single payments market for cash already exists nor to payment transactions based on paper cheques since, by their nature, they cannot be processed as efficiently as other means of payment. Good practice in this area should, however, be based on the principles set out in this Directive.

(20) As consumers and enterprises are not in the same position, they do not need the same level of protection. While it is important to guarantee consumers' rights by provisions which cannot be derogated from by contract, it is reasonable to let enterprises and organisations agree otherwise. However, Member States should have the possibility to provide that micro-enterprises, as defined by Commission Recommendation 2003/361/EC of 6 May 2003 concerning the definition of micro, small and medium-sized enterprises[2], should be treated in the same way

1 OJ L 166, 11.6.1998, p. 45.

2 OJ L 124, 20.5.2003, p. 36.

as consumers. In any case, certain core provisions of this Directive should always be applicable irrespective of the status of the user.

(21) This Directive should specify the obligations on payment service providers as regards the provision of information to the payment service users who should receive the same high level of clear information about payment services in order to make well-informed choices and be able to shop around within the EU. In the interest of transparency this Directive should lay down the harmonised requirements needed to ensure that necessary and sufficient information is given to the payment service users with regard to the payment service contract and the payment transactions. In order to promote smooth functioning of the single market in payment services, Member States should be able to adopt only those information provisions laid down in this Directive.

(22) Consumers should be protected against unfair and misleading practices in line with Directive 2005/29/EC of the European Parliament and the Council of 11 May 2005 concerning unfair business-to-consumer commercial practices in the Internal Market[1] as well as Directive 2000/31/EC of the European Parliament and the Council of 8 June 2000 on certain legal aspects of information society services, in particular electronic commerce, in the Internal Market (Directive on electronic commerce)[2] and Directive 2002/65/EC of the European Parliament and the Council of 23 September 2002 concerning the distance marketing of consumer financial services[3]. The additional provisions in those Directives continue to be applicable. However, the relationship of the pre-contractual information requirements between this Directive and Directive 2002/65/EC should, in particular, be clarified.

(23) The information required should be proportionate to the needs of users and communicated in a standard manner. However, the information requirements for a single payment transaction should be different from those of a framework contract which provides for the series of payment transactions.

(24) In practice, framework contracts and the payment transactions covered by them are far more common and economically important than single payment transactions. If there is a payment account or a specific payment instrument, a framework contract is required. Therefore, the requirements for prior information on framework contracts should be quite comprehensive and information should always be provided on paper or on another durable medium, such as printouts by account printers, floppy disks, CD-ROMs, DVDs and hard drives of personal computers on which electronic mail can be stored, and Internet sites, as long as such sites are accessible for future reference for a period of time adequate for the purposes of information and allow the unchanged reproduction of the information stored. However, it should be possible for the payment service provider and the payment service user to agree in the framework contract on the manner in which subsequent information on

[1] OJ L 149, 11.6.2005, p. 22.

[2] OJ L 178, 17.7.2000, p. 1.

[3] OJ L 271, 9.10.2002, p. 16. Directive as amended by Directive 2005/29/EC.

executed payment transactions is given, for instance, that in Internet banking all information on the payment account is made available online.

(25) In single payment transactions only the essential information should always be given on the payment service provider's own initiative. As the payer is usually present when he gives the payment order, it is not necessary to require that information should in every case be provided on paper or on another durable medium. The payment service provider may give information orally over the counter or make it otherwise easily accessible, for example by keeping the conditions on a notice board on the premises. Information should also be given on where other more detailed information is available (e.g. the address of the website). However, if the consumer so requests, the essential information should be given on paper or on another durable medium.

(26) This Directive should provide for the consumer's right to receive relevant information free of charge before he is bound by any payment service contract. The consumer should also be able to request prior information as well as the framework contract, on paper, free of charge at any time during the contractual relationship, so as to enable him to compare payment service providers' services and their conditions and in case of any dispute verify his contractual rights and obligations. Those provisions should be compatible with Directive 2002/65/EC. The explicit provisions on free information in this Directive should not have the effect of allowing charges to be imposed for the provision of information to consumers under other applicable Directives.

(27) The way in which the required information is to be given by the payment service provider to the payment service user should take into account the needs of the latter as well as practical technical aspects and cost-efficiency depending on the situation with regard to the agreement in the respective payment service contract. Thus, this Directive should distinguish between two ways in which information is to be given by the payment service provider: either the information should be provided, i.e. actively communicated by the payment service provider at the appropriate time as required by this Directive without further prompting by the payment service user, or the information should be made available to the payment service user, taking into account any request he may have for further information. In the latter case, the payment service user should take some active steps in order to obtain the information, such as requesting it explicitly from the payment service provider, logging into bank account mail box or inserting a bank card into printer for account statements. For such purposes the payment service provider should ensure that access to the information is possible and that the information is available to the payment service user.

(28) In addition, the consumer should receive basic information on executed payment transactions for no additional charge. In the case of a single payment transaction the payment service provider should not charge separately for this information. Similarly, the subsequent monthly information on payment transactions under a framework contract should be given free of charge.

However, taking into account the importance of transparency in pricing and differing customer needs, the parties should be able to agree on charges for more frequent or additional information. In order to take into account different national practices, Member States should be allowed to set rules requiring that monthly paper-based statements of payment accounts are always to be given free of charge.

(29) In order to facilitate customer mobility, it should be possible for consumers to terminate a framework contract after the expiry of a year without incurring charges. For consumers, the period of notice agreed should be no longer than a month, and for payment service providers no shorter than two months. This Directive should be without prejudice to the payment service provider's obligation to terminate the payment service contract in exceptional circumstances under other relevant Community or national legislation, such as legislation on money laundering and terrorist financing, any action targeting the freezing of funds, or any specific measure linked to the prevention and investigation of crimes.

(30) Low value payment instruments should be a cheap and easy-to-use alternative in the case of low-priced goods and services and should not be overburdened by excessive requirements. The relevant information requirements and rules on their execution should therefore be limited to essential information, taking also into account technical capabilities that can justifiably be expected from instruments dedicated to low value payments. Despite the lighter regime payment service users should benefit from adequate protection considering the limited risks posed by those payment instruments, especially with regard to prepaid payment instruments.

(31) In order to reduce the risks and consequences of unauthorised or incorrectly executed payment transactions the payment service user should inform the payment service provider as soon as possible about any contestations concerning allegedly unauthorised or incorrectly executed payment transactions provided that the payment service provider has fulfilled his information obligations under this Directive. If the notification deadline is met by the payment service user, he should be able to pursue those claims within the prescription periods pursuant to national law. This Directive should not affect other claims between payment service users and payment service providers.

(32) In order to provide an incentive for the payment service user to notify, without undue delay, his provider of any theft or loss of a payment instrument and thus to reduce the risk of unauthorised payment transactions, the user should be liable only for a limited amount, unless the payment service user has acted fraudulently or with gross negligence. Moreover, once a user has notified a payment service provider that his payment instrument may have been compromised, the user should not be required to cover any further losses stemming from unauthorised use of that instrument. This Directive should be without prejudice to the payment service providers' responsibility for technical security of their own products.

(33) In order to assess possible negligence by the payment service user, account should be taken of all the circumstances. The evidence and degree of alleged negligence should be evaluated according to national law. Contractual terms and conditions relating to the provision and use of a payment instrument, the effect of which would be to increase the burden of proof on the consumer or to reduce the burden of proof on the issuer should be considered null and void.

(34) However, Member States should be able to establish less stringent rules than mentioned above in order to maintain existing levels of consumer protection and promote trust in the safe usage of electronic payment instruments. The fact that different payment instruments involve different risks should be taken into account accordingly thus promoting the issuance of safer instruments. Member States should be allowed to reduce or completely waive the payer's liability except where the payer has acted fraudulently.

(35) Provisions should be made for the allocation of losses in the case of unauthorised payment transactions. Different provisions may apply to payment service users who are not consumers, since such users are normally in a better position to assess the risk of fraud and take countervailing measures.

(36) This Directive should lay down rules for a refund to protect the consumer when the executed payment transaction exceeds the amount which could reasonably have been expected. Payment service providers should be able to provide even more favourable terms to their customers and, for example, refund any disputed payment transactions. In cases where the user makes a claim for the refund of a payment transaction refund rights should affect neither the liability of the payer vis-à-vis the payee from the underlying relationship, e.g. for goods or services ordered, consumed or legitimately charged, nor the users rights with regard to revocation of a payment order.

(37) For financial planning and the fulfilment of payment obligations in due time, consumers and enterprises need to have certainty on the length of time that the execution of a payment order takes. Therefore, this Directive should introduce a point in time at which rights and obligations take effect, namely, when the payment service provider receives the payment order, including when he has had the opportunity to receive it through the means of communication agreed in the payment service contract, notwithstanding any prior involvement in the process leading up to the creation and transmission of the payment order, e.g. security and availability of funds checks, information on the use of the personal identity number or issuance of a payment promise. Furthermore, the receipt of a payment order should occur when the payer's payment service provider receives the payment order to be debited from the payer's account. The day or moment in time when a payee transmits to his service provider payment orders for the collection e.g. of card payment or of direct debits or when the payee is granted a pre-financing on the related amounts by his payment service provider (by way of a contingent credit to his account) should have no relevance in this respect. Users should be able to rely on the proper execution of a complete and valid payment order if the payment service provider has no contractual or statutory

ground for refusal. If the payment service provider refuses a payment order, the refusal and the reason therefor should be communicated to the payment service user at the earliest opportunity subject to the requirements of Community and national law.

(38) In view of the speed with which modern fully automated payment systems process payment transactions, which means that after a certain point in time payment orders cannot be revoked without high manual intervention costs, it is necessary to specify a clear deadline for payment revocations. However, depending on the type of the payment service and the payment order, the point in time may be varied by agreement between the parties. Revocation, in this context, is applicable only to the relationship between a payment service user and payment service provider, thus being without prejudice to the irrevocability and finality of payment transactions in payment systems.

(39) Such irrevocability should not affect a payment service provider's right or obligation under the laws of some Member States, based on the payer's framework contract or national laws, regulations, administrative provisions or guidelines, to reimburse the payer with the amount of the executed payment transaction in the event of a dispute between the payer and the payee. Such reimbursement should be considered to be a new payment order. Except for those cases, legal disputes arising within the relationship underlying the payment order should be settled only between the payer and the payee.

(40) It is essential, for the fully integrated straight-through processing of payments and for legal certainty with respect to the fulfilment of any underlying obligation between payment service users, that the full amount transferred by the payer should be credited to the account of the payee. Accordingly, it should not be possible for any of the intermediaries involved in the execution of payment transactions to make deductions from the amount transferred. However, it should be possible for the payee to enter into an agreement with his payment service provider under which the latter may deduct his own charges. Nevertheless, in order to enable the payee to verify that the amount due is correctly paid, subsequent information provided on the payment transaction should indicate not only the full amount of funds transferred but also the amount of any charges.

(41) With regard to charges, experience has shown that the sharing of charges between a payer and a payee is the most efficient system since it facilitates the straight-through processing of payments. Provision should therefore be made for charges to be levied, in the normal course, directly on the payer and the payee by their respective payment service providers. However, that should apply only where the payment transaction does not require currency exchange. The amount of any charges levied may also be zero as the provisions of this Directive do not affect the practice whereby the payment service provider does not charge consumers for crediting their accounts. Similarly, depending on the contract terms, a payment service provider may charge only the payee (merchant) for the use of the payment service, which has the effect that no charges are imposed on

the payer. The charging of the payment systems may be in the form of a subscription fee. The provisions on the amount transferred or any charges levied have no direct impact on pricing between payment service providers or any intermediaries.

(42) In order to promote transparency and competition, the payment service provider should not prevent the payee from requesting a charge from the payer for using a specific payment instrument. While the payee should be free to levy charges for the use of a certain payment instrument, Member States may decide whether they forbid or limit any such practice where, in their view, this may be warranted in view of abusive pricing or pricing which may have a negative impact on the use of a certain payment instrument taking into account the need to encourage competition and the use of efficient payment instruments.

(43) In order to improve the efficiency of payments throughout the Community, all payment orders initiated by the payer and denominated in euro or the currency of a Member State outside the euro area, including credit transfers and money remittances, should be subject to a maximum one-day execution time. For all other payments, such as payments initiated by or through a payee, including direct debits and card payments, in the absence of an explicit agreement between the payment service provider and the payer setting a longer execution time, the same one-day execution time should apply. The periods above could be extended by an additional business day, if a payment order is given on paper. This allows the continued provision of payment services for those consumers who are used to paper documents only. When a direct debit scheme is used the payee's payment service provider should transmit the collection order within the time limits agreed between the payee and his payment service provider, enabling settlement at the agreed due date. In view of the fact that national payment infrastructures are often highly efficient and in order to prevent any deterioration in current service levels, Member States should be allowed to maintain or set rules specifying an execution time shorter than one business day, where appropriate.

(44) The provisions on execution for the full amount and execution time should constitute good practice where one of the service providers is not located in the Community.

(45) It is essential for payment service users to know the real costs and charges of payment services in order to make their choice. Accordingly, the use of non-transparent pricing methods should not be allowed, since it is commonly accepted that those methods make it extremely difficult for users to establish the real price of the payment service. Specifically, the use of value dating to the disadvantage of the user should not be permitted.

(46) The smooth and efficient functioning of the payment system depends on the user being able to rely on the payment service provider executing the payment transaction correctly and within the agreed time. Usually, the provider is in the position to assess the risks involved in the payment transaction. It is the provider that provides the payments system, makes arrangements to recall misplaced or

wrongly allocated funds and decides in most cases on the intermediaries involved in the execution of a payment transaction. In view of all those considerations, it is entirely appropriate, except under abnormal and unforeseeable circumstances, to impose liability on the payment service provider in respect of execution of a payment transaction accepted from the user, except for the payee's payment service provider's acts and omissions for whose selection solely the payee is responsible. However, in order not to leave the payer unprotected in unlikely constellations where it may remain open (non liquet) whether the payment amount was duly received by the payee's payment service provider or not, the corresponding burden of proof should lie upon the payer's payment service provider. As a rule, it can be expected that the intermediary institution, usually a "neutral" body like a central bank or a clearing house, transferring the payment amount from the sending to the receiving payment service provider will store the account data and be able to furnish the latter whenever this may be necessary. Whenever the payment amount has been credited to the receiving payment service provider's account, the payee should immediately have a claim against his payment service provider for credit to his account.

(47) The payer's payment service provider should assume liability for correct payment execution, including, in particular the full amount of the payment transaction and execution time, and full responsibility for any failure by other parties in the payment chain up to the account of the payee. As a result of that liability the payment service provider of the payer should, where the full amount is not credited to the payee's payment service provider, correct the payment transaction or without undue delay refund to the payer the relevant amount of that transaction, without prejudice to any other claims which may be made in accordance with national law. This Directive should concern only contractual obligations and responsibilities between the payment service user and his payment service provider. However, the proper functioning of credit transfers and other payment services requires that payment service providers and their intermediaries, such as processors, have contracts where their mutual rights and obligations are agreed upon. Questions related to liabilities form an essential part of these uniform contracts. To ensure the reliability among payment service providers and intermediaries taking part in a payment transaction, legal certainty is necessary to the effect that a non-responsible payment service provider is compensated for losses incurred or sums paid under the provisions of this Directive relating to liability. Further rights and details of content of recourse and how to handle claims towards the payment service provider or intermediary attributable to a defective payment transaction should be left to be defined by contractual arrangements.

(48) It should be possible for the payment service provider to specify unambiguously the information required to execute a payment order correctly. On the other hand, however, in order to avoid fragmentation and jeopardising the setting-up of integrated payment systems in the Community, Member States

should not be allowed to require a particular identifier to be used for payment transactions. However, this should not prevent Member States from requiring the payment service provider of the payer to act in due diligence and verify, where technically possible and without requiring manual intervention, the coherence of the unique identifier, and where the unique identifier is found to be incoherent, to refuse the payment order and inform the payer thereof. The liability of the payment service provider should be limited to the correct execution of the payment transaction in accordance with the payment order of the payment service user.

(49) In order to facilitate effective fraud prevention and combat payment fraud across the Community, provision should be made for the efficient exchange of data between payment service providers who should be allowed to collect, process and exchange personal data relating to persons involved in payment fraud. All those activities should be conducted in compliance with Directive 95/46/EC of the European Parliament and of the Council of 24 October 1995 on the protection of individuals with regard to the processing of personal data and on the free movement of such data[1].

(50) It is necessary to ensure the effective enforcement of the provisions of national law adopted pursuant to this Directive. Appropriate procedures should therefore be established by means of which it will be possible to pursue complaints against payment service providers which do not comply with those provisions and to ensure that, where appropriate, effective, proportionate and dissuasive penalties are imposed.

(51) Without prejudice to the right of customers to bring action in the courts, Member States should ensure an easily accessible and cost-sensitive out-of-court resolution of conflicts between payment service providers and consumers arising from the rights and obligations set out in this Directive. Article 5(2) of the Rome Convention on the law applicable to contractual obligations[2] ensures that the protection afforded to consumers by the mandatory rules of the law of the country in which they have their habitual residence may not be undermined by any contractual terms on law applicable.

(52) Member States should determine whether the competent authorities designated for granting authorisation to payment institutions might also be the competent authorities with regard to out-of-court complaint and redress procedures.

(53) This Directive should be without prejudice to provisions of national law relating to the consequences as regards liability of inaccuracy in the expression or transmission of a statement.

(54) Since it is necessary to review the efficient functioning of this Directive and to monitor progress on the establishment of a single payment market, the Commission should be required to produce a report three years after the end of

1 OJ L 281, 23.11.1995, p. 31. Directive as amended by Regulation (EC) No 1882/2003 (OJ L 284, 31.10.2003, p. 1).

2 OJ C 27, 26.1.1998, p. 34.

the transposition period of this Directive. With regard to the global integration of financial services and harmonised consumer protection also beyond the efficient functioning of this Directive focal points of the review should be the possible need to expand the scope of application with regard to non-EU currencies and to payment transactions where only one payment service provider concerned is located in the Community.

(55) Since the provisions of this Directive replace those of Directive 97/5/EC, that Directive should be repealed.

(56) It is necessary to lay down more detailed rules concerning the fraudulent use of payment cards, an area currently covered by Directive 97/7/EC of the European Parliament and of the Council of 20 May 1997 on the protection of consumers in respect of distance contracts[1] and Directive 2002/65/EC. Those Directives should therefore be amended accordingly.

(57) Since, pursuant to Directive 2006/48/EC, financial institutions are not subject to the rules applicable to credit institutions, they should be made subject to the same requirements as payment institutions so that they are able to provide payment services throughout the Community. Directive 2006/48/EC should therefore be amended accordingly.

(58) Since money remittance is defined in this Directive as a payment service which requires an authorisation for a payment institution or a registration for some natural or legal persons benefiting from a waiver clause under certain circumstances specified in the provisions of this Directive, Directive 2005/60/EC of the European Parliament and of the Council of 26 October 2005 on the prevention of the use of the financial system for the purpose of money laundering and terrorist financing[2] should be amended accordingly.

(59) In the interests of legal certainty, it is appropriate to make transitional arrangements in accordance with which persons who have commenced the activities of payment institutions in accordance with the national law in force before the entry into force of this Directive may continue those activities within the Member State concerned for a specified period.

(60) Since the objective of this Directive, namely, the establishment of a single market in payment services, cannot be sufficiently achieved by the Member States because it requires the harmonisation of a multitude of different rules currently existing in the legal systems of the various Member States and can therefore be better achieved at Community level, the Community may adopt measures, in accordance with the principle of subsidiarity as set out in Article 5 of the Treaty. In accordance with the principle of proportionality, as set out in that Article, this Directive does not go beyond what is necessary in order to achieve that objective.

(61) The measures necessary for the implementation of this Directive should be adopted in accordance with Council Decision 1999/468/EC of 28 June 1999

---

1 OJ L 144, 4.6.1997, p. 19. Directive as last amended by Directive 2005/29/EC.

2 OJ L 309, 25.11.2005, p. 15.

laying down the procedures for the exercise of implementing powers conferred on the Commission[1].

(62) In particular, the Commission should be empowered to adopt implementing provisions in order to take account of technological and market developments. Since those measures are of general scope and are designed to amend non-essential elements of this Directive, they must be adopted in accordance with the regulatory procedure with scrutiny provided for in Article 5a of Decision 1999/468/EC.

(63) In accordance with point 34 of the Interinstitutional Agreement on better law-making[2], Member States are encouraged to draw up, for themselves and in the interest of the Community, their own tables illustrating, as far as possible, the correlation between this Directive and the transposition measures, and to make them public,

HAVE ADOPTED THIS DIRECTIVE:

TITLE I : SUBJECT MATTER, SCOPE AND DEFINITIONS

Article 1 Subject matter

1. This Directive lays down the rules in accordance with which Member States shall distinguish the following six categories of payment service provider:
   (a) credit institutions within the meaning of Article 4(1)(a) of Directive 2006/48/EC;
   (b) electronic money institutions within the meaning of Article 1(3)(a) of Directive 2000/46/EC;
   (c) post office giro institutions which are entitled under national law to provide payment services;
   (d) payment institutions within the meaning of this Directive;
   (e) the European Central Bank and national central banks when not acting in their capacity as monetary authority or other public authorities;
   (f) Member States or their regional or local authorities when not acting in their capacity as public authorities.
2. This Directive also lays down rules concerning transparency of conditions and information requirements for payment services, and the respective rights and obligations of payment service users and payment service providers in relation to the provision of payment services as a regular occupation or business activity.

Article 2 Scope

1. This Directive shall apply to payment services provided within the Community. However, with the exception of Article 73, Titles III and IV shall apply only where both the payer's payment service provider and the payee's payment

[1] OJ L 184, 17.7.1999, p. 23. Decision as amended by Decision 2006/512/EC (OJ L 200, 22.7.2006, p. 11).
[2] OJ C 321, 31.12.2003, p. 1.

service provider are, or the sole payment service provider in the payment transaction is, located in the Community.

2. Titles III and IV shall apply to payment services made in euro or the currency of a Member State outside the euro area.
3. Member States may waive the application of all or part of the provisions of this Directive to the institutions referred to in Article 2 of Directive 2006/48/EC, with the exception of those referred to in the first and second indent of that article.

Article 3 Negative scope

This Directive shall apply to none of the following:

(a) payment transactions made exclusively in cash directly from the payer to the payee, without any intermediary intervention;
(b) payment transactions from the payer to the payee through a commercial agent authorised to negotiate or conclude the sale or purchase of goods or services on behalf of the payer or the payee;
(c) professional physical transport of banknotes and coins, including their collection, processing and delivery;
(d) payment transactions consisting of the non-professional cash collection and delivery within the framework of a non-profit or charitable activity;
(e) services where cash is provided by the payee to the payer as part of a payment transaction following an explicit request by the payment service user just before the execution of the payment transaction through a payment for the purchase of goods or services;
(f) money exchange business, that is to say, cash-to-cash operations, where the funds are not held on a payment account;
(g) payment transactions based on any of the following documents drawn on the payment service provider with a view to placing funds at the disposal of the payee:
   (i) paper cheques in accordance with the Geneva Convention of 19 March 1931 providing a uniform law for cheques;
   (ii) paper cheques similar to those referred to in point (i) and governed by the laws of Member States which are not party to the Geneva Convention of 19 March 1931 providing a uniform law for cheques;
   (iii) paper-based drafts in accordance with the Geneva Convention of 7 June 1930 providing a uniform law for bills of exchange and promissory notes;
   (iv) paper-based drafts similar to those referred to in point (iii) and governed by the laws of Member States which are not party to the Geneva Convention of 7 June 1930 providing a uniform law for bills of exchange and promissory notes;
   (v) paper-based vouchers;
   (vi) paper-based traveller's cheques; or
   (vii) paper-based postal money orders as defined by the Universal Postal Union;

(h) payment transactions carried out within a payment or securities settlement system between settlement agents, central counterparties, clearing houses and/or central banks and other participants of the system, and payment service providers, without prejudice to Article 28;
(i) payment transactions related to securities asset servicing, including dividends, income or other distributions, or redemption or sale, carried out by persons referred to in point (h) or by investment firms, credit institutions, collective investment undertakings or asset management companies providing investment services and any other entities allowed to have the custody of financial instruments;
(j) services provided by technical service providers, which support the provision of payment services, without them entering at any time into possession of the funds to be transferred, including processing and storage of data, trust and privacy protection services, data and entity authentication, information technology (IT) and communication network provision, provision and maintenance of terminals and devices used for payment services;
(k) services based on instruments that can be used to acquire goods or services only in the premises used by the issuer or under a commercial agreement with the issuer either within a limited network of service providers or for a limited range of goods or services;
(l) payment transactions executed by means of any telecommunication, digital or IT device, where the goods or services purchased are delivered to and are to be used through a telecommunication, digital or IT device, provided that the telecommunication, digital or IT operator does not act only as an intermediary between the payment service user and the supplier of the goods and services;
(m) payment transactions carried out between payment service providers, their agents or branches for their own account;
(n) payment transactions between a parent undertaking and its subsidiary or between subsidiaries of the same parent undertaking, without any intermediary intervention by a payment service provider other than an undertaking belonging to the same group; or
(o) services by providers to withdraw cash by means of automated teller machines acting on behalf of one or more card issuers, which are not a party to the framework contract with the customer withdrawing money from a payment account, on condition that these providers do not conduct other payment services as listed in the Annex.

Article 4 Definitions

For the purposes of this Directive, the following definitions shall apply:

1. "home Member State" means either of the following:
   (i) the Member State in which the registered office of the payment service provider is situated; or
   (ii) if the payment service provider has, under its national law, no registered office, the Member State in which its head office is situated;

2. "host Member State" means the Member State other than the home Member State in which a payment service provider has an agent or a branch or provides payment services;
3. "payment service" means any business activity listed in the Annex;
4. "payment institution" means a legal person that has been granted authorisation in accordance with Article 10 to provide and execute payment services throughout the Community;
5. "payment transaction" means an act, initiated by the payer or by the payee, of placing, transferring or withdrawing funds, irrespective of any underlying obligations between the payer and the payee;
6. "payment system" means a funds transfer system with formal and standardised arrangements and common rules for the processing, clearing and/or settlement of payment transactions;
7. "payer" means a natural or legal person who holds a payment account and allows a payment order from that payment account, or, where there is no payment account, a natural or legal person who gives a payment order;
8. "payee" means a natural or legal person who is the intended recipient of funds which have been the subject of a payment transaction;
9. "payment service provider" means bodies referred to in Article 1(1) and legal and natural persons benefiting from the waiver under Article 26;
10. "payment service user" means a natural or legal person making use of a payment service in the capacity of either payer or payee, or both;
11. "consumer" means a natural person who, in payment service contracts covered by this Directive, is acting for purposes other than his trade, business or profession;
12. "framework contract" means a payment service contract which governs the future execution of individual and successive payment transactions and which may contain the obligation and conditions for setting up a payment account;
13. "money remittance" means a payment service where funds are received from a payer, without any payment accounts being created in the name of the payer or the payee, for the sole purpose of transferring a corresponding amount to a payee or to another payment service provider acting on behalf of the payee, and/or where such funds are received on behalf of and made available to the payee;
14. "payment account" means an account held in the name of one or more payment service users which is used for the execution of payment transactions;
15. "funds" means banknotes and coins, scriptural money and electronic money as defined in Article 1(3)(b) of Directive 2000/46/EC;
16. "payment order" means any instruction by a payer or payee to his payment service provider requesting the execution of a payment transaction;

17. "value date" means a reference time used by a payment service provider for the calculation of interest on the funds debited from or credited to a payment account;
18. "reference exchange rate" means the exchange rate which is used as the basis to calculate any currency exchange and which is made available by the payment service provider or comes from a publicly available source;
19. "authentication" means a procedure which allows the payment service provider to verify the use of a specific payment instrument, including its personalised security features;
20. "reference interest rate" means the interest rate which is used as the basis for calculating any interest to be applied and which comes from a publicly available source which can be verified by both parties to a payment service contract;
21. "unique identifier" means a combination of letters, numbers or symbols specified to the payment service user by the payment service provider and to be provided by the payment service user to identify unambiguously the other payment service user and/or his payment account for a payment transaction;
22. "agent" means a natural or legal person which acts on behalf of a payment institution in providing payment services;
23. "payment instrument" means any personalised device(s) and/or set of procedures agreed between the payment service user and the payment service provider and used by the payment service user in order to initiate a payment order;
24. "means of distance communication" refers to any means which, without the simultaneous physical presence of the payment service provider and the payment service user, may be used for the conclusion of a payment services contract;
25. "durable medium" means any instrument which enables the payment service user to store information addressed personally to him in a way accessible for future reference for a period of time adequate to the purposes of the information and which allows the unchanged reproduction of the information stored;
26. "micro-enterprise" means an enterprise, which at the time of conclusion of the payment service contract, is an enterprise as defined in Article 1 and Article 2(1) and (3) of the Annex to Recommendation 2003/361/EC;
27. "business day" means a day on which the relevant payment service provider of the payer or the payment service provider of the payee involved in the execution of a payment transaction is open for business as required for the execution of a payment transaction;
28. "direct debit" means a payment service for debiting a payer's payment account, where a payment transaction is initiated by the payee on the basis of the payer's consent given to the payee, to the payee's payment service provider or to the payer's own payment service provider;
29. "branch" means a place of business other than the head office which is a part of a payment institution, which has no legal personality and which carries out

directly some or all of the transactions inherent in the business of a payment institution; all the places of business set up in the same Member State by a payment institution with a head office in another Member State shall be regarded as a single branch;

30. "group" means a group of undertakings, which consists of a parent undertaking, its subsidiaries and the entities in which the parent undertaking or its subsidiaries have a holding as well as undertakings linked to each other by a relationship referred to in Article 12(1) of Directive 83/349/EEC.

TITLE II : PAYMENT SERVICE PROVIDERS

CHAPTER 1 : PAYMENT INSTITUTIONS

Section 1 : **General rules**

Article 5 Applications for authorisation

For authorisation as a payment institution, an application shall be submitted to the competent authorities of the home Member State, together with the following:

(a) a programme of operations, setting out in particular the type of payment services envisaged;
(b) a business plan including a forecast budget calculation for the first three financial years which demonstrates that the applicant is able to employ the appropriate and proportionate systems, resources and procedures to operate soundly;
(c) evidence that the payment institution holds initial capital provided for in Article 6;
(d) for the payment institutions referred to in Article 9(1), a description of the measures taken for safeguarding payment service users' funds in accordance with Article 9;
(e) a description of the applicant's governance arrangements and internal control mechanisms, including administrative, risk management and accounting procedures, which demonstrates that these governance arrangements, control mechanisms and procedures are proportionate, appropriate, sound and adequate;
(f) a description of the internal control mechanisms which the applicant has established in order to comply with obligations in relation to money laundering and terrorist financing under Directive 2005/60/EC and Regulation (EC) No 1781/2006 of the European Parliament and of the Council of 15 November 2006 on information on the payer accompanying transfers of funds[1];
(g) a description of the applicant's structural organisation, including, where applicable, a description of the intended use of agents and branches and a description of outsourcing arrangements, and of its participation in a national or international payment system;

[1] OJ L 345, 8.12.2006, p. 1.

(h) the identity of persons holding in the applicant, directly or indirectly, qualifying holdings within the meaning of Article 4(11) of Directive 2006/48/EC, the size of their holdings and evidence of their suitability taking into account the need to ensure the sound and prudent management of a payment institution;
(i) the identity of directors and persons responsible for the management of the payment institution and, where relevant, persons responsible for the management of the payment services activities of the payment institution, as well as evidence that they are of good repute and possess appropriate knowledge and experience to perform payment services as determined by the home Member State of the payment institution;
(j) where applicable, the identity of statutory auditors and audit firms as defined in Directive 2006/43/EC of the European Parliament and of the Council of 17 May 2006 on statutory audits of annual accounts and consolidated accounts[1];
(k) the applicant's legal status and articles of association;
(l) the address of the applicant's head office.

For the purposes of points (d), (e) and (g), the applicant shall provide a description of its audit arrangements and the organisational arrangements it has set up with a view to taking all reasonable steps to protect the interests of its users and to ensure continuity and reliability in the performance of payment services.

Article 6 Initial capital

Member States shall require payment institutions to hold, at the time of authorisation, initial capital, comprised of the items defined in Article 57(a) and (b) of Directive 2006/48/EC as follows:

(a) where the payment institution provides only the payment service listed in point 6 of the Annex, its capital shall at no time be less than EUR 20000;
(b) where the payment institution provides the payment service listed in point 7 of the Annex, its capital shall at no time be less than EUR 50000; and
(c) where the payment institution provides any of the payment services listed in points 1 to 5 of the Annex, its capital shall at no time be less than EUR 125000.

Article 7 Own funds

1. The payment institution's own funds, as defined in Articles 57 to 61, 63, 64 and 66 of Directive 2006/48/EC, may not fall below the amount required under Articles 6 or 8 of this Directive, whichever the higher.
2. Member States shall take the necessary measures to prevent the multiple use of elements eligible for own funds where the payment institution belongs to the same group as another payment institution, credit institution, investment firm, asset management company or insurance undertaking. This paragraph shall also

[1] OJ L 157, 9.6.2006, p. 87.

apply where a payment institution has a hybrid character and carries out activities other than providing payment services listed in the Annex.

3. If the conditions laid down in Article 69 of Directive 2006/48/EC are met, Member States or their competent authorities may choose not to apply Article 8 of this Directive to payment institutions which are included in the consolidated supervision of the parent credit institution pursuant to Directive 2006/48/EC.

Article 8 Calculation of own funds

1. Notwithstanding the initial capital requirements set out in Article 6, Member States shall require payment institutions to hold, at all times, own funds calculated in accordance with one of the following three methods, as determined by the competent authorities in accordance with national legislation:

Method A

The payment institution's own funds shall amount to at least 10 % of its fixed overheads of the preceding year. The competent authorities may adjust that requirement in the event of a material change in a payment institution's business since the preceding year. Where a payment institution has not completed a full year's business at the date of the calculation, the requirement shall be that its own funds amount to at least 10 % of the corresponding fixed overheads as projected in its business plan, unless an adjustment to that plan is required by the competent authorities.

Method B

The payment institution's own funds shall amount to at least the sum of the following elements multiplied by the scaling factor k defined in paragraph 2, where payment volume (PV) represents one twelfth of the total amount of payment transactions executed by the payment institution in the preceding year:

(a) 4,0 % of the slice of PV up to EUR 5 million,
plus
(b) 2,5 % of the slice of PV above EUR 5 million up to EUR 10 million,
plus
(c) 1 % of the slice of PV above EUR 10 million up to EUR 100 million,
plus
(d) 0,5 % of the slice of PV above EUR 100 million up to EUR 250 million,
plus
(e) 0,25 % of the slice of PV above EUR 250 million.

Method C

The payment institution's own funds shall amount to at least the relevant indicator defined in point (a), multiplied by the multiplication factor defined in point (b) and by the scaling factor k defined in paragraph 2.

(a) The relevant indicator is the sum of the following:
- interest income,
- interest expenses,
- commissions and fees received, and

- other operating income.

Each element shall be included in the sum with its positive or negative sign. Income from extraordinary or irregular items may not be used in the calculation of the relevant indicator. Expenditure on the outsourcing of services rendered by third parties may reduce the relevant indicator if the expenditure is incurred from an undertaking subject to supervision under this Directive. The relevant indicator is calculated on the basis of the twelve-monthly observation at the end of the previous financial year. The relevant indicator shall be calculated over the previous financial year. Nevertheless own funds calculated according to Method C shall not fall below 80 % of the average of the previous three financial years for the relevant indicator. When audited figures are not available, business estimates may be used.

(b) The multiplication factor shall be:

(i) 10 % of the slice of the relevant indicator up to EUR 2,5 million;

(ii) 8 % of the slice of the relevant indicator from EUR 2,5 million up to EUR 5 million;

(iii) 6 % of the slice of the relevant indicator from EUR 5 million up to EUR 25 million;

(iv) 3 % of the slice of the relevant indicator from EUR 25 million up to 50 million;

(v) 1,5 % above EUR 50 million.

2. The scaling factor k to be used in Methods B and C shall be:

(a) 0,5 where the payment institution provides only the payment service listed in point 6 of the Annex;

(b) 0,8 where the payment institution provides the payment service listed in point 7 of the Annex;

(c) 1 where the payment institution provides any of the payment services listed in points 1 to 5 of the Annex.

3. The competent authorities may, based on an evaluation of the risk-management processes, risk loss data base and internal control mechanisms of the payment institution, require the payment institution to hold an amount of own funds which is up to 20 % higher than the amount which would result from the application of the method chosen in accordance with paragraph 1, or permit the payment institution to hold an amount of own funds which is up to 20 % lower than the amount which would result from the application of the method chosen in accordance with paragraph 1.

Article 9 Safeguarding requirements

1. The Member States or competent authorities shall require a payment institution which provides any of the payment services listed in the Annex and, at the same time, is engaged in other business activities referred to in Article 16(1)(c) to safeguard funds which have been received from the payment service users or through another payment service provider for the execution of payment transactions, as follows:

   either:

(a) they shall not be commingled at any time with the funds of any natural or legal person other than payment service users on whose behalf the funds are held and, where they are still held by the payment institution and not yet delivered to the payee or transferred to another payment service provider by the end of the business day following the day when the funds have been received, they shall be deposited in a separate account in a credit institution or invested in secure, liquid low-risk assets as defined by the competent authorities of the home Member State; and

(b) they shall be insulated in accordance with national law in the interest of the payment service users against the claims of other creditors of the payment institution, in particular in the event of insolvency;

or

(c) they shall be covered by an insurance policy or some other comparable guarantee from an insurance company or a credit institution, which does not belong to the same group as the payment institution itself, for an amount equivalent to that which would have been segregated in the absence of the insurance policy or other comparable guarantee, payable in the event that the payment institution is unable to meet its financial obligations.

2. Where a payment institution is required to safeguard funds under paragraph 1 and a portion of those funds is to be used for future payment transactions with the remaining amount to be used for non-payment services, that portion of the funds to be used for future payment transactions shall also be subject to the requirements under paragraph 1. Where that portion is variable or unknown in advance, Member States may allow payment institutions to apply this paragraph on the basis of a representative portion assumed to be used for payment services provided such a representative portion can be reasonably estimated on the basis of historical data to the satisfaction of the competent authorities.

3. The Member States or competent authorities may require that payment institutions which are not engaged in other business activities referred to in Article 16(1)(c) shall also comply with the safeguarding requirements under paragraph 1 of this Article.

4. The Member States or competent authorities may also limit such safeguarding requirements to funds of those payment service users whose funds individually exceed a threshold of EUR 600.

Article 10 Granting of authorisation

1. Member States shall require undertakings other than those referred to in Article 1(1)(a) to (c), (e) and (f) and other than legal or natural persons benefiting from a waiver under Article 26, who intend to provide payment services, to obtain authorisation as a payment institution before commencing the provision of payment services. An authorisation shall only be granted to a legal person established in a Member State.

2. An authorisation shall be granted if the information and evidence accompanying the application complies with all the requirements under Article 5 and if the

competent authorities' overall assessment, having scrutinised the application, is favourable. Before an authorisation is granted, the competent authorities may, where relevant, consult the national central bank or other relevant public authorities.

3. A payment institution which under the national law of its home Member State is required to have a registered office, shall have its head office in the same Member State as its registered office.
4. The competent authorities shall grant an authorisation only if, taking into account the need to ensure the sound and prudent management of a payment institution, the payment institution has robust governance arrangements for its payment services business, which include a clear organisational structure with well-defined, transparent and consistent lines of responsibility, effective procedures to identify, manage, monitor and report the risks to which it is or might be exposed, and adequate internal control mechanisms, including sound administrative and accounting procedures; those arrangements, procedures and mechanisms shall be comprehensive and proportionate to the nature, scale and complexity of the payment services provided by the payment institution.
5. Where a payment institution provides any of the payment services listed in the Annex and, at the same time, is engaged in other business activities, the competent authorities may require the establishment of a separate entity for the payment services business, where the non-payment services activities of the payment institution impair or are likely to impair either the financial soundness of the payment institution or the ability of the competent authorities to monitor the payment institution's compliance with all obligations laid down by this Directive.
6. The competent authorities shall refuse to grant an authorisation if, taking into account the need to ensure the sound and prudent management of a payment institution, they are not satisfied as to the suitability of the shareholders or members that have qualifying holdings.
7. Where close links as defined in Article 4(46) of Directive 2006/48/EC exist between the payment institution and other natural or legal persons, the competent authorities shall grant an authorisation only if those links do not prevent the effective exercise of their supervisory functions.
8. The competent authorities shall grant an authorisation only if the laws, regulations or administrative provisions of a third country governing one or more natural or legal persons with which the payment institution has close links, or difficulties involved in the enforcement of those laws, regulations or administrative provisions, do not prevent the effective exercise of their supervisory functions.
9. An authorisation shall be valid in all Member States and shall allow the payment institution concerned to provide payment services throughout the Community, either under the freedom to provide services or the freedom of establishment, provided that such services are covered by the authorisation.

Article 11 Communication of the decision

Within three months of receipt of an application or, should the application be incomplete, of all the information required for the decision, the competent authorities shall inform the applicant whether the authorisation has been granted or refused. Reasons shall be given whenever an authorisation is refused.

Article 12 Withdrawal of authorisation

1. The competent authorities may withdraw an authorisation issued to a payment institution only where the institution:
   (a) does not make use of the authorisation within 12 months, expressly renounces the authorisation or has ceased to engage in business for more than six months, if the Member State concerned has made no provision for the authorisation to lapse in such cases;
   (b) has obtained the authorisation through false statements or any other irregular means;
   (c) no longer fulfils the conditions for granting the authorisation;
   (d) would constitute a threat to the stability of the payment system by continuing its payment services business; or
   (e) falls within one of the other cases where national law provides for withdrawal of an authorisation.
2. Reasons shall be given for any withdrawal of an authorisation and those concerned shall be informed accordingly.
3. The withdrawal of an authorisation shall be made public.

Article 13 Registration

Member States shall establish a public register of authorised payment institutions, their agents and branches, as well as of natural and legal persons, their agents and branches, benefiting from a waiver under Article 26, and of the institutions referred to in Article 2(3) that are entitled under national law to provide payment services. They shall be entered in the register of the home Member State.

This register shall identify the payment services for which the payment institution is authorised or for which the natural or legal person has been registered. Authorised payment institutions shall be listed in the register separately from natural and legal persons that have been registered in accordance with Article 26. The register shall be publicly available for consultation, accessible online, and updated on a regular basis.

Article 14 Maintenance of authorisation

Where any change affects the accuracy of information and evidence provided in accordance with Article 5, the payment institution shall without undue delay inform the competent authorities of its home Member State accordingly.

Article 15 Accounting and statutory audit

1. Directive 78/660/EEC and, where applicable, Directives 83/349/EEC and 86/635/EEC and Regulation (EC) 1606/2002 of the European Parliament and of the Council of 19 July 2002 on the application of international accounting standards[1] shall apply to payment institutions mutatis mutandis.
2. Unless exempted under Directive 78/660/EEC and, where applicable, Directives 83/349/EEC and 86/635/EEC, the annual accounts and consolidated accounts of payment institutions shall be audited by statutory auditors or audit firms within the meaning of Directive 2006/43/EC.
3. For supervisory purposes, Member States shall require that payment institutions provide separate accounting information for payment services listed in the Annex and activities referred to in Article 16(1), which shall be subject to an auditor's report. That report shall be prepared, where applicable, by the statutory auditors or an audit firm.
4. The obligations established in Article 53 of Directive 2006/48/EC shall apply mutatis mutandis to the statutory auditors or audit firms of payment institutions in respect of payment services activities.

Article 16 Activities

1. Apart from the provision of payment services listed in the Annex payment institutions shall be entitled to engage in the following activities:
   (a) the provision of operational and closely related ancillary services such as ensuring the execution of payment transactions, foreign exchange services, safekeeping activities, and the storage and processing of data;
   (b) the operation of payment systems, without prejudice to Article 28;
   (c) business activities other than the provision of payment services, having regard to applicable Community and national law.
2. When payment institutions engage in the provision of one or more of the payment services listed in the Annex, they may hold only payment accounts used exclusively for payment transactions. Any funds received by payment institutions from payment service users with a view to the provision of payment services shall not constitute a deposit or other repayable funds within the meaning of Article 5 of Directive 2006/48/EC, or electronic money within the meaning of Article 1(3) of Directive 2000/46/EC.
3. Payment institutions may grant credit related to payment services referred to in points 4, 5 or 7 of the Annex only if the following conditions are met:
   (a) the credit shall be ancillary and granted exclusively in connection with the execution of a payment transaction;
   (b) notwithstanding national rules on providing credit by credit cards, the credit granted in connection with a payment and executed in accordance with

1 OJ L 243, 11.9.2002, p. 1.

Article 10(9) and Article 25 shall be repaid within a short period which shall in no case exceed twelve months;

(c) such credit shall not be granted from the funds received or held for the purpose of executing a payment transaction; and

(d) the own funds of the payment institution shall at all times and to the satisfaction of the supervisory authorities be appropriate in view of the overall amount of credit granted.

4. Payment institutions shall not conduct the business of taking deposits or other repayable funds within the meaning of Article 5 of Directive 2006/48/EC.

5. This Directive shall be without prejudice to national measures implementing Directive 87/102/EEC. This Directive shall also be without prejudice to other relevant Community or national legislation regarding conditions for granting credit to consumers not harmonised by this Directive that are in conformity with Community law.

Section 2 : **Other requirements**

Article 17 Use of agents, branches or entities to which activities are outsourced

1. When a payment institution intends to provide payment services through an agent it shall communicate the following information to the competent authorities in its home Member State:

   (a) the name and address of the agent;

   (b) a description of the internal control mechanisms that will be used by agents in order to comply with the obligations in relation to money laundering and terrorist financing under Directive 2005/60/EC; and

   (c) the identity of directors and persons responsible for the management of the agent to be used in the provision of payment services and evidence that they are fit and proper persons.

2. When the competent authorities receive the information in accordance with paragraph 1 then they may list the agent in the register provided for in Article 13.

3. Before listing the agent in the register, the competent authorities may, if they consider that the information provided to them is incorrect, take further action to verify the information.

4. If, after taking action to verify the information, the competent authorities are not satisfied that the information provided to them pursuant to paragraph 1 is correct, they shall refuse to list the agent in the register provided for in Article 13.

5. If the payment institution wishes to provide payment services in another Member State by engaging an agent it shall follow the procedures set out in Article 25. In that case, before the agent may be registered under this Article, the competent authorities of the home Member State shall inform the competent authorities of the host Member State of their intention to register the agent and take their opinion into account.

6. If the competent authorities of the host Member State have reasonable grounds to suspect that, in connection with the intended engagement of the agent or establishment of the branch, money laundering or terrorist financing within the meaning of Directive 2005/60/EC is taking place, has taken place or been attempted, or that the engagement of such agent or establishment of such branch could increase the risk of money laundering or terrorist financing, they shall so inform the competent authorities of the home Member State, which may refuse to register the agent or branch, or may withdraw the registration, if already made, of the agent or branch.
7. Where a payment institution intends to outsource operational functions of payment services, it shall inform the competent authorities of its home Member State accordingly.

   Outsourcing of important operational functions may not be undertaken in such way as to impair materially the quality of the payment institution's internal control and the ability of the competent authorities to monitor the payment institution's compliance with all obligations laid down in this Directive.

   For the purposes of the second subparagraph, an operational function shall be regarded as important if a defect or failure in its performance would materially impair the continuing compliance of a payment institution with the requirements of its authorisation requested under this Title or its other obligations under this Directive, or its financial performance, or the soundness or the continuity of its payment services. Member States shall ensure that when payment institutions outsource important operational functions, the payment institutions comply with the following conditions:

   (a) the outsourcing shall not result in the delegation by senior management of its responsibility;
   (b) the relationship and obligations of the payment institution towards its payment service users under this Directive shall not be altered;
   (c) the conditions with which the payment institution is to comply in order to be authorised and remain so in accordance with this Title shall not be undermined; and
   (d) none of the other conditions subject to which the payment institution's authorisation was granted shall be removed or modified.
8. Payment institutions shall ensure that agents or branches acting on their behalf inform payment service users of this fact.

Article 18 Liability

1. Member States shall ensure that, where payment institutions rely on third parties for the performance of operational functions, those payment institutions take reasonable steps to ensure that the requirements of this Directive are complied with.

2. Member States shall require that payment institutions remain fully liable for any acts of their employees, or any agent, branch or entity to which activities are outsourced.

Article 19 Record-keeping

Member States shall require payment institutions to keep all appropriate records for the purpose of this Title for at least five years, without prejudice to Directive 2005/60/EC or other relevant Community or national legislation.

Section 3 : **Competent authorities and supervision**

Article 20 Designation of competent authorities

1. Member States shall designate as the competent authorities responsible for the authorisation and prudential supervision of payment institutions which are to carry out the duties provided for under this Title either public authorities, or bodies recognised by national law or by public authorities expressly empowered for that purpose by national law, including national central banks.

   The competent authorities shall guarantee independence from economic bodies and avoid conflicts of interest. Without prejudice to the first subparagraph, payment institutions, credit institutions, electronic money institutions, or post office giro institutions shall not be designated as competent authorities.

   The Member States shall inform the Commission accordingly.
2. Member States shall ensure that the competent authorities designated under paragraph 1 possess all the powers necessary for the performance of their duties.
3. Where there is more than one competent authority for matters covered by this Title on its territory, Member States shall ensure that those authorities cooperate closely so that they can discharge their respective duties effectively. The same applies in cases where the authorities competent for matters covered by this Title are not the competent authorities responsible for the supervision of credit institutions.
4. The tasks of the competent authorities designated under paragraph 1 shall be the responsibility of the competent authorities of the home Member State.
5. Paragraph 1 shall not imply that the competent authorities are required to supervise business activities of the payment institutions other than the provision of payment services listed in the Annex and the activities listed in Article 16(1)(a).

Article 21 Supervision

1. Member States shall ensure that the controls exercised by the competent authorities for checking continued compliance with this Title are proportionate, adequate and responsive to the risks to which payment institutions are exposed.

   In order to check compliance with this Title, the competent authorities shall be entitled to take the following steps, in particular:

(a) to require the payment institution to provide any information needed to monitor compliance;
(b) to carry out on-site inspections at the payment institution, at any agent or branch providing payment services under the responsibility of the payment institution, or at any entity to which activities are outsourced;
(c) to issue recommendations, guidelines and, if applicable, binding administrative provisions; and
(d) to suspend or withdraw authorisation in cases referred to in Article 12.

2. Without prejudice to the procedures for the withdrawal of authorisations and the provisions of criminal law, the Member States shall provide that their respective competent authorities, may, as against payment institutions or those who effectively control the business of payment institutions which breach laws, regulations or administrative provisions concerning the supervision or pursuit of their payment service business, adopt or impose in respect of them penalties or measures aimed specifically at ending observed breaches or the causes of such breaches.
3. Notwithstanding the requirements of Article 6, Article 7(1) and (2) and Article 8, Member States shall ensure that the competent authorities are entitled to take steps described under paragraph 1 of this Article to ensure sufficient capital for payment services, in particular where the non-payment services activities of the payment institution impair or are likely to impair the financial soundness of the payment institution.

Article 22 Professional secrecy

1. Member States shall ensure that all persons working or who have worked for the competent authorities, as well as experts acting on behalf of the competent authorities, are bound by the obligation of professional secrecy, without prejudice to cases covered by criminal law.
2. In the exchange of information in accordance with Article 24, professional secrecy shall be strictly applied to ensure the protection of individual and business rights.
3. Member States may apply this Article taking into account, mutatis mutandis, Articles 44 to 52 of Directive 2006/48/EC.

Article 23 Right to apply to the courts

1. Member States shall ensure that decisions taken by the competent authorities in respect of a payment institution pursuant to the laws, regulations and administrative provisions adopted in accordance with this Directive may be contested before the courts.
2. Paragraph 1 shall apply also in respect of failure to act.

Article 24 Exchange of information

1. The competent authorities of the different Member States shall cooperate with each other and, where appropriate, with the European Central Bank and the

national central banks of the Member States and other relevant competent authorities designated under Community or national legislation applicable to payment service providers.

2. Member States shall, in addition, allow the exchange of information between their competent authorities and the following:
   (a) the competent authorities of other Member States responsible for the authorisation and supervision of payment institutions;
   (b) the European Central Bank and the national central banks of Member States, in their capacity as monetary and oversight authorities, and, where appropriate, other public authorities responsible for overseeing payment and settlement systems;
   (c) other relevant authorities designated under this Directive, Directive 95/46/EC, Directive 2005/60/EC and other Community legislation applicable to payment service providers, such as legislation applicable to the protection of individuals with regard to the processing of personal data as well as money laundering and terrorist financing.

Article 25 Exercise of the right of establishment and freedom to provide services

1. Any authorised payment institution wishing to provide payment services for the first time in a Member State other than its home Member State, in exercise of the right of establishment or the freedom to provide services, shall so inform the competent authorities in its home Member State.

   Within one month of receiving that information, the competent authorities of the home Member State shall inform the competent authorities of the host Member State of the name and address of the payment institution, the names of those responsible for the management of the branch, its organisational structure and of the kind of payment services it intends to provide in the territory of the host Member State.

2. In order to carry out the controls and take the necessary steps provided for in Article 21 in respect of the agent, branch or entity to which activities are outsourced of a payment institution located in the territory of another Member State, the competent authorities of the home Member State shall cooperate with the competent authorities of the host Member State.

3. By way of cooperation in accordance with paragraphs 1 and 2, the competent authorities of the home Member State shall notify the competent authorities of the host Member State whenever they intend to carry out an on-site inspection in the territory of the latter.

   However, if they so wish, the competent authorities of the home Member State may delegate to the competent authorities of the host Member State the task of carrying out on-site inspections of the institution concerned.

4. The competent authorities shall provide each other with all essential and/or relevant information, in particular in the case of infringements or suspected

infringements by an agent, a branch or an entity to which activities are outsourced. In this regard, the competent authorities shall communicate, upon request, all relevant information and, on their own initiative, all essential information.

5. Paragraphs 1 to 4 shall be without prejudice to the obligation of competent authorities under Directive 2005/60/EC and Regulation (EC) No 1781/2006, in particular under Article 37(1) of Directive 2005/60/EC and Article 15(3) of Regulation (EC) No 1781/2006 to supervise or monitor the compliance with the requirements laid down in those instruments.

Section 4 : **Waiver**

Article 26 Conditions

1. Notwithstanding Article 13, Member States may waive or allow their competent authorities to waive the application of all or part of the procedure and conditions set out in Sections 1 to 3, with the exception of Articles 20, 22, 23 and 24, and allow natural or legal persons to be entered in the register provided for in Article 13, where:
   (a) the average of the preceding 12 months' total amount of payment transactions executed by the person concerned, including any agent for which it assumes full responsibility, does not exceed EUR 3 million per month. That requirement shall be assessed on the projected total amount of payment transactions in its business plan, unless an adjustment to that plan is required by the competent authorities; and
   (b) none of the natural persons responsible for the management or operation of the business has been convicted of offences relating to money laundering or terrorist financing or other financial crimes.
2. Any natural or legal person registered in accordance with paragraph 1 shall be required to have its head office or place of residence in the Member State in which it actually carries on its business.
3. The persons referred to in paragraph 1 shall be treated as payment institutions, save that Article 10(9) and Article 25 shall not apply to them.
4. Member States may also provide that any natural or legal person registered in accordance with paragraph 1 may engage only in certain activities listed in Article 16.
5. The persons referred to in paragraph 1 shall notify the competent authorities of any change in their situation which is relevant to the conditions specified in that paragraph. Member States shall take the necessary steps to ensure that where the conditions set out in paragraphs 1, 2 and 4 are no longer fulfilled, the persons concerned shall seek authorisation within 30 calendar days in accordance with the procedure laid down in Article 10.
6. This Article shall not be applied in respect of provisions of Directive 2005/60/EC or national anti-money-laundering provisions.

Article 27 Notification and information

If a Member State avails itself of the waiver provided for in Article 26, it shall notify the Commission accordingly by 1 November 2009 and it shall notify the Commission forthwith of any subsequent change. In addition, the Member State shall inform the Commission of the number of natural and legal persons concerned and, on an annual basis, of the total amount of payment transactions executed as of 31 December of each calendar year, as referred to in Article 26(1)(a).

CHAPTER 2 : COMMON PROVISIONS

Article 28 Access to payment systems

1. Member States shall ensure that the rules on access of authorised or registered payment service providers that are legal persons to payment systems shall be objective, non-discriminatory and proportionate and that those rules do not inhibit access more than is necessary to safeguard against specific risks such as settlement risk, operational risk and business risk and to protect the financial and operational stability of the payment system.

   Payment systems shall impose on payment service providers, on payment service users or on other payment systems none of the following requirements:

   (a) any restrictive rule on effective participation in other payment systems;
   (b) any rule which discriminates between authorised payment service providers or between registered payment service providers in relation to the rights, obligations and entitlements of participants; or
   (c) any restriction on the basis of institutional status.

2. Paragraph 1 shall not apply to:

   (a) payment systems designated under Directive 98/26/EC;
   (b) payment systems composed exclusively of payment service providers belonging to a group composed of entities linked by capital where one of the linked entities enjoys effective control over the other linked entities; or
   (c) payment systems where a sole payment service provider (whether as a single entity or as a group):
      - acts or can act as the payment service provider for both the payer and the payee and is exclusively responsible for the management of the system, and
      - licenses other payment service providers to participate in the system and the latter have no right to negotiate fees between or amongst themselves in relation to the payment system although they may establish their own pricing in relation to payers and payees.

Article 29 Prohibition for persons other than payment service providers to provide payment services

Member States shall prohibit natural or legal persons that are neither payment service providers nor explicitly excluded from the scope of this Directive from providing the payment services listed in the Annex.

TITLE III : TRANSPARENCY OF CONDITIONS AND INFORMATION REQUIREMENTS FOR PAYMENT SERVICES

CHAPTER 1 : GENERAL RULES

Article 30 Scope

1. This Title shall apply to single payment transactions, framework contracts and payment transactions covered by them. The parties may agree that it shall not apply in whole or in part when the payment service user is not a consumer.
2. Member States may provide that the provisions in this Title shall be applied to micro enterprises in the same way as to consumers.
3. This Directive shall be without prejudice to national measures implementing Directive 87/102/EEC. This Directive shall also be without prejudice to other relevant Community or national legislation regarding conditions for granting credit to consumers not harmonised by this Directive that are in conformity with Community law.

Article 31 Other provisions in Community legislation

The provisions of this Title are without prejudice to any Community legislation containing additional requirements on prior information.

However, where Directive 2002/65/EC is also applicable, the information requirements set out in Article 3(1) of that Directive, with the exception of points (2)(c) to (g), (3)(a), (d) and (e), and (4)(b) of that paragraph shall be replaced by Articles 36, 37, 41 and 42 of this Directive.

Article 32 Charges for information

1. The payment service provider shall not charge the payment service user for providing information under this Title.
2. The payment service provider and the payment service user may agree on charges for additional or more frequent information, or transmission by means of communication other than those specified in the framework contract, provided at the payment service user's request.
3. Where the payment service provider may impose charges for information in accordance with paragraph 2, they shall be appropriate and in line with the payment service provider's actual costs.

Article 33 Burden of proof on information requirements

Member States may stipulate that the burden of proof shall lie with the payment service provider to prove that it has complied with the information requirements set out in this Title.

Article 34 Derogation from information requirements for low-value payment instruments and electronic money

1. In cases of payment instruments which, according to the framework contract, concern only individual payment transactions that do not exceed EUR 30 or that either have a spending limit of EUR 150 or store funds that do not exceed EUR 150 at any time:
   (a) by way of derogation from Articles 41, 42 and 46, the payment service provider shall provide the payer only with information on the main characteristics of the payment service, including the way in which the payment instrument can be used, liability, charges levied and other material information needed to take an informed decision as well as an indication of where any other information and conditions specified in Article 42 are made available in an easily accessible manner;
   (b) it may be agreed that, by way of derogation from Article 44, the payment service provider shall not be required to propose changes in the conditions of the framework contract in the same way as provided for in Article 41(1);
   (c) it may be agreed that, by way of derogation from Articles 47 and 48, after the execution of a payment transaction:
      (i) the payment service provider shall provide or make available only a reference enabling the payment service user to identify the payment transaction, the amount of the payment transaction, any charges and/or, in the case of several payment transactions of the same kind made to the same payee, information on the total amount and charges for those payment transactions;
      (ii) the payment service provider shall not be required to provide or make available information referred to in point (i) if the payment instrument is used anonymously or if the payment service provider is not otherwise technically in a position to provide it. However, the payment service provider shall provide the payer with a possibility to verify the amount of funds stored.
2. For national payment transactions, Member States or their competent authorities may reduce or double the amounts referred to in paragraph 1. For prepaid payment instruments, Member States may increase those amounts up to EUR 500.

CHAPTER 2 : SINGLE PAYMENT TRANSACTIONS

Article 35 Scope

1. This Chapter shall apply to single payment transactions not covered by a framework contract.

2. When a payment order for a single payment transaction is transmitted by a payment instrument covered by a framework contract, the payment service provider shall not be obliged to provide or make available information which is already given to the payment service user on the basis of a framework contract with another payment service provider or which will be given to him according to that framework contract.

Article 36 Prior general information

1. Member States shall require that before the payment service user is bound by any single payment service contract or offer, the payment service provider, in an easily accessible manner, makes available to the payment service user the information and conditions specified in Article 37. At the payment service user's request, the payment service provider shall provide the information and conditions on paper or on another durable medium. The information and conditions shall be given in easily understandable words and in a clear and comprehensible form, in an official language of the Member State where the payment service is offered or in any other language agreed between the parties.
2. If the single payment service contract has been concluded at the request of the payment service user using a means of distance communication which does not enable the payment service provider to comply with paragraph 1, the payment service provider shall fulfil its obligations under that paragraph immediately after the execution of the payment transaction.
3. The obligations under paragraph 1 may also be discharged by supplying a copy of the draft single payment service contract or the draft payment order including the information and conditions specified in Article 37.

Article 37 Information and conditions

1. Member States shall ensure that the following information and conditions are provided or made available to the payment service user:
   (a) a specification of the information or unique identifier that has to be provided by the payment service user in order for a payment order to be properly executed;
   (b) the maximum execution time for the payment service to be provided;
   (c) all charges payable by the payment service user to his payment service provider and, where applicable, the breakdown of the amounts of any charges;
   (d) where applicable, the actual or reference exchange rate to be applied to the payment transaction.
2. Where applicable, any other relevant information and conditions specified in Article 42 shall be made available to the payment service user in an easily accessible manner.

Article 38 Information for the payer after receipt of the payment order

Immediately after receipt of the payment order, the payer's payment service provider shall provide or make available to the payer, in the same way as provided for in Article 36(1), the following information:

(a) a reference enabling the payer to identify the payment transaction and, where appropriate, information relating to the payee;
(b) the amount of the payment transaction in the currency used in the payment order;
(c) the amount of any charges for the payment transaction payable by the payer and, where applicable, a breakdown of the amounts of such charges;
(d) where applicable, the exchange rate used in the payment transaction by the payer's payment service provider or a reference thereto, when different from the rate provided in accordance with Article 37(1)(d), and the amount of the payment transaction after that currency conversion; and

Article 39 Information for the payee after execution

Immediately after the execution of the payment transaction, the payee's payment service provider shall provide or make available to the payee, in the same way as provided for in Article 36(1), the following information:

(a) the reference enabling the payee to identify the payment transaction and, where appropriate, the payer and any information transferred with the payment transaction;
(b) the amount of the payment transaction in the currency in which the funds are at the payee's disposal;
(c) the amount of any charges for the payment transaction payable by the payee and, where applicable, a breakdown of the amount of such charges;
(d) where applicable, the exchange rate used in the payment transaction by the payee's payment service provider, and the amount of the payment transaction before that currency conversion; and
(e) the credit value date.

CHAPTER 3 : FRAMEWORK CONTRACTS

Article 40 Scope

This Chapter applies to payment transactions covered by a framework contract.

Article 41 Prior general information

1. Member States shall require that, in good time before the payment service user is bound by any framework contract or offer, the payment service provider provide the payment service user on paper or on another durable medium with the information and conditions specified in Article 42. The information and conditions shall be given in easily understandable words and in a clear and

comprehensible form, in an official language of the Member State where the payment service is offered or in any other language agreed between the parties.

2. If the framework contract has been concluded at the request of the payment service user using a means of distance communication which does not enable the payment service provider to comply with paragraph 1, the payment service provider shall fulfil its obligations under that paragraph immediately after the conclusion of the framework contract.
3. The obligations under paragraph 1 may also be discharged by supplying a copy of the draft framework contract including the information and conditions specified in Article 42.

Article 42 Information and conditions

Member States shall ensure that the following information and conditions are provided to the payment service user:

1. on the payment service provider:
   (a) the name of the payment service provider, the geographical address of its head office and, where applicable, the geographical address of its agent or branch established in the Member State where the payment service is offered, and any other address, including electronic mail address, relevant for communication with the payment service provider; and
   (b) the particulars of the relevant supervisory authorities and of the register provided for in Article 13 or of any other relevant public register of authorisation of the payment service provider and the registration number, or equivalent means of identification in that register;
2. on use of the payment service:
   (a) a description of the main characteristics of the payment service to be provided;
   (b) a specification of the information or unique identifier that has to be provided by the payment service user in order for a payment order to be properly executed;
   (c) the form of and procedure for giving consent to execute a payment transaction and withdrawal of such consent in accordance with Articles 54 and 66;
   (d) a reference to the point in time of receipt of a payment order as defined in Article 64 and the cut-off time, if any, established by the payment service provider;
   (e) the maximum execution time for the payment services to be provided; and
   (f) whether there is a possibility to agree on spending limits for the use of the payment instrument in accordance with Article 55(1);
3. on charges, interest and exchange rates:
   (a) all charges payable by the payment service user to the payment service provider and, where applicable, the breakdown of the amounts of any charges;

(b) where applicable, the interest and exchange rates to be applied or, if reference interest and exchange rates are to be used, the method of calculating the actual interest, and the relevant date and index or base for determining such reference interest or exchange rate; and

(c) if agreed, the immediate application of changes in reference interest or exchange rate and information requirements related to the changes in accordance with Article 44(2);

4. on communication:

(a) where applicable, the means of communication, including the technical requirements for the payment service user's equipment, agreed between the parties for the transmission of information or notifications under this Directive;

(b) the manner in and frequency with which information under this Directive is to be provided or made available;

(c) the language or languages in which the framework contract will be concluded and communication during this contractual relationship undertaken; and

(d) the payment service user's right to receive the contractual terms of the framework contract and information and conditions in accordance with Article 43;

5. on safeguards and corrective measures:

(a) where applicable, a description of steps that the payment service user is to take in order to keep safe a payment instrument and how to notify the payment service provider for the purposes of Article 56(1)(b);

(b) if agreed, the conditions under which the payment service provider reserves the right to block a payment instrument in accordance with Article 55;

(c) the liability of the payer in accordance with Article 61, including information on the relevant amount;

(d) how and within what period of time the payment service user is to notify the payment service provider of any unauthorised or incorrectly executed payment transaction in accordance with Article 58 as well as the payment service provider's liability for unauthorised payment transactions in accordance with Article 60;

(e) the liability of the payment service provider for the execution of payment transactions in accordance with Article 75; and

(f) the conditions for refund in accordance with Articles 62 and 63;

6. on changes in and termination of framework contract:

(a) if agreed, information that the payment service user will be deemed to have accepted changes in the conditions in accordance with Article 44, unless he notifies the payment service provider that he does not accept them before the date of their proposed date of entry into force;

(b) the duration of the contract; and

(c) the right of the payment service user to terminate the framework contract and any agreements relating to termination in accordance with Article 44(1) and Article 45;

7. on redress:

(a) any contractual clause on the law applicable to the framework contract and/or the competent courts; and

(b) the out-of-court complaint and redress procedures available to the payment service user in accordance with Articles 80 to 83.

Article 43 Accessibility of information and conditions of the framework contract

At any time during the contractual relationship the payment service user shall have a right to receive, on request, the contractual terms of the framework contract as well as the information and conditions specified in Article 42 on paper or on another durable medium.

Article 44 Changes in conditions of the framework contract

1. Any changes in the framework contract as well as the information and conditions specified in Article 42, shall be proposed by the payment service provider in the same way as provided for in Article 41(1) and no later than two months before their proposed date of application.

   Where applicable in accordance with point (6)(a) of Article 42, the payment service provider shall inform the payment service user that he is to be deemed to have accepted these changes if he does not notify the payment service provider that he does not accept them before the proposed date of their entry into force. In this case, the payment service provider shall also specify that the payment service user has the right to terminate the framework contract immediately and without charge before the date of the proposed application of the changes.

2. Changes in the interest or exchange rates may be applied immediately and without notice, provided that such a right is agreed upon in the framework contract and that the changes are based on the reference interest or exchange rates agreed on in accordance with Article 42(3)(b) and (c). The payment service user shall be informed of any change in the interest rate at the earliest opportunity in the same way as provided for in Article 41(1), unless the parties have agreed on a specific frequency or manner in which the information is to be provided or made available. However, changes in interest or exchange rates which are more favourable to the payment service users, may be applied without notice.

3. Changes in the interest or exchange rate used in payment transactions shall be implemented and calculated in a neutral manner that does not discriminate against payment service users.

Article 45 Termination

1. The payment service user may terminate the framework contract at any time, unless the parties have agreed on a period of notice. Such a period may not exceed one month.
2. Termination of a framework contract concluded for a fixed period exceeding 12 months or for an indefinite period shall be free of charge for the payment service user after the expiry of 12 months. In all other cases charges for the termination shall be appropriate and in line with costs.
3. If agreed in the framework contract, the payment service provider may terminate a framework contract concluded for an indefinite period by giving at least two months' notice in the same way as provided for in Article 41(1).
4. Charges for payment services levied on a regular basis shall be payable by the payment service user only proportionally up to the termination of the contract. If such charges are paid in advance, they shall be reimbursed proportionally.
5. The provisions of this Article are without prejudice to the Member States' laws and regulations governing the rights of the parties to declare the framework contract unenforceable or void.
6. Member States may provide more favourable provisions for payment service users.

Article 46 Information before execution of individual payment transactions

In the case of an individual payment transaction under a framework contract initiated by the payer, a payment service provider shall, at the payer's request for this specific payment transaction, provide explicit information on the maximum execution time and the charges payable by the payer and, where applicable, a breakdown of the amounts of any charges.

Article 47 Information for the payer on individual payment transactions

1. After the amount of an individual payment transaction is debited from the payer's account or, where the payer does not use a payment account, after the receipt of the payment order, the payer's payment service provider shall provide the payer without undue delay in the same way as laid down in Article 41(1) with the following information:
   (a) a reference enabling the payer to identify each payment transaction and, where appropriate, information relating to the payee;
   (b) the amount of the payment transaction in the currency in which the payer's payment account is debited or in the currency used for the payment order;
   (c) the amount of any charges for the payment transaction and, where applicable, a breakdown thereof, or the interest payable by the payer;

(d) where applicable, the exchange rate used in the payment transaction by the payer's payment service provider, and the amount of the payment transaction after that currency conversion; and
(e) the debit value date or the date of receipt of the payment order.

2. A framework contract may include a condition that the information referred to in paragraph 1 is to be provided or made available periodically at least once a month and in an agreed manner which allows the payer to store and reproduce information unchanged.
3. However, Member States may require payment service providers to provide information on paper once a month free of charge.

Article 48 Information for the payee on individual payment transactions

1. After the execution of an individual payment transaction, the payee's payment service provider shall provide the payee without undue delay in the same way as laid down in Article 41(1) with the following information:
   (a) the reference enabling the payee to identify the payment transaction and, where appropriate, the payer, and any information transferred with the payment transaction;
   (b) the amount of the payment transaction in the currency in which the payee's payment account is credited;
   (c) the amount of any charges for the payment transaction and, where applicable, a breakdown thereof, or the interest payable by the payee;
   (d) where applicable, the exchange rate used in the payment transaction by the payee's payment service provider, and the amount of the payment transaction before that currency conversion; and
   (e) the credit value date.
2. A framework contract may include a condition that the information referred to in paragraph 1 is to be provided or made available periodically at least once a month and in an agreed manner which allows the payee to store and reproduce information unchanged.
3. However, Member States may require payment service providers to provide information on paper once a month free of charge.

CHAPTER 4 : COMMON PROVISIONS

Article 49 Currency and currency conversion

1. Payments shall be made in the currency agreed between the parties.
2. Where a currency conversion service is offered prior to the initiation of the payment transaction and where that currency conversion service is offered at the point of sale or by the payee, the party offering the currency conversion service to the payer shall disclose to the payer all charges as well as the exchange rate to be used for converting the payment transaction.

   The payer shall agree to the currency conversion service on that basis.

Article 50 Information on additional charges or reductions

1. Where, for the use of a given payment instrument, the payee requests a charge or offers a reduction, the payee shall inform the payer thereof prior to the initiation of the payment transaction.
2. Where, for the use of a given payment instrument, a payment service provider or a third party requests a charge, he shall inform the payment service user thereof prior to the initiation of the payment transaction.

TITLE IV : RIGHTS AND OBLIGATIONS IN RELATION TO THE PROVISION AND USE OF PAYMENT SERVICES

CHAPTER 1 : COMMON PROVISIONS

Article 51 Scope

1. Where the payment service user is not a consumer, the parties may agree that Article 52(1), the second subparagraph of Article 54(2), and Articles 59, 61, 62, 63, 66 and 75 shall not apply in whole or in part. The parties may also agree on a time period different from that laid down in Article 58.
2. Member States may provide that Article 83 does not apply where the payment service user is not a consumer.
3. Member States may provide that provisions in this Title are applied to micro enterprises in the same way as to consumers.
4. This Directive shall be without prejudice to national measures implementing Directive 87/102/EEC. This Directive shall also be without prejudice to other relevant Community or national legislation regarding conditions for granting credit to consumers not harmonised by this Directive that are in conformity with Community law.

Article 52 Charges applicable

1. The payment service provider may not charge the payment service user for fulfilment of its information obligations or corrective and preventive measures under this Title, unless otherwise specified in Articles 65(1), 66(5) and 74(2). Those charges shall be agreed between the payment service user and the payment service provider and shall be appropriate and in line with the payment service provider's actual costs.
2. Where a payment transaction does not involve any currency conversion, Member States shall require that the payee pays the charges levied by his payment service provider, and the payer pays the charges levied by his payment service provider.
3. The payment service provider shall not prevent the payee from requesting from the payer a charge or from offering him a reduction for the use of a given payment instrument. However, Member States may forbid or limit the right to request charges taking into account the need to encourage competition and promote the use of efficient payment instruments.

Article 53 Derogation for low value payment instruments and electronic money

1. In the case of payment instruments which according to the framework contract, solely concern individual payment transactions not exceeding EUR 30 or which either have a spending limit of EUR 150 or store funds which do not exceed EUR 150 at any time payment service providers may agree with their payment service users that:
   (a) Article 56(1)(b) and Article 57(1)(c) and (d) as well as Article 61(4) and (5) do not apply if the payment instrument does not allow its blocking or prevention of its further use;
   (b) Articles 59, 60 and Article 61(1) and (2) do not apply if the payment instrument is used anonymously or the payment service provider is not in a position for other reasons which are intrinsic to the payment instrument to prove that a payment transaction was authorised;
   (c) by way of derogation from Article 65(1), the payment service provider is not required to notify the payment service user of the refusal of a payment order, if the non-execution is apparent from the context;
   (d) by way of derogation from Article 66, the payer may not revoke the payment order after transmitting the payment order or giving his consent to execute the payment transaction to the payee;
   (e) by way of derogation from Articles 69 and 70, other execution periods apply.
2. For national payment transactions, Member States or their competent authorities may reduce or double the amounts referred to in paragraph 1. They may increase them for prepaid payment instruments up to EUR 500.
3. Articles 60 and 61 shall apply also to electronic money within the meaning of Article 1(3)(b) of Directive 2000/46/EC, except where the payer's payment service provider does not have the ability to freeze the payment account or block the payment instrument. Member States may limit that derogation to payment accounts or payment instruments of a certain value.

CHAPTER 2 : AUTHORISATION OF PAYMENT TRANSACTIONS

Article 54 Consent and withdrawal of consent

1. Member States shall ensure that a payment transaction is considered to be authorised only if the payer has given consent to execute the payment transaction. A payment transaction may be authorised by the payer prior to or, if agreed between the payer and his payment service provider, after the execution of the payment transaction.
2. Consent to execute a payment transaction or a series of payment transactions shall be given in the form agreed between the payer and his payment service provider.

   In the absence of such consent, a payment transaction shall be considered to be unauthorised.

3. Consent may be withdrawn by the payer at any time, but no later than the point in time of irrevocability under Article 66. Consent to execute a series of payment transactions may also be withdrawn with the effect that any future payment transaction is to be considered as unauthorised.
4. The procedure for giving consent shall be agreed between the payer and the payment service provider.

Article 55 Limits of the use of the payment instrument

1. In cases where a specific payment instrument is used for the purposes of giving consent, the payer and his payment service provider may agree on spending limits for payment transactions executed through that payment instrument.
2. If agreed in the framework contract, the payment service provider may reserve the right to block the payment instrument for objectively justified reasons related to the security of the payment instrument, the suspicion of unauthorised or fraudulent use of the payment instrument or, in the case of a payment instrument with a credit line, a significantly increased risk that the payer may be unable to fulfil his liability to pay.
3. In such cases the payment service provider shall inform the payer of the blocking of the payment instrument and the reasons for it in an agreed manner, where possible, before the payment instrument is blocked and at the latest immediately thereafter, unless giving such information would compromise objectively justified security reasons or is prohibited by other relevant Community or national legislation.
4. The payment service provider shall unblock the payment instrument or replace it with a new payment instrument once the reasons for blocking no longer exist.

Article 56 Obligations of the payment service user in relation to payment instruments

1. The payment service user entitled to use a payment instrument shall have the following obligations:
   - (a) to use the payment instrument in accordance with the terms governing the issue and use of the payment instrument; and
   - (b) to notify the payment service provider, or the entity specified by the latter, without undue delay on becoming aware of loss, theft or misappropriation of the payment instrument or of its unauthorised use.
2. For the purposes of paragraph 1(a), the payment service user shall, in particular, as soon as he receives a payment instrument, take all reasonable steps to keep its personalised security features safe.

Article 57 Obligations of the payment service provider in relation to payment instruments

1. The payment service provider issuing a payment instrument shall have the following obligations:

(a) to make sure that the personalised security features of the payment instrument are not accessible to parties other than the payment service user entitled to use the payment instrument, without prejudice to the obligations on the payment service user set out in Article 56;
(b) to refrain from sending an unsolicited payment instrument, except where a payment instrument already given to the payment service user is to be replaced;
(c) to ensure that appropriate means are available at all times to enable the payment service user to make a notification pursuant to Article 56(1)(b) or request unblocking pursuant to Article 55(4); on request, the payment service provider shall provide the payment service user with the means to prove, for 18 months after notification, that he made such notification; and
(d) to prevent all use of the payment instrument once notification pursuant to Article 56(1)(b) has been made.

2. The payment service provider shall bear the risk of sending a payment instrument to the payer or of sending any personalised security features of it.

Article 58 Notification of unauthorised or incorrectly executed payment transactions

The payment service user shall obtain rectification from the payment service provider only if he notifies his payment service provider without undue delay on becoming aware of any unauthorised or incorrectly executed payment transactions giving rise to a claim, including that under Article 75, and no later than 13 months after the debit date, unless, where applicable, the payment service provider has failed to provide or make available the information on that payment transaction in accordance with Title III.

Article 59 Evidence on authentication and execution of payment transactions

1. Member States shall require that, where a payment service user denies having authorised an executed payment transaction or claims that the payment transaction was not correctly executed, it is for his payment service provider to prove that the payment transaction was authenticated, accurately recorded, entered in the accounts and not affected by a technical breakdown or some other deficiency.
2. Where a payment service user denies having authorised an executed payment transaction, the use of a payment instrument recorded by the payment service provider shall in itself not necessarily be sufficient to prove either that the payment transaction was authorised by the payer or that the payer acted fraudulently or failed with intent or gross negligence to fulfil one or more of his obligations under Article 56.

Article 60 **Payment service provider's liability for unauthorised payment transactions**

1. Member States shall ensure that, without prejudice to Article 58, in the case of an unauthorised payment transaction, the payer's payment service provider refunds to the payer immediately the amount of the unauthorised payment transaction and, where applicable, restores the debited payment account to the state in which it would have been had the unauthorised payment transaction not taken place.
2. Further financial compensation may be determined in accordance with the law applicable to the contract concluded between the payer and his payment service provider.

Article 61 **Payer's liability for unauthorised payment transactions**

1. By way of derogation from Article 60 the payer shall bear the losses relating to any unauthorised payment transactions, up to a maximum of EUR 150, resulting from the use of a lost or stolen payment instrument or, if the payer has failed to keep the personalised security features safe, from the misappropriation of a payment instrument.
2. The payer shall bear all the losses relating to any unauthorised payment transactions if he incurred them by acting fraudulently or by failing to fulfil one or more of his obligations under Article 56 with intent or gross negligence. In such cases, the maximum amount referred to in paragraph 1 of this Article shall not apply.
3. In cases where the payer has neither acted fraudulently nor with intent failed to fulfil his obligations under Article 56, Member States may reduce the liability referred to in paragraphs 1 and 2 of this Article, taking into account, in particular, the nature of the personalised security features of the payment instrument and the circumstances under which it was lost, stolen or misappropriated.
4. The payer shall not bear any financial consequences resulting from use of the lost, stolen or misappropriated payment instrument after notification in accordance with Article 56(1)(b), except where he has acted fraudulently.
5. If the payment service provider does not provide appropriate means for the notification at all times of a lost, stolen or misappropriated payment instrument, as required under Article 57(1)(c), the payer shall not be liable for the financial consequences resulting from use of that payment instrument, except where he has acted fraudulently.

Article 62 **Refunds for payment transactions initiated by or through a payee**

1. Member States shall ensure that a payer is entitled to a refund from his payment service provider of an authorised payment transaction initiated by or through a payee which has already been executed, if the following conditions are met:

(a) the authorisation did not specify the exact amount of the payment transaction when the authorisation was made; and

(b) the amount of the payment transaction exceeded the amount the payer could reasonably have expected taking into account his previous spending pattern, the conditions in his framework contract and relevant circumstances of the case.

At the payment service provider's request, the payer shall provide factual elements relating to such conditions.

The refund consists of the full amount of the executed payment transaction.

For direct debits the payer and his payment service provider may agree in the framework contract that the payer is entitled to a refund from his payment service provider even though the conditions for refund in the first subparagraph are not met.

2. However, for the purposes of point (b) of the first subparagraph of paragraph 1, the payer may not rely on currency exchange reasons if the reference exchange rate agreed with his payment service provider in accordance with Articles 37(1)(d) and 42(3)(b) was applied.

3. It may be agreed in the framework contract between the payer and the payment service provider that the payer has no right to a refund where he has given his consent to execute the payment transaction directly to his payment service provider and, where applicable, information on the future payment transaction was provided or made available in an agreed manner to the payer for at least four weeks before the due date by the payment service provider or by the payee.

Article 63 Requests for refunds for payment transactions initiated by or through a payee

1. Member States shall ensure that the payer can request the refund referred to in Article 62 of an authorised payment transaction initiated by or through a payee for a period of eight weeks from the date on which the funds were debited.

2. Within ten business days of receiving a request for a refund, the payment service provider shall either refund the full amount of the payment transaction or provide justification for refusing the refund, indicating the bodies to which the payer may refer the matter in accordance with Articles 80 to 83 if he does not accept the justification provided.

The payment service provider's right under the first subparagraph to refuse the refund shall not apply in the case set out in the fourth subparagraph of Article 62(1).

CHAPTER 3 : EXECUTION OF PAYMENT TRANSACTIONS

Section 1 : **Payment orders and amounts transferred**

Article 64 Receipt of payment orders

1. Member States shall ensure that the point in time of receipt is the time when the payment order transmitted directly by the payer or indirectly by or through a payee is received by the payer's payment service provider. If the point in time of receipt is not on a business day for the payer's payment service provider, the payment order shall be deemed to have been received on the following business day. The payment service provider may establish a cut-off time near the end of a business day beyond which any payment order received shall be deemed to have been received on the following business day.
2. If the payment service user initiating a payment order and his payment service provider agree that execution of the payment order shall start on a specific day or at the end of a certain period or on the day on which the payer has set funds at his payment service provider's disposal, the point in time of receipt for the purposes of Article 69 is deemed to be the agreed day. If the agreed day is not a business day for the payment service provider, the payment order received shall be deemed to have been received on the following business day.

Article 65 Refusal of payment orders

1. Where the payment service provider refuses to execute a payment order, the refusal and, if possible, the reasons for it and the procedure for correcting any factual mistakes that led to the refusal shall be notified to the payment service user, unless prohibited by other relevant Community or national legislation.

   The payment service provider shall provide or make available the notification in an agreed manner at the earliest opportunity, and in any case, within the periods specified in Article 69.

   The framework contract may include a condition that the payment service provider may charge for such a notification if the refusal is objectively justified.
2. In cases where all the conditions set out in the payer's framework contract are met, the payer's payment service provider shall not refuse to execute an authorised payment order irrespective of whether the payment order is initiated by a payer or by or through a payee, unless prohibited by other relevant Community or national legislation.
3. For the purposes of Articles 69 and 75 a payment order of which execution has been refused shall be deemed not to have been received.

Article 66 Irrevocability of a payment order

1. Member States shall ensure that the payment service user may not revoke a payment order once it has been received by the payer's payment service provider, unless otherwise specified in this Article.

2. Where the payment transaction is initiated by or through the payee, the payer may not revoke the payment order after transmitting the payment order or giving his consent to execute the payment transaction to the payee.
3. However, in the case of a direct debit and without prejudice to refund rights the payer may revoke the payment order at the latest by the end of the business day preceding the day agreed for debiting the funds.
4. In the case referred to in Article 64(2) the payment service user may revoke a payment order at the latest by the end of the business day preceding the agreed day.
5. After the time limits specified in paragraphs 1 to 4, the payment order may be revoked only if agreed between the payment service user and his payment service provider. In the case referred to in paragraphs 2 and 3, the payee's agreement shall also be required. If agreed in the framework contract, the payment service provider may charge for revocation.

Article 67 Amounts transferred and amounts received

1. Member States shall require the payment service provider of the payer, the payment service provider of the payee and any intermediaries of the payment service providers to transfer the full amount of the payment transaction and refrain from deducting charges from the amount transferred.
2. However, the payee and his payment service provider may agree that the payment service provider deduct its charges from the amount transferred before crediting it to the payee. In such a case, the full amount of the payment transaction and charges shall be separated in the information given to the payee.
3. If any charges other than those referred to in paragraph 2 are deducted from the amount transferred, the payment service provider of the payer shall ensure that the payee receives the full amount of the payment transaction initiated by the payer. In cases where the payment transaction is initiated by or through the payee, his payment service provider shall ensure that the full amount of the payment transaction is received by the payee.

Section 2 : **Execution time and value date**

Article 68 Scope

1. This Section shall apply to:
   (a) payment transactions in euro;
   (b) national payment transactions in the currency of the Member State outside the euro area concerned; and
   (c) payment transactions involving only one currency conversion between the euro and the currency of a Member State outside the euro area, provided that the required currency conversion is carried out in the Member State outside the euro area concerned and, in the case of cross-border payment transactions, the cross-border transfer takes place in euro.

2. This Section shall apply to other payment transactions, unless otherwise agreed between the payment service user and his payment service provider, with the exception of Article 73, which is not at the disposal of the parties. However, when the payment service user and his payment service provider agree on a longer period than those laid down in Article 69, for intra-Community payment transactions such period shall not exceed 4 business days following the point in time of receipt in accordance with Article 64.

Article 69 Payment transactions to a payment account

1. Member States shall require the payer's payment service provider to ensure that, after the point in time of receipt in accordance with Article 64, the amount of the payment transaction is credited to the payee's payment service provider's account at the latest by the end of the next business day. Until 1 January 2012, a payer and his payment service provider may agree on a period no longer than three business days. These periods may be extended by a further business day for paper-initiated payment transactions.
2. Member States shall require the payment service provider of the payee to value date and make available the amount of the payment transaction to the payee's payment account after the payment service provider has received the funds in accordance with Article 73.
3. Member States shall require the payee's payment service provider to transmit a payment order initiated by or through the payee to the payer's payment service provider within the time limits agreed between the payee and his payment service provider, enabling settlement, as far as direct debit is concerned, on the agreed due date.

Article 70 Absence of payee's payment account with the payment service provider

Where the payee does not have a payment account with the payment service provider, the funds shall be made available to the payee by the payment service provider who receives the funds for the payee within the period specified in Article 69.

Article 71 Cash placed on a payment account

Where a consumer places cash on a payment account with that payment service provider in the currency of that payment account, the payment service provider shall ensure that the amount is made available and value dated immediately after the point of time of the receipt of the funds. Where the payment service user is not a consumer, the amount shall be made available and value dated at the latest on the next business day after the receipt of the funds.

Article 72 National payment transactions

For national payment transactions, Member States may provide for shorter maximum execution times than those provided for in this Section.

Article 73 Value date and availability of funds

1. Member States shall ensure that the credit value date for the payee's payment account is no later than the business day on which the amount of the payment transaction is credited to the payee's payment service provider's account.

   The payment service provider of the payee shall ensure that the amount of the payment transaction is at the payee's disposal immediately after that amount is credited to the payee's payment service provider's account.
2. Member States shall ensure that the debit value date for the payer's payment account is no earlier than the point in time at which the amount of the payment transaction is debited to that payment account.

Section 3 : **Liability**

Article 74 Incorrect unique identifiers

1. If a payment order is executed in accordance with the unique identifier, the payment order shall be deemed to have been executed correctly with regard to the payee specified by the unique identifier.
2. If the unique identifier provided by the payment service user is incorrect, the payment service provider shall not be liable under Article 75 for non-execution or defective execution of the payment transaction.

   However the payer's payment service provider shall make reasonable efforts to recover the funds involved in the payment transaction.

   If agreed in the framework contract, the payment service provider may charge the payment service user for recovery.
3. If the payment service user provides information additional to that specified in Articles 37(1)(a) or 42(2)(b), the payment service provider shall be liable only for the execution of payment transactions in accordance with the unique identifier provided by the payment service user.

Article 75 Non-execution or defective execution

1. Where a payment order is initiated by the payer, his payment service provider shall, without prejudice to Article 58, Article 74(2) and (3), and Article 78, be liable to the payer for correct execution of the payment transaction, unless he can prove to the payer and, where relevant, to the payee's payment service provider that the payee's payment service provider received the amount of the payment transaction in accordance with Article 69(1), in which case, the payee's payment service provider shall be liable to the payee for the correct execution of the payment transaction.

   Where the payer's payment service provider is liable under the first subparagraph, he shall without undue delay refund to the payer the amount of the non-executed or defective payment transaction and, where applicable, restore the debited payment account to the state in which it would have been had the defective payment transaction not taken place.

Where the payee's payment service provider is liable under the first subparagraph, he shall immediately place the amount of the payment transaction at the payee's disposal and, where applicable, credit the corresponding amount to the payee's payment account.

In the case of a non-executed or defectively executed payment transaction where the payment order is initiated by the payer, his payment service provider shall regardless of liability under this paragraph, on request, make immediate efforts to trace the payment transaction and notify the payer of the outcome.

2. Where a payment order is initiated by or through the payee, his payment service provider shall, without prejudice to Article 58, Article 74(2) and (3), and Article 78, be liable to the payee for correct transmission of the payment order to the payment service provider of the payer in accordance with Article 69(3). Where the payee's payment service provider is liable under this subparagraph, he shall immediately re-transmit the payment order in question to the payment service provider of the payer.

   In addition, the payment service provider of the payee shall, without prejudice to Article 58, Article 74(2) and (3), and Article 78, be liable to the payee for handling the payment transaction in accordance with its obligations under Article 73. Where the payee's payment service provider is liable under this subparagraph, he shall ensure that the amount of the payment transaction is at the payee's disposal immediately after that amount is credited to the payee's payment service provider's account.

   In the case of a non-executed or defectively executed payment transaction for which the payee's payment service provider is not liable under the first and second subparagraphs, the payer's payment service provider shall be liable to the payer. Where the payer's payment service provider is so liable he shall, as appropriate and without undue delay, refund to the payer the amount of the non-executed or defective payment transaction and restore the debited payment account to the state in which it would have been had the defective payment transaction not taken place.

   In the case of a non-executed or defectively executed payment transaction where the payment order is initiated by or through the payee, his payment service provider shall, regardless of liability under this paragraph, on request, make immediate efforts to trace the payment transaction and notify the payee of the outcome.

3. In addition, payment service providers shall be liable to their respective payment service users for any charges for which they are responsible, and for any interest to which the payment service user is subject as a consequence of non-execution or defective execution of the payment transaction.

Article 76 Additional financial compensation

Any financial compensation additional to that provided for under this Section may be determined in accordance with the law applicable to the contract concluded between the payment service user and his payment service provider.

Article 77 Right of recourse

1. Where the liability of a payment service provider under Article 75 is attributable to another payment service provider or to an intermediary, that payment service provider or intermediary shall compensate the first payment service provider for any losses incurred or sums paid under Article 75.
2. Further financial compensation may be determined in accordance with agreements between payment service providers and/or intermediaries and the law applicable to the agreement concluded between them.

Article 78 No liability

Liability under Chapter 2 and 3 shall not apply in cases of abnormal and unforeseeable circumstances beyond the control of the party pleading for the application of those circumstances, the consequences of which would have been unavoidable despite all efforts to the contrary, or where a payment service provider is bound by other legal obligations covered by national or Community legislation.

CHAPTER 4 : DATA PROTECTION

Article 79 Data protection

Member States shall permit the processing of personal data by payment systems and payment service providers when this is necessary to safeguard the prevention, investigation and detection of payment fraud. The processing of such personal data shall be carried out in accordance with Directive 95/46/EC.

CHAPTER 5 : OUT-OF-COURT COMPLAINT AND REDRESS PROCEDURES FOR THE SETTLEMENT OF DISPUTES

Section 1 : **Complaint procedures**

Article 80 Complaints

1. Member States shall ensure that procedures are set up which allow payment service users and other interested parties, including consumer associations, to submit complaints to the competent authorities with regard to payment service providers' alleged infringements of the provisions of national law implementing the provisions of this Directive.
2. Where appropriate and without prejudice to the right to bring proceedings before a court in accordance with national procedural law, the reply from the competent authorities shall inform the complainant of the existence of the out-of-court complaint and redress procedures set up in accordance with Article 83.

Article 81 Penalties

1. Member States shall lay down the rules on penalties applicable to infringements of the national provisions adopted pursuant to this Directive and shall take all measures necessary to ensure that they are implemented. Such penalties shall be effective, proportionate and dissuasive.
2. Member States shall notify the Commission of the rules referred to in paragraph 1 and of the competent authorities referred to in Article 82 by 1 November 2009 and shall notify it without delay of any subsequent amendment affecting them.

Article 82 Competent authorities

1. Member States shall take all the measures necessary to ensure that the complaints procedures and penalties provided for in Articles 80(1) and 81(1) respectively are administered by the authorities empowered to ensure compliance with the provisions of national law adopted pursuant to the requirements laid down in this Section.
2. In the event of infringement or suspected infringement of the provisions of national law adopted pursuant to Titles III and IV, the competent authorities referred to in paragraph 1 shall be those of the home Member State of the payment service provider, except for agents and branches conducted under the right of establishment where the competent authorities shall be those of the host Member State.

Section 2 : **Out-of-court redress procedures**

Article 83 Out-of-court redress

1. Member States shall ensure that adequate and effective out-of-court complaint and redress procedures for the settlement of disputes between payment service users and their payment service providers are put in place for disputes concerning rights and obligations arising under this Directive, using existing bodies where appropriate.
2. In the case of cross-border disputes, Member States shall make sure that those bodies cooperate actively in resolving them.

TITLE V : IMPLEMENTING MEASURES AND PAYMENTS COMMITTEE

Article 84 Implementing measures

In order to take account of technological and market developments in payment services and to ensure the uniform application of this Directive, the Commission may, in accordance with the regulatory procedure with scrutiny referred to in Article 85(2), adopt implementing measures designed to amend non-essential elements of this Directive and relating to the following:

(a) adapting the list of activities in the Annex, in accordance with Articles 2 to 4 and 16;

(b) changing the definition of micro enterprise within the meaning of Article 4(26) in accordance with an amendment of Recommendation 2003/361/EC;
(c) updating the amounts specified in Articles 26(1) and 61(1) in order to take account of inflation and significant market developments.

Article 85 Committee

1. The Commission shall be assisted by a Payments Committee.
2. Where reference is made to this paragraph, Article 5a(1) to (4) and Article 7 of Decision 1999/468/EC shall apply, having regard to the provisions of Article 8 thereof.

TITLE VI : FINAL PROVISIONS

Article 86 Full harmonisation

1. Without prejudice to Article 30(2), Article 33, Article 34(2), Article 45(6), Article 47(3), Article 48(3), Article 51(2), Article 52(3), Article 53(2), Article 61(3), and Articles 72 and 88 insofar as this Directive contains harmonised provisions, Member States shall not maintain or introduce provisions other than those laid down in this Directive.
2. Where a Member State makes use of any of the options referred to in paragraph 1, it shall inform the Commission thereof as well as of any subsequent changes. The Commission shall make the information public on a web-site or other easily accessible means.
3. Member States shall ensure that payment service providers do not derogate, to the detriment of payment service users, from the provisions of national law implementing or corresponding to provisions of this Directive except where explicitly provided for therein.

   However, payment service providers may decide to grant more favourable terms to payment service users.

Article 87 Review

No later than 1 November 2012, the Commission shall present to the European Parliament, the Council, the European Economic and Social Committee and the European Central Bank a report on the implementation and impact of this Directive, in particular on:

- the possible need to extend the scope of the Directive to payment transactions in all currencies and to payment transactions where only one of the payment service providers is located in the Community,
- the application of Articles 6, 8 and 9 concerning prudential requirements for payment institutions, in particular as regards own funds requirements and safeguarding requirements (ringfencing),
- the possible impact of the granting of credit by payment institutions related to payments services, as set out in Article 16(3),

- the possible impact of the authorisation requirements of payment institutions on competition between payment institutions and other payment service providers as well as on barriers to market entry by new payment service providers,
- the application of Articles 34 and 53 and the possible need to revise the scope of this Directive with respect to low value payment instruments and electronic money, and
- the application and functioning of Articles 69 and 75 for all kinds of payment instruments,

accompanied, where appropriate, by a proposal for its revision.

Article 88 Transitional provision

1. Without prejudice to Directive 2005/60/EC or other relevant Community legislation, Member States shall allow legal persons who have commenced before 25 December 2007 the activities of payment institutions within the meaning of this Directive, in accordance with the national law in force to continue those activities within the Member State concerned until 30 April 2011, without authorisation under Article 10. Any such persons who have not been granted authorisation within this period shall be prohibited in accordance with Article 29 to provide payment services.
2. Notwithstanding paragraph 1, an exemption to the authorisation requirement under Article 10 shall be granted to financial institutions that have commenced activities listed in point 4 of Annex I to Directive 2006/48/EC and meet the conditions of point (e) of the first subparagraph of Article 24(1), of that Directive in accordance with national law before 25 December 2007. However, they shall notify the competent authorities of the home Member State of these activities by 25 December 2007. Furthermore, this notification shall include the information demonstrating that they have complied with Article 5(a), (d), (g) to (i), (k) and (l) of this Directive. Where the competent authorities are satisfied that those requirements are complied with, the financial institutions concerned shall be registered in accordance with Article 13 of this Directive. Member States may allow their competent authorities to exempt those financial institutions from the requirements under Article 5.
3. Member States may provide that legal persons referred to in paragraph 1 shall be automatically granted authorisation and entered into the register provided for in Article 13 if the competent authorities already have evidence that the requirements laid down in Articles 5 and 10 are complied with. The competent authorities shall inform the entities concerned before the authorisation is granted.
4. Without prejudice to Directive 2005/60/EC or other relevant Community legislation, Member States may allow natural or legal persons who have commenced the activities of payment institutions within the meaning of this Directive, in accordance with the national law in force before 25 December 2007 and who are eligible for waiver under Article 26 to continue those activities within the Member State concerned for a transitional period not longer than 3 years without being waived in accordance with Article 26 and entered into the

register provided for in Article 13. Any such persons who are not waived within this period shall be prohibited in accordance with Article 29 to provide payment services.

Article 89 Amendment of Directive 97/7/EC

Article 8 of Directive 97/7/EC shall be deleted.

Article 90 Amendments of Directive 2002/65/EC

Directive 2002/65/EC is hereby amended as follows:

1. in Article 4 the following paragraph shall be added:

   "5. Where Directive 2007/64/EC of the European Parliament and of the Council of 13 November 2007 on payment services in the internal market[1] is also applicable, the information provisions under Article 3(1) of this Directive, with the exception of paragraphs (2)(c) to (g), (3)(a), (d) and (e), and (4)(b), shall be replaced with Articles 36, 37, 41 and 42 of that Directive.

2. Article 8 shall be deleted.

Article 91 Amendments of Directive 2005/60/EC

Directive 2005/60/EC is hereby amended as follows:

1. Article 3(2)(a) shall be replaced by the following:

   "(a) an undertaking other than a credit institution which carries out one or more of the activities listed in points 2 to 12 and 14 of Annex I to Directive 2006/48/EC, including the activities of currency exchange offices (bureaux de change)";

2. in Article 15 paragraphs 1 and 2 shall be replaced by the following:

   "1. Where a Member State permits credit and financial institutions referred to in Article 2(1)(1) or (2) situated in its territory to be relied on as a third party domestically, that Member State shall in any case permit institutions and persons referred to in Article 2(1) situated in its territory to recognise and accept, in accordance with Article 14, the outcome of the customer due diligence requirements laid down in Article 8(1)(a) to (c), carried out in accordance with this Directive by an institution referred to in Article 2(1)(1) or (2) in another Member State, with the exception of currency exchange offices and payment institutions as defined in Article 4(4) of Directive 2007/64/EC of the European Parliament and of the Council of 13 November 2007 on payment services in the internal market[2], which mainly provide the payment service listed in point 6 of the Annex to that Directive, including natural and legal persons benefiting from a waiver under Article 26 of that Directive, and meeting the requirements laid down in Articles 16 and 18 of this Directive, even if the documents or data on which these requirements have been based are different to those required in the Member State to which the customer is being referred.

---

1 OJ L 319, 5.12.2007, p. 1

2 OJ L 319, 5.12.2007, p. 1

Where a Member State permits currency exchange offices referred to in Article 3(2)(a) and payment institutions as defined in Article 4(4) of Directive 2007/64/EC, which mainly provide the payment service listed in point 6 of the Annex to that Directive, situated in its territory to be relied on as a third party domestically, that Member State shall in any case permit them to recognise and accept, in accordance with Article 14 of this Directive, the outcome of the customer due diligence requirements laid down in Article 8(1)(a) to (c), carried out in accordance with this Directive by the same category of institution in another Member State and meeting the requirements laid down in Articles 16 and 18 of this Directive, even if the documents or data on which these requirements have been based are different to those required in the Member State to which the customer is being referred.

3. the second sentence of Article 36(1) shall be deleted.

Article 92 Amendments of Directive 2006/48/EC

Annex I to Directive 2006/48/EC is hereby amended as follows:

1. point 4 shall be replaced by the following:

"(4) Payment services as defined in Article 4(3) of Directive 2007/64/EC of the European Parliament and of the Council of 13 November 2007 on payment services in the internal market[1]

2. point 5 shall be replaced by the following:

"(5) Issuing and administering other means of payment (e.g. travellers' cheques and bankers' drafts) insofar as this activity is not covered by point 4".

Article 93 Repeal

Directive 97/5/EC shall be repealed with effect from 1 November 2009.

Article 94 Transposition

1. Member States shall bring into force the laws, regulations and administrative provisions necessary to comply with this Directive before 1 November 2009. They shall forthwith inform the Commission thereof.

   When they are adopted by Member States, those measures shall contain a reference to this Directive or shall be accompanied by such reference on the occasion of their official publication. The methods of making such reference shall be laid down by Member States.

2. Member States shall communicate to the Commission the text of the main provisions of national law which they adopt in the field covered by this Directive.

Article 95 Entry into force

This Directive shall enter into force on the 20th day following its publication in the Official Journal of the European Union.

[1] OJ L 319, 5.12.2007, p. 1

Article 96 Addressees

This Directive is addressed to the Member States.

Done at Strasbourg, 13 November 2007.

For the European Parliament

The President

H.-G. Pöttering

For the Council

The President

M. Lobo Antunes

ANNEX

PAYMENT SERVICES (DEFINITION 3 IN ARTICLE 4)

1. Services enabling cash to be placed on a payment account as well as all the operations required for operating a payment account.
2. Services enabling cash withdrawals from a payment account as well as all the operations required for operating a payment account.
3. Execution of payment transactions, including transfers of funds on a payment account with the user's payment service provider or with another payment service provider:
   - execution of direct debits, including one-off direct debits,
   - execution of payment transactions through a payment card or a similar device,
   - execution of credit transfers, including standing orders.
4. Execution of payment transactions where the funds are covered by a credit line for a payment service user:
   - execution of direct debits, including one-off direct debits,
   - execution of payment transactions through a payment card or a similar device,
   - execution of credit transfers, including standing orders.
5. Issuing and/or acquiring of payment instruments.
6. Money remittance.
7. Execution of payment transactions where the consent of the payer to execute a payment transaction is given by means of any telecommunication, digital or IT device and the payment is made to the telecommunication, IT system or network operator, acting only as an intermediary between the payment service user and the supplier of the goods and services.

17.Directive 2008/48/EC of the European Parliament and of the Council of 23 April 2008 on credit agreements for consumers and repealing Council Directive 87/102/EEC

(OJ L 133 , 22/05/2008 p. 66 – 92)

THE EUROPEAN PARLIAMENT AND THE COUNCIL OF THE EUROPEAN UNION,

Having regard to the Treaty establishing the European Community, and in particular Article 95 thereof,

Having regard to the proposal from the Commission,

Having regard to the opinion of the European Economic and Social Committee[1],

Acting in accordance with the procedure laid down in Article 251 of the Treaty[2],

Whereas:

(1) Council Directive 87/102/EEC of 22 December 1986 for the approximation of the laws, regulations and administrative provisions of the Member States concerning consumer credit[3] lays down rules at Community level concerning consumer credit agreements.

(2) In 1995, the Commission presented a report on the operation of Directive 87/102/EEC and undertook a broad consultation of the interested parties. In 1997, the Commission presented a summary report of reactions to the 1995 report. A second report was produced in 1996 on the operation of Directive 87/102/EEC.

(3) Those reports and consultations revealed substantial differences between the laws of the various Member States in the field of credit for natural persons in general and consumer credit in particular. An analysis of the national laws transposing Directive 87/102/EEC shows that Member States use a variety of consumer protection mechanisms, in addition to Directive 87/102/EEC, on account of differences in the legal or economic situation at national level.

(4) The de facto and de jure situation resulting from those national differences in some cases leads to distortions of competition among creditors in the Community and creates obstacles to the internal market where Member States have adopted different mandatory provisions more stringent than those provided for in Directive 87/102/EEC. It restricts consumers' ability to make direct use of the gradually increasing availability of cross-border credit. Those distortions and

---

1 OJ C 234, 30.9.2003, p. 1.

2 Opinion of the European Parliament of 20 April 2004 (OJ C 104 E, 30.4.2004, p. 233), Council common position of 20 September 2007 (OJ C 270 E, 13.11.2007, p. 1) and Position of the European Parliament of 16 January 2008 (not yet published in the Official Journal). Council Decision of 7 April 2008.

3 OJ L 42, 12.2.1987, p. 48. Directive as last amended by Directive 98/7/EC of the European Parliament and of the Council (OJ L 101, 1.4.1998, p. 17).

restrictions may in turn have consequences in terms of the demand for goods and services.

(5) In recent years the types of credit offered to and used by consumers have evolved considerably. New credit instruments have appeared, and their use continues to develop. It is therefore necessary to amend existing provisions and to extend their scope, where appropriate.

(6) In accordance with the Treaty, the internal market comprises an area without internal frontiers in which the free movement of goods and services and freedom of establishment are ensured. The development of a more transparent and efficient credit market within the area without internal frontiers is vital in order to promote the development of cross-border activities.

(7) In order to facilitate the emergence of a well-functioning internal market in consumer credit, it is necessary to make provision for a harmonised Community framework in a number of core areas. In view of the continuously developing market in consumer credit and the increasing mobility of European citizens, forward-looking Community legislation which is able to adapt to future forms of credit and which allows Member States the appropriate degree of flexibility in their implementation should help to establish a modern body of law on consumer credit.

(8) It is important that the market should offer a sufficient degree of consumer protection to ensure consumer confidence. Thus, it should be possible for the free movement of credit offers to take place under optimum conditions for both those who offer credit and those who require it, with due regard to specific situations in the individual Member States.

(9) Full harmonisation is necessary in order to ensure that all consumers in the Community enjoy a high and equivalent level of protection of their interests and to create a genuine internal market. Member States should therefore not be allowed to maintain or introduce national provisions other than those laid down in this Directive. However, such restriction should only apply where there are provisions harmonised in this Directive. Where no such harmonised provisions exist, Member States should remain free to maintain or introduce national legislation. Accordingly, Member States may, for instance, maintain or introduce national provisions on joint and several liability of the seller or the service provider and the creditor. Another example of this possibility for Member States could be the maintenance or introduction of national provisions on the cancellation of a contract for the sale of goods or supply of services if the consumer exercises his right of withdrawal from the credit agreement. In this respect Member States, in the case of open-end credit agreements, should be allowed to fix a minimum period needing to elapse between the time when the creditor asks for reimbursement and the day on which the credit has to be reimbursed.

(10) The definitions contained in this Directive determine the scope of harmonisation. The obligation on Member States to implement the provisions of

this Directive should therefore be limited to its scope as determined by those definitions. However, this Directive should be without prejudice to the application by Member States, in accordance with Community law, of the provisions of this Directive to areas not covered by its scope. A Member State could thereby maintain or introduce national legislation corresponding to the provisions of this Directive or certain of its provisions on credit agreements outside the scope of this Directive, for instance on credit agreements involving amounts less than EUR 200 or more than EUR 75000. Furthermore, Member States could also apply the provisions of this Directive to linked credit which does not fall within the definition of a linked credit agreement as contained in this Directive. Thus, the provisions on linked credit agreements could be applied to credit agreements that serve only partially to finance a contract for the supply of goods or provision of a service.

(11) In the case of specific credit agreements to which only some provisions of this Directive are applicable, Member States should not be allowed to adopt national legislation implementing other provisions of this Directive. However, Member States should remain free to regulate, in their national legislation, such types of credit agreements as regards other aspects not harmonised by this Directive.

(12) Agreements for the provision on a continuing basis of services or for the supply of goods of the same kind, where the consumer pays for them for the duration of their provision by means of instalments, may differ considerably, in terms of the interests of the contractual parties involved, and the modalities and performance of the transactions, from credit agreements covered by this Directive. Therefore, it should be clarified that such agreements are not regarded as credit agreements for the purposes of this Directive. Such types of agreement include, for example, an insurance contract where the insurance is paid for in monthly instalments.

(13) This Directive should not apply to certain types of credit agreement, such as deferred debit cards, under the terms of which the credit has to be repaid within three months and only insignificant charges are payable.

(14) Credit agreements covering the granting of credit secured by real estate should be excluded from the scope of this Directive. That type of credit is of a very specific nature. Also, credit agreements the purpose of which is to finance the acquisition or retention of property rights in land or in an existing or projected building should be excluded from the scope of this Directive. However, credit agreements should not be excluded from the scope of this Directive only because their purpose is the renovation or increase of value of an existing building.

(15) The provisions of this Directive apply irrespective of whether the creditor is a legal person or a natural person. However, this Directive does not affect the right of Member States to limit, in conformity with Community law, the provision of credit for consumers to legal persons only or to certain legal persons.

(16) Certain provisions of this Directive should apply to natural and legal persons (credit intermediaries) who, in the course of their trade, business or profession,

for a fee, present or offer credit agreements to consumers, assist consumers by undertaking preparatory work in respect of credit agreements or conclude credit agreements with consumers on behalf of the creditor. Organisations which allow their identity to be used in promoting credit products, such as credit cards, and which may also recommend those products to their members should not be regarded as credit intermediaries for the purposes of this Directive.

(17) This Directive regulates only certain obligations of credit intermediaries in relation to consumers. Member States should therefore remain free to maintain or introduce additional obligations incumbent on credit intermediaries, including the conditions under which a credit intermediary may receive fees from a consumer who has requested his service.

(18) Consumers should be protected against unfair or misleading practices, in particular with respect to the disclosure of information by the creditor, in line with Directive 2005/29/EC of the European Parliament and of the Council of 11 May 2005 concerning unfair business-to-consumer commercial practices in the internal market ("Unfair Commercial Practices Directive)[1]. However, this Directive should contain specific provisions on advertising concerning credit agreements as well as certain items of standard information to be provided to consumers in order to enable them, in particular, to compare different offers. Such information should be given in a clear, concise and prominent way by means of a representative example. A ceiling should be provided where it is not possible to indicate the total amount of credit as the total sums made available, in particular where a credit agreement gives the consumer freedom of drawdown with a limitation with regard to the amount. The ceiling should indicate the upper limit of credit which can be made available to the consumer. In addition, Member States should remain free to regulate information requirements in their national law regarding advertising which does not contain information on the cost of the credit.

(19) In order to enable consumers to make their decisions in full knowledge of the facts, they should receive adequate information, which the consumer may take away and consider, prior to the conclusion of the credit agreement, on the conditions and cost of the credit and on their obligations. To ensure the fullest possible transparency and comparability of offers, such information should, in particular, include the annual percentage rate of charge applicable to the credit, determined in the same way throughout the Community. As the annual percentage rate of charge can at this stage be indicated only through an example, such example should be representative. Therefore, it should correspond, for instance, to the average duration and total amount of credit granted for the type of credit agreement under consideration and, if applicable, to the goods purchased. When determining the representative example, the frequency of certain types of credit agreement in a specific market should also be taken into account. As regards the borrowing rate, the frequency of instalments and the

[1] OJ L 149, 11.6.2005, p. 22.

capitalisation of interest, creditors should use their conventional method of calculation for the consumer credit concerned.

(20) The total cost of the credit to the consumer should comprise all the costs, including interest, commissions, taxes, fees for credit intermediaries and any other fees which the consumer has to pay in connection with the credit agreement, except for notarial costs. Creditors" actual knowledge of the costs should be assessed objectively, taking into account the requirements of professional diligence.

(21) Credit agreements in which a borrowing rate is periodically revised in line with changes occurring in a reference rate referred to in the credit agreement should not be regarded as credit agreements with a fixed borrowing rate.

(22) Member States should remain free to maintain or introduce national provisions prohibiting the creditor from requiring the consumer, in connection with the credit agreement, to open a bank account or conclude an agreement in respect of another ancillary service, or to pay the expenses or fees for such bank accounts or other ancillary services. In those Member States where such combined offers are allowed, consumers should be informed before the conclusion of the credit agreement about any ancillary services which are compulsory in order for the credit to be obtained in the first place or on the terms and conditions marketed. The costs payable in respect of those ancillary services should be included in the total cost of the credit; alternatively, if the amount of such costs cannot be determined in advance, consumers should receive adequate information about the existence of costs at a pre-contractual stage. The creditor must be presumed to have knowledge of the costs of the ancillary services which he offers to the consumer himself, or on behalf of a third party, unless the price thereof depends on the specific characteristics or situation of the consumer.

(23) For specific types of credit agreements, however, it is appropriate, in order to ensure an adequate level of consumer protection without placing an excessive burden on creditors or, where applicable, credit intermediaries, to restrict the pre-contractual information requirements of this Directive, taking into account the specific character of such types of agreements.

(24) The consumer needs to be given comprehensive information before he concludes the credit agreement, regardless of whether or not a credit intermediary is involved in the marketing of the credit. Therefore, in general, the pre-contractual information requirements should also apply to credit intermediaries. However, where suppliers of goods and services act as credit intermediaries in an ancillary capacity, it is not appropriate to burden them with the legal obligation to provide the pre-contractual information in accordance with this Directive. Suppliers of goods and services may be deemed, for example, to be acting as credit intermediaries in an ancillary capacity if their activity as credit intermediaries is not the main purpose of their trade, business or profession. In those cases, a sufficient level of consumer protection is still achieved since the creditor is responsible for ensuring that the consumer receives

the full pre-contractual information, either from the intermediary, if the creditor and the intermediary so agree, or in some other appropriate manner.

(25) The potentially binding character of the information to be provided to the consumer prior to the conclusion of the credit agreement and the period of time during which the creditor is to be bound by it may be regulated by the Member States.

(26) Member States should take appropriate measures to promote responsible practices during all phases of the credit relationship, taking into account the specific features of their credit market. Those measures may include, for instance, the provision of information to, and the education of, consumers, including warnings about the risks attaching to default on payment and to over-indebtedness. In the expanding credit market, in particular, it is important that creditors should not engage in irresponsible lending or give out credit without prior assessment of creditworthiness, and the Member States should carry out the necessary supervision to avoid such behaviour and should determine the necessary means to sanction creditors in the event of their doing so. Without prejudice to the credit risk provisions of Directive 2006/48/EC of the European Parliament and of the Council of 14 June 2006 relating to the taking up and pursuit of the business of credit institutions[1], creditors should bear the responsibility of checking individually the creditworthiness of the consumer. To that end, they should be allowed to use information provided by the consumer not only during the preparation of the credit agreement in question, but also during a long-standing commercial relationship. The Member States' authorities could also give appropriate instructions and guidelines to creditors. Consumers should also act with prudence and respect their contractual obligations.

(27) Despite the pre-contractual information to be provided, the consumer may still need additional assistance in order to decide which credit agreement, within the range of products proposed, is the most appropriate for his needs and financial situation. Therefore, Member States should ensure that creditors provide such assistance in relation to the credit products which they offer to the consumer. Where appropriate, the relevant pre-contractual information, as well as the essential characteristics of the products proposed, should be explained to the consumer in a personalised manner so that the consumer can understand the effects which they may have on his economic situation. Where applicable, this duty to assist the consumer should also apply to credit intermediaries. Member States could determine when and to what extent such explanations are to be given to the consumer, taking into account the particular circumstances in which the credit is offered, the consumer's need for assistance and the nature of individual credit products.

(28) To assess the credit status of a consumer, the creditor should also consult relevant databases; the legal and actual circumstances may require that such consultations vary in scope. To prevent any distortion of competition among

1 OJ L 177, 30.6.2006, p. 1. Directive as last amended by Directive 2008/24/EC (OJ L 81, 20.3.2008, p. 38).

creditors, it should be ensured that creditors have access to private or public databases concerning consumers in a Member State where they are not established under non-discriminatory conditions compared with creditors in that Member State.

(29) Where a decision to reject an application for credit is based on the consultation of a database, the creditor should inform the consumer of this fact and of the particulars of the database consulted. However, the creditor should not be obliged to give such information when this is prohibited by other Community legislation, for example legislation on money laundering or the financing of terrorism. Furthermore, such information should not be given if this would be contrary to objectives of public policy or public security, such as the prevention, investigation, detection or prosecution of criminal offences.

(30) This Directive does not regulate contract law issues related to the validity of credit agreements. Therefore, in that area, the Member States may maintain or introduce national provisions which are in conformity with Community law. Member States may regulate the legal regime governing the offer to conclude the credit agreement, in particular when it is to be given and the period during which it is to be binding on the creditor. If such an offer is made at the same time as the pre-contractual information provided for by this Directive is given, it should, like any additional information the creditor may wish to give to the consumer, be provided in a separate document which may be annexed to the Standard European Consumer Credit Information.

(31) In order to enable the consumer to know his rights and obligations under the credit agreement, it should contain all necessary information in a clear and concise manner.

(32) In order to ensure full transparency, the consumer should be provided with information concerning the borrowing rate, both at a pre-contractual stage and when the credit agreement is concluded. During the contractual relationship, the consumer should further be informed of changes to the variable borrowing rate and changes to the payments caused thereby. This is without prejudice to provisions of national law not related to consumer information which lay down conditions for, or prescribe the consequences of, changes, other than changes concerning payments, in borrowing rates and other economic conditions governing the credit, for instance rules providing that the creditor may change the borrowing rate only where there is a valid reason for such change or that the consumer may terminate the contract should there be a change in the borrowing rate or in some other economic condition concerning the credit.

(33) The contracting parties should have the right to effect a standard termination of an open-end credit agreement. In addition, if agreed in the credit agreement, the creditor should have the right to suspend the consumer's right to draw down on an open-end credit agreement for objectively justified reasons. Such reasons may include, for instance, suspicion of an unauthorised or fraudulent use of the credit or a significantly increased risk of the consumer being unable to fulfil his obligation to repay the credit. This Directive does not affect national law in the

area of contract law regulating the rights of the contracting parties to terminate the credit agreement on the basis of a breach of contract.

(34) In order to approximate the procedures for exercising the right of withdrawal in similar areas, it is necessary to make provision for a right of withdrawal without penalty and with no obligation to provide justification, under conditions similar to those provided for by Directive 2002/65/EC of the European Parliament and of the Council of 23 September 2002 concerning the distance marketing of consumer financial services[1].

(35) Where a consumer withdraws from a credit agreement in connection with which he has received goods, in particular from a purchase in instalments or from a hiring or leasing agreement providing for an obligation to purchase, this Directive should be without prejudice to any regulation by Member States of questions concerning the return of the goods or any related questions.

(36) In some cases, national legislation already provides that funds cannot be made available to the consumer before the expiry of a specific deadline. In these cases, consumers may wish to ensure that they receive the goods or services purchased early. Therefore, in the case of linked credit agreements, Member States may exceptionally provide that, if the consumer explicitly wishes early receipt, the deadline for the exercise of the right of withdrawal could be reduced to the same deadline before which funds cannot be made available.

(37) In the case of linked credit agreements, a relationship of interdependence exists between the purchase of goods or services and the credit agreement concluded for that purpose. Therefore, where the consumer exercises his right of withdrawal in respect of the purchase agreement, based on Community law, he should no longer be bound by the linked credit agreement. This should not affect national law applicable to linked credit agreements in cases where a purchase agreement has been voided or where the consumer has exercised his right of withdrawal based on national law. Nor should this affect the rights of consumers granted by national provisions according to which no commitment may be entered into between the consumer and a supplier of goods or services, nor any payment made between those persons, as long as the consumer has not signed the credit agreement to finance the purchase of the goods or services.

(38) Under certain conditions, the consumer should be allowed to pursue remedies against the creditor in the event of problems related to the purchase agreement. However, Member States should determine to what extent and under what conditions the consumer is required to pursue his remedies against the supplier, in particular by bringing an action against the latter, before being in a position to pursue them against the creditor. This Directive should not deprive consumers of their rights under national provisions attaching joint and several liability to the seller or supplier of services and to the creditor.

---

1 OJ L 271, 9.10.2002, p. 16. Directive as last amended by Directive 2007/64/EC (OJ L 319, 5.12.2007, p. 1).

(39) The consumer should have the right to discharge his obligations before the date agreed in the credit agreement. In the case of early repayment, either in part or in full, the creditor should be entitled to compensation for the costs directly linked to the early repayment, taking into account also any savings thereby made by the creditor. However, in order to determine the method of calculating the compensation, it is important to respect several principles. The calculation of the compensation due to the creditor should be transparent and comprehensible to consumers already at the pre-contractual stage and in any case during the performance of the credit agreement. In addition, the calculation method should be easy for creditors to apply, and supervisory control of the compensation by the responsible authorities should be facilitated. Therefore, and due to the fact that consumer credit is, given its duration and volume, not financed by long-term funding mechanisms, the ceiling for the compensation should be fixed in terms of a flat-rate amount. This approach reflects the special nature of credits for consumers and should not prejudice the possibly different approach in respect of other products which are financed by long-term funding mechanisms, such as fixed-rate mortgage loans.

(40) Member States should have the right to provide that compensation for early repayment may be claimed by the creditor only on condition that the amount repaid over a 12-month period exceeds a threshold defined by Member States. When fixing that threshold, which should not exceed EUR 10000, Member States should for instance take into account the average amount of consumer credits in their market.

(41) Assignment of the creditor's rights under a credit agreement should not have the effect of placing the consumer in a less favourable position. The consumer should also be properly informed when the credit agreement is assigned to a third party. However, where the initial creditor, in agreement with the assignee, continues to service the credit vis-à-vis the consumer, the consumer has no significant interest in being informed of the assignment. Therefore, a requirement at EU level that the consumer be informed of the assignment in such cases would be excessive.

(42) Member States should remain free to maintain or introduce national rules providing for collective forms of communication when this is necessary for purposes relating to the effectiveness of complex transactions such as securitisations or liquidation of assets that take place in the compulsory administrative liquidation of banks.

(43) In order to promote the establishment and functioning of the internal market and to ensure a high degree of protection for consumers throughout the Community, it is necessary to ensure the comparability of information relating to annual percentage rates of charge throughout the Community. Despite the uniform mathematical formula for its calculation, the annual percentage rate of charge provided for in Directive 87/102/EEC is not yet fully comparable throughout the Community. In individual Member States different cost factors

are taken into account in the calculation thereof. This Directive should therefore clearly and comprehensively define the total cost of a credit to the consumer.

(44) In order to ensure market transparency and stability, and pending further harmonisation, Member States should ensure that appropriate measures for the regulation or supervision of creditors are in place.

(45) This Directive respects fundamental rights and observes the principles recognised in particular by the Charter of Fundamental Rights of the European Union. In particular, this Directive seeks to ensure full respect for the rules on protection of personal data, the right to property, non-discrimination, protection of family and professional life, and consumer protection pursuant to the Charter of Fundamental Rights of the European Union.

(46) Since the objective of this Directive, namely the establishment of common rules for certain aspects of the laws, regulations and administrative provisions of the Member States concerning consumer credit, cannot be sufficiently achieved by the Member States and can therefore be better achieved at Community level, the Community may adopt measures, in accordance with the principle of subsidiarity as set out in Article 5 of the Treaty. In accordance with the principle of proportionality, as set out in that Article, this Directive does not go beyond what is necessary in order to achieve that objective.

(47) Member States should lay down rules on penalties applicable to infringements of the national provisions adopted pursuant to this Directive and ensure that they are implemented. While the choice of penalties remains within the discretion of the Member States, the penalties provided for should be effective, proportionate and dissuasive.

(48) The measures necessary for the implementation of this Directive should be adopted in accordance with Council Decision 1999/468/EC of 28 June 1999 laying down the procedures for the exercise of implementing powers conferred on the Commission[1].

(49) In particular, the Commission should be empowered to adopt additional assumptions for the calculation of the annual percentage rate of charge. Since those measures are of general scope and are designed to amend non-essential elements of this Directive, they must be adopted in accordance with the regulatory procedure with scrutiny provided for in Article 5a of Decision 1999/468/EC.

(50) In accordance with point 34 of the Interinstitutional Agreement on better law-making[2], Member States are encouraged to draw up, for themselves and in the interests of the Community, their own tables illustrating, as far as possible, the correlation between this Directive and the transposition measures, and to make them public.

(51) Accordingly, taking account of the number of amendments that need to be made to Directive 87/102/EEC due to the evolution of the consumer credit sector

1 OJ L 184, 17.7.1999, p. 23. Decision as amended by Decision 2006/512/EC (OJ L 200, 22.7.2006, p. 11).

2 OJ C 321, 31.12.2003, p. 1.

and in the interests of the clarity of Community legislation, that Directive should be repealed and replaced by this Directive,

HAVE ADOPTED THIS DIRECTIVE:

CHAPTER I : SUBJECT MATTER, SCOPE AND DEFINITIONS

Article 1 Subject matter

The purpose of this Directive is to harmonise certain aspects of the laws, regulations and administrative provisions of the Member States concerning agreements covering credit for consumers.

Article 2 Scope

1. This Directive shall apply to credit agreements.
2. This Directive shall not apply to the following:
   (a) credit agreements which are secured either by a mortgage or by another comparable security commonly used in a Member State on immovable property or secured by a right related to immovable property;
   (b) credit agreements the purpose of which is to acquire or retain property rights in land or in an existing or projected building;
   (c) credit agreements involving a total amount of credit less than EUR 200 or more than EUR 75000;
   (d) hiring or leasing agreements where an obligation to purchase the object of the agreement is not laid down either by the agreement itself or by any separate agreement; such an obligation shall be deemed to exist if it is so decided unilaterally by the creditor;
   (e) credit agreements in the form of an overdraft facility and where the credit has to be repaid within one month;
   (f) credit agreements where the credit is granted free of interest and without any other charges and credit agreements under the terms of which the credit has to be repaid within three months and only insignificant charges are payable;
   (g) credit agreements where the credit is granted by an employer to his employees as a secondary activity free of interest or at annual percentage rates of charge lower than those prevailing on the market and which are not offered to the public generally;
   (h) credit agreements which are concluded with investment firms as defined in Article 4(1) of Directive 2004/39/EC of the European Parliament and of the Council of 21 April 2004 on markets in financial instruments[1] or with credit institutions as defined in Article 4 of Directive 2006/48/EC for the purposes of allowing an investor to carry out a transaction relating to one or more of the instruments listed in Section C of Annex I to Directive 2004/39/EC,

[1] OJ L 145, 30.4.2004, p. 1. Directive as last amended by Directive 2008/10/EC (OJ L 76, 19.3.2008, p. 33).

where the investment firm or credit institution granting the credit is involved in such transaction;

(i) credit agreements which are the outcome of a settlement reached in court or before another statutory authority;

(j) credit agreements which relate to the deferred payment, free of charge, of an existing debt;

(k) credit agreements upon the conclusion of which the consumer is requested to deposit an item as security in the creditor's safe-keeping and where the liability of the consumer is strictly limited to that pledged item;

(l) credit agreements which relate to loans granted to a restricted public under a statutory provision with a general interest purpose, and at lower interest rates than those prevailing on the market or free of interest or on other terms which are more favourable to the consumer than those prevailing on the market and at interest rates not higher than those prevailing on the market.

3. In the case of credit agreements in the form of an overdraft facility and where the credit has to be repaid on demand or within three months, only Articles 1 to 3, Article 4(1), Article 4(2)(a) to (c), Article 4(4), Articles 6 to 9, Article 10(1), Article 10(4), Article 10(5), Articles 12, 15, 17 and Articles 19 to 32 shall apply.

4. In the case of credit agreements in the form of overrunning, only Articles 1 to 3, 18, 20 and 22 to 32 shall apply.

5. Member States may determine that only Articles 1 to 4, 6, 7 and 9, Article 10(1), points (a) to (h) and (l) of Article 10(2), Article 10(4) and Articles 11, 13 and 16 to 32 shall apply to credit agreements which are concluded by an organisation which:

(a) is established for the mutual benefit of its members;

(b) does not make profits for any other person than its members;

(c) fulfils a social purpose required by domestic legislation;

(d) receives and manages the savings of, and provides sources of credit to, its members only; and

(e) provides credit on the basis of an annual percentage rate of charge which is lower than that prevailing on the market or subject to a ceiling laid down by national law,

and whose membership is restricted to persons residing or employed in a particular location or employees and retired employees of a particular employer, or to persons meeting other qualifications laid down under national law as the basis for the existence of a common bond between the members.

Member States may exempt from the application of this Directive credit agreements concluded by such an organisation where the total value of all existing credit agreements entered into by the organisation is insignificant in relation to the total value of all existing credit agreements in the Member State in which the organisation is based and the total value of all existing credit agreements entered into by all such organisations in the Member State is less than 1 % of the total value of all existing credit agreements entered into in that Member State.

Member States shall each year review whether the conditions for the application of any such exemption continue to exist and shall take action to withdraw the exemption where they consider that the conditions are no longer met.

6. Member States may determine that only Articles 1 to 4, 6, 7, 9, Article 10(1), points (a) to (i), (l) and (r) of Article 10(2), Article 10(4), Articles 11, 13, 16 and Articles 18 to 32 shall apply to credit agreements which provide for arrangements to be agreed by the creditor and the consumer in respect of deferred payment or repayment methods, where the consumer is already in default on the initial credit agreement and where:
   (a) such arrangements would be likely to avert the possibility of legal proceedings concerning such default; and
   (b) the consumer would not thereby be subject to terms less favourable than those laid down in the initial credit agreement.

   However, if the credit agreement falls within the scope of paragraph 3, only the provisions of that paragraph shall apply.

Article 3 Definitions

For the purposes of this Directive, the following definitions shall apply:

(a) "consumer" means a natural person who, in transactions covered by this Directive, is acting for purposes which are outside his trade, business or profession;

(b) "creditor" means a natural or legal person who grants or promises to grant credit in the course of his trade, business or profession;

(c) "credit agreement" means an agreement whereby a creditor grants or promises to grant to a consumer credit in the form of a deferred payment, loan or other similar financial accommodation, except for agreements for the provision on a continuing basis of services or for the supply of goods of the same kind, where the consumer pays for such services or goods for the duration of their provision by means of instalments;

(d) "overdraft facility" means an explicit credit agreement whereby a creditor makes available to a consumer funds which exceed the current balance in the consumer's current account;

(e) "overrunning" means a tacitly accepted overdraft whereby a creditor makes available to a consumer funds which exceed the current balance in the consumer's current account or the agreed overdraft facility;

(f) "credit intermediary" means a natural or legal person who is not acting as a creditor and who, in the course of his trade, business or profession, for a fee, which may take a pecuniary form or any other agreed form of financial consideration:

   (i) presents or offers credit agreements to consumers;

(ii) assists consumers by undertaking preparatory work in respect of credit agreements other than as referred to in (i); or

(iii) concludes credit agreements with consumers on behalf of the creditor;

(g) "total cost of the credit to the consumer" means all the costs, including interest, commissions, taxes and any other kind of fees which the consumer is required to pay in connection with the credit agreement and which are known to the creditor, except for notarial costs; costs in respect of ancillary services relating to the credit agreement, in particular insurance premiums, are also included if, in addition, the conclusion of a service contract is compulsory in order to obtain the credit or to obtain it on the terms and conditions marketed;

(h) "total amount payable by the consumer" means the sum of the total amount of the credit and the total cost of the credit to the consumer;

(i) "annual percentage rate of charge" means the total cost of the credit to the consumer, expressed as an annual percentage of the total amount of credit, where applicable including the costs referred to in Article 19(2);

(j) "borrowing rate" means the interest rate expressed as a fixed or variable percentage applied on an annual basis to the amount of credit drawn down;

(k) "fixed borrowing rate" means that the creditor and the consumer agree in the credit agreement on one borrowing rate for the entire duration of the credit agreement or on several borrowing rates for partial periods using exclusively a fixed specific percentage. If not all borrowing rates are determined in the credit agreement, the borrowing rate shall be deemed to be fixed only for the partial periods for which the borrowing rates are determined exclusively by a fixed specific percentage agreed on the conclusion of the credit agreement;

(l) "total amount of credit" means the ceiling or the total sums made available under a credit agreement;

(m) "durable medium" means any instrument which enables the consumer to store information addressed personally to him in a way accessible for future reference for a period of time adequate for the purposes of the information and which allows the unchanged reproduction of the information stored;

(n) "linked credit agreement" means a credit agreement where

(i) the credit in question serves exclusively to finance an agreement for the supply of specific goods or the provision of a specific service, and

(ii) those two agreements form, from an objective point of view, a commercial unit; a commercial unit shall be deemed to exist where the supplier or service provider himself finances the credit for the consumer or, if it is financed by a third party, where the creditor uses the services of the supplier or service provider in connection with the conclusion or preparation of the credit agreement, or where the specific goods or the provision of a specific service are explicitly specified in the credit agreement.

CHAPTER II : INFORMATION AND PRACTICES PRELIMINARY TO THE CONCLUSION OF THE CREDIT AGREEMENT

Article 4 Standard information to be included in advertising

1. Any advertising concerning credit agreements which indicates an interest rate or any figures relating to the cost of the credit to the consumer shall include standard information in accordance with this Article.

   This obligation shall not apply where national legislation requires the indication of the annual percentage rate of charge in advertising concerning credit agreements which does not indicate an interest rate or any figures relating to any cost of credit to the consumer within the meaning of the first subparagraph.

2. The standard information shall specify in a clear, concise and prominent way by means of a representative example:
   (a) the borrowing rate, fixed or variable or both, together with particulars of any charges included in the total cost of the credit to the consumer;
   (b) the total amount of credit;
   (c) the annual percentage rate of charge; in the case of a credit agreement of the kind referred to in Article 2(3), Member States may decide that the annual percentage rate of charge need not be provided;
   (d) if applicable, the duration of the credit agreement;
   (e) in the case of a credit in the form of deferred payment for a specific good or service, the cash price and the amount of any advance payment; and
   (f) if applicable, the total amount payable by the consumer and the amount of the instalments.

3. Where the conclusion of a contract regarding an ancillary service relating to the credit agreement, in particular insurance, is compulsory in order to obtain the credit or to obtain it on the terms and conditions marketed, and the cost of that service cannot be determined in advance, the obligation to enter into that contract shall also be stated in a clear, concise and prominent way, together with the annual percentage rate of charge.

4. This Article shall be without prejudice to Directive 2005/29/EC.

Article 5 Pre-contractual information

1. In good time before the consumer is bound by any credit agreement or offer, the creditor and, where applicable, the credit intermediary shall, on the basis of the credit terms and conditions offered by the creditor and, if applicable, the preferences expressed and information supplied by the consumer, provide the consumer with the information needed to compare different offers in order to take an informed decision on whether to conclude a credit agreement. Such information, on paper or on another durable medium, shall be provided by means of the Standard European Consumer Credit Information form set out in Annex II. The creditor shall be deemed to have fulfilled the information requirements in this paragraph and in Article 3, paragraphs (1) and (2) of Directive 2002/65/EC if he has supplied the Standard European Consumer Credit Information.

The information in question shall specify:

(a) the type of credit;

(b) the identity and the geographical address of the creditor as well as, if applicable, the identity and geographical address of the credit intermediary involved;

(c) the total amount of credit and the conditions governing the drawdown;

(d) the duration of the credit agreement;

(e) in the case of a credit in the form of deferred payment for a specific good or service and linked credit agreements, that good or service and its cash price;

(f) the borrowing rate, the conditions governing the application of the borrowing rate and, where available, any index or reference rate applicable to the initial borrowing rate, as well as the periods, conditions and procedure for changing the borrowing rate; if different borrowing rates apply in different circumstances, the abovementioned information on all the applicable rates;

(g) the annual percentage rate of charge and the total amount payable by the consumer, illustrated by means of a representative example mentioning all the assumptions used in order to calculate that rate; where the consumer has informed the creditor of one or more components of his preferred credit, such as the duration of the credit agreement and the total amount of credit, the creditor shall take those components into account; if a credit agreement provides different ways of drawdown with different charges or borrowing rates and the creditor uses the assumption set out in point (b) of Part II of Annex I, he shall indicate that other drawdown mechanisms for this type of credit agreement may result in higher annual percentage rates of charge;

(h) the amount, number and frequency of payments to be made by the consumer and, where appropriate, the order in which payments will be allocated to different outstanding balances charged at different borrowing rates for the purposes of reimbursement;

(i) where applicable, the charges for maintaining one or several accounts recording both payment transactions and drawdowns, unless the opening of an account is optional, together with the charges for using a means of payment for both payment transactions and drawdowns, any other charges deriving from the credit agreement and the conditions under which those charges may be changed;

(j) where applicable, the existence of costs payable by the consumer to a notary on conclusion of the credit agreement;

(k) the obligation, if any, to enter into an ancillary service contract relating to the credit agreement, in particular an insurance policy, where the conclusion of such a contract is compulsory in order to obtain the credit or to obtain it on the terms and conditions marketed;

(l) the interest rate applicable in the case of late payments and the arrangements for its adjustment, and, where applicable, any charges payable for default;
(m) a warning regarding the consequences of missing payments;
(n) where applicable, the sureties required;
(o) the existence or absence of a right of withdrawal;
(p) the right of early repayment, and, where applicable, information concerning the creditor's right to compensation and the way in which that compensation will be determined in accordance with Article 16;
(q) the consumer's right to be informed immediately and free of charge, pursuant to Article 9(2), of the result of a database consultation carried out for the purposes of assessing his creditworthiness;
(r) the consumer's right to be supplied, on request and free of charge, with a copy of the draft credit agreement. This provision shall not apply if the creditor is at the time of the request unwilling to proceed to the conclusion of the credit agreement with the consumer; and
(s) if applicable, the period of time during which the creditor is bound by the pre-contractual information.

Any additional information which the creditor may provide to the consumer shall be given in a separate document which may be annexed to the Standard European Consumer Credit Information form.

2. However, in the case of voice telephony communications, as referred to in Article 3(3) of Directive 2002/65/EC, the description of the main characteristics of the financial service to be provided pursuant to the second indent of Article 3(3)(b) of that Directive shall include at least the items referred to in points (c), (d), (e), (f) and (h) of paragraph (1) of this Article, together with the annual percentage rate of charge illustrated by means of a representative example and the total amount payable by the consumer.
3. If the agreement has been concluded at the consumer's request using a means of distance communication which does not enable the information to be provided in accordance with paragraph 1, in particular in the case referred to in paragraph 2, the creditor shall provide the consumer with the full pre-contractual information using the Standard European Consumer Credit Information form immediately after the conclusion of the credit agreement.
4. Upon request, the consumer shall, in addition to receiving the Standard European Consumer Credit Information, be supplied free of charge with a copy of the draft credit agreement. This provision shall not apply if the creditor is at the time of the request unwilling to proceed to the conclusion of the credit agreement with the consumer.
5. In the case of a credit agreement under which payments made by the consumer do not give rise to an immediate corresponding amortisation of the total amount of credit, but are used to constitute capital during periods and under conditions laid down in the credit agreement or in an ancillary agreement, the pre-contractual information required under paragraph 1 shall include a clear and

concise statement that such credit agreements do not provide for a guarantee of repayment of the total amount of credit drawn down under the credit agreement, unless such a guarantee is given.

6. Member States shall ensure that creditors and, where applicable, credit intermediaries provide adequate explanations to the consumer, in order to place the consumer in a position enabling him to assess whether the proposed credit agreement is adapted to his needs and to his financial situation, where appropriate by explaining the pre-contractual information to be provided in accordance with paragraph 1, the essential characteristics of the products proposed and the specific effects they may have on the consumer, including the consequences of default in payment by the consumer. Member States may adapt the manner by which and the extent to which such assistance is given, as well as by whom it is given, to the particular circumstances of the situation in which the credit agreement is offered, the person to whom it is offered and the type of credit offered.

Article 6 Pre-contractual information requirements for certain credit agreements in the form of an overdraft facility and for certain specific credit agreements

1. In good time before the consumer becomes bound by any credit agreement or offer concerning a credit agreement as referred to in Article 2(3), (5) or (6), the creditor and, where applicable, the credit intermediary shall, on the basis of the credit terms and conditions offered by the creditor and, if applicable, the preferences expressed and information supplied by the consumer, provide the consumer with the information needed to compare different offers in order to take an informed decision on whether to conclude a credit agreement.

   The information in question shall specify:

   (a) the type of credit;
   (b) the identity and geographical address of the creditor as well as, if applicable, the identity and geographical address of the credit intermediary involved;
   (c) the total amount of credit;
   (d) the duration of the credit agreement;
   (e) the borrowing rate; the conditions governing the application of that rate, any index or reference rate applicable to the initial borrowing rate, the charges applicable from the time the credit agreement is concluded, and, where applicable, the conditions under which those charges may be changed;
   (f) the annual percentage rate of charge, illustrated by means of representative examples mentioning all the assumptions used in order to calculate that rate;
   (g) the conditions and procedure for terminating the credit agreement;

(h) in the case of credit agreements as referred to in Article 2(3), where applicable, an indication that the consumer may be requested to repay the amount of credit in full at any time;

(i) the interest rate applicable in the case of late payments and the arrangements for its adjustment, and, where applicable, any charges payable for default;

(j) the consumer's right to be informed immediately and free of charge, pursuant to Article 9(2), of the result of a database consultation carried out for the purposes of assessing his creditworthiness;

(k) in the case of credit agreements as referred to in Article 2(3), information about the charges applicable from the time such agreements are concluded and, if applicable, the conditions under which those charges may be changed;

(l) if applicable, the period of time during which the creditor is bound by the pre-contractual information.

Such information shall be provided on paper or on another durable medium and all information shall be equally prominent. It may be provided by means of the European Consumer Credit Information form set out in Annex III. The creditor shall be deemed to have fulfilled the information requirements in this paragraph and in Article 3(1) and (2) of Directive 2002/65/EC if he has supplied the European Consumer Credit Information.

2. In the case of a credit agreement of the kind referred to in Article 2(3), Member States may decide that the annual percentage rate of charge need not be provided.

3. In the case of a credit agreement as referred to in Article 2(5) and (6), the information provided to the consumer in accordance with paragraph 1 of this Article shall also include:

(a) the amount, number and frequency of payments to be made by the consumer and, where appropriate, the order in which payments will be allocated to different outstanding balances charged at different borrowing rates for the purposes of reimbursement; and

(b) the right of early repayment, and, where applicable, information concerning the creditor's right to compensation and the way in which that compensation will be determined.

However, if the credit agreement falls within the scope of Article 2(3), only the provisions of paragraph 1 of this Article shall apply.

4. However, in the case of voice telephony communications and where the consumer requests that the overdraft facility be made available with immediate effect, the description of the main characteristics of the financial service shall include at least the items referred to in points (c), (e), (f) and (h) of paragraph 1. In addition, in credit agreements of the kind referred to in paragraph 3, the description of the main characteristics shall include a specification of the duration of the credit agreement.

5. Notwithstanding the exclusion provided for in Article 2(2)(e), the Member States shall apply at least the requirements of the first sentence of paragraph 4 of this Article to credit agreements in the form of an overdraft facility and where the credit has to be repaid within one month.
6. Upon request, the consumer shall, in addition to receiving the information referred to in paragraphs 1 to 4, be supplied free of charge with a copy of the draft credit agreement containing the contractual information provided for by Article 10 insofar as that Article is applicable. This provision shall not apply if the creditor is at the time of the request unwilling to proceed to the conclusion of the credit agreement with the consumer.
7. If the agreement has been concluded at the consumer's request using a means of distance communication which does not enable the information to be provided in accordance with paragraphs 1 and 3, including in the cases referred to in paragraph 4, the creditor shall immediately after the conclusion of the credit agreement fulfil his obligations under paragraphs 1 and 3 by providing the contractual information pursuant to Article 10 insofar as that Article is applicable.

Article 7 Exemptions from the pre-contractual information requirements

Articles 5 and 6 shall not apply to suppliers of goods or services acting as credit intermediaries in an ancillary capacity. This is without prejudice to the creditor's obligation to ensure that the consumer receives the pre-contractual information referred to in those Articles.

Article 8 Obligation to assess the creditworthiness of the consumer

1. Member States shall ensure that, before the conclusion of the credit agreement, the creditor assesses the consumer's creditworthiness on the basis of sufficient information, where appropriate obtained from the consumer and, where necessary, on the basis of a consultation of the relevant database. Member States whose legislation requires creditors to assess the creditworthiness of consumers on the basis of a consultation of the relevant database may retain this requirement.
2. Member States shall ensure that, if the parties agree to change the total amount of credit after the conclusion of the credit agreement, the creditor updates the financial information at his disposal concerning the consumer and assesses the consumer's creditworthiness before any significant increase in the total amount of credit.

CHAPTER III : DATABASE ACCESS

Article 9 Database access

1. Each Member State shall in the case of cross-border credit ensure access for creditors from other Member States to databases used in that Member State for

assessing the creditworthiness of consumers. The conditions for access shall be non-discriminatory.

2. If the credit application is rejected on the basis of consultation of a database, the creditor shall inform the consumer immediately and without charge of the result of such consultation and of the particulars of the database consulted.
3. The information shall be provided unless the provision of such information is prohibited by other Community legislation or is contrary to objectives of public policy or public security.
4. This Article shall be without prejudice to the application of Directive 95/46/EC of the European Parliament and of the Council of 24 October 1995 on the protection of individuals with regard to the processing of personal data and on the free movement of such data[1].

CHAPTER IV : INFORMATION AND RIGHTS CONCERNING CREDIT AGREEMENTS

Article 10 Information to be included in credit agreements

1. Credit agreements shall be drawn up on paper or on another durable medium.

   All the contracting parties shall receive a copy of the credit agreement. This Article shall be without prejudice to any national rules regarding the validity of the conclusion of credit agreements which are in conformity with Community law.
2. The credit agreement shall specify in a clear and concise manner:
   (a) the type of credit;
   (b) the identities and geographical addresses of the contracting parties as well as, if applicable, the identity and geographical address of the credit intermediary involved;
   (c) the duration of the credit agreement;
   (d) the total amount of credit and the conditions governing the drawdown;
   (e) in case of a credit in the form of deferred payment for a specific good or service or in the case of linked credit agreements, that good or service and its cash price;
   (f) the borrowing rate, the conditions governing the application of that rate and, where available, any index or reference rate applicable to the initial borrowing rate, as well as the periods, conditions and procedures for changing the borrowing rate and, if different borrowing rates apply in different circumstances, the abovementioned information in respect of all the applicable rates;
   (g) the annual percentage rate of charge and the total amount payable by the consumer, calculated at the time the credit agreement is concluded; all the assumptions used in order to calculate that rate shall be mentioned;

[1] OJ L 281, 23.11.1995, p. 31. Directive as amended by Regulation (EC) No 1882/2003 (OJ L 284, 31.10.2003, p. 1).

(h) the amount, number and frequency of payments to be made by the consumer and, where appropriate, the order in which payments will be allocated to different outstanding balances charged at different borrowing rates for the purposes of reimbursement;

(i) where capital amortisation of a credit agreement with a fixed duration is involved, the right of the consumer to receive, on request and free of charge, at any time throughout the duration of the credit agreement, a statement of account in the form of an amortisation table.
The amortisation table shall indicate the payments owing and the periods and conditions relating to the payment of such amounts; the table shall contain a breakdown of each repayment showing capital amortisation, the interest calculated on the basis of the borrowing rate and, where applicable, any additional costs; where the interest rate is not fixed or the additional costs may be changed under the credit agreement, the amortisation table shall indicate, clearly and concisely, that the data contained in the table will remain valid only until such time as the borrowing rate or the additional costs are changed in accordance with the credit agreement;

(j) if charges and interest are to be paid without capital amortisation, a statement showing the periods and conditions for the payment of the interest and of any associated recurrent and non-recurrent charges;

(k) where applicable, the charges for maintaining one or several accounts recording both payment transactions and drawdowns, unless the opening of an account is optional, together with the charges for using a means of payment for both payment transactions and drawdowns, and any other charges deriving from the credit agreement and the conditions under which those charges may be changed;

(l) the interest rate applicable in the case of late payments as applicable at the time of the conclusion of the credit agreement and the arrangements for its adjustment and, where applicable, any charges payable for default;

(m) a warning regarding the consequences of missing payments;

(n) where applicable, a statement, that notarial fees will be payable;

(o) the sureties and insurance required, if any;

(p) the existence or absence of a right of withdrawal, the period during which that right may be exercised and other conditions governing the exercise thereof, including information concerning the obligation of the consumer to pay the capital drawn down and the interest in accordance with Article 14(3)(b) and the amount of interest payable per day;

(q) information concerning the rights resulting from Article 15 as well as the conditions for the exercise of those rights;

(r) the right of early repayment, the procedure for early repayment, as well as, where applicable, information concerning the creditor's right to compensation and the way in which that compensation will be determined;

(s) the procedure to be followed in exercising the right of termination of the credit agreement;

(t) whether or not there is an out-of-court complaint and redress mechanism for the consumer and, if so, the methods for having access to it;
(u) where applicable, other contractual terms and conditions;
(v) where applicable, the name and address of the competent supervisory authority.

3. Where paragraph 2(i) applies, the creditor shall make available to the consumer, free of charge and at any time throughout the duration of the credit agreement, a statement of account in the form of an amortisation table.
4. In the case of a credit agreement under which payments made by the consumer do not give rise to an immediate corresponding amortisation of the total amount of credit, but are used to constitute capital during periods and under conditions laid down in the credit agreement or in an ancillary agreement, the information required under paragraph 2 shall include a clear and concise statement that such credit agreements do not provide for a guarantee of repayment of the total amount of credit drawn down under the credit agreement, unless such a guarantee is given.
5. In the case of credit agreements in the form of overdraft facilities as referred to in Article 2(3), the following shall be specified in a clear and concise manner:

(a) the type of credit;
(b) the identities and geographical addresses of the contracting parties as well as, if applicable, the identity and geographical address of the credit intermediary involved;
(c) the duration of the credit agreement;
(d) the total amount of the credit and the conditions governing the drawdown;
(e) the borrowing rate, the conditions governing the application of the borrowing rate and, where available, any index or reference rate applicable to the initial borrowing rate, as well as the periods, conditions and procedure for changing the borrowing rate and, if different borrowing rates apply in different circumstances, the abovementioned information in respect of all the applicable rates;
(f) the annual percentage rate of charge and the total cost of the credit to the consumer, calculated at the time the credit agreement is concluded; all the assumptions used in order to calculate that rate as referred to in Article 19(2) in conjunction with Article 3(g) and (i) shall be mentioned; Member States may decide that the annual percentage rate of charge need not be provided;
(g) an indication that the consumer may be requested to repay the amount of credit in full on demand at any time;
(h) conditions governing the exercise of the right of withdrawal from the credit agreement; and
(i) information concerning the charges applicable from the time such agreements are concluded and, if applicable, the conditions under which those charges may be changed.

Article 11 Information concerning the borrowing rate

1. Where applicable, the consumer shall be informed of any change in the borrowing rate, on paper or another durable medium, before the change enters into force. The information shall state the amount of the payments to be made after the entry into force of the new borrowing rate and, if the number or frequency of the payments changes, particulars thereof.
2. However, the parties may agree in the credit agreement that the information referred to in paragraph 1 is to be given to the consumer periodically in cases where the change in the borrowing rate is caused by a change in a reference rate, the new reference rate is made publicly available by appropriate means and the information concerning the new reference rate is also kept available in the premises of the creditor.

Article 12 Obligations in connection with credit agreement in the form of an overdraft facility

1. Where a credit agreement covers credit in the form of an overdraft facility, the consumer shall be kept regularly informed by means of a statement of account, on paper or on another durable medium, containing the following particulars:
   (a) the precise period to which the statement of account relates;
   (b) the amounts and dates of drawdowns;
   (c) the balance from the previous statement, and the date thereof;
   (d) the new balance;
   (e) the dates and amounts of payments made by the consumer;
   (f) the borrowing rate applied;
   (g) any charges that have been applied;
   (h) where applicable, the minimum amount to be paid.
2. In addition, the consumer shall be informed on paper or another durable medium of increases in the borrowing rate, or in any charges payable, before the change in question enters into force.

   However, the parties may agree in the credit agreement that information concerning changes in the borrowing rate is to be given in the manner provided for in paragraph 1 in cases where the change in the borrowing rate is caused by a change in a reference rate, the new reference rate is made publicly available by appropriate means and the information concerning the new reference rate is also kept available in the premises of the creditor.

Article 13 Open-end credit agreements

1. The consumer may effect standard termination of an open-end credit agreement free of charge at any time unless the parties have agreed on a period of notice. Such a period may not exceed one month.

   If agreed in the credit agreement, the creditor may effect standard termination of an open-end credit agreement by giving the consumer at least two months' notice drawn up on paper or on another durable medium.

2. If agreed in the credit agreement, the creditor may, for objectively justified reasons, terminate the consumer's right to draw down on an open-end credit agreement. The creditor shall inform the consumer of the termination and the reasons for it on paper or on another durable medium, where possible before the termination and at the latest immediately thereafter, unless the provision of such information is prohibited by other Community legislation or is contrary to objectives of public policy or public security.

Article 14 Right of withdrawal

1. The consumer shall have a period of 14 calendar days in which to withdraw from the credit agreement without giving any reason.

   That period of withdrawal shall begin

   (a) either from the day of the conclusion of the credit agreement, or

   (b) from the day on which the consumer receives the contractual terms and conditions and information in accordance with Article 10, if that day is later than the date referred to in point (a) of this subparagraph.

2. Where in the case of a linked credit agreement, as defined in Article 3(n), national legislation at the time of the entry into force of this Directive already provides that funds cannot be made available to the consumer before the expiry of a specific period, Member States may exceptionally provide that the period referred to in paragraph 1 of this Article may be reduced to this specific period at the explicit request of the consumer.

3. If the consumer exercises his right of withdrawal, he shall:

   (a) in order to give effect to the withdrawal before the expiry of the deadline referred to in paragraph 1, notify this to the creditor in line with the information given by the creditor pursuant to Article 10(2)(p) by means which can be proven in accordance with national law. The deadline shall be deemed to have been met if that notification, if it is on paper or on another durable medium that is available and accessible to the creditor, is dispatched before the deadline expires; and

   (b) pay to the creditor the capital and the interest accrued thereon from the date the credit was drawn down until the date the capital is repaid, without any undue delay and no later than 30 calendar days after the despatch by him to the creditor of notification of the withdrawal. The interest shall be calculated on the basis of the agreed borrowing rate. The creditor shall not be entitled to any other compensation from the consumer in the event of withdrawal, except compensation for any non-returnable charges paid by the creditor to any public administrative body.

4. If an ancillary service relating to the credit agreement is provided by the creditor or by a third party on the basis of an agreement between the third party and the creditor, the consumer shall no longer be bound by the ancillary service contract if the consumer exercises his right of withdrawal from the credit agreement in accordance with this Article.

5. If the consumer has a right of withdrawal under paragraphs 1, 3 and 4, Articles 6 and 7 of Directive 2002/65/EC and Article 5 of Council Directive 85/577/EEC of 20 December 1985 to protect the consumer in respect of contracts negotiated away from business premises[1] shall not apply.
6. Member States may provide that paragraphs 1 to 4 of this Article shall not apply to credit agreements which by law are required to be concluded through the services of a notary, provided that the notary confirms that the consumer is guaranteed the rights provided for under Articles 5 and 10.
7. This Article shall be without prejudice to any rule of national law establishing a period of time during which the performance of the contract may not begin.

Article 15 Linked credit agreements

1. Where the consumer has exercised a right of withdrawal, based on Community law, concerning a contract for the supply of goods or services, he shall no longer be bound by a linked credit agreement.
2. Where the goods or services covered by a linked credit agreement are not supplied, or are supplied only in part, or are not in conformity with the contract for the supply thereof, the consumer shall have the right to pursue remedies against the creditor if the consumer has pursued his remedies against the supplier but has failed to obtain the satisfaction to which he is entitled according to the law or the contract for the supply of goods or services. Member States shall determine to what extent and under what conditions those remedies shall be exercisable.
3. This Article shall be without prejudice to any national rules rendering the creditor jointly and severally liable in respect of any claim which the consumer may have against the supplier where the purchase of goods or services from the supplier has been financed by a credit agreement.

Article 16 Early repayment

1. The consumer shall be entitled at any time to discharge fully or partially his obligations under a credit agreement. In such cases, he shall be entitled to a reduction in the total cost of the credit, such reduction consisting of the interest and the costs for the remaining duration of the contract.
2. In the event of early repayment of credit the creditor shall be entitled to fair and objectively justified compensation for possible costs directly linked to early repayment of credit provided that the early repayment falls within a period for which the borrowing rate is fixed.

   Such compensation may not exceed 1 % of the amount of credit repaid early, if the period of time between the early repayment and the agreed termination of the credit agreement exceeds one year. If the period does not exceed one year, the compensation may not exceed 0,5 % of the amount of credit repaid early.
3. Compensation for early repayment shall not be claimed:

[1] OJ L 372, 31.12.1985, p. 31.

(a) if the repayment has been made under an insurance contract intended to provide a credit repayment guarantee;
(b) in the case of overdraft facilities; or
(c) if the repayment falls within a period for which the borrowing rate is not fixed.

4. Member States may provide that:
(a) such compensation may be claimed by the creditor only on condition that the amount of the early repayment exceeds the threshold defined by national law. That threshold shall not exceed EUR 10000 within any period of 12 months;
(b) the creditor may exceptionally claim higher compensation if he can prove that the loss he suffered from early repayment exceeds the amount determined under paragraph 2.
If the compensation claimed by the creditor exceeds the loss actually suffered, the consumer may claim a corresponding reduction.
In this case, the loss shall consist of the difference between the initially agreed interest rate and the interest rate at which the creditor can lend out the amount repaid early on the market at the time of early repayment, and shall take into account the impact of early repayment on administrative costs.

5. Any compensation shall not exceed the amount of interest the consumer would have paid during the period between the early repayment and the agreed date of termination of the credit agreement.

Article 17 Assignment of rights

1. In the event of assignment to a third party of the creditor's rights under a credit agreement or the agreement itself, the consumer shall be entitled to plead against the assignee any defence which was available to him against the original creditor, including set-off where the latter is permitted in the Member State concerned.
2. The consumer shall be informed of the assignment referred to in paragraph 1 except where the original creditor, by agreement with the assignee, continues to service the credit vis-à-vis the consumer.

Article 18 Overrunning

1. In the case of an agreement to open a current account, where there is a possibility that the consumer is allowed an overrun, the agreement shall contain in addition the information referred to in Article 6(1)(e). The creditor shall in any case provide that information on paper or another durable medium on a regular basis.
2. In the event of a significant overrunning exceeding a period of one month, the creditor shall inform the consumer without delay, on paper or on another durable medium,
(a) of the overrunning;
(b) of the amount involved;

(c) of the borrowing rate;
(d) of any penalties, charges or interest on arrears applicable.

3. This Article shall be without prejudice to any rule of national law requiring the creditor to offer another kind of credit product when the duration of the overrunning is significant.

CHAPTER V : ANNUAL PERCENTAGE RATE OF CHARGE

Article 19 Calculation of the annual percentage rate of charge

1. The annual percentage rate of charge, equating, on an annual basis, to the present value of all commitments (drawdowns, repayments and charges), future or existing, agreed by the creditor and the consumer, shall be calculated in accordance with the mathematical formula set out in Part I of Annex I.
2. For the purpose of calculating the annual percentage rate of charge, the total cost of the credit to the consumer shall be determined, with the exception of any charges payable by the consumer for non-compliance with any of his commitments laid down in the credit agreement and charges other than the purchase price which, for purchases of goods or services, he is obliged to pay whether the transaction is effected in cash or on credit.

   The costs of maintaining an account recording both payment transactions and drawdowns, the costs of using a means of payment for both payment transactions and drawdowns, and other costs relating to payment transactions shall be included in the total cost of credit to the consumer unless the opening of the account is optional and the costs of the account have been clearly and separately shown in the credit agreement or in any other agreement concluded with the consumer.
3. The calculation of the annual percentage rate of charge shall be based on the assumption that the credit agreement is to remain valid for the period agreed and that the creditor and the consumer will fulfil their obligations under the terms and by the dates specified in the credit agreement.
4. In the case of credit agreements containing clauses allowing variations in the borrowing rate and, where applicable, charges contained in the annual percentage rate of charge but unquantifiable at the time of calculation, the annual percentage rate of charge shall be calculated on the assumption that the borrowing rate and other charges will remain fixed in relation to the initial level and will remain applicable until the end of the credit agreement.
5. Where necessary, the additional assumptions set out in Annex I may be used in calculating the annual percentage rate of charge.

   If the assumptions set out in this Article and in Part II of Annex I do not suffice to calculate the annual percentage rate of charge in a uniform manner or are not adapted any more to the commercial situation at the market, the Commission may determine the necessary additional assumptions for the calculation of the annual percentage rate of charge, or modify existing ones. These measures, designed to amend non-essential elements of this Directive, shall be adopted in accordance with the regulatory procedure with scrutiny referred to in Article 25(2).

CHAPTER VI : CREDITORS AND CREDIT INTERMEDIARIES

Article 20 Regulation of creditors

Member States shall ensure that creditors are supervised by a body or authority independent from financial institutions, or regulated. This shall be without prejudice to Directive 2006/48/EC.

Article 21 Certain obligations of credit intermediaries vis-à-vis consumers

Member States shall ensure that:

(a) a credit intermediary indicates in advertising and documentation intended for consumers the extent of his powers, in particular whether he works exclusively with one or more creditors or as an independent broker;

(b) the fee, if any, payable by the consumer to the credit intermediary for his services is disclosed to the consumer, and agreed between the consumer and the credit intermediary on paper or another durable medium before the conclusion of the credit agreement;

(c) the fee, if any, payable by the consumer to the credit intermediary for his services is communicated to the creditor by the credit intermediary, for the purpose of calculation of the annual percentage rate of charge.

CHAPTER VII : IMPLEMENTING MEASURES

Article 22 Harmonisation and imperative nature of this Directive

1. Insofar as this Directive contains harmonised provisions, Member States may not maintain or introduce in their national law provisions diverging from those laid down in this Directive.
2. Member States shall ensure that consumers may not waive the rights conferred on them by the provisions of national law implementing or corresponding to this Directive.
3. Member States shall further ensure that the provisions they adopt in implementation of this Directive cannot be circumvented as a result of the way in which agreements are formulated, in particular by integrating drawdowns or credit agreements falling within the scope of this Directive into credit agreements the character or purpose of which would make it possible to avoid its application.
4. Member States shall take the necessary measures to ensure that consumers do not lose the protection granted by this Directive by virtue of the choice of the law of a third country as the law applicable to the credit agreement, if the credit agreement has a close link with the territory of one or more Member States.

Article 23 Penalties

Member States shall lay down the rules on penalties applicable to infringements of the national provisions adopted pursuant to this Directive and shall take all measures necessary to ensure that they are implemented. The penalties provided for must be effective, proportionate and dissuasive.

Article 24 Out-of-court dispute resolution

1. Member States shall ensure that adequate and effective out-of-court dispute resolution procedures for the settlement of consumer disputes concerning credit agreements are put in place, using existing bodies where appropriate.
2. Member States shall encourage those bodies to cooperate in order to also resolve cross-border disputes concerning credit agreements.

Article 25 Committee procedure

1. The Commission shall be assisted by a Committee.
2. Where reference is made to this paragraph, Article 5a(1) to (4) and Article 7 of Decision 1999/468/EC shall apply, having regard to the provisions of Article 8 thereof.

Article 26 Information to be supplied to the Commission

Where a Member State makes use of any of the regulatory choices referred to in Article 2(5) and 2(6), Article 4(1), Article 4(2)(c), Article 6(2), Article 10(1), Article 10(5)(f), Article 14(2) and Article 16(4), it shall inform the Commission thereof as well as of any subsequent changes. The Commission shall make that information public on a website or in another easily accessible way. Member States shall take the appropriate measures to diffuse that information amongst national creditors and consumers.

Article 27 Transposition

1. Before 11 June 2010 Member States shall adopt and publish the provisions necessary to comply with this Directive. They shall forthwith inform the Commission thereof.

   They shall apply those provisions from 11 June 2010.

   When Member States adopt these provisions, they shall contain a reference to this Directive or be accompanied by such reference on the occasion of their official publication. The methods of making such reference shall be laid down by Member States.
2. The Commission shall undertake, every five years and for the first time 11 June 2013, a review of the thresholds laid down in this Directive and its annexes and the percentages used to calculate the compensation payable in the event of early repayment, assessing them in the light of economic trends in the Community and the situation of the market concerned.

The Commission shall also monitor the effect of the existence of the regulatory choices referred to in Article 2(5) and 2(6), Article 4(1), Article 4(2)(c), Article 6(2), Article 10(1), Article 10(5)(f), Article 14(2) and Article 16(4) on the internal market and consumers.. The results shall be made known to the European Parliament and the Council, accompanied where appropriate by a proposal to modify the thresholds and percentages as well as the abovementioned regulatory choices accordingly.

Article 28 Conversion of amounts expressed in euro into national currency

1. For the purposes of this Directive, those Member States who convert the amounts expressed in euro into their national currency shall initially use in the conversion the exchange rate prevailing on the date of adoption of this Directive.
2. Member States may round off the amounts resulting from the conversion provided that such rounding off does not exceed EUR 10.

CHAPTER VIII : TRANSITIONAL AND FINAL PROVISIONS

Article 29 Repeal

Directive 87/102/EEC shall be repealed with effect from 11 June 2010.

Article 30 Transitional measures

1. This Directive shall not apply to credit agreements existing on the date when the national implementing measures enter into force.
2. However, Member States shall ensure that Articles 11, 12, 13 and 17, the second sentence of Article 18(1), and Article 18(2) are applied also to open-end credit agreements existing on the date when the national implementing measures enter into force.

Article 31 Entry into force

This Directive shall enter into force on the 20th day following its publication in the Official Journal of the European Union.

Article 32 Addressees

This Directive is addressed to the Member States.

Done at Strasbourg, 23 April 2008.

For the European Parliament

The President

H.-G. Pöttering

For the Council

The President

J. Lenarčič

ANNEX I

I. The basic equation expressing the equivalence of drawdowns on the one hand and repayments and charges on the other.

The basic equation, which establishes the annual percentage rate of charge (APR), equates, on an annual basis, the total present value of drawdowns on the one hand and the total present value of repayments and payments of charges on the other hand, i.e.:

$$\sum_{k=1}^{m} C_k(1+X)^{-t_k} = \sum_{l=1}^{m'} D_l(1+X)^{-S_l}$$

where:

- X : is the APR,
- m : is the number of the last drawdown,
- k : is the number of a drawdown, thus $1 \leq k \leq m$,
- Ck : is the amount of drawdown k,
- tk : is the interval, expressed in years and fractions of a year, between the date of the first drawdown and the date of each subsequent drawdown, thus t1 = 0,
- m': is the number of the last repayment or payment of charges,
- l : is the number of a repayment or payment of charges,
- Dl : is the amount of a repayment or payment of charges,
- sl : is the interval, expressed in years and fractions of a year, between the date of the first drawdown and the date of each repayment or payment of charges.

Remarks:

(a) The amounts paid by both parties at different times shall not necessarily be equal and shall not necessarily be paid at equal intervals.

(b) The starting date shall be that of the first drawdown.

(c) Intervals between dates used in the calculations shall be expressed in years or in fractions of a year. A year is presumed to have 365 days (or 366 days for leap years), 52 weeks or 12 equal months. An equal month is presumed to have 30,41666 days (i.e. 365/12) regardless of whether or not it is a leap year.

(d) The result of the calculation shall be expressed with an accuracy of at least one decimal place. If the figure at the following decimal place is greater than or equal to 5, the figure at that particular decimal place shall be increased by one.

(e) The equation can be rewritten using a single sum and the concept of flows (Ak), which will be positive or negative, in other words either paid or received during periods 1 to k, expressed in years, i.e.:

$$S = \sum_{k=1}^{n} A_k(1+X)^{-t_k},$$

S being the present balance of flows. If the aim is to maintain the equivalence of flows, the value will be zero.

II. Additional assumptions for the calculation of the annual percentage rate of charge

(a) if a credit agreement gives the consumer freedom of drawdown, the total amount of credit shall be deemed to be drawn down immediately and in full;

(b) if a credit agreement provides different ways of drawdown with different charges or borrowing rates, the total amount of credit shall be deemed to be drawn down at the highest charge and borrowing rate applied to the most common drawdown mechanism for this type of credit agreement;

(c) if a credit agreement gives the consumer freedom of drawdown in general but imposes, amongst the different ways of drawdown, a limitation with regard to the amount and period of time, the amount of credit shall be deemed to be drawn down on the earliest date provided for in the agreement and in accordance with those drawdown limits;

(d) if there is no fixed timetable for repayment, it shall be assumed:

  (i) that the credit is provided for a period of one year; and

  (ii) that the credit will be repaid in 12 equal instalments and at monthly intervals;

(e) if there is a fixed timetable for repayment but the amount of such repayments is flexible, the amount of each repayment shall be deemed to be the lowest for which the agreement provides;

(f) unless otherwise specified, where the credit agreement provides for more than one repayment date, the credit is to be made available and the repayments made on the earliest date provided for in the agreement;

(g) if the ceiling applicable to the credit has not yet been agreed, that ceiling is assumed to be EUR 1500;

(h) in the case of an overdraft facility the total amount of credit shall be deemed to be drawn down in full and for the whole duration of the credit agreement. If the duration of the credit agreement is not known the annual percentage rate of charge shall be calculated on the assumption that the duration of the credit is three months;

(i) if different interest rates and charges are offered for a limited period or amount, the interest rate and the charges shall be deemed to be the highest rate for the whole duration of the credit agreement;

(j) for consumer credit agreements for which a fixed borrowing rate is agreed in relation to the initial period, at the end of which a new borrowing rate is determined and subsequently periodically adjusted according to an agreed indicator, the calculation of the annual percentage rate shall be based on the assumption that, at the end of the fixed borrowing rate period, the borrowing rate is the same as at the time of calculating the annual percentage rate, based on the value of the agreed indicator at that time.

ANNEX II
STANDARD EUROPEAN CONSUMER CREDIT INFORMATION

1. Identity and contact details of the creditor/credit intermediary

Creditor Address Telephone number [*] E-mail address [*] Fax number [*] Web address [*]	[Identity] [Geographical address to be used by the consumer]
If applicable Credit intermediary Address Telephone number [*] E-mail address [*] Fax number [*] Web address [*]	 [Identity] [Geographical address to be used by the consumer]

Wherever "if applicable" is indicated, the creditor must fill in the box if the information is relevant to the credit product or delete the respective information or the entire row if the information is not relevant for the type of credit considered.

Indications between square brackets provide explanations for the creditor and must be replaced with the corresponding information.

2. Description of the main features of the credit product

The type of credit	
The total amount of credit This means the ceiling or the total sums made available under the credit agreement	
The conditions governing the drawdown This means how and when you will obtain the money.	
The duration of the credit agreement	
Instalments and, where appropriate, the order in which instalments will be allocated	You will have to pay the following: [The amount, number and frequency of payments to be made by the consumer] Interest and/or charges will be payable in the following manner

The total amount you will have to pay This means the amount of borrowed capital plus interest and possible costs related to your credit.	[Sum of total amount of credit and total cost of credit]
If applicable The credit is granted in the form of a deferred payment for a good or service or is linked to the supply of specific goods or the provision of a service Name of good/service Cash price	
If applicable Sureties required This is a description of the security to be provided by you in relation to the credit agreement.	[Kind of sureties]
If applicable Repayments do not give rise to immediate amortisation of the capital.	

3. Costs of the credit

The borrowing rate or, if applicable, different borrowing rates which apply to the credit agreement	[% fixed or, variable (with the index or reference rate applicable to the initial borrowing rate), periods],
Annual Percentage Rate of Charge (APR) This is the total cost expressed as an annual percentage of the total amount of credit. The APR is there to help you compare different offers.	[% A representative example mentioning all the assumptions used for calculating the rate to be set out here]
Is it compulsory, in order to obtain the credit or to obtain it on the terms and conditions marketed, to take out an insurance policy securing the credit, or another ancillary service contract If the costs of these services are not	Yes/no [if yes, specify the kind of insurance] Yes/no [if yes, specify the kind of

known by the creditor they are not included in the APR	ancillary service]
Related costs	
If applicable Maintaining one or more accounts is required for recording both payment transactions and drawdowns	
If applicable Amount of costs for using a specific means of payment (e.g. a credit card)	
If applicable Any other costs deriving from the credit agreement	
If applicable Conditions under which the abovementioned costs related to the credit agreement can be changed	
If applicable Conditions under which the abovementioned costs related to the credit agreement can be changed	
If applicable Obligation to pay notarial fees	
Costs in the case of late payments Missing payments could have severe consequences for you (e.g. forced sale) and make obtaining credit more difficult. |	You will be charged [...... (applicable interest rate and arrangements for its adjustment and, where applicable, default charges)] for late payments.

4. Other important legal aspects

Right of withdrawal *You have the right to withdraw from the credit agreement within a period of 14 calendar days.*	Yes/no
Early repayment *You have the right to repay the credit early at any time in full or partially.*	

If applicable The creditor is entitled to compensation in the case of early repayment	[Determination of the compensation (calculation method) in accordance with the provisions implementing Article 16 of Directive 2008/48/EC]
Consultation of a database *The creditor must inform you immediately and without charge of the result of a consultation of a database, if a credit application is rejected on the basis of such a consultation. This does not apply if the provision of such information is prohibited by European Community law or is contrary to objectives of public policy or public security.*	
Right to a draft credit agreement *You have the right, upon request, to obtain a copy of the draft credit agreement free of charge. This provision does not apply if the creditor is at the time of the request unwilling to proceed to the conclusion of the credit agreement with you.*	
If applicable The period of time during which the creditor is bound by the pre-contractual information	This information is valid from … until …

If applicable

5. Additional information in the case of distance marketing of financial services

(a)concerning the creditor	
If applicable Representative of the creditor in your Member State of residence Address Telephone number [**] E-mail address [**] Fax number [**] Web address [**]	[Identity] [Geographical address to be used by the consumer]
If applicable Registration	[The trade register in which the creditor

	is entered and his registration number or an equivalent means of identification in that register]
If applicable The supervisory authority	
(b)concerning the credit agreement	
If applicable Exercise of the right of withdrawal	[Practical instructions for exercising the right of withdrawal indicating, inter alia, the period for exercising the right, the address to which notification of exercise of the right of withdrawal should be sent and the consequences of non-exercise of that right]
If applicable The law taken by the creditor as a basis for the establishment of relations with you before the conclusion of the credit contract	
If applicable Clause stipulating the governing law applicable to the credit agreement and/or the competent court	[Relevant clause to be set out here]
If applicable Language regime	Information and contractual terms will be supplied in [specific language]. With your consent, we intend to communicate in [specific language/languages] during the duration of the credit agreement.
(c)concerning redress	
Existence of and access to out-of-court complaint and redress mechanism	[Whether or not there is an out-of-court complaint and redress mechanism for the consumer who is party to the distance contract and, if so, the methods of access to it]

[*] This information is optional for the creditor.

[**] This information is optional for the creditor.

ANNEX III

EUROPEAN CONSUMER CREDIT INFORMATION FOR

(1) overdrafts

(2) consumer credit offered by certain credit organisations (Article 2(5) of Directive 2008/48/EC)

(3) debt conversion

1. Identity and contact details of the creditor/credit intermediary

Creditor Address Telephone number [*] E-mail address [*] Fax number [*] Web address [*]	[Identity] [Geographical address to be used by the consumer]
If applicable Credit intermediary Address Telephone number [*] E-mail address [*] Fax number [*] Web address [*]	 [Identity] [Geographical address to be used by the consumer]

Wherever "if applicable" is indicated, the creditor must fill in the box if the information is relevant to the credit product or delete the respective information or the entire row if the information is not relevant for the type of credit considered.

Indications between square brackets provide explanations for the creditor and must be replaced with the corresponding information.

2. Description of the main features of the credit product

The type of credit	
The total amount of credit This means the ceiling or the total sums made available under the credit agreement.	
The duration of the credit agreement	
If applicable You may be requested to repay the amount of credit in full on demand at any time.	

3. Costs of the credit

The borrowing rate or, if applicable, different borrowing rates which apply to the credit agreement	[% fixed or, variable (with the index or reference rate applicable to the initial borrowing rate)],
If applicable The annual percentage rate of charge (APR) [**] This is the total cost of credit expressed as an annual percentage of the total amount of credit. The APR is there to help you compare different offers.	[% A representative example mentioning all the assumptions used for calculating the rate to be set out here]
If applicable Costs If applicable The conditions under which those costs may be changed	[The costs applicable from the time the credit agreement is concluded]
Costs in the case of late payments	You will be charged [...... (applicable interest rate and arrangements for its adjustment and, where applicable, default charges)] for late payments.

4. Other important legal aspects

Termination of the credit agreement	[The conditions and procedure for terminating the credit agreement]
Consultation of a database The creditor must inform you immediately and without charge of the result of a consultation of a database if a credit application is rejected on the basis of such a consultation. This does not apply if the provision of such information is prohibited by European Community law or is contrary to objectives of public policy or public security.	
If applicable The period of time during which the creditor is bound by the pre-contractual information	This information is valid from … until…

If applicable

5. Additional information to be given where the pre-contractual information is provided by certain credit organisations (Article 2(5) of Directive 2008/48/EC or relates to a consumer credit for debt conversion

Instalments and, where appropriate, the order in which instalments will be allocated	You will have to pay the following: [Representative example of an instalment table including the amount, number and frequency of payments to be made by the consumer]
The total amount you will have to pay	
Early repayment You have the right to repay the credit early at any time in full or partially. If applicable	
The creditor is entitled to compensation in the case of early repayment	[Determination of the compensation (calculation method) in accordance with the provisions implementing Article 16 of Directive 2008/48/EC]

If applicable

6. Additional information to be given in the case of distance marketing of financial services

(a)concerning the creditor	
If applicable Representative of the creditor in your Member State of residence Address Telephone number [***] E-mail address [***] Fax number [***] Web address [***]	 [Identity] [Geographical address to be used by the consumer]
If applicable Registration	 [The trade register in which the creditor is entered and his registration number or an equivalent means of identification in that register]
If applicable The supervisory authority	
(b)concerning the credit agreement	
Right of withdrawal You have the right to withdraw from the credit agreement within a period of 14 calendar days. If applicable Exercise of the right of withdrawal	Yes/no
If applicable The law taken by the creditor as a basis for the establishment of relations with you before the conclusion of the credit contract	
If applicable Clause stipulating the law applicable to the credit agreement and/or the competent court	 [Relevant clause to be set out here]
If applicable	

Language regime	Information and contractual terms will be supplied in [specific language]. With your consent, we intend to communicate in [specific language/languages] during the duration of the credit agreement.
(c)concerning redress	
Existence of and access to out-of-court complaint and redress mechanism	[Whether or not there is an out-of-court complaint and redress mechanism for the consumer who is party to the distance contract and, if so, the methods of access to it]

[*] This information is optional for the creditor.

[**] Not applicable to European Consumer Credit Information for overdrafts in those Member States which decide on the basis of Article 6(2) of Directive 2008/48/EC that the APR need not be provided for overdrafts.

[***] This information is optional for the creditor.

18. Directive 2008/122/EC of the European Parliament and of the Council of 14 January 2009 on the protection of consumers in respect of certain aspects of timeshare, long-term holiday product, resale and exchange contracts Text with EEA relevance

(OJ L 033 , 03/02/2009 p. 10 – 30)

THE EUROPEAN PARLIAMENT AND THE COUNCIL OF THE EUROPEAN UNION,

Having regard to the Treaty establishing the European Community, and in particular Article 95 thereof,

Having regard to the proposal from the Commission,

Having regard to the opinion of the European Economic and Social Committee[1],

Acting in accordance with the procedure laid down in Article 251 of the Treaty[2],

Whereas:

(1) Since the adoption of Directive 94/47/EC of the European Parliament and of the Council of 26 October 1994 on the protection of purchasers in respect of certain aspects of contracts relating to the purchase of the right to use immovable properties on a timeshare basis[3], timeshare has evolved and new holiday products similar to it have appeared on the market. These new holiday products and certain transactions related to timeshare, such as resale contracts and exchange contracts, are not covered by Directive 94/47/EC. In addition, experience with the application of Directive 94/47/EC has shown that some subjects already covered need to be updated or clarified, in order to prevent the development of products aiming at circumventing this Directive.

(2) The existing regulatory gaps create appreciable distortions of competition and cause serious problems for consumers, thus hindering the smooth functioning of the internal market. Directive 94/47/EC should therefore be replaced by a new up-to-date directive. Since tourism plays an increasingly important role in the economies of the Member States, greater growth and productivity in the timeshare and long-term holiday product industries should be encouraged by adopting certain common rules.

(3) In order to enhance legal certainty and fully achieve the benefits of the internal market for consumers and businesses, the relevant laws of the Member States need to be approximated further. Therefore, certain aspects of the marketing, sale and resale of timeshares and long-term holiday products as well as the exchange of rights deriving from timeshare contracts should be fully harmonised. Member States should not be allowed to maintain or introduce in

[1] OJ C 44, 16.2.2008, p. 27.

[2] Opinion of the European Parliament of 22 October 2008 (not yet published in the Official Journal) and Council Decision of 18 December 2008.

[3] OJ L 280, 29.10.1994, p. 83.

their national legislation provisions diverging from those laid down in this Directive. Where no such harmonised provisions exist, Member States should remain free to maintain or introduce national legislation in conformity with Community law. Thus, Member States should, for instance, be able to maintain or introduce provisions on the effects of exercising the right of withdrawal in legal relationships falling outside the scope of this Directive or provisions according to which no commitment may be entered into between a consumer and a trader of a timeshare or long-term holiday product, nor any payment made between those persons, as long as the consumer has not signed a credit agreement to finance the purchase of those services.

(4) This Directive should be without prejudice to the application by Member States, in accordance with Community law, of the provisions of this Directive to areas not within its scope. Member States could therefore maintain or introduce national legislation corresponding to the provisions of this Directive or certain of its provisions in relation to transactions that fall outside the scope of this Directive.

(5) The different contracts covered by this Directive should be clearly defined in such a way as to preclude circumvention of its provisions.

(6) For the purposes of this Directive, timeshare contracts should not be understood as covering multiple reservations of accommodation, including hotel rooms, in so far as multiple reservations do not imply rights and obligations beyond those arising from separate reservations. Nor should timeshare contracts be understood as covering ordinary lease contracts since the latter refer to one single continuous period of occupation and not to multiple periods.

(7) For the purposes of this Directive, long-term holiday product contracts should not be understood as covering ordinary loyalty schemes which provide discounts on future stays in the hotels of a hotel chain, since membership in the scheme is not obtained for consideration nor is the consideration paid by the consumer primarily for the purpose of obtaining discounts or other benefits in respect of accommodation.

(8) This Directive should not affect the provisions of Council Directive 90/314/EEC of 13 June 1990 on package travel, package holidays and package tours [1].

(9) Directive 2005/29/EC of the European Parliament and of the Council of 11 May 2005 concerning unfair business-to-consumer commercial practices in the internal market (Unfair Commercial Practices Directive)[2] prohibits misleading, aggressive and other unfair commercial business-to-consumer practices. Given the nature of the products and the commercial practices related to timeshares, long-term holiday products, resale and exchange, it is appropriate to adopt more detailed and specific provisions regarding information requirements and sales events. The commercial purpose of invitations to sales events should be made

---

1 OJ L 158, 23.6.1990, p. 59.

2 OJ L 149, 11.6.2005, p. 22.

clear to consumers. The provisions concerning pre-contractual information and the contract should be clarified and updated. In order to give consumers the possibility to acquaint themselves with the information before the conclusion of the contract, it should be provided by means which are easily accessible to them at that time.

(10) Consumers should have the right, which should not be refused by traders, to be provided with pre-contractual information and the contract in a language, of their choice, with which they are familiar. In addition, in order to facilitate the execution and the enforcement of the contract, Member States should be allowed to determine that further language versions of the contract should be provided to consumers.

(11) In order to provide consumers with the opportunity of fully understanding their rights and obligations under the contract, they should be allowed a period during which they may withdraw from the contract without having to justify the withdrawal and without bearing any cost. Currently the length of this period varies between Member States, and experience shows that the length prescribed in Directive 94/47/EC is not sufficiently long. The period should therefore be extended in order to achieve a high level of consumer protection and more clarity for consumers and traders. The length of the period, the modalities for and the effects of exercising the right of withdrawal should be harmonised.

(12) Consumers should have effective remedies in the event that traders do not comply with the provisions regarding pre-contractual information or the contract, in particular those laying down that the contract should include all the information required and that the consumer should receive a copy of the contract at the time of its conclusion. In addition to the remedies existing under national law, consumers should benefit from an extended withdrawal period where information has not been provided by traders. The exercise of the right of withdrawal should remain free of charge during that extended period regardless of what services consumers may have enjoyed. The expiration of the withdrawal period does not preclude consumers from seeking remedies in accordance with national law for breaches of the information requirements.

(13) Council Regulation (EEC, Euratom) No 1182/71 of 3 June 1971 determining the rules applicable to periods, dates and time limits[1] should apply to the calculation of the periods set out in this Directive.

(14) The prohibition on advance payments to traders or any third party before the end of the withdrawal period should be clarified in order to improve consumer protection. For resale contracts, the prohibition of advance payment should apply until the actual sale takes place or the resale contract is terminated, but Member States should remain free to regulate the possibility and modalities of final payments to intermediaries where resale contracts are terminated.

(15) For long-term holiday product contracts, the price to be paid in the context of a staggered payment schedule could take into consideration the possibility that

[1] OJ L 124, 8.6.1971, p. 1.

subsequent amounts could be adjusted after the first year in order to ensure that the real value of those instalments is maintained, for instance to take account of inflation.

(16) In the event of a consumer withdrawing from a contract where the price is entirely or partly covered by credit granted to the consumer by the trader or by a third party on the basis of an arrangement between that third party and the trader, the credit agreement should be terminated at no cost to the consumer. The same should apply to contracts for other related services provided by the trader or by a third party on the basis of an arrangement between that third party and the trader.

(17) Consumers should not be deprived of the protection granted by this Directive where the law applicable to the contract is that of a Member State. The law applicable to a contract should be determined in accordance with the Community rules on private international law, in particular Regulation (EC) No 593/2008 of the European Parliament and of the Council of 17 June 2008 on the law applicable to contractual obligations (Rome I)[1]. Under that Regulation, the law of a third country may be applicable, in particular where consumers are targeted by traders whilst on holiday in a country other than their country of residence. Given that such commercial practices are common in the area covered by this Directive and that the contracts involve considerable amounts of money, an additional safeguard should be provided in certain specific situations, in particular where the courts of any Member State have jurisdiction over the contract, to ensure that the consumer is not deprived of the protection granted by this Directive. This concept reflects the particular needs of consumer protection arising from the typical complexity, long-term nature and financial relevance of the contracts falling within the scope of this Directive.

(18) It should be determined in accordance with Council Regulation (EC) No 44/2001 of 22 December 2000 on jurisdiction and the recognition and enforcement of judgments in civil and commercial matters[2] which courts have jurisdiction in proceedings which have as their object matters covered by this Directive.

(19) In order to ensure that the protection afforded to consumers under this Directive is fully effective, in particular as regards compliance by traders with the information requirements both at the pre-contractual stage and in the contract, it is necessary that the Member States lay down effective, proportionate and dissuasive penalties for infringements of this Directive.

(20) It is necessary to ensure that persons or organisations having, under national law, a legitimate interest in the matter have legal remedies for initiating proceedings against infringements of this Directive.

(21) It is necessary to develop suitable and effective redress procedures in the Member States for settling disputes between consumers and traders. To this end,

1 OJ L 177, 4.7.2008, p. 6.
2 OJ L 12, 16.1.2001, p. 1.

Member States should encourage the establishment of public or private bodies for settling disputes out of court.

(22) Member States should ensure that consumers are effectively informed of the national provisions transposing this Directive and encourage traders and code owners to inform consumers about their codes of conduct in this field. With the aim of pursuing a high level of consumer protection, consumer organisations could be informed of, and involved in, the drafting of codes of conduct.

(23) Since the objectives of this Directive cannot be sufficiently achieved by the Member States and can therefore be better achieved at Community level, the Community may adopt measures in accordance with the principle of subsidiarity as set out in Article 5 of the Treaty. In accordance with the principle of proportionality, as set out in that Article, this Directive does not go beyond what is necessary in order to eliminate the internal market barriers and achieve a high common level of consumer protection.

(24) This Directive respects the fundamental rights and observes the principles recognised in particular by the European Convention on Human Rights and Fundamental Freedoms and the Charter of Fundamental Rights of the European Union.

(25) In accordance with point 34 of the Interinstitutional agreement on better law-making[1], Member States are encouraged to draw up, for themselves and in the interests of the Community, their own tables, which will, as far as possible, illustrate the correlation between this Directive and the transposition measures, and to make them public,

HAVE ADOPTED THIS DIRECTIVE:

Article 1 Purpose and scope

1. The purpose of this Directive is to contribute to the proper functioning of the internal market and to achieve a high level of consumer protection, by approximating the laws, regulations and administrative provisions of the Member States in respect of certain aspects of the marketing, sale and resale of timeshares and long-term holiday products as well as exchange contracts.
2. This Directive applies to trader-to-consumer transactions.

   This Directive is without prejudice to national legislation which:

   (a) provides for general contract law remedies;

   (b) relates to the registration of immovable or movable property and conveyance of immovable property;

   (c) relates to conditions of establishment or authorisation regimes or licensing requirements; and

   (d) relates to the determination of the legal nature of the rights which are the subject of the contracts covered by this Directive.

[1] OJ C 321, 31.12.2003, p. 1.

Article 2 Definitions

1. For the purposes of this Directive, the following definitions shall apply:
   (a) "timeshare contract" means a contract of a duration of more than one year under which a consumer, for consideration, acquires the right to use one or more overnight accommodation for more than one period of occupation;
   (b) "long-term holiday product contract" means a contract of a duration of more than one year under which a consumer, for consideration, acquires primarily the right to obtain discounts or other benefits in respect of accommodation, in isolation or together with travel or other services;
   (c) "resale contract" means a contract under which a trader, for consideration, assists a consumer to sell or buy a timeshare or a long-term holiday product;
   (d) "exchange contract" means a contract under which a consumer, for consideration, joins an exchange system which allows that consumer access to overnight accommodation or other services in exchange for granting to other persons temporary access to the benefits of the rights deriving from that consumer's timeshare contract;
   (e) "trader" means a natural or legal person who is acting for purposes relating to that person's trade, business, craft or profession and anyone acting in the name of or on behalf of a trader;
   (f) "consumer" means a natural person who is acting for purposes which are outside that person's trade, business, craft or profession;
   (g) "ancillary contract" means a contract under which the consumer acquires services which are related to a timeshare contract or long-term holiday product contract and which are provided by the trader or a third party on the basis of an arrangement between that third party and the trader;
   (h) "durable medium" means any instrument which enables the consumer or the trader to store information addressed personally to him in a way which is accessible for future reference for a period of time adequate for the purposes of the information and which allows the unchanged reproduction of the information stored;
   (i) "code of conduct" means an agreement or set of rules not imposed by law, regulation or administrative provision of a Member State which defines the behaviour of traders who undertake to be bound by the code in relation to one or more particular commercial practices or business sectors;
   (j) "code owner" means any entity, including a trader or group of traders, which is responsible for the formulation and revision of a code of conduct and/or for monitoring compliance with the code by those who have undertaken to be bound by it.
2. In calculating the duration of a timeshare contract or a long-term holiday product contract, as defined in points (a) and (b) of paragraph 1 respectively, any provision in the contract allowing for tacit renewal or prolongation shall be taken into account.

Article 3 Advertising

1. Member States shall ensure that any advertising specifies the possibility of obtaining the information referred to in Article 4(1) and indicates where it can be obtained.
2. Where a timeshare, long-term holiday product, resale or exchange contract is to be offered to a consumer in person at a promotion or sales event, the trader shall clearly indicate in the invitation the commercial purpose and the nature of the event.
3. The information referred to in Article 4(1) shall be available to the consumer at any time during the event.
4. A timeshare or a long-term holiday product shall not be marketed or sold as an investment.

Article 4 Pre-contractual information

1. In good time before the consumer is bound by any contract or offer, the trader shall provide the consumer, in a clear and comprehensible manner, with accurate and sufficient information, as follows:
   (a) in the case of a timeshare contract: by means of the standard information form as set out in Annex I and information as listed in Part 3 of that form;
   (b) in the case of a long-term holiday product contract: by means of the standard information form as set out in Annex II and information as listed in Part 3 of that form;
   (c) in the case of a resale contract: by means of the standard information form as set out in Annex III and information as listed in Part 3 of that form;
   (d) in the case of an exchange contract: by means of the standard information form as set out in Annex IV and information as listed in Part 3 of that form.
2. The information referred to in paragraph 1 shall be provided, free of charge, by the trader on paper or on another durable medium which is easily accessible to the consumer.
3. Member States shall ensure that the information referred to in paragraph 1 is drawn up in the language or one of the languages of the Member State in which the consumer is resident or a national, at the choice of the consumer, provided it is an official language of the Community.

Article 5 The timeshare, long-term holiday product, resale or exchange contract

1. Member States shall ensure that the contract is in writing, on paper or on another durable medium, and drawn up in the language or one of the languages of the Member State in which the consumer is resident or a national, at the choice of the consumer, provided it is an official language of the Community.

   However, the Member State in which the consumer is resident may require that in addition:

(a) in every instance, the contract be provided to the consumer in the language or one of the languages of that Member State, provided it is an official language of the Community;

(b) in the case of a timeshare contract concerning one specific immovable property, the trader provide the consumer with a certified translation of the contract in the language or one of the languages of the Member State in which the property is situated, provided it is an official language of the Community.

The Member State on whose territory the trader carries out sale activities may require that, in every instance, the contract be provided to the consumer in the language or one of the languages of that Member State, provided it is an official language of the Community.

2. The information referred to in Article 4(1) shall form an integral part of the contract and shall not be altered unless the parties expressly agree otherwise or the changes result from unusual and unforeseeable circumstances beyond the trader's control, the consequences of which could not have been avoided even if all due care had been exercised.

These changes shall be communicated to the consumer on paper or on another durable medium easily accessible to him, before the contract is concluded.

The contract shall expressly mention any such changes.

3. In addition to the information referred to in Article 4(1), the contract shall include:

(a) the identity, place of residence and signature of each of the parties; and

(b) the date and place of the conclusion of the contract.

4. Before the conclusion of the contract, the trader shall explicitly draw the consumer's attention to the existence of the right of withdrawal, the length of the withdrawal period referred to in Article 6, and the ban on advance payments during the withdrawal period referred to in Article 9.

The corresponding contractual clauses shall be signed separately by the consumer.

The contract shall include a separate standard withdrawal form, as set out in Annex V, intended to facilitate the exercise of the right of withdrawal in accordance with Article 6.

5. The consumer shall receive a copy or copies of the contract at the time of its conclusion.

Article 6 Right of withdrawal

1. In addition to the remedies available to the consumer under national law in the event of breach of the provisions of this Directive, Member States shall ensure that the consumer is given a period of 14 calendar days to withdraw from the timeshare, long-term holiday product, resale or exchange contract, without giving any reason.

2. The withdrawal period shall be calculated:

(a) from the day of the conclusion of the contract or of any binding preliminary contract; or

(b) from the day when the consumer receives the contract or any binding preliminary contract if it is later than the date referred to in point (a).

3. The withdrawal period shall expire:

(a) after one year and 14 calendar days from the day referred to in paragraph 2 of this Article, where a separate standard withdrawal form as required by Article 5(4) has not been filled in by the trader and provided to the consumer in writing, on paper or on another durable medium;

(b) after three months and 14 calendar days from the day referred to in paragraph 2 of this Article, where the information referred to in Article 4(1), including the applicable standard information form set out in Annexes I to IV, has not been provided to the consumer in writing, on paper or on another durable medium.

In addition, Member States shall provide for appropriate penalties in accordance with Article 15, in particular in the event that, on expiry of the withdrawal period, the trader has failed to comply with the information requirements set out in this Directive.

4. Where a separate standard withdrawal form as required by Article 5(4) has been filled in by the trader and provided to the consumer in writing, on paper or on another durable medium, within one year from the day referred to in paragraph 2 of this Article, the withdrawal period shall start from the day the consumer receives that form. Similarly, where the information referred to in Article 4(1), including the applicable standard information form set out in Annexes I to IV, has been provided to the consumer in writing, on paper or on another durable medium, within three months from the day referred to in paragraph 2 of this Article, the withdrawal period shall start from the day the consumer receives such information.

5. In the event that the exchange contract is offered to the consumer together with and at the same time as the timeshare contract, only a single withdrawal period in accordance with paragraph 1 shall apply to both contracts. The withdrawal period for both contracts shall be calculated according to the provisions of paragraph 2 as they apply to the timeshare contract.

Article 7 Modalities for exercising the right of withdrawal

Where the consumer intends to exercise the right of withdrawal the consumer shall, before the expiry of the withdrawal period, notify the trader on paper or on another durable medium of the decision to withdraw. The consumer may use the standard withdrawal form set out in Annex V and provided by the trader in accordance with Article 5(4). The deadline is met if the notification is sent before the withdrawal period has expired.

Article 8 **Effects of exercising the right of withdrawal**

1. The exercise of the right of withdrawal by the consumer terminates the obligation of the parties to perform the contract.
2. Where the consumer exercises the right of withdrawal, the consumer shall neither bear any cost nor be liable for any value corresponding to the service which may have been performed before withdrawal.

Article 9 **Advance payment**

1. Member States shall ensure that in relation to timeshare, long-term holiday product and exchange contracts any advance payment, provision of guarantees, reservation of money on accounts, explicit acknowledgement of debt or any other consideration to the trader or to any third party by the consumer before the end of the withdrawal period according to Article 6, is prohibited.
2. Member States shall ensure that in relation to resale contracts any advance payment, provision of guarantees, reservation of money on accounts, explicit acknowledgement of debt or any other consideration to the trader or to any third party by the consumer before the actual sale takes place or the resale contract is otherwise terminated, is prohibited.

Article 10 **Specific provisions relating to long-term holiday product contracts**

1. For long-term holiday product contracts, payment shall be made according to a staggered payment schedule. Any payment of the price specified in the contract otherwise than in accordance with the staggered payment schedule shall be prohibited. The payments, including any membership fee, shall be divided into yearly instalments, each of which shall be of equal value. The trader shall send a written request for payment, on paper or on another durable medium, at least fourteen calendar days in advance of each due date.
2. From the second instalment payment onwards, the consumer may terminate the contract without incurring any penalty by giving notice to the trader within fourteen calendar days of receiving the request for payment of each instalment. This right shall not affect rights to terminate the contract under existing national legislation.

Article 11 **Termination of ancillary contracts**

1. Member States shall ensure that, where the consumer exercises the right to withdraw from the timeshare or long-term holiday product contract, any exchange contract ancillary to it or any other ancillary contract is automatically terminated, at no cost to the consumer.
2. Without prejudice to Article 15 of Directive 2008/48/EC of the European Parliament and of the Council of 23 April 2008 on credit agreements for consumers[1], where the price is fully or partly covered by a credit granted to the

[1] OJ L 133, 22.5.2008, p. 66.

consumer by the trader, or by a third party on the basis of an arrangement between the third party and the trader, the credit agreement shall be terminated, at no cost to the consumer, where the consumer exercises the right to withdraw from the timeshare, long-term holiday product, resale or exchange contract.

3. The Member States shall lay down detailed rules on the termination of such contracts.

Article 12 Imperative nature of the Directive and application in international cases

1. Member States shall ensure that, where the law applicable to the contract is the law of a Member State, consumers may not waive the rights conferred on them by this Directive.
2. Where the applicable law is that of a third country, consumers shall not be deprived of the protection granted by this Directive, as implemented in the Member State of the forum if:

Article 13 Judicial and administrative redress

1. Member States shall ensure that, in the interests of consumers, adequate and effective means exist to ensure compliance by traders with this Directive.
2. The means referred to in paragraph 1 shall include provisions whereby one or more of the following bodies, as determined by national law, shall be entitled to take action in accordance with national law before the courts or competent administrative bodies to ensure that the national provisions for implementing this Directive are applied:
   (a) public bodies and authorities or their representatives;
   (b) consumer organisations with a legitimate interest in protecting consumers;
   (c) professional organisations with a legitimate interest in taking such action.

Article 14 Consumer information and out-of-court redress

1. Member States shall take appropriate measures to inform consumers of the national law transposing this Directive and shall encourage, where appropriate, traders and code owners to inform consumers of their codes of conduct.

   The Commission shall encourage the drawing up at Community level, particularly by professional bodies, organisations and associations, of codes of conduct aimed at facilitating the implementation of this Directive, in conformity with Community law. It shall also encourage traders and their branch organisations to inform consumers of any such codes, including, where appropriate, by means of a specific marking.
2. Member States shall encourage the setting up or development of adequate and effective out-of-court complaints and redress procedures for the settlement of consumer disputes under this Directive and shall, where appropriate, encourage traders and their branch organisations to inform consumers of the availability of such procedures.

Article 15 Penalties

1. Member States shall provide for appropriate penalties in the event of a trader's failure to comply with the national provisions adopted pursuant to this Directive.
2. Those penalties shall be effective, proportionate and dissuasive.

Article 16 Transposition

1. Member States shall adopt and publish, by 23 February 2011, the laws, regulations and administrative provisions necessary to comply with this Directive. They shall forthwith communicate to the Commission the text of those provisions.

   They shall apply those provisions from 23 February 2011.

   When Member States adopt those provisions, they shall contain a reference to this Directive or be accompanied by such a reference on the occasion of their official publication. Member States shall determine how such reference is to be made.
2. Member States shall communicate to the Commission the text of the main provisions of national law which they adopt in the field covered by this Directive.

Article 17 Review

The Commission shall review this Directive and report to the European Parliament and the Council no later than 23 February 2014.

If necessary, it shall make further proposals to adapt it to developments in the area.

The Commission may request information from the Member States and the national regulatory authorities.

Article 18 Repeal

Directive 94/47/EC shall be repealed.

References to the repealed Directive shall be construed as references to this Directive and shall be read in accordance with the correlation table in Annex VI.

Article 19 Entry into force

This Directive shall enter into force on the 20th day following its publication in the Official Journal of the European Union.

Article 20 Addressees

This Directive is addressed to the Member States.

Done at Strasbourg, 14 January 2009.

For the European Parliament

The President

H.-G. Pöttering

For the Council

The President

A. Vondra

ANNEX I

STANDARD INFORMATION FORM FOR TIMESHARE CONTRACTS

PART 1:

Identity, place of residence and legal status of the trader(s) which will be party to the contract
Short description of the product (e.g. description of the immovable property): Exact nature and content of the right(s):
Exact period within which the right which is the subject of the contract may be exercised and, if necessary, its duration: Date on which the consumer may start to exercise the contractual right: If the contract concerns a specific property under construction, date when the accommodation and services/facilities will be completed/available:
Price to be paid by the consumer for acquiring the right(s): Outline of additional obligatory costs imposed under the contract; type of costs and indication of amounts (e.g. annual fees, other recurrent fees, special levies, local taxes):
A summary of key services available to the consumer (e.g. electricity, water, maintenance refuse collection) and an indication of the amount to be paid by the consumer for such services: A summary of facilities available to the consumer (e.g. swimming pool or sauna): Are these facilities included in the costs indicated above? If not, specify what is included and what has to be paid for:
Is it possible to join an exchange scheme? If yes, specify the name of the exchange scheme: Indication of costs for membership/exchange:
Has the trader signed a code/codes of conduct and, if yes, where can it/they be found?

PART 2:

General information: - The consumer has the right to withdraw from this contract without giving any reason within 14 calendar days from the conclusion of the contract or any binding preliminary contract or receipt of those contracts if that takes place later. - During this withdrawal period, any advance payment by the consumer is prohibited. The prohibition concerns any consideration, including payment, provision of guarantees, reservation of money on accounts, explicit

acknowledgement of debt etc. It includes not only payment to the trader, but also to third parties.

- The consumer shall not bear any costs or obligations other than those specified in the contract.

- In accordance with international private law, the contract may be governed by a law other than the law of the Member State in which the consumer is resident or is habitually domiciled and possible disputes may be referred to courts other than those of the Member State in which the consumer is resident or is habitually domiciled.

Signature of the consumer:

PART 3:

Additional information to which the consumer is entitled and where it can be obtained specifically (for instance, under which chapter of a general brochure) if not provided below:

1. INFORMATION ABOUT THE RIGHTS ACQUIRED

- conditions governing the exercise of the right which is the subject of the contract within the territory of the Member States(s) in which the property or properties concerned are situated and information on whether those conditions have been fulfilled or, if they have not, what conditions remain to be fulfilled,

- where the contract provides rights to occupy accommodation to be selected from a pool of accommodation, information on restrictions on the consumer's ability to use any accommodation in the pool at any time.

2. INFORMATION ON THE PROPERTIES

- where the contract concerns a specific immovable property, an accurate and detailed description of that property and its location; where the contract concerns a number of properties (multi-resorts), an appropriate description of the properties and their location; where the contract concerns accommodation other than immovable property, an appropriate description of the accommodation and the facilities,

- the services (e.g. electricity, water, maintenance, refuse collection) to which the consumer has or will have access to and under what conditions,

- where applicable, the common facilities, such as swimming pool, sauna, etc., to which the consumer has or may have access and under what conditions.

3. ADDITIONAL REQUIREMENTS FOR ACCOMMODATION UNDER CONSTRUCTION (where applicable)

- the state of completion of the accommodation and of the services rendering the accommodation fully operational (gas, electricity, water and telephone connections) and any facilities to which the consumer will have access,

- the deadline for completion of the accommodation and of the services rendering it fully operational (gas, electricity, water and telephone connections) and a reasonable estimate of the deadline for the completion of any facilities to which the consumer will have access,

- the number of the building permit and the name(s) and full address(es) of the competent authority or authorities,

- a guarantee regarding completion of the accommodation or a guarantee regarding reimbursement of any payment made if the accommodation is not completed and, where appropriate, the conditions governing the operation of such guarantees.

4. INFORMATION ON THE COSTS

- an accurate and appropriate description of all costs associated with the timeshare contract; how these costs will be allocated to the consumer and how and when such costs may be increased; the method for the calculation of the amount of charges relating to occupation of the property, the mandatory statutory charges (for example, taxes and fees) and the administrative overheads (for example, management, maintenance and repairs),

- where applicable, information on whether there are any charges, mortgages, encumbrances or any other liens recorded against title to the accommodation.

5. INFORMATION ON TERMINATION OF THE CONTRACT

- where appropriate, information on the arrangements for the termination of ancillary contracts and the consequences of such termination,

- conditions for terminating the contract, the consequences of termination, and information on any liability of the consumer for any costs which might result from such termination.

6. ADDITIONAL INFORMATION

- information on how maintenance and repairs of the property and its administration and management are arranged, including whether and how consumers may influence and participate in the decisions regarding these issues,

- information on whether or not it is possible to join a system for the resale of the contractual rights, information about the relevant system and an indication of costs related to resale through this system,

- indication of the language(s) available for communication with the trader in relation to the contract, for instance in relation to management decisions, increase of costs and the handling of queries and complaints,

where applicable, the possibility for out-of-court dispute resolution.

Acknowledgement of receipt of information:

Signature of the consumer:

ANNEX II

STANDARD INFORMATION FORM FOR LONG-TERM HOLIDAY PRODUCT CONTRACTS

PART 1:

Identity, place of residence and legal status of the trader(s) which will be party to the contract:
Short description of the product: Exact nature and content of the right(s):
Exact period within which the right which is the subject of the contract may be exercised and, if necessary, its duration: Date on which the consumer may start to exercise the contractual right:
Price to be paid by the consumer for acquiring the right(s), including any recurring costs the consumer can expect to incur resulting from the right to obtain access to the accommodation, travel and any related products or services as specified: The staggered payment schedule setting out equal amounts of instalments of this price for each year of the length of the contract and the dates on which they are due to be paid: After year 1, subsequent amounts may be adjusted to ensure that the real value of those instalments is maintained, for instance to take account of inflation. Outline of additional obligatory costs imposed under the contract; type of costs and indication of amounts (e.g. annual membership fees):
A summary of key services available to the consumer (e.g. discounted hotel stays and flights): Are they included in the costs indicated above? If not, specify what is included and what has to be paid for (e.g. three-night stay included in annual membership fee, all other accommodation must be paid for separately):
Has the trader signed a code/codes of conduct and, if yes, where can it/they be found?

PART 2:

General information: - The consumer has the right to withdraw from this contract without giving any reason within 14 calendar days from the conclusion of the contract or any binding preliminary contract or receipt of those contracts if that takes place later. - During this withdrawal period, any advance payment by the consumer is prohibited. The prohibition concerns any consideration, including payment, provision of guarantees, reservation of money on accounts, explicit

acknowledgement of debt etc. It includes not only payment to the trader, but also to third parties.

- The consumer has the right to terminate the contract without incurring any penalty by giving notice to the trader within 14 calendar days of receiving the request for payment for each annual instalment.

- The consumer shall not bear any costs or obligations other than those specified in the contract.

- In accordance with international private law, the contract may be governed by a law other than the law of the Member State in which the consumer is resident or is habitually domiciled and possible disputes may be referred to courts other than those of the Member State in which the consumer is resident or is habitually domiciled.

Signature of the consumer:

PART 3:

Additional information to which the consumer is entitled and where it can be obtained specifically (for instance, under which chapter of a general brochure) if not provided below:

1. INFORMATION ABOUT THE RIGHTS ACQUIRED

- an appropriate and correct description of discounts available for future bookings, illustrated by a set of examples of recent offers,

- information on the restrictions on the consumer's ability to use the rights, such as limited availability or offers provided on a first-come-first-served basis, time limits on particular promotions and special discounts.

2. INFORMATION ON THE TERMINATION OF THE CONTRACT

- where appropriate, information on the arrangements for the termination of ancillary contracts and the consequences of such termination,

- conditions for terminating the contract, the consequences of termination, and information on any liability of the consumer for any costs which might result from such termination.

3. ADDITIONAL INFORMATION

- indication of the language(s) available for communication with the trader in relation to the contract, for instance in relation to the handling of queries and complaints,

where applicable, the possibility for out-of-court dispute resolution.

Acknowledgement of receipt of information:

Signature of the consumer:

ANNEX III

STANDARD INFORMATION FORM FOR RESALE CONTRACTS

PART 1:

Identity, place of residence and legal status of the trader(s) which will be party to the contract:
Short description of the services (e.g. marketing):
Duration of the contract:
Price to be paid by the consumer for acquiring the services: Outline of additional obligatory costs imposed under the contract; type of costs and indication of amounts (e.g. local taxes, notary fees, cost of advertising): Has the trader signed a code/codes of conduct and, if yes, where can it/they be found?

PART 2:

General information: - The consumer has the right to withdraw from this contract without giving any reason within 14 calendar days from the conclusion of the contract or any binding preliminary contract or receipt of those contracts if that takes place later. - Any advance payment by the consumer is prohibited until the actual sale has taken place or the resale contract otherwise is terminated. The prohibition concerns any consideration, including payment, provision of guarantees, reservation of money on accounts, explicit acknowledgement of debt etc. It includes not only payment to the trader, but also to third parties. - The consumer shall not bear any costs or obligations other than those specified in the contract. - In accordance with international private law, the contract may be governed by a law other than the law of the Member State in which the consumer is resident or is habitually domiciled and possible disputes may be referred to courts other than those of the Member State in which the consumer is resident or is habitually domiciled. Signature of the consumer:

PART 3:

Additional information to which the consumer is entitled and where it can be obtained specifically (for instance, under which chapter of a general brochure) if not provided below:
- conditions for terminating the contract, the consequences of termination, and information on any liability of the consumer for any costs which might result from such termination,
- indication of the language(s) available for communication with the trader in relation to the contract, for instance in relation to the handling of queries and complaints,
- where applicable, the possibility for out-of-court dispute resolution.

Acknowledgement of receipt of information:

Signature of the consumer:

ANNEX IV

STANDARD INFORMATION FORM FOR EXCHANGE CONTRACTS

PART 1:

Identity, place of residence and legal status of the trader(s) which will be party to the contract:
Short description of the product: Exact nature and content of the right(s):
Exact period within which the right which is the subject of the contract may be exercised and, if necessary, its duration: Date on which the consumer may start to exercise the contractual right:
Price to be paid by the consumer for the exchange membership fees: Outline of additional obligatory costs imposed under the contract; type of costs and indication of amounts (e.g. renewal fees, other recurrent fees, special levies, local taxes):
A summary of key services available to the consumer: Are they included in the costs indicated above? If not, specify what is included and what has to be paid for (type of costs and indication of amounts; e.g. an estimate of the price to be paid for individual exchange transactions, including any additional charges):
Has the trader signed a code/codes of conduct and, if yes, where can it/they be found?

PART 2:

General information:

- The consumer has the right to withdraw from this contract without giving any reason within 14 calendar days from the conclusion of the contract or any binding preliminary contract or receipt of those contracts if that takes place later. In cases where the exchange contract is offered together with and at the same time as the timeshare contract, only a single withdrawal period shall apply to both contracts.

- During this withdrawal period, any advance payment by the consumer is prohibited. The prohibition concerns any consideration, including payment, provision of guarantees, reservation of money on accounts, explicit acknowledgement of debt etc. It includes not only payment to the trader, but also to third parties.

- The consumer shall not bear any costs or obligations other than those specified in the contract,

- In accordance with international private law, the contract may be governed by a law other than the law of the Member State in which the consumer is resident or is habitually domiciled and possible disputes may be referred to courts other than those of the Member State in which the consumer is resident or is habitually domiciled.

Signature of the consumer:

PART 3:

Additional information to which the consumer is entitled and where it can be obtained specifically (for instance, under which chapter of a general brochure) if not provided below:

1. INFORMATION ABOUT THE RIGHTS ACQUIRED

- explanation of how the exchange system works; the possibilities and modalities for exchange; an indication of the value allotted to the consumer's timeshare in the exchange system and a set of examples of concrete exchange possibilities,

- an indication of the number of resorts available and the number of members in the exchange system, including any limitations on the availability of particular accommodation selected by the consumer, for example, as the result of peak periods of demand, the potential need to book a long time in advance, and indications of any restrictions on the choice resulting from the timeshare rights deposited into the exchange system by the consumer.

2. INFORMATION ON THE PROPERTIES

- a brief and appropriate description of the properties and their location; where the contract concerns accommodation other than immovable property, an appropriate description of the accommodation and the facilities; description of where the consumer can obtain further information.

3. INFORMATION ON THE COSTS

- information on the obligation on the trader to provide details before an exchange is arranged, in respect of each proposed exchange, of any additional charges for which the consumer is liable in respect of the exchange.

4. INFORMATION ON THE TERMINATION OF THE CONTRACT

- where appropriate, information on the arrangements for the termination of ancillary contracts and the consequences of such termination,

- conditions for terminating the contract, the consequences of termination, and information on any liability of the consumer for any costs which might result from such termination.

5. ADDITIONAL INFORMATION

- indication of the language(s) available for communication with the trader in relation to the contract, for instance in relation to the handling of queries and complaints,

- where applicable, the possibility for out-of-court dispute resolution.

Acknowledgement of receipt of information:

Signature of the consumer:

ANNEX V

SEPARATE STANDARD WITHDRAWAL FORM TO FACILITATE THE RIGHT OF WITHDRAWAL

Right of withdrawal

The consumer has the right to withdraw from this contract within 14 calendar days without giving any reason.

The right of withdrawal starts from … (to be filled in by the trader before providing the form to the consumer).

Where the consumer has not received this form, the withdrawal period starts when the consumer has received this form, but expires in any case after one year and 14 calendar days.

Where the consumer has not received all the required information, the withdrawal period starts when the consumer has received that information, but expires in any case after three months and 14 calendar days.

To exercise the right of withdrawal, the consumer shall notify the trader using the name and address indicated below by using a durable medium (e.g. written letter sent by post, e-mail). The consumer may use this form, but it is not obligatory.

Where the consumer exercises the right of withdrawal, the consumer shall not be liable for any costs.

In addition to the right of withdrawal, national contract law rules may provide for consumer rights, e.g. to terminate the contract in case of omission of information.

<table>
<tr><td>Ban on advance payment
During the withdrawal period any advance payment by the consumer is prohibited. The prohibition concerns any consideration, including payment, provision of guarantees, reservation of money on accounts, explicit acknowledgement of debt, etc.
It includes not only payment to the trader, but also to third parties.</td></tr>
<tr><td>Notice of withdrawal
- To (Name and address of the trader) (*):
- I/We (**) hereby give notice that I/We (**) withdraw from the contract,
- Date of conclusion of contract (*):
- Name(s) of consumer(s) (***):
- Address(es) of consumer(s) (***):
- Signature(s) of consumer(s) (only if this form is notified on paper) (***):
- Date (***):
(*) To be filled in by the trader before providing the form to the consumer.
(**) Delete as appropriate.
(***) To be filled in by the consumer(s) where this form is used to withdraw from the contract.</td></tr>
</table>

Acknowledgement of receipt of information:

Signature of the consumer:

ANNEX VI

CORRELATION TABLE BETWEEN PROVISIONS OF THIS DIRECTIVE AND DIRECTIVE 94/47/EC

Directive 94/47/EC	This Directive
Article 1, first paragraph	Article 1(1) and Article 1(2), first subparagraph
Article 1, second paragraph	-
Article 1, third paragraph	Article 1(2), second subparagraph
Article 2, first indent	Article 2(1)(a)
-	Article 2(1)(b) (new)
	Article 2(1)(c) (new)

Directive 94/47/EC	This Directive
	Article 2(1)(d) (new)
Article 2, second indent	-
Article 2, third indent	Article 2(1)(e)
Article 2, fourth indent	Article 2(1)(f)
-	Article 2(1)(g) (new)
-	Article 2(1)(h) (new)
-	Article 2(1)(i) (new)
-	Article 2(1)(j) (new)
-	Article 2(2) (new)
Article 3(1)	Article 4(1)
Article 3(2)	Article 5(2)
Article 3(3)	Article 3(1)
-	Article 3(2) (new)
-	Article 3(3) (new)
-	Article 3(4) (new)
Article 4, first indent	Article 5(1), first subparagraph, and Article 5(2), first subparagraph
Article 4, second indent	Article 4(3) and Article 5(1)
-	Article 4(2) (new)
-	Article 5(4) (new)
-	Article 5(5) (new)
Article 5(1), introductory sentence	Article 6(1)
Article 5(1), first indent	Article 6(1) and Article 6(2)
Article 5(1), second indent	Article 6(3) and Article 6(4)
Article 5(1), third indent	Article 6(3)
-	Article 6(5) (new)
Article 5(2)	Article 7
-	Article 8(1) (new)
Article 5(3)	Article 8(2)
Article 5(4)	Article 8(2)
Article 6	Article 9(1)
-	Article 9(2) (new)
-	Article 10(1) (new)

Directive 94/47/EC	This Directive
-	Article 10(2) (new)
-	Article 11(1) (new)
Article 7, first paragraph	Article 11(2)
Article 7, second paragraph	Article 11(3)
Article 8	Article 12(1)
Article 9	Article 12(2)
Article 10	Articles 13 and 15
Article 11	-
-	Article 14(1) (new)
-	Article 14(2) (new)
Article 12	Article 16
-	Article 17 (new)
-	Article 18 (new)
-	Article 19 (new)
Article 13	Article 20
Annex	Annex I
Annex, point (a)	Article 5(3)(a), and Annex I, Part 1, first box
Annex, point (b)	Annex I, Part 1, third box, and Annex I, Part 3, point 1, first indent
Annex, point (c)	Annex I, Part 1, second box, and Annex I, Part 3, point 2, first indent
Annex, point (d)(1)	Annex I, Part 3, point 3, first indent
Annex, point (d)(2)	Annex I, Part 1, fourth box, and Annex I, Part 3, point 3, second indent
Annex, point (d)(3)	Annex I, Part 3, point 3, third indent
Annex, point (d)(4)	Annex I, Part 3, point 3, first indent
Annex, point (d)(5)	Annex I, Part 3, point 3, fourth indent
Annex, point (e)	Annex I, Part 1, sixth box, and Annex I, Part 3, point 2, second indent
Annex, point (f)	Annex I, Part 1, sixth box, and Annex I, Part 3, point 2, third indent
Annex, point (g)	Annex I, Part 3, point 6, first indent
Annex, point (h)	Annex I, Part 1, fourth box
Annex, point (i)	Annex I, Part 1, fifth and sixth boxes, and Annex I, Part 3, point 4, first indent

Directive 94/47/EC	This Directive
Annex, point (j)	Annex I, Part 2, third indent
Annex, point (k)	Annex I, Part 2, seventh box, and Annex I, Part 3, point 6, second indent
Annex, point (l)	Annex I, Part 2, first and third indents, Annex I, Part 3, point 5, first indent, and Annex V (new)
Annex, point (m)	Article 5(3)(b)
-	Annex I, Part 1, eighth box (new)
-	Annex I, Part 2, second indent (new)
-	Annex I, Part 2, fourth indent (new)
-	Annex I, Part 3, point 1, second indent (new)
-	Annex I, Part 3, point 4, second indent (new)
-	Annex I, Part 3, point 5, second indent (new)
-	Annex I, Part 3, point 6, third indent (new)
-	Annex I, Part 3, point 6, fourth indent (new)
-	Annexes II to V (new)

19. Directive 2009/22/EC of the European Parliament and of the Council of 23 April 2009 on injunctions for the protection of consumers' interests (Codified version) Text with EEA relevance

(OJ L 110 , 01/05/2009 p. 30 – 36)

THE EUROPEAN PARLIAMENT AND THE COUNCIL OF THE EUROPEAN UNION,

Having regard to the Treaty establishing the European Community, and in particular Article 95 thereof,

Having regard to the proposal from the Commission,

Having regard to the opinion of the European Economic and Social Committee[1],

Acting in accordance with the procedure laid down in Article 251 of the Treaty[2],

Whereas:

(1) Directive 98/27/EC of the European Parliament and of the Council of 19 May 1998 on injunctions for the protection of consumers' interests[3] has been substantially amended several times[4]. In the interests of clarity and rationality the said Directive should be codified.

(2) Certain Directives, listed in Annex I to this Directive, lay down rules with regard to the protection of consumers' interests.

(3) Current mechanisms available for ensuring compliance with those Directives, both at national and at Community level, do not always allow infringements harmful to the collective interests of consumers to be terminated in good time. Collective interests means interests which do not include the cumulation of interests of individuals who have been harmed by an infringement. This is without prejudice to individual actions brought by individuals who have been harmed by an infringement.

(4) As far as the purpose of bringing about the cessation of practices that are unlawful under the national provisions applicable is concerned, the effectiveness of national measures transposing the Directives in question, including protective measures that go beyond the level required by those Directives, provided they are compatible with the Treaty and allowed by those Directives, may be thwarted where those practices produce effects in a Member State other than that in which they originate.

(5) Those difficulties can disrupt the smooth functioning of the internal market, their consequence being that it is sufficient to move the source of an unlawful

1 OJ C 161, 13.7.2007, p. 39.

2 Opinion of the European Parliament of 19 June 2007 (OJ C 146 E, 12.6.2008, p. 73) and Council Decision of 23 March 2009.

3 OJ L 166, 11.6.1998, p. 51.

4 See Annex II, Part A.

practice to another country in order to place it out of reach of all forms of enforcement. This constitutes a distortion of competition.

(6) Those difficulties are likely to diminish consumer confidence in the internal market and may limit the scope for action by organisations representing the collective interests of consumers or independent public bodies responsible for protecting the collective interests of consumers, adversely affected by practices that infringe Community law.

(7) Those practices often extend beyond the frontiers between the Member States. There is an urgent need for some degree of approximation of national provisions designed to enjoin the cessation of the unlawful practices irrespective of the Member State in which the unlawful practice has produced its effects. With regard to jurisdiction, this is without prejudice to the rules of private international law and the Conventions in force between Member States, while respecting the general obligations of the Member States deriving from the Treaty, in particular those related to the smooth functioning of the internal market.

(8) The objective of the action envisaged can only be attained by the Community. It is therefore incumbent on the Community to act.

(9) The third paragraph of Article 5 of the Treaty makes it incumbent on the Community not to go beyond what is necessary to achieve the objectives of the Treaty. In accordance with that Article, the specific features of national legal systems must be taken into account to every extent possible by leaving Member States free to choose between different options having equivalent effect. The courts or administrative authorities competent to rule on the proceedings referred to in this Directive should have the right to examine the effects of previous decisions.

(10) One option should consist in requiring one or more independent public bodies, specifically responsible for the protection of the collective interests of consumers, to exercise the rights of action set out in this Directive. Another option should provide for the exercise of those rights by organisations whose purpose is to protect the collective interests of consumers, in accordance with criteria laid down by national law.

(11) Member States should be able to choose between or combine these two options in designating at national level the bodies and/or organisations qualified for the purposes of this Directive.

(12) For the purposes of intra-Community infringements the principle of mutual recognition should apply to these bodies and/or organisations. The Member States should, at the request of their national entities, communicate to the Commission the name and purpose of their national entities which are qualified to bring an action in their own country according to the provisions of this Directive.

(13) It is the business of the Commission to ensure the publication of a list of these qualified entities in the Official Journal of the European Union. Until a

statement to the contrary is published, a qualified entity is assumed to have legal capacity if its name is included in that list.

(14) Member States should be able to require that a prior consultation be undertaken by the party that intends to bring an action for an injunction, in order to give the defendant an opportunity to bring the contested infringement to an end. Member States should be able to require that this prior consultation take place jointly with an independent public body designated by those Member States.

(15) Where the Member States have established that there should be prior consultation, a deadline of two weeks after the request for consultation is received should be set after which, should the cessation of the infringement not be achieved, the applicant shall be entitled to bring an action, without any further delay, before the competent court or administrative authority.

(16) It is appropriate that the Commission report on the functioning of this Directive and in particular on its scope and on the operation of prior consultation.

(17) The application of this Directive should not prejudice the application of Community competition rules.

(18) This Directive should be without prejudice to the obligations of the Member States concerning the time limits for transposition and application in national law of the Directives set out in Annex II, Part B,

HAVE ADOPTED THIS DIRECTIVE:

Article 1 Scope

1. The purpose of this Directive is to approximate the laws, regulations and administrative provisions of the Member States relating to actions for an injunction referred to in Article 2 aimed at the protection of the collective interests of consumers included in the Directives listed in Annex I, with a view to ensuring the smooth functioning of the internal market.
2. For the purposes of this Directive, an infringement means any act contrary to the Directives listed in Annex I as transposed into the internal legal order of the Member States which harms the collective interests referred to in paragraph 1.

Article 2 Actions for an injunction

1. Member States shall designate the courts or administrative authorities competent to rule on proceedings commenced by qualified entities within the meaning of Article 3 seeking:
   (a) an order with all due expediency, where appropriate by way of summary procedure, requiring the cessation or prohibition of any infringement;
   (b) where appropriate, measures such as the publication of the decision, in full or in part, in such form as deemed adequate and/or the publication of a corrective statement with a view to eliminating the continuing effects of the infringement;

(c) in so far as the legal system of the Member State concerned so permits, an order against the losing defendant for payments into the public purse or to any beneficiary designated in or under national legislation, in the event of failure to comply with the decision within a time limit specified by the courts or administrative authorities, of a fixed amount for each day's delay or any other amount provided for in national legislation, with a view to ensuring compliance with the decisions.

2. This Directive shall be without prejudice to the rules of private international law with respect to the applicable law, that is, normally, either the law of the Member State where the infringement originated or the law of the Member State where the infringement has its effects.

Article 3 Entities qualified to bring an action

For the purposes of this Directive, a "qualified entity" means any body or organisation which, being properly constituted according to the law of a Member State, has a legitimate interest in ensuring that the provisions referred to in Article 1 are complied with, in particular:

(a) one or more independent public bodies, specifically responsible for protecting the interests referred to in Article 1, in Member States in which such bodies exist; and/or

(b) organisations whose purpose is to protect the interests referred to in Article 1, in accordance with the criteria laid down by the national law.

Article 4 Intra-Community infringements

1. Each Member State shall take the measures necessary to ensure that, in the event of an infringement originating in that Member State, any qualified entity from another Member State where the interests protected by that qualified entity are affected by the infringement, may apply to the court or administrative authority referred to in Article 2, on presentation of the list provided for in paragraph 3 of this Article. The courts or administrative authorities shall accept this list as proof of the legal capacity of the qualified entity without prejudice to their right to examine whether the purpose of the qualified entity justifies its taking action in a specific case.

2. For the purposes of intra-Community infringements, and without prejudice to the rights granted to other entities under national legislation, the Member States shall, at the request of their qualified entities, communicate to the Commission that these entities are qualified to bring an action under Article 2. The Member States shall inform the Commission of the name and purpose of these qualified entities.

3. The Commission shall draw up a list of the qualified entities referred to in paragraph 2, with the specification of their purpose. This list shall be published in the Official Journal of the European Union; changes to this list shall be published without delay and the updated list shall be published every six months.

Article 5 Prior consultation

1. Member States may introduce or maintain in force provisions whereby the party that intends to seek an injunction can only start this procedure after it has tried to achieve the cessation of the infringement in consultation either with the defendant or with both the defendant and a qualified entity within the meaning of Article 3(a) of the Member State in which the injunction is sought. It shall be for the Member State to decide whether the party seeking the injunction must consult the qualified entity. If the cessation of the infringement is not achieved within two weeks after the request for consultation is received, the party concerned may bring an action for an injunction without any further delay.
2. The rules governing prior consultation adopted by Member States shall be notified to the Commission and shall be published in the Official Journal of the European Union.

Article 6 Reports

1. Every three years and for the first time no later than 2 July 2003 the Commission shall submit to the European Parliament and to the Council a report on the application of this Directive.
2. In its first report the Commission shall examine in particular:
   (a) the scope of this Directive in relation to the protection of the collective interests of persons exercising a commercial, industrial, craft or professional activity;
   (b) the scope of this Directive as determined by the Directives listed in Annex I;
   (c) whether the prior consultation provided for in Article 5 has contributed to the effective protection of consumers.

Where appropriate, this report shall be accompanied by proposals with a view to amending this Directive.

Article 7 Provisions for wider action

This Directive shall not prevent Member States from adopting or maintaining in force provisions designed to grant qualified entities and any other person concerned more extensive rights to bring action at national level.

Article 8 Implementation

Member States shall communicate to the Commission the provisions of national law which they adopt in the field covered by this Directive.

Article 9 Repeal

Directive 98/27/EC, as amended by the Directives set out in Annex II, Part A, is repealed, without prejudice to the obligations of the Member States concerning the time limits for transposition into national law and application of the Directives set out in Annex II, Part B.

References to the repealed Directive shall be construed as references to this Directive and shall be read in accordance with the correlation table in Annex III.

Article 10 Entry into force

This Directive shall enter into force on 29 December 2009.

Article 11 Addressees

This Directive is addressed to the Member States.

Done at Strasbourg, 23 April 2009.

For the European Parliament

The President

H.-G. Pöttering

For the Council

The President

P. Nečas

ANNEX I

LIST OF DIRECTIVES REFERRED TO IN ARTICLE 1[1]

1. Council Directive 85/577/EEC of 20 December 1985 to protect the consumer in respect of contracts negotiated away from business premises (OJ L 372, 31.12.1985, p. 31).
2. Council Directive 87/102/EEC of 22 December 1986 for the approximation of the laws, regulations and administrative provisions of the Member States concerning consumer credit (OJ L 42, 12.2.1987, p. 48)[2].
3. Council Directive 89/552/EEC of 3 October 1989 on the coordination of certain provisions laid down by law, regulation or administrative action in Member States concerning the pursuit of television broadcasting activities: Articles 10 to 21 (OJ L 298, 17.10.1989, p. 23).
4. Council Directive 90/314/EEC of 13 June 1990 on package travel, package holidays and package tours (OJ L 158, 23.6.1990, p. 59).
5. Council Directive 93/13/EEC of 5 April 1993 on unfair terms in consumer contracts (OJ L 95, 21.4.1993, p. 29).
6. Directive 97/7/EC of the European Parliament and of the Council of 20 May 1997 on the protection of consumers in respect of distance contracts (OJ L 144, 4.6.1997, p. 19).
7. Directive 1999/44/EC of the European Parliament and of the Council of 25 May 1999 on certain aspects of the sale of consumer goods and associated guarantees (OJ L 171, 7.7.1999, p. 12).
8. Directive 2000/31/EC of the European Parliament and of the Council of 8 June 2000 on certain legal aspects on information society services, in particular electronic commerce, in the internal market (Directive on electronic commerce) (OJ L 178, 17.7.2000, p. 1).
9. Directive 2001/83/EC of the European Parliament and of the Council of 6 November 2001 on the Community code relating to medicinal products for human use: Articles 86 to 100 (OJ L 311, 28.11.2001, p. 67).
10. Directive 2002/65/EC of the European Parliament and of the Council of 23 September 2002 concerning the distance marketing of consumer financial services (OJ L 271, 9.10.2002, p. 16).
11. Directive 2005/29/EC of the European Parliament and of the Council of 11 May 2005 concerning unfair business-to-consumer commercial practices in the internal market (OJ L 149, 11.6.2005, p. 22).
12. Directive 2006/123/EC of the European Parliament and of the Council of 12 December 2006 on services in the internal market (OJ L 376, 27.12.2006, p. 36).

[1] The Directives referred to in points 5, 6, 9 and 11 contain specific provisions concerning injunctions.

[2] The said Directive was repealed and replaced, with effect from 12 May 2010, by Directive 2008/48/EC of the European Parliament and of the Council of 23 April 2008 on credit agreements for consumers (OJ L 133, 22.5.2008, p. 66).

13. Directive 2008/122/EC of the European Parliament and of the Council of 14 January 2009 on the protection of consumers in respect of certain aspects of timeshare, long-term holiday product, resale and exchange contracts (OJ L 33, 3.2.2009, p. 10).

ANNEX II

PART A

Repealed Directive and its amendments (referred to in Article 9)

Directive 98/27/EC of the European Parliament and of the Council (OJ L 166, 11.6.1998, p. 51)	
Directive 1999/44/EC of the European Parliament and of the Council (OJ L 171, 7.7.1999, p. 12)	Article 10 only
Directive 2000/31/EC of the European Parliament and of the Council (OJ L 178, 17.7.2000, p. 1)	Article 18(2) only
Directive 2002/65/EC of the European Parliament and of the Council (OJ L 271, 9.10.2002, p. 16)	Article 19 only
Directive 2005/29/EC of the European Parliament and of the Council (OJ L 149, 11.6.2005, p. 22)	Article 16(1) only
Directive 2006/123/EC of the European Parliament and of the Council (OJ L 376, 27.12.2006, p. 36)	Article 42 only

PART B

List of time limits for transposition into national law and application (referred to in Article 9)

Directive	Time limit for transposition	Date of application
98/27/EC	1 January 2001	-
1999/44/EC	1 January 2002	-
2000/31/EC	16 January 2002	-
2002/65/EC	9 October 2004	-
2005/29/EC	12 June 2007	12 December 2007
2006/123/EC	28 December 2009	-

ANNEX III

CORRELATION TABLE

Directive 98/27/EC	This Directive
Articles 1 to 5	Articles 1 to 5
Article 6(1)	Article 6(1)
Article 6(2), first subparagraph, first indent	Article 6(2), first subparagraph, point (a)
Article 6(2), first subparagraph, second indent	Article 6(2), first subparagraph, point (b)
Article 6(2), first subparagraph, third indent	Article 6(2), first subparagraph, point (c)
Article 6(2), second subparagraph	Article 6(2), second subparagraph
Article 7	Article 7
Article 8(1)	-
Article 8(2)	Article 8
-	Article 9
Article 9	Article 10
Article 10	Article 11
Annex	Annex I
-	Annex II
-	Annex III

TORT

20. Council Directive 85/374/EEC of 25 July 1985 on the approximation of the laws, regulations and administrative provisions of the Member States concerning liability for defective products

(OJ L 210 , 07/08/1985 p. 29 – 33)

THE COUNCIL OF THE EUROPEAN COMMUNITIES,

Having regard to the Treaty establishing the European Economic Community, and in particular Article 100 thereof,

Having regard to the proposal from the Commission[1],

Having regard to the opinion of the European Parliament[2],

Having regard to the opinion of the Economic and Social Committee[3],

Whereas approximation of the laws of the Member States concerning the liability of the producer for damage caused by the defectiveness of his products is necessary because the existing divergences may distort competition and affect the movement of goods within the common market and entail a differing degree of protection of the consumer against damage caused by a defective product to his health or property;

Whereas liability without fault on the part of the producer is the sole means of adequately solving the problem, peculiar to our age of increasing technicality, of a fair apportionment of the risks inherent in modern technological production;

Whereas libility without fault should apply only to movables which have been industrially produced; whereas, as a result, it is appropriate to exclude liability for agricultural products and game, except where they have undergone a processing of an industrial nature which could cause a defect in these products; whereas the liability provided for in this Directive should also apply to movables which are used in the construction of immovables or are installed in immovables;

Whereas protection of the consumer requires that all producers involved in the production process should be made liable, in so far as their finished product, component part or any raw material supplied by them was defective; whereas, for the same reason, liability should extend to importers of products into the Community and to persons who present themselves as producers by affixing their name, trade mark or other distinguishing feature or who supply a product the producer of which cannot be identified;

Whereas, in situations where several persons are liable for the same damage, the protection of the consumer requires that the injured person should be able to claim full compensation for the damage from any one of them;

---

1 OJ No C 241, 14. 10. 1976, p. 9 and OJ No C 271, 26. 10. 1979, p. 3.

2 OJ No C 127, 21. 5. 1979, p. 61.

3 OJ No C 114, 7. 5. 1979, p. 15.

whereas, to protect the physical well-being and property of the consumer, the defectiveness of the product should be determined by reference not to its fitness for use but to the lack of the safety which the public at large is entitled to expect; whereas the safety is assessed by excluding any misuse of the product not reasonable under the circumstances;

Whereas a fair apportionment of risk between the injured person and the producer implies that the producer should be able to free himself from liability if he furnishes proof as to the existence of certain exonerating circumstances;

Whereas the protection of the consumer requires that the liability of the producer remains unaffacted by acts or omissions of other persons having contributed to cause the damage; whereas, however, the contributory negligence of the injured person may be taken into account to reduce or disallow such liability;

Whereas the protection of the consumer requires compensation for death and personal injury as well as compensation for damage to property; whereas the latter should nevertheless be limited to goods for private use or consumption and be subject to a deduction of a lower threshold of a fixed amount in order to avoid litigation in an excessive number of cases; whereas this Directive should not prejudice compensation for pain and suffering and other non-material damages payable, where appropriate, under the law applicable to the case;

Whereas a uniform period of limitation for the bringing of action for compensation is in the interests both of the injured person and of the producer;

Whereas products age in the course of time, higher safety standards are developed and the state of science and technology progresses; whereas, therefore, it would not be reasonable to make the producer liable for an unlimited period for the defectiveness of his product; whereas, therefore, liability should expire after a reasonable length of time, without prejudice to claims pending at law;

Whereas, to achieve effective protection of consumers, no contractual derogation should be permitted as regards the liability of the producer in relation to the injured person;

Whereas under the legal systems of the Member States an injured party may have a claim for damages based on grounds of contractual liability or on grounds of non-contractual liability other than that provided for in this Directive; in so far as these provisions also serve to attain the objective of effective protection of consumers, they should remain unaffected by this Directive; whereas, in so far as effective protection of consumers in the sector of pharmaceutical products is already also attained in a Member State under a special liability system, claims based on this system should similarly remain possible;

Whereas, to the extent that liability for nuclear injury or damage is already covered in all Member States by adequate special rules, it has been possible to exclude damage of this type from the scope of this Directive;

Whereas, since the exclusion of primary agricultural products and game from the scope of this Directive may be felt, in certain Member States, in view of what is expected for the protection of consumers, to restrict unduly such protection, it should be possible for a Member State to extend liability to such products;

Whereas, for similar reasons, the possibility offered to a producer to free himself from liability if he proves that the state of scientific and technical knowledge at the time when he put the product into circulation was not such as to enable the existence of a defect to be discovered may be felt in certain Member States to restrict unduly the protection of the consumer; whereas it should therefore be possible for a Member State to maintain in its legislation or to provide by new legislation that this exonerating circumstance is not admitted; whereas, in the case of new legislation, making use of this derogation should, however, be subject to a Community stand-still procedure, in order to raise, if possible, the level of protection in a uniform manner throughout the Community;

Whereas, taking into account the legal traditions in most of the Member States, it is inappropriate to set any financial ceiling on the producer's liability without fault; whereas, in so far as there are, however, differing traditions, it seems possible to admit that a Member State may derogate from the principle of unlimited liability by providing a limit for the total liability of the producer for damage resulting from a death or personal injury and caused by identical items with the same defect, provided that this limit is established at a level sufficiently high to guarantee adequate protection of the consumer and the correct functioning of the common market;

Whereas the harmonization resulting from this cannot be total at the present stage, but opens the way towards greater harmonization; whereas it is therefore necessary that the Council receive at regular intervals, reports from the Commission on the application of this Directive, accompanied, as the case may be, by appropriate proposals;

Whereas it is particularly important in this respect that a re-examination be carried out of those parts of the Directive relating to the derogations open to the Member States, at the expiry of a period of sufficient length to gather practical experience on the effects of these derogations on the protection of consumers and on the functioning of the common market,

HAS ADOPTED THIS DIRECTIVE:

Article 1

The producer shall be liable for damage caused by a defect in his product.

Article 2

For the purpose of this Directive, 'product' means all movables even if incorporated into another movable or into an immovable. 'Product' includes electricity.

Article 3

1. 'Producer' means the manufacturer of a finished product, the producer of any raw material or the manufacturer of a component part and any person who, by

putting his name, trade mark or other distinguishing feature on the product presents himself as its producer.

2. Without prejudice to the liability of the producer, any person who imports into the Community a product for sale, hire, leasing or any form of distribution in the course of his business shall be deemed to be a producer within the meaning of this Directive and shall be responsible as a producer.
3. Where the producer of the product cannot be identified, each supplier of the product shall be treated as its producer unless he informs the injured person, within a reasonable time, of the identity of the producer or of the person who supplied him with the product. The same shall apply, in the case of an imported product, if this product does not indicate the identity of the importer referred to in paragraph 2, even if the name of the producer is indicated.

Article 4

The injured person shall be required to prove the damage, the defect and the causal relationship between defect and damage.

Article 5

Where, as a result of the provisions of this Directive, two or more persons are liable for the same damage, they shall be liable jointly and severally, without prejudice to the provisions of national law concerning the rights of contribution or recourse.

Article 6

1. A product is defective when it does not provide the safety which a person is entitled to expect, taking all circumstances into account, including:
   (a) the presentation of the product;
   (b) the use to which it could reasonably be expected that the product would be put;
   (c) the time when the product was put into circulation.
2. A product shall not be considered defective for the sole reason that a better product is subsequently put into circulation.

Article 7

The producer shall not be liable as a result of this Directive if he proves:

(a) that he did not put the product into circulation; or

(b) that, having regard to the circumstances, it is probable that the defect which caused the damage did not exist at the time when the product was put into circulation by him or that this defect came into being afterwards; or

(c) that the product was neither manufactured by him for sale or any form of distribution for economic purpose nor manufactured or distributed by him in the course of his business; or

(d) that the defect is due to compliance of the product with mandatory regulations issued by the public authorities; or

(e) that the state of scientific and technical knowledge at the time when he put the product into circulation was not such as to enable the existence of the defect to be discovered; or

(f) in the case of a manufacturer of a component, that the defect is attributable to the design of the product in which the component has been fitted or to the instructions given by the manufacturer of the product.

Article 8

1. Without prejudice to the provisions of national law concerning the right of contribution or recourse, the liability of the producer shall not be reduced when the damage is caused both by a defect in product and by the act or omission of a third party.
2. The liability of the producer may be reduced or disallowed when, having regard to all the circumstances, the damage is caused both by a defect in the product and by the fault of the injured person or any person for whom the injured person is responsible.

Article 9

For the purpose of Article 1, 'damage' means:

(a) damage caused by death or by personal injuries;

(b) damage to, or destruction of, any item of property other than the defective product itself, with a lower threshold of 500 ECU, provided that the item of property:

(i) is of a type ordinarily intended for private use or consumption, and

(ii) was used by the injured person mainly for his own private use or consumption.

This Article shall be without prejudice to national provisions relating to non-material damage.

Article 10

1. Member States shall provide in their legislation that a limitation period of three years shall apply to proceedings for the recovery of damages as provided for in this Directive. The limitation period shall begin to run from the day on which the plaintiff became aware, or should reasonably have become aware, of the damage, the defect and the identity of the producer.
2. The laws of Member States regulating suspension or interruption of the limitation period shall not be affected by this Directive. Article 11

   Member States shall provide in their legislation that the rights conferred upon the injured person pursuant to this Directive shall be extinguished upon the expiry of a period of 10 years from the date on which the producer put into circulation the actual product which caused the damage, unless the injured person has in the meantime instituted proceedings against the producer.

Article 12

The liability of the producer arising from this Directive may not, in relation to the injured person, be limited or excluded by a provision limiting his liability or exempting him from liability.

Article 13

This Directive shall not affect any rights which an injured person may have according to the rules of the law of contractual or non-contractual liability or a special liability system existing at the moment when this Directive is notified.

Article 14

This Directive shall not apply to injury or damage arising from nuclear accidents and covered by international conventions ratified by the Member States.

Article 15

1. Each Member State may:
   (a) (Deleted)[1]
   (b) by way of derogation from Article 7 (e), maintain or, subject to the procedure set out in paragraph 2 of this Article, provide in this legislation that the producer shall be liable even if he proves that the state of scientific and technical knowledge at the time when he put the product into circulation was not such as to enable the existence of a defect to be discovered.
2. A Member State wishing to introduce the measure specified in paragraph 1 (b) shall communicate the text of the proposed measure to the Commission. The Commission shall inform the other Member States thereof.

   The Member State concerned shall hold the proposed measure in abeyance for nine months after the Commission is informed and provided that in the meantime the Commission has not submitted to the Council a proposal amending this Directive on the relevant matter. However, if within three months of receiving the said information, the Commission does not advise the Member State concerned that it intends submitting such a proposal to the Council, the Member State may take the proposed measure immediately.

   If the Commission does submit to the Council such a proposal amending this Directive within the aforementioned nine months, the Member State concerned shall hold the proposed measure in abeyance for a further period of 18 months from the date on which the proposal is submitted.
3. Ten years after the date of notification of this Directive, the Commission shall submit to the Council a report on the effect that rulings by the courts as to the application of Article 7 (e) and of paragraph 1 (b) of this Article have on consumer protection and the functioning of the common market. In the light of this report the Council, acting on a proposal from the Commission and pursuant

[1] OJ L 141 20 4.6.1999

to the terms of Article 100 of the Treaty, shall decide whether to repeal Article 7 (e).

Article 16

1. Any Member State may provide that a producer's total liability for damage resulting from a death or personal injury and caused by identical items with the same defect shall be limited to an amount which may not be less than 70 million ECU.
2. Ten years after the date of notification of this Directive, the Commission shall submit to the Council a report on the effect on consumer protection and the functioning of the common market of the implementation of the financial limit on liability by those Member States which have used the option provided for in paragraph 1. In the light of this report the Council, acting on a proposal from the Commission and pursuant to the terms of Article 100 of the Treaty, shall decide whether to repeal paragraph 1.

Article 17

This Directive shall not apply to products put into circulation before the date on which the provisions referred to in Article 19 enter into force.

Article 18

1. For the purposes of this Directive, the ECU shall be that defined by Regulation (EEC) No 3180/78[1], as amended by Regulation (EEC) No 2626/84[2]. The equivalent in national currency shall initially be calculated at the rate obtaining on the date of adoption of this Directive.
2. Every five years the Council, acting on a proposal from the Commission, shall examine and, if need be, revise the amounts in this Directive, in the light of economic and monetary trends in the Community.

Article 19

1. Member States shall bring into force, not later than three years from the date of notification of this Directive, the laws, regulations and administrative provisions necessary to comply with this Directive. They shall forthwith inform the Commission thereof[3].
2. The procedure set out in Article 15 (2) shall apply from the date of notification of this Directive.

Article 20

Member States shall communicate to the Commission the texts of the main provisions of national law which they subsequently adopt in the field governed by this Directive.

---

1 OJ No L 379, 30. 12. 1978, p. 1.

2 OJ No L 379, 30. 12. 1978, p. 1.

3 This Directive was notified to the Member States on 30 July 1985.

Article 21

Every five years the Commission shall present a report to the Council on the application of this Directive and, if necessary, shall submit appropriate proposals to it.

Article 22

This Directive is addressed to the Member States.

Done at Brussels, 25 July 1985.

For the Council

The President

J. POOS

21.Council Directive 96/82/EC of 9 December 1996 on the control of major-accident hazards involving dangerous substances

(OJ L 010 , 14/01/1997 P.13 -33)

THE COUNCIL OF THE EUROPEAN UNION,

Having regard to the Treaty establishing the European Community, and in particular Article 130s (1) thereof,

Having regard to the proposal from the Commission[1],

Having regard to the opinion of the Economic and Social Committee[2],

Acting in accordance with the procedure laid down in Article 189c of the Treaty[3],

(1) Whereas Council Directive 82/501/EEC of 24 June 1982 on the major-accident hazards of certain industrial activities[4] is concerned with the prevention of major accidents which might result from certain industrial activities and with the limitation of their consequences for man and the environment;

(2) Whereas the objectives and principles of the Community's environment policy, as set out in Article 130r (1) and (2) of the Treaty and detailed in the European Community's action programmes on the environment[5], aim, in particular, at preserving and protecting the quality of the environment, and protecting human health, through preventive action;

(3) Whereas the Council and the representatives of the Governments of the Member States, meeting within the Council, in their accompanying resolution concerning the fourth Action Programme on the Environment[6], highlighted the need for more effective implementation of Directive 82/501/EEC and called for a review of the Directive to include, if necessary, a possible widening of its scope and a greater exchange of information on the matter between Member States; whereas the fifth Action Programme, the general approach of which was approved by the Council and the representatives of the Governments of the Member States, meeting within the Council, in their resolution of 1 February 1993[7], also presses for better risk-and-accident management;

(4) Whereas, in the light of the accidents at Bhopal and Mexico City, which demonstrated the hazard which arises when dangerous sites and dwellings are

---

1 OJ No C 106, 14. 4. 1994, p. 4 and OJ No C 238, 13. 9. 1995, p. 4.

2 OJ No C 295, 22. 10. 1994, p. 83.

3 Opinion of the European Parliament of 16 February 1995 (OJ No C 56, 6. 3. 1995, p. 80), Council common position of 19 March 1996 (OJ No C 120, 24. 4. 1996, p. 20) and Decision of the European Parliament of 15 July 1996 (OJ No C 261, 9. 9. 1996, p. 24).

4 OJ No L 230, 5. 8. 1982, p. 1. Directive as last amended by Directive 91/692/EEC (OJ No L 377, 31. 12. 1991, p. 48).

5 OJ No C 112, 20. 12. 1973, p. 1. OJ No C 139, 13. 6. 1977, p. 1. OJ No C 46, 17. 2. 1983, p. 1. OJ No C 70, 18. 3. 1987, p. 1. OJ No C 138, 17. 5. 1993, p. 1.

6 OJ No C 328, 7. 12. 1987, p. 3.

7 OJ No C 138, 17. 5. 1993.

close together, the Council Resolution of 16 October 1989 called on the Commission to include in Directive 82/501/EEC provisions concerning controls on land-use planning when new installations are authorized and when urban development takes place around existing installations;

(5) Whereas the said Council resolution invited the Commission to work with Member States towards greater mutual understanding and harmonization of national principles and practices regarding safety reports;

(6) Whereas it is desirable to pool the experience gained through different approaches to the control of major-accident hazards; whereas the Commission and the Member States should develop their relations with the relevant international bodies and seek to establish measures equivalent to those set out in this Directive for use in third countries;

(7) Whereas the Convention on the Transboundary Effects of Industrial Accidents of the United Nations Economic Commission for Europe provides for measures regarding the prevention of, preparedness for and response to industrial accidents capable of causing transboundary effects as well as for international cooperation in this field;

(8) Whereas Directive 82/501/EEC constituted a first stage in the harmonization process; whereas the said Directive should be revised and supplemented in order to ensure high levels of protection throughout the Community in a consistent and efficient manner; whereas the present harmonization is limited to the measures which are necessary to put in place a more effective system for preventing major accidents with widespread effects and for limiting their consequences;

(9) Whereas major accidents can have consequences beyond frontiers; whereas the ecological and economic cost of an accident is borne not only by the establishment affected but also by the Member States concerned; whereas it is therefore necessary to take measures ensuring a high level of protection throughout the Community;

(10) Whereas the provisions of this Directive must apply without prejudice to Community provisions as regards health and safety at work;

(11) Whereas use of a list specifying certain installations while excluding others with identical hazards is not an appropriate practice, and may allow potential sources of major accidents to escape regulation; whereas the scope of Directive 82/501/EEC must be altered to make the provisions applicable to all establishments where dangerous substances are present in sufficiently large quantities to create a major-accident hazard;

(12) Whereas, with due regard for the Treaty and in compliance with the relevant Community legislation, Member States may retain or adopt appropriate measures for transport-related activities at docks, wharves and marshalling yards, which are excluded from this Directive, in order to ensure a level of safety equivalent to that established by this Directive;

(13) Whereas the transmission of dangerous substances through pipelines also has a potential to produce major accidents; whereas the Commission should, after collecting and evaluating information about existing mechanisms within the Community for regulating such activities and the occurrence of relevant incidents, prepare a communication setting out the case, and most appropriate instrument, for action in this area if necessary;

(14) Whereas, with due regard for the Treaty and in compliance with the relevant Community legislation, Member States may retain or adopt measures on waste land-fill, which do not come within the scope of this Directive;

(15) Whereas analysis of the major accidents reported in the Community indicates that the majority of them are the result of managerial and/or organizational shortcomings; whereas it is therefore necessary to lay down at Community level basic principles for management systems, which must be suitable for preventing and controlling major-accident hazards and limiting the consequences thereof;

(16) Whereas differences in the arrangements for the inspection of establishments by the competent authorities may give rise to differing levels of protection; whereas it is necessary to lay down at Community level the essential requirements with which the systems for inspection established by the Member States must comply;

(17) Whereas, in order to demonstrate that all that is necessary has been done to prevent major accidents, to prepare contingency plans and response measures, the operator should, in the case of establishments where dangerous substances are present in significant quantities, provide the competent authority with information in the form of a safety report containing details of the establishment, the dangerous substances present, the installation or storage facilities, possible major accidents and the management systems available, in order to prevent and reduce the risk of major accidents and to enable the necessary steps to be taken to limit the consequences thereof;

(18) Whereas, in order to reduce the risk of domino effects, where establishments are sited in such a way or so close together as to increase the probability and possibility of major accidents, or aggravate their consequences, there should be provision for the exchange of appropriate information and cooperation on public information;

(19) Whereas, in order to promote access to information on the environment, the public should have access to safety reports produced by operators, and persons likely to be affected by a major accident should be given information sufficient to inform them of the correct action to be taken in that event;

(20) Whereas, in order to provide against emergencies, in the case of establishments where dangerous substances are present in significant quantities it is necessary to establish external and internal emergency plans and to create systems to ensure those plans are tested and revised as necessary and implemented in the event of a major accident or the likelihood thereof;

(21) Whereas the staff of an establishment must be consulted on the internal emergency plan and the public must be consulted on the external emergency plan;

(22) Whereas, in order to provide greater protection for residential areas, areas of substantial public use and areas of particular natural interest or sensitivity, it is necessary for land-use and/or other relevant policies applied in the Member States to take account of the need, in the long term, to keep a suitable distance between such areas and establishments presenting such hazards and, where existing establishments are concerned, to take account of additional technical measures so that the risk to persons is not increased;

(23) Whereas, in order to ensure that adequate response measures are taken if a major accident occurs, the operator must immediately inform the competent authorities and communicate the information necessary for them to assess the impact of that accident;

(24) Whereas, in order to provide for an information exchange and to prevent future accidents of a similar nature, Member States should forward information to the Commission regarding major accidents occurring in their territory, so that the Commission can analyze the hazards involved, and operate a system for the distribution of information concerning, in particular, major accidents and the lessons learned from them; whereas this information exchange should also cover 'near misses` which Member States regard as being of particular technical interest for preventing major accidents and limiting their consequences,

HAS ADOPTED THIS DIRECTIVE:

Article 1 Aim

This Directive is aimed at the prevention of major accidents which involve dangerous substances, and the limitation of their consequences for man and the environment, with a view to ensuring high levels of protection throughout the Community in a consistent and effective manner.

Article 2 Scope

1. The Directive shall apply to establishments where dangerous substances are present in quantities equal to or in excess of the quantities listed in Annex I, Parts 1 and 2, column 2, with the exception of Articles 9, 11 and 13 which shall apply to any establishment where dangerous substances are present in quantities equal to or in excess of the quantities listed in Annex I, Parts 1 and 2, column 3.

   For the purposes of this Directive, the 'presence of dangerous substances` shall mean the actual or anticipated presence of such substances in the establishment, or the presence of those which it is believed may be generated during loss of control of an industrial chemical process, in quantities equal to or in excess of the thresholds in Parts 1 and 2 of Annex I.

2. The provisions of this Directive shall apply without prejudice to Community provisions concerning the working environment, and, in particular, without

prejudice to Council Directive 89/391/EEC of 12 June 1989 on the introduction of measures to encourage improvements in the safety and health of workers at work[1].

Article 3 Definitions

For the purposes of this Directive:

1. 'establishment` shall mean the whole area under the control of an operator where dangerous substances are present in one or more installations, including common or related infrastructures or activities;
2. 'installation` shall mean a technical unit within an establishment in which dangerous substances are produced, used, handled or stored. It shall include all the equipment, structures, pipework, machinery, tools, private railway sidings, docks, unloading quays serving the installation, jetties, warehouses or similar structures, floating or otherwise, necessary for the operation of the installation;
3. 'operator` shall mean any individual or corporate body who operates or holds an establishment or installation or, if provided for by national legislation, has been given decisive economic power in the technical operation thereof;
4. 'dangerous substance` shall mean a substance, mixture or preparation listed in Annex 1, Part 1, or fulfilling the criteria laid down in Annex 1, Part 2, and present as a raw material, product, by-product, residue or intermediate, including those substances which it is reasonable to suppose may be generated in the event of accident;
5. 'major accident` shall mean an occurrence such as a major emission, fire, or explosion resulting from uncontrolled developments in the course of the operation of any establishment covered by this Directive, and leading to serious danger to human health and/or the environment, immediate or delayed, inside or outside the establishment, and involving one or more dangerous substances;
6. 'hazard` shall mean the intrinsic property of a dangerous substance or physical situation, with a potential for creating damage to human health and/or the environment;
7. 'risk` shall mean the likelihood of a specific effect occurring within a specified period or in specified circumstances;
8. 'storage` shall mean the presence of a quantity of dangerous substances for the purposes of warehousing, depositing in safe custody or keeping in stock.

Article 4 Exclusions

This Directive shall not apply to the following:

(a) military establishments, installations or storage facilities;

(b) hazards created by ionizing radiation;

---

[1] OJ No L 183, 29. 6. 1989, p. 1.

(c) the transport of dangerous substances and intermediate temporary storage by road, rail, internal waterways, sea or air, outside the establishments covered by this Directive, including loading and unloading and transport to and from another means of transport at docks, wharves or marshalling yards;
(d) the transport of dangerous substances in pipelines, including pumping stations, outside establishments covered by this Directive;
(e) the exploitation (exploration, extraction and processing) of minerals in mines, quarries, or by means of boreholes, with the exception of chemical and thermal processing operations and storage related to those operations which involve dangerous substances, as defined in Annex I;
(f) the offshore exploration and exploitation of minerals, including hydrocarbons;
(g) waste land-fill sites, with the exception of operational tailings disposal facilities, including tailing ponds or dams, containing dangerous substances as defined in Annex I, in particular when used in connection with the chemical and thermal processing of minerals.

Article 5 General obligations of the operator

1. Member States shall ensure that the operator is obliged to take all measures necessary to prevent major accidents and to limit their consequences for man and the environment.
2. Member States shall ensure that the operator is required to prove to the competent authority referred to in Article 16, hereinafter referred to as the 'competent authority`, at any time, in particular for the purposes of the inspections and controls referred to in Article 18, that he has taken all the measures necessary as specified in this Directive.

Article 6 Notification

1. Member States shall require the operator to send the competent authority a notification within the following time-limits:
   - for new establishments, a reasonable period of time prior to the start of construction or operation,
   - for establishments which subsequently fall within the scope of this Directive, within three months after the date on which this Directive applies to the establishment concerned, as laid down in the first subparagraph of Article 2(1).
2. The notification required by paragraph 1 shall contain the following details:
   (a) the name or trade name of the operator and the full address of the establishment concerned;
   (b) the registered place of business of the operator, with the full address;
   (c) the name or position of the person in charge of the establishment, if different from (a);
   (d) information sufficient to identify the dangerous substances or category of substances involved;

(e) the quantity and physical form of the dangerous substance or substances involved;
(f) the activity or proposed activity of the installation or storage facility;
(g) the immediate environment of the establishment (elements liable to cause a major accident or to aggravate the consequences thereof).

3. In the case of existing establishments for which the operator has already provided all the information under paragraph 2 to the competent authority under the requirements of national law at the date of entry into force of this Directive, notification under paragraph 1 is not required.
4. In the event of:
   - any significant increase in the quantity or significant change in the nature or physical form of the dangerous substance present, as indicated in the notification provided by the operator pursuant to paragraph 2, or any change in the processes employing it,
   - modification of an establishment or an installation which could have significant repercussions on major accide
   - permanent closure of the installation,

   the operator shall immediately inform the competent authority of the change in the situation.

Article 7 Major-accident prevention policy

1. Member States shall require the operator to draw up a document setting out his major-accident prevention policy and to ensure that it is properly implemented. The major-accident prevention policy established by the operator shall be designed to guarantee a high level of protection for man and the environment by appropriate means, structures and management systems.

1a. For establishments which subsequently fall within the scope of this Directive, the document referred to in paragraph 1 shall be drawn up without delay, but at all events within three months after the date on which this Directive applies to the establishment concerned, as laid down in the first subparagraph of Article 2(1).

2. The document must take account of the principles contained in Annex III and be made available to the competent authorities for the purposes of, amongst other things, implementation of Articles 5 (2) and 18.
3. This Article shall not apply to the establishments referred to in Article 9.

Article 8 Domino effect

1. Member States shall ensure that the competent authority, using the information received from the operators in compliance with Articles 6 and 9, identifies establishments or groups of establishments where the likelihood and the possibility or consequences of a major accident may be increased because of the location and the proximity of such establishments, and their inventories of dangerous substances.

2. Member States must ensure that in the case of the establishments thus identified:
   (a) suitable information is exchanged in an appropriate manner to enable these establishments to take account of the nature and extent of the overall hazard of a major accident in their major accident prevention policies, safety management systems, safety reports and internal emergency plans;
   (b) provision is made for cooperation in informing the public and in supplying information to the authority responsible for the preparation of external emergency plans.

Article 9 Safety report

1. Member States shall require the operator to produce a safety report for the purposes of:
   (a) demonstrating that a major-accident prevention policy and a safety management system for implementing it have been put into effect in accordance with the information set out in Annex III;
   (b) demonstrating that major-accident hazards have been identified and that the necessary measures have been taken to prevent such accidents and to limit their consequences for man and the environment;
   (c) demonstrating that adequate safety and reliability have been incorporated into the design, construction, operation and maintenance of any installation, storage facility, equipment and infrastructure connected with its operation which are linked to major-accident hazards inside the establishment;
   (d) demonstrating that internal emergency plans have been drawn up and supplying information to enable the external plan to be drawn up in order to take the necessary measures in the event of a major accident;
   (e) providing sufficient information to the competent authorities to enable decisions to be made in terms of the siting of new activities or developments around existing establishments.
2. The safety report shall contain at least the data and information listed in Annex II. It shall name the relevant organisations involved in the drawing up of the report. It shall also contain an updated inventory of the dangerous substances present in the establishment.

   Safety reports, or parts of reports, or any other equivalent reports produced in response to other legislation, may be combined to form a single safety report for the purposes of this Article, where such a format obviates the unnecessary duplication of information and the repetition of work by the operator or competent authority, on condition that all the requirements of this Article are complied with.
3. The safety report provided for in paragraph 1 shall be sent to the competent authority within the following time limits:
   - for new establishments, a reasonable period of time prior to the start of construction or of operation,

- for existing establishments not previously covered by Directive 82/501/EEC, three years from the date laid down in Article 24 (1),
- for other establishments, two years from the date laid down in Article 24 (1),
- for establishments which subsequently fall within the scope of this Directive, without delay, but at all events within one year after the date on which this Directive applies to the establishment concerned, as laid down in the first subparagraph of Article 2(1),

4. Before the operator commences construction or operation, or in the cases referred to in the second, third, fourth and fifth indents of paragraph 3, the competent authority shall within a reasonable period of receipt of the report:
   - communicate the conclusions of its examination of the safety report to the operator, if necessary after requesting further information, or
   - prohibit the bringing into use, or the continued use, of the establishment concerned, in accordance with the powers and procedures laid down in Article 17.
5. The safety report shall be periodically reviewed and where necessary updated:
   - at least every five years,
   - at any other time at the initiative of the operator or the request of the competent authority, where justified by new facts or to take account of new technical knowledge about safety matters, for example arising from analysis of accidents or, as far as possible, 'near misses`, and of developments in knowledge concerning the assessment of hazards.
6. (a) Where it is demonstrated to the satisfaction of the competent authority that particular substances present at the establishment, or any part thereof, are in a state incapable of creating a major-accident hazard, then the Member State may, in accordance with the criteria referred to in subparagraph (b), limit the information required in safety reports to those matters which are relevant to the prevention of residual major-accident hazards and the limitation of their consequences for man and the environment.
   (b) The Commission shall establish harmonised criteria for decisions of the competent authority that an establishment is in a state incapable of creating a major accident hazard within the meaning of subparagraph (a). Those measures, designed to amend non-essential elements of this Directive by supplementing it, shall be adopted in accordance with the regulatory procedure with scrutiny referred to in Article 22(3).
   (c) Member States shall ensure that the competent authority communicates a list of the establishments concerned to the Commission, giving reasons. The Commission shall forward the lists annually to the Committee referred to in Article 22.
   (d) The Commission is invited to review by 31 December 2006 in close cooperation with the Member States, the existing 'Guidance on the Preparation of a Safety Report'.

Article 10 Modification of an installation, an establishment or a storage facility

In the event of the modification of an installation, establishment, storage facility, or process or of the nature or quantity of dangerous substances which could have significant repercussions on major-accident hazards, the Member States shall ensure that the operator:

- reviews and where necessary revises the major-accident prevention policy, and the management systems and procedures referred to in Articles 7 and 9,
- reviews, and where necessary revises, the safety report and informs the competent authority referred to in Article 16 of the details of such revision in advance of such modification.

Article 11 Emergency plans

1. Member States shall ensure that, for all establishments to which Article 9 applies:
   (a) the operator draws up an internal emergency plan for the measures to be taken inside the establishment,
      - for new establishments, prior to commencing operation,
      - for existing establishments not previously covered by Directive 82/501/EEC, three years from the date laid down in Article 24 (1),
      - for other establishments, two years from the date laid down in Article 24 (1);
      - for establishments which subsequently fall within the scope of this Directive, without delay, but at all events within one year after the date on which this Directive applies to the establishment concerned, as laid down in the first subparagraph of Article 2(1);
   (b) the operator supplies to the competent authorities, to enable the latter to draw up external emergency plans, the necessary information within the following periods of time:
      - for new establishments, prior to the start of operation,
      - for existing establishments not previously covered by Directive 82/501/EEC, three years from the date laid down in Article 24 (1),
      - for other establishments, two years from the date laid down in Article 24 (1);
      - for establishments which subsequently fall within the scope of this Directive, without delay, but at all events within one year after the date on which this Directive applies to the establishment concerned, as laid down in the first subparagraph of Article 2(1);
   (c) the authorities designated for that purpose by the Member State draw up an external emergency plan for the measures to be taken outside the establishment.
2. The emergency plans must be established with the objectives of:

- containing and controlling incidents so as to minimize the effects, and to limit damage to man, the environment and property,
- implementing the measures necessary to protect man and the environment from the effects of major accidents,
- communicating the necessary information to the public and to the services or authorities concerned in the area,
- providing for the restoration and clean-up of the environment following a major accident.

Emergency plans shall contain the information set out in Annex IV.

3. Without prejudice to the obligations of the competent authorities, Member States shall ensure that the internal emergency plans provided for in this Directive are drawn up in consultation with the personnel working inside the establishment, including long-term relevant subcontracted personnel, and that the public is consulted on external emergency plans when they are established or updated.
4. Member States shall ensure that internal and external emergency plans are reviewed, tested, and where necessary revised and updated by the operators and designated authorities at suitable intervals of no longer than three years. The review shall take into account changes occurring in the establishments concerned or within the emergency services concerned, new technical knowledge, and knowledge concerning the response to major accidents.

4a. With regard to external emergency plans, Member States should take into account the need to facilitate enhanced cooperation in civil protection assistance in major emergencies.

5. Member States shall ensure that emergency plans are put into effect without delay by the operator and, if necessary by the competent authority designated for this purpose:
   - when a major accident occurs, or
   - when an uncontrolled event occurs which by its nature could reasonably be expected to lead to a major accident.
6. The competent authority may decide, giving reasons for its decision, in view of the information contained in the safety report, that the requirement to produce an external emergency plan under paragraph 1 shall not apply.

Article 12 Land-use planning

1. Member States shall ensure that the objectives of preventing major accidents and limiting the consequences of such accidents are taken into account in their land-use policies and/or other relevant policies. They shall pursue those objectives through controls on:
   (a) the siting of new establishments,
   (b) modifications to existing establishments covered by Article 10,
   (c) new developments such as transport links, locations frequented by the public and residential areas in the vicinity of existing establishments, where

the siting or developments are such as to increase the risk or consequences of a major accident.

Member States shall ensure that their land-use and/or other relevant policies and the procedures for implementing those policies take account of the need, in the long term, to maintain appropriate distances between establishments covered by this Directive and residential areas, buildings and areas of public use, major transport routes as far as possible, recreational areas and areas of particular natural sensitivity or interest and, in the case of existing establishments, of the need for additional technical measures in accordance with Article 5 so as not to increase the risks to people.

1a. The Commission is invited by 31 December 2006, in close cooperation with the Member States, to draw up guidelines defining a technical database including risk data and risk scenarios, to be used for assessing the compatibility between the establishments covered by this Directive and the areas described in paragraph 1. The definition of this database shall as far as possible take account of the evaluations made by the competent authorities, the information obtained from operators and all other relevant information such as the socioeconomic benefits of development and the mitigating effects of emergency plans.

2. Member States shall ensure that all competent authorities and planning authorities responsible for decisions in this area set up appropriate consultation procedures to facilitate implementation of the policies established under paragraph 1. The procedures shall be designed to ensure that technical advice on the risks arising from the establishment is available, either on a case-by-case or on a generic basis, when decisions are taken.

Article 13 Information on safety measures

1. Member States shall ensure that information on safety measures and on the requisite behaviour in the event of an accident is supplied regularly and in the most appropriate form, without their having to request it, to all persons and all establishments serving the public (such as schools and hospitals) liable to be affected by a major accident originating in an establishment covered by Article 9.

   The information shall be reviewed every three years and, where necessary, repeated and updated, at least if there is any modification within the meaning of Article 10. It shall also be made permanently available to the public. The maximum period between the repetition of

   the information to the public shall, in any case, be no longer than five years.

   Such information shall contain, at least, the information listed in Annex V.

2. Member States shall, with respect to the possibility of a major accident with transboundary effects originating in an establishment under Article 9, provide sufficient information to the potentially affected Member States so that all relevant provisions contained in Articles 11, 12 and this Article can be applied, where applicable, by the affected Member State.

3. Where the Member State concerned has decided that an establishment close to the territory of another Member State is incapable of creating a major-accident hazard beyond its boundary for the purposes of Article 11 (6) and is not therefore required to produce an external emergency plan under Article 11 (1), it shall so inform the other Member State.
4. Member States shall ensure that the safety report is made available to the public. The operator may ask the competent authority not to disclose to the public certain parts of the report, for reasons of industrial, commercial or personal confidentiality, public security or national defence. In such cases, on the approval of the competent authority, the operator shall supply to the authority, and make available to the public, an amended report excluding those matters.
5. Member States shall ensure that the public is able to give its opinion in the following cases:
   - planning for new establishments covered by Article 9,
   - modifications to existing establishments under Article 10, where such modifications are subject to obligations provided for in this Directive as to planning,
   - developments around such existing establishments.
6. In the case of establishments subject to the provisions of Article 9, Member States shall ensure that the inventory of dangerous substances provided for in Article 9(2) is made available to the public subject to the provisions of paragraph 4 of this Article and Article 20.

Article 14 Information to be supplied by the operator following a major accident

1. Member States shall ensure that, as soon as practicable following a major accident, the operator shall be required, using the most appropriate means:
   (a) to inform the competent authorities;
   (b) to provide them with the following information as soon as it becomes available:
      - the circumstances of the accident,
      - the dangerous substances involved,
      - the data available for assessing the effects of the accident on man and the environment, and
      - the emergency measures taken;
   (c) to inform them of the steps envisaged:
      - to alleviate the medium- and long-term effects of the accident,
      - to prevent any recurrence of such an accident;
   (d) to update the information provided if further investigation reveals additional facts which alter that information or the conclusions drawn.
2. Member States shall require the competent authority:
   (a) to ensure that any urgent, medium- and long-term measures which may prove necessary are taken;

(b) to collect, by inspection, investigation or other appropriate means, the information necessary for a full analysis of the technical, organizational and managerial aspects of the major accident;
(c) to take appropriate action to ensure that the operator takes any necessary remedial measures; and
(d) to make recommendations on future preventive measures.

Article 15 Information to be supplied by the Member States to the Commission

1. For the purpose of prevention and mitigation of major accidents, Member States shall inform the Commission as soon as practicable of major accidents meeting the criteria of Annex VI which have occurred within their territory. They shall provide it with the following details:
   (a) the Member State, the name and address of the authority responsible for the report;
   (b) the date, time and place of the major accident, including the full name of the operator and the address of the establishment involved;
   (c) a brief description of the circumstances of the accident, including the dangerous substances involved, and the immediate effects on man and the environment;
   (d) a brief description of the emergency measures taken and of the immediate precautions necessary to prevent recurrence.
2. Member States shall, as soon as the information provided for in Article 14 is collected, inform the Commission of the result of their analysis and recommendations using a report form established and kept under review by means of the regulatory procedure referred to in Article 22(2).

   Reporting of this information by Member States may be delayed only to allow for the completion of legal proceedings where such reporting is liable to affect those proceedings.
3. Member States shall inform the Commission of the name and address of any body which might have relevant information on major accidents and which is able to advise the competent authorities of other Member States which have to intervene in the event of such an accident.

Article 16 Competent authority

Without prejudice to the operator's responsibilities, Member States shall set up or appoint the competent authority or authorities responsible for carrying out the duties laid down in this Directive and, if necessary, bodies to assist the competent authority or authorities at technical level.

Article 17 Prohibition of use

1. Member States shall prohibit the use or bringing into use of any establishment, installation or storage facility, or any part thereof where the measures taken by

the operator for the prevention and mitigation of major accidents are seriously deficient.

Member States may prohibit the use or bringing into use of any establishment, installation or storage facility, or any part thereof if the operator has not submitted the notification, reports or other information required by this Directive within the specified period.

2. Member States shall ensure that operators may appeal against a prohibition order by a competent authority under paragraph 1 to an appropriate body determined by national law and procedures.

Article 18 Inspections

1. Member States shall ensure that the competent authorities organize a system of inspections, or other measures of control appropriate to the type of establishment concerned. Those inspections or control measures shall not be dependent upon receipt of the safety report or any other report submitted. Such inspections or other control measures shall be sufficient for a planned and systematic examination of the systems being employed at the establishment, whether of a technical, organizational or managerial nature, so as to ensure in particular:
   - that the operator can demonstrate that he has taken appropriate measures, in connection with the various activities involved in the establishment, to prevent major accidents,
   - that the operator can demonstrate that he has provided appropriate means for limiting the consequences of major accidents, on site and off site,
   - that the data and information contained in the safety report, or any other report submitted, adequately reflects the conditions in the establishment,
   - that information has been supplied to the public pursuant to Article 13 (1).
2. The system of inspection specified in paragraph 1 shall comply with the following conditions:
   (a) there shall be a programme of inspections for all establishments. Unless the competent authority has established a programme of inspections based upon a systematic appraisal of major-accident hazards of the particular establishment concerned, the programme shall entail at least one on-site inspection made by the competent authority every twelve months of each establishment covered by Article 9;
   (b) following each inspection, a report shall be prepared by the competent authority;
   (c) where necessary, every inspection carried out by the competent authority shall be followed up with the management of the establishment, within a reasonable period following the inspection.
3. The competent authority may require the operator to provide any additional information necessary to allow the authority fully to assess the possibility of a major accident and to determine the scope of possible increased probability

and/or aggravation of major accidents, to permit the preparation of an external emergency plan, and to take substances into account which, due to their physical form, particular conditions or location, may require additional consideration.

Article 19 Information system and exchanges

1. Member States and the Commission shall exchange information on the experience acquired with regard to the prevention of major accidents and the limitation of their consequences. This information shall concern, in particular, the functioning of the measures provided for in this Directive.

1a. For establishments covered by this Directive, Member States shall supply the Commission with at least the following information:

(a) the name or trade name of the operator and the full address of the establishment concerned; and

(b) the activity or activities of the establishment.

The Commission shall set up and keep up to date a database containing the information supplied by the Member States. Access to the database shall be reserved to persons authorised by the Commission or the competent authorities of the Member States.

2. The Commission shall set up and keep at the disposal of Member States a register and information system containing, in particular, details of the major accidents which have occurred within the territory of Member States, for the purpose of:

(a) the rapid dissemination of the information supplied by Member States pursuant to Article 15 (1) among all competent authorities;

(b) distribution to competent authorities of an analysis of the causes of major accidents and the lessons learned from them;

(c) supply of information to competent authorities on preventive measures;

(d) provision of information on organizations able to provide advice or relevant information on the occurrence, prevention and mitigation of major accidents.

The register and information system shall contain, at least:

(a) the information supplied by Member States in compliance with Article 15 (1);

(b) an analysis of the causes of the accidents;

(c) the lessons learned from the accidents;

(d) the preventive measures necessary to prevent a recurrence.

3. Without prejudice to Article 20, access to the register and information system shall be open to government departments of the Member States, industry or trade associations, trade unions, non-governmental organizations in the field of the protection of the environment and other international or research organizations working in the field.

4. Member States shall provide the Commission with a three-yearly report in accordance with the procedure laid down in Council Directive 91/692/EEC of

23 December 1991 standardizing and rationalizing reports on the implementation of certain Directives relating to the environment[1] for establishments covered by Articles 6 and 9. The Commission shall publish a summary of this information every three years.

Article 20 Confidentiality

1. Member States shall ensure, in the interests of transparency, that the competent authorities are required to make information received pursuant to this Directive available to any natural or legal person who so requests.

   Information obtained by the competent authorities or the Commission may, where national provisions so require, be kept confidential if it calls into question:

   - the confidentiality of the deliberations of the competent authorities and the Commission,
   - the confidentiality of international relations and national defence,
   - public security,
   - the confidentiality of preliminary investigation proceedings or of current legal proceedings,
   - commercial and industrial secrets, including intellectual property,
   - personal data and/or files,
   - data supplied by a third party if that party asks for them to be kept confidential.

2. This Directive shall not preclude the conclusion by a Member State of agreements with third countries on the exchange of information to which it is privy at internal level.

Article 21 Terms of reference of the Committee

1. The Commission shall adapt the criteria referred to in Article 9(6)(b) and Annexes II to VI to technical progress. Those measures, designed to amend non-essential elements of this Directive, shall be adopted in accordance with the regulatory procedure with scrutiny referred to in Article 22(3).
2. The measure to draw up the report form referred to in Article 15(2) shall be adopted in accordance with the regulatory procedure referred to in Article 22(2).

Article 22 Committee procedure

1. The Commission shall be assisted by a Committee.
2. Where reference is made to this paragraph, Articles 5 and 7 of Decision 1999/468/EC shall apply, having regard to the provisions of Article 8 thereof. The period laid down in Article 5(6) of Decision 1999/468/EC shall be set at three months.

[1] OJ No L 377, 31. 12. 1991, p. 48.

3. Where reference is made to this paragraph, Article 5a(1) to (4) and Article 7 of Decision 1999/468/EC shall apply, having regard to the provisions of Article 8 thereof.

Article 23 Repeal of Directive 82/501/EEC

1. Directive 82/501/EEC shall be repealed 24 months after the entry into force of this Directive.
2. Notifications, emergency plans and information for the public presented or drawn up pursuant to Directive 82/501/EEC shall remain in force until such time as they are replaced under the corresponding provisions of this Directive.

Article 24 Implementation

1. Member States shall bring into force the laws, regulations and administrative provisions necessary to comply with this Directive not later than 24 months after its entry into force. They shall forthwith inform the Commission thereof.

   When Member States adopt these measures, they shall contain a reference to this Directive or shall be accompanied by such reference on the occasion of their official publication. The methods of making such reference shall be laid down by Member States.
2. Member States shall communicate to the Commission the main provisions of domestic law which they adopt in the field governed by this Directive.

Article 25 Entry into force

This Directive shall enter into force on the 20th day following that of its publication in the Official Journal of the European Communities.

Article 26 This Directive is addressed to the Member States.

Done at Brussels, 9 December 1996.

For the Council

The President

B. HOWLIN

List of Annexes

ANNEX I

APPLICATION OF THE DIRECTIVE

INTRODUCTION

1. This Annex applies to the presence of dangerous substances at any establishment within the meaning of Article 3 of this Directive and determines the application of the relevant Articles thereof.
2. Mixtures and preparations shall be treated in the same way as pure substances provided they remain within concentration limits set according to their properties under the relevant Directives given in Part 2, Note 1, or their latest adaptation to technical progress, unless a percentage composition or other description is specifically given.
3. The qualifying quantities set out below relate to each establishment.
4. The quantities to be considered for the application of the relevant Articles are the maximum quantities which are present or are likely to be present at any one time. Dangerous substances present at an establishment only in quantities equal to or less than 2 % of the relevant qualifying quantity shall be ignored for the purposes of calculating the total quantity present if their location within an establishment is such that it cannot act as an initiator of a major accident elsewhere on the site.
5. The rules given in Part 2, Note 4 governing the addition of dangerous substances, or categories of dangerous substances, shall apply where appropriate.
6. For the purposes of this Directive, a gas is any substance that has an absolute vapour pressure equal to or greater than 101,3 kPa at a temperature of 20 °C.
7. For the purposes of this Directive, a liquid is any substance that is not defined as a gas and that is not in the solid state at a temperature of 20 °C and at a standard pressure of 101,3 kPa.

PART 1

Named substances

Where a substance or group of substances listed in Part 1 also falls within a category of Part 2, the qualifying quantities set out in Part 1 must be used.

Column 1	Column 2	Column 3
Dangerous substances	Qualifying quantity (tonnes) for the application of 001	
	Articles 6 and 7	Articles 9
Ammonium nitrate (see note 1)	5 000	10 000
Ammonium nitrate (see note 2)	1 250	5 000
Ammonium nitrate (see note 3)	350	2 500
Ammonium nitrate (see note 4)	10	50
Potassium nitrate (see note 5)	5 000	10 000
Potassium nitrate (see note 6)	1 250	5 000
Bromine	20	100
Chlorine	10	25
Nickel compounds in inhalable powder form (nickel monoxide, nickel dioxide, nickel sulphide, trinickel disulphide, dinickel trioxide)		1
Ethyleneimine	10	20
Fluorine	10	20
Formaldehyde (concentration ≥ 90 %)	5	50

Column 1	Column 2	Column 3
Dangerous substances	Qualifying quantity (tonnes) for the application of 001	
	Articles 6 and 7	Articles 9
Hydrogen	5	50
Hydrogen chloride (liquefied gas)	25	250
Lead alkyls	5	50
Liquefied extremely flammable gases (including LPG) and natural gas	50	200
Acetylen	5	50
Ethylene oxide	5	50
Propylene oxide	5	50
Methanol	500	5000
4, 4-Methylenebis (2-chloraniline) and/or salts, in powder form		0.01
Methylisocyanate		0.15
Oxygen	200	2000
Toluene diisocyanate	10	100
Carbonyl dichloride (phosgene)	0.3	0.75
Arsenic trihydride (arsine)	0.2	1
Phosphorus trihydride (phosphine)	0.2	1
Sulphur dichloride	1	1
Sulphur trioxide	15	75

Column 1	Column 2	Column 3
Dangerous substances	Qualifying quantity (tonnes) for the application of 0.01	
	Articles 6 and 7	Articles 9
Petroleum products: (a) gasolines and naphthas, (b) kerosenes (including jet fuels), (c) gas oils (including diesel fuels, home heating oils and gas oil blending streams)	2500	25000

NOTES

1. Ammonium nitrate (5 000/10 000): fertilisers capable of self-sustaining decomposition

   This applies to ammonium nitrate-based compound/composite fertilisers (compound/composite fertilisers containing ammonium nitrate with phosphate and/or potash) in which the nitrogen content as a result of ammonium nitrate is

   - between 15,75 %[1] and 24,5 %[2] by weight, and either with not more than 0,4 % total combustible/organic materials or which fulfil the requirements of Annex II of Directive 80/876/EEC,
   - 15,75 %[3] by weight or less and unrestricted combustible materials, and which are capable of self-sustaining decomposition according to the UN Trough Test (see United Nations Recommendations on the Transport of Dangerous Goods: Manual of Tests and Criteria, Part III, subsection 38.2).

2. Ammonium nitrate (1 250/5 000): fertiliser grade

   This applies to straight ammonium nitrate-based fertilisers and to ammonium nitrate-based compound/composite fertilisers in which the nitrogen content as a result of ammonium nitrate is

   - more than 24,5 % by weight, except for mixtures of ammonium nitrate with dolomite, limestone and/or calcium carbonate with a purity of at least 90 %,
   - more than 15,75 % by weight for mixtures of ammonium nitrate and ammonium sulphate,

1 15,75 % nitrogen content by weight as a result of ammonium nitrate corresponds to 45 % ammonium nitrate.

2 24,5 % nitrogen content by weight as a result of ammonium nitrate corresponds to 70 % ammonium nitrate.

3 15,75 % nitrogen content by weight as a result of ammonium nitrate corresponds to 45 % ammonium nitrate

- more than 28 %[1] by weight for mixtures of ammonium nitrate with dolomite, limestone and/or calcium carbonate with a purity of at least 90 %, and which fulfil the requirements of Annex II of Directive 80/876/EEC.

3. Ammonium nitrate (350/2500): technical grade

   This applies to:

   - ammonium nitrate and preparations of ammonium nitrate in which the nitrogen content as a result of the ammonium nitrate is
   - between 24,5 % and 28 % by weight, and which contain not more than 0,4 % combustible substances,
   - more than 28 % by weight, and which contain not more than 0,2 % combustible substances,
   - aqueous ammonium nitrate solutions in which the concentration of ammonium nitrate is more than 80 % by weight.

4. Ammonium nitrate (10/50): 'off-specs' material and fertilisers not fulfilling the detonation test

   This applies to:

   - material rejected during the manufacturing process and to ammonium nitrate and preparations of ammonium nitrate, straight ammonium nitrate-based fertilisers and ammonium nitrate-based compound/ - composite fertilisers referred to in notes 2 and 3, that are being or have been returned from the final user to a manufacturer, temporary storage or reprocessing plant for reworking, recycling or treatment for safe use, because they no longer comply with the specifications of Notes 2 and 3;
   - fertilisers referred to in note 1, first indent, and Note 2 which do not fulfil the requirements of Annex II of Directive 80/876/EEC.

5. Potassium nitrate (5 000/10 000): composite potassium-nitrate based fertilisers composed of potassium nitrate in prilled/granular form

6. Potassium nitrate (1 250/5 000): composite potassium-nitrate based fertilisers composed of potassium nitrate in crystalline form

7. Polychlorodibenzofurans and polychlorodibenzodioxins1. Ammonium nitrate (350/2 500)

[1] 28 % nitrogen content by weight as a result of ammonium nitrate corresponds to 80 % ammonium nitrate.

The quantities of polychlorodibenzofurans and polychlorodibenzodioxins are calculated using the following factors:

International Toxic Equivalent Factors (ITEF) for the congeners of concern (NATO/CCMS)					
2,3,7,8-TCDD		1	1 2,3,7,8-TCDF		0.1
1,2,3,7,8-PeDD		0.5	2,3,4,7,8-PeCDF		0.5
1,2,3,4,7,8-HxCDD 1,2,3,6,7,8-HxCDD 1,2,3,7,8,9-HxCDD	}	0.1	1,2,3,4,7,8-HxCDF 1,2,3,7,8,9-HxCDF 1,2,3,6,7,8-HxCDF 2,3,4,6,7,8-HxCDF	}	0.1
1,2,3,4,6,7,8-HpCDD		0.01			
OCDD		0.001	1,2,3,4,6,7,8-HpCDD 1,2,3,4,6,7,8-HpCDF	}	0.01
(T = tetra, P = penta, Hx = hexa, HP = hepta, O = octa)					

PART 2

Categories of substances and preparations not specifically named in Part 1

Column 1	Column 2	Column 3
Categories of dangerous substances	Qualifying quantity (tonnes) of dangerous substances as delivered in Article 3 (4), for the application of	
	Articles 6 and 7	Articles 9
1. VERY TOXIC	5	20
2. TOXIC	50	200

3. OXIDIZING	50	200
4. EXPLOSIVE (see note 2) where the substance, preparation or article falls under UN/ADR Division 1.4	50	200
5. EXPLOSIVE (see note 2) where the substance, preparation or article falls under any of: UN/ADR Divisions 1.1, 1.2, 1.3, 1.5 or 1.6 or risk phrase R2 or R3	10	50
6. FLAMMABLE (where the substance or preparation falls within the definition given in Note 3 (a))	5000	50000
7 a. HIGHLY FLAMMABLE (where the substance or preparation falls within the definition given in Note 3 (b) (1))	50	200
7 b. HIGHLY FLAMMABLE liquids (where the substance or preparation falls within the definition given in Note 3 (b) (2))	5000	50000
8. EXTREMELY FLAMMABLE (where the substance or preparation falls within the definition given in Note 3 (c))	10	50
9. DANGEROUS FOR THE ENVIRONMENT risk phrases: i) R50: 'Very toxic to aquatic organisms' (including R50/53) ii) R51/53: 'Toxic to aquatic organisms; may cause long term adverse effects in the aquatic environment	100 200	200 500
10. ANY CLASSIFICATION not covered by those given above in combination with risk phrases: (i) R14: 'Reacts violenty with water' (including R14/15) (ii) R29: 'in contact with water, liberates toxic gas'	100 50	500 200

NOTES

1. Substances and preparations are classified according to the following Directives and their current adaptation to technical progress: Council Directive 67/548/EEC of 27 June 1967 on the approximation of the laws, regulations and administrative provisions relating to the classification, packaging and labelling of dangerous substances[1],

   Directive 1999/45/EC of the European Parliament and of the Council of 31 May 1999 concerning the approximation of laws, regulations and administrative provisions of the Member States relating to the classification, packaging and labelling of dangerous preparations[2].

   In the case of substances and preparations which are not classified as dangerous according to either of the above directives, for example waste, but which nevertheless are present, or are likely to be present, in an establishment and which possess or are likely to possess, under the conditions found at the establishment, equivalent properties in terms of major-accident potential the procedures for provisional classification shall be followed in accordance with the relevant article of the appropriate Directive.

   In the case of substances and preparations with properties giving rise to more than one classification, for the purposes of this Directive the lowest qualifying quantities shall apply. However, for the application of the rule in Note 4, the qualifying quantity used shall always be the one corresponding to the classification concerned.

   For the purposes of this Directive, the Commission shall establish and keep up to date a list of substances which have been classified into the above categories by a harmonised Decision in accordance with Directive 67/548/EEC.

2. An 'explosive' means:
   - a substance or preparation which creates the risk of an explosion by shock, friction, fire or other sources of ignition (risk phrase R2),
   - a substance or preparation which creates extreme risks of explosion by shock, friction, fire or other sources of ignition (risk phrase R3), or
   - a substance, preparation or article covered by Class 1 of the European. Agreement concerning the International Carriage of Dangerous Goods by Road (UN/ADR), concluded on 30 September 1957, as amended, as transposed by Council Directive 94/55/EC of 21 November 1994 on the approximation of the laws of the Member States with regard to the transport of dangerous goods by road.

   Included in this definition are pyrotechnics, which for the purposes of this Directive are defined as substances (or mixtures of substances) designated to produce heat, light, sound, gas or smoke or a combination of such effects

[1] OJ L 196, 16.8.1967, p. 1. Directive as last amended by Regulation (EC) No 807/2003 (OJ L 122, 16.5.2003, p. 36).

[2] OJ L 200, 30.7.1999, p. 1. Directive as amended by Commission Directive 2001/60/ECm (OJ L 226, 22.8.2001, p. 5).

through self-sustained exothermic chemical reactions. Where a substance or preparation is classified by both UN/ADR and risk phase R2 or R3, the UN/ADR classification shall take precedence over assignment of risk phrases.

Substances and articles of Class 1 are classified in any of the divisions 1.1 to 1.6 in accordance with the UN/ADR classification scheme. The divisions concerned are:

Division 1.1: 'Substances and articles which have a mass explosion hazard (a mass explosion is an explosion which affects almost the entire load virtually instantaneously).'

Division 1.2: 'Substances and articles which have a projection hazard but not a mass explosion hazard.'

Division 1.3: 'Substances and articles which have a fire hazard and either a minor blast hazard or a minor projection hazard or both, but not a mass explosion hazard:

(a) combustion of which gives rise to considerable radiant heat; or
(b) which burn one after another, producing minor blast or projection effects or both.'

Division 1.4: 'Substances and articles which present only a slight risk in the event of ignition or initiation during carriage. The effects are largely confined to the package and no projection of fragments of appreciable size or range is to be expected. An external fire shall not cause virtually instantaneous explosion of virtually the entire contents of the package.'

Division 1.5: 'Very insensitive substances having a mass explosion hazard which are so insensitive that there is very little probability of initiation or of transition from burning to detonation under normal conditions of carriage. As a minimum requirement they shall not explode in the external fire test.'

Division 1.6: 'Extremely insensitive articles which do not have a mass explosion hazard. The articles contain only extremely insensitive detonating substances and demonstrate a negligible probability of accidental initiation or propagation. The risk is limited to the explosion of a single article.'

Included in this definition are also explosive or pyrotechnic substances or preparations contained in articles. In the case of articles containing explosive or pyrotechnic substances or preparations, if the quantity of the substance or preparation contained is known, that quantity shall be considered for the purposes of this Directive. If the quantity is not known, then, for the purposes of this Directive, the whole article shall be treated as explosive.

3. 'Flammable`, 'highly flammable`, and 'extremely flammable` in categories 6, 7 and 8 mean:
   (a) flammable liquids:
   substances and preparations having a flash point equal to or greater than 21 °C and less than or equal to 55 °C (risk phrase R 10), supporting combustion;

(b) highly flammable liquids:

1. - substances and preparations which may become hot and finally catch fire in contact with air at ambient temperature without any input of energy (risk phrase R 17),
   - substances which have a flash point lower than 55 °C and which remain liquid under pressure, where particular processing conditions, such as high pressure or high temperature, may create major-accident hazards;
2. - substances and preparations having a flash point lower than 21 °C and which are not extremely flammable (risk phrase R 11, second indent);
   - substances and preparations which have a flash point lower than 55 °C and which remain liquid under pressure, where particular processing conditions, such as high pressure or high temperature, may create major-accident hazards;

(c) extremely flammable gases and liquids:

1. liquid substances and preparations which have a flash point lower than 0 °C and the boiling point (or, in the case of a boiling range, the initial boiling point) of which at normal pressure is less than or equal to 35 °C (risk phrase R 12, first indent), and
2. gases which are flammable in contact with air at ambient temperature and pressure (risk phrase R12, second indent), which are in a gaseous or supercritical state, and
3. flammable and highly flammable liquid substances and preparations maintained at a temperature above their boiling point
4. In the case of an establishment where no individual substance or preparation is present in a quantity above or equal to the relevant qualifying quantities, the following rule shall be applied to determine whether the establishment is covered by the relevant requirements of this Directive.

This Directive shall apply if the sum :

q1/QU1 + q2/QU2 + q3/QU3 + q4/QU4 + q5/QU5 +… is greater than or equal to 1,

where qx = the quantity of dangerous substance x (or category of dangerous substances) falling within Parts 1 or 2 of this Annex,

and QUX = the relevant qualifying quantity for substance or category x from column 3 of Parts 1 or 2.

This Directive shall apply, with the exception of Articles 9, 11 and 13, if the sum

q1/QL1 + q2/QL2 + q3/QL3 + q4/QL4 + q5/QL5 +… is greater than or equal to 1,

where qx = the quantity of dangerous substance x (or category of dangerous substances) falling within Parts 1 or 2 of this Annex,

and QLX = the relevant qualifying quantity for substance or category x from column 2 of Parts 1 or 2.

This rule shall be used to assess the overall hazards associated with toxicity, flammability, and eco-toxicity. It must therefore be applied three times:

(a) for the addition of substances and preparations named in Part 1 and classified as toxic or very toxic, together with substances and preparations falling into categories 1 or 2;

(b) for the addition of substances and preparations named in Part 1 and classified as oxidising, explosive, flammable, highly flammable, or extremely flammable, together with substances and preparations falling into categories 3, 4, 5, 6, 7a, 7b or 8;

(c) for the addition of substances and preparations named in Part 1 and classified as dangerous for the environment (R50 (including R50/53) or R51/53), together with substances and preparations falling into categories 9(i) or 9(ii);

The relevant provisions of this Directive apply if any of the sums obtained by (a), (b) or (c) is greater than or equal to 1.

ANNEX II

MINIMUM DATA AND INFORMATION TO BE CONSIDERED IN THE SAFETY REPORT SPECIFIED IN ARTICLE 9

I. Information on the management system and on the organization of the establishment with a view to major accident prevention

This information shall contain the elements given in Annex III.

II. Presentation of the environment of the establishment

A. description of the site and its environment including the geographical location, meteorological, geological, hydrographic conditions and, if necessary, its history;

B. identification of installations and other activities of the establishment which could present a major-accident hazard;

C. description of areas where a major accident may occur.

III. Description of the installation

A. description of the main activities and products of the parts of the establishment which are important from the point of view of safety, sources of major-accident risks and conditions under which such a major accident could happen, together with a description of proposed preventive measures;

B. description of processes, in particular the operating methods;

C. description of dangerous substances:

1. inventory of dangerous substances including:
   - the identification of dangerous substances: chemical name, CAS number, name according to IUPAC nomenclature,
   - the maximum quantity of dangerous substances present or likely to be present;

2. physical, chemical, toxicological characteristics and indication of the hazards, both immediate and delayed for man and the environment;
3. physical and chemical behaviour under normal conditions of use or under foreseeable accidental conditions.

IV. Identification and accidental risks analysis and prevention methods

A. detailed description of the possible major-accident scenarios and their probability or the conditions under which they occur including a summary of the events which may play a role in triggering each of these scenarios, the causes being internal or external to the installation;

B. assessment of the extent and severity of the consequences of identified major accidents including maps, images or, as appropriate, equivalent descriptions, showing areas which are liable to be affected by such accidents arising from the establishment, subject to the provisions of Articles 13(4) and 20

C. description of technical parameters and equipment used for the safety of installations.

V. Measures of protection and intervention to limit the consequences of an accident

A. description of the equipment installed in the plant to limit the consequences of major accidents;

B. organization of alert and intervention;

C. description of mobilizable resources, internal or external;

D. summary of elements described in A, B, and C above necessary for drawing up the internal emergency plan prepared in compliance with Article 11.

ANNEX III

PRINCIPLES REFERRED TO IN ARTICLE 7 AND INFORMATION REFERRED TO IN ARTICLE 9 ON THE MANAGEMENT SYSTEM AND THE ORGANIZATION OF THE ESTABLISHMENT WITH A VIEW TO THE PREVENTION OF MAJOR ACCIDENTS

For the purpose of implementing the operator's major-accident prevention policy and safety management system account shall be taken of the following elements. The requirements laid down in the document referred to in Article 7 should be proportionate to the major-accident hazards presented by the establishment:

(a) the major accident prevention policy should be established in writing and should include the operator's overall aims and principles of action with respect to the control of major-accident hazards;

(b) the safety management system should include the part of the general management system which includes the organizational structure, responsibilities, practices, procedures, processes and resources for determining and implementing the major-accident prevention policy;

(c) the following issues shall be addressed by the safety management system:

(i) organisation and personnel - the roles and responsibilities of personnel involved in the management of major hazards at all levels in the organisation. The identification of training needs of such personnel and the provision of the training so identified. The involvement of employees and of subcontracted personnel working in the establishment;

(ii) identification and evaluation of major hazards - adoption and implementation of procedures for systematically identifying major hazards arising from normal and abnormal operation and the assessment of their likelihood and severity;

(iii) operational control - adoption and implementation of procedures and instructions for safe operation, including maintenance, of plant, processes, equipment and temporary stoppages;

(iv) management of change - adoption and implementation of procedures for planning modifications to, or the design of new installations, processes or storage facilities;

(v) planning for emergencies - adoption and implementation of procedures to identify foreseeable emergencies by systematic analysis, to prepare, test and review emergency plans to respond to such emergencies and to provide specific training for the staff concerned. Such training shall be given to all personnel working in the establishment, including relevant subcontracted personnel;

(vi) monitoring performance - adoption and implementation of procedures for the ongoing assessment of compliance with the objectives set by the operator's major-accident prevention policy and safety management system, and the mechanisms for investigation and taking corrective action in case of non-compliance. The procedures should cover the operator's system for reporting major accidents of near misses, particularly those involving failure of protective measures, and their investigation and follow-up on the basis of lessons learnt;

(vii) audit and review - adoption and implementation of procedures for periodic systematic assessment of the major-accident prevention policy and the effectiveness and suitability of the safety management system; the documented review of performance of the policy and safety management system and its updating by senior management.

ANNEX IV

DATA AND INFORMATION TO BE INCLUDED IN THE EMERGENCY PLANS SPECIFIED UNDER ARTICLE 11

1. Internal emergency plans

(a) Names or positions of persons authorized to set emergency procedures in motion and the person in charge of and coordinating the on-site mitigatory action.

(b) Name or position of the person with responsibility for liaising with the authority responsible for the external emergency plan.
(c) For foreseeable conditions or events which could be significant in bringing about a major accident, a description of the action which should be taken to control the conditions or events and to limit their consequences, including a description of the safety equipment and the resources available.
(d) Arrangements for limiting the risks to persons on site including how warnings are to be given and the actions persons are expected to take on receipt of a warning.
(e) Arrangements for providing early warning of the incident to the authority responsible for setting the external emergency plan in motion, the type of information which should be contained in an initial warning and the arrangements for the provision of more detailed information as it becomes available.
(f) Arrangements for training staff in the duties they will be expected to perform, and where necessary coordinating this with off-site emergency services.
(g) Arrangements for providing assistance with off-site mitigatory action.

2. External emergency plans
(a) Names or positions of persons authorized to set emergency procedures in motion and of persons authorized to take charge of and coordinate off-site action.
(b) Arrangements for receiving early warning of incidents, and alert and call-out procedures.
(c) Arrangements for coordinating resources necessary to implement the external emergency plan.
(d) Arrangements for providing assistance with on-site mitigatory action.
(e) Arrangements for off-site mitigatory action.
(f) Arrangements for providing the public with specific information relating to the accident and the behaviour which it should adopt.
(g) Arrangements for the provision of information to the emergency services of other Member States in the event of a major accident with possible transboundary consequences.

ANNEX V

ITEMS OF INFORMATION TO BE COMMUNICATED TO THE PUBLIC AS PROVIDED FOR IN ARTICLE 13 (1)

1. Name of operator and address of the establishment.
2. Identification, by position held, of the person giving the information.
3. Confirmation that the establishment is subject to the regulations and/or administrative provisions implementing this Directive and that the notification referred to in Article 6 (3), or the safety report referred to in Article 9 (1) has been submitted to the competent authority.

4. An explanation in simple terms of the activity or activities undertaken at the establishment.
5. The common names or, in the case of dangerous substances covered by Part 2 of Annex I, the generic names or the general danger classification of the substances and preparations involved at the establishment which could give rise to a major accident, with an indication of their principal dangerous characteristics.
6. General information relating to the nature of the major-accident hazards, including their potential effects on the population and the environment.
7. Adequate information on how the population concerned will be warned and kept informed in the event of a major accident.
8. Adequate information on the actions the population concerned should take, and on the behaviour they should adopt, in the event of a major accident.
9. Confirmation that the operator is required to make adequate arrangements on site, in particular liaison with the emergency services, to deal with major accidents and to minimize their effects.
10. A reference to the external emergency plan drawn up to cope with any off-site effects from an accident. This should include advice to cooperate with any instructions or requests from the emergency services at the time of an accident.
11. Details of where further relevant information can be obtained, subject to the requirements of confidentiality laid down in national legislation.

ANNEX VI

CRITERIA FOR THE NOTIFICATION OF AN ACCIDENT TO THE COMMISSION AS PROVIDED FOR IN ARTICLE 15 (1)

I. Any accident covered by paragraph 1 or having at least one of the consequences described in paragraphs 2, 3, 4 and 5 must be notified to the Commission.

1. Substances involved

   Any fire or explosion or accidental discharge of a dangerous substance involving, a quantity of at least 5 % of the qualifying quantity laid down in column 3 of Annex I.

2. Injury to persons and damage to real estate

   An accident directly involving a dangerous substance and giving rise to one of the following events:

   - a death,
   - six persons injured within the establishment and hospitalized for at least 24 hours,
   - one person outside the establishment hospitalized for at least 24 hours,
   - dwelling(s) outside the establishment damaged and unusable as a result of the accident,
   - the evacuation or confinement of persons for more than 2 hours (persons × hours): the value is at least 500,

- the interruption of drinking water, electricity, gas or telephone services for more than 2 hours (persons × hours): the value is at least 1 000.

3. Immediate damage to the environment
   - permanent or long-term damage to terrestrial habitats:
   - 0,5 ha or more of a habitat of environmental or conservation importance protected by legislation,
   - 10 or more hectares of more widespread habitat, including agricultural land,
   - significant or long-term damage to freshwater and marine habitats[1]- 10 km or more of river or canal,
   - 1 ha or more of a lake or pond,
   - 2 ha or more of delta,
   - 2 ha or more of a coastline or open sea,
   - significant damage to an aquifer or underground water (2*)
   - 1 ha or more.
4. Damage to property
   - damage to property in the establishment: at least ECU 2 million,
   - damage to property outside the establishment: at least ECU 0,5 million.
5. Cross-border damage

   Any accident directly involving a dangerous substance giving rise to effects outside the territory of the Member State concerned.

II. Accidents or 'near misses` which Member States regard as being of particular technical interest for preventing major accidents and limiting their consequences and which do not meet the quantitative criteria above should be notified to the Commission.

[1] In assessing damage, reference could be made where appropriate to Directives 75/440/EEC, 76/464/EEC and Directives adopted for its application in relation to certain substances, namely, Directives 76/160/EEC, 78/659/EEC, 79/923/EEC, or to the Lethal Concentration (LC) for 50 % of the species representative of the environment affected as defined by Directive 92/32/EEC for the criterion 'dangerous for the environment`.

22. Directive 2001/95/EC of the European Parliament and of the Council of 3 December 2001 on general product safety (Text with EEA relevance)

(OJ L 011 , 15/01/2002 p. 4 – 17)

THE EUROPEAN PARLIAMENT AND THE COUNCIL OF THE EUROPEAN UNION,

Having regard to the Treaty establishing the European Community, and in particular Article 95 thereof,

Having regard to the proposal from the Commission[1],

Having regard to the opinion of the Economic and Social Committee[2],

Acting in accordance with the procedure referred to in Article 251 of the Treaty[3], in the light of the joint text approved by the Conciliation Committee on 2 August 2001,

Whereas:

(1) Under Article 16 of Council Directive 92/59/EEC of 29 June 1992 on general product safety[4], the Council was to decide, four years after the date set for the implementation of the said Directive, on the basis of a report of the Commission on the experience acquired, together with appropriate proposals, whether to adjust Directive 92/59/EEC. It is necessary to amend Directive 92/59/EEC in several respects, in order to complete, reinforce or clarify some of its provisions in the light of experience as well as new and relevant developments on consumer product safety, together with the changes made to the Treaty, especially in Articles 152 concerning public health and 153 concerning consumer protection, and in the light of the precautionary principle. Directive 92/59/EEC should therefore be recast in the interest of clarity. This recasting leaves the safety of services outside the scope of this Directive, since the Commission intends to identify the needs, possibilities and priorities for Community action on the safety of services and liability of service providers, with a view to presenting appropriate proposals.

(2) It is important to adopt measures with the aim of improving the functioning of the internal market, comprising an area without internal frontiers in which the free movement of goods, persons, services and capital is assured.

(3) In the absence of Community provisions, horizontal legislation of the Member States on product safety, imposing in particular a general obligation on economic operators to market only safe products, might differ in the level of

1 OJ C 337 E, 28.11.2000, p. 109 and OJ C 154 E, 29.5.2000, p. 265.

2 OJ C 367, 20.12.2000, p. 34.

3 Opinion of the European Parliament of 15.11.2000 (OJ C 223, 8.8.2001, p. 154), Council Common Position of 12.2.2001 (OJ C 93, 23.3.2001, p. 24) and Decision of the European Parliament of 16.5.2001 (not yet published in the Official Journal). Decision of the European Parliament of 4.10.2001 and Council Decision of 27.9.2001.

4 OJ L 228, 11.8.1992, p. 24.

protection afforded to consumers. Such disparities, and the absence of horizontal legislation in some Member States, would be liable to create barriers to trade and distortion of competition within the internal market.

(4) In order to ensure a high level of consumer protection, the Community must contribute to protecting the health and safety of consumers. Horizontal Community legislation introducing a general product safety requirement, and containing provisions on the general obligations of producers and distributors, on the enforcement of Community product safety requirements and on rapid exchange of information and action at Community level in certain cases, should contribute to that aim.

(5) It is very difficult to adopt Community legislation for every product which exists or which may be developed; there is a need for a broad-based, legislative framework of a horizontal nature to deal with such products, and also to cover lacunae, in particular pending revision of the existing specific legislation, and to complement provisions in existing or forthcoming specific legislation, in particular with a view to ensuring a high level of protection of safety and health of consumers, as required by Article 95 of the Treaty.

(6) It is therefore necessary to establish at Community level a general safety requirement for any product placed on the market, or otherwise supplied or made available to consumers, intended for consumers, or likely to be used by consumers under reasonably foreseeable conditions even if not intended for them. In all these cases the products under consideration can pose risks for the health and safety of consumers which must be prevented. Certain second-hand goods should nevertheless be excluded by their very nature.

(7) This Directive should apply to products irrespective of the selling techniques, including distance and electronic selling.

(8) The safety of products should be assessed taking into account all the relevant aspects, in particular the categories of consumers which can be particularly vulnerable to the risks posed by the products under consideration, in particular children and the elderly.

(9) This Directive does not cover services, but in order to secure the attainment of the protection objectives in question, its provisions should also apply to products that are supplied or made available to consumers in the context of service provision for use by them. The safety of the equipment used by service providers themselves to supply a service to consumers does not come within the scope of this Directive since it has to be dealt with in conjunction with the safety of the service provided. In particular, equipment on which consumers ride or travel which is operated by a service provider is excluded from the scope of this Directive.

(10) Products which are designed exclusively for professional use but have subsequently migrated to the consumer market should be subject to the requirements of this Directive because they can pose risks to consumer health and safety when used under reasonably foreseeable conditions.

(11) In the absence of more specific provisions, within the framework of Community legislation covering safety of the products concerned, all the provisions of this Directive should apply in order to ensure consumer health and safety.

(12) If specific Community legislation sets out safety requirements covering only certain risks or categories of risks, with regard to the products concerned the obligations of economic operators in respect of these risks are those determined by the provisions of the specific legislation, while the general safety requirement of this Directive should apply to the other risks.

(13) The provisions of this Directive relating to the other obligations of producers and distributors, the obligations and powers of the Member States, the exchanges of information and rapid intervention situations and dissemination of information and confidentiality apply in the case of products covered by specific rules of Community law, if those rules do not already contain such obligations.

(14) In order to facilitate the effective and consistent application of the general safety requirement of this Directive, it is important to establish European voluntary standards covering certain products and risks in such a way that a product which conforms to a national standard transposing a European standard is to be presumed to be in compliance with the said requirement.

(15) With regard to the aims of this Directive, European standards should be established by European standardisation bodies, under mandates set by the Commission assisted by appropriate Committees. In order to ensure that products in compliance with the standards fulfil the general safety requirement, the Commission assisted by a committee composed of representatives of the Member States, should fix the requirements that the standards must meet. These requirements should be included in the mandates to the standardisation bodies.

(16) In the absence of specific regulations and when the European standards established under mandates set by the Commission are not available or recourse is not made to such standards, the safety of products should be assessed taking into account in particular national standards transposing any other relevant European or international standards, Commission recommendations or national standards, international standards, codes of good practice, the state of the art and the safety which consumers may reasonably expect. In this context, the Commission's recommendations may facilitate the consistent and effective application of this Directive pending the introduction of European standards or as regards the risks and/or products for which such standards are deemed not to be possible or appropriate.

(17) Appropriate independent certification recognised by the competent authorities may facilitate proof of compliance with the applicable product safety criteria.

(18) It is appropriate to supplement the duty to observe the general safety requirement by other obligations on economic operators because action by such operators is necessary to prevent risks to consumers under certain circumstances.

(19) The additional obligations on producers should include the duty to adopt measures commensurate with the characteristics of the products, enabling them to be informed of the risks that these products may present, to supply consumers with information enabling them to assess and prevent risks, to warn consumers of the risks posed by dangerous products already supplied to them, to withdraw those products from the market and, as a last resort, to recall them when necessary, which may involve, depending on the provisions applicable in the Member States, an appropriate form of compensation, for example exchange or reimbursement.

(20) Distributors should help in ensuring compliance with the applicable safety requirements. The obligations placed on distributors apply in proportion to their respective responsibilities. In particular, it may prove impossible, in the context of charitable activities, to provide the competent authorities with information and documentation on possible risks and origin of the product in the case of isolated used objects provided by private individuals.

(21) Both producers and distributors should cooperate with the competent authorities in action aimed at preventing risks and inform them when they conclude that certain products supplied are dangerous. The conditions regarding the provision of such information should be set in this Directive to facilitate its effective application, while avoiding an excessive burden for economic operators and the authorities.

(22) In order to ensure the effective enforcement of the obligations incumbent on producers and distributors, the Member States should establish or designate authorities which are responsible for monitoring product safety and have powers to take appropriate measures, including the power to impose effective, proportionate and dissuasive penalties, and ensure appropriate coordination between the various designated authorities.

(23) It is necessary in particular for the appropriate measures to include the power for Member States to order or organise, immediately and efficiently, the withdrawal of dangerous products already placed on the market and as a last resort to order, coordinate or organise the recall from consumers of dangerous products already supplied to them. Those powers should be applied when producers and distributors fail to prevent risks to consumers in accordance with their obligations. Where necessary, the appropriate powers and procedures should be available to the authorities to decide and apply any necessary measures rapidly.

(24) The safety of consumers depends to a great extent on the active enforcement of Community product safety requirements. The Member States should, therefore, establish systematic approaches to ensure the effectiveness of market surveillance and other enforcement activities and should ensure their openness to the public and interested parties.

(25) Collaboration between the enforcement authorities of the Member States is necessary in ensuring the attainment of the protection objectives of this

Directive. It is, therefore, appropriate to promote the operation of a European network of the enforcement authorities of the Member States to facilitate, in a coordinated manner with other Community procedures, in particular the Community Rapid Information System (RAPEX), improved collaboration at operational level on market surveillance and other enforcement activities, in particular risk assessment, testing of products, exchange of expertise and scientific knowledge, execution of joint surveillance projects and tracing, withdrawing or recalling dangerous products.

(26) It is necessary, for the purpose of ensuring a consistent, high level of consumer health and safety protection and preserving the unity of the internal market, that the Commission be informed of any measure restricting the placing on the market of a product or requiring its withdrawal or recall from the market. Such measures should be taken in compliance with the provisions of the Treaty, and in particular Articles 28, 29 and 30 thereof.

(27) Effective supervision of product safety requires the setting-up at national and Community levels of a system of rapid exchange of information in situations of serious risk requiring rapid intervention in respect of the safety of a product. It is also appropriate in this Directive to set out detailed procedures for the operation of the system and to give the Commission, assisted by an advisory committee, power to adapt them.

(28) This Directive provides for the establishment of non-binding guidelines aimed at indicating simple and clear criteria and practical rules which may change, in particular for the purpose of allowing efficient notification of measures restricting the placing on the market of products in the cases referred to in this Directive, whilst taking into account the range of situations dealt with by Member States and economic operators. The guidelines should in particular include criteria for the application of the definition of serious risks in order to facilitate consistent implementation of the relevant provisions in case of such risks.

(29) It is primarily for Member States, in compliance with the Treaty and in particular with Articles 28, 29 and 30 thereof, to take appropriate measures with regard to dangerous products located within their territory.

(30) However, if the Member States differ as regards the approach to dealing with the risk posed by certain products, such differences could entail unacceptable disparities in consumer protection and constitute a barrier to intra-Community trade.

(31) It may be necessary to deal with serious product-safety problems requiring rapid intervention which affect or could affect, in the immediate future, all or a significant part of the Community and which, in view of the nature of the safety problem posed by the product, cannot be dealt with effectively in a manner commensurate with the degree of urgency, under the procedures laid down in the specific rules of Community law applicable to the products or category of products in question.

(32) It is therefore necessary to provide for an adequate mechanism allowing, as a last resort, for the adoption of measures applicable throughout the Community, in the form of a decision addressed to the Member States, to cope with situations created by products presenting a serious risk. Such a decision should entail a ban on the export of the product in question, unless in the case in point exceptional circumstances allow a partial ban or even no ban to be decided upon, particularly when a system of prior consent is established. In addition, the banning of exports should be examined with a view to preventing risks to the health and safety of consumers. Since such a decision is not directly applicable to economic operators, Member States should take all necessary measures for its implementation. Measures adopted under such a procedure are interim measures, save when they apply to individually identified products or batches of products. In order to ensure the appropriate assessment of the need for, and the best preparation of such measures, they should be taken by the Commission, assisted by a committee, in the light of consultations with the Member States, and, if scientific questions are involved falling within the competence of a Community scientific committee, with the scientific committee competent for the risk concerned.

(33) The measures necessary for the implementation of this Directive should be adopted in accordance with Council Decision 1999/468/EC of 28 June 1999 laying down the procedures for the exercise of implementing powers conferred on the Commission[1].

(34) In order to facilitate effective and consistent application of this Directive, the various aspects of its application may need to be discussed within a committee.

(35) Public access to the information available to the authorities on product safety should be ensured. However, professional secrecy, as referred to in Article 287 of the Treaty, must be protected in a way which is compatible with the need to ensure the effectiveness of market surveillance activities and of protection measures.

(36) This Directive should not affect victims' rights within the meaning of Council Directive 85/374/EEC of 25 July 1985 on the approximation of the laws, regulations and administrative provisions of the Member States concerning liability for defective products[2].

(37) It is necessary for Member States to provide for appropriate means of redress before the competent courts in respect of measures taken by the competent authorities which restrict the placing on the market of a product or require its withdrawal or recall.

(38) In addition, the adoption of measures concerning imported products, like those concerning the banning of exports, with a view to preventing risks to the safety

[1] OJ L 184, 17.7.1999, p. 23.

[2] OJ L 210, 7.8.1985, p. 29. Directive as amended by Directive 1999/34/EC of the European Parliament and of the Council (OJ L 141, 4.6.1999, p. 20).

and health of consumers must comply with the Community's international obligations.

(39) The Commission should periodically examine the manner in which this Directive is applied and the results obtained, in particular in relation to the functioning of market surveillance systems, the rapid exchange of information and measures adopted at Community level, together with other issues relevant for consumer product safety in the Community, and submit regular reports to the European Parliament and the Council on the subject.

(40) This Directive should not affect the obligations of Member States concerning the deadline for transposition and application of Directive 92/59/EEC,

HAVE ADOPTED THIS DIRECTIVE:

CHAPTER I : OBJECTIVE - SCOPE - DEFINITIONS

Article 1

1. The purpose of this Directive is to ensure that products placed on the market are safe.
2. This Directive shall apply to all the products defined in Article 2(a). Each of its provisions shall apply in so far as there are no specific provisions with the same objective in rules of Community law governing the safety of the products concerned.

   Where products are subject to specific safety requirements imposed by Community legislation, this Directive shall apply only to the aspects and risks or categories of risks not covered by those requirements. This means that:

   (a) Articles 2(b) and (c), 3 and 4 shall not apply to those products insofar as concerns the risks or categories of risks covered by the specific legislation;

   (b) Articles 5 to 18 shall apply except where there are specific provisions governing the aspects covered by the said Articles with the same objective.

Article 2

For the purposes of this Directive:

(a) "product" shall mean any product - including in the context of providing a service - which is intended for consumers or likely, under reasonably foreseeable conditions, to be used by consumers even if not intended for them, and is supplied or made available, whether for consideration or not, in the course of a commercial activity, and whether new, used or reconditioned.

This definition shall not apply to second-hand products supplied as antiques or as products to be repaired or reconditioned prior to being used, provided that the supplier clearly informs the person to whom he supplies the product to that effect;

(b) "safe product" shall mean any product which, under normal or reasonably foreseeable conditions of use including duration and, where applicable, putting into service, installation and maintenance requirements, does not present any risk or only the minimum risks compatible with the product's use, considered to be acceptable and consistent with a high level of protection for the safety and health of persons, taking into account the following points in particular:

(i) the characteristics of the product, including its composition, packaging, instructions for assembly and, where applicable, for installation and maintenance;

(ii) the effect on other products, where it is reasonably foreseeable that it will be used with other products;

(iii) the presentation of the product, the labelling, any warnings and instructions for its use and disposal and any other indication or information regarding the product;

(iv) the categories of consumers at risk when using the product, in particular children and the elderly.

The feasibility of obtaining higher levels of safety or the availability of other products presenting a lesser degree of risk shall not constitute grounds for considering a product to be "dangerous";

(c) "dangerous product" shall mean any product which does not meet the definition of "safe product" in (b);

(d) "serious risk" shall mean any serious risk, including those the effects of which are not immediate, requiring rapid intervention by the public authorities;

(e) "producer" shall mean:

(i) the manufacturer of the product, when he is established in the Community, and any other person presenting himself as the manufacturer by affixing to the product his name, trade mark or other distinctive mark, or the person who reconditions the product;

(ii) the manufacturer's representative, when the manufacturer is not established in the Community or, if there is no representative established in the Community, the importer of the product;

(iii) other professionals in the supply chain, insofar as their activities may affect the safety properties of a product;

(f) "distributor" shall mean any professional in the supply chain whose activity does not affect the safety properties of a product;

(g) "recall" shall mean any measure aimed at achieving the return of a dangerous product that has already been supplied or made available to consumers by the producer or distributor;

(h) "withdrawal" shall mean any measure aimed at preventing the distribution, display and offer of a product dangerous to the consumer.

CHAPTER II : GENERAL SAFETY REQUIREMENT, CONFORMITY ASSESSMENT CRITERIA AND EUROPEAN STANDARDS

Article 3

1. Producers shall be obliged to place only safe products on the market.

2. A product shall be deemed safe, as far as the aspects covered by the relevant national legislation are concerned, when, in the absence of specific Community provisions governing the safety of the product in question, it conforms to the specific rules of national law of the Member State in whose territory the product is marketed, such rules being drawn up in conformity with the Treaty, and in particular Articles 28 and 30 thereof, and laying down the health and safety requirements which the product must satisfy in order to be marketed.

   A product shall be presumed safe as far as the risks and risk categories covered by relevant national standards are concerned when it conforms to voluntary national standards transposing European standards, the references of which have been published by the Commission in the Official Journal of the European Communities in accordance with Article 4. The Member States shall publish the references of such national standards.

3. In circumstances other than those referred to in paragraph 2, the conformity of a product to the general safety requirement shall be assessed by taking into account the following elements in particular, where they exist:
   (a) voluntary national standards transposing relevant European standards other than those referred to in paragraph 2;
   (b) the standards drawn up in the Member State in which the product is marketed;
   (c) Commission recommendations setting guidelines on product safety assessment;
   (d) product safety codes of good practice in force in the sector concerned;
   (e) the state of the art and technology;
   (f) reasonable consumer expectations concerning safety.

4. Conformity of a product with the criteria designed to ensure the general safety requirement, in particular the provisions mentioned in paragraphs 2 or 3, shall not bar the competent authorities of the Member States from taking appropriate measures to impose restrictions on its being placed on the market or to require its withdrawal from the market or recall where there is evidence that, despite such conformity, it is dangerous.

Article 4

1. For the purposes of this Directive, the European standards referred to in the second subparagraph of Article 3(2) shall be drawn up as follows:
   (a) the requirements intended to ensure that products which conform to those standards satisfy the general safety requirement shall be determined by the Commission. Those measures, designed to amend non-essential elements of this Directive by supplementing it, shall be adopted in accordance with the regulatory procedure with scrutiny referred to in Article 15(4);
   (b) on the basis of those requirements, the Commission shall, in accordance with Directive 98/34/EC of the European Parliament and of the Council of 22 June 1998 laying down a procedure for the provision of information in the field of technical standards and regulations and of rules on information society

services[1] call on the European standardisation bodies to draw up standards which satisfy these requirements;

(c) on the basis of those mandates, the European standardisation bodies shall adopt the standards in accordance with the principles contained in the general guidelines for cooperation between the Commission and those bodies;

(d) the Commission shall report every three years to the European Parliament and the Council, within the framework of the report referred to in Article 19(2), on its programmes for setting the requirements and the mandates for standardisation provided for in subparagraphs (a) and (b) above. This report will, in particular, include an analysis of the decisions taken regarding requirements and mandates for standardisation referred to in subparagraphs (a) and (b) and regarding the standards referred to in subparagraph (c). It will also include information on the products for which the Commission intends to set the requirements and the mandates in question, the product risks to be considered and the results of any preparatory work launched in this area.

2. The Commission shall publish in the Official Journal of the European Communities the references of the European standards adopted in this way and drawn up in accordance with the requirements referred to in paragraph 1.

If a standard adopted by the European standardisation bodies before the entry into force of this Directive ensures compliance with the general safety requirement, the Commission shall decide to publish its references in the Official Journal of the European Communities.

If a standard does not ensure compliance with the general safety requirement, the Commission shall withdraw reference to the standard from publication in whole or in part.

In the cases referred to in the second and third subparagraphs, the Commission shall, on its own initiative or at the request of a Member State, decide in accordance with the procedure laid down in Article 15(2) whether the standard in question meets the general safety requirement. The Commission shall decide to publish or withdraw after consulting the Committee established by Article 5 of Directive 98/34/EC. The Commission shall notify the Member States of its decision.

CHAPTER III : OTHER OBLIGATIONS OF PRODUCERS AND OBLIGATIONS OF DISTRIBUTORS

Article 5

1. Within the limits of their respective activities, producers shall provide consumers with the relevant information to enable them to assess the risks inherent in a product throughout the normal or reasonably foreseeable period of its use, where such risks are not immediately obvious without adequate warnings, and to take precautions against those risks.

[1] OJ L 204, 21.7.1998, p. 37. Directive amended by Directive 98/48/EC (OJ L 217, 5.8.1998, p. 18).

The presence of warnings does not exempt any person from compliance with the other requirements laid down in this Directive.

Within the limits of their respective activities, producers shall adopt measures commensurate with the characteristics of the products which they supply, enabling them to:

(a) be informed of risks which these products might pose;
(b) choose to take appropriate action including, if necessary to avoid these risks, withdrawal from the market, adequately and effectively warning consumers or recall from consumers.

The measures referred to in the third subparagraph shall include, for example:

(a) an indication, by means of the product or its packaging, of the identity and details of the producer and the product reference or, where applicable, the batch of products to which it belongs, except where not to give such indication is justified and
(b) in all cases where appropriate, the carrying out of sample testing of marketed products, investigating and, if necessary, keeping a register of complaints and keeping distributors informed of such monitoring.

Action such as that referred to in (b) of the third subparagraph shall be undertaken on a voluntary basis or at the request of the competent authorities in accordance with Article 8(1)(f). Recall shall take place as a last resort, where other measures would not suffice to prevent the risks involved, in instances where the producers consider it necessary or where they are obliged to do so further to a measure taken by the competent authority. It may be effected within the framework of codes of good practice on the matter in the Member State concerned, where such codes exist.

2. Distributors shall be required to act with due care to help to ensure compliance with the applicable safety requirements, in particular by not supplying products which they know or should have presumed, on the basis of the information in their possession and as professionals, do not comply with those requirements. Moreover, within the limits of their respective activities, they shall participate in monitoring the safety of products placed on the market, especially by passing on information on product risks, keeping and providing the documentation necessary for tracing the origin of products, and cooperating in the action taken by producers and competent authorities to avoid the risks. Within the limits of their respective activities they shall take measures enabling them to cooperate efficiently.

3. Where producers and distributors know or ought to know, on the basis of the information in their possession and as professionals, that a product that they have placed on the market poses risks to the consumer that are incompatible with the general safety requirement, they shall immediately inform the competent authorities of the Member States thereof under the conditions laid down in Annex I, giving details, in particular, of action taken to prevent risk to the consumer.

The Commission shall adapt the specific requirements relating to the obligation to provide information laid down in Annex I. Those measures, designed to amend non-essential elements of this Directive by supplementing it, shall be adopted in accordance with the regulatory procedure with scrutiny referred to in Article 15(5).

4. Producers and distributors shall, within the limits of their respective activities, cooperate with the competent authorities, at the request of the latter, on action taken to avoid the risks posed by products which they supply or have supplied. The procedures for such cooperation, including procedures for dialogue with the producers and distributors concerned on issues related to product safety, shall be established by the competent authorities.

CHAPTER IV : SPECIFIC OBLIGATIONS AND POWERS OF THE MEMBER STATES

Article 6

1. Member States shall ensure that producers and distributors comply with their obligations under this Directive in such a way that products placed on the market are safe.
2. Member States shall establish or nominate authorities competent to monitor the compliance of products with the general safety requirements and arrange for such authorities to have and use the necessary powers to take the appropriate measures incumbent upon them under this Directive.
3. Member States shall define the tasks, powers, organisation and cooperation arrangements of the competent authorities. They shall keep the Commission informed, and the Commission shall pass on such information to the other Member States.

Article 7

Member States shall lay down the rules on penalties applicable to infringements of the national provisions adopted pursuant to this Directive and shall take all measures necessary to ensure that they are implemented. The penalties provided for shall be effective, proportionate and dissuasive. Member States shall notify those provisions to the Commission by 15 January 2004 and shall also notify it, without delay, of any amendment affecting them.

Article 8

1. For the purposes of this Directive, and in particular of Article 6 thereof, the competent authorities of the Member States shall be entitled to take, inter alia, the measures in (a) and in (b) to (f) below, where appropriate:

   (a) for any product:

      (i) to organise, even after its being placed on the market as being safe, appropriate checks on its safety properties, on an adequate scale, up to the final stage of use or consumption;

  (ii) to require all necessary information from the parties concerned;
  (iii) to take samples of products and subject them to safety checks;
- (b) for any product that could pose risks in certain conditions:
  - (i) to require that it be marked with suitable, clearly worded and easily comprehensible warnings, in the official languages of the Member State in which the product is marketed, on the risks it may present;
  - (ii) to make its marketing subject to prior conditions so as to make it safe;
- (c) for any product that could pose risks for certain persons:
  to order that they be given warning of the risk in good time and in an appropriate form, including the publication of special warnings;
- (d) for any product that could be dangerous:
  for the period needed for the various safety evaluations, checks and controls, temporarily to ban its supply, the offer to supply it or its display;
- (e) for any dangerous product:
  to ban its marketing and introduce the accompanying measures required to ensure the ban is complied with;
- (f) for any dangerous product already on the market:
  - (i) to order or organise its actual and immediate withdrawal, and alert consumers to the risks it presents;
  - (ii) to order or coordinate or, if appropriate, to organise together with producers and distributors its recall from consumers and its destruction in suitable conditions.

2. When the competent authorities of the Member States take measures such as those provided for in paragraph 1, in particular those referred to in (d) to (f), they shall act in accordance with the Treaty, and in particular Articles 28 and 30 thereof, in such a way as to implement the measures in a manner proportional to the seriousness of the risk, and taking due account of the precautionary principle.

   In this context, they shall encourage and promote voluntary action by producers and distributors, in accordance with the obligations incumbent on them under this Directive, and in particular Chapter III thereof, including where applicable by the development of codes of good practice.

   If necessary, they shall organise or order the measures provided for in paragraph 1(f) if the action undertaken by the producers and distributors in fulfilment of their obligations is unsatisfactory or insufficient. Recall shall take place as a last resort. It may be effected within the framework of codes of good practice on the matter in the Member State concerned, where such codes exist.

3. In the case of products posing a serious risk, the competent authorities shall with due dispatch take the appropriate measures referred to in paragraph 1(b) to (f). The existence of a serious risk shall be determined by the Member States, assessing each individual case on its merits and taking into account the guidelines referred to in point 8 of Annex II.

4. The measures to be taken by the competent authorities under this Article shall be addressed, as appropriate, to:

(a) the producer;
(b) within the limits of their respective activities, distributors and in particular the party responsible for the first stage of distribution on the national market;
(c) any other person, where necessary, with a view to cooperation in action taken to avoid risks arising from a product.

Article 9

1. In order to ensure effective market surveillance, aimed at guaranteeing a high level of consumer health and safety protection, which entails cooperation between their competent authorities, Member States shall ensure that approaches employing appropriate means and procedures are put in place, which may include in particular:
   (a) establishment, periodical updating and implementation of sectoral surveillance programmes by categories of products or risks and the monitoring of surveillance activities, findings and results;
   (b) follow-up and updating of scientific and technical knowledge concerning the safety of products;
   (c) periodical review and assessment of the functioning of the control activities and their effectiveness and, if necessary, revision of the surveillance approach and organisation put in place.
2. Member States shall ensure that consumers and other interested parties are given an opportunity to submit complaints to the competent authorities on product safety and on surveillance and control activities and that these complaints are followed up as appropriate. Member States shall actively inform consumers and other interested parties of the procedures established to that end.

Article 10

1. The Commission shall promote and take part in the operation in a European network of the authorities of the Member States competent for product safety, in particular in the form of administrative cooperation.
2. This network operation shall develop in a coordinated manner with the other existing Community procedures, particularly RAPEX. Its objective shall be, in particular, to facilitate:
   (a) the exchange of information on risk assessment, dangerous products, test methods and results, recent scientific developments as well as other aspects relevant for control activities;
   (b) the establishment and execution of joint surveillance and testing projects;
   (c) the exchange of expertise and best practices and cooperation in training activities;
   (d) improved cooperation at Community level with regard to the tracing, withdrawal and recall of dangerous products.

CHAPTER V : EXCHANGES OF INFORMATION AND RAPID INTERVENTION SITUATIONS

Article 11

1. Where a Member State takes measures which restrict the placing on the market of products - or require their withdrawal or recall - such as those provided for in Article 8(1)(b) to (f), the Member State shall, to the extent that such notification is not required under Article 12 or any specific Community legislation, inform the Commission of the measures, specifying its reasons for adopting them. It shall also inform the Commission of any modification or lifting of such measures.

   If the notifying Member State considers that the effects of the risk do not or cannot go beyond its territory, it shall notify the measures concerned insofar as they involve information likely to be of interest to Member States from the product safety standpoint, and in particular if they are in response to a new risk which has not yet been reported in other notifications.

   In accordance with the procedure laid down in Article 15(3) of this Directive, the Commission shall, while ensuring the effectiveness and proper functioning of the system, adopt the guidelines referred to in point 8 of Annex II. These shall propose the content and standard form for the notifications provided for in this Article, and, in particular, shall provide precise criteria for determining the conditions for which notification is relevant for the purposes of the second subparagraph.
2. The Commission shall forward the notification to the other Member States, unless it concludes, after examination on the basis of the information contained in the notification, that the measure does not comply with Community law. In such a case, it shall immediately inform the Member State which initiated the action.

Article 12

1. Where a Member State adopts or decides to adopt, recommend or agree with producers and distributors, whether on a compulsory or voluntary basis, measures or actions to prevent, restrict or impose specific conditions on the possible marketing or use, within its own territory, of products by reason of a serious risk, it shall immediately notify the Commission thereof through RAPEX. It shall also inform the Commission without delay of modification or withdrawal of any such measure or action.

   If the notifying Member State considers that the effects of the risk do not or cannot go beyond its territory, it shall follow the procedure laid down in Article 11, taking into account the relevant criteria proposed in the guidelines referred to in point 8 of Annex II.

   Without prejudice to the first subparagraph, before deciding to adopt such measures or to take such action, Member States may pass on to the Commission any information in their possession regarding the existence of a serious risk.

In the case of a serious risk, they shall notify the Commission of the voluntary measures laid down in Article 5 of this Directive taken by producers and distributors.

2. On receiving such notifications, the Commission shall check whether they comply with this Article and with the requirements applicable to the functioning of RAPEX, and shall forward them to the other Member States, which, in turn, shall immediately inform the Commission of any measures adopted.
3. Detailed procedures for RAPEX are set out in Annex II. They shall be adapted by the Commission. Those measures, designed to amend non-essential elements of this Directive by supplementing it, shall be adopted in accordance with the regulatory procedure with scrutiny referred to in Article 15(5).
4. Access to RAPEX shall be open to applicant countries, third countries or international organisations, within the framework of agreements between the Community and those countries or international organisations, according to arrangements defined in these agreements. Any such agreements shall be based on reciprocity and include provisions on confidentiality corresponding to those applicable in the Community.

Article 13

1. If the Commission becomes aware of a serious risk from certain products to the health and safety of consumers in various Member States, it may, after consulting the Member States, and, if scientific questions arise which fall within the competence of a Community Scientific Committee, the Scientific Committee competent to deal with the risk concerned, adopt a decision in the light of the result of those consultations, in accordance with the procedure laid down in Article 15(2), requiring Member States to take measures from among those listed in Article 8(1)(b) to (f) if, at one and the same time:
   (a) it emerges from prior consultations with the Member States that they differ significantly on the approach adopted or to be adopted to deal with the risk; and
   (b) the risk cannot be dealt with, in view of the nature of the safety issue posed by the product, in a manner compatible with the degree of urgency of the case, under other procedures laid down by the specific Community legislation applicable to the products concerned; and
   (c) the risk can be eliminated effectively only by adopting appropriate measures applicable at Community level, in order to ensure a consistent and high level of protection of the health and safety of consumers and the proper functioning of the internal market.
2. The decisions referred to in paragraph 1 shall be valid for a period not exceeding one year and may be confirmed, under the same procedure, for additional periods none of which shall exceed one year.

   However, decisions concerning specific, individually identified products or batches of products shall be valid without a time limit.

3. Export from the Community of dangerous products which have been the subject of a decision referred to in paragraph 1 shall be prohibited unless the decision provides otherwise.
4. Member States shall take all necessary measures to implement the decisions referred to in paragraph 1 within less than 20 days, unless a different period is specified in those decisions.
5. The competent authorities responsible for carrying out the measures referred to in paragraph 1 shall, within one month, give the parties concerned an opportunity to submit their views and shall inform the Commission accordingly.

CHAPTER VI : COMMITTEE PROCEDURES

Article 14

1. The measures necessary for the implementation of this Directive relating to the matters referred to below shall be adopted in accordance with the regulatory procedure provided for in Article 15(2):
   (a) the measures referred to in Article 4 concerning standards adopted by the European standardisation bodies;
   (b) the decisions referred to in Article 13 requiring Member States to take measures as listed in Article 8(1)(b) to (f).
2. The measures necessary for the implementation of this Directive in respect of all other matters shall be adopted in accordance with the advisory procedure provided for in Article 15(3).

Article 15

1. The Commission shall be assisted by a Committee.
2. Where reference is made to this paragraph, Articles 5 and 7 of Decision 1999/468/EC shall apply, having regard to the provisions of Article 8 thereof. The period laid down in Article 5(6) of Decision 1999/468/EC shall be set at 15 days.
3. Where reference is made to this paragraph, Articles 3 and 7 of Decision 1999/468/EC shall apply, having regard to the provisions of Article 8 thereof.
4. Where reference is made to this paragraph, Article 5a(1) to (4) and Article 7 of Decision 1999/468/EC shall apply, having regard to the provisions of Article 8 thereof.
5. Where reference is made to this paragraph, Article 5a(1) to (4) and (5)(b) and Article 7 of Decision 1999/468/EC shall apply, having regard to the provisions of Article 8 thereof.

The time-limits laid down in Article 5a(3)(c) and (4)(b) and (e) of Decision 1999/468/EC shall be set at two months, one month and two months respectively.

CHAPTER VII : FINAL PROVISIONS

Article 16

1. Information available to the authorities of the Member States or the Commission relating to risks to consumer health and safety posed by products shall in general be available to the public, in accordance with the requirements of transparency and without prejudice to the restrictions required for monitoring and investigation activities. In particular the public shall have access to information on product identification, the nature of the risk and the measures taken.

   However, Member States and the Commission shall take the steps necessary to ensure that their officials and agents are required not to disclose information obtained for the purposes of this Directive which, by its nature, is covered by professional secrecy in duly justified cases, except for information relating to the safety properties of products which must be made public if circumstances so require, in order to protect the health and safety of consumers.
2. Protection of professional secrecy shall not prevent the dissemination to the competent authorities of information relevant for ensuring the effectiveness of market monitoring and surveillance activities. The authorities receiving information covered by professional secrecy shall ensure its protection.

Article 17

This Directive shall be without prejudice to the application of Directive 85/374/EEC.

Article 18

1. Any measure adopted under this Directive and involving restrictions on the placing of a product on the market or requiring its withdrawal or recall must state the appropriate reasons on which it is based. It shall be notified as soon as possible to the party concerned and shall indicate the remedies available under the provisions in force in the Member State in question and the time limits applying to such remedies.

   The parties concerned shall, whenever feasible, be given an opportunity to submit their views before the adoption of the measure. If this has not been done in advance because of the urgency of the measures to be taken, they shall be given such opportunity in due course after the measure has been implemented.

   Measures requiring the withdrawal of a product or its recall shall take into consideration the need to encourage distributors, users and consumers to contribute to the implementation of such measures.
2. Member States shall ensure that any measure taken by the competent authorities involving restrictions on the placing of a product on the market or requiring its withdrawal or recall can be challenged before the competent courts.
3. Any decision taken by virtue of this Directive and involving restrictions on the placing of a product on the market or requiring its withdrawal or its recall shall

be without prejudice to assessment of the liability of the party concerned, in the light of the national criminal law applying in the case in question.

Article 19

1. The Commission may bring before the Committee referred to in Article 15 any matter concerning the application of this Directive and particularly those relating to market monitoring and surveillance activities.
2. Every three years, following 15 January 2004, the Commission shall submit a report on the implementation of this Directive to the European Parliament and the Council.

   The report shall in particular include information on the safety of consumer products, in particular on improved traceability of products, the functioning of market surveillance, standardisation work, the functioning of RAPEX and Community measures taken on the basis of Article 13. To this end the Commission shall conduct assessments of the relevant issues, in particular the approaches, systems and practices put in place in the Member States, in the light of the requirements of this Directive and the other Community legislation relating to product safety. The Member States shall provide the Commission with all the necessary assistance and information for carrying out the assessments and preparing the reports.

Article 20

The Commission shall identify the needs, possibilities and priorities for Community action on the safety of services and submit to the European Parliament and the Council, before 1 January 2003, a report, accompanied by proposals on the subject as appropriate.

Article 21

1. Member States shall bring into force the laws, regulations and administrative provisions necessary in order to comply with this Directive with effect from 15 January 2004. They shall forthwith inform the Commission thereof.

   When Member States adopt those measures, they shall contain a reference to this Directive or be accompanied by such reference on the occasion of their official publication. The methods of making such reference shall be laid down by Member States.
2. Member States shall communicate to the Commission the provisions of national law which they adopt in the field covered by this Directive.

Article 22

Directive 92/59/EEC is hereby repealed from 15 January 2004, without prejudice to the obligations of Member States concerning the deadlines for transposition and application of the said Directive as indicated in Annex III.

References to Directive 92/59/EEC shall be construed as references to this Directive and shall be read in accordance with the correlation table in Annex IV.

Article 23

This Directive shall enter into force on the day of its publication in the Official Journal of the European Communities.

Article 24

This Directive is addressed to the Member States.

Done at Brussels, 3 December 2001.

For the European Parliament

The President

N. Fontaine

For the Council

The President

F. Vandenbroucke

ANNEX I

REQUIREMENTS CONCERNING INFORMATION ON PRODUCTS THAT DO NOT COMPLY WITH THE GENERAL SAFETY REQUIREMENT TO BE PROVIDED TO THE COMPETENT AUTHORITIES BY PRODUCERS AND DISTRIBUTORS

1. The information specified in Article 5(3), or where applicable by specific requirements of Community rules on the product concerned, shall be passed to the competent authorities appointed for the purpose in the Member States where the products in question are or have been marketed or otherwise supplied to consumers.
2. The Commission, assisted by the Committee referred to in Article 15, shall define the content and draw up the standard form of the notifications provided for in this Annex, while ensuring the effectiveness and proper functioning of the system. In particular, it shall put forward, possibly in the form of a guide, simple and clear criteria for determining the special conditions, particularly those concerning isolated circumstances or products, for which notification is not relevant in relation to this Annex.
3. In the event of serious risks, this information shall include at least the following:
   (a) information enabling a precise identification of the product or batch of products in question;
   (b) a full description of the risk that the products in question present;
   (c) all available information relevant for tracing the product;
   (d) a description of the action undertaken to prevent risks to consumers.

ANNEX II

PROCEDURES FOR THE APPLICATION OF RAPEX AND GUIDELINES FOR NOTIFICATIONS

1. RAPEX covers products as defined in Article 2(a) that pose a serious risk to the health and safety of consumers.

   Pharmaceuticals, which come under Directives 75/319/EEC[1] and 81/851/EEC[2], are excluded from the scope of RAPEX.
2. RAPEX is essentially aimed at a rapid exchange of information in the event of a serious risk. The guidelines referred to in point 8 define specific criteria for identifying serious risks.

[1] OJ L 147, 9.6.1975, p. 13. Directive as last amended by Commission Directive 2000/38/EC (OJ L 139, 10.6.2000, p. 28).

[2] OJ L 317, 6.11.1981, p. 1. Directive as last amended by Commission Directive 2000/37/EC (OJ L 139, 10.6.2000, p. 25).

3. Member States notifying under Article 12 shall provide all available details. In particular, the notification shall contain the information stipulated in the guidelines referred to in point 8 and at least:
   (a) information enabling the product to be identified;
   (b) a description of the risk involved, including a summary of the results of any tests/analyses and of their conclusions which are relevant to assessing the level of risk;
   (c) the nature and the duration of the measures or action taken or decided on, if applicable;
   (d) information on supply chains and distribution of the product, in particular on destination countries.

   Such information must be transmitted using the special standard notification form and by the means stipulated in the guidelines referred to in point 8.

   When the measure notified pursuant to Article 11 or Article 12 seeks to limit the marketing or use of a chemical substance or preparation, the Member States shall provide as soon as possible either a summary or the references of the relevant data relating to the substance or preparation considered and to known and available substitutes, where such information is available. They will also communicate the anticipated effects of the measure on consumer health and safety together with the assessment of the risk carried out in accordance with the general principles for the risk evaluation of chemical substances as referred to in Article 10(4) of Regulation (EEC) No 793/93[1] in the case of an existing substance or in Article 3(2) of Directive 67/548/EEC[2] in the case of a new substance. The guidelines referred to in point 8 shall define the details and procedures for the information requested in that respect.
4. When a Member State has informed the Commission, in accordance with Article 12(1), third subparagraph, of a serious risk before deciding to adopt measures, it must inform the Commission within 45 days whether it confirms or modifies this information.
5. The Commission shall, in the shortest time possible, verify the conformity with the provisions of the Directive of the information received under RAPEX and, may, when it considers it to be necessary and in order to assess product safety, carry out an investigation on its own initiative. In the case of such an investigation, Member States shall supply the Commission with the requested information to the best of their ability.

---

1 OJ L 84, 5.4.1993, p. 1.

2 OJ 196, 16.8.1967, p. 1/67. Directive as last amended by Commission Directive 2000/33/EC (OJ L 136, 8.6.2000, p. 90).

6. Upon receipt of a notification referred to in Article 12, the Member States are requested to inform the Commission, at the latest within the set period of time stipulated in the guidelines referred to in point 8, of the following:
   (a) whether the product has been marketed in their territory;
   (b) what measures concerning the product in question they may be adopting in the light of their own circumstances, stating the reasons, including any differing assessment of risk or any other special circumstance justifying their decision, in particular lack of action or of follow-up;
   (c) any relevant supplementary information they have obtained on the risk involved, including the results of any tests or analyses carried out.

   The guidelines referred to in point 8 shall provide precise criteria for notifying measures limited to national territory and shall specify how to deal with notifications concerning risks which are considered by the Member State not to go beyond its territory.
7. Member States shall immediately inform the Commission of any modification or lifting of the measure(s) or action(s) in question.
8. The Commission shall prepare and regularly update, in accordance with the procedure laid down in Article 15(3), guidelines concerning the management of RAPEX by the Commission and the Member States.
9. The Commission may inform the national contact points regarding products posing serious risks, imported into or exported from the Community and the European Economic Area.
10. Responsibility for the information provided lies with the notifying Member State.
11. The Commission shall ensure the proper functioning of the system, in particular classifying and indexing notifications according to the degree of urgency. Detailed procedures shall be laid down by the guidelines referred to in point 8.

ANNEX III

PERIOD FOR THE TRANSPOSITION AND APPLICATION OF THE REPEALED DIRECTIVE

(REFERRED TO IN THE FIRST SUBPARAGRAPHE OF ARTICLE 22)

Directive	Period for transposition	Period for bringing into application
Directive 92/59/EEC	29 June 1994	29 June 1994

ANNEX IV
CORRELATION TABLE
(REFERRED TO IN THE SECOND SUBPARAGRAPH OF ARTICLE 22)

This Directive	Directive 92/59/EEC
Article 1	Article 1
Article 2	Article 2
Article 3	Article 4
Article 4	-
Article 5	Article 3
Article 6	Article 5
Article 7	Article 5(2)
Article 8	Article 6
Article 9	-
Article 10	-
Article 11	Article 7
Article 12	Article 8
Article 13	Article 9
Articles 14 and 15	Article 10
Article 16	Article 12
Article 17	Article 13
Article 18	Article 14
Article 19	Article 15
Article 20	-
Article 21	Article 17
Article 22	Article 18
Article 23	Article 19
Annex I	-
Annex II	Annex
Annex III	-
Annex IV	-

23. Directive 2005/29/EC of the European Parliament and of the Council of 11 May 2005 concerning unfair business-to-consumer commercial practices in the internal market and amending Council Directive 84/450/EEC, Directives 97/7/EC, 98/27/EC and 2002/65/EC of the European Parliament and of the Council and Regulation (EC) No 2006/2004 of the European Parliament and of the Council ('Unfair Commercial Practices Directive') (Text with EEA relevance)

(OJ L 149 , 11/06/2005 p. 22 – 39)

THE EUROPEAN PARLIAMENT AND THE COUNCIL OF THE EUROPEAN UNION,

Having regard to the Treaty establishing the European Community, and in particular Article 95 thereof,

Having regard to the proposal from the Commission,

Having regard to the opinion of the European Economic and Social Committee[1],

Acting in accordance with the procedure laid down in Article 251 of the Treaty[2],

Whereas:

(1) Article 153(1) and (3)(a) of the Treaty provides that the Community is to contribute to the attainment of a high level of consumer protection by the measures it adopts pursuant to Article 95 thereof.

(2) In accordance with Article 14(2) of the Treaty, the internal market comprises an area without internal frontiers in which the free movement of goods and services and freedom of establishment are ensured. The development of fair commercial practices within the area without internal frontiers is vital for the promotion of the development of cross-border activities.

(3) The laws of the Member States relating to unfair commercial practices show marked differences which can generate appreciable distortions of competition and obstacles to the smooth functioning of the internal market. In the field of advertising, Council Directive 84/450/EEC of 10 September 1984 concerning misleading and comparative advertising[3] establishes minimum criteria for harmonising legislation on misleading advertising, but does not prevent the Member States from retaining or adopting measures which provide more extensive protection for consumers. As a result, Member States' provisions on misleading advertising diverge significantly.

---

1 OJ C 108, 30.4.2004, p. 81.

2 Opinion of the European Parliament of 20 April 2004 (OJ C 104 E, 30.4.2004, p. 260), Council Common Position of 15 November 2004 (OJ C 38 E, 15.2.2005, p. 1), Position of the European Parliament of 24 February 2005 (not yet published in the Official Journal) and Council Decision of 12 April 2005.

3 OJ L 250, 19.9.1984, p. 17. Directive as amended by Directive 97/55/EC of the European Parliament and of the Council (OJ L 290, 23.10.1997, p. 18).

(4) These disparities cause uncertainty as to which national rules apply to unfair commercial practices harming consumers' economic interests and create many barriers affecting business and consumers. These barriers increase the cost to business of exercising internal market freedoms, in particular when businesses wish to engage in cross border marketing, advertising campaigns and sales promotions. Such barriers also make consumers uncertain of their rights and undermine their confidence in the internal market.

(5) In the absence of uniform rules at Community level, obstacles to the free movement of services and goods across borders or the freedom of establishment could be justified in the light of the case-law of the Court of Justice of the European Communities as long as they seek to protect recognised public interest objectives and are proportionate to those objectives. In view of the Community's objectives, as set out in the provisions of the Treaty and in secondary Community law relating to freedom of movement, and in accordance with the Commission's policy on commercial communications as indicated in the Communication from the Commission entitled "The follow-up to the Green Paper on Commercial Communications in the Internal Market", such obstacles should be eliminated. These obstacles can only be eliminated by establishing uniform rules at Community level which establish a high level of consumer protection and by clarifying certain legal concepts at Community level to the extent necessary for the proper functioning of the internal market and to meet the requirement of legal certainty.

(6) This Directive therefore approximates the laws of the Member States on unfair commercial practices, including unfair advertising, which directly harm consumers' economic interests and thereby indirectly harm the economic interests of legitimate competitors. In line with the principle of proportionality, this Directive protects consumers from the consequences of such unfair commercial practices where they are material but recognises that in some cases the impact on consumers may be negligible. It neither covers nor affects the national laws on unfair commercial practices which harm only competitors' economic interests or which relate to a transaction between traders; taking full account of the principle of subsidiarity, Member States will continue to be able to regulate such practices, in conformity with Community law, if they choose to do so. Nor does this Directive cover or affect the provisions of Directive 84/450/EEC on advertising which misleads business but which is not misleading for consumers and on comparative advertising. Further, this Directive does not affect accepted advertising and marketing practices, such as legitimate product placement, brand differentiation or the offering of incentives which may legitimately affect consumers' perceptions of products and influence their behaviour without impairing the consumer's ability to make an informed decision.

(7) This Directive addresses commercial practices directly related to influencing consumers' transactional decisions in relation to products. It does not address commercial practices carried out primarily for other purposes, including for

example commercial communication aimed at investors, such as annual reports and corporate promotional literature. It does not address legal requirements related to taste and decency which vary widely among the Member States. Commercial practices such as, for example, commercial solicitation in the streets, may be undesirable in Member States for cultural reasons. Member States should accordingly be able to continue to ban commercial practices in their territory, in conformity with Community law, for reasons of taste and decency even where such practices do not limit consumers' freedom of choice. Full account should be taken of the context of the individual case concerned in applying this Directive, in particular the general clauses thereof.

(8) This Directive directly protects consumer economic interests from unfair business-to-consumer commercial practices. Thereby, it also indirectly protects legitimate businesses from their competitors who do not play by the rules in this Directive and thus guarantees fair competition in fields coordinated by it. It is understood that there are other commercial practices which, although not harming consumers, may hurt competitors and business customers. The Commission should carefully examine the need for Community action in the field of unfair competition beyond the remit of this Directive and, if necessary, make a legislative proposal to cover these other aspects of unfair competition.

(9) This Directive is without prejudice to individual actions brought by those who have been harmed by an unfair commercial practice. It is also without prejudice to Community and national rules on contract law, on intellectual property rights, on the health and safety aspects of products, on conditions of establishment and authorisation regimes, including those rules which, in conformity with Community law, relate to gambling activities, and to Community competition rules and the national provisions implementing them. The Member States will thus be able to retain or introduce restrictions and prohibitions of commercial practices on grounds of the protection of the health and safety of consumers in their territory wherever the trader is based, for example in relation to alcohol, tobacco or pharmaceuticals. Financial services and immovable property, by reason of their complexity and inherent serious risks, necessitate detailed requirements, including positive obligations on traders. For this reason, in the field of financial services and immovable property, this Directive is without prejudice to the right of Member States to go beyond its provisions to protect the economic interests of consumers. It is not appropriate to regulate here the certification and indication of the standard of fineness of articles of precious metal.

(10) It is necessary to ensure that the relationship between this Directive and existing Community law is coherent, particularly where detailed provisions on unfair commercial practices apply to specific sectors. This Directive therefore amends Directive 84/450/EEC, Directive 97/7/EC of the European Parliament and of the Council of 20 May 1997 on the protection of consumers in respect of

distance contracts[1], Directive 98/27/EC of the European Parliament and of the Council of 19 May 1998 on injunctions for the protection of consumers' interests[2] and Directive 2002/65/EC of the European Parliament and of the Council of 23 September 2002 concerning the distance marketing of consumer financial services[3]. This Directive accordingly applies only in so far as there are no specific Community law provisions regulating specific aspects of unfair commercial practices, such as information requirements and rules on the way the information is presented to the consumer. It provides protection for consumers where there is no specific sectoral legislation at Community level and prohibits traders from creating a false impression of the nature of products. This is particularly important for complex products with high levels of risk to consumers, such as certain financial services products. This Directive consequently complements the Community acquis, which is applicable to commercial practices harming consumers' economic interests.

(11) The high level of convergence achieved by the approximation of national provisions through this Directive creates a high common level of consumer protection. This Directive establishes a single general prohibition of those unfair commercial practices distorting consumers' economic behaviour. It also sets rules on aggressive commercial practices, which are currently not regulated at Community level.

(12) Harmonisation will considerably increase legal certainty for both consumers and business. Both consumers and business will be able to rely on a single regulatory framework based on clearly defined legal concepts regulating all aspects of unfair commercial practices across the EU. The effect will be to eliminate the barriers stemming from the fragmentation of the rules on unfair commercial practices harming consumer economic interests and to enable the internal market to be achieved in this area.

(13) In order to achieve the Community's objectives through the removal of internal market barriers, it is necessary to replace Member States' existing, divergent general clauses and legal principles. The single, common general prohibition established by this Directive therefore covers unfair commercial practices distorting consumers' economic behaviour. In order to support consumer confidence the general prohibition should apply equally to unfair commercial practices which occur outside any contractual relationship between a trader and a consumer or following the conclusion of a contract and during its execution. The general prohibition is elaborated by rules on the two types of commercial practices which are by far the most common, namely misleading commercial practices and aggressive commercial practices.

(14) It is desirable that misleading commercial practices cover those practices, including misleading advertising, which by deceiving the consumer prevent him from making an informed and thus efficient choice. In conformity with the laws

---

1 OJ L 144, 4.6.1997, p. 19. Directive as amended by Directive 2002/65/EC (OJ L 271, 9.10.2002, p. 16).

2 OJ L 166, 11.6.1998, p. 51. Directive as last amended by Directive 2002/65/EC.

3 OJ L 271, 9.10.2002, p. 16.

and practices of Member States on misleading advertising, this Directive classifies misleading practices into misleading actions and misleading omissions. In respect of omissions, this Directive sets out a limited number of key items of information which the consumer needs to make an informed transactional decision. Such information will not have to be disclosed in all advertisements, but only where the trader makes an invitation to purchase, which is a concept clearly defined in this Directive. The full harmonisation approach adopted in this Directive does not preclude the Member States from specifying in national law the main characteristics of particular products such as, for example, collectors' items or electrical goods, the omission of which would be material when an invitation to purchase is made. It is not the intention of this Directive to reduce consumer choice by prohibiting the promotion of products which look similar to other products unless this similarity confuses consumers as to the commercial origin of the product and is therefore misleading. This Directive should be without prejudice to existing Community law which expressly affords Member States the choice between several regulatory options for the protection of consumers in the field of commercial practices. In particular, this Directive should be without prejudice to Article 13(3) of Directive 2002/58/EC of the European Parliament and of the Council of 12 July 2002 concerning the processing of personal data and the protection of privacy in the electronic communications sector[1].

(15) Where Community law sets out information requirements in relation to commercial communication, advertising and marketing that information is considered as material under this Directive. Member States will be able to retain or add information requirements relating to contract law and having contract law consequences where this is allowed by the minimum clauses in the existing Community law instruments. A non-exhaustive list of such information requirements in the acquis is contained in Annex II. Given the full harmonisation introduced by this Directive only the information required in Community law is considered as material for the purpose of Article 7(5) thereof. Where Member States have introduced information requirements over and above what is specified in Community law, on the basis of minimum clauses, the omission of that extra information will not constitute a misleading omission under this Directive. By contrast Member States will be able, when allowed by the minimum clauses in Community law, to maintain or introduce more stringent provisions in conformity with Community law so as to ensure a higher level of protection of consumers' individual contractual rights.

(16) The provisions on aggressive commercial practices should cover those practices which significantly impair the consumer's freedom of choice. Those are practices using harassment, coercion, including the use of physical force, and undue influence.

---

[1] OJ L 201, 31.7.2002, p. 37.

(17) It is desirable that those commercial practices which are in all circumstances unfair be identified to provide greater legal certainty. Annex I therefore contains the full list of all such practices. These are the only commercial practices which can be deemed to be unfair without a case-by-case assessment against the provisions of Articles 5 to 9. The list may only be modified by revision of the Directive.

(18) It is appropriate to protect all consumers from unfair commercial practices; however the Court of Justice has found it necessary in adjudicating on advertising cases since the enactment of Directive 84/450/EEC to examine the effect on a notional, typical consumer. In line with the principle of proportionality, and to permit the effective application of the protections contained in it, this Directive takes as a benchmark the average consumer, who is reasonably well-informed and reasonably observant and circumspect, taking into account social, cultural and linguistic factors, as interpreted by the Court of Justice, but also contains provisions aimed at preventing the exploitation of consumers whose characteristics make them particularly vulnerable to unfair commercial practices. Where a commercial practice is specifically aimed at a particular group of consumers, such as children, it is desirable that the impact of the commercial practice be assessed from the perspective of the average member of that group. It is therefore appropriate to include in the list of practices which are in all circumstances unfair a provision which, without imposing an outright ban on advertising directed at children, protects them from direct exhortations to purchase. The average consumer test is not a statistical test. National courts and authorities will have to exercise their own faculty of judgement, having regard to the case-law of the Court of Justice, to determine the typical reaction of the average consumer in a given case.

(19) Where certain characteristics such as age, physical or mental infirmity or credulity make consumers particularly susceptible to a commercial practice or to the underlying product and the economic behaviour only of such consumers is likely to be distorted by the practice in a way that the trader can reasonably foresee, it is appropriate to ensure that they are adequately protected by assessing the practice from the perspective of the average member of that group.

(20) It is appropriate to provide a role for codes of conduct, which enable traders to apply the principles of this Directive effectively in specific economic fields. In sectors where there are specific mandatory requirements regulating the behaviour of traders, it is appropriate that these will also provide evidence as to the requirements of professional diligence in that sector. The control exercised by code owners at national or Community level to eliminate unfair commercial practices may avoid the need for recourse to administrative or judicial action and should therefore be encouraged. With the aim of pursuing a high level of consumer protection, consumers' organisations could be informed and involved in the drafting of codes of conduct.

(21) Persons or organisations regarded under national law as having a legitimate interest in the matter must have legal remedies for initiating proceedings against

unfair commercial practices, either before a court or before an administrative authority which is competent to decide upon complaints or to initiate appropriate legal proceedings. While it is for national law to determine the burden of proof, it is appropriate to enable courts and administrative authorities to require traders to produce evidence as to the accuracy of factual claims they have made.

(22) It is necessary that Member States lay down penalties for infringements of the provisions of this Directive and they must ensure that these are enforced. The penalties must be effective, proportionate and dissuasive.

(23) Since the objectives of this Directive, namely to eliminate the barriers to the functioning of the internal market represented by national laws on unfair commercial practices and to provide a high common level of consumer protection, by approximating the laws, regulations and administrative provisions of the Member States on unfair commercial practices, cannot be sufficiently achieved by the Member States and can therefore be better achieved at Community level, the Community may adopt measures, in accordance with the principle of subsidiarity as set out in Article 5 of the Treaty. In accordance with the principle of proportionality, as set out in that Article, this Directive does not go beyond what is necessary in order to eliminate the internal market barriers and achieve a high common level of consumer protection.

(24) It is appropriate to review this Directive to ensure that barriers to the internal market have been addressed and a high level of consumer protection achieved. The review could lead to a Commission proposal to amend this Directive, which may include a limited extension to the derogation in Article 3(5), and/or amendments to other consumer protection legislation reflecting the Commission's Consumer Policy Strategy commitment to review the existing acquis in order to achieve a high, common level of consumer protection.

(25) This Directive respects the fundamental rights and observes the principles recognised in particular by the Charter of Fundamental Rights of the European Union,

HAVE ADOPTED THIS DIRECTIVE:

CHAPTER 1 : GENERAL PROVISIONS

Article 1 Purpose

The purpose of this Directive is to contribute to the proper functioning of the internal market and achieve a high level of consumer protection by approximating the laws, regulations and administrative provisions of the Member States on unfair commercial practices harming consumers' economic interests.

Article 2 Definitions

For the purposes of this Directive:

(a) "consumer" means any natural person who, in commercial practices covered by this Directive, is acting for purposes which are outside his trade, business, craft or profession;

(b) "trader" means any natural or legal person who, in commercial practices covered by this Directive, is acting for purposes relating to his trade, business, craft or profession and anyone acting in the name of or on behalf of a trader;
(c) "product" means any goods or service including immovable property, rights and obligations;
(d) "business-to-consumer commercial practices" (hereinafter also referred to as commercial practices) means any act, omission, course of conduct or representation, commercial communication including advertising and marketing, by a trader, directly connected with the promotion, sale or supply of a product to consumers;
(e) "to materially distort the economic behaviour of consumers" means using a commercial practice to appreciably impair the consumer's ability to make an informed decision, thereby causing the consumer to take a transactional decision that he would not have taken otherwise;
(f) "code of conduct" means an agreement or set of rules not imposed by law, regulation or administrative provision of a Member State which defines the behaviour of traders who undertake to be bound by the code in relation to one or more particular commercial practices or business sectors;
(g) "code owner" means any entity, including a trader or group of traders, which is responsible for the formulation and revision of a code of conduct and/or for monitoring compliance with the code by those who have undertaken to be bound by it;
(h) "professional diligence" means the standard of special skill and care which a trader may reasonably be expected to exercise towards consumers, commensurate with honest market practice and/or the general principle of good faith in the trader's field of activity;
(i) "invitation to purchase" means a commercial communication which indicates characteristics of the product and the price in a way appropriate to the means of the commercial communication used and thereby enables the consumer to make a purchase;
(j) "undue influence" means exploiting a position of power in relation to the consumer so as to apply pressure, even without using or threatening to use physical force, in a way which significantly limits the consumer's ability to make an informed decision;
(k) "transactional decision" means any decision taken by a consumer concerning whether, how and on what terms to purchase, make payment in whole or in part for, retain or dispose of a product or to exercise a contractual right in relation to the product, whether the consumer decides to act or to refrain from acting;
(l) "regulated profession" means a professional activity or a group of professional activities, access to which or the pursuit of which, or one of the modes of pursuing which, is conditional, directly or indirectly, upon possession of specific professional qualifications, pursuant to laws, regulations or administrative provisions.

Article 3 **Scope**

1. This Directive shall apply to unfair business-to-consumer commercial practices, as laid down in Article 5, before, during and after a commercial transaction in relation to a product.
2. This Directive is without prejudice to contract law and, in particular, to the rules on the validity, formation or effect of a contract.
3. This Directive is without prejudice to Community or national rules relating to the health and safety aspects of products.
4. In the case of conflict between the provisions of this Directive and other Community rules regulating specific aspects of unfair commercial practices, the latter shall prevail and apply to those specific aspects.
5. For a period of six years from 12 June 2007, Member States shall be able to continue to apply national provisions within the field approximated by this Directive which are more restrictive or prescriptive than this Directive and which implement directives containing minimum harmonisation clauses. These measures must be essential to ensure that consumers are adequately protected against unfair commercial practices and must be proportionate to the attainment of this objective. The review referred to in Article 18 may, if considered appropriate, include a proposal to prolong this derogation for a further limited period.
6. Member States shall notify the Commission without delay of any national provisions applied on the basis of paragraph 5.
7. This Directive is without prejudice to the rules determining the jurisdiction of the courts.
8. This Directive is without prejudice to any conditions of establishment or of authorisation regimes, or to the deontological codes of conduct or other specific rules governing regulated professions in order to uphold high standards of integrity on the part of the professional, which Member States may, in conformity with Community law, impose on professionals.
9. In relation to "financial services", as defined in Directive 2002/65/EC, and immovable property, Member States may impose requirements which are more restrictive or prescriptive than this Directive in the field which it approximates.
10. This Directive shall not apply to the application of the laws, regulations and administrative provisions of Member States relating to the certification and indication of the standard of fineness of articles of precious metal.

Article 4 **Internal market**

Member States shall neither restrict the freedom to provide services nor restrict the free movement of goods for reasons falling within the field approximated by this Directive.

CHAPTER 2 : UNFAIR COMMERCIAL PRACTICES

Article 5 Prohibition of unfair commercial practices

1. Unfair commercial practices shall be prohibited.
2. A commercial practice shall be unfair if:
   (a) it is contrary to the requirements of professional diligence,
   and
   (b) it materially distorts or is likely to materially distort the economic behaviour with regard to the product of the average consumer whom it reaches or to whom it is addressed, or of the average member of the group when a commercial practice is directed to a particular group of consumers.
3. Commercial practices which are likely to materially distort the economic behaviour only of a clearly identifiable group of consumers who are particularly vulnerable to the practice or the underlying product because of their mental or physical infirmity, age or credulity in a way which the trader could reasonably be expected to foresee, shall be assessed from the perspective of the average member of that group. This is without prejudice to the common and legitimate advertising practice of making exaggerated statements or statements which are not meant to be taken literally.
4. In particular, commercial practices shall be unfair which:
   (a) are misleading as set out in Articles 6 and 7,
   or
   (b) are aggressive as set out in Articles 8 and 9.
5. Annex I contains the list of those commercial practices which shall in all circumstances be regarded as unfair. The same single list shall apply in all Member States and may only be modified by revision of this Directive.

Section 1 : **Misleading commercial practices**

Article 6 Misleading actions

1. A commercial practice shall be regarded as misleading if it contains false information and is therefore untruthful or in any way, including overall presentation, deceives or is likely to deceive the average consumer, even if the information is factually correct, in relation to one or more of the following elements, and in either case causes or is likely to cause him to take a transactional decision that he would not have taken otherwise:
   (a) the existence or nature of the product;
   (b) the main characteristics of the product, such as its availability, benefits, risks, execution, composition, accessories, after-sale customer assistance and complaint handling, method and date of manufacture or provision, delivery, fitness for purpose, usage, quantity, specification, geographical or commercial origin or the results to be expected from its use, or the results and material features of tests or checks carried out on the product;

(c) the extent of the trader's commitments, the motives for the commercial practice and the nature of the sales process, any statement or symbol in relation to direct or indirect sponsorship or approval of the trader or the product;
(d) the price or the manner in which the price is calculated, or the existence of a specific price advantage;
(e) the need for a service, part, replacement or repair;
(f) the nature, attributes and rights of the trader or his agent, such as his identity and assets, his qualifications, status, approval, affiliation or connection and ownership of industrial, commercial or intellectual property rights or his awards and distinctions;
(g) the consumer's rights, including the right to replacement or reimbursement under Directive 1999/44/EC of the European Parliament and of the Council of 25 May 1999 on certain aspects of the sale of consumer goods and associated guarantees[1], or the risks he may face.

2. A commercial practice shall also be regarded as misleading if, in its factual context, taking account of all its features and circumstances, it causes or is likely to cause the average consumer to take a transactional decision that he would not have taken otherwise, and it involves:
   (a) any marketing of a product, including comparative advertising, which creates confusion with any products, trade marks, trade names or other distinguishing marks of a competitor;
   (b) non-compliance by the trader with commitments contained in codes of conduct by which the trader has undertaken to be bound, where:
      (i) the commitment is not aspirational but is firm and is capable of being verified,
      and
      (ii) the trader indicates in a commercial practice that he is bound by the code.

Article 7 Misleading omissions

1. A commercial practice shall be regarded as misleading if, in its factual context, taking account of all its features and circumstances and the limitations of the communication medium, it omits material information that the average consumer needs, according to the context, to take an informed transactional decision and thereby causes or is likely to cause the average consumer to take a transactional decision that he would not have taken otherwise.
2. It shall also be regarded as a misleading omission when, taking account of the matters described in paragraph 1, a trader hides or provides in an unclear, unintelligible, ambiguous or untimely manner such material information as referred to in that paragraph or fails to identify the commercial intent of the commercial practice if not already apparent from the context, and where, in

[1] OJ L 171, 7.7.1999, p. 12.

either case, this causes or is likely to cause the average consumer to take a transactional decision that he would not have taken otherwise.

3. Where the medium used to communicate the commercial practice imposes limitations of space or time, these limitations and any measures taken by the trader to make the information available to consumers by other means shall be taken into account in deciding whether information has been omitted.
4. In the case of an invitation to purchase, the following information shall be regarded as material, if not already apparent from the context:
   (a) the main characteristics of the product, to an extent appropriate to the medium and the product;
   (b) the geographical address and the identity of the trader, such as his trading name and, where applicable, the geographical address and the identity of the trader on whose behalf he is acting;
   (c) the price inclusive of taxes, or where the nature of the product means that the price cannot reasonably be calculated in advance, the manner in which the price is calculated, as well as, where appropriate, all additional freight, delivery or postal charges or, where these charges cannot reasonably be calculated in advance, the fact that such additional charges may be payable;
   (d) the arrangements for payment, delivery, performance and the complaint handling policy, if they depart from the requirements of professional diligence;
   (e) for products and transactions involving a right of withdrawal or cancellation, the existence of such a right.
5. Information requirements established by Community law in relation to commercial communication including advertising or marketing, a non-exhaustive list of which is contained in Annex II, shall be regarded as material.

Section 2 : **Aggressive commercial practices**

Article 8 Aggressive commercial practices

A commercial practice shall be regarded as aggressive if, in its factual context, taking account of all its features and circumstances, by harassment, coercion, including the use of physical force, or undue influence, it significantly impairs or is likely to significantly impair the average consumer's freedom of choice or conduct with regard to the product and thereby causes him or is likely to cause him to take a transactional decision that he would not have taken otherwise.

Article 9 Use of harassment, coercion and undue influence

In determining whether a commercial practice uses harassment, coercion, including the use of physical force, or undue influence, account shall be taken of:

(a) its timing, location, nature or persistence;
(b) the use of threatening or abusive language or behaviour;

(c) the exploitation by the trader of any specific misfortune or circumstance of such gravity as to impair the consumer's judgement, of which the trader is aware, to influence the consumer's decision with regard to the product;
(d) any onerous or disproportionate non-contractual barriers imposed by the trader where a consumer wishes to exercise rights under the contract, including rights to terminate a contract or to switch to another product or another trader;
(e) any threat to take any action that cannot legally be taken.

CHAPTER 3 : CODES OF CONDUCT

Article 10 Codes of conduct

This Directive does not exclude the control, which Member States may encourage, of unfair commercial practices by code owners and recourse to such bodies by the persons or organisations referred to in Article 11 if proceedings before such bodies are in addition to the court or administrative proceedings referred to in that Article.

Recourse to such control bodies shall never be deemed the equivalent of foregoing a means of judicial or administrative recourse as provided for in Article 11.

CHAPTER 4 : FINAL PROVISIONS

Article 11 Enforcement

1. Member States shall ensure that adequate and effective means exist to combat unfair commercial practices in order to enforce compliance with the provisions of this Directive in the interest of consumers.

   Such means shall include legal provisions under which persons or organisations regarded under national law as having a legitimate interest in combating unfair commercial practices, including competitors, may:

   (a) take legal action against such unfair commercial practices;
   and/or
   (b) bring such unfair commercial practices before an administrative authority competent either to decide on complaints or to initiate appropriate legal proceedings.

   It shall be for each Member State to decide which of these facilities shall be available and whether to enable the courts or administrative authorities to require prior recourse to other established means of dealing with complaints, including those referred to in Article 10. These facilities shall be available regardless of whether the consumers affected are in the territory of the Member State where the trader is located or in another Member State.

   It shall be for each Member State to decide:

   (a) whether these legal facilities may be directed separately or jointly against a number of traders from the same economic sector;

and

(b) whether these legal facilities may be directed against a code owner where the relevant code promotes non-compliance with legal requirements.

2. Under the legal provisions referred to in paragraph 1, Member States shall confer upon the courts or administrative authorities powers enabling them, in cases where they deem such measures to be necessary taking into account all the interests involved and in particular the public interest:

(a) to order the cessation of, or to institute appropriate legal proceedings for an order for the cessation of, unfair commercial practices;

or

(b) if the unfair commercial practice has not yet been carried out but is imminent, to order the prohibition of the practice, or to institute appropriate legal proceedings for an order for the prohibition of the practice,

even without proof of actual loss or damage or of intention or negligence on the part of the trader.

Member States shall also make provision for the measures referred to in the first subparagraph to be taken under an accelerated procedure:

- either with interim effect,

or

- with definitive effect,

on the understanding that it is for each Member State to decide which of the two options to select.

Furthermore, Member States may confer upon the courts or administrative authorities powers enabling them, with a view to eliminating the continuing effects of unfair commercial practices the cessation of which has been ordered by a final decision:

(a) to require publication of that decision in full or in part and in such form as they deem adequate;

(b) to require in addition the publication of a corrective statement.

3. The administrative authorities referred to in paragraph 1 must:

(a) be composed so as not to cast doubt on their impartiality;

(b) have adequate powers, where they decide on complaints, to monitor and enforce the observance of their decisions effectively;

(c) normally give reasons for their decisions.

Where the powers referred to in paragraph 2 are exercised exclusively by an administrative authority, reasons for its decisions shall always be given. Furthermore, in this case, provision must be made for procedures whereby improper or unreasonable exercise of its powers by the administrative authority or improper or unreasonable failure to exercise the said powers can be the subject of judicial review.

Article 12 Courts and administrative authorities: substantiation of claims

Member States shall confer upon the courts or administrative authorities powers enabling them in the civil or administrative proceedings provided for in Article 11:

(a) to require the trader to furnish evidence as to the accuracy of factual claims in relation to a commercial practice if, taking into account the legitimate interest of the trader and any other party to the proceedings, such a requirement appears appropriate on the basis of the circumstances of the particular case;
and

(b) to consider factual claims as inaccurate if the evidence demanded in accordance with (a) is not furnished or is deemed insufficient by the court or administrative authority.

Article 13 Penalties

Member States shall lay down penalties for infringements of national provisions adopted in application of this Directive and shall take all necessary measures to ensure that these are enforced. These penalties must be effective, proportionate and dissuasive.

Article 14 Amendments to Directive 84/450/EEC

Directive 84/450/EEC is hereby amended as follows:

1. Article 1 shall be replaced by the following:

"Article 1

The purpose of this Directive is to protect traders against misleading advertising and the unfair consequences thereof and to lay down the conditions under which comparative advertising is permitted."

;

2. in Article 2:

- point 3 shall be replaced by the following:
"3. "trader" means any natural or legal person who is acting for purposes relating to his trade, craft, business or profession and any one acting in the name of or on behalf of a trader."

,

- the following point shall be added:
"4. "code owner" means any entity, including a trader or group of traders, which is responsible for the formulation and revision of a code of conduct and/or for monitoring compliance with the code by those who have undertaken to be bound by it."

;

3. Article 3a shall be replaced by the following:

"Article 3a

1. Comparative advertising shall, as far as the comparison is concerned, be permitted when the following conditions are met:
(a) it is not misleading within the meaning of Articles 2(2), 3 and 7(1) of this Directive or Articles 6 and 7 of Directive 2005/29/EC of the European Parliament and of the Council of 11 May 2005 concerning unfair business-to-consumer commercial practices in the internal market[1];
(b) it compares goods or services meeting the same needs or intended for the same purpose;
(c) it objectively compares one or more material, relevant, verifiable and representative features of those goods and services, which may include price;
(d) it does not discredit or denigrate the trade marks, trade names, other distinguishing marks, goods, services, activities, or circumstances of a competitor;
(e) for products with designation of origin, it relates in each case to products with the same designation;
(f) it does not take unfair advantage of the reputation of a trade mark, trade name or other distinguishing marks of a competitor or of the designation of origin of competing products;
(g) it does not present goods or services as imitations or replicas of goods or services bearing a protected trade mark or trade name;
(h) it does not create confusion among traders, between the advertiser and a competitor or between the advertiser's trade marks, trade names, other distinguishing marks, goods or services and those of a competitor.

4. Article 4(1) shall be replaced by the following:

"1. Member States shall ensure that adequate and effective means exist to combat misleading advertising in order to enforce compliance with the provisions on comparative advertising in the interest of traders and competitors. Such means shall include legal provisions under which persons or organisations regarded under national law as having a legitimate interest in combating misleading advertising or regulating comparative advertising may:

(a) take legal action against such advertising;

or

(b) bring such advertising before an administrative authority competent either to decide on complaints or to initiate appropriate legal proceedings.

It shall be for each Member State to decide which of these facilities shall be available and whether to enable the courts or administrative authorities to require prior recourse to other established means of dealing with complaints, including those referred to in

Article 5.

It shall be for each Member State to decide:

[1] OJ L 149, 11.6.2005, p. 22.";

(a) whether these legal facilities may be directed separately or jointly against a number of traders from the same economic sector;

and

(b) whether these legal facilities may be directed against a code owner where the relevant code promotes non-compliance with legal requirements."

;

5. Article 7(1) shall be replaced by the following:

"1. This Directive shall not preclude Member States from retaining or adopting provisions with a view to ensuring more extensive protection, with regard to misleading advertising, for traders and competitors."

Article 15 Amendments to Directives 97/7/EC and 2002/65/EC

1. Article 9 of Directive 97/7/EC shall be replaced by the following:

"Article 9

Inertia selling

Given the prohibition of inertia selling practices laid down in Directive 2005/29/EC of 11 May 2005of the European Parliament and of the Council concerning unfair business-to-consumer commercial practices in the internal market[1], Member States shall take the measures necessary to exempt the consumer from the provision of any consideration in cases of unsolicited supply, the absence of a response not constituting consent.

2. Article 9 of Directive 2002/65/EC shall be replaced by the following:

"Article 9

Given the prohibition of inertia selling practices laid down in Directive 2005/29/EC of 11 May 2005 of the European Parliament and of the Council concerning unfair business-to-consumer commercial practices in the internal market[2] and without prejudice to the provisions of Member States' legislation on the tacit renewal of distance contracts, when such rules permit tacit renewal, Member States shall take measures to exempt the consumer from any obligation in the event of unsolicited supplies, the absence of a reply not constituting consent.

Article 16 Amendments to Directive 98/27/EC and Regulation (EC) No 2006/2004

1. In the Annex to Directive 98/27/EC, point 1 shall be replaced by the following:

"1. Directive 2005/29/EC of the European Parliament and of the Council of 11 May 2005 concerning unfair business-to-consumer commercial practices in the internal market (OJ L 149, 11.6.2005, p. 22)."

2. In the Annex to Regulation (EC) No 2006/2004 of the European Parliament and of the Council of 27 October 2004 on cooperation between national authorities

[1] OJ L 149, 11.6.2005, p. 22.";

[2] OJ L 149, 11.6.2005, p. 22.";

responsible for the enforcement of the consumer protection law (the Regulation on consumer protection cooperation)[1] the following point shall be added:

"16. Directive 2005/29/EC of the European Parliament and of the Council of 11 May 2005 concerning unfair business-to-consumer commercial practices in the internal market (OJ L 149, 11.6.2005, p. 22)."

Article 17 Information

Member States shall take appropriate measures to inform consumers of the national law transposing this Directive and shall, where appropriate, encourage traders and code owners to inform consumers of their codes of conduct.

Article 18 Review

1. By 12 June 2011 the Commission shall submit to the European Parliament and the Council a comprehensive report on the application of this Directive, in particular of Articles 3(9) and 4 and Annex I, on the scope for further harmonisation and simplification of Community law relating to consumer protection, and, having regard to Article 3(5), on any measures that need to be taken at Community level to ensure that appropriate levels of consumer protection are maintained. The report shall be accompanied, if necessary, by a proposal to revise this Directive or other relevant parts of Community law.
2. The European Parliament and the Council shall endeavour to act, in accordance with the Treaty, within two years of the presentation by the Commission of any proposal submitted under paragraph 1.

Article 19 Transposition

Member States shall adopt and publish the laws, regulations and administrative provisions necessary to comply with this Directive by 12 June 2007. They shall forthwith inform the Commission thereof and inform the Commission of any subsequent amendments without delay.

They shall apply those measures by 12 December 2007. When Member States adopt those measures, they shall contain a reference to this Directive or be accompanied by such a reference on the occasion of their official publication. Member States shall determine how such reference is to be made.

Article 20 Entry into force

This Directive shall enter into force on the day following its publication in the Official Journal of the European Union.

[1] OJ L 364, 9.12.2004, p. 1.

Article 21 Addressees

This Directive is addressed to the Member States.

Done at Strasbourg, 11 May 2005.

For the European Parliament

The President

J. P. Borrell Fontelles

For the Council

The President

N. Schmit

ANNEX I

COMMERCIAL PRACTICES WHICH ARE IN ALL CIRCUMSTANCES CONSIDERED UNFAIR

Misleading commercial practices

1. Claiming to be a signatory to a code of conduct when the trader is not.
2. Displaying a trust mark, quality mark or equivalent without having obtained the necessary authorisation.
3. Claiming that a code of conduct has an endorsement from a public or other body which it does not have.
4. Claiming that a trader (including his commercial practices) or a product has been approved, endorsed or authorised by a public or private body when he/it has not or making such a claim without complying with the terms of the approval, endorsement or authorisation.
5. Making an invitation to purchase products at a specified price without disclosing the existence of any reasonable grounds the trader may have for believing that he will not be able to offer for supply or to procure another trader to supply, those products or equivalent products at that price for a period that is, and in quantities that are, reasonable having regard to the product, the scale of advertising of the product and the price offered (bait advertising).
6. Making an invitation to purchase products at a specified price and then:

   (a) refusing to show the advertised item to consumers;

   or

   (b) refusing to take orders for it or deliver it within a reasonable time;

   or

   (c) demonstrating a defective sample of it,

   with the intention of promoting a different product (bait and switch)
7. Falsely stating that a product will only be available for a very limited time, or that it will only be available on particular terms for a very limited time, in order to elicit an immediate decision and deprive consumers of sufficient opportunity or time to make an informed choice.
8. Undertaking to provide after-sales service to consumers with whom the trader has communicated prior to a transaction in a language which is not an official language of the Member State where the trader is located and then making such service available only in another language without clearly disclosing this to the consumer before the consumer is committed to the transaction.
9. Stating or otherwise creating the impression that a product can legally be sold when it cannot.
10. Presenting rights given to consumers in law as a distinctive feature of the trader's offer.
11. Using editorial content in the media to promote a product where a trader has paid for the promotion without making that clear in the content or by images or

sounds clearly identifiable by the consumer (advertorial). This is without prejudice to Council Directive 89/552/EEC[1].

12. Making a materially inaccurate claim concerning the nature and extent of the risk to the personal security of the consumer or his family if the consumer does not purchase the product.
13. Promoting a product similar to a product made by a particular manufacturer in such a manner as deliberately to mislead the consumer into believing that the product is made by that same manufacturer when it is not.
14. Establishing, operating or promoting a pyramid promotional scheme where a consumer gives consideration for the opportunity to receive compensation that is derived primarily from the introduction of other consumers into the scheme rather than from the sale or consumption of products.
15. Claiming that the trader is about to cease trading or move premises when he is not.
16. Claiming that products are able to facilitate winning in games of chance.
17. Falsely claiming that a product is able to cure illnesses, dysfunction or malformations.
18. Passing on materially inaccurate information on market conditions or on the possibility of finding the product with the intention of inducing the consumer to acquire the product at conditions less favourable than normal market conditions.
19. Claiming in a commercial practice to offer a competition or prize promotion without awarding the prizes described or a reasonable equivalent.
20. Describing a product as "gratis", "free", "without charge" or similar if the consumer has to pay anything other than the unavoidable cost of responding to the commercial practice and collecting or paying for delivery of the item.
21. Including in marketing material an invoice or similar document seeking payment which gives the consumer the impression that he has already ordered the marketed product when he has not.
22. Falsely claiming or creating the impression that the trader is not acting for purposes relating to his trade, business, craft or profession, or falsely representing oneself as a consumer.
23. Creating the false impression that after-sales service in relation to a product is available in a Member State other than the one in which the product is sold.

Aggressive commercial practices

24. Creating the impression that the consumer cannot leave the premises until a contract is formed.

[1] Council Directive 89/552/EEC of 3 October 1989 on the coordination of certain provisions laid down by Law, Regulation or Administrative Action in Member States concerning the pursuit of television broadcasting activities (OJ L 298, 17.10.1989, p. 23). Directive as amended by Directive 97/36/EC of the European Parliament and of the Council (OJ L 202, 30.7.1997, p. 60).

25. Conducting personal visits to the consumer's home ignoring the consumer's request to leave or not to return except in circumstances and to the extent justified, under national law, to enforce a contractual obligation.
26. Making persistent and unwanted solicitations by telephone, fax, e-mail or other remote media except in circumstances and to the extent justified under national law to enforce a contractual obligation. This is without prejudice to Article 10 of Directive 97/7/EC and Directives 95/46/EC[1] and 2002/58/EC.
27. Requiring a consumer who wishes to claim on an insurance policy to produce documents which could not reasonably be considered relevant as to whether the claim was valid, or failing systematically to respond to pertinent correspondence, in order to dissuade a consumer from exercising his contractual rights.
28. Including in an advertisement a direct exhortation to children to buy advertised products or persuade their parents or other adults to buy advertised products for them. This provision is without prejudice to Article 16 of Directive 89/552/EEC on television broadcasting.
29. Demanding immediate or deferred payment for or the return or safekeeping of products supplied by the trader, but not solicited by the consumer except where the product is a substitute supplied in conformity with Article 7(3) of Directive 97/7/EC (inertia selling).
30. Explicitly informing a consumer that if he does not buy the product or service, the trader's job or livelihood will be in jeopardy.
31. Creating the false impression that the consumer has already won, will win, or will on doing a particular act win, a prize or other equivalent benefit, when in fact either:
    - there is no prize or other equivalent benefit,

    or

    - taking any action in relation to claiming the prize or other equivalent benefit is subject to the consumer paying money or incurring a cost.

ANNEX II

COMMUNITY LAW PROVISIONS SETTING OUT RULES FOR ADVERTISING AND COMMERCIAL COMMUNICATION

Articles 4 and 5 of Directive 97/7/EC

Article 3 of Council Directive 90/314/EEC of 13 June 1990 on package travel, package holidays and package tours[2]

---

[1] Directive 95/46/EC of the European Parliament and of the Council of 24 October 1995 on the protection of individuals with regard to the processing of personal data and on the free movement of such data (OJ L 281, 23.11.1995, p. 31). Directive as amended by Regulation (EC) No 1882/2003 (OJ L 284, 31.10.2003, p. 1).

[2] OJ L 158, 23.6.1990, p. 59.

Article 3(3) of Directive 94/47/EC of the European Parliament and of the Council of 26 October 1994 on the protection of purchasers in respect of certain aspects of contracts relating to the purchase of a right to use immovable properties on a timeshare basis[1]

Article 3(4) of Directive 98/6/EC of the European Parliament and of the Council of 16 February 1998 on consumer protection in the indication of the prices of products offered to consumers[2]

Articles 86 to 100 of Directive 2001/83/EC of the European Parliament and of the Council of 6 November 2001 on the Community code relating to medicinal products for human use[3]

Articles 5 and 6 of Directive 2000/31/EC of the European Parliament and of the Council of 8 June 2000 on certain legal aspects of information society services, in particular electronic commerce, in the Internal Market (Directive on electronic commerce)[4]

Article 1(d) of Directive 98/7/EC of the European Parliament and of the Council of 16 February 1998 amending Council Directive 87/102/EEC for the approximation of the laws, regulations and administrative provisions of the Member States concerning consumer credit[5]

Articles 3 and 4 of Directive 2002/65/EC

Article 1(9) of Directive 2001/107/EC of the European Parliament and of the Council of 21 January 2002 amending Council Directive 85/611/EEC on the coordination of laws, regulations and administrative provisions relating to undertakings for collective investment in transferable securities (UCITS) with a view to regulating management companies and simplified prospectuses[6]

Articles 12 and 13 of Directive 2002/92/EC of the European Parliament and of the Council of 9 December 2002 on insurance mediation[7]

Article 36 of Directive 2002/83/EC of the European Parliament and of the Council of 5 November 2002 concerning life assurance[8]

Article 19 of Directive 2004/39/EC of the European Parliament and of the Council of 21 April 2004 on markets in financial instruments[9]

Articles 31 and 43 of Council Directive 92/49/EEC of 18 June 1992 on the coordination of laws, regulations and administrative provisions relating to direct insurance other than life assurance[1] (third non-life insurance Directive)

---

1 OJ L 280, 29.10.1994, p. 83.

2 OJ L 80, 18.3.1998, p. 27.

3 OJ L 311, 28.11.2001, p. 67. Directive as last amended by Directive 2004/27/EC (OJ L 136, 30.4.2004, p. 34).

4 OJ L 178, 17.7.2000, p. 1.

5 OJ L 101, 1.4.1998, p. 17.

6 OJ L 41, 13.2.2002, p. 20.

7 OJ L 9, 15.1.2003, p. 3.

8 OJ L 345, 19.12.2002, p. 1. Directive as amended by Council Directive 2004/66/EC. (OJ L 168, 1.5.2004, p. 35).

9 OJ L 145, 30.4.2004, p. 1.

Articles 5, 7 and 8 of Directive 2003/71/EC of the European Parliament and of the Council of 4 November 2003 on the prospectus to be published when securities are offered to the public or admitted to trading[2]

[1] OJ L 228, 11.8.1992, p. 1. Directive as last amended by Directive 2002/87/EC of the European Parliament and of the Council (OJ L 35, 11.2.2003, p. 1).

[2] OJ L 345, 31.12.2003, p. 64.

24. Directive 2006/123/EC of the European Parliament and of the Council of 12 December 2006 on services in the internal market

(OJ L 376 , 27/12/2006 p. 36 -68)

THE EUROPEAN PARLIAMENT AND THE COUNCIL OF THE EUROPEAN UNION,

Having regard to the Treaty establishing the European Community, and in particular the first and third sentence of Article 47(2) and Article 55 thereof,

Having regard to the proposal from the Commission,

Having regard to the Opinion of the European Economic and Social Committee[1],

Having regard to the opinion of the Committee of the Regions[2],

Acting in accordance with the procedure laid down in Article 251 of the Treaty[3],

Whereas:

(1) The European Community is seeking to forge ever closer links between the States and peoples of Europe and to ensure economic and social progress. In accordance with Article 14(2) of the Treaty, the internal market comprises an area without internal frontiers in which the free movement of services is ensured. In accordance with Article 43 of the Treaty the freedom of establishment is ensured. Article 49 of the Treaty establishes the right to provide services within the Community. The elimination of barriers to the development of service activities between Member States is essential in order to strengthen the integration of the peoples of Europe and to promote balanced and sustainable economic and social progress. In eliminating such barriers it is essential to ensure that the development of service activities contributes to the fulfilment of the task laid down in Article 2 of the Treaty of promoting throughout the Community a harmonious, balanced and sustainable development of economic activities, a high level of employment and of social protection, equality between men and women, sustainable and non-inflationary growth, a high degree of competitiveness and convergence of economic performance, a high level of protection and improvement of the quality of the environment, the raising of the standard of living and quality of life and economic and social cohesion and solidarity among Member States.

(2) A competitive market in services is essential in order to promote economic growth and create jobs in the European Union. At present numerous barriers within the internal market prevent providers, particularly small and medium-sized enterprises (SMEs), from extending their operations beyond their national

1 OJ C 221, 8.9.2005, p. 113.

2 OJ C 43, 18.2.2005, p. 18.

3 Opinion of the European Parliament of 16 February 2006 (not yet published in the Official Journal), Council Common Position of 24 July 2006 (OJ C 270 E, 7.11.2006, p. 1) and Position of the European Parliament of 15 November 2006. Council Decision of 11 December 2006.

borders and from taking full advantage of the internal market. This weakens the worldwide competitiveness of European Union providers. A free market which compels the Member States to eliminate restrictions on cross-border provision of services while at the same time increasing transparency and information for consumers would give consumers wider choice and better services at lower prices.

(3) The report from the Commission on "The State of the Internal Market for Services" drew up an inventory of a large number of barriers which are preventing or slowing down the development of services between Member States, in particular those provided by SMEs, which are predominant in the field of services. The report concludes that a decade after the envisaged completion of the internal market, there is still a huge gap between the vision of an integrated European Union economy and the reality as experienced by European citizens and providers. The barriers affect a wide variety of service activities across all stages of the provider's activity and have a number of common features, including the fact that they often arise from administrative burdens, the legal uncertainty associated with cross-border activity and the lack of mutual trust between Member States.

(4) Since services constitute the engine of economic growth and account for 70 % of GDP and employment in most Member States, this fragmentation of the internal market has a negative impact on the entire European economy, in particular on the competitiveness of SMEs and the movement of workers, and prevents consumers from gaining access to a greater variety of competitively priced services. It is important to point out that the services sector is a key employment sector for women in particular, and that they therefore stand to benefit greatly from new opportunities offered by the completion of the internal market for services. The European Parliament and the Council have emphasised that the removal of legal barriers to the establishment of a genuine internal market is a matter of priority for achieving the goal set by the European Council in Lisbon of 23 and 24 March 2000 of improving employment and social cohesion and achieving sustainable economic growth so as to make the European Union the most competitive and dynamic knowledge-based economy in the world by 2010, with more and better jobs. Removing those barriers, while ensuring an advanced European social model, is thus a basic condition for overcoming the difficulties encountered in implementing the Lisbon Strategy and for reviving the European economy, particularly in terms of employment and investment. It is therefore important to achieve an internal market for services, with the right balance between market opening and preserving public services and social and consumer rights.

(5) It is therefore necessary to remove barriers to the freedom of establishment for providers in Member States and barriers to the free movement of services as between Member States and to guarantee recipients and providers the legal certainty necessary for the exercise in practice of those two fundamental freedoms of the Treaty. Since the barriers in the internal market for services

affect operators who wish to become established in other Member States as well as those who provide a service in another Member State without being established there, it is necessary to enable providers to develop their service activities within the internal market either by becoming established in a Member State or by making use of the free movement of services. Providers should be able to choose between those two freedoms, depending on their strategy for growth in each Member State.

(6) Those barriers cannot be removed solely by relying on direct application of Articles 43 and 49 of the Treaty, since, on the one hand, addressing them on a case-by-case basis through infringement procedures against the Member States concerned would, especially following enlargement, be extremely complicated for national and Community institutions, and, on the other hand, the lifting of many barriers requires prior coordination of national legal schemes, including the setting up of administrative cooperation. As the European Parliament and the Council have recognised, a Community legislative instrument makes it possible to achieve a genuine internal market for services.

(7) This Directive establishes a general legal framework which benefits a wide variety of services while taking into account the distinctive features of each type of activity or profession and its system of regulation. That framework is based on a dynamic and selective approach consisting in the removal, as a matter of priority, of barriers which may be dismantled quickly and, for the others, the launching of a process of evaluation, consultation and complementary harmonisation of specific issues, which will make possible the progressive and coordinated modernisation of national regulatory systems for service activities which is vital in order to achieve a genuine internal market for services by 2010. Provision should be made for a balanced mix of measures involving targeted harmonisation, administrative cooperation, the provision on the freedom to provide services and encouragement of the development of codes of conduct on certain issues. That coordination of national legislative regimes should ensure a high degree of Community legal integration and a high level of protection of general interest objectives, especially protection of consumers, which is vital in order to establish trust between Member States. This Directive also takes into account other general interest objectives, including the protection of the environment, public security and public health as well as the need to comply with labour law.

(8) It is appropriate that the provisions of this Directive concerning the freedom of establishment and the free movement of services should apply only to the extent that the activities in question are open to competition, so that they do not oblige Member States either to liberalise services of general economic interest or to privatise public entities which provide such services or to abolish existing monopolies for other activities or certain distribution services.

(9) This Directive applies only to requirements which affect the access to, or the exercise of, a service activity. Therefore, it does not apply to requirements, such as road traffic rules, rules concerning the development or use of land, town and

country planning, building standards as well as administrative penalties imposed for non-compliance with such rules which do not specifically regulate or specifically affect the service activity but have to be respected by providers in the course of carrying out their economic activity in the same way as by individuals acting in their private capacity.

(10) This Directive does not concern requirements governing access to public funds for certain providers. Such requirements include notably those laying down conditions under which providers are entitled to receive public funding, including specific contractual conditions, and in particular quality standards which need to be observed as a condition for receiving public funds, for example for social services.

(11) This Directive does not interfere with measures taken by Member States, in accordance with Community law, in relation to the protection or promotion of cultural and linguistic diversity and media pluralism, including the funding thereof. This Directive does not prevent Member States from applying their fundamental rules and principles relating to the freedom of press and freedom of expression. This Directive does not affect Member State laws prohibiting discrimination on grounds of nationality or on grounds such as those set out in Article 13 of the Treaty.

(12) This Directive aims at creating a legal framework to ensure the freedom of establishment and the free movement of services between the Member States and does not harmonise or prejudice criminal law. However, Member States should not be able to restrict the freedom to provide services by applying criminal law provisions which specifically affect the access to or the exercise of a service activity in circumvention of the rules laid down in this Directive.

(13) It is equally important that this Directive fully respect Community initiatives based on Article 137 of the Treaty with a view to achieving the objectives of Article 136 thereof concerning the promotion of employment and improved living and working conditions.

(14) This Directive does not affect terms and conditions of employment, including maximum work periods and minimum rest periods, minimum paid annual holidays, minimum rates of pay as well as health, safety and hygiene at work, which Member States apply in compliance with Community law, nor does it affect relations between social partners, including the right to negotiate and conclude collective agreements, the right to strike and to take industrial action in accordance with national law and practices which respect Community law, nor does it apply to services provided by temporary work agencies. This Directive does not affect Member States' social security legislation.

(15) This Directive respects the exercise of fundamental rights applicable in the Member States and as recognised in the Charter of fundamental Rights of the European Union and the accompanying explanations, reconciling them with the fundamental freedoms laid down in Articles 43 and 49 of the Treaty. Those

fundamental rights include the right to take industrial action in accordance with national law and practices which respect Community law.

(16) This Directive concerns only providers established in a Member State and does not cover external aspects. It does not concern negotiations within international organisations on trade in services, in particular in the framework of the General Agreement on Trade in Services (GATS).

(17) This Directive covers only services which are performed for an economic consideration. Services of general interest are not covered by the definition in Article 50 of the Treaty and therefore do not fall within the scope of this Directive. Services of general economic interest are services that are performed for an economic consideration and therefore do fall within the scope of this Directive. However, certain services of general economic interest, such as those that may exist in the field of transport, are excluded from the scope of this Directive and certain other services of general economic interest, for example, those that may exist in the area of postal services, are the subject of a derogation from the provision on the freedom to provide services set out in this Directive. This Directive does not deal with the funding of services of general economic interest and does not apply to systems of aids granted by Member States, in particular in the social field, in accordance with Community rules on competition. This Directive does not deal with the follow-up to the Commission White Paper on Services of General Interest.

(18) Financial services should be excluded from the scope of this Directive since these activities are the subject of specific Community legislation aimed, as is this Directive, at achieving a genuine internal market for services. Consequently, t his exclusion should cover all financial services such as banking, credit, insurance, including reinsurance, occupational or personal pensions, securities, investment funds, payments and investment advice, including the services listed in Annex I to Directive 2006/48/EC of the European Parliament and of the Council of 14 June 2006 relating to the taking up and pursuit of the business of credit institutions[1].

(19) In view of the adoption in 2002 of a package of legislative instruments relating to electronic communications networks and services, as well as to associated resources and services, which has established a regulatory framework facilitating access to those activities within the internal market, notably through the elimination of most individual authorisation schemes, it is necessary to exclude issues dealt with by those instruments from the scope of this Directive.

(20) The exclusion from the scope of this Directive as regards matters of electronic communications services as covered by Directives 2002/19/EC of the European Parliament and of the Council of 7 March 2002 on access to, and interconnection of, electronic communications networks and associated facilities (Access Directive)[2], 2002/20/EC of the European Parliament and of the Council

---

1 OJ L 177, 30.6.2006, p. 1.

2 OJ L 108, 24.4.2002, p. 7.

of 7 March 2002 on the authorisation of electronic communications networks and services (Authorisation Directive)[1], 2002/21/EC of the European Parliament and of the Council of 7 March 2002 on a common regulatory framework for electronic communications networks and services (Framework Directive)[2], 2002/22/EC of the European Parliament and of the Council of 7 March 2002 on universal service and users' rights relating to electronic communications networks and services (Universal Service Directive)[3] and 2002/58/EC of the European Parliament and of the Council of 12 July 2002 concerning the processing of personal data and the protection of privacy in the electronic communications sector (Directive on privacy and electronic communications)[4] should apply not only to questions specifically dealt with in these Directives but also to matters for which the Directives explicitly leave to Member States the possibility of adopting certain measures at national level.

(21) Transport services, including urban transport, taxis and ambulances as well as port services, should be excluded from the scope of this Directive.

(22) The exclusion of healthcare from the scope of this Directive should cover healthcare and pharmaceutical services provided by health professionals to patients to assess, maintain or restore their state of health where those activities are reserved to a regulated health profession in the Member State in which the services are provided.

(23) This Directive does not affect the reimbursement of healthcare provided in a Member State other than that in which the recipient of the care is resident. This issue has been addressed by the Court of Justice on numerous occasions, and the Court has recognised patients' rights. It is important to address this issue in another Community legal instrument in order to achieve greater legal certainty and clarity to the extent that this issue is not already addressed in Council Regulation (EEC) No 1408/71 of 14 June 1971 on the application of social security schemes to employed persons, to self-employed persons and to members of their families moving within the Community[5].

(24) Audiovisual services, whatever their mode of transmission, including within cinemas, should also be excluded from the scope of this Directive. Furthermore, this Directive should not apply to aids granted by Member States in the audiovisual sector which are covered by Community rules on competition.

(25) Gambling activities, including lottery and betting transactions, should be excluded from the scope of this Directive in view of the specific nature of these activities, which entail implementation by Member States of policies relating to public policy and consumer protection.

---

[1] OJ L 108, 24.4.2002, p. 21.

[2] OJ L 108, 24.4.2002, p. 33.

[3] OJ L 108, 24.4.2002, p. 51.

[4] OJ L 201, 31.7.2002, p. 37. Directive as amended by Directive 2006/24/EC (OJ L 105, 13.4.2006, p. 54)

[5] OJ L 149, 5.7.1971, p. 2. Regulation as last amended by Regulation (EC) No 629/2006 of the European Parliament and of the Council (OJ L 114, 27.4.2006, p. 1).

(26) This Directive is without prejudice to the application of Article 45 of the Treaty.

(27) This Directive should not cover those social services in the areas of housing, childcare and support to families and persons in need which are provided by the State at national, regional or local level by providers m andated by the State or by charities recognised as such by the State with the objective of ensuring support for those who are permanently or temporarily in a particular state of need because of their insufficient family income or total or partial lack of independence and for those who risk being marginalised. These services are essential in order to guarantee the fundamental right to human dignity and integrity and are a manifestation of the principles of social cohesion and solidarity and should not be affected by this Directive.

(28) This Directive does not deal with the funding of, or the system of aids linked to, social services. Nor does it affect the criteria or conditions set by Member States to ensure that social services effectively carry out a function to the benefit of the public interest and social cohesion. In addition, this Directive should not affect the principle of universal service in Member States' social services.

(29) Given that the Treaty provides specific legal bases for taxation matters and given the Community instruments already adopted in that field, it is necessary to exclude the field of taxation from the scope of this Directive.

(30) There is already a considerable body of Community law on service activities. This Directive builds on, and thus complements, the Community acquis. Conflicts between this Directive and other Community instruments have been identified and are addressed by this Directive, including by means of derogations. However, it is necessary to provide a rule for any residual and exceptional cases where there is a conflict between a provision of this Directive and a provision of another Community instrument. The existence of such a conflict should be determined in compliance with the rules of the Treaty on the right of establishment and the free movement of services.

(31) This Directive is consistent with and does not affect Directive 2005/36/EC of the European Parliament and of the Council of 7 September 2005 on the recognition of professional qualifications[1]. It deals with questions other than those relating to professional qualifications, for example professional liability insurance, commercial communications, multidisciplinary activities and administrative simplification. With regard to temporary cross-border service provision, a derogation from the provision on the freedom to provide services in this Directive ensures that Title II on the free provision of services of Directive 2005/36/EC is not affected. Therefore, none of the measures applicable under that Directive in the Member State where the service is provided is affected by the provision on the freedom to provide services.

(32) This Directive is consistent with Community legislation on consumer protection, such as Directive 2005/29/EC of the European Parliament and of the

[1] OJ L 255, 30.9.2005, p. 22.

Council of 11 May 2005 concerning unfair business-to-consumer commercial practices in the internal market (the Unfair Commercial Practices Directive)[1] and Regulation (EC) No 2006/2004 of the European Parliament and of the Council of 27 October 2004 on cooperation between national authorities responsible for the enforcement of consumer protection laws (the Regulation on consumer protection cooperation)[2].

(33) The services covered by this Directive concern a wide variety of ever-changing activities, including business services such as management consultancy, certification and testing; facilities management, including office maintenance; advertising; recruitment services; and the services of commercial agents. The services covered are also services provided both to businesses and to consumers, such as legal or fiscal advice; real estate services such as estate agencies; construction, including the services of architects; distributive trades; the organisation of trade fairs; car rental; and travel agencies. Consumer services are also covered, such as those in the field of tourism, including tour guides; leisure services, sports centres and amusement parks; and, to the extent that they are not excluded from the scope of application of the Directive, household support services, such as help for the elderly. Those activities may involve services requiring the proximity of provider and recipient, services requiring travel by the recipient or the provider and services which may be provided at a distance, including via the Internet.

(34) According to the case-law of the Court of Justice, the assessment of whether certain activities, in particular activities which are publicly funded or provided by public entities, constitute a "service" has to be carried out on a case by case basis in the light of all their characteristics, in particular the way they are provided, organised and financed in the Member State concerned. The Court of Justice has held that the essential characteristic of remuneration lies in the fact that it constitutes consideration for the services in question and has recognised that the characteristic of remuneration is absent in the case of activities performed, for no consideration, by the State or on behalf of the State in the context of its duties in the social, cultural, educational and judicial fields, such as courses provided under the national education system, or the management of social security schemes which do not engage in economic activity. The payment of a fee by recipients, for example, a tuition or enrolment fee paid by students in order to make a certain contribution to the operating expenses of a system, does not in itself constitute remuneration because the service is still essentially financed by public funds. These activities are, therefore, not covered by the definition of service in Article 50 of the Treaty and do not therefore fall within the scope of this Directive.

(35) Non-profit making amateur sporting activities are of considerable social importance. They often pursue wholly social or recreational objectives. Thus,

1 OJ L 149, 11.6.2005, p. 22.

2 OJ L 364, 9.12.2004, p. 1. Regulation as amended by Directive 2005/29/EC.

they might not constitute economic activities within the meaning of Community law and should fall outside the scope of this Directive.

(36) The concept of "provider" should cover any natural person who is a national of a Member State or any legal person engaged in a service activity in a Member State, in exercise either of the freedom of establishment or of the free movement of services. The concept of provider should thus not be limited solely to cross-border service provision within the framework of the free movement of services but should also cover cases in which an operator establishes itself in a Member State in order to develop its service activities there. On the other hand, the concept of a provider should not cover the case of branches in a Member State of companies from third countries because, under Article 48 of the Treaty, the freedom of establishment and free movement of services may benefit only companies constituted in accordance with the laws of a Member State and having their registered office, central administration or principal place of business within the Community. The concept of "recipient" should also cover third country nationals who already benefit from rights conferred upon them by Community acts such as Regulation (EEC) No 1408/71, Council Directive 2003/109/EC of 25 November 2003 concerning the status of third-country nationals who are long-term residents[1], Council Regulation (EC) No 859/2003 of 14 May 2003 extending the provisions of Regulation (EEC) No 1408/71 and Regulation (EEC) No 574/72 to nationals of third countries who are not already covered by those provisions solely on the ground of their nationality[2] and Directive 2004/38/ECof the European Parliament and of the Council of 29 April 2004 on the right of citizens of the Union and their family members to move and reside freely within the territory of the Member States[3]. Furthermore, Member States may extend the concept of recipient to other third country nationals that are present within their territory.

(37) The place at which a provider is established should be determined in accordance with the case law of the Court of Justice according to which the concept of establishment involves the actual pursuit of an economic activity through a fixed establishment for an indefinite period. This requirement may also be fulfilled where a company is constituted for a given period or where it rents the building or installation through which it pursues its activity. It may also be fulfilled where a Member State grants authorisations for a limited duration only in relation to particular services. An establishment does not need to take the form of a subsidiary, branch or agency, but may consist of an office managed by a provider's own staff or by a person who is independent but authorised to act on a permanent basis for the undertaking, as would be the case with an agency. According to this definition, which requires the actual pursuit of an economic activity at the place of establishment of the provider, a mere letter box does not constitute an establishment. Where a provider has several places of

1 OJ L 16, 23.1.2004, p. 44.

2 OJ L 124, 20.5.2003, p. 1.

3 OJ L 158, 30.4.2004, p. 77.

establishment, it is important to determine the place of establishment from which the actual service concerned is provided. Where it is difficult to determine from which of several places of establishment a given service is provided, the location of the provider's centre of activities relating to this particular service should be that place of establishment.

(38) The concept of "legal persons", according to the Treaty provisions on establishment, leaves operators free to choose the legal form which they deem suitable for carrying out their activity. Accordingly, "legal persons", within the meaning of the Treaty, means all entities constituted under, or governed by, the law of a Member State, irrespective of their legal form.

(39) The concept of "authorisation scheme" should cover, inter alia, the administrative procedures for granting authorisations, licences, approvals or concessions, and also the obligation, in order to be eligible to exercise the activity, to be registered as a member of a profession or entered in a register, roll or database, to be officially appointed to a body or to obtain a card attesting to membership of a particular profession. Authorisation may be granted not only by a formal decision but also by an implicit decision arising, for example, from the silence of the competent authority or from the fact that the interested party must await acknowledgement of receipt of a declaration in order to commence the activity in question or for the latter to become lawful.

(40) The concept of "overriding reasons relating to the public interest" to which reference is made in certain provisions of this Directive has been developed by the Court of Justice in its case law in relation to Articles 43 and 49 of the Treaty and may continue to evolve. The notion as recognised in the case law of the Court of Justice covers at least the following grounds: public policy, public security and public health, within the meaning of Articles 46 and 55 of the Treaty; the maintenance of order in society; social policy objectives; the protection of the recipients of services; consumer protection; the protection of workers, including the social protection of workers; animal welfare; the preservation of the financial balance of the social security system; the prevention of fraud; the prevention of unfair competition; the protection of the environment and the urban environment, including town and country planning; the protection of creditors; safeguarding the sound administration of justice; road safety; the protection of intellectual property; cultural policy objectives, including safeguarding the freedom of expression of various elements, in particular social, cultural, religious and philosophical values of society; the need to ensure a high level of education, the maintenance of press diversity and the promotion of the national language; the preservation of national historical and artistic heritage; and veterinary policy.

(41) The concept of "public policy", as interpreted by the Court of Justice, covers the protection against a genuine and sufficiently serious threat affecting one of the fundamental interests of society and may include, in particular, issues relating to human dignity, the protection of minors and vulnerable adults and

animal welfare. Similarly, the concept of public security includes issues of public safety.

(42) The rules relating to administrative procedures should not aim at harmonising administrative procedures but at removing overly burdensome authorisation schemes, procedures and formalities that hinder the freedom of establishment and the creation of new service undertakings therefrom.

(43) One of the fundamental difficulties faced, in particular by SMEs, in accessing service activities and exercising them is the complexity, length and legal uncertainty of administrative procedures. For this reason, following the example of certain modernising and good administrative practice initiatives undertaken at Community and national level, it is necessary to establish principles of administrative simplification, inter alia through the limitation of the obligation of prior authorisation to cases in which it is essential and the introduction of the principle of tacit authorisation by the competent authorities after a certain period of time elapsed. Such modernising action, while maintaining the requirements on transparency and the updating of information relating to operators, is intended to eliminate the delays, costs and dissuasive effects which arise, for example, from unnecessary or excessively complex and burdensome procedures, the duplication of procedures, the "red tape" involved in submitting documents, the arbitrary use of powers by the competent authorities, indeterminate or excessively long periods before a response is given, the limited duration of validity of authorisations granted and disproportionate fees and penalties. Such practices have particularly significant dissuasive effects on providers wishing to develop their activities in other Member States and require coordinated modernisation within an enlarged internal market of twenty-five Member States.

(44) Member States should introduce, where appropriate, forms harmonised at Community level, as established by the Commission, which will serve as an equivalent to certificates, attestations or any other document in relation to establishment.

(45) In order to examine the need for simplifying procedures and formalities, Member States should be able, in particular, to take into account their necessity, number, possible duplication, cost, clarity and accessibility, as well as the delay and practical difficulties to which they could give rise for the provider concerned.

(46) In order to facilitate access to service activities and the exercise thereof in the internal market, it is necessary to establish an objective, common to all Member States, of administrative simplification and to lay down provisions concerning, inter alia, the right to information, procedures by electronic means and the establishment of a framework for authorisation schemes. Other measures adopted at national level to meet that objective could involve reduction of the number of procedures and formalities applicable to service activities and the restriction of such procedures and formalities to those which are essential in order to achieve a general interest objective and which do not duplicate each other in terms of content or purpose.

(47) With the aim of administrative simplification, general formal requirements, such as presentation of original documents, certified copies or a certified translation, should not be imposed, except where objectively justified by an overriding reason relating to the public interest, such as the protection of workers, public health, the protection of the environment or the protection of consumers. It is also necessary to ensure that an authorisation as a general rule permits access to, or exercise of, a service activity throughout the national territory, unless a new authorisation for each establishment, for example for each new hypermarket, or an authorisation that is restricted to a specific part of the national territory is objectively justified by an overriding reason relating to the public interest.

(48) In order to further simplify administrative procedures, it is appropriate to ensure that each provider has a single point through which he can complete all procedures and formalities (hereinafter referred to as "points of single contact"). The number of points of single contact per Member State may vary according to regional or local competencies or according to the activities concerned. The creation of points of single contact should not interfere with the allocation of functions among competent authorities within each national system. Where several authorities at regional or local level are competent, one of them may assume the role of point of single contact and coordinator. Points of single contact may be set up not only by administrative authorities but also by chambers of commerce or crafts, or by the professional organisations or private bodies to which a Member State decides to entrust that function. Points of single contact have an important role to play in providing assistance to providers either as the authority directly competent to issue the documents necessary to access a service activity or as an intermediary between the provider and the authorities which are directly competent.

(49) The fee which may be charged by points of single contact should be proportionate to the cost of the procedures and formalities with which they deal. This should not prevent Member States from entrusting the points of single contact with the collection of other administrative fees, such as the fee of supervisory bodies.

(50) It is necessary for providers and recipients of services to have easy access to certain types of information It should be for each Member State to determine, within the framework of this Directive, the way in which providers and recipients are provided with information. In particular, the obligation on Member States to ensure that relevant information is easily accessible to providers and recipients and that it can be accessed by the public without obstacle could be fulfilled by making this information accessible through a website. Any information given should be provided in a clear and unambiguous manner.

(51) The information provided to providers and recipients of services should include, in particular, information on procedures and formalities, contact details of the competent authorities, conditions for access to public registers and data

bases and information concerning available remedies and the contact details of associations and organisations from which providers or recipients can obtain practical assistance. The obligation on competent authorities to assist providers and recipients should not include the provision of legal advice in individual cases. Nevertheless, general information on the way in which requirements are usually interpreted or applied should be given. Issues such as liability for providing incorrect or misleading information should be determined by Member States.

(52) The setting up, in the reasonably near future, of electronic means of completing procedures and formalities will be vital for administrative simplification in the field of service activities, for the benefit of providers, recipients and competent authorities. In order to meet that obligation as to results, national laws and other rules applicable to services may need to be adapted. This obligation should not prevent Member States from providing other means of completing such procedures and formalities, in addition to electronic means. The fact that it must be possible to complete those procedures and formalities at a distance means, in particular, that Member States must ensure that they may be completed across borders. The obligation as to results does not cover procedures or formalities which by their very nature are impossible to complete at a distance. Furthermore, this does not interfere with Member States' legislation on the use of languages.

(53) The granting of licences for certain service activities may require an interview with the applicant by the competent authority in order to assess the applicant's personal integrity and suitability for carrying out the service in question. In such cases, the completion of formalities by electronic means may not be appropriate.

(54) The possibility of gaining access to a service activity should be made subject to authorisation by the competent authorities only if that decision satisfies the criteria of non-discrimination, necessity and proportionality. That means, in particular, that authorisation schemes should be permissible only where an a posteriori inspection would not be effective because of the impossibility of ascertaining the defects of the services concerned a posteriori, due account being taken of the risks and dangers which could arise in the absence of a prior inspection. However, the provision to that effect made by this Directive cannot be relied upon in order to justify authorisation schemes which are prohibited by other Community instruments such as Directive 1999/93/EC of the European Parliament and the Council of 13 December 1999 on a Community framework for electronic signatures[1], or Directive 2000/31/EC of the European Parliament and of the Council of 8 June 2000 on certain legal aspects of information society services, in particular electronic commerce, in the internal market (Directive on electronic commerce)[2]. The results of the process of mutual evaluation will make it possible to determine, at Community level, the types of activity for which authorisation schemes should be eliminated.

---

[1] OJ L 13, 19.1.2000, p. 12.

[2] OJ L 178, 17.7.2000, p. 1.

(55) This Directive should be without prejudice to the possibility for Member States to withdraw authorisations after they have been issued, if the conditions for the granting of the authorisation are no longer fulfilled.

(56) According to the case law of the Court of Justice, public health, consumer protection, animal health and the protection of the urban environment constitute overriding reasons relating to the public interest. Such overriding reasons may justify the application of authorisation schemes and other restrictions. However, no such authorisation scheme or restriction should discriminate on grounds of nationality. Further, the principles of necessity and proportionality should always be respected.

(57) The provisions of this Directive relating to authorisation schemes should concern cases where the access to or exercise of a service activity by operators requires a decision by a competent authority. This concerns neither decisions by competent authorities to set up a public or private entity for the provision of a particular service nor the conclusion of contracts by competent authorities for the provision of a particular service which is governed by rules on public procurement, since this Directive does not deal with rules on public procurement.

(58) In order to facilitate access to and exercise of service activities, it is important to evaluate and report on authorisation schemes and their justification. This reporting obligation concerns only the existence of authorisation schemes and not the criteria and conditions for the granting of an authorisation.

(59) The authorisation should as a general rule enable the provider to have access to the service activity, or to exercise that activity, throughout the national territory, unless a territorial limit is justified by an overriding reason relating to the public interest. For example, environmental protection may justify the requirement to obtain an individual authorisation for each installation on the national territory. This provision should not affect regional or local competences for the granting of authorisations within the Member States.

(60) This Directive, and in particular the provisions concerning authorisation schemes and the territorial scope of an authorisation, should not interfere with the division of regional or local competences within the Member States, including regional and local self-government and the use of official languages.

(61) The provision relating to the non-duplication of conditions for the granting of an authorisation should not prevent Member States from applying their own conditions as specified in the authorisation scheme. It should only require that competent authorities, when considering whether these conditions are met by the applicant, take into account the equivalent conditions which have already been satisfied by the applicant in another Member State. This provision should not require the application of the conditions for the granting of an authorisation provided for in the authorisation scheme of another Member State.

(62) Where the number of authorisations available for an activity is limited because of scarcity of natural resources or technical capacity, a procedure for

selection from among several potential candidates should be adopted with the aim of developing through open competition the quality and conditions for supply of services available to users. Such a procedure should provide guarantees of transparency and impartiality and the authorisation thus granted should not have an excessive duration, be subject to automatic renewal or confer any advantage on the provider whose authorisation has just expired. In particular, the duration of the authorisation granted should be fixed in such a way that it does not restrict or limit free competition beyond what is necessary in order to enable the provider to recoup the cost of investment and to make a fair return on the capital invested. This provision should not prevent Member States from limiting the number of authorisations for reasons other than scarcity of natural resources or technical capacity. These authorisationsshould remain in any case subject to the other provisions of this Directive relating to authorisation schemes.

(63) In the absence of different arrangements, failing a response within a time period, an authorisation should be deemed to have been granted. However, different arrangements may be put in place in respect of certain activities, where objectively justified by overriding reasons relating to the public interest, including a legitimate interest of third parties. Such different arrangements could include national rules according to which, in the absence of a response of the competent authority, the application is deemed to have been rejected, this rejection being open to challenge before the courts.

(64) In order to establish a genuine internal market for services, it is necessary to abolish any restrictions on the freedom of establishment and the free movement of services which are still enshrined in the laws of certain Member States and which are incompatible with Articles 43 and 49 of the Treaty respectively. The restrictions to be prohibited particularly affect the internal market for services and should be systematically dismantled as soon as possible.

(65) Freedom of establishment is predicated, in particular, upon the principle of equal treatment, which entails the prohibition not only of any discrimination on grounds of nationality but also of any indirect discrimination based on other grounds but capable of producing the same result. Thus, access to a service activity or the exercise thereof in a Member State, either as a principal or secondary activity, should not be made subject to criteria such as place of establishment, residence, domicile or principal provision of the service activity. However, these criteria should not include requirements according to which a provider or one of his employees or a representative must be present during the exercise of the activity when this is justified by an overriding reason relating to the public interest. Furthermore, a Member State should not restrict the legal capacity or the right of companies, incorporated in accordance with the law of another Member State on whose territory they have their primary establishment, to bring legal proceedings. Moreover, a Member State should not be able to confer any advantages on providers having a particular national or local socio-economic link; nor should it be able to restrict, on grounds of place of

establishment, the provider's freedom to acquire, exploit or dispose of rights and goods or to access different forms of credit or accommodation in so far as those choices are useful for access to his activity or for the effective exercise thereof.

(66) Access to or the exercise of a service activity in the territory of a Member State should not be subject to an economic test. The prohibition of economic tests as a prerequisite for the grant of authorisation should cover economic tests as such, but not requirements which are objectively justified by overriding reasons relating to the public interest, such as the protection of the urban environment, social policy or public health. The prohibition should not affect the exercise of the powers of the authorities responsible for applying competition law.

(67) With respect to financial guarantees or insurance, the prohibition of requirements should concern only the obligation that the requested financial guarantees or insurance must be obtained from a financial institution established in the Member State concerned.

(68) With respect to pre-registration, the prohibition of requirements should concern only the obligation that the provider, prior to the establishment, be pre-registered for a given period in a register held in the Member State concerned.

(69) In order to coordinate the modernisation of national rules and regulations in a manner consistent with the requirements of the internal market, it is necessary to evaluate certain non-discriminatory national requirements which, by their very nature, could severely restrict or even prevent access to an activity or the exercise thereof under the freedom of establishment. This evaluation process should be limited to the compatibility of these requirements with the criteria already established by the Court of Justice on the freedom of establishment. It should not concern the application of Community competition law. Where such requirements are discriminatory or not objectively justified by an overriding reason relating to the public interest, or where they are disproportionate, they must be abolished or amended. The outcome of this assessment will be different according to the nature of the activity and the public interest concerned. In particular, such requirements could be fully justified when they pursue social policy objectives.

(70) For the purposes of this Directive, and without prejudice to Article 16 of the Treaty, services may be considered to be services of general economic interest only if they are provided in application of a special task in the public interest entrusted to the provider by the Member State concerned. This assignment should be made by way of one or more acts, the form of which is determined by the Member State concerned, and should specify the precise nature of the special task.

(71) The mutual evaluation process provided for in this Directive should not affect the freedom of Member States to set in their legislation a high level of protection of the public interest, in particular in relation to social policy objectives. Furthermore, it is necessary that the mutual evaluation process take

fully into account the specificity of services of general economic interest and of the particular tasks assigned to them. This may justify certain restrictions on the freedom of establishment, in particular where such restrictions pursue the protection of public health and social policy objectives and where they satisfy the conditions set out in Article 15(3)(a), (b) and (c). For example, with regard to the obligation to take a specific legal form in order to exercise certain services in the social field, the Court of Justice has already recognised that it may be justified to subject the provider to a requirement to be non-profit making.

(72) Services of a general economic interest are entrusted with important tasks relating to social and territorial cohesion. The performance of these tasks should not be obstructed as a result of the evaluation process provided for in this Directive. Requirements which are necessary for the fulfilment of such tasks should not be affected by this process while, at the same time, unjustified restrictions on the freedom of establishment should be addressed.

(73) The requirements to be examined include national rules which, on grounds other than those relating to professional qualifications, reserve access to certain activities to particular providers. These requirements also include obligations on a provider to take a specific legal form, in particular to be a legal person, to be a company with individual ownership, to be a non-profit making organisation or a company owned exclusively by natural persons, and requirements which relate to the shareholding of a company, in particular obligations to hold a minimum amount of capital for certain service activities or to have a specific qualification in order to hold share capital in or to manage certain companies. The evaluation of the compatibility of fixed minimum and/or maximum tariffs with the freedom of establishment concerns only tariffs imposed by competent authorities specifically for the provision of certain services and not, for example, general rules on price determination, such as for the renting of houses.

(74) The mutual evaluation process means that during the transposition period Member States will first have to conduct a screening of their legislation in order to ascertain whether any of the above mentioned requirements exists in their legal systems. At the latest by the end of the transposition period, Member States should draw up a report on the results of this screening. Each report will be submitted to all other Member States and interested parties. Member States will then have six months in which to submit their observations on these reports. At the latest by one year after the date of transposition of this Directive, the Commission should draw up a summary report, accompanied where appropriate by proposals for further initiatives. If necessary the Commission, in cooperation with the Member States, could assist them to design a common method.

(75) The fact that this Directive specifies a number of requirements to be abolished or evaluated by the Member States during the transposition period is without prejudice to any infringement proceedings against a Member State for failure to fulfil its obligations under Articles 43 or 49 of the Treaty.

(76) This Directive does not concern the application of Articles 28 to 30 of the Treaty relating to the free movement of goods. The restrictions prohibited

pursuant to the provision on the freedom to provide services cover the requirements applicable to access to service activities or to the exercise thereof and not those applicable to goods as such.

(77) Where an operator travels to another Member State to exercise a service activity there, a distinction should be made between situations covered by the freedom of establishment and those covered, due to the temporary nature of the activities concerned, by the free movement of services. As regards the distinction between the freedom of establishment and the free movement of services, according to the case law of the Court of Justice the key element is whether or not the operator is established in the Member State where it provides the service concerned. If the operator is established in the Member State where it provides its services, it should come under the scope of application of the freedom of establishment. If, by contrast, the operator is not established in the Member State where the service is provided, its activities should be covered by the free movement of services. The Court of Justice has consistently held that the temporary nature of the activities in question should be determined in the light not only of the duration of the provision of the service, but also of its regularity, periodical nature or continuity. The fact that the activity is temporary should not mean that the provider may not equip itself with some forms of infrastructure in the Member State where the service is provided, such as an office, chambers or consulting rooms, in so far as such infrastructure is necessary for the purposes of providing the service in question.

(78) In order to secure effective implementation of the free movement of services and to ensure that recipients and providers can benefit from and supply services throughout the Community regardless of borders, it is necessary to clarify the extent to which requirements of the Member State where the service is provided can be imposed. It is indispensable to provide that the provision on the freedom to provide services does not prevent the Member State where the service is provided from imposing, in compliance with the principles set out in Article 16(1)(a) to (c), its specific requirements for reasons of public policy or public security or for the protection of public health or the environment.

(79) The Court of Justice has consistently held that Member States retain the right to take measures in order to prevent providers from abusively taking advantage of the internal market principles. Abuse by a provider should be established on a case by case basis.

(80) It is necessary to ensure that providers are able to take equipment which is integral to the provision of their service with them when they travel to provide services in another Member State. In particular, it is important to avoid cases in which the service could not be provided without the equipment or situations in which providers incur additional costs, for example, by hiring or purchasing different equipment to that which they habitually use or by needing to deviate significantly from the way they habitually carry out their activity.

(81) The concept of equipment does not refer to physical objects which are either supplied by the provider to the client or become part of a physical object as a

result of the service activity, such as building materials or spare parts, or which are consumed or left in situ in the course of the service provision, such as combustible fuels, explosives, fireworks, pesticides, poisons or medicines.

(82) The provisions of this Directive should not preclude the application by a Member State of rules on employment conditions. Rules laid down by law, regulation or administrative provisions should, in accordance with the Treaty, be justified for reasons relating to the protection of workers and be non-discriminatory, necessary, and proportionate, as interpreted by the Court of Justice, and comply with other relevant Community law.

(83) It is necessary to ensure that the provision on the freedom to provide services may be departed from only in the areas covered by derogations. Those derogations are necessary in order to take into account the level of integration of the internal market or certain Community instruments relating to services pursuant to which a provider is subject to the application of a law other than that of the Member State of establishment. Moreover, by way of exception, measures against a given provider should also be adopted in certain individual cases and under certain strict procedural and substantive conditions. In addition, any restriction of the free movement of services should be permitted, by way of exception, only if it is consistent with fundamental rights which form an integral part of the general principles of law enshrined in the Community legal order.

(84) The derogation from the provision on the freedom to provide services concerning postal services should cover both activities reserved to the universal service provider and other postal services.

(85) The derogation from the provision on the freedom to provide services relating to the judicial recovery of debts and the reference to a possible future harmonisation instrument should concern only the access to and the exercise of activities which consist, notably, in bringing actions before a court relating to the recovery of debts.

(86) This Directive should not affect terms and conditions of employment which, pursuant to Directive 96/71/ECof the European Parliament and of the Council of 16 December 1996 concerning the posting of workers in the framework of the provision of services[1], apply to workers posted to provide a service in the territory of another Member State. In such cases, Directive 96/71/EC stipulates that providers have to comply with terms and conditions of employment in a listed number of areas applicable in the Member State where the service is provided. These are: maximum work periods and minimum rest periods, minimum paid annual holidays, minimum rates of pay, including overtime rates, the conditions of hiring out of workers, in particular the protection of workers hired out by temporary employment undertakings, health, safety and hygiene at work, protective measures with regard to the terms and conditions of employment of pregnant women or women who have recently given birth and of children and young people and equality of treatment between men and women

[1] OJ L 18, 21.1.1997, p. 1.

and other provisions on non-discrimination. This not only concerns terms and conditions of employment which are laid down by law but also those laid down in collective agreements or arbitration awards that are officially declared or de facto universally applicable within the meaning of Directive 96/71/EC. Moreover, this Directive should not prevent Member States from applying terms and conditions of employment on matters other than those listed in Article 3(1) of Directive 96/71/EC on the grounds of public policy.

(87) Neither should this Directive affect terms and conditions of employment in cases where the worker employed for the provision of a cross-border service is recruited in the Member State where the service is provided. Furthermore, this Directive should not affect the right for the Member State where the service is provided to determine the existence of an employment relationship and the distinction between self-employed persons and employed persons, including "false self-employed persons". In that respect the essential characteristic of an employment relationship within the meaning of Article 39 of the Treaty should be the fact that for a certain period of time a person provides services for and under the direction of another person in return for which he receives remuneration. Any activity which a person performs outside a relationship of subordination must be classified as an activity pursued in a self-employed capacity for the purposes of Articles 43 and 49 of the Treaty.

(88) The provision on the freedom to provide services should not apply in cases where, in conformity with Community law, an activity is reserved in a Member State to a particular profession, for example requirements which reserve the provision of legal advice to lawyers.

(89) The derogation from the provision on the freedom to provide services concerning matters relating to the registration of vehicles leased in a Member State other than that in which they are used follows from the case law of the Court of Justice, which has recognised that a Member State may impose such an obligation, in accordance with proportionate conditions, in the case of vehicles used on its territory. That exclusion does not cover occasional or temporary rental.

(90) Contractual relations between the provider and the client as well as between an employer and employee should not be subject to this Directive. The applicable law regarding the contractual or non contractual obligations of the provider should be determined by the rules of private international law.

(91) It is necessary to afford Member States the possibility, exceptionally and on a case-by-case basis, of taking measures which derogate from the provision on the freedom to provide services in respect of a provider established in another Member State on grounds of the safety of services. However, it should be possible to take such measures only in the absence of harmonisation at Community level.

(92) Restrictions on the free movement of services, contrary to this Directive, may arise not only from measures applied to providers, but also from the many

barriers to the use of services by recipients, especially consumers. This Directive mentions, by way of illustration, certain types of restriction applied to a recipient wishing to use a service performed by a provider established in another Member State. This also includes cases where recipients of a service are under an obligation to obtain authorisation from or to make a declaration to their competent authorities in order to receive a service from a provider established in another Member State. This does not concern general authorisation schemes which also apply to the use of a service supplied by a provider established in the same Member State.

(93) The concept of financial assistance provided for the use of a particular service should not apply to systems of aids granted by Member States, in particular in the social field or in the cultural sector, which are covered by Community rules on competition, nor to general financial assistance not linked to the use of a particular service, for example grants or loans to students.

(94) In accordance with the Treaty rules on the free movement of services, discrimination on grounds of the nationality of the recipient or national or local residence is prohibited. Such discrimination could take the form of an obligation, imposed only on nationals of another Member State, to supply original documents, certified copies, a certificate of nationality or official translations of documents in order to benefit from a service or from more advantageous terms or prices. However, the prohibition of discriminatory requirements should not preclude the reservation of advantages, especially as regards tariffs, to certain recipients, if such reservation is based on legitimate and objective criteria.

(95) The principle of non-discrimination within the internal market means that access by a recipient, and especially by a consumer, to a service on offer to the public may not be denied or restricted by application of a criterion, included in general conditions made available to the public, relating to the recipient's nationality or place of residence. It does not follow that it will be unlawful discrimination if provision were made in such general conditions for different tariffs and conditions to apply to the provision of a service, where those tariffs, prices and conditions are justified for objective reasons that can vary from country to country, such as additional costs incurred because of the distance involved or the technical characteristics of the provision of the service, or different market conditions, such as higher or lower demand influenced by seasonality, different vacation periods in the Member States and pricing by different competitors, or extra risks linked to rules differing from those of the Member State of establishment. Neither does it follow that the non-provision of a service to a consumer for lack of the required intellectual property rights in a particular territory would constitute unlawful discrimination.

(96) It is appropriate to provide that, as one of the means by which the provider may make the information which he is obliged to supply easily accessible to the recipient, he supply his electronic address, including that of his website. Furthermore, the obligation to make available certain information in the

provider's information documents which present his services in detail should not cover commercial communications of a general nature, such as advertising, but rather documents giving a detailed description of the services proposed, including documents on a website.

(97) It is necessary to provide in this Directive for certain rules on high quality of services, ensuring in particular information and transparency requirements. These rules should apply both in cases of cross border provision of services between Member States and in cases of services provided in a Member State by a provider established there, without imposing unnecessary burdens on SMEs. They should not in any way prevent Member States from applying, in conformity with this Directive and other Community law, additional or different quality requirements.

(98) Any operator providing services involving a direct and particular health, safety or financial risk for the recipient or a third person should, in principle, be covered by appropriate professional liability insurance, or by another form of guarantee which is equivalent or comparable, which means, in particular, that such an operator should as a general rule have adequate insurance cover for services provided in one or more Member States other than the Member State of establishment.

(99) The insurance or guarantee should be appropriate to the nature and extent of the risk. Therefore it should be necessary for the provider to have cross-border cover only if that provider actually provides services in other Member States. Member States should not lay down more detailed rules concerning the insurance cover and fix for example minimum thresholds for the insured sum or limits on exclusions from the insurance cover. Providers and insurance companies should maintain the necessary flexibility to negotiate insurance policies precisely targeted to the nature and extent of the risk. Furthermore, it is not necessary for an obligation of appropriate insurance to be laid down by law. It should be sufficient if an insurance obligation is part of the ethical rules laid down by professional bodies. Finally, there should be no obligation for insurance companies to provide insurance cover.

(100) It is necessary to put an end to total prohibitions on commercial communications by the regulated professions, not by removing bans on the content of a commercial communication but rather by removing those bans which, in a general way and for a given profession, forbid one or more forms of commercial communication, such as a ban on all advertising in one or more given media. As regards the content and methods of commercial communication, it is necessary to encourage professionals to draw up, in accordance with Community law, codes of conduct at Community level.

(101) It is necessary and in the interest of recipients, in particular consumers, to ensure that it is possible for providers to offer multidisciplinary services and that restrictions in this regard be limited to what is necessary to ensure the impartiality, independence and integrity of the regulated professions. This does not affect restrictions or prohibitions on carrying out particular activities which

aim at ensuring independence in cases in which a Member State entrusts a provider with a particular task, notably in the area of urban development, nor should it affect the application of competition rules.

(102) In order to increase transparency and promote assessments based on comparable criteria with regard to the quality of the services offered and supplied to recipients, it is important that information on the meaning of quality labels and other distinctive marks relating to these services be easily accessible. That obligation of transparency is particularly important in areas such as tourism, especially the hotel business, in which the use of a system of classification is widespread. Moreover, it is appropriate to examine the extent to which European standardisation could facilitate compatibility and quality of services. European standards are drawn up by the European standards-setting bodies, the European Committee for Standardisation (CEN), the European Committee for Electrotechnical Standardisation (CENELEC) and the European Telecommunications Standards Institute (ETSI). Where appropriate, the Commission may, in accordance with the procedures laid down in Directive 98/34/EC of the European Parliament and of the Council of 22 June 1998 laying down a procedure for the provision of information in the field of technical standards and regulations[1] and of rules on Information Society services, issue a mandate for the drawing up of specific European standards.

(103) In order to solve potential problems with compliance with judicial decisions, it is appropriate to provide that Member States recognise equivalent guarantees lodged with institutions or bodies such as banks, insurance providers or other financial services providers established in another Member State.

(104) The development of a network of Member States' consumer protection authorities, which is the subject of Regulation (EC) No 2006/2004, complements the cooperation provided for in this Directive. The application of consumer protection legislation in cross-border cases, in particular with regard to new marketing and selling practices, as well as the need to remove certain specific obstacles to cooperation in this field, necessitates a greater degree of cooperation between Member States. In particular, it is necessary in this area to ensure that Member States require the cessation of illegal practices by operators in their territory who target consumers in another Member State.

(105) Administrative cooperation is essential to make the internal market in services function properly. Lack of cooperation between Member States results in proliferation of rules applicable to providers or duplication of controls for cross-border activities, and can also be used by rogue traders to avoid supervision or to circumvent applicable national rules on services. It is, therefore, essential to provide for clear, legally binding obligations for Member States to cooperate effectively.

[1] OJ L 204, 21.7.1998, p. 37. Directive as last amended by the 2003 Act of Accession.

(106) For the purposes of the Chapter on administrative cooperation, "supervision" should cover activities such as monitoring and fact finding, problem solving, enforcement and imposition of sanctions and subsequent follow-up activities.

(107) In normal circumstances mutual assistance should take place directly between competent authorities. The liaison points designated by Member States should be required to facilitate this process only in the event of difficulties being encountered, for instance if assistance is required to identify the relevant competent authority.

(108) Certain obligations of mutual assistance should apply to all matters covered by this Directive, including those relating to cases where a provider establishes in another Member State. Other obligations of mutual assistance should apply only in cases of cross-border provision of services, where the provision on the freedom to provide services applies. A further set of obligations should apply in all cases of cross-border provision of services, including areas not covered by the provision on the freedom to provide services. Cross-border provision of services should include cases where services are provided at a distance and where the recipient travels to the Member State of establishment of the provider in order to receive services.

(109) In cases where a provider moves temporarily to a Member State other than the Member State of establishment, it is necessary to provide for mutual assistance between those two Member States so that the former can carry out checks, inspections and enquiries at the request of the Member State of establishment or carry out such checks on its own initiative if these are merely factual checks.

(110) It should not be possible for Member States to circumvent the rules laid down in this Directive, including the provision on the freedom to provide services, by conducting checks, inspections or investigations which are discriminatory or disproportionate.

(111) The provisions of this Directive concerning exchange of information regarding the good repute of providers should not pre-empt initiatives in the area of police and judicial cooperation in criminal matters, in particular on the exchange of information between law enforcement authorities of the Member States and on criminal records.

(112) Cooperation between Member States requires a well-functioning electronic information system in order to allow competent authorities easily to identify their relevant interlocutors in other Member States and to communicate in an efficient way.

(113) It is necessary to provide that the Member States, in cooperation with the Commission, are to encourage interested parties to draw up codes of conduct at Community level, aimed, in particular, at promoting the quality of services and taking into account the specific nature of each profession. Those codes of conduct should comply with Community law, especially competition law. They

should be compatible with legally binding rules governing professional ethics and conduct in the Member States.

(114) Member States should encourage the setting up of codes of conduct, in particular, by professional bodies, organisations and associations at Community level. These codes of conduct should include, as appropriate to the specific nature of each profession, rules for commercial communications relating to the regulated professions and rules of professional ethics and conduct of the regulated professions which aim, in particular, at ensuring independence, impartiality and professional secrecy. In addition, the conditions to which the activities of estate agents are subject should be included in such codes of conduct. Member States should take accompanying measures to encourage professional bodies, organisations and associations to implement at national level the codes of conduct adopted at Community level.

(115) Codes of conduct at Community level are intended to set minimum standards of conduct and are complementary to Member States' legal requirements. They do not preclude Member States, in accordance with Community law, from taking more stringent measures in law or national professional bodies from providing for greater protection in their national codes of conduct.

(116) Since the objectives of this Directive, namely the elimination of barriers to the freedom of establishment for providers in the Member States and to the free provision of services between Member States, cannot be sufficiently achieved by the Member States and can therefore, by reason of the scale of the action, be better achieved at Community level, the Community may adopt measures, in accordance with the principle of subsidiarity as set out in Article 5 of the Treaty. In accordance with the principle of proportionality, as set out in that Article, this Directive does not go beyond what is necessary in order to achieve those objectives.

(117) The measures necessary for the implementation of this Directive should be adopted in accordance with Council Decision 1999/468/EC of 28 June 1999 laying down the procedures for the exercise of implementing powers conferred on the Commission[1].

(118) In accordance with paragraph 34 of the Interinstitutional Agreement on better law-making[2], Member States are encouraged to draw up, for themselves and in the interest of the Community, their own tables, which will, as far as possible, illustrate the correlation between the Directive and the transposition measures, and to make them public,

HAVE ADOPTED THIS DIRECTIVE:

[1] OJ L 184, 17.7.1999, p. 23. Decision as amended by Decision 2006/512/EC (OJ L 200, 22.7.2006, p. 11).

[2] OJ C 321, 31.12.2003, p. 1.

CHAPTER I : GENERAL PROVISIONS

Article 1 Subject matter

1. This Directive establishes general provisions facilitating the exercise of the freedom of establishment for service providers and the free movement of services, while maintaining a high quality of services.
2. This Directive does not deal with the liberalisation of services of general economic interest, reserved to public or private entities, nor with the privatisation of public entities providing services.
3. This Directive does not deal with the abolition of monopolies providing services nor with aids granted by Member States which are covered by Community rules on competition.

   This Directive does not affect the freedom of Member States to define, in conformity with Community law, what they consider to be services of general economic interest, how those services should be organised and financed, in compliance with the State aid rules, and what specific obligations they should be subject to.
4. This Directive does not affect measures taken at Community level or at national level, in conformity with Community law, to protect or promote cultural or linguistic diversity or media pluralism.
5. This Directive does not affect Member States' rules of criminal law. However, Member States may not restrict the freedom to provide services by applying criminal law provisions which specifically regulate or affect access to or exercise of a service activity in circumvention of the rules laid down in this Directive.
6. This Directive does not affect labour law, that is any legal or contractual provision concerning employment conditions, working conditions, including health and safety at work and the relationship between employers and workers, which Member States apply in accordance with national law which respects Community law. Equally, this Directive does not affect the social security legislation of the Member States.
7. This Directive does not affect the exercise of fundamental rights as recognised in the Member States and by Community law. Nor does it affect the right to negotiate, conclude and enforce collective agreements and to take industrial action in accordance with national law and practices which respect Community law.

Article 2 Scope

1. This Directive shall apply to services supplied by providers established in a Member State.
2. This Directive shall not apply to the following activities:
   (a) non-economic services of general interest;

(b) financial services, such as banking, credit, insurance and re-insurance, occupational or personal pensions, securities, investment funds, payment and investment advice, including the services listed in Annex I to Directive 2006/48/EC;
(c) electronic communications services and networks, and associated facilities and services, with respect to matters covered by Directives 2002/19/EC, 2002/20/EC, 2002/21/EC, 2002/22/EC and 2002/58/EC;
(d) services in the field of transport, including port services, falling within the scope of Title V of the Treaty;
(e) services of temporary work agencies;
(f) healthcare services whether or not they are provided via healthcare facilities, and regardless of the ways in which they are organised and financed at national level or whether they are public or private;
(g) audiovisual services, including cinematographic services, whatever their mode of production, distribution and transmission, and radio broadcasting;
(h) gambling activities which involve wagering a stake with pecuniary value in games of chance, including lotteries, gambling in casinos and betting transactions;
(i) activities which are connected with the exercise of official authority as set out in Article 45 of the Treaty;
(j) social services relating to social housing, childcare and support of families and persons permanently or temporarily in need which are provided by the State, by providers mandated by the State or by charities recognised as such by the State;
(k) private security services;
(l) services provided by notaries and bailiffs, who are appointed by an official act of government.

3. This Directive shall not apply to the field of taxation.

Article 3 Relationship with other provisions of Community law

1. If the provisions of this Directive conflict with a provision of another Community act governing specific aspects of access to or exercise of a service activity in specific sectors or for specific professions, the provision of the other Community act shall prevail and shall apply to those specific sectors or professions. These include:
   (a) Directive 96/71/EC;
   (b) Regulation (EEC) No 1408/71;
   (c) Council Directive 89/552/EEC of 3 October 1989 on the coordination of certain provisions laid down by law, regulation or administrative action in Member States concerning the pursuit of television broadcasting activities[1];
   (d) Directive 2005/36/EC.

---

[1] OJ L 298, 17.10.1989, p. 23. Directive as amended by Directive 97/36/EC of the European Parliament and of the Council (OJ L 202, 30.7.1997, p. 60).

2. This Directive does not concern rules of private international law, in particular rules governing the law applicable to contractual and non contractual obligations, including those which guarantee that consumers benefit from the protection granted to them by the consumer protection rules laid down in the consumer legislation in force in their Member State.
3. Member States shall apply the provisions of this Directive in compliance with the rules of the Treaty on the right of establishment and the free movement of services.

Article 4 Definitions

For the purposes of this Directive, the following definitions shall apply:

1) "service" means any self-employed economic activity, normally provided for remuneration, as referred to in Article 50 of the Treaty;
2) "provider" means any natural person who is a national of a Member State, or any legal person as referred to in Article 48 of the Treaty and established in a Member State, who offers or provides a service;
3) "recipient" means any natural person who is a national of a Member State or who benefits from rights conferred upon him by Community acts, or any legal person as referred to in Article 48 of the Treaty and established in a Member State, who, for professional or non-professional purposes, uses, or wishes to use, a service;
4) "Member State of establishment" means the Member State in whose territory the provider of the service concerned is established;
5) "establishment" means the actual pursuit of an economic activity, as referred to in Article 43 of the Treaty, by the provider for an indefinite period and through a stable infrastructure from where the business of providing services is actually carried out;
6) "authorisation scheme" means any procedure under which a provider or recipient is in effect required to take steps in order to obtain from a competent authority a formal decision, or an implied decision, concerning access to a service activity or the exercise thereof;
7) "requirement" means any obligation, prohibition, condition or limit provided for in the laws, regulations or administrative provisions of the Member States or in consequence of case-law, administrative practice, the rules of professional bodies, or the collective rules of professional associations or other professional organisations, adopted in the exercise of their legal autonomy; rules laid down in collective agreements negotiated by the social partners shall not as such be seen as requirements within the meaning of this Directive;
8) "overriding reasons relating to the public interest" means reasons recognised as such in the case law of the Court of Justice, including the following grounds: public policy; public security; public safety; public health; preserving the financial equilibrium of the social security system; the protection of consumers, recipients of services and workers; fairness of trade transactions; combating fraud; the protection of the environment and the urban environment; the health

of animals; intellectual property; the conservation of the national historic and artistic heritage; social policy objectives and cultural policy objectives;

9) "competent authority" means any body or authority which has a supervisory or regulatory role in a Member State in relation to service activities, including, in particular, administrative authorities, including courts acting as such, professional bodies, and those professional associations or other professional organisations which, in the exercise of their legal autonomy, regulate in a collective manner access to service activities or the exercise thereof;
10) "Member State where the service is provided" means the Member State where the service is supplied by a provider established in another Member State;
11) "regulated profession" means a professional activity or a group of professional activities as referred to in Article 3(1)(a) of Directive 2005/36/EC;
12) "commercial communication" means any form of communication designed to promote, directly or indirectly, the goods, services or image of an undertaking, organisation or person engaged in commercial, industrial or craft activity or practising a regulated profession. The following do not in themselves constitute commercial communications:
    (a) information enabling direct access to the activity of the undertaking, organisation or person, including in particular a domain name or an electronic-mailing address;
    (b) communications relating to the goods, services or image of the undertaking, organisation or person, compiled in an independent manner, particularly when provided for no financial consideration.

CHAPTER II : ADMINISTRATIVE SIMPLIFICATION

Article 5 Simplification of procedures

1. Member States shall examine the procedures and formalities applicable to access to a service activity and to the exercise thereof. Where procedures and formalities examined under this paragraph are not sufficiently simple, Member States shall simplify them.
2. The Commission may introduce harmonised forms at Community level, in accordance with the procedure referred to in Article 40(2). These forms shall be equivalent to certificates, attestations and any other documents required of a provider.
3. Where Member States require a provider or recipient to supply a certificate, attestation or any other document proving that a requirement has been satisfied, they shall accept any document from another Member State which serves an equivalent purpose or from which it is clear that the requirement in question has been satisfied. They may not require a document from another Member State to be produced in its original form, or as a certified copy or as a certified translation, save in the cases provided for in other Community instruments or where such a requirement is justified by an overriding reason relating to the public interest, including public order and security.

The first subparagraph shall not affect the right of Member States to require non-certified translations of documents in one of their official languages.

4. Paragraph 3 shall not apply to the documents referred to in Article 7(2) and 50 of Directive 2005/36/EC, in Articles 45(3), 46, 49 and 50 of Directive 2004/18/EC of the European Parliament and of the Council of 31 March 2004 on the coordination of procedures for the award of public works contracts, public supply contracts and public service contracts[1], in Article 3(2) of Directive 98/5/EC of the European Parliament and of the Council of 16 February 1998 to facilitate practice of the profession of lawyer on a permanent basis in a Member State other than that in which the qualification was obtained[2], in the First Council Directive 68/151/EEC of 9 March 1968 on coordination of safeguards which, for the protection of the interests of members and others, are required by Member States of companies within the meaning of the second paragraph of Article 58 of the Treaty, with a view to making such safeguards equivalent throughout the Community[3] and in the Eleventh Council Directive 89/666/EECof 21 December 1989 concerning disclosure requirements in respect of branches opened in a Member State by certain types of company governed by the law of another State[4].

Article 6 Points of single contact

1. Member States shall ensure that it is possible for providers to complete the following procedures and formalities through points of single contact:
   (a) all procedures and formalities needed for access to his service activities, in particular, all declarations, notifications or applications necessary for authorisation from the competent authorities, including applications for inclusion in a register, a roll or a database, or for registration with a professional body or association;
   (b) any applications for authorisation needed to exercise his service activities.
2. The establishment of points of single contact shall be without prejudice to the allocation of functions and powers among the authorities within national systems.

Article 7 Right to information

1. Member States shall ensure that the following information is easily accessible to providers and recipients through the points of single contact:

[1] OJ L 134, 30.4.2004, p. 114. Directive as last amended by Commission Regulation (EC) No 2083/2005 (OJ L 333, 20.12.2005, p. 28).

[2] OJ L 77, 14.3.1998, p. 36. Directive as amended by the 2003 Act of Accession.

[3] OJ L 65, 14.3.1968, p. 8. Directive as last amended by Directive 2003/58/EC of the European Parliament and of the Council (OJ L 221, 4.9.2003, p. 13).

[4] OJ L 395, 30.12.1989, p. 36.

(a) requirements applicable to providers established in their territory, in particular those requirements concerning the procedures and formalities to be completed in order to access and to exercise service activities;
(b) the contact details of the competent authorities enabling the latter to be contacted directly, including the details of those authorities responsible for matters concerning the exercise of service activities;
(c) the means of, and conditions for, accessing public registers and databases on providers and services;
(d) the means of redress which are generally available in the event of dispute between the competent authorities and the provider or the recipient, or between a provider and a recipient or between providers;
(e) the contact details of the associations or organisations, other than the competent authorities, from which providers or recipients may obtain practical assistance.

2. Member States shall ensure that it is possible for providers and recipients to receive, at their request, assistance from the competent authorities, consisting in information on the way in which the requirements referred to in point (a) of paragraph 1 are generally interpreted and applied. Where appropriate, such advice shall include a simple step-by-step guide. The information shall be provided in plain and intelligible language.
3. Member States shall ensure that the information and assistance referred to in paragraphs 1 and 2 are provided in a clear and unambiguous manner, that they are easily accessible at a distance and by electronic means and that they are kept up to date.
4. Member States shall ensure that the points of single contact and the competent authorities respond as quickly as possible to any request for information or assistance as referred to in paragraphs 1 and 2 and, in cases where the request is faulty or unfounded, inform the applicant accordingly without delay.
5. Member States and the Commission shall take accompanying measures in order to encourage points of single contact to make the information provided for in this Article available in other Community languages. This does not interfere with Member States' legislation on the use of languages.
6. The obligation for competent authorities to assist providers and recipients does not require those authorities to provide legal advice in individual cases but concerns only general information on the way in which requirements are usually interpreted or applied.

Article 8 Procedures by electronic means

1. Member States shall ensure that all procedures and formalities relating to access to a service activity and to the exercise thereof may be easily completed, at a distance and by electronic means, through the relevant point of single contact and with the relevant competent authorities.

2. Paragraph 1 shall not apply to the inspection of premises on which the service is provided or of equipment used by the provider or to physical examination of the capability or of the personal integrity of the provider or of his responsible staff.
3. The Commission shall, in accordance with the procedure referred to in Article 40(2), adopt detailed rules for the implementation of paragraph 1 of this Article with a view to facilitating the interoperability of information systems and use of procedures by electronic means between Member States, taking into account common standards developed at Community level.

CHAPTER III : FREEDOM OF ESTABLISHMENT FOR PROVIDERS

Section 1 : **Authorisations**

Article 9 Authorisation schemes

1. Member States shall not make access to a service activity or the exercise thereof subject to an authorisation scheme unless the following conditions are satisfied:
   (a) the authorisation scheme does not discriminate against the provider in question;
   (b) the need for an authorisation scheme is justified by an overriding reason relating to the public interest;
   (c) the objective pursued cannot be attained by means of a less restrictive measure, in particular because an a posteriori inspection would take place too late to be genuinely effective.
2. In the report referred to in Article 39(1), Member States shall identify their authorisation schemes and give reasons showing their compatibility with paragraph 1 of this Article.
3. This section shall not apply to those aspects of authorisation schemes which are governed directly or indirectly by other Community instruments.

Article 10 Condiations for the granting of authorisation

1. Authorisation schemes shall be based on criteria which preclude the competent authorities from exercising their power of assessment in an arbitrary manner.
2. The criteria referred to in paragraph 1 shall be:
   (a) non-discriminatory;
   (b) justified by an overriding reason relating to the public interest;
   (c) proportionate to that public interest objective;
   (d) clear and unambiguous;
   (e) objective;
   (f) made public in advance;
   (g) transparent and accessible.
3. The conditions for granting authorisation for a new establishment shall not duplicate requirements and controls which are equivalent or essentially comparable as regards their purpose to which the provider is already subject in another Member State or in the same Member State. The liaison points referred

to in Article 28(2) and the provider shall assist the competent authority by providing any necessary information regarding those requirements.

4. The authorisation shall enable the provider to have access to the service activity, or to exercise that activity, throughout the national territory, including by means of setting up agencies, subsidiaries, branches or offices, except where an authorisation for each individual establishment or a limitation of the authorisation to a certain part of the territory is justified by an overriding reason relating to the public interest.
5. The authorisation shall be granted as soon as it is established, in the light of an appropriate examination, that the conditions for authorisation have been met.
6. Except in the case of the granting of an authorisation, any decision from the competent authorities, including refusal or withdrawal of an authorisation, shall be fully reasoned and shall be open to challenge before the courts or other instances of appeal.
7. This Article shall not call into question the allocation of the competences, at local or regional level, of the Member States' authorities granting authorisations.

Article 11 Duration of authorisation

1. An authorisation granted to a provider shall not be for a limited period, except where:
   (a) the authorisation is being automatically renewed or is subject only to the continued fulfilment of requirements;
   (b) the number of available authorisations is limited by an overriding reason relating to the public interest;
   or
   (c) a limited authorisation period can be justified by an overriding reason relating to the public interest.
2. Paragraph 1 shall not concern the maximum period before the end of which the provider must actually commence his activity after receiving authorisation.
3. Member States shall require a provider to inform the relevant point of single contact provided for in Article 6 of the following changes:
   (a) the creation of subsidiaries whose activities fall within the scope of the authorisation scheme;
   (b) changes in his situation which result in the conditions for authorisation no longer being met.
4. This Article shall be without prejudice to the Member States' ability to revoke authorisations, when the conditions for authorisation are no longer met.

Article 12 Selection from among several candidates

1. Where the number of authorisations available for a given activity is limited because of the scarcity of available natural resources or technical capacity, Member States shall apply a selection procedure to potential candidates which provides full guarantees of impartiality and transparency, including, in

particular, adequate publicity about the launch, conduct and completion of the procedure.

2. In the cases referred to in paragraph 1, authorisation shall be granted for an appropriate limited period and may not be open to automatic renewal nor confer any other advantage on the provider whose authorisation has just expired or on any person having any particular links with that provider.
3. Subject to paragraph 1 and to Articles 9 and 10, Member States may take into account, in establishing the rules for the selection procedure, considerations of public health, social policy objectives, the health and safety of employees or self-employed persons, the protection of the environment, the preservation of cultural heritage and other overriding reasons relating to the public interest, in conformity with Community law.

Article 13 Authorisation procedures

1. Authorisation procedures and formalities shall be clear, made public in advance and be such as to provide the applicants with a guarantee that their application will be dealt with objectively and impartially.
2. Authorisation procedures and formalities shall not be dissuasive and shall not unduly complicate or delay the provision of the service. They shall be easily accessible and any charges which the applicants may incur from their application shall be reasonable and proportionate to the cost of the authorisation procedures in question and shall not exceed the cost of the procedures.
3. Authorisation procedures and formalities shall provide applicants with a guarantee that their application will be processed as quickly as possible and, in any event, within a reasonable period which is fixed and made public in advance. The period shall run only from the time when all documentation has been submitted. When justified by the complexity of the issue, the time period may be extended once, by the competent authority, for a limited time. The extension and its duration shall be duly motivated and shall be notified to the applicant before the original period has expired.
4. Failing a response within the time period set or extended in accordance with paragraph 3, authorisation shall be deemed to have been granted. Different arrangements may nevertheless be put in place, where justified by overriding reasons relating to the public interest, including a legitimate interest of third parties.
5. All applications for authorisation shall be acknowledged as quickly as possible. The acknowledgement must specify the following:
   (a) the period referred to in paragraph 3;
   (b) the available means of redress;
   (c) where applicable, a statement that in the absence of a response within the period specified, the authorisation shall be deemed to have been granted.

6. In the case of an incomplete application, the applicant shall be informed as quickly as possible of the need to supply any additional documentation, as well as of any possible effects on the period referred to in paragraph 3.
7. When a request is rejected because it fails to comply with the required procedures or formalities, the applicant shall be informed of the rejection as quickly as possible.

Section 2 : **Requirements prohibited or subject to evaluation**

Article 14 Prohibited requirements

Member States shall not make access to, or the exercise of, a service activity in their territory subject to compliance with any of the following:

1) discriminatory requirements based directly or indirectly on nationality or, in the case of companies, the location of the registered office, including in particular:
   (a) nationality requirements for the provider, his staff, persons holding the share capital or members of the provider's management or supervisory bodies;
   (b) a requirement that the provider, his staff, persons holding the share capital or members of the provider's management or supervisory bodies be resident within the territory;
2) a prohibition on having an establishment in more than one Member State or on being entered in the registers or enrolled with professional bodies or associations of more than one Member State;
3) restrictions on the freedom of a provider to choose between a principal or a secondary establishment, in particular an obligation on the provider to have its principal establishment in their territory, or restrictions on the freedom to choose between establishment in the form of an agency, branch or subsidiary;
4) conditions of reciprocity with the Member State in which the provider already has an establishment, save in the case of conditions of reciprocity provided for in Community instruments concerning energy;
5) the case-by-case application of an economic test making the granting of authorisation subject to proof of the existence of an economic need or market demand, an assessment of the potential or current economic effects of the activity or an assessment of the appropriateness of the activity in relation to the economic planning objectives set by the competent authority; this prohibition shall not concern planning requirements which do not pursue economic aims but serve overriding reasons relating to the public interest;
6) the direct or indirect involvement of competing operators, including within consultative bodies, in the granting of authorisations or in the adoption of other decisions of the competent authorities, with the exception of professional bodies and associations or other organisations acting as the competent authority; this prohibition shall not concern the consultation of organisations, such as chambers of commerce or social partners, on matters other than individual applications for authorisation, or a consultation of the public at large;

7) an obligation to provide or participate in a financial guarantee or to take out insurance from a provider or body established in their territory. This shall not affect the possibility for Member States to require insurance or financial guarantees as such, nor shall it affect requirements relating to the participation in a collective compensation fund, for instance for members of professional bodies or organisations;
8) an obligation to have been pre-registered, for a given period, in the registers held in their territory or to have previously exercised the activity for a given period in their territory.

Article 15 Requirements to be evaluated

1. Member States shall examine whether, under their legal system, any of the requirements listed in paragraph 2 are imposed and shall ensure that any such requirements are compatible with the conditions laid down in paragraph 3. Member States shall adapt their laws, regulations or administrative provisions so as to make them compatible with those conditions.
2. Member States shall examine whether their legal system makes access to a service activity or the exercise of it subject to compliance with any of the following non-discriminatory requirements:
   (a) quantitative or territorial restrictions, in particular in the form of limits fixed according to population or of a minimum geographical distance between providers;
   (b) an obligation on a provider to take a specific legal form;
   (c) requirements which relate to the shareholding of a company;
   (d) requirements, other than those concerning matters covered by Directive 2005/36/EC or provided for in other Community instruments, which reserve access to the service activity in question to particular providers by virtue of the specific nature of the activity;
   (e) a ban on having more than one establishment in the territory of the same State;
   (f) requirements fixing a minimum number of employees;
   (g) fixed minimum and/or maximum tariffs with which the provider must comply;
   (h) an obligation on the provider to supply other specific services jointly with his service.
3. Member States shall verify that the requirements referred to in paragraph 2 satisfy the following conditions:
   (a) non-discrimination: requirements must be neither directly nor indirectly discriminatory according to nationality nor, with regard to companies, according to the location of the registered office;
   (b) necessity: requirements must be justified by an overriding reason relating to the public interest;
   (c) proportionality: requirements must be suitable for securing the attainment of the objective pursued; they must not go beyond what is necessary to

attain that objective and it must not be possible to replace those requirements with other, less restrictive measures which attain the same result.

4. Paragraphs 1, 2 and 3 shall apply to legislation in the field of services of general economic interest only insofar as the application of these paragraphs does not obstruct the performance, in law or in fact, of the particular task assigned to them.
5. In the mutual evaluation report provided for in Article 39(1), Member States shall specify the following:
   (a) the requirements that they intend to maintain and the reasons why they consider that those requirements comply with the conditions set out in paragraph 3;
   (b) the requirements which have been abolished or made less stringent.
6. From 28 December 2006 Member States shall not introduce any new requirement of a kind listed in paragraph 2, unless that requirement satisfies the conditions laid down in paragraph 3.
7. Member States shall notify the Commission of any new laws, regulations or administrative provisions which set requirements as referred to in paragraph 6, together with the reasons for those requirements. The Commission shall communicate the provisions concerned to the other Member States. Such notification shall not prevent Member States from adopting the provisions in question.

   Within a period of 3 months from the date of receipt of the notification, the Commission shall examine the compatibility of any new requirements with Community law and, where appropriate, shall adopt a decision requesting the Member State in question to refrain from adopting them or to abolish them.

   The notification of a draft national law in accordance with Directive 98/34/EC shall fulfil the obligation of notification provided for in this Directive.

CHAPTER IV : FREE MOVEMENT OF SERVICES

Section 1 : **Freedom to provide services and related derogations**

Article 16 Freedom to provide services

1. Member States shall respect the right of providers to provide services in a Member State other than that in which they are established.

   The Member State in which the service is provided shall ensure free access to and free exercise of a service activity within its territory.

   Member States shall not make access to or exercise of a service activity in their territory subject to compliance with any requirements which do not respect the following principles:

   (a) non-discrimination: the requirement may be neither directly nor indirectly discriminatory with regard to nationality or, in the case of legal persons, with regard to the Member State in which they are established;

(b) necessity: the requirement must be justified for reasons of public policy, public security, public health or the protection of the environment;
(c) proportionality: the requirement must be suitable for attaining the objective pursued, and must not go beyond what is necessary to attain that objective.

2. Member States may not restrict the freedom to provide services in the case of a provider established in another Member State by imposing any of the following requirements:
   (a) an obligation on the provider to have an establishment in their territory;
   (b) an obligation on the provider to obtain an authorisation from their competent authorities including entry in a register or registration with a professional body or association in their territory, except where provided for in this Directive or other instruments of Community law;
   (c) a ban on the provider setting up a certain form or type of infrastructure in their territory, including an office or chambers, which the provider needs in order to supply the services in question;
   (d) the application of specific contractual arrangements between the provider and the recipient which prevent or restrict service provision by the self-employed;
   (e) an obligation on the provider to possess an identity document issued by its competent authorities specific to the exercise of a service activity;
   (f) requirements, except for those necessary for health and safety at work, which affect the use of equipment and material which are an integral part of the service provided;
   (g) restrictions on the freedom to provide the services referred to in Article 19.
3. The Member State to which the provider moves shall not be prevented from imposing requirements with regard to the provision of a service activity, where they are justified for reasons of public policy, public security, public health or the protection of the environment and in accordance with paragraph 1. Nor shall that Member State be prevented from applying, in accordance with Community law, its rules on employment conditions, including those laid down in collective agreements.
4. By 28 December 2011 the Commission shall, after consultation of the Member States and the social partners at Community level, submit to the European Parliament and the Council a report on the application of this Article, in which it shall consider the need to propose harmonisation measures regarding service activities covered by this Directive.

Article 17 Additional derogations from the freedom to provide services

Article 16 shall not apply to:

1) services of general economic interest which are provided in another Member State, inter alia:

(a) in the postal sector, services covered by Directive 97/67/EC of the European Parliament and of the Council of 15 December 1997 on common rules for the development of the internal market of Community postal services and the improvement of quality of service[1];
(b) in the electricity sector, services covered by Directive 2003/54/EC[2] of the European Parliament and of the Council of 26 June 2003 concerning common rules for the internal market in electricity;
(c) in the gas sector, services covered by Directive 2003/55/EC of the European Parliament and of the Council of 26 June 2003 concerning common rules for the internal market in natural gas[3];
(d) water distribution and supply services and waste water services;
(e) treatment of waste;

2) matters covered by Directive 96/71/EC;

3) matters covered by Directive 95/46/EC of the European Parliament and of the Council of 24 October 1995 on the protection of individuals with regard to the processing of personal data and on the free movement of such data[4];

4) matters covered by Council Directive 77/249/EEC of 22 March 1977to facilitate the effective exercise by lawyers of freedom to provide services[5];

5) the activity of judicial recovery of debts;

6) matters covered by Title II of Directive 2005/36/EC, as well as requirements in the Member State where the service is provided which reserve an activity to a particular profession;

7) matters covered by Regulation (EEC) No 1408/71;

8) as regards administrative formalities concerning the free movement of persons and their residence, matters covered by the provisions of Directive 2004/38/EC that lay down administrative formalities of the competent authorities of the Member Statewhere the service is provided with which beneficiaries must comply;

9) as regards third country nationals who move to another Member State in the context of the provision of a service, the possibility for Member States to require visa or residence permits for third country nationals who are not covered by the mutual recognition regime provided for in Article 21 of the Convention implementing the Schengen Agreement of 14 June 1985 on the gradual abolition of checks at the common borders[6] or the possibility to oblige third country

---

1 OJ L 15, 21.1.1998, p. 14. Directive as last amended by Regulation (EC) No 1882/2003 (OJ L 284, 31.10.2003, p. 1).

2 OJ L 176, 15.7.2003, p. 37. Directive as last amended by Commission Decision 2006/653/EC (OJ L 270, 29.9.2006, p. 72).

3 OJ L 176, 15.7.2003, p. 57.

4 OJ L 281, 23.11.1995, p. 31. Directive as amended by Regulation (EC) No 1882/2003.

5 OJ L 78, 26.3.1977, p. 17. Directive as last amended by the 2003 Act of Accession.

6 OJ L 239, 22.9.2000, p. 19. Convention as last amended by Regulation (EC) No 1160/2005 of the European Parliament and of the Council (OJ L 191, 22.7.2005, p. 18).

nationals to report to the competent authorities of the Member State in which the service is provided on or after their entry;

10) as regards the shipment of waste, matters covered by Council Regulation (EEC) No 259/93 of 1 February 1993 on the supervision and control of shipments of waste within, into and out of the European Community[1];

11) copyright, neighbouring rights and rights covered by Council Directive 87/54/EEC of 16 December 1986 on the legal protection of topographies of semiconductor products[2] and by Directive 96/9/EC of the European Parliament and of the Council of 11 March 1996 on the legal protection of databases[3], as well as industrial property rights;

12) acts requiring by law the involvement of a notary;

13) matters covered by Directive 2006/43/EC of the European Parliament and of the Council of 17 May 2006 on statutory audit of annual accounts and consolidated accounts[4];

14) the registration of vehicles leased in another Member State;

15) provisions regarding contractual and non-contractual obligations, including the form of contracts, determined pursuant to the rules of private international law.

Article 18 Case-by-case derogations

1. By way of derogation from Article 16, and in exceptional circumstances only, a Member State may, in respect of a provider established in another Member State, take measures relating to the safety of services.
2. The measures provided for in paragraph 1 may be taken only if the mutual assistance procedure laid down in Article 35 is complied with and the following conditions are fulfilled:
   (a) the national provisions in accordance with which the measure is taken have not been subject to Community harmonisation in the field of the safety of services;
   (b) the measures provide for a higher level of protection of the recipient than would be the case in a measure taken by the Member State of establishment in accordance with its national provisions;
   (c) the Member State of establishment has not taken any measures or has taken measures which are insufficient as compared with those referred to in Article 35(2);
   (d) the measures are proportionate.
3. Paragraphs 1 and 2 shall be without prejudice to provisions, laid down in Community instruments, which guarantee the freedom to provide services or which allow derogations therefrom.

---

1 OJ L 30, 6.2.1993, p. 1. Regulation as last amended by Commission Regulation (EC) No 2557/2001 (OJ L 349, 31.12.2001, p. 1).

2 OJ L 24, 27.1.1987, p. 36.

3 OJ L 77, 27.3.1996, p. 20.

4 OJ L 157, 9.6.2006, p. 87.

Section 3 : **Rights of recipients of services**

Article 19 Prohibited restrictions

Member States may not impose on a recipient requirements which restrict the use of a service supplied by a provider established in another Member State, in particular the following requirements:

(a) an obligation to obtain authorisation from or to make a declaration to their competent authorities;

(b) discriminatory limits on the grant of financial assistance by reason of the fact that the provider is established in another Member State or by reason of the location of the place at which the service is provided.

Article 20 Non-discrimination

1. Member States shall ensure that the recipient is not made subject to discriminatory requirements based on his nationality or place of residence.
2. Member States shall ensure that the general conditions of access to a service, which are made available to the public at large by the provider, do not contain discriminatory provisions relating to the nationality or place of residence of the recipient, but without precluding the possibility of providing for differences in the conditions of access where those differences are directly justified by objective criteria.

Article 21 Assistance for recipients

1. Member States shall ensure that recipients can obtain, in their Member State of residence, the following information:

   (a) general information on the requirements applicable in other Member States relating to access to, and exercise of, service activities, in particular those relating to consumer protection;

   (b) general information on the means of redress available in the case of a dispute between a provider and a recipient;

   (c) the contact details of associations or organisations, including the centres of the European Consumer Centres Network, from which providers or recipients may obtain practical assistance.

   Where appropriate, advice from the competent authorities shall include a simple step-by-step guide. Information and assistance shall be provided in a clear and unambiguous manner, shall be easily accessible at a distance, including by electronic means, and shall be kept up to date.

2. Member States may confer responsibility for the task referred to in paragraph 1 on points of single contact or on any other body, such as the centres of the European Consumer Centres Network, consumer associations or Euro Info Centres.

   Member States shall communicate to the Commission the names and contact details of the designated bodies. The Commission shall transmit them to all Member States.

3. In fulfilment of the requirements set out in paragraphs 1 and 2, the body approached by the recipient shall, if necessary, contact the relevant body for the Member State concerned. The latter shall send the information requested as soon as possible to the requesting body which shall forward the information to the recipient. Member States shall ensure that those bodies give each other mutual assistance and shall put in place all possible measures for effective cooperation. Together with the Commission, Member States shall put in place practical arrangements necessary for the implementation of paragraph 1.
4. The Commission shall, in accordance with the procedure referred to in Article 40(2), adopt measures for the implementation of paragraphs 1, 2 and 3 of this Article, specifying the technical mechanisms for the exchange of information between the bodies of the various Member States and, in particular, the interoperability of information systems, taking into account common standards.

CHAPTER V : QUALITY OF SERVICES

Article 22 Information on providers and their services

1. Member States shall ensure that providers make the following information available to the recipient:
   (a) the name of the provider, his legal status and form, the geographic address at which he is established and details enabling him to be contacted rapidly and communicated with directly and, as the case may be, by electronic means;
   (b) where the provider is registered in a trade or other similar public register, the name of that register and the provider's registration number, or equivalent means of identification in that register;
   (c) where the activity is subject to an authorisation scheme, the particulars of the relevant competent authority or the single point of contact;
   (d) where the provider exercises an activity which is subject to VAT, the identification number referred to in Article 22(1) of Sixth Council Directive 77/388/EEC of 17 May 1977 on the harmonisation of the laws of the Member States relating to turnover taxes – Common system of value added tax: uniform basis of assessment[1];
   (e) in the case of the regulated professions, any professional body or similar institution with which the provider is registered, the professional title and the Member State in which that title has been granted;
   (f) the general conditions and clauses, if any, used by the provider;
   (g) the existence of contractual clauses, if any, used by the provider concerning the law applicable to the contract and/or the competent courts;
   (h) the existence of an after-sales guarantee, if any, not imposed by law;
   (i) the price of the service, where a price is pre-determined by the provider for a given type of service;
   (j) the main features of the service, if not already apparent from the context;

[1] OJ L 145, 13.6.1977, p. 1. Directive as last amended by Directive 2006/18/EC (OJ L 51, 22.2.2006, p. 12).

(k) the insurance or guarantees referred to in Article 23(1), and in particular the contact details of the insurer or guarantor and the territorial coverage.

2. Member States shall ensure that the information referred to in paragraph 1, according to the provider's preference:
   (a) is supplied by the provider on his own initiative;
   (b) is easily accessible to the recipient at the place where the service is provided or the contract concluded;
   (c) can be easily accessed by the recipient electronically by means of an address supplied by the provider;
   (d) appears in any information documents supplied to the recipient by the provider which set out a detailed description of the service he provides.

3. Member States shall ensure that, at the recipient's request, providers supply the following additional information:
   (a) where the price is not pre-determined by the provider for a given type of service, the price of the service or, if an exact price cannot be given, the method for calculating the price so that it can be checked by the recipient, or a sufficiently detailed estimate;
   (b) as regards the regulated professions, a reference to the professional rules applicable in the Member State of establishment and how to access them;
   (c) information on their multidisciplinary activities and partnerships which are directly linked to the service in question and on the measures taken to avoid conflicts of interest. That information shall be included in any information document in which providers give a detailed description of their services;
   (d) any codes of conduct to which the provider is subject and the address at which these codes may be consulted by electronic means, specifying the language version available;
   (e) where a provider is subject to a code of conduct, or member of a trade association or professional body which provides for recourse to a non-judicial means of dispute settlement, information in this respect. The provider shall specify how to access detailed information on the characteristics of, and conditions for, the use of non-judicial means of dispute settlement.

4. Member States shall ensure that the information which a provider must supply in accordance with this Chapter is made available or communicated in a clear and unambiguous manner, and in good time before conclusion of the contract or, where there is no written contract, before the service is provided.

5. The information requirements laid down in this Chapter are in addition to requirements already provided for in Community law and do not prevent Member States from imposing additional information requirements applicable to providers established in their territory.

6. The Commission may, in accordance with the procedure referred to in Article 40(2), specify the content of the information provided for in paragraphs 1 and 3

of this Article according to the specific nature of certain activities and may specify the practical means of implementing paragraph 2 of this Article.

Article 23 Professional liability insurance and guarantees

1. Member States may ensure that providers whose services present a direct and particular risk to the health or safety of the recipient or a third person, or to the financial security of the recipient, subscribe to professional liability insurance appropriate to the nature and extent of the risk, or provide a guarantee or similar arrangement which is equivalent or essentially comparable as regards its purpose.
2. When a provider establishes himself in their territory, Member States may not require professional liability insurance or a guarantee from the provider where he is already covered by a guarantee which is equivalent, or essentially comparable as regards its purpose and the cover it provides in terms of the insured risk, the insured sum or a ceiling for the guarantee and possible exclusions from the cover, in another Member State in which the provider is already established. Where equivalence is only partial, Member States may require a supplementary guarantee to cover those aspects not already covered.

   When a Member State requires a provider established in its territory to subscribe to professional liability insurance or to provide another guarantee, that Member State shall accept as sufficient evidence attestations of such insurance cover issued by credit institutions and insurers established in other Member States.
3. Paragraphs 1 and 2 shall not affect professional insurance or guarantee arrangements provided for in other Community instruments.
4. For the implementation of paragraph 1, the Commission may, in accordance with the regulatory procedure referred to in Article 40(2), establish a list of services which exhibit the characteristics referred to in paragraph 1 of this Article. The Commission may also, in accordance with the procedure referred to in Article 40(3), adopt measures designed to amend non-essential elements of this Directive by supplementing it by establishing common criteria for defining, for the purposes of the insurance or guarantees referred to in paragraph 1 of this Article, what is appropriate to the nature and extent of the risk.
5. For the purpose of this Article
   - "direct and particular risk" means a risk arising directly from the provision of the service,
   - "health and safety" means, in relation to a recipient or a third person, the prevention of death or serious personal injury,
   - "financial security" means, in relation to a recipient, the prevention of substantial losses of money or of value of property,
   - "professional liability insurance" means insurance taken out by a provider in respect of potential liabilities to recipients and, where applicable, third parties arising out of the provision of the service.

Article 24 Commercial communications by the regulated professions

1. Member States shall remove all total prohibitions on commercial communications by the regulated professions.
2. Member States shall ensure that commercial communications by the regulated professions comply with professional rules, in conformity with Community law, which relate, in particular, to the independence, dignity and integrity of the profession, as well as to professional secrecy, in a manner consistent with the specific nature of each profession. Professional rules on commercial communications shall be non-discriminatory, justified by an overriding reason relating to the public interest and proportionate.

Article 25 Multidisciplinary activities

1. Member States shall ensure that providers are not made subject to requirements which oblige them to exercise a given specific activity exclusively or which restrict the exercise jointly or in partnership of different activities.

   However, the following providers may be made subject to such requirements:

   (a) the regulated professions, in so far as is justified in order to guarantee compliance with the rules governing professional ethics and conduct, which vary according to the specific nature of each profession, and is necessary in order to ensure their independence and impartiality;

   (b) providers of certification, accreditation, technical monitoring, test or trial services, in so far as is justified in order to ensure their independence and impartiality.
2. Where multidisciplinary activities between providers referred to in points (a) and (b) of paragraph 1 are authorised, Member States shall ensure the following:

   (a) that conflicts of interest and incompatibilities between certain activities are prevented;

   (b) that the independence and impartiality required for certain activities is secured;

   (c) that the rules governing professional ethics and conduct for different activities are compatible with one another, especially as regards matters of professional secrecy.
3. In the report referred to in Article 39(1), Member States shall indicate which providers are subject to the requirements laid down in paragraph 1 of this Article, the content of those requirements and the reasons for which they consider them to be justified.

Article 26 Policy on quality of services

1. Member States shall, in cooperation with the Commission, take accompanying measures to encourage providers to take action on a voluntary basis in order to ensure the quality of service provision, in particular through use of one of the following methods:

(a) certification or assessment of their activities by independent or accredited bodies;
(b) drawing up their own quality charter or participation in quality charters or labels drawn up by professional bodies at Community level.

2. Member States shall ensure that information on the significance of certain labels and the criteria for applying labels and other quality marks relating to services can be easily accessed by providers and recipients.
3. Member States shall, in cooperation with the Commission, take accompanying measures to encourage professional bodies, as well as chambers of commerce and craft associationsand consumer associations, in their territory to cooperate at Community level in order to promote the quality of service provision, especially by making it easier to assess the competence of a provider.
4. Member States shall, in cooperation with the Commission, take accompanying measures to encourage the development of independent assessments, notably by consumer associations, in relation to the quality and defects of service provision, and, in particular, the development at Community level of comparative trials or testing and the communication of the results.
5. Member States, in cooperation with the Commission, shall encourage the development of voluntary European standards with the aim of facilitating compatibility between services supplied by providers in different Member States, information to the recipient and the quality of service provision.

Article 27 Settlement of disputes

1. Member States shall take the general measures necessary to ensure that providers supply contact details, in particular a postal address, fax number or e-mail addressand telephone number to which all recipients, including those resident in another Member State, can send a complaint or a request for information about the service provided. Providers shall supply their legal address if this is not their usual address for correspondence.

   Member States shall take the general measures necessary to ensure that providers respond to the complaints referred to in the first subparagraph in the shortest possible time and make their best efforts to find a satisfactory solution.
2. Member States shall take the general measures necessary to ensure that providers are obliged to demonstrate compliance with the obligations laid down in this Directive as to the provision of information and to demonstrate that the information is accurate.
3. Where a financial guarantee is required for compliance with a judicial decision, Member States shall recognise equivalent guarantees lodged with a credit institution or insurer established in another Member State. Such credit institutions must be authorised in a Member State in accordance with Directive 2006/48/EC and such insurers in accordance, as appropriate, with First Council Directive 73/239/EEC of 24 July 1973 on the coordination of laws, regulations and administrative provisions relating to the taking-up and pursuit of the

business of direct insurance other than life assurance[1] and Directive 2002/83/EC of the European Parliament and of the Council of 5 November 2002 concerning life assurance [2].

4. Member States shall take the general measures necessary to ensure that providers who are subject to a code of conduct, or are members of a trade association or professional body, which provides for recourse to a non-judicial means of dispute settlement inform the recipient thereof and mention that fact in any document which presents their services in detail, specifying how to access detailed information on the characteristics of, and conditions for, the use of such a mechanism.

CHAPTER VI : ADMINISTRATIVE COOPERATION

Article 28 Mutual assistance – general obligations

1. Member States shall give each other mutual assistance, and shall put in place measures for effective cooperation with one another, in order to ensure the supervision of providers and the services they provide.
2. For the purposes of this Chapter, Member States shall designate one or more liaison points, the contact details of which shall be communicated to the other Member States and the Commission. The Commission shall publish and regularly update the list of liaison points.
3. Information requests and requests to carry out any checks, inspections and investigations under this Chapter shall be duly motivated, in particular by specifying the reason for the request. Information exchanged shall be used only in respect of the matter for which it was requested.
4. In the event of receiving a request for assistance from competent authorities in another Member State, Member States shall ensure that providers established in their territory supply their competent authorities with all the information necessary for supervising their activities in compliance with their national laws.
5. In the event of difficulty in meeting a request for information or in carrying out checks, inspections or investigations, the Member State in question shall rapidly inform the requesting Member State with a view to finding a solution.
6. Member States shall supply the information requested by other Member States or the Commission by electronic means and within the shortest possible period of time.
7. Member States shall ensure that registers in which providers have been entered, and which may be consulted by the competent authorities in their territory, may also be consulted, in accordance with the same conditions, by the equivalent competent authorities of the other Member States.

[1] OJ L 228, 16.8.1973, p. 3. Directive as last amended by Directive 2005/68/EC of the European Parliament and of the Council (OJ L 323, 9.12.2005, p. 1).

[2] OJ L 345, 19.12.2002, p. 1. Directive as last amended by Directive 2005/68/EC.

8. Member States shall communicate to the Commission information on cases where other Member States do not fulfil their obligation of mutual assistance. Where necessary, the Commission shall take appropriate steps, including proceedings provided for in Article 226 of the Treaty, in order to ensure that the Member States concerned comply with their obligation of mutual assistance. The Commission shall periodically inform Member States about the functioning of the mutual assistance provisions.

Article 29 Mutual assistance – general obligations for the Member State of establishment

1. With respect to providers providing services in another Member State, the Member State of establishment shall supply information on providers established in its territory when requested to do so by another Member State and, in particular, confirmation that a provider is established in its territory and, to its knowledge, is not exercising his activities in an unlawful manner.
2. The Member State of establishment shall undertake the checks, inspections and investigations requested by another Member State and shall inform the latter of the results and, as the case may be, of the measures taken. In so doing, the competent authorities shall act to the extent permitted by the powers vested in them in their Member State. The competent authorities can decide on the most appropriate measures to be taken in each individual case in order to meet the request by another Member State.
3. Upon gaining actual knowledge of any conduct or specific acts by a provider established in its territory which provides services in other Member States, that, to its knowledge, could cause serious damage to the health or safety of persons or to the environment, the Member State of establishment shall inform all other Member States and the Commission within the shortest possible period of time.

Article 30 Supervision by the Member State of establishment in the event of the temporary movement of a provider to another Member State

1. With respect to cases not covered by Article 31(1), the Member State of establishment shall ensure that compliance with its requirementsis supervised in conformity with the powers of supervision provided for in its national law, in particular through supervisory measures at the place of establishment of the provider.
2. The Member State of establishment shall not refrain from taking supervisory or enforcement measures in its territory on the grounds that the service has been provided or caused damage in another Member State.
3. The obligation laid down in paragraph 1 shall not entail a duty on the part of the Member State of establishment to carry out factual checks and controls in the territory of the Member State where the service is provided. Such checks and controls shall be carried out by the authorities of the Member State where the

provider is temporarily operating at the request of the authorities of the Member State of establishment, in accordance with Article 31.

Article 31 Supervision by the Member State where the service is provided in the event of the temporary movement of the provider

1. With respect to national requirements which may be imposed pursuant to Articles 16 or 17, the Member State where the service is provided is responsible for the supervision of the activity of the provider in its territory. In conformity with Community law, the Member State where the service is provided:
   (a) shall take all measures necessary to ensure the provider complies with those requirements as regards the access to and the exercise of the activity;
   (b) shall carry out the checks, inspections and investigations necessary to supervise the service provided.
2. With respect to requirements other than those referred to in paragraph 1, where a provider moves temporarily to another Member State in order to provide a service without being established there, the competent authorities of that Member State shall participate in the supervision of the provider in accordance with paragraphs 3 and 4.
3. At the request of the Member State of establishment, the competent authorities of the Member State where the service is provided shall carry out any checks, inspections and investigations necessary for ensuring the effective supervision by the Member State of establishment. In so doing, the competent authorities shall act to the extent permitted by the powers vested in them in their Member State. The competent authorities may decide on the most appropriate measures to be taken in each individual case in order to meet the request by the Member State of establishment.
4. On their own initiative, the competent authorities of the Member State where the service is provided may conduct checks, inspections and investigations on the spot, provided that those checks, inspections or investigations are not discriminatory, are not motivated by the fact that the provider is established in another Member State and are proportionate.

Article 32 Alert mechanism

1. Where a Member State becomes aware of serious specific acts or circumstances relating to a service activity that could cause serious damage to the health or safety of persons or to the environment in its territory or in the territory of other Member States, that Member State shall inform the Member State of establishment, the other Member States concerned and the Commission within the shortest possible period of time.
2. The Commission shall promote and take part in the operation of a European network of Member States' authorities in order to implement paragraph 1.

3. The Commission shall adopt and regularly update, in accordance with the procedure referred to in Article 40(2), detailed rules concerning the management of the network referred to in paragraph 2 of this Article.

Article 33 Information on the good repute of providers

1. Member States shall, at the request of a competent authority in another Member State, supply information, in conformity with their national law, on disciplinary or administrative actions or criminal sanctions and decisions concerning insolvency or bankruptcy involving fraud taken by their competent authorities in respect of the provider which are directly relevant to the provider's competence or professional reliability. The Member State which supplies the information shall inform the provider thereof.

   A request made pursuant to the first subparagraph must be duly substantiated, in particular as regards the reasons for the request for information.

2. Sanctions and actions referred to in paragraph 1 shall only be communicated if a final decision has been taken. With regard to other enforceable decisions referred to in paragraph 1, the Member State which supplies the information shall specify whether a particular decision is final or whether an appeal has been lodged in respect of it, in which case the Member State in question should provide an indication of the date when the decision on appeal is expected.

   Moreover, that Member State shall specify the provisions of national law pursuant to which the provider was found guilty or penalised.

3. Implementation of paragraphs 1and 2 must comply with rules on the provision of personal dataand with rights guaranteed to persons found guilty or penalised in the Member States concerned, including by professional bodies. Any information in question which is public shall be accessible to consumers.

Article 34 Accompanying measures

1. The Commission, in cooperation with Member States, shall establish an electronic system for the exchange of information between Member States, taking into account existing information systems.
2. Member States shall, with the assistance of the Commission, take accompanying measures to facilitate the exchange of officials in charge of the implementation of mutual assistance and training of such officials, including language and computer training.
3. The Commission shall assess the need to establish a multi-annual programme in order to organise relevant exchanges of officials and training.

Article 35 Mutual assistance in the event of case-by-case derogations

1. Where a Member State intends to take a measure pursuant to Article 18, the procedure laid down in paragraphs 2 to 6 of this Article shall apply without prejudice to court proceedings, including preliminary proceedings and acts carried out in the framework of a criminal investigation.

2. The Member State referred to in paragraph 1 shall ask the Member State of establishment to take measures with regard to the provider, supplying all relevant information on the service in question and the circumstances of the case.

   The Member State of establishment shall check, within the shortest possible period of time, whether the provider is operating lawfully and verify the facts underlying the request. It shall inform the requesting Member State within the shortest possible period of time of the measures taken or envisaged or, as the case may be, the reasons why it has not taken any measures.

3. Following communication by the Member State of establishment as provided for in the second subparagraph of paragraph 2, the requesting Member State shall notify the Commission and the Member State of establishment of its intention to take measures, stating the following:

   (a) the reasons why it believes the measures taken or envisaged by the Member State of establishment are inadequate;

   (b) the reasons why it believes the measures it intends to take fulfil the conditions laid down in Article 18.

4. The measures may not be taken until fifteen working days after the date of notification provided for in paragraph 3.

5. Without prejudice to the possibility for the requesting Member State to take the measures in question upon expiry of the period specified in paragraph 4, the Commission shall, within the shortest possible period of time, examine the compatibility with Community law of the measures notified.

   Where the Commission concludes that the measure is incompatible with Community law, it shall adopt a decision asking the Member State concerned to refrain from taking the proposed measures or to put an end to the measures in question as a matter of urgency.

6. In the case of urgency, a Member State which intends to take a measure may derogate from paragraphs 2, 3 and 4. In such cases, the measures shall be notified within the shortest possible period of time to the Commission and the Member State of establishment, stating the reasons for which the Member State considers that there is urgency.

Article 36 Implementing measures

In accordance with the procedure referred to in Article 40(3), the Commission shall adopt the implementing measures designed to amend non-essential elements of this Chapter by supplementing it by specifying the time-limits provided for in Articles 28 and 35. The Commission shall also adopt, in accordance with the procedure referred to in Article 40(2), the practical arrangements for the exchange of information by electronic means between Member States, and in particular the interoperability provisions for information systems.

CHAPTER VII : CONVERGENCE PROGRAMME

Article 37 Codes of conduct at Community level

1. Member States shall, in cooperation with the Commission, take accompanying measures to encourage the drawing up at Community level, particularly by professional bodies, organisations and associations, of codes of conduct aimed at facilitating the provision of services or the establishment of a provider in another Member State, in conformity with Community law.
2. Member States shall ensure that the codes of conduct referred to in paragraph 1 are accessible at a distance, by electronic means.

Article 38 Additional harmonisation

The Commission shall assess, by 28 December 2010 the possibility of presenting proposals for harmonisation instruments on the following subjects:

(a) access to the activity of judicial recovery of debts;

(b) private security services and transport of cash and valuables.

Article 39 Mutual evaluation

1. By 28 December 2009 at the latest, Member States shall present a report to the Commission, containing the information specified in the following provisions:
   (a) Article 9(2), on authorisation schemes;
   (b) Article 15(5), on requirements to be evaluated;
   (c) Article 25(3), on multidisciplinary activities.
2. The Commission shall forward the reports provided for in paragraph 1 to the Member States, which shall submit their observations on each of the reports within six months of receipt. Within the same period, the Commission shall consult interested parties on those reports.
3. The Commission shall present the reports and the Member States' observations to the Committee referred to in Article 40(1), which may make observations.
4. In the light of the observations provided for in paragraphs 2 and 3, the Commission shall, by 28 December 2010 at the latest, present a summary report to the European Parliament and to the Council, accompanied where appropriate by proposals for additional initiatives.
5. By 28 December 2009 at the latest, Member States shall present a report to the Commission on the national requirements whose application could fall under the third subparagraph of Article 16(1) and the first sentence of Article 16(3), providing reasons why they consider that the application of those requirements fulfil the criteria referred to in the third subparagraph of Article 16(1) and the first sentence of Article 16(3).

   Thereafter, Member States shall transmit to the Commission any changes in their requirements, including new requirements, as referred to above, together with the reasons for them.

The Commission shall communicate the transmitted requirements to other Member States. Such transmission shall not prevent the adoption by Member States of the provisions in question. The Commission shall on an annual basis thereafter provide analyses and orientations on the application of these provisions in the context of this Directive.

Article 40 Committee procedure

1. The Commission shall be assisted by a Committee.
2. Where reference is made to this paragraph, Articles 5 and 7 of Decision 1999/468/EC shall apply, having regard to the provisions of Article 8 thereof. The period laid down in Article 5(6) of Decision 1999/468/EC shall be set at three months.
3. Where reference is made to this paragraph, Article 5a(1) to (4), and Article 7 of Decision 1999/468/EC shall apply, having regard to the provisions of Article 8 thereof.

Article 41 Review clause

The Commission, by 28 December 2011 and every three years thereafter, shall present to the European Parliament and to the Council a comprehensive report on the application of this Directive. This report shall, in accordance with Article 16(4), address in particular the application of Article 16. It shall also consider the need for additional measures for matters excluded from the scope of application of this Directive. It shall be accompanied, where appropriate, by proposals for amendment of this Directive with a view to completing the Internal Market for services.

Article 42 Amendment of Directive 98/27/EC

In the Annex to Directive 98/27/EC of the European Parliament and of the Council of 19 May 1998 on injunctions for the protection of consumers' interests[1], the following point shall be added:

"13. Directive 2006/123/EC of the European Parliament and of the Council of 12 December 2006 on services in the internal market (OJ L 376, 27.12.2006, p. 36)"

Article 43 Protection of personal data

The implementation and application of this Directive and, in particular, the provisions on supervision shall respect the rules on the protection of personal data as provided for in Directives 95/46/EC and 2002/58/EC.

CHAPTER VIII : FINAL PROVISIONS

Article 44 Transposition

1. Member States shall bring into force the laws, regulations and administrative provisions necessary to comply with this Directive before 28 December 2009.

   They shall forthwith communicate to the Commission the text of those measures.

[1] OJ L 166, 11.6.1998, p. 51. Directive as last amended by Directive 2005/29/EC.

When Member States adopt these measures, they shall contain a reference to this Directive or shall be accompanied by such a reference on the occasion of their official publication. The methods of making such reference shall be laid down by Member States.

2. Member States shall communicate to the Commission the text of the main provisions of national law which they adopt in the field covered by this Directive.

Article 45 Entry into force

This Directive shall enter into force on the day following that of its publication in the Official Journal of the European Union.

Article 46 Addressees

This Directive is addressed to the Member States.

Done at Strasbourg, 12 December 2006.

For the European Parliament

The President

J. Borrell Fontelles

For the Council

The President

M. Pekkarinen

25. Directive 2009/20/EC of the European Parliament and of the Council of 23 April 2009 on the insurance of shipowners for maritime claims Text with EEA relevance

(OJ L 131 , 28/05/2009 p. 128 – 131)

THE EUROPEAN PARLIAMENT AND THE COUNCIL OF THE EUROPEAN UNION,

Having regard to the Treaty establishing the European Community, and in particular Article 80(2) thereof,

Having regard to the proposal from the Commission,

Having regard to the opinion of the European Economic and Social Committee[1],

Having regard to the opinion of the Committee of the Regions[2],

Acting in accordance with the procedure laid down in Article 251 of the Treaty[3],

Whereas:

(1) One element of Community maritime transport policy is to improve the quality of merchant shipping by making all economic operators act more responsibly.

(2) Dissuasive measures have already been adopted under Directive 2005/35/EC of the European Parliament and of the Council of 7 September 2005 on ship source pollution and on the introduction of penalties for infringements[4].

(3) On 9 October 2008, the Member States adopted a statement in which they unanimously recognised the importance of the application of the 1996 Protocol to the 1976 Convention on Limitation of Liability for Maritime Claims by all Member States.

(4) The obligation to have insurance should make it possible to ensure better protection for victims. It should also help to eliminate substandard ships and make it possible to reestablish competition between operators. Furthermore, in Resolution A.898(21), the International Maritime Organisation invited States to urge shipowners to be properly insured.

(5) Non compliance with the provisions of this Directive should be rectified. Directive 2009/16/EC of the European Parliament and of the Council of 23 April 2009 on port State control (recast)[5] already provides for the detention of ships in the case of absence of certificates which have to be carried on board. However, it is appropriate to provide for the possibility of expelling a ship

1 OJ C 318, 23.12.2006, p. 195.

2 OJ C 229, 22.9.2006, p. 38.

3 Opinion of the European Parliament of 29 March 2007 (OJ C 27 E, 31.1.2008, p. 166), Council Common Position of 9 December 2008 (OJ C 330 E, 30.12.2008, p. 7) and Position of the European Parliament of 11 March 2009 (not yet published in the Official Journal).

4 OJ L 255, 30.9.2005, p. 11.

5 See page 57 of this Official Journal.

which does not carry a certificate of insurance. The modalities of the expulsion should allow the situation to be rectified within a reasonable time period.

(6) Since the objectives of this Directive, namely the introduction and implementation of appropriate measures in the field of maritime transport policy, cannot be sufficiently achieved by the Member States and can therefore, by reason of its scale and effects, be better achieved at Community level, the Community may adopt measures, in accordance with the principle of subsidiarity as set out in Article 5 of the Treaty. In accordance with the principle of proportionality, as set out in that Article, this Directive does not go beyond what is necessary in order to achieve those objectives,

HAVE ADOPTED THIS DIRECTIVE:

Article 1 Subject matter

This Directive lays down rules applicable to certain aspects of the obligations on shipowners as regards their insurance for maritime claims.

Article 2 Scope

1. This Directive shall apply to ships of 300 gross tonnage or more.
2. This Directive shall not apply to warships, auxiliary warships or other State owned or operated ships used for a non commercial public service.
3. This Directive shall be without prejudice to the regimes established by the instruments in force in the Member State concerned and listed in the Annex hereto.

Article 3 Definitions

For the purpose of this Directive, the following definitions shall apply:

(a) "shipowner" means the registered owner of a seagoing ship, or any other person such as the bareboat charterer who is responsible for the operation of the ship;

(b) "insurance" means insurance with or without deductibles, and comprises, for example, indemnity insurance of the type currently provided by members of the International Group of P & I Clubs, and other effective forms of insurance (including proved self insurance) and financial security offering similar conditions of cover;

(c) "1996 Convention" means the consolidated text of the 1976 Convention on Limitation of Liability for Maritime Claims, adopted by the International Maritime Organisation (IMO), as amended by the 1996 Protocol.

Article 4 Insurance for maritime claims

1. Each Member State shall require that shipowners of ships flying its flag have insurance covering such ships.
2. Each Member State shall require shipowners of ships flying a flag other than its own to have insurance in place when such ships enter a port under the Member State's jurisdiction. This shall not prevent Member States, if in conformity with

international law, from requiring compliance with that obligation when such ships are operating in their territorial waters.

3. The insurance referred to in paragraphs 1 and 2 shall cover maritime claims subject to limitation under the 1996 Convention. The amount of the insurance for each and every ship per incident shall be equal to the relevant maximum amount for the limitation of liability as laid down in the 1996 Convention.

Article 5 Inspections, compliance, expulsion from ports and denial of access to ports

1. Each Member State shall ensure that any inspection of a ship in a port under its jurisdiction in accordance with Directive 2009/16/EC, includes verification that a certificate referred to in Article 6 is carried on board.
2. If the certificate referred to in Article 6 is not carried on board, and without prejudice to Directive 2009/16/EC providing for detention of ships when safety issues are at stake, the competent authority may issue an expulsion order to the ship which shall be notified to the Commission, the other Member States and the flag State concerned. As a result of the issuing of such an expulsion order, every Member State shall refuse entry of this ship into any of its ports until the shipowner notifies the certificate referred to in Article 6.

Article 6 Insurance certificates

1. The existence of the insurance referred to in Article 4 shall be proved by one or more certificates issued by its provider and carried on board the ship.
2. The certificates issued by the insurance provider shall include the following information:
   (a) name of ship, its IMO number, and port of registry;
   (b) shipowner's name and principal place of business;
   (c) type and duration of the insurance;
   (d) name and principal place of business of the provider of the insurance and, where appropriate, the place of business where the insurance is established.
3. If the language used in the certificates is neither English nor French nor Spanish, the text shall include a translation into one of these languages.

Article 7 Penalties

For the purposes of Article 4(1), Member States shall lay down a system of penalties for the breach of national provisions adopted pursuant to this Directive and shall take all the measures necessary to ensure that those penalties are applied. The penalties provided for shall be effective, proportionate and dissuasive.

Article 8 Reports

Every three years, and for the first time before 1 January 2015, the Commission shall present a report to the European Parliament and to the Council on the application of this Directive.

Article 9 Transposition

1. Member States shall bring into force the laws, regulations and administrative provisions necessary to comply with this Directive before 1 January 2012. They shall forthwith inform the Commission thereof.

   When Member States adopt these measures, they shall contain a reference to this Directive or shall be accompanied by such a reference on the occasion of their official publication. The methods of making such reference shall be laid down by Member States.

2. Member States shall communicate to the Commission the text of the main provisions of national law which they adopt in the field covered by this Directive.

Article 10 Entry into force

This Directive shall enter into force on the day following its publication in the Official Journal of the European Union.

Article 11 Addressees

This Directive is addressed to the Member States.

Done at Strasbourg, 23 April 2009.

For the European Parliament

The President

H.-G. Pöttering

For the Council

The President

P. Nečas

ANNEX

- The International Convention on Civil Liability for Oil Pollution Damage, 1992.
- The International Convention on Liability and Compensation for Damage in Connection with the Carriage of Hazardous and Noxious Substances by Sea, 1996 (HNS Convention).
- The International Convention on Civil Liability for Bunker Oil Pollution Damage, 2001 ("Bunker Oil" Convention).
- The Nairobi International Convention on the Removal of Wrecks, 2007 ("Wrecks Removal" Convention).
- Regulation (EC) No 392/2009 of the European Parliament and of the Council of 23 April 2009 on the liability of carriers of passengers by sea in the event of accidents.

26. Directive 2009/103/EC of the European Parliament and of the Council of 16 September 2009 relating to insurance against civil liability in respect of the use of motor vehicles, and the enforcement of the obligation to insure against such liability Text with EEA relevance

(OJ L 263 , 07/10/2009 p. 11 – 31)

THE EUROPEAN PARLIAMENT AND THE COUNCIL OF THE EUROPEAN UNION,

Having regard to the Treaty establishing the European Community, and in particular Article 95(1) thereof,

Having regard to the proposal from the Commission,

Having regard to the opinion of the European Economic and Social Committee[1],

Acting in accordance with the procedure laid down in Article 251 of the Treaty[2],

Whereas:

(1) Council Directive 72/166/EEC of 24 April 1972 on the approximation of the laws of Member States relating to insurance against civil liability in respect of the use of motor vehicles, and to the enforcement of the obligation to insure against such liability[3], Second Council Directive 84/5/EEC of 30 December 1983 on the approximation of the laws of the Member States relating to insurance against civil liability in respect of the use of motor vehicles[4], Third Council Directive 90/232/EEC of 14 May 1990 on the approximation of the laws of the Member States relating to insurance against civil liability in respect of the use of motor vehicles[5] and Directive 2000/26/EC of the European Parliament and of the Council of 16 May 2000 on the approximation of the laws of the Member States relating to insurance against civil liability in respect of the use of motor vehicles (Fourth motor insurance Directive)[6] have been substantially amended several times[7]. In the interests of clarity and rationality those four Directives should be codified, as well as Directive 2005/14/EC of the European Parliament and of the Council of 11 May 2005 amending Council Directives 72/166/EEC, 84/5/EEC, 88/357/EEC and 90/232/EEC and Directive 2000/26/EC of the European Parliament and of the Council relating to insurance against civil liability in respect of the use of motor vehicles[8].

---

1 OJ C 224, 30.8.2008, p. 39.

2 Opinion of the European Parliament of 21 October 2008 (not yet published in the Official Journal) and Council Decision of 13 July 2009.

3 OJ L 103, 2.5.1972, p. 1.

4 OJ L 8, 11.1.1984, p. 17.

5 OJ L 129, 19.5.1990, p. 33.

6 OJ L 181, 20.7.2000, p. 65.

7 See Annex I, Part A.

8 OJ L 149, 11.6.2005, p. 14.

(2) Insurance against civil liability in respect of the use of motor vehicles (motor insurance) is of special importance for European citizens, whether they are policyholders or victims of an accident. It is also a major concern for insurance undertakings as it constitutes an important part of non-life insurance business in the Community. Motor insurance also has an impact on the free movement of persons and vehicles. It should therefore be a key objective of Community action in the field of financial services to reinforce and consolidate the internal market in motor insurance.

(3) Each Member State must take all appropriate measures to ensure that civil liability in respect of the use of vehicles normally based in its territory is covered by insurance. The extent of the liability covered and the terms and conditions of the insurance cover are to be determined on the basis of those measures.

(4) In order to exclude any possible misinterpretation of this Directive and to make it easier to obtain insurance cover for vehicles bearing temporary plates, the definition of the territory in which the vehicle is normally based should refer to the territory of the State of which the vehicle bears a registration plate, irrespective of whether such a plate is permanent or temporary.

(5) While respecting the general criterion of the registration plate to determine the territory in which the vehicle is normally based, a special rule should be laid down for accidents caused by vehicles without a registration plate or bearing a registration plate which does not correspond or no longer corresponds to the vehicle. In this case and for the sole purpose of settling the claim, the territory in which the vehicle is normally based should be deemed to be the territory in which the accident took place.

(6) A prohibition of systematic checks on motor insurance should apply to vehicles normally based in the territory of another Member State as well as to vehicles normally based in the territory of a third country but entering from the territory of another Member State. Only non-systematic checks which are not discriminatory and are carried out as part of a control not aimed exclusively at insurance verification may be permitted.

(7) The abolition of checks on green cards for vehicles normally based in a Member State which enter the territory of another Member State can be effected by means of an agreement between the national insurers' bureaux, whereby each national bureau would guarantee compensation in accordance with the provisions of national law in respect of any loss or injury giving entitlement to compensation caused in its territory by one of those vehicles, whether or not insured.

(8) Such a guarantee agreement presupposes that all Community motor vehicles travelling in Community territory are covered by insurance. The national law of each Member State should, therefore, provide for the compulsory insurance of vehicles against civil liability, such insurance to be valid throughout Community territory.

(9) The system provided for in this Directive could be extended to vehicles normally based in the territory of any third country in respect of which the national bureaux of the Member States have concluded a similar agreement.

(10) Each Member State should be able to act in derogation from the general obligation to take out compulsory insurance in respect of vehicles belonging to certain natural or legal persons, public or private. For accidents caused by such vehicles, the Member State so derogating should designate an authority or body to compensate for the damage to victims of accidents caused in another Member State. Steps should be taken to ensure that due compensation is paid not only to the victims of accidents caused by these vehicles abroad but also the victims of accidents occurring in the Member State in which the vehicle is normally based, whether or not they are resident in its territory. Furthermore, Member States should ensure that the list of persons exempt from compulsory insurance and the authorities or bodies responsible for compensation of victims of accidents caused by such vehicles is communicated to the Commission for publication.

(11) Each Member State should be able to act in derogation from the general obligation to take out compulsory insurance in respect of certain types of vehicles or certain vehicles having a special plate. In that case, the other Member States are allowed to require, at the entry into their territory, a valid green card or a frontier insurance contract, in order to ensure the provision of compensation to victims of any accident which may be caused by those vehicles in their territories. However, since the elimination of border controls within the Community means that it is not possible to ensure that vehicles crossing frontiers are covered by insurance, compensation for victims of accidents caused abroad cannot be guaranteed. Steps should also be taken to ensure that due compensation is awarded to the victims of accidents caused by those vehicles not only abroad but also in the Member State in which the vehicle is normally based. For this purpose, Member States should treat the victims of accidents caused by those vehicles in the same way as victims of accidents caused by uninsured vehicles. Indeed, compensation to victims of accidents caused by uninsured vehicles should be paid by the compensation body of the Member State in which the accident took place. Where payments are made to victims of accidents caused by vehicles subject to the derogation, the compensation body should have a claim against the body of the Member State in which the vehicle is normally based. After a certain period to allow for the implementation and application of this possibility of derogation, and taking into account the lessons drawn therefrom, the Commission should, when appropriate, submit proposals for its replacement or repeal.

(12) Member States' obligations to guarantee insurance cover at least in respect of certain minimum amounts constitute an important element in ensuring the protection of victims. The minimum amount of cover for personal injury should be calculated so as to compensate fully and fairly all victims who have suffered very serious injuries, while taking into account the low frequency of accidents involving several victims and the small number of accidents in which several

victims suffer very serious injuries in the course of one and the same event. A minimum amount of cover per victim or per claim should be provided for. With a view to facilitating the introduction of these minimum amounts, a transitional period should be established. However, a period shorter than the transitional period should be provided for, in which Member States should increase these amounts to at least half the levels provided for.

(13) In order to ensure that the minimum amount of cover is not eroded over time, a periodic review clause should be provided using as a benchmark the European Index of Consumer Prices (EICP) published by Eurostat, as provided for in Council Regulation (EC) No 2494/95 of 23 October 1995 concerning harmonised indices of consumer prices[1]. Procedural rules governing such a review should also be laid down.

(14) It is necessary to make provision for a body to guarantee that the victim will not remain without compensation where the vehicle which caused the accident is uninsured or unidentified. It is important to provide that the victim of such an accident should be able to apply directly to that body as a first point of contact. However, Member States should be given the possibility of applying certain limited exclusions as regards the payment of compensation by that body and of providing that compensation for damage to property caused by an unidentified vehicle may be limited or excluded in view of the danger of fraud.

(15) It is in the interest of victims that the effects of certain exclusion clauses be limited to the relationship between the insurer and the person responsible for the accident. However, in the case of vehicles stolen or obtained by violence, Member States may specify that compensation will be payable by the abovementioned body.

(16) In order to alleviate the financial burden on that body, Member States may make provision for the application of certain excesses where the body provides compensation for damage to property caused by uninsured vehicles or, as the case may be, vehicles stolen or obtained by violence.

(17) The option of limiting or excluding legitimate compensation for victims on the basis that the vehicle is unidentified should not apply where the body has paid compensation for significant personal injuries to any victim of the accident in which damage to property was caused. Member States may provide for an excess, up to the limit prescribed in this Directive, to be borne by the victim of the damage to property. The conditions in which personal injuries are to be considered significant should be determined by the national legislation or administrative provisions of the Member State where the accident takes place. In establishing those conditions, the Member State may take into account, inter alia, whether the injury has required hospital care.

(18) In the case of an accident caused by an uninsured vehicle, the body which compensates victims of accidents caused by uninsured or unidentified vehicles is better placed than the victim to bring an action against the party liable.

[1] OJ L 257, 27.10.1995, p. 1.

Therefore, it should be provided that that body cannot require that victim, if he is to be compensated, to establish that the party liable is unable or refuses to pay.

(19) In the event of a dispute between the body referred to above and a civil liability insurer as to which of them should compensate the victim of an accident, Member States, to avoid any delay in the payment of compensation to the victim, should ensure that one of those parties is designated as being responsible in the first instance for paying compensation pending resolution of the dispute.

(20) Motor vehicle accident victims should be guaranteed comparable treatment irrespective of where in the Community accidents occur.

(21) The members of the family of the policyholder, driver or any other person liable should be afforded protection comparable to that of other third parties, in any event in respect of their personal injuries.

(22) Personal injuries and damage to property suffered by pedestrians, cyclists and other non-motorised road users, who are usually the weakest party in an accident, should be covered by the compulsory insurance of the vehicle involved in the accident where they are entitled to compensation under national civil law. This provision does not prejudge the issue of civil liability, or the level of awards of damages in respect of a given accident, under national legislation.

(23) The inclusion within the insurance cover of any passenger in the vehicle is a major achievement of the existing legislation. This objective would be placed in jeopardy if national legislation or any contractual clause contained in an insurance policy excluded passengers from insurance cover because they knew or should have known that the driver of the vehicle was under the influence of alcohol or of any other intoxicating agent at the time of the accident. The passenger is not usually in a position to assess properly the level of intoxication of the driver. The objective of discouraging persons from driving while under the influence of intoxicating agents is not achieved by reducing the insurance cover for passengers who are victims of motor vehicle accidents. Cover of such passengers under the vehicle's compulsory motor insurance does not prejudge any liability they might incur pursuant to the applicable national legislation, nor the level of any award of damages in a specific accident.

(24) All compulsory motor insurance policies should cover the entire territory of the Community.

(25) Some insurance undertakings insert into insurance policies clauses to the effect that the contract will be cancelled if the vehicle remains outside the Member State of registration for longer than a specified period. This practice is in conflict with the principle set out in this Directive, according to which compulsory motor insurance should cover, on the basis of a single premium, the entire territory of the Community. It should therefore be specified that the insurance cover is to remain valid during the whole term of the contract, irrespective of whether the vehicle remains in another Member State for a

particular period, without prejudice to the obligations under Member States' national legislation with respect to the registration of vehicles.

(26) In the interests of the party insured, every insurance policy should guarantee for a single premium, in each Member State, the cover required by its law or the cover required by the law of the Member State where the vehicle is normally based, when that cover is higher.

(27) Steps should be taken to make it easier to obtain insurance cover for vehicles imported from one Member State into another, even though the vehicle is not yet registered in the Member State of destination. A temporary derogation from the general rule determining the Member State where the risk is situated should be made available. For a period of 30 days from the date when the vehicle is delivered, made available or dispatched to the purchaser, the Member State of destination should be considered to be the Member State where the risk is situated.

(28) Any person wishing to take out a new motor insurance contract with another insurer should be in a position to justify his accident and claims record under the old contract. The policyholder should have the right to request at any time a statement concerning the claims, or the absence of claims, involving the vehicle or vehicles covered by the insurance contract at least during the preceding five years of the contractual relationship. The insurance undertaking, or any body which may have been appointed by a Member State to provide compulsory insurance or to supply such statements, should provide this statement to the policyholder within 15 days of the request.

(29) In order to ensure due protection for victims of motor vehicle accidents, Member States should not permit insurance undertakings to rely on excesses against an injured party.

(30) The right to invoke the insurance contract and to claim against the insurance undertaking directly is of great importance for the protection of victims of motor vehicle accidents. In order to facilitate an efficient and speedy settlement of claims and to avoid as far as possible costly legal proceedings, a right of direct action against the insurance undertaking covering the person responsible against civil liability should be provided for victims of any motor vehicle accident.

(31) In order to obtain an adequate level of protection for victims of motor vehicle accidents, a "reasoned offer" procedure should be extended to any kind of motor vehicle accident. This same procedure should also apply mutatis mutandis where the accident is settled by the system of national insurers' bureaux.

(32) Under Article 11(2) read in conjunction with Article 9(1)(b) of Council Regulation (EC) No 44/2001 of 22 December 2000 on jurisdiction and the recognition and enforcement of judgments in civil and commercial matters[1], injured parties may bring legal proceedings against the civil liability insurance provider in the Member State in which they are domiciled.

[1] OJ L 12, 16.1.2001, p. 1.

(33) The green card bureau system ensures the ready settlement of claims in the injured party's country of residence even where the other party comes from a different European country.

(34) Parties injured as a result of a motor vehicle accident falling within the scope of this Directive and occurring in a State other than that of their residence should be entitled to claim in their Member State of residence against a claims representative appointed there by the insurance undertaking of the responsible party. This solution would enable damage suffered by injured parties outside their Member State of residence to be dealt with under procedures which are familiar to them.

(35) This system of having claims representatives in the injured party's Member State of residence affects neither the substantive law to be applied in each individual case nor the matter of jurisdiction.

(36) The existence of a direct right of action for the injured party against the insurance undertaking is a logical supplement to the appointment of such representatives and moreover improves the legal position of parties injured as a result of motor vehicle accidents occurring outside their Member State of residence.

(37) It should be provided that the Member State where the insurance undertaking is authorised should require that undertaking to appoint claims representatives resident or established in the other Member States to collect all necessary information in relation to claims resulting from such accidents and to take appropriate action to settle the claims on behalf and for the account of the insurance undertaking, including the payment of compensation. Claims representatives should have sufficient powers to represent the insurance undertaking in relation to persons suffering damage from such accidents, and also to represent the insurance undertaking before national authorities including, where necessary, before the courts, in so far as this is compatible with the rules of private international law on the conferral of jurisdiction.

(38) The activities of the claims representative are not sufficient in order to confer jurisdiction on the courts in the injured party's Member State of residence if the rules of private international law on the conferral of jurisdiction do not so provide.

(39) The appointment of representatives responsible for settling claims should be one of the conditions for access to and carrying on the activity of insurance listed in class 10 of point A of the Annex to First Council Directive 73/239/EEC of 24 July 1973 on the coordination of laws, regulations and administrative provisions relating to the taking-up and pursuit of the business of direct insurance other than life assurance[1], except for carriers' liability. That condition should therefore be covered by the single official authorisation issued by the authorities of the Member State where the insurance undertaking establishes its head office, as specified in Title II of Council Directive 92/49/EEC of 18 June

[1] OJ L 228, 16.8.1973, p. 3.

1992 on the coordination of laws, regulations and administrative provisions relating to direct insurance other than life assurance and amending Directives 73/239/EEC and 88/357/EEC (third non-life insurance Directive)[1]. That condition should also apply to insurance undertakings having their head office outside the Community which have secured an authorisation granting them access to the activity of insurance in a Member State of the Community.

(40) In addition to ensuring that the insurance undertaking has a representative in the State where the injured party resides, it is appropriate to guarantee the specific right of the injured party to have the claim settled promptly. It is therefore necessary to include in national law appropriate effective and systematic financial or equivalent administrative penalties — such as injunctions combined with administrative fines, reporting to supervisory authorities on a regular basis, on-the-spot checks, publications in the national official journal and in the press, suspension of the activities of the company (prohibition on the conclusion of new contracts for a certain period), designation of a special representative of the supervisory authorities responsible for verifying that the business is run in line with insurance laws, withdrawal of the authorisation for this business line, sanctions to be imposed on directors and management staff — in the event that the insurance undertaking or its representative fails to fulfil its obligation to make an offer of compensation within a reasonable period of time. This should not prejudice the application of any other measure, especially under the law applicable to supervisory matters, which may be considered appropriate. However, it is a condition that liability and the damage and injury sustained should not be in dispute, so that the insurance undertaking is able to make a reasoned offer within the prescribed period of time. The reasoned offer of compensation should be in writing and should contain the grounds on the basis of which liability and damages have been assessed.

(41) In addition to those sanctions, it is appropriate to provide that interest should be payable on the amount of compensation offered by the insurance undertaking or awarded by the court to the injured party when the offer has not been made within the prescribed time limit. If Member States have existing national rules which cover the requirement for late-payment interest, this provision could be implemented by a reference to those rules.

(42) Injured parties suffering loss or injury as a result of motor vehicle accidents sometimes have difficulty in establishing the name of the insurance undertaking providing insurance against civil liability in respect of the use of motor vehicles involved in an accident.

(43) In the interests of such injured parties, Member States should set up information centres to ensure that such information concerning any accident involving a motor vehicle is made available promptly. Those information centres should also make available to injured parties information concerning claims representatives. It is necessary that such centres should cooperate with

[1] OJ L 228, 11.8.1992, p. 1.

each other and respond rapidly to requests for information about claims representatives made by centres in other Member States. It seems appropriate that such centres should collect information about the actual termination date of the insurance cover but not about the expiry of the original validity of the policy if the duration of the contract is extended owing to non-cancellation.

(44) Specific provision should be made with respect to vehicles (for example, government or military vehicles) which fall within the exemptions from the obligation to be insured against civil liability.

(45) The injured party may have a legitimate interest in being informed about the identity of the owner or usual driver or the registered keeper of the vehicle, for example if he can obtain compensation only from those persons because the vehicle is not duly insured or the damage exceeds the sum insured, in which event this information should also be provided.

(46) Certain information provided, such as the name and address of the owner or usual driver of the vehicle and the number of the insurance policy or the registration number of the vehicle, constitutes personal data within the meaning of Directive 95/46/EC of the European Parliament and of the Council of 24 October 1995 on the protection of individuals with regard to the processing of personal data and on the free movement of such data[1]. The processing of such data which is required for the purposes of this Directive should therefore comply with the national measures taken pursuant to Directive 95/46/EC. The name and address of the usual driver should be communicated only if national legislation provides for such communication.

(47) In order to ensure that the injured party will not remain without the compensation to which he is entitled, it is necessary to make provision for a compensation body to which the injured party may apply where the insurance undertaking has failed to appoint a representative or is manifestly dilatory in settling a claim or where the insurance undertaking cannot be identified. The intervention of the compensation body should be limited to rare individual cases where the insurance undertaking has failed to comply with its duties in spite of the deterrent effect of the potential imposition of penalties.

(48) The role played by the compensation body is that of settling the claim in respect of any loss or injury suffered by the injured party only in cases which are capable of objective determination and therefore the compensation body should limit its activity to verifying that an offer of compensation has been made in accordance with the time limits and procedures laid down, without any assessment of the merits.

(49) Legal persons who are subrogated by law to the injured party in his claims against the person responsible for the accident or the latter's insurance undertaking (such as, for example, other insurance undertakings or social security bodies) should not be entitled to present the corresponding claim to the compensation body.

1 OJ L 281, 23.11.1995, p. 31.

(50) The compensation body should have a right of subrogation in so far as it has compensated the injured party. In order to facilitate enforcement of the compensation body's claim against the insurance undertaking where the latter has failed to appoint a claims representative or is manifestly dilatory in settling a claim, the body providing compensation in the injured party's State should also enjoy an automatic right of reimbursement with subrogation to the rights of the injured party on the part of the corresponding body in the State where the insurance undertaking is established. This body is the best placed to institute proceedings for recourse against the insurance undertaking.

(51) Even though Member States may provide that the claim against the compensation body is to be subsidiary, the injured person should not be obliged to present his claim to the person responsible for the accident before presenting it to the compensation body. In such a case the injured party should be in at least the same position as in the case of a claim against the guarantee fund.

(52) This system can be made to function by means of an agreement between the compensation bodies established or approved by the Member States, defining their functions and obligations and the procedures for reimbursement.

(53) Where it is impossible to identify the insurer of a vehicle, it should be provided that the ultimate debtor in respect of the damages to be paid to the injured party is the guarantee fund provided for this purpose situated in the Member State where the uninsured vehicle, the use of which has caused the accident, is normally based. Where it is impossible to identify the vehicle, it should be provided that the ultimate debtor is the guarantee fund provided for this purpose situated in the Member State in which the accident occurred.

(54) This Directive should be without prejudice to the obligations of the Member States relating to the time limits for transposition into national law and application of the Directives set out in Annex I, Part B,

HAVE ADOPTED THIS DIRECTIVE:

CHAPTER 1 : GENERAL PROVISIONS

Article 1 Definitions

For the purposes of this Directive:

1. "vehicle" means any motor vehicle intended for travel on land and propelled by mechanical power, but not running on rails, and any trailer, whether or not coupled;
2. "injured party" means any person entitled to compensation in respect of any loss or injury caused by vehicles;
3. "national insurers' bureau" means a professional organisation which is constituted in accordance with Recommendation No 5 adopted on 25 January 1949 by the Road Transport Sub-committee of the Inland Transport Committee of the United Nations Economic Commission for Europe and which groups

together insurance undertakings which, in a State, are authorised to conduct the business of motor vehicle insurance against civil liability;

4. "territory in which the vehicle is normally based" means:
   (a) the territory of the State of which the vehicle bears a registration plate, irrespective of whether the plate is permanent or temporary; or
   (b) in cases where no registration is required for a type of vehicle but the vehicle bears an insurance plate, or a distinguishing sign analogous to the registration plate, the territory of the State in which the insurance plate or the sign is issued; or
   (c) in cases where neither a registration plate nor an insurance plate nor a distinguishing sign is required for certain types of vehicle, the territory of the State in which the person who has custody of the vehicle is permanently resident; or
   (d) in cases where the vehicle does not bear any registration plate or bears a registration plate which does not correspond or no longer corresponds to the vehicle and has been involved in an accident, the territory of the State in which the accident took place, for the purpose of settling the claim as provided for in the first indent of Article 2(a) or in Article 10;
5. "green card" means an international certificate of insurance issued on behalf of a national bureau in accordance with Recommendation No 5 adopted on 25 January 1949 by the Road Transport Sub-committee of the Inland Transport Committee of the United Nations Economic Commission for Europe;
6. "insurance undertaking" means an undertaking which has received its official authorisation in accordance with Article 6 or Article 23(2) of Directive 73/239/EEC;
7. "establishment" means the head office, agency or branch of an insurance undertaking as defined in Article 2(c) of Second Council Directive 88/357/EEC of 22 June 1988 on the coordination of laws, regulations and administrative provisions relating to direct insurance other than life assurance and laying down provisions to facilitate the effective exercise of freedom to provide services[1].

Article 2 Scope

The provisions of Articles 4, 6, 7 and 8 shall apply to vehicles normally based on the territory of one of the Member States:

(a) after an agreement has been concluded between the national insurers' bureaux under the terms of which each national bureau guarantees the settlement, in accordance with the provisions of national law on compulsory insurance, of claims in respect of accidents occurring in its territory, caused by vehicles normally based in the territory of another Member State, whether or not such vehicles are insured;

[1] OJ L 172, 4.7.1988, p. 1.

(b) from the date fixed by the Commission, upon its having ascertained in close cooperation with the Member States that such an agreement has been concluded;

(c) for the duration of that agreement.

Article 3 Compulsory insurance of vehicles

Each Member State shall, subject to Article 5, take all appropriate measures to ensure that civil liability in respect of the use of vehicles normally based in its territory is covered by insurance.

The extent of the liability covered and the terms and conditions of the cover shall be determined on the basis of the measures referred to in the first paragraph.

Each Member State shall take all appropriate measures to ensure that the contract of insurance also covers:

(a) according to the law in force in other Member States, any loss or injury which is caused in the territory of those States;

(b) any loss or injury suffered by nationals of Member States during a direct journey between two territories in which the Treaty is in force, if there is no national insurers' bureau responsible for the territory which is being crossed; in such a case, the loss or injury shall be covered in accordance with the national laws on compulsory insurance in force in the Member State in whose territory the vehicle is normally based.

The insurance referred to in the first paragraph shall cover compulsorily both damage to property and personal injuries.

Article 4 Checks on insurance

Member States shall refrain from making checks on insurance against civil liability in respect of vehicles normally based in the territory of another Member State and in respect of vehicles normally based in the territory of a third country entering their territory from the territory of another Member State. However, they may carry out non-systematic checks on insurance provided that those checks are not discriminatory and are carried out as part of a control which is not aimed exclusively at insurance verification.

Article 5 Derogation from the obligation in respect of compulsory insurance of vehicles

1. A Member State may derogate from Article 3 in respect of certain natural or legal persons, public or private; a list of such persons shall be drawn up by the State concerned and communicated to the other Member States and to the Commission.

   A Member State so derogating shall take the appropriate measures to ensure that compensation is paid in respect of any loss or injury caused in its territory and in the territory of other Member States by vehicles belonging to such persons.

It shall in particular designate an authority or body in the country where the loss or injury occurs responsible for compensating injured parties in accordance with the laws of that State in cases where Article 2(a) is not applicable.

It shall communicate to the Commission the list of persons exempt from compulsory insurance and the authorities or bodies responsible for compensation.

The Commission shall publish that list.

2. A Member State may derogate from Article 3 in respect of certain types of vehicle or certain vehicles having a special plate; the list of such types or of such vehicles shall be drawn up by the State concerned and communicated to the other Member States and to the Commission.

   Any Member State so derogating shall ensure that vehicles referred to in the first subparagraph are treated in the same way as vehicles for which the insurance obligation provided for in Article 3 has not been satisfied.

   The guarantee fund of the Member State in which the accident has taken place shall then have a claim against the guarantee fund in the Member State where the vehicle is normally based.

   From 11 June 2010 Member States shall report to the Commission on the implementation and practical application of this paragraph.

   The Commission, after examining those reports, shall, if appropriate, submit proposals for the replacement or repeal of this derogation.

Article 6 National insurers' bureaux

Each Member State shall ensure that, where an accident is caused in its territory by a vehicle normally based in the territory of another Member State, the national insurers' bureau shall, without prejudice to the obligation referred to in Article 2(a), obtain information:

(a) as to the territory in which the vehicle is normally based, and as to its registration mark, if any;

(b) in so far as is possible, as to the details of the insurance of the vehicle, as they normally appear on the green card, which are in the possession of the person having custody of the vehicle, to the extent that those details are required by the Member State in whose territory the vehicle is normally based.

Each Member State shall also ensure that the bureau communicates the information referred to in points (a) and (b) to the national insurers' bureau of the State in whose territory the vehicle referred to in the first paragraph is normally based.

CHAPTER 2 : PROVISIONS CONCERNING VEHICLES NORMALLY BASED IN THE TERRITORY OF THIRD COUNTRIES

Article 7 National measures concerning vehicles normally based on the territory of third countries

Each Member State shall take all appropriate measures to ensure that vehicles normally based in the territory of a third country which enter the territory in which the Treaty is in force shall not be used in its territory unless any loss or injury caused by those vehicles is covered, in accordance with the requirements of the laws of the various Member States on compulsory insurance against civil liability in respect of the use of vehicles, throughout the territory in which the Treaty is in force.

Article 8 Documentation concerning vehicles normally based in the territory of third countries

1. Every vehicle normally based in the territory of a third country must, before entering the territory in which the Treaty is in force, be provided either with a valid green card or with a certificate of frontier insurance establishing that the vehicle is insured in accordance with Article 7.

   However, vehicles normally based in a third country shall be treated as vehicles normally based in the Community if the national bureaux of all the Member States severally guarantee, each in accordance with the provisions of its own national law on compulsory insurance, settlement of claims in respect of accidents occurring in their territory caused by such vehicles.
2. Having ascertained, in close cooperation with the Member States, that the obligations referred to in the second subparagraph of paragraph 1 have been assumed, the Commission shall fix the date from which and the types of vehicles for which Member States shall no longer require production of the documents referred to in the first subparagraph of paragraph 1.

CHAPTER 3 : MINIMUM AMOUNTS COVERED BY COMPULSORY INSURANCE

Article 9 Minimum amounts

1. Without prejudice to any higher guarantees which Member States may prescribe, each Member State shall require the insurance referred to in Article 3 to be compulsory at least in respect of the following amounts:
   (a) in the case of personal injury, a minimum amount of cover of EUR 1000000 per victim or EUR 5000000 per claim, whatever the number of victims;
   (b) in the case of damage to property, EUR 1000000 per claim, whatever the number of victims.

If necessary, Member States may establish a transitional period extending until 11 June 2012 at the latest within which to adapt their minimum amounts of cover to the amounts provided for in the first subparagraph.

Member States establishing such a transitional period shall inform the Commission thereof and indicate the duration of the transitional period.

However, until 11 December 2009 at the latest, Member States shall increase guarantees to at least a half of the levels provided for in the first subparagraph.

2. Every five years after 11 June 2005 or the end of any transitional period as referred to in the second subparagraph of paragraph 1, the amounts referred to in that paragraph shall be reviewed in line with the European Index of Consumer Prices (EICP) established pursuant to Regulation (EC) No 2494/95.

   The amounts shall be adjusted automatically. Such amounts shall be increased by the percentage change indicated by the EICP for the relevant period, that is to say, the five years immediately preceding the review referred to in the first subparagraph, and rounded up to a multiple of EUR 10000.

   The Commission shall communicate the adjusted amounts to the European Parliament and to the Council and shall ensure their publication in the Official Journal of the European Union.

CHAPTER 4 : COMPENSATION FOR DAMAGE CAUSED BY AN UNIDENTIFIED VEHICLE OR A VEHICLE FOR WHICH THE INSURANCE OBLIGATION PROVIDED FOR IN ARTICLE 3 HAS NOT BEEN SATISFIED

Article 10 Body responsible for compensation

1. Each Member State shall set up or authorise a body with the task of providing compensation, at least up to the limits of the insurance obligation for damage to property or personal injuries caused by an unidentified vehicle or a vehicle for which the insurance obligation provided for in Article 3 has not been satisfied.

   The first subparagraph shall be without prejudice to the right of the Member States to regard compensation by the body as subsidiary or non-subsidiary and the right to make provision for the settlement of claims between the body and the person or persons responsible for the accident and other insurers or social security bodies required to compensate the victim in respect of the same accident. However, Member States may not allow the body to make the payment of compensation conditional on the victim establishing in any way that the person liable is unable or refuses to pay.

2. The victim may in any event apply directly to the body which, on the basis of information provided at its request by the victim, shall be obliged to give him a reasoned reply regarding the payment of any compensation.

Member States may, however, exclude the payment of compensation by that body in respect of persons who voluntarily entered the vehicle which caused the damage or injury when the body can prove that they knew it was uninsured.

3. Member States may limit or exclude the payment of compensation by the body in the event of damage to property by an unidentified vehicle.

   However, where the body has paid compensation for significant personal injuries to any victim of the same accident in which damage to property was caused by an unidentified vehicle, Member States may not exclude the payment of compensation for damage to property on the basis that the vehicle is unidentified. Nevertheless, Member States may provide for an excess of not more than EUR 500 to be borne by the victim of such damage to property.

   The conditions in which personal injuries are to be regarded as significant shall be determined in accordance with the legislation or administrative provisions of the Member State in which the accident takes place. In this regard, Member States may take into account, inter alia, whether the injury required hospital care.

4. Each Member State shall apply its laws, regulations and administrative provisions to the payment of compensation by the body, without prejudice to any other practice which is more favourable to the victim.

Article 11 Disputes

In the event of a dispute between the body referred to in Article 10(1) and the civil liability insurer as to which must compensate the victim, the Member States shall take the appropriate measures so that one of those parties is designated to be responsible in the first instance for paying compensation to the victim without delay.

If it is ultimately decided that the other party should have paid all or part of the compensation, that other party shall reimburse accordingly the party which has paid.

CHAPTER 5 : SPECIAL CATEGORIES OF VICTIM, EXCLUSION CLAUSES, SINGLE PREMIUM, VEHICLES DISPATCHED FROM ONE MEMBER STATE TO ANOTHER

Article 12 Special categories of victim

1. Without prejudice to the second subparagraph of Article 13(1), the insurance referred to in Article 3 shall cover liability for personal injuries to all passengers, other than the driver, arising out of the use of a vehicle.
2. The members of the family of the policyholder, driver or any other person who is liable under civil law in the event of an accident, and whose liability is covered by the insurance referred to in Article 3, shall not be excluded from insurance in respect of their personal injuries by virtue of that relationship.
3. The insurance referred to in Article 3 shall cover personal injuries and damage to property suffered by pedestrians, cyclists and other non-motorised users of the roads who, as a consequence of an accident in which a motor vehicle is involved, are entitled to compensation in accordance with national civil law.

This Article shall be without prejudice either to civil liability or to the quantum of damages.

Article 13 Exclusion clauses

1. Each Member State shall take all appropriate measures to ensure that any statutory provision or any contractual clause contained in an insurance policy issued in accordance with Article 3 shall be deemed to be void in respect of claims by third parties who have been victims of an accident where that statutory provision or contractual clause excludes from insurance the use or driving of vehicles by:
   (a) persons who do not have express or implied authorisation to do so;
   (b) persons who do not hold a licence permitting them to drive the vehicle concerned;
   (c) persons who are in breach of the statutory technical requirements concerning the condition and safety of the vehicle concerned.

   However, the provision or clause referred to in point (a) of the first subparagraph may be invoked against persons who voluntarily entered the vehicle which caused the damage or injury, when the insurer can prove that they knew the vehicle was stolen.

   Member States shall have the option — in the case of accidents occurring on their territory — of not applying the provision in the first subparagraph if and in so far as the victim may obtain compensation for the damage suffered from a social security body.
2. In the case of vehicles stolen or obtained by violence, Member States may provide that the body specified in Article 10(1) is to pay compensation instead of the insurer under the conditions set out in paragraph 1 of this Article. Where the vehicle is normally based in another Member State, that body can make no claim against any body in that Member State.

   Member States which, in the case of vehicles stolen or obtained by violence, provide that the body referred to in Article 10(1) is to pay compensation may fix in respect of damage to property an excess of not more than EUR 250 to be borne by the victim.
3. Member States shall take the necessary measures to ensure that any statutory provision or any contractual clause contained in an insurance policy which excludes a passenger from such cover on the basis that he knew or should have known that the driver of the vehicle was under the influence of alcohol or of any other intoxicating agent at the time of an accident, shall be deemed to be void in respect of the claims of such passenger.

Article 14 Single premium

Member States shall take the necessary steps to ensure that all compulsory policies of insurance against civil liability arising out of the use of vehicles:

(a) cover, on the basis of a single premium and during the whole term of the contract, the entire territory of the Community, including for any period in which the vehicle remains in other Member States during the term of the contract; and

(b) guarantee, on the basis of that single premium, in each Member State, the cover required by its law or the cover required by the law of the Member State where the vehicle is normally based when that cover is higher.

Article 15 Vehicles dispatched from one Member State to another

1. By way of derogation from the second indent of Article 2(d) of Directive 88/357/EEC, where a vehicle is dispatched from one Member State to another, the Member State where the risk is situated shall be considered to be the Member State of destination, immediately upon acceptance of delivery by the purchaser, for a period of 30 days, even though the vehicle has not formally been registered in the Member State of destination.
2. In the event that the vehicle is involved in an accident during the period mentioned in paragraph 1 of this Article while being uninsured, the body referred to in Article 10(1) in the Member State of destination shall be liable for the compensation provided for in Article 9.

CHAPTER 6 : STATEMENT, EXCESS, DIRECT ACTION

Article 16 Statement relating to the third party liability claims

Member States shall ensure that the policyholder has the right to request at any time a statement relating to the third party liability claims involving the vehicle or vehicles covered by the insurance contract at least during the preceding five years of the contractual relationship, or to the absence of such claims.

The insurance undertaking, or a body which may have been appointed by a Member State to provide compulsory insurance or to supply such statements, shall provide that statement to the policyholder within 15 days of the request.

Article 17 Excess

Insurance undertakings shall not require any party injured as a result of an accident to bear any excess as far as the insurance referred to in Article 3 is concerned.

Article 18 Direct right of action

Member States shall ensure that any party injured as a result of an accident caused by a vehicle covered by insurance as referred to in Article 3 enjoys a direct right of action against the insurance undertaking covering the person responsible against civil liability.

CHAPTER 7 : SETTLEMENT OF CLAIMS ARISING FROM ANY ACCIDENT CAUSED BY A VEHICLE COVERED BY INSURANCE AS REFERRED TO IN ARTICLE 3

Article 19 Procedure for the settlement of claims

Member States shall establish the procedure referred to in Article 22 for the settlement of claims arising from any accident caused by a vehicle covered by insurance as referred to in Article 3.

In the case of claims which may be settled by the system of national insurers' bureaux provided for in Article 2 Member States shall establish the same procedure as in Article 22.

For the purpose of applying this procedure, any reference to an insurance undertaking shall be understood as a reference to national insurers' bureaux.

Article 20 Special provisions concerning compensation for injured parties following an accident in a Member State other than that of their residence

1. The object of Articles 20 to 26 is to lay down special provisions applicable to injured parties entitled to compensation in respect of any loss or injury resulting from accidents occurring in a Member State other than the Member State of residence of the injured party which are caused by the use of vehicles insured and normally based in a Member State.

   Without prejudice to the legislation of third countries on civil liability and private international law, these provisions shall also apply to injured parties resident in a Member State and entitled to compensation in respect of any loss or injury resulting from accidents occurring in third countries whose national insurer's bureaux have joined the green card system whenever such accidents are caused by the use of vehicles insured and normally based in a Member State.
2. Articles 21 and 24 shall apply only in the case of accidents caused by the use of a vehicle:
   (a) insured through an establishment in a Member State other than the State of residence of the injured party; and
   (b) normally based in a Member State other than the State of residence of the injured party.

Article 21 Claims representatives

1. Each Member State shall take all measures necessary to ensure that all insurance undertakings covering the risks classified in class 10 of point A of the Annex to Directive 73/239/EEC, other than carrier's liability, appoint a claims representative in each Member State other than that in which they have received their official authorisation.

   The claims representative shall be responsible for handling and settling claims arising from an accident in the cases referred to in Article 20(1).

The claims representative shall be resident or established in the Member State where he is appointed.

2. The choice of its claims representative shall be at the discretion of the insurance undertaking.

   The Member States may not restrict this freedom of choice.

3. The claims representative may act for one or more insurance undertakings.

4. The claims representative shall, in relation to such claims, collect all information necessary in connection with the settlement of the claims and shall take the measures necessary to negotiate a settlement of claims.

   The requirement of appointing a claims representative shall not preclude the right of the injured party or his insurance undertaking to institute proceedings directly against the person who caused the accident or his insurance undertaking.

5. Claims representatives shall possess sufficient powers to represent the insurance undertaking in relation to injured parties in the cases referred to in Article 20(1) and to meet their claims in full.

   They must be capable of examining cases in the official language(s) of the Member State of residence of the injured party.

6. The appointment of a claims representative shall not in itself constitute the opening of a branch within the meaning of Article 1(b) of Directive 92/49/EEC and the claims representative shall not be regarded as an establishment within the meaning of Article 2(c) of Directive 88/357/EEC or an establishment within the meaning of Regulation (EC) No 44/2001.

Article 22 Compensation procedure

The Member States shall create a duty, backed by appropriate, effective and systematic financial or equivalent administrative penalties, whereby, within three months of the date when the injured party presented his claim for compensation either directly to the insurance undertaking of the person who caused the accident or to its claims representative,

(a) the insurance undertaking of the person who caused the accident or its claims representative is required to make a reasoned offer of compensation in cases where liability is not contested and the damages have been quantified; or

(b) the insurance undertaking to whom the claim for compensation has been addressed or its claims representative is required to provide a reasoned reply to the points made in the claim in cases where liability is denied or has not been clearly determined or the damages have not been fully quantified.

Member States shall adopt provisions to ensure that, where the offer is not made within the three-month time limit, interest shall be payable on the amount of compensation offered by the insurance undertaking or awarded by the court to the injured party.

Article 23 Information centres

1. In order to enable the injured party to seek compensation, each Member State shall establish or approve an information centre responsible:
   (a) for keeping a register containing the following information:
      (i) the registration numbers of motor vehicles normally based in the territory of the State in question;
      (ii) the numbers of the insurance policies covering the use of those vehicles for the risks classified in class 10 of point A of the Annex to Directive 73/239/EEC, other than carrier's liability and, where the period of validity of the policy has expired, the date of termination of the insurance cover;
      (iii) insurance undertakings covering the use of vehicles for the risks classified in class 10 of point A of the Annex to Directive 73/239/EEC, other than carrier's liability, and claims representatives appointed by such insurance undertakings in accordance with Article 21 of this Directive whose names are to be notified to the information centre in accordance with paragraph 2 of this Article;
      (iv) the list of vehicles which, in each Member State, benefit from the derogation from the requirement for civil liability insurance cover in accordance with Article 5(1) and (2);
      (v) as regards the vehicles provided for in point (iv):
         - the name of the authority or body designated in accordance with the third subparagraph of Article 5(1) as responsible for compensating injured parties in the cases where the procedure provided for in Article 2(2)(a) is not applicable, if the vehicle benefits from the derogation provided for in the first subparagraph of Article 5(1),
         - the name of the body covering the vehicle in the Member State where it is normally based if the vehicle benefits from the derogation provided for in Article 5(2);
   (b) or for coordinating the compilation and dissemination of that information; and
   (c) for assisting entitled persons to be apprised of the information mentioned in points (a)(i) to (v).

   The information under points (a)(i), (ii) and (iii) must be preserved for a period of seven years after the termination of the registration of the vehicle or the termination of the insurance contract.
2. Insurance undertakings referred to in point (a)(iii) of paragraph 1 shall notify to the information centres of all Member States the name and address of the claims representative appointed by them in accordance with Article 21 in each of the Member States.
3. Member States shall ensure that the injured party is entitled for a period of seven years after the accident to obtain without delay from the information centre of the Member State where he resides, the Member State where the vehicle is

normally based or the Member State where the accident occurred the following information:

(a) the name and address of the insurance undertaking;
(b) the number of the insurance policy; and
(c) the name and address of the insurance undertaking's claims representative in the State of residence of the injured party.

Information centres shall cooperate with each other.

4. The information centre shall provide the injured party with the name and address of the owner or usual driver or registered keeper of the vehicle if the injured party has a legitimate interest in obtaining this information. For the purposes of this provision, the information centre shall address itself in particular:

   (a) to the insurance undertaking; or
   (b) to the vehicle registration agency.

   If the vehicle benefits from the derogation provided for in the first subparagraph of Article 5(1) the information centre shall inform the injured party of the name of the authority or body designated in accordance with the third subparagraph of Article 5(1) as responsible for compensating injured parties in cases where the procedure provided for in Article 2(a) is not applicable.

   If the vehicle benefits from the derogation provided for in Article 5(2) the information centre shall inform the injured party of the name of the body covering the vehicle in the country where it is normally based.

5. Member States shall ensure that, without prejudice to their obligations under paragraphs 1 and 4, the information centres provide the information specified in these paragraphs to any party involved in any traffic accident caused by a vehicle covered by insurance as referred to in Article 3.

6. The processing of personal data resulting from paragraphs 1 to 5 must be carried out in accordance with national measures taken pursuant to Directive 95/46/EC.

Article 24 Compensation bodies

1. Each Member State shall establish or approve a compensation body responsible for providing compensation to injured parties in the cases referred to in Article 20(1).

   Such injured parties may present a claim to the compensation body in their Member State of residence:

   (a) if, within three months of the date when the injured party presented his claim for compensation to the insurance undertaking of the vehicle the use of which caused the accident or to its claims representative, the insurance undertaking or its claims representative has not provided a reasoned reply to the points made in the claim; or
   (b) if the insurance undertaking has failed to appoint a claims representative in the Member State of residence of the injured party in accordance with Article 20(1); in such a case, injured parties may not present a claim to the

compensation body if they have presented a claim for compensation directly to the insurance undertaking of the vehicle the use of which caused the accident and if they have received a reasoned reply within three months of presenting the claim.

Injured parties may not however present a claim to the compensation body if they have taken legal action directly against the insurance undertaking.

The compensation body shall take action within two months of the date when the injured party presents a claim for compensation to it but shall terminate its action if the insurance undertaking, or its claims representative, subsequently makes a reasoned reply to the claim.

The compensation body shall immediately inform:

(a) the insurance undertaking of the vehicle the use of which caused the accident or the claims representative;
(b) the compensation body in the Member State in which the insurance undertaking which issued the policy is established;
(c) if known, the person who caused the accident;

that it has received a claim from the injured party and that it will respond to that claim within two months of the presentation of that claim.

This provision shall be without prejudice to the right of the Member States to regard compensation by that body as subsidiary or non-subsidiary and the right to make provision for the settlement of claims between that body and the person or persons who caused the accident and other insurance undertakings or social security bodies required to compensate the injured party in respect of the same accident. However, Member States may not allow the body to make the payment of compensation subject to any conditions other than those laid down in this Directive, in particular the injured party's establishing in any way that the person liable is unable or refuses to pay.

2. The compensation body which has compensated the injured party in his Member State of residence shall be entitled to claim reimbursement of the sum paid by way of compensation from the compensation body in the Member State in which the insurance undertaking which issued the policy is established.

   The latter body shall be subrogated to the injured party in his rights against the person who caused the accident or his insurance undertaking in so far as the compensation body in the Member State of residence of the injured party has provided compensation for the loss or injury suffered.

   Each Member State shall be obliged to acknowledge this subrogation as provided for by any other Member State.

3. This Article shall take effect:

   (a) after an agreement has been concluded between the compensation bodies established or approved by the Member States relating to their functions and obligations and the procedures for reimbursement;

(b) from the date fixed by the Commission upon its having ascertained in close cooperation with the Member States that such an agreement has been concluded.

Article 25 Compensation

1. If it is impossible to identify the vehicle or if, within two months of the date of the accident, it is impossible to identify the insurance undertaking, the injured party may apply for compensation from the compensation body in the Member State where he resides. The compensation shall be provided in accordance with the provisions of Articles 9 and 10. The compensation body shall then have a claim, on the conditions laid down in Article 24(2):
   (a) where the insurance undertaking cannot be identified: against the guarantee fund in the Member State where the vehicle is normally based;
   (b) in the case of an unidentified vehicle: against the guarantee fund in the Member State in which the accident took place;
   (c) in the case of a third-country vehicle: against the guarantee fund in the Member State in which the accident took place.
2. This Article shall apply to accidents caused by third-country vehicles covered by Articles 7 and 8.

Article 26 Central body

Member States shall take all appropriate measures to facilitate the timely provision to the victims, their insurers or their legal representatives of the basic data necessary for the settlement of claims.

Those basic data shall, where appropriate, be made available in electronic form in a central repository in each Member State, and be accessible by parties involved in the case at their express request.

Article 27 Penalties

Member States shall fix penalties for breaches of the national provisions which they adopt in implementation of this Directive and shall take the steps necessary to secure the application thereof. The penalties shall be effective, proportional and dissuasive. The Member States shall notify to the Commission as soon as possible any amendments concerning provisions adopted pursuant to this Article.

CHAPTER 8 : FINAL PROVISIONS

Article 28 National provisions

1. Member States may, in accordance with the Treaty, maintain or bring into force provisions which are more favourable to injured parties than the provisions needed to comply with this Directive.
2. Member States shall communicate to the Commission the text of the main provisions of domestic law which they adopt in the field governed by this Directive.

Article 29 Repeal

Directives 72/166/EEC, 84/5/EEC, 90/232/EEC, 2000/26/EC and 2005/14/EC, as amended by the Directives listed in Annex I, Part A, are hereby repealed, without prejudice to the obligations of the Member States relating to the time limits for transposition into national law and application of the Directives set out in Annex I, Part B.

References to the repealed Directives shall be construed as references to this Directive and shall be read in accordance with the correlation table in Annex II.

Article 30 Entry into force

This Directive shall enter into force on the 20th day following its publication in the Official Journal of the European Union.

Article 31 Addressees

This Directive is addressed to the Member States.

Done at Strasbourg, 16 September 2009.

For the European Parliament

The President

J. Buzek

For the Council

The President

C. Malmström

ANNEX I

PART A

Repealed Directive with list of its successive amendments (referred to in Article 29)

Council Directive 72/166/EEC (OJ L 103, 2.5.1972, p. 1)	
Council Directive 72/430/EEC (OJ L 291, 28.12.1972, p. 162)	
Council Directive 84/5/EEC (OJ L 8, 11.1.1984, p. 17)	Only Article 4
Directive 2005/14/EC of the European Parliament and Council (OJ L 149, 11.6.2005, p. 14)	Only Article 1
Council Directive 84/5/EEC (OJ L 8, 11.1.1984, p. 17)	
Annex I, point IX.F of the 1985 Act of Accession (OJ L 302, 15.11.1985, p. 218)	
Council Directive 90/232/EEC (OJ L 129, 19.5.1990, p. 33)	Only Article 4
Directive 2005/14/EC of the European Parliament and Council (OJ L 149, 11.6.2005, p. 14)	Only Article 2
Council Directive 90/232/EEC (OJ L 129, 19.5.1990, p. 33)	
Directive 2005/14/EC of the European Parliament and Council (OJ L 149, 11.6.2005, p. 14)	Only Article 4
Directive 2000/26/EC of the European Parliament and Council (OJ L 181, 20.7.2000, p. 65)	
Directive 2005/14/EC of the European Parliament and Council (OJ L 149, 11.6.2005, p. 14)	Only Article 5
Directive 2005/14/EC of the European Parliament and Council (OJ L 149, 11.6.2005, p. 14)	

PART B

List of time limits for transposition into national law and application (referred to in Article 29)

Directive	Time limit for transposition	Date of application
72/166/EEC	31 December 1973	
72/430/EEC	-	1 January 1973
84/5/EEC	31 December 1987	31 December 1988
90/232/EEC	31 December 1992	-
2000/26/EC	19 July 2002	19 January 2003
2005/14/EC	11 June 2007	-

ANNEX II

CORRELATION TABLE

Directive 72/166/EEC	Directive 84/5/EEC	Directive 90/232/EEC	Directive 2000/26/EC	This Directive
Article 1, points (1) to (3)				Article 1, points (1) to (3)
Article 1, point (4), first indent				Article 1, point (4)(a)
Article 1, point (4), second indent				Article 1, point (4)(b)
Article 1, point (4), third indent				Article 1, point (4)(c)
Article 1, point (4), fourth indent				Article 1, point (4)(d)
Article 1, point (5)				Article 1, point (5)
Article 2(1)				Article 4
Article 2(2), introductory wording				Article 2, introductory wording

Directive 72/166/EEC	Directive 84/5/EEC	Directive 90/232/EEC	Directive 2000/26/EC	This Directive
Article 2(2), first indent				Article 2, point (a)
Article 2(2), second indent				Article 2, point (b)
Article 2(2), third indent				Article 2, point (c)
Article 3(1), first sentence				Article 3, first paragraph
Article 3(1), second sentence				Article 3, second paragraph
Article 3(2), introductory wording				Article 3, third paragraph, introductory wording
Article 3(2), first indent				Article 3, third paragraph, point (a)
Article 3(2), second indent				Article 3, third paragraph, point (b)
Article 4, introductory wording				Article 5(1), first subparagraph
Article 4, point (a), first subparagraph				Article 5(1), first subparagraph
Article 4, point (a), second subparagraph, first sentence				Article 5(1), second subparagraph
Article 4, point (a), second subparagraph, second sentence				Article 5(1), third subparagraph
Article 4, point (a), second subparagraph, third sentence				Article 5(1), fourth subparagraph

Directive 72/166/EEC	Directive 84/5/EEC	Directive 90/232/EEC	Directive 2000/26/EC	This Directive
Article 4, point (a), second subparagraph, fourth sentence				Article 5(1), fifth subparagraph
Article 4, point (b), first subparagraph				Article 5(2), first subparagraph
Article 4, point (b), second subparagraph, first sentence				Article 5(2), second subparagraph
Article 4, point (b), second subparagraph, second sentence				Article 5(2), third subparagraph
Article 4, point (b), third subparagraph, first sentence				Article 5(2), fourth subparagraph
Article 4, point (b), third subparagraph, second sentence				Article 5(2), fifth subparagraph
Article 5, introductory wording				Article 6, first subparagraph, introductory wording
Article 5, first indent				Article 6, first paragraph, point (a)
Article 5, second indent				Article 6, first paragraph, point (b)
Article 5, final wording				Article 6, second paragraph
Article 6				Article 7
Article 7(1)				Article 8(1), first subparagraph

Directive 72/166/EEC	Directive 84/5/EEC	Directive 90/232/EEC	Directive 2000/26/EC	This Directive
Article 7(2)				Article 8(1), second subparagraph
Article 7(3)				Article 8(2)
Article 8				-
	Article 1(1)			Article 3, fourth paragraph
	Article 1(2)			Article 9(1)
	Article 1(3)			Article 9(2)
	Article 1(4)			Article 10(1)
	Article 1(5)			Article 10(2)
	Article 1(6)			Article 10(3)
	Article 1(7)			Article 10(4)
	Article 2(1), first subparagraph, introductory wording			Article 13(1), first subparagraph, introductory wording
	Article 2(1), first indent			Article 13(1), first subparagraph, point (a)
	Article 2(1), second indent			Article 13(1), first subparagraph, point (b)
	Article 2(1), third indent			Article 13(1), first subparagraph, point (c)
	Article 2(1), first subparagraph, final wording			Article 13(1), first subparagraph, introductory wording
	Article 2(1), second and third subparagraphs			Article 13(1), second and third subparagraphs

Directive 72/166/EEC	Directive 84/5/EEC	Directive 90/232/EEC	Directive 2000/26/EC	This Directive
	Article 2(2)			Article 13(2)
	Article 3			Article 12(2)
	Article 4			-
	Article 5			-
	Article 6			-
		Article 1, first paragraph		Article 12(1)
		Article 1, second paragraph		Article 13(3)
		Article 1, third paragraph		-
		Article 1a, first sentence		Article 12(3), first subparagraph
		Article 1a, second sentence		Article 12(3), second subparagraph
		Article 2, introductory wording		Article 14, introductory wording
		Article 2, first indent		Article 14, point (a)
		Article 2, second indent		Article 14, point (b)
		Article 3		-
		Article 4		Article 11
		Article 4a		Article 15
		Article 4b, first sentence		Article 16, first paragraph
		Article 4b, second sentence		Article 16, second paragraph
		Article 4c		Article 17
		Article 4d	Article 3	Article 18
		Article 4e, first paragraph		Article 19, first paragraph

Directive 72/166/EEC	Directive 84/5/EEC	Directive 90/232/EEC	Directive 2000/26/EC	This Directive
		Article 4e, second paragraph, first sentence		Article 19, second paragraph
		Article 4e, second paragraph, second sentence		Article 19, third paragraph
		Article 5(1)		Article 23(5)
		Article 5(2)		-
		Article 6		-
			Article 1(1)	Article 20(1)
			Article 1(2)	Article 20(2)
			Article 1(3)	Article 25(2)
			Article 2, introductory wording	-
			Article 2, point (a)	Article 1, point (6)
			Article 2, point (b)	Article 1, point (7)
			Article 2, points (c), (d) and (e)	-
			Article 4(1), first sentence	Article 21(1), first subparagraph
			Article 4(1), second sentence	Article 21(1), second subparagraph
			Article 4(1), third sentence	Article 21(1), third subparagraph
			Article 4(2), first sentence	Article 21(2), first subparagraph
			Article 4(2), second sentence	Article 21(2), second subparagraph

Directive 72/166/EEC	Directive 84/5/EEC	Directive 90/232/EEC	Directive 2000/26/EC	This Directive
			Article 4(3)	Article 21(3)
			Article 4(4), first sentence	Article 21(4), first subparagraph
			Article 4(4), second sentence	Article 21(4), second subparagraph
			Article 4(5), first sentence	Article 21(5), first subparagraph
			Article 4(5), second sentence	Article 21(5), second subparagraph
			Article 4(6)	Article 22
			Article 4(7)	-
			Article 4(8)	Article 21(6)
			Article 5(1), first subparagraph, introductory wording	Article 23(1), first subparagraph, introductory wording
			Article 5(1), first subparagraph, point (a), introductory wording	Article 23(1), first subparagraph, point (a), introductory wording
			Article 5(1), first subparagraph, point (a)(1)	Article 23(1), first subparagraph, point (a)(i)
			Article 5(1), first subparagraph, point (a)(2)	Article 23(1), first subparagraph, point (a)(ii)
			Article 5(1), first subparagraph, point (a)(3)	Article 23(1), first subparagraph, point (a)(iii)

Directive 72/166/EEC	Directive 84/5/EEC	Directive 90/232/EEC	Directive 2000/26/EC	This Directive
			Article 5(1), first subparagraph, point (a)(4)	Article 23(1), first subparagraph, point (a)(iv)
			Article 5(1), first subparagraph, point (a)(5), introductory wording	Article 23(1), first subparagraph, point (a)(v), introductory wording
			Article 5(1), first subparagraph, point (a)(5)(i)	Article 23(1), first subparagraph, point (a)(v), first indent
			Article 5(1), first subparagraph, point (a)(5)(ii)	Article 23(1), first subparagraph, point (a)(v), second indent
			Article 5(1), second subparagraph	Article 23(1), second subparagraph
			Article 5(2), (3) and (4)	Article 23(2), (3) and (4)
			Article 5(5)	Article 23(6)
			Article 6(1)	Article 24(1)
			Article 6(2), first subparagraph	Article 24(2), first subparagraph
			Article 6(2), second subparagraph, first sentence	Article 24(2), second subparagraph
			Article 6(2), second subparagraph, second sentence	Article 24(2), third subparagraph
			Article 6(3), first subparagraph	Article 24(3)

Directive 72/166/EEC	Directive 84/5/EEC	Directive 90/232/EEC	Directive 2000/26/EC	This Directive
			Article 6(3), second subparagraph	-
			Article 6a	Article 26
			Article 7, introductory wording	Article 25(1), introductory wording
			Article 7, point (a)	Article 25(1), point (a)
			Article 7, point (b)	Article 25(1), point (b)
			Article 7, point (c)	Article 25(1), point (c)
			Article 8	-
			Article 9	-
			Article 10(1) to (3)	-
			Article 10(4)	Article 28(1)
			Article 10(5)	Article 28(2)
				Article 29
			Article 11	Article 30
			Article 12	Article 27
Article 9	Article 7	Article 7	Article 13	Article 31
				Annex I
				Annex II

CIVIL PROCEDURE AND PRIVATE INTERNATIONAL LAW

27. Directive 98/26/EC of the European Parliament and of the Council of 19 May 1998 on settlement finality in payment and securities settlement systems

(OJ L 166 , 11/06/1998 p. 45 – 50)

THE EUROPEAN PARLIAMENT AND THE COUNCIL OF THE EUROPEAN UNION,

Having regard to the Treaty establishing the European Community, and in particular Article 100a thereof,

Having regard to the proposal from the Commission [1],

Having regard to the opinion of the European Monetary Institute[2],

Having regard to the opinion of the Economic and Social Committee[3],

Acting in accordance with the procedure laid down in Article 189b of the Treaty[4],

(1) Whereas the Lamfalussy report of 1990 to the Governors of the central banks of the Group of Ten Countries demonstrated the important systemic risk inherent in payment systems which operate on the basis of several legal types of payment netting, in particular multilateral netting; whereas the reduction of legal risks associated with participation in real time gross settlement systems is of paramount importance, given the increasing development of these systems;

(2) Whereas it is also of the utmost importance to reduce the risk associated with participation in securities settlement systems, in particular where there is a close connection between such systems and payment systems;

(3) Whereas this Directive aims at contributing to the efficient and cost effective operation of cross-border payment and securities settlement arrangements in the Community, which reinforces the freedom of movement of capital in the internal market; whereas this Directive thereby follows up the progress made towards completion of the internal market, in particular towards the freedom to provide services and liberalisation of capital movements, with a view to the realisation of Economic and Monetary Union;

(4) Whereas it is desirable that the laws of the Member States should aim to minimise the disruption to a system caused by insolvency proceedings against a participant in that system;

---

1. OJ C 207, 18. 7. 1996, p. 13, and OJ C 259, 26. 8. 1997, p. 6.
2. Opinion delivered on 21 November 1996.
3. OJ C 56, 24. 2. 1997, p. 1.
4. Opinion of the European Parliament of 9 April 1997 (OJ C 132, 28. 4. 1997, p. 74), Council Common Position of 13 October 1997 (OJ C 375, 10. 12. 1997, p. 34) and Decision of the European Parliament of 29 January 1998 (OJ C 56, 23. 2. 1998). Council Decision of 27 April 1998.

(5) Whereas a proposal for a Directive on the reorganisation and winding-up of credit institutions submitted in 1985 and amended on 8 February 1988 is still pending before the Council; whereas the Convention on Insolvency Proceedings drawn up on 23 November 1995 by the Member States meeting within the Council explicitly excludes insurance undertakings, credit institutions and investment firms;

(6) Whereas this Directive is intended to cover payment and securities settlement systems of a domestic as well as of a cross-border nature; whereas the Directive is applicable to Community systems and to collateral security constituted by their participants, be they Community or third country participants, in connection with participation in these systems;

(7) Whereas Member States may apply the provisions of this Directive to their domestic institutions which participate directly in third country systems and to collateral security provided in connection with participation in such systems;

(8) Whereas Member States should be allowed to designate as a system covered by this Directive a system whose main activity is the settlement of securities even if the system to a limited extent also deals with commodity derivatives;

(9) Whereas the reduction of systemic risk requires in particular the finality of settlement and the enforceability of collateral security; whereas collateral security is meant to comprise all means provided by a participant to the other participants in the payment and/or securities settlement systems to secure rights and obligations in connection with that system, including repurchase agreements, statutory liens and fiduciary transfers; whereas regulation in national law of the kind of collateral security which can be used should not be affected by the definition of collateral security in this Directive;

(10) Whereas this Directive, by covering collateral security provided in connection with operations of the central banks of the Member States functioning as central banks, including monetary policy operations, assists the European Monetary Institute in its task of promoting the efficiency of cross-border payments with a view to the preparation of the third stage of Economic and Monetary Union and thereby contributes to developing the necessary legal framework in which the future European central bank may develop its policy;

(11) Whereas transfer orders and their netting should be legally enforceable under all Member States' jurisdictions and binding on third parties;

(12) Whereas rules on finality of netting should not prevent systems testing, before the netting takes place, whether orders that have entered the system comply with the rules of that system and allow the settlement of that system to take place;

(13) Whereas nothing in this Directive should prevent a participant or a third party from exercising any right or claim resulting from the underlying transaction which they may have in law to recovery or restitution in respect of a transfer order which has entered a system, e.g. in case of fraud or technical error, as long as this leads neither to the unwinding of netting nor to the revocation of the transfer order in the system;

(14) Whereas it is necessary to ensure that transfer orders cannot be revoked after a moment defined by the rules of the system;

(15) Whereas it is necessary that a Member State should immediately notify other Member States of the opening of insolvency proceedings against a participant in the system;

(16) Whereas insolvency proceedings should not have a retroactive effect on the rights and obligations of participants in a system;

(17) Whereas, in the event of insolvency proceedings against a participant in a system, this Directive furthermore aims at determining which insolvency law is applicable to the rights and obligations of that participant in connection with its participation in a system;

(18) Whereas collateral security should be insulated from the effects of the insolvency law applicable to the insolvent participant;

(19) Whereas the provisions of Article 9(2) should only apply to a register, account or centralized deposit system which evidences the existence of proprietary rights in or for the delivery or transfer of the securities concerned;

(20) Whereas the provisions of Article 9(2) are intended to ensure that if the participant, the central bank of a Member State or the future European central bank has a valid and effective collateral security as determined under the law of the Member State where the relevant register, account or centralized deposit system is located, then the validity and enforceability of that collateral security as against that system (and the operator thereof) and against any other person claiming directly or indirectly through it, should be determined solely under the law of that Member State;

(21) Whereas the provisions of Article 9(2) are not intended to prejudice the operation and effect of the law of the Member State under which the securities are constituted or of the law of the Member State where the securities may otherwise be located (including, without limitation, the law concerning the creation, ownership or transfer of such securities or of rights in such securities) and should not be interpreted to mean that any such collateral security will be directly enforceable or be capable of being recognised in any such Member State otherwise than in accordance with the law of that Member State;

(22) Whereas it is desirable that Member States endeavour to establish sufficient links between all the securities settlement systems covered by this Directive with a view towards promoting maximum transparency and legal certainty of transactions relating to securities;

(23) Whereas the adoption of this Directive constitutes the most appropriate way of realising the abovementioned objectives and does not go beyond what is necessary to achieve them,

HAVE ADOPTED THIS DIRECTIVE:

Section I : **Scope and definitions**

Article 1

The provisions of this Directive shall apply to:

(a) any system as defined in Article 2(a), governed by the law of a Member State and operating in any currency, the ecu or in various currencies which the system converts one against another;

(b) any participant in such a system;

(c) collateral security provided in connection with:
- participation in a system, or
- operations of the central banks of the Member States in their functions as central banks.

Article 2

For the purpose of this Directive:

(a) 'system` shall mean a formal arrangement:
- between three or more participants, without counting a possible settlement agent, a possible central counterparty, a possible clearing house or a possible indirect participant, with common rules and standardised arrangements for the execution of transfer orders between the participants,
- governed by the law of a Member State chosen by the participants; the participants may, however, only choose the law of a Member State in which at least one of them has its head office, and
- designated, without prejudice to other more stringent conditions of general application laid down by national law, as a system and notified to the Commission by the Member State whose law is applicable, after that Member State is satisfied as to the adequacy of the rules of the system.

Subject to the conditions in the first subparagraph, a Member State may designate as a system such a formal arrangement whose business consists of the execution of transfer orders as defined in the second indent of (i) and which to a limited extent executes orders relating to other financial instruments, when that Member State considers that such a designation is warranted on grounds of systemic risk.

A Member State may also on a case-by-case basis designate as a system such a formal arrangement between two participants, without counting a possible settlement agent, a possible central counterparty, a possible clearing house or a possible indirect participant, when that Member State considers that such a designation is warranted on grounds of systemic risk;

(b) 'institution` shall mean:
- a credit institution as defined in the first indent of Article 1 of Directive 77/780/EEC[1] including the institutions set out in the list in Article 2(2) thereof, or
- an investment firm as defined in point 2 of Article 1 of Directive 93/22/EEC[2] excluding the institutions set out in the list in Article 2(2)(a) to (k) thereof, or
- public authorities and publicly guaranteed undertakings, or
- any undertaking whose head office is outside the Community and whose functions correspond to those of the Community credit institutions or investment firms as defined in the first and second indent,

which participates in a system and which is responsible for discharging the financial obligations arising from transfer orders within that system.

If a system is supervised in accordance with national legislation and only executes transfer orders as defined in the second indent of (i), as well as payments resulting from such orders, a Member State may decide that undertakings which participate in such a system and which have responsibility for discharging the financial obligations arising from transfer orders within this system, can be considered institutions, provided that at least three participants of this system are covered by the categories referred to in the first subparagraph and that such a decision is warranted on grounds of systemic risk;

(c) 'central counterparty` shall mean an entity which is interposed between the institutions in a system and which acts as the exclusive counterparty of these institutions with regard to their transfer orders;

(d) 'settlement agent` shall mean an entity providing to institutions and/or a central counterparty participating in systems, settlement accounts through which transfer orders within such systems are settled and, as the case may be, extending credit to those institutions and/or central counterparties for settlement purposes;

(e) 'clearing house` shall mean an entity responsible for the calculation of the net positions of institutions, a possible central counterparty and/or a possible settlement agent;

(f) 'participant` shall mean an institution, a central counterparty, a settlement agent or a clearing house.

According to the rules of the system, the same participant may act as a central counterparty, a settlement agent or a clearing house or carry out part or all of these tasks.

A Member State may decide that for the purposes of this Directive an indirect participant may be considered a participant if it is warranted on the grounds of

---

1 First Council Directive 77/780/EEC of 12 December 1977 on the coordination of the laws, regulations and administrative provisions relating to the taking up and pursuit of the business of credit institutions (OJ L 322, 17. 12. 1977, p. 30). Directive as last amended by Directive 96/13/EC (OJ L 66, 16. 3. 1996, p. 15).

2 Council Directive 93/22/EEC of 10 May 1993 on investment services in the securities field (OJ L 141, 11. 6. 1993, p. 27). Directive as last amended by Directive 97/9/EC (OJ L 84, 26. 3. 1997, p. 22).

systemic risk and on condition that the indirect participant is known to the system;

(g) 'indirect participant` shall mean a credit institution as defined in the first indent of (b) with a contractual relationship with an institution participating in a system executing transfer orders as defined in the first indent of (i) which enables the abovementioned credit institution to pass transfer orders through the system;

(h) 'securities` shall mean all instruments referred to in section B of the Annex to Directive 93/22/EEC;

(i) 'transfer order` shall mean:

- any instruction by a participant to place at the disposal of a recipient an amount of money by means of a book entry on the accounts of a credit institution, a central bank or a settlement agent, or any instruction which results in the assumption or discharge of a payment obligation as defined by the rules of the system, or
- an instruction by a participant to transfer the title to, or interest in, a security or securities by means of a book entry on a register, or otherwise;

(j) 'insolvency proceedings` shall mean any collective measure provided for in the law of a Member State, or a third country, either to wind up the participant or to reorganise it, where such measure involves the suspending of, or imposing limitations on, transfers or payments;

(k) 'netting` shall mean the conversion into one net claim or one net obligation of claims and obligations resulting from transfer orders which a participant or participants either issue to, or receive from, one or more other participants with the result that only a net claim can be demanded or a net obligation be owed;

(l) 'settlement account` shall mean an account at a central bank, a settlement agent or a central counterparty used to hold funds and securities and to settle transactions between participants in a system;

(m) 'collateral security` shall mean all realisable assets provided under a pledge (including money provided under a pledge), a repurchase or similar agreement, or otherwise, for the purpose of securing rights and obligations potentially arising in connection with a system, or provided to central banks of the Member States or to the future European central bank.

Section II : **Netting and transfer orders**

Article 3

1. Transfer orders and netting shall be legally enforceable and, even in the event of insolvency proceedings against a participant, shall be binding on third parties, provided that transfer orders were entered into a system before the moment of opening of such insolvency proceedings as defined in Article 6(1).

   Where, exceptionally, transfer orders are entered into a system after the moment of opening of insolvency proceedings and are carried out on the day of opening of such proceedings, they shall be legally enforceable and binding on third parties only if, after the time of settlement, the settlement agent, the central counterparty or the clearing house can prove that they were not aware, nor should have been aware, of the opening of such proceedings.

2. No law, regulation, rule or practice on the setting aside of contracts and transactions concluded before the moment of opening of insolvency proceedings, as defined in Article 6(1) shall lead to the unwinding of a netting.
3. The moment of entry of a transfer order into a system shall be defined by the rules of that system. If there are conditions laid down in the national law governing the system as to the moment of entry, the rules of that system must be in accordance with such conditions.

Article 4

Member States may provide that the opening of insolvency proceedings against a participant shall not prevent funds or securities available on the settlement account of that participant from being used to fulfil that participant's obligations in the system on the day of the opening of the insolvency proceedings. Furthermore, Member States may also provide that such a participant's credit facility connected to the system be used against available, existing collateral security to fulfil that participant's obligations in the system.

Article 5

A transfer order may not be revoked by a participant in a system, nor by a third party, from the moment defined by the rules of that system.

Section III : **Provision concerning insolvency proceedings**

Article 6

1. For the purpose of this Directive, the moment of opening of insolvency proceedings shall be the moment when the relevant judicial or administrative authority handed down its decision.
2. When a decision has been taken in accordance with paragraph 1, the relevant judicial or administrative authority shall immediately notify that decision to the appropriate authority chosen by its Member State.
3. The Member State referred to in paragraph 2 shall immediately notify other Member States.

Article 7

Insolvency proceedings shall not have retroactive effects on the rights and obligations of a participant arising from, or in connection with, its participation in a system earlier than the moment of opening of such proceedings as defined in Article 6(1).

Article 8

In the event of insolvency proceedings being opened against a participant in a system, the rights and obligations arising from, or in connection with, the participation of that participant shall be determined by the law governing that system.

Section IV : **Insulation of the rights of holders of collateral security from the effects of the insolvency of the provider.**

Article 9

1. The rights of:
   - a participant to collateral security provided to it in connection with a system, and
   - central banks of the Member States or the future European central bank to collateral security provided to them,

   shall not be affected by insolvency proceedings against the participant or counterparty to central banks of the Member States or the future European central bank which provided the collateral security. Such collateral security may be realised for the satisfaction of these rights.
2. Where securities (including rights in securities) are provided as collateral security to participants and/or central banks of the Member States or the future European central bank as described in paragraph 1, and their right (or that of any nominee, agent or third party acting on their behalf) with respect to the securities is legally recorded on a register, account or centralised deposit system located in a Member State, the determination of the rights of such entities as holders of collateral security in relation to those securities shall be governed by the law of that Member State.

Section V : **Final provisions**

Article 10

Member States shall specify the systems which are to be included in the scope of this Directive and shall notify them to the Commission and inform the Commission of the authorities they have chosen in accordance with Article 6(2).

The system shall indicate to the Member State whose law is applicable the participants in the system, including any possible indirect participants, as well as any change in them.

In addition to the indication provided for in the second subparagraph, Member States may impose supervision or authorisation requirements on systems which fall under their jurisdiction.

Anyone with a legitimate interest may require an institution to inform him of the systems in which it participates and to provide information about the main rules governing the functioning of those systems.

Article 11

1. Member States shall bring into force the laws, regulations and administrative provisions necessary to comply with this Directive before 11 December 1999. They shall forthwith inform the Commission thereof.

   When Member States adopt these measures, they shall contain a reference to this Directive or shall be accompanied by such reference on the occasion of their official publication. The methods of making such a reference shall be laid down by the Member States.
2. Member States shall communicate to the Commission the text of the provisions of domestic law which they adopt in the field governed by this Directive. In this Communication, Member States shall provide a table of correspondence showing the national provisions which exist or are introduced in respect of each Article of this Directive.

Article 12

No later than three years after the date mentioned in Article 11(1), the Commission shall present a report to the European Parliament and the Council on the application of this Directive, accompanied where appropriate by proposals for its revision.

Article 13

This Directive shall enter into force on the day of its publication in the Official Journal of the European Communities.

Article 14

This Directive is addressed to the Member States.

Done at Brussels, 19 May 1998.

For the European Parliament

The President

J.M. GIL-ROBLES

For the Council

The President

G. BROWN

28. Directive 2000/35/EC of the European Parliament and of the Council of 29 June 2000 on combating late payment in commercial transactions

(OJ L 200 , 08/08/2000 p. 35 – 38)

THE EUROPEAN PARLIAMENT AND THE COUNCIL OF THE EUROPEAN UNION,

Having regard to the Treaty establishing the European Community, and in particular Article 95 thereof,

Having regard to the proposal from the Commission[1],

Having regard to the opinion of the Economic and Social Committee[2],

Acting in accordance with the procedure laid down in Article 251 of the Treaty[3], in the light of the joint text approved by the Conciliation Committee on 4 May 2000,

Whereas:

(1) In its resolution on the integrated programme in favour of SMEs and the craft sector[4], the European Parliament urged the Commission to submit proposals to deal with the problem of late payment.

(2) On 12 May 1995 the Commission adopted a recommendation on payment periods in commercial transactions[5].

(3) In its resolution on the Commission recommendation on payment periods in commercial transactions[6], the European Parliament called on the Commission to consider transforming its recommendation into a proposal for a Council directive to be submitted as soon as possible.

(4) On 29 May 1997 the Economic and Social Committee adopted an opinion on the Commission's Green Paper on Public procurement in the European Union: Exploring the way forward[7].

(5) On 4 June 1997 the Commission published an action plan for the single market, which underlined that late payment represents an increasingly serious obstacle for the success of the single market.

(6) On 17 July 1997 the Commission published a report on late payments in commercial transactions[8], summarising the results of an evaluation of the effects of the Commission's recommendation of 12 May 1995.

---

1 OJ C 168, 3.6.1998, p. 13, andOJ C 374, 3.12.1998, p. 4.

2 OJ C 407, 28.12.1998, p. 50.

3 Opinion of the European Parliament of 17 September 1998 (OJ C 313, 12.10.1998, p. 142), Council Common Position of 29 July 1999 (OJ C 284, 6.10.1999, p. 1) and decision of the European Parliament of 16 December 1999 (not yet published in the Official Journal). Decision of the European Parliament of 15 June 2000 and Decision of the Council of 18 May 2000.

4 OJ C 323, 21.11.1994, p. 19.

5 OJ L 127, 10.6.1995, p. 19.

6 OJ C 211, 22.7.1996, p. 43.

7 OJ C 287, 22.9.1997, p. 92.

8 OJ C 216, 17.7.1997, p. 10.

(7) Heavy administrative and financial burdens are placed on businesses, particularly small and medium-sized ones, as a result of excessive payment periods and late payment. Moreover, these problems are a major cause of insolvencies threatening the survival of businesses and result in numerous job losses.

(8) In some Member States contractual payment periods differ significantly from the Community average.

(9) The differences between payment rules and practices in the Member States constitute an obstacle to the proper functioning of the internal market.

(10) This has the effect of considerably limiting commercial transactions between Member States. This is in contradiction with Article 14 of the Treaty as entrepreneurs should be able to trade throughout the internal market under conditions which ensure that transborder operations do not entail greater risks than domestic sales. Distortions of competition would ensue if substantially different rules applied to domestic and transborder operations.

(11) The most recent statistics indicate that there has been, at best, no improvement in late payments in many Member States since the adoption of the recommendation of 12 May 1995.

(12) The objective of combating late payments in the internal market cannot be sufficiently achieved by the Member States acting individually and can, therefore, be better achieved by the Community. This Directive does not go beyond what is necessary to achieve that objective. This Directive complies therefore, in its entirety, with the requirements of the principles of subsidiarity and proportionality as laid down in Article 5 of the Treaty.

(13) This Directive should be limited to payments made as remuneration for commercial transactions and does not regulate transactions with consumers, interest in connection with other payments, e.g. payments under the laws on cheques and bills of exchange, payments made as compensation for damages including payments from insurance companies.

(14) The fact that the liberal professions are covered by this Directive does not mean that Member States have to treat them as undertakings or merchants for purposes not covered by this Directive.

(15) This Directive only defines the term "enforceable title" but does not regulate the various procedures of forced execution of such a title and the conditions under which forced execution of such a title can be stopped or suspended.

(16) Late payment constitutes a breach of contract which has been made financially attractive to debtors in most Member States by low interest rates on late payments and/or slow procedures for redress. A decisive shift, including compensation of creditors for the costs incurred, is necessary to reverse this trend and to ensure that the consequences of late payments are such as to discourage late payment.

(17) The reasonable compensation for the recovery costs has to be considered without prejudice to national provisions according to which a national judge can

award to the creditor any additional damage caused by the debtor's late payment, taking also into account that such incurred costs may be already compensated for by the interest for late payment.

(18) This Directive takes into account the issue of long contractual payment periods and, in particular, the existence of certain categories of contracts where a longer payment period in combination with a restriction of freedom of contract or a higher interest rate can be justified.

(19) This Directive should prohibit abuse of freedom of contract to the disadvantage of the creditor. Where an agreement mainly serves the purpose of procuring the debtor additional liquidity at the expense of the creditor, or where the main contractor imposes on his suppliers and subcontractors terms of payment which are not justified on the grounds of the terms granted to himself, these may be considered to be factors constituting such an abuse. This Directive does not affect national provisions relating to the way contracts are concluded or regulating the validity of contractual terms which are unfair to the debtor.

(20) The consequences of late payment can be dissuasive only if they are accompanied by procedures for redress which are rapid and effective for the creditor. In conformity with the principle of non-discrimination contained in Article 12 of the Treaty, those procedures should be available to all creditors who are established in the Community.

(21) It is desirable to ensure that creditors are in a position to exercise a retention of title on a non-discriminatory basis throughout the Community, if the retention of title clause is valid under the applicable national provisions designated by private international law.

(22) This Directive should regulate all commercial transactions irrespective of whether they are carried out between private or public undertakings or between undertakings and public authorities, having regard to the fact that the latter handle a considerable volume of payments to business. It should therefore also regulate all commercial transactions between main contractors and their suppliers and subcontractors.

(23) Article 5 of this Directive requires that the recovery procedure for unchallenged claims be completed within a short period of time in conformity with national legislation, but does not require Member States to adopt a specific procedure or to amend their existing legal procedures in a specific way,

HAVE ADOPTED THIS DIRECTIVE:

Article 1 Scope

This Directive shall apply to all payments made as remuneration for commercial transactions.

Article 2 Definitions

For the purposes of this Directive:

1. "commercial transactions" means transactions between undertakings or between undertakings and public authorities which lead to the delivery of goods or the provision of services for remuneration,

   "public authority" means any contracting authority or entity, as defined by the Public Procurement Directives (92/50/EEC[1], 93/36/EEC[2], 93/37/EEC[3] and 93/38/EEC[4]),

   "undertaking" means any organisation acting in the course of its independent economic or professional activity, even where it is carried on by a single person;
2. "late payment" means exceeding the contractual or statutory period of payment;
3. "retention of title" means the contractual agreement according to which the seller retains title to the goods in question until the price has been paid in full;
4. "interest rate applied by the European Central Bank to its main refinancing operations" means the interest rate applied to such operations in the case of fixed-rate tenders. In the event that a main refinancing operation was conducted according to a variable-rate tender procedure, this interest rate refers to the marginal interest rate which resulted from that tender. This applies both in the case of single-rate and variable-rate auctions;
5. "enforceable title" means any decision, judgment or order for payment issued by a court or other competent authority, whether for immediate payment or payment by instalments, which permits the creditor to have his claim against the debtor collected by means of forced execution; it shall include a decision, judgment or order for payment that is provisionally enforceable and remains so even if the debtor appeals against it.

Article 3 Interest in case of late payment

1. Member States shall ensure that:
   (a) interest in accordance with point (d) shall become payable from the day following the date or the end of the period for payment fixed in the contract;
   (b) if the date or period for payment is not fixed in the contract, interest shall become payable automatically without the necessity of a reminder:
      (i) 30 days following the date of receipt by the debtor of the invoice or an equivalent request for payment; or
      (ii) if the date of the receipt of the invoice or the equivalent request for payment is uncertain, 30 days after the date of receipt of the goods or services; or

[1] OJ L 209, 24.7.1992, p. 1.
[2] OJ L 199, 9.8.1993, p. 1.
[3] OJ L 199, 9.8.1993, p. 54.
[4] OJ L 199, 9.8.1993, p. 84.

(iii) if the debtor receives the invoice or the equivalent request for payment earlier than the goods or the services, 30 days after the receipt of the goods or services; or

(iv) if a procedure of acceptance or verification, by which the conformity of the goods or services with the contract is to be ascertained, is provided for by statute or in the contract and if the debtor receives the invoice or the equivalent request for payment earlier or on the date on which such acceptance or verification takes place, 30 days after this latter date;

(c) the creditor shall be entitled to interest for late payment to the extent that:

(i) he has fulfilled his contractual and legal obligations; and

(ii) he has not received the amount due on time, unless the debtor is not responsible for the delay;

(d) the level of interest for late payment ("the statutory rate"), which the debtor is obliged to pay, shall be the sum of the interest rate applied by the European Central Bank to its most recent main refinancing operation carried out before the first calendar day of the half-year in question ("the reference rate"), plus at least seven percentage points ("the margin"), unless otherwise specified in the contract. For a Member State which is not participating in the third stage of economic and monetary union, the reference rate referred to above shall be the equivalent rate set by its national central bank. In both cases, the reference rate in force on the first calendar day of the half-year in question shall apply for the following six months;

(e) unless the debtor is not responsible for the delay, the creditor shall be entitled to claim reasonable compensation from the debtor for all relevant recovery costs incurred through the latter's late payment. Such recovery costs shall respect the principles of transparency and proportionality as regards the debt in question. Member States may, while respecting the principles referred to above, fix maximum amounts as regards the recovery costs for different levels of debt.

2. For certain categories of contracts to be defined by national law, Member States may fix the period after which interest becomes payable to a maximum of 60 days provided that they either restrain the parties to the contract from exceeding this period or fix a mandatory interest rate that substantially exceeds the statutory rate.

3. Member States shall provide that an agreement on the date for payment or on the consequences of late payment which is not in line with the provisions of paragraphs 1(b) to (d) and 2 either shall not be enforceable or shall give rise to a claim for damages if, when all circumstances of the case, including good commercial practice and the nature of the product, are considered, it is grossly unfair to the creditor. In determining whether an agreement is grossly unfair to the creditor, it will be taken, inter alia, into account whether the debtor has any objective reason to deviate from the provisions of paragraphs 1(b) to (d) and 2. If such an agreement is determined to be grossly unfair, the statutory terms will apply, unless the national courts determine different conditions which are fair.

4. Member States shall ensure that, in the interests of creditors and of competitors, adequate and effective means exist to prevent the continued use of terms which are grossly unfair within the meaning of paragraph 3.
5. The means referred to in paragraph 4 shall include provisions whereby organisations officially recognised as, or having a legitimate interest in, representing small and medium-sized enterprises may take action according to the national law concerned before the courts or before competent administrative bodies on the grounds that contractual terms drawn up for general use are grossly unfair within the meaning of paragraph 3, so that they can apply appropriate and effective means to prevent the continued use of such terms.

Article 4 Retention of title

1. Member States shall provide in conformity with the applicable national provisions designated by private international law that the seller retains title to goods until they are fully paid for if a retention of title clause has been expressly agreed between the buyer and the seller before the delivery of the goods.
2. Member States may adopt or retain provisions dealing with down payments already made by the debtor.

Article 5 Recovery procedures for unchallenged claims

1. Member States shall ensure that an enforceable title can be obtained, irrespective of the amount of the debt, normally within 90 calendar days of the lodging of the creditor's action or application at the court or other competent authority, provided that the debt or aspects of the procedure are not disputed. This duty shall be carried out by Member States in conformity with their respective national legislation, regulations and administrative provisions.
2. The respective national legislation, regulations and administrative provisions shall apply the same conditions for all creditors who are established in the European Community.
3. The 90 calendar day period referred to in paragraph 1 shall not include the following:
   (a) periods for service of documents;
   (b) any delays caused by the creditor, such as periods devoted to correcting applications.
4. This Article shall be without prejudice to the provisions of the Brussels Convention on jurisdiction and enforcement of judgments in civil and commercial matters(13).

Article 6 Transposition

1. Member States shall bring into force the laws, regulations and administrative provisions necessary to comply with this Directive before 8 August 2002. They shall forthwith inform the Commission thereof.

When Member States adopt these measures, they shall contain a reference to this Directive or shall be accompanied by such reference on the occasion of their official publication. The methods of making such reference shall be laid down by Member States.

2. Member States may maintain or bring into force provisions which are more favourable to the creditor than the provisions necessary to comply with this Directive.
3. In transposing this Directive, Member States may exclude:
   (a) debts that are subject to insolvency proceedings instituted against the debtor;
   (b) contracts that have been concluded prior to 8 August 2002; and
   (c) claims for interest of less than EUR 5.
4. Member States shall communicate to the Commission the text of the main provisions of national law which they adopt in the field covered by this Directive.
5. The Commission shall undertake two years after 8 August 2002 a review of, inter alia, the statutory rate, contractual payment periods and late payments, to assess the impact on commercial transactions and the operation of the legislation in practice. The results of this review and of other reviews will be made known to the European Parliament and the Council, accompanied where appropriate by proposals for improvement of this Directive.

Article 7 Entry into force

This Directive shall enter into force on the day of its publication in the Official Journal of the European Communities.

Article 8 Addressees

This Directive is addressed to the Member States.

Done at Luxembourg, 29 June 2000.

For the European Parliament

The President

N. Fontaine

For the Council

The President

M. Marques da Costa

29. Council Regulation (EC) No 44/2001 of 22 December 2000 on jurisdiction and the recognition and enforcement of judgments in civil and commercial matters (Brussels I)

(OJ L 012 , 16/01/2001 p. 1 – 23)

THE COUNCIL OF THE EUROPEAN UNION,

Having regard to the Treaty establishing the European Community, and in particular Article 61(c) and Article 67(1) thereof,

Having regard to the proposal from the Commission[1],

Having regard to the opinion of the European Parliament[2],

Having regard to the opinion of the Economic and Social Committee[3],

Whereas:

(1) The Community has set itself the objective of maintaining and developing an area of freedom, security and justice, in which the free movement of persons is ensured. In order to establish progressively such an area, the Community should adopt, amongst other things, the measures relating to judicial cooperation in civil matters which are necessary for the sound operation of the internal market.

(2) Certain differences between national rules governing jurisdiction and recognition of judgments hamper the sound operation of the internal market. Provisions to unify the rules of conflict of jurisdiction in civil and commercial matters and to simplify the formalities with a view to rapid and simple recognition and enforcement of judgments from Member States bound by this Regulation are essential.

(3) This area is within the field of judicial cooperation in civil matters within the meaning of Article 65 of the Treaty.

(4) In accordance with the principles of subsidiarity and proportionality as set out in Article 5 of the Treaty, the objectives of this Regulation cannot be sufficiently achieved by the Member States and can therefore be better achieved by the Community. This Regulation confines itself to the minimum required in order to achieve those objectives and does not go beyond what is necessary for that purpose.

(5) On 27 September 1968 the Member States, acting under Article 293, fourth indent, of the Treaty, concluded the Brussels Convention on Jurisdiction and the Enforcement of Judgments in Civil and Commercial Matters, as amended by Conventions on the Accession of the New Member States to that Convention (hereinafter referred to as the "Brussels Convention")[4]. On 16 September 1988

1 OJ C 376, 28.12.1999, p. 1.

2 Opinion delivered on 21 September 2000 (not yet published in the Official Journal).

3 OJ C 117, 26.4.2000, p. 6.

4 OJ L 299, 31.12.1972, p. 32.
OJ L 304, 30.10.1978, p. 1.

Member States and EFTA States concluded the Lugano Convention on Jurisdiction and the Enforcement of Judgments in Civil and Commercial Matters, which is a parallel Convention to the 1968 Brussels Convention. Work has been undertaken for the revision of those Conventions, and the Council has approved the content of the revised texts. Continuity in the results achieved in that revision should be ensured.

(6) In order to attain the objective of free movement of judgments in civil and commercial matters, it is necessary and appropriate that the rules governing jurisdiction and the recognition and enforcement of judgments be governed by a Community legal instrument which is binding and directly applicable.

(7) The scope of this Regulation must cover all the main civil and commercial matters apart from certain well-defined matters.

(8) There must be a link between proceedings to which this Regulation applies and the territory of the Member States bound by this Regulation. Accordingly common rules on jurisdiction should, in principle, apply when the defendant is domiciled in one of those Member States.

(9) A defendant not domiciled in a Member State is in general subject to national rules of jurisdiction applicable in the territory of the Member State of the court seised, and a defendant domiciled in a Member State not bound by this Regulation must remain subject to the Brussels Convention.

(10) For the purposes of the free movement of judgments, judgments given in a Member State bound by this Regulation should be recognised and enforced in another Member State bound by this Regulation, even if the judgment debtor is domiciled in a third State.

(11) The rules of jurisdiction must be highly predictable and founded on the principle that jurisdiction is generally based on the defendant's domicile and jurisdiction must always be available on this ground save in a few well-defined situations in which the subject-matter of the litigation or the autonomy of the parties warrants a different linking factor. The domicile of a legal person must be defined autonomously so as to make the common rules more transparent and avoid conflicts of jurisdiction.

(12) In addition to the defendant's domicile, there should be alternative grounds of jurisdiction based on a close link between the court and the action or in order to facilitate the sound administration of justice.

(13) In relation to insurance, consumer contracts and employment, the weaker party should be protected by rules of jurisdiction more favourable to his interests than the general rules provide for.

(14) The autonomy of the parties to a contract, other than an insurance, consumer or employment contract, where only limited autonomy to determine the courts

---

OJ L 388, 31.12.1982, p. 1.
OJ L 285, 3.10.1989, p. 1.
OJ C 15, 15.1.1997, p. 1.
For a consolidated text, see OJ C 27, 26.1.1998, p. 1.

having jurisdiction is allowed, must be respected subject to the exclusive grounds of jurisdiction laid down in this Regulation.

(15) In the interests of the harmonious administration of justice it is necessary to minimise the possibility of concurrent proceedings and to ensure that irreconcilable judgments will not be given in two Member States. There must be a clear and effective mechanism for resolving cases of lis pendens and related actions and for obviating problems flowing from national differences as to the determination of the time when a case is regarded as pending. For the purposes of this Regulation that time should be defined autonomously.

(16) Mutual trust in the administration of justice in the Community justifies judgments given in a Member State being recognised automatically without the need for any procedure except in cases of dispute.

(17) By virtue of the same principle of mutual trust, the procedure for making enforceable in one Member State a judgment given in another must be efficient and rapid. To that end, the declaration that a judgment is enforceable should be issued virtually automatically after purely formal checks of the documents supplied, without there being any possibility for the court to raise of its own motion any of the grounds for non-enforcement provided for by this Regulation.

(18) However, respect for the rights of the defence means that the defendant should be able to appeal in an adversarial procedure, against the declaration of enforceability, if he considers one of the grounds for non-enforcement to be present. Redress procedures should also be available to the claimant where his application for a declaration of enforceability has been rejected.

(19) Continuity between the Brussels Convention and this Regulation should be ensured, and transitional provisions should be laid down to that end. The same need for continuity applies as regards the interpretation of the Brussels Convention by the Court of Justice of the European Communities and the 1971 Protocol[1] should remain applicable also to cases already pending when this Regulation enters into force.

(20) The United Kingdom and Ireland, in accordance with Article 3 of the Protocol on the position of the United Kingdom and Ireland annexed to the Treaty on European Union and to the Treaty establishing the European Community, have given notice of their wish to take part in the adoption and application of this Regulation.

(21) Denmark, in accordance with Articles 1 and 2 of the Protocol on the position of Denmark annexed to the Treaty on European Union and to the Treaty establishing the European Community, is not participating in the adoption of this Regulation, and is therefore not bound by it nor subject to its application.

---

[1] OJ L 204, 2.8.1975, p. 28.
OJ L 304, 30.10.1978, p. 1.
OJ L 388, 31.12.1982, p. 1.
OJ L 285, 3.10.1989, p. 1.
OJ C 15, 15.1.1997, p. 1.

(22) Since the Brussels Convention remains in force in relations between Denmark and the Member States that are bound by this Regulation, both the Convention and the 1971 Protocol continue to apply between Denmark and the Member States bound by this Regulation.

(23) The Brussels Convention also continues to apply to the territories of the Member States which fall within the territorial scope of that Convention and which are excluded from this Regulation pursuant to Article 299 of the Treaty.

(24) Likewise for the sake of consistency, this Regulation should not affect rules governing jurisdiction and the recognition of judgments contained in specific Community instruments.

(25) Respect for international commitments entered into by the Member States means that this Regulation should not affect conventions relating to specific matters to which the Member States are parties.

(26) The necessary flexibility should be provided for in the basic rules of this Regulation in order to take account of the specific procedural rules of certain Member States. Certain provisions of the Protocol annexed to the Brussels Convention should accordingly be incorporated in this Regulation.

(27) In order to allow a harmonious transition in certain areas which were the subject of special provisions in the Protocol annexed to the Brussels Convention, this Regulation lays down, for a transitional period, provisions taking into consideration the specific situation in certain Member States.

(28) No later than five years after entry into force of this Regulation the Commission will present a report on its application and, if need be, submit proposals for adaptations.

(29) The Commission will have to adjust Annexes I to IV on the rules of national jurisdiction, the courts or competent authorities and redress procedures available on the basis of the amendments forwarded by the Member State concerned; amendments made to Annexes V and VI should be adopted in accordance with Council Decision 1999/468/EC of 28 June 1999 laying down the procedures for the exercise of implementing powers conferred on the Commission[1],

HAS ADOPTED THIS REGULATION:

CHAPTER I : SCOPE

Article 1

1. This Regulation shall apply in civil and commercial matters whatever the nature of the court or tribunal. It shall not extend, in particular, to revenue, customs or administrative matters.
2. The Regulation shall not apply to:

[1] OJ L 184, 17.7.1999, p. 23.

(a) the status or legal capacity of natural persons, rights in property arising out of a matrimonial relationship, wills and succession;
(b) bankruptcy, proceedings relating to the winding-up of insolvent companies or other legal persons, judicial arrangements, compositions and analogous proceedings;
(c) social security;
(d) arbitration.

3. In this Regulation, the term "Member State" shall mean Member States with the exception of Denmark.

CHAPTER II : JURISDICTION

Section 1 : **General provisions**

Article 2

1. Subject to this Regulation, persons domiciled in a Member State shall, whatever their nationality, be sued in the courts of that Member State.
2. Persons who are not nationals of the Member State in which they are domiciled shall be governed by the rules of jurisdiction applicable to nationals of that State.

Article 3

1. Persons domiciled in a Member State may be sued in the courts of another Member State only by virtue of the rules set out in Sections 2 to 7 of this Chapter.
2. In particular the rules of national jurisdiction set out in Annex I shall not be applicable as against them.

Article 4

1. If the defendant is not domiciled in a Member State, the jurisdiction of the courts of each Member State shall, subject to Articles 22 and 23, be determined by the law of that Member State.
2. As against such a defendant, any person domiciled in a Member State may, whatever his nationality, avail himself in that State of the rules of jurisdiction there in force, and in particular those specified in Annex I, in the same way as the nationals of that State.

Section 2 : **Special jurisdiction**

Article 5

A person domiciled in a Member State may, in another Member State, be sued:

1.(a) in matters relating to a contract, in the courts for the place of performance of the obligation in question;
(b) for the purpose of this provision and unless otherwise agreed, the place of performance of the obligation in question shall be:

- in the case of the sale of goods, the place in a Member State where, under the contract, the goods were delivered or should have been delivered,
- in the case of the provision of services, the place in a Member State where, under the contract, the services were provided or should have been provided,

(c) if subparagraph (b) does not apply then subparagraph (a) applies;

2. in matters relating to maintenance, in the courts for the place where the maintenance creditor is domiciled or habitually resident or, if the matter is ancillary to proceedings concerning the status of a person, in the court which, according to its own law, has jurisdiction to entertain those proceedings, unless that jurisdiction is based solely on the nationality of one of the parties;
3. in matters relating to tort, delict or quasi-delict, in the courts for the place where the harmful event occurred or may occur;
4. as regards a civil claim for damages or restitution which is based on an act giving rise to criminal proceedings, in the court seised of those proceedings, to the extent that that court has jurisdiction under its own law to entertain civil proceedings;
5. as regards a dispute arising out of the operations of a branch, agency or other establishment, in the courts for the place in which the branch, agency or other establishment is situated;
6. as settlor, trustee or beneficiary of a trust created by the operation of a statute, or by a written instrument, or created orally and evidenced in writing, in the courts of the Member State in which the trust is domiciled;
7. as regards a dispute concerning the payment of remuneration claimed in respect of the salvage of a cargo or freight, in the court under the authority of which the cargo or freight in question:
   (a) has been arrested to secure such payment, or
   (b) could have been so arrested, but bail or other security has been given;
   provided that this provision shall apply only if it is claimed that the defendant has an interest in the cargo or freight or had such an interest at the time of salvage.

Article 6

A person domiciled in a Member State may also be sued:

1. where he is one of a number of defendants, in the courts for the place where any one of them is domiciled, provided the claims are so closely connected that it is expedient to hear and determine them together to avoid the risk of irreconcilable judgments resulting from separate proceedings;
2. as a third party in an action on a warranty or guarantee or in any other third party proceedings, in the court seised of the original proceedings, unless these were instituted solely with the object of removing him from the jurisdiction of the court which would be competent in his case;

3. on a counter-claim arising from the same contract or facts on which the original claim was based, in the court in which the original claim is pending;
4. in matters relating to a contract, if the action may be combined with an action against the same defendant in matters relating to rights in rem in immovable property, in the court of the Member State in which the property is situated.

Article 7

Where by virtue of this Regulation a court of a Member State has jurisdiction in actions relating to liability from the use or operation of a ship, that court, or any other court substituted for this purpose by the internal law of that Member State, shall also have jurisdiction over claims for limitation of such liability.

Section 3 : **Jurisdiction in matters relating to insurance**

Article 8

In matters relating to insurance, jurisdiction shall be determined by this Section, without prejudice to Article 4 and point 5 of Article 5.

Article 9

1. An insurer domiciled in a Member State may be sued:
   (a) in the courts of the Member State where he is domiciled, or
   (b) in another Member State, in the case of actions brought by the policyholder, the insured or a beneficiary, in the courts for the place where the plaintiff is domiciled,
   (c) if he is a co-insurer, in the courts of a Member State in which proceedings are brought against the leading insurer.
2. An insurer who is not domiciled in a Member State but has a branch, agency or other establishment in one of the Member States shall, in disputes arising out of the operations of the branch, agency or establishment, be deemed to be domiciled in that Member State.

Article 10

In respect of liability insurance or insurance of immovable property, the insurer may in addition be sued in the courts for the place where the harmful event occurred. The same applies if movable and immovable property are covered by the same insurance policy and both are adversely affected by the same contingency.

Article 11

1. In respect of liability insurance, the insurer may also, if the law of the court permits it, be joined in proceedings which the injured party has brought against the insured.
2. Articles 8, 9 and 10 shall apply to actions brought by the injured party directly against the insurer, where such direct actions are permitted.

3. If the law governing such direct actions provides that the policyholder or the insured may be joined as a party to the action, the same court shall have jurisdiction over them.

Article 12

1. Without prejudice to Article 11(3), an insurer may bring proceedings only in the courts of the Member State in which the defendant is domiciled, irrespective of whether he is the policyholder, the insured or a beneficiary.
2. The provisions of this Section shall not affect the right to bring a counter-claim in the court in which, in accordance with this Section, the original claim is pending.

Article 13

The provisions of this Section may be departed from only by an agreement:

1. which is entered into after the dispute has arisen, or
2. which allows the policyholder, the insured or a beneficiary to bring proceedings in courts other than those indicated in this Section, or
3. which is concluded between a policyholder and an insurer, both of whom are at the time of conclusion of the contract domiciled or habitually resident in the same Member State, and which has the effect of conferring jurisdiction on the courts of that State even if the harmful event were to occur abroad, provided that such an agreement is not contrary to the law of that State, or
4. which is concluded with a policyholder who is not domiciled in a Member State, except in so far as the insurance is compulsory or relates to immovable property in a Member State, or
5. which relates to a contract of insurance in so far as it covers one or more of the risks set out in Article 14.

Article 14

The following are the risks referred to in Article 13(5):

1. any loss of or damage to:
   (a) seagoing ships, installations situated offshore or on the high seas, or aircraft, arising from perils which relate to their use for commercial purposes;
   (b) goods in transit other than passengers' baggage where the transit consists of or includes carriage by such ships or aircraft;
2. any liability, other than for bodily injury to passengers or loss of or damage to their baggage:
   (a) arising out of the use or operation of ships, installations or aircraft as referred to in point 1(a) in so far as, in respect of the latter, the law of the Member State in which such aircraft are registered does not prohibit agreements on jurisdiction regarding insurance of such risks;
   (b) for loss or damage caused by goods in transit as described in point 1(b);

3. any financial loss connected with the use or operation of ships, installations or aircraft as referred to in point 1(a), in particular loss of freight or charter-hire;
4. any risk or interest connected with any of those referred to in points 1 to 3;
5. notwithstanding points 1 to 4, all "large risks" as defined in Council Directive 73/239/EEC[1], as amended by Council Directives 88/357/EEC[2] and 90/618/EEC[3], as they may be amended.

Section 4 : **Jurisdiction over consumer contracts**

Article 15

1. In matters relating to a contract concluded by a person, the consumer, for a purpose which can be regarded as being outside his trade or profession, jurisdiction shall be determined by this Section, without prejudice to Article 4 and point 5 of Article 5, if:
   (a) it is a contract for the sale of goods on instalment credit terms; or
   (b) it is a contract for a loan repayable by instalments, or for any other form of credit, made to finance the sale of goods; or
   (c) in all other cases, the contract has been concluded with a person who pursues commercial or professional activities in the Member State of the consumer's domicile or, by any means, directs such activities to that Member State or to several States including that Member State, and the contract falls within the scope of such activities.
2. Where a consumer enters into a contract with a party who is not domiciled in the Member State but has a branch, agency or other establishment in one of the Member States, that party shall, in disputes arising out of the operations of the branch, agency or establishment, be deemed to be domiciled in that State.
3. This Section shall not apply to a contract of transport other than a contract which, for an inclusive price, provides for a combination of travel and accommodation.

Article 16

1. A consumer may bring proceedings against the other party to a contract either in the courts of the Member State in which that party is domiciled or in the courts for the place where the consumer is domiciled.
2. Proceedings may be brought against a consumer by the other party to the contract only in the courts of the Member State in which the consumer is domiciled.
3. This Article shall not affect the right to bring a counter-claim in the court in which, in accordance with this Section, the original claim is pending.

---

1 OJ L 228, 16.8.1973, p. 3. Directive as last amended by Directive 2000/26/EC of the European Parliament and of the Council (OJ L 181, 20.7.2000, p. 65).

2 OJ L 172, 4.7.1988, p. 1. Directive as last amended by Directive 2000/26/EC.

3 OJ L 330, 29.11.1990, p. 44.

Article 17

The provisions of this Section may be departed from only by an agreement:

1. which is entered into after the dispute has arisen; or
2. which allows the consumer to bring proceedings in courts other than those indicated in this Section; or
3. which is entered into by the consumer and the other party to the contract, both of whom are at the time of conclusion of the contract domiciled or habitually resident in the same Member State, and which confers jurisdiction on the courts of that Member State, provided that such an agreement is not contrary to the law of that Member State.

Section 5 : **Jurisdiction over individual contracts of employment**

Article 18

1. In matters relating to individual contracts of employment, jurisdiction shall be determined by this Section, without prejudice to Article 4 and point 5 of Article 5.
2. Where an employee enters into an individual contract of employment with an employer who is not domiciled in a Member State but has a branch, agency or other establishment in one of the Member States, the employer shall, in disputes arising out of the operations of the branch, agency or establishment, be deemed to be domiciled in that Member State.

Article 19

An employer domiciled in a Member State may be sued:

1. in the courts of the Member State where he is domiciled; or
2. in another Member State:
   (a) in the courts for the place where the employee habitually carries out his work or in the courts for the last place where he did so, or
   (b) if the employee does not or did not habitually carry out his work in any one country, in the courts for the place where the business which engaged the employee is or was situated.

Article 20

1. An employer may bring proceedings only in the courts of the Member State in which the employee is domiciled.
2. The provisions of this Section shall not affect the right to bring a counter-claim in the court in which, in accordance with this Section, the original claim is pending.

Article 21

The provisions of this Section may be departed from only by an agreement on jurisdiction:

1. which is entered into after the dispute has arisen; or
2. which allows the employee to bring proceedings in courts other than those indicated in this Section.

Section 6 : **Exclusive jurisdiction**

Article 22

The following courts shall have exclusive jurisdiction, regardless of domicile:

1. in proceedings which have as their object rights in rem in immovable property or tenancies of immovable property, the courts of the Member State in which the property is situated.

   However, in proceedings which have as their object tenancies of immovable property concluded for temporary private use for a maximum period of six consecutive months, the courts of the Member State in which the defendant is domiciled shall also have jurisdiction, provided that the tenant is a natural person and that the landlord and the tenant are domiciled in the same Member State;
2. in proceedings which have as their object the validity of the constitution, the nullity or the dissolution of companies or other legal persons or associations of natural or legal persons, or of the validity of the decisions of their organs, the courts of the Member State in which the company, legal person or association has its seat. In order to determine that seat, the court shall apply its rules of private international law;
3. in proceedings which have as their object the validity of entries in public registers, the courts of the Member State in which the register is kept;
4. in proceedings concerned with the registration or validity of patents, trade marks, designs, or other similar rights required to be deposited or registered, the courts of the Member State in which the deposit or registration has been applied for, has taken place or is under the terms of a Community instrument or an international convention deemed to have taken place.

   Without prejudice to the jurisdiction of the European Patent Office under the Convention on the Grant of European Patents, signed at Munich on 5 October 1973, the courts of each Member State shall have exclusive jurisdiction, regardless of domicile, in proceedings concerned with the registration or validity of any European patent granted for that State;
5. in proceedings concerned with the enforcement of judgments, the courts of the Member State in which the judgment has been or is to be enforced.

Section 7 : **Prorogation of jurisdiction**

Article 23

1. If the parties, one or more of whom is domiciled in a Member State, have agreed that a court or the courts of a Member State are to have jurisdiction to settle any disputes which have arisen or which may arise in connection with a particular

legal relationship, that court or those courts shall have jurisdiction. Such jurisdiction shall be exclusive unless the parties have agreed otherwise. Such an agreement conferring jurisdiction shall be either:

(a) in writing or evidenced in writing; or
(b) in a form which accords with practices which the parties have established between themselves; or
(c) in international trade or commerce, in a form which accords with a usage of which the parties are or ought to have been aware and which in such trade or commerce is widely known to, and regularly observed by, parties to contracts of the type involved in the particular trade or commerce concerned.

2. Any communication by electronic means which provides a durable record of the agreement shall be equivalent to "writing".
3. Where such an agreement is concluded by parties, none of whom is domiciled in a Member State, the courts of other Member States shall have no jurisdiction over their disputes unless the court or courts chosen have declined jurisdiction.
4. The court or courts of a Member State on which a trust instrument has conferred jurisdiction shall have exclusive jurisdiction in any proceedings brought against a settlor, trustee or beneficiary, if relations between these persons or their rights or obligations under the trust are involved.
5. Agreements or provisions of a trust instrument conferring jurisdiction shall have no legal force if they are contrary to Articles 13, 17 or 21, or if the courts whose jurisdiction they purport to exclude have exclusive jurisdiction by virtue of Article 22.

Article 24

Apart from jurisdiction derived from other provisions of this Regulation, a court of a Member State before which a defendant enters an appearance shall have jurisdiction. This rule shall not apply where appearance was entered to contest the jurisdiction, or where another court has exclusive jurisdiction by virtue of Article 22.

Section 8 : **Examination as to jurisdiction and admissibility**

Article 25

Where a court of a Member State is seised of a claim which is principally concerned with a matter over which the courts of another Member State have exclusive jurisdiction by virtue of Article 22, it shall declare of its own motion that it has no jurisdiction.

Article 26

1. Where a defendant domiciled in one Member State is sued in a court of another Member State and does not enter an appearance, the court shall declare of its

own motion that it has no jurisdiction unless its jurisdiction is derived from the provisions of this Regulation.

2. The court shall stay the proceedings so long as it is not shown that the defendant has been able to receive the document instituting the proceedings or an equivalent document in sufficient time to enable him to arrange for his defence, or that all necessary steps have been taken to this end.
3. Article 19 of Council Regulation (EC) No 1348/2000 of 29 May 2000 on the service in the Member States of judicial and extrajudicial documents in civil or commercial matters[1] shall apply instead of the provisions of paragraph 2 if the document instituting the proceedings or an equivalent document had to be transmitted from one Member State to another pursuant to this Regulation.
4. Where the provisions of Regulation (EC) No 1348/2000 are not applicable, Article 15 of the Hague Convention of 15 November 1965 on the Service Abroad of Judicial and Extrajudicial Documents in Civil or Commercial Matters shall apply if the document instituting the proceedings or an equivalent document had to be transmitted pursuant to that Convention.

Section 9 : **Lis pendens - related actions**

Article 27

1. Where proceedings involving the same cause of action and between the same parties are brought in the courts of different Member States, any court other than the court first seised shall of its own motion stay its proceedings until such time as the jurisdiction of the court first seised is established.
2. Where the jurisdiction of the court first seised is established, any court other than the court first seised shall decline jurisdiction in favour of that court.

Article 28

1. Where related actions are pending in the courts of different Member States, any court other than the court first seised may stay its proceedings.
2. Where these actions are pending at first instance, any court other than the court first seised may also, on the application of one of the parties, decline jurisdiction if the court first seised has jurisdiction over the actions in question and its law permits the consolidation thereof.
3. For the purposes of this Article, actions are deemed to be related where they are so closely connected that it is expedient to hear and determine them together to avoid the risk of irreconcilable judgments resulting from separate proceedings.

Article 29

Where actions come within the exclusive jurisdiction of several courts, any court other than the court first seised shall decline jurisdiction in favour of that court.

[1] OJ L 160, 30.6.2000, p. 37.

Article 30

For the purposes of this Section, a court shall be deemed to be seised:

1. at the time when the document instituting the proceedings or an equivalent document is lodged with the court, provided that the plaintiff has not subsequently failed to take the steps he was required to take to have service effected on the defendant, or
2. if the document has to be served before being lodged with the court, at the time when it is received by the authority responsible for service, provided that the plaintiff has not subsequently failed to take the steps he was required to take to have the document lodged with the court.

Section 10 : **Provisional, including protective, measures**

Article 31

Application may be made to the courts of a Member State for such provisional, including protective, measures as may be available under the law of that State, even if, under this Regulation, the courts of another Member State have jurisdiction as to the substance of the matter.

CHAPTER III : RECOGNITION AND ENFORCEMENT

Article 32

For the purposes of this Regulation, "judgment" means any judgment given by a court or tribunal of a Member State, whatever the judgment may be called, including a decree, order, decision or writ of execution, as well as the determination of costs or expenses by an officer of the court.

Section 1 : **Recognition**

Article 33

1. A judgment given in a Member State shall be recognised in the other Member States without any special procedure being required.
2. Any interested party who raises the recognition of a judgment as the principal issue in a dispute may, in accordance with the procedures provided for in Sections 2 and 3 of this Chapter, apply for a decision that the judgment be recognised.
3. If the outcome of proceedings in a court of a Member State depends on the determination of an incidental question of recognition that court shall have jurisdiction over that question.

Article 34

A judgment shall not be recognised:

1. if such recognition is manifestly contrary to public policy in the Member State in which recognition is sought;

2. where it was given in default of appearance, if the defendant was not served with the document which instituted the proceedings or with an equivalent document in sufficient time and in such a way as to enable him to arrange for his defence, unless the defendant failed to commence proceedings to challenge the judgment when it was possible for him to do so;
3. if it is irreconcilable with a judgment given in a dispute between the same parties in the Member State in which recognition is sought;
4. if it is irreconcilable with an earlier judgment given in another Member State or in a third State involving the same cause of action and between the same parties, provided that the earlier judgment fulfils the conditions necessary for its recognition in the Member State addressed.

Article 35

1. Moreover, a judgment shall not be recognised if it conflicts with Sections 3, 4 or 6 of Chapter II, or in a case provided for in Article 72.
2. In its examination of the grounds of jurisdiction referred to in the foregoing paragraph, the court or authority applied to shall be bound by the findings of fact on which the court of the Member State of origin based its jurisdiction.
3. Subject to the paragraph 1, the jurisdiction of the court of the Member State of origin may not be reviewed. The test of public policy referred to in point 1 of Article 34 may not be applied to the rules relating to jurisdiction.

Article 36

Under no circumstances may a foreign judgment be reviewed as to its substance.

Article 37

1. A court of a Member State in which recognition is sought of a judgment given in another Member State may stay the proceedings if an ordinary appeal against the judgment has been lodged.
2. A court of a Member State in which recognition is sought of a judgment given in Ireland or the United Kingdom may stay the proceedings if enforcement is suspended in the State of origin, by reason of an appeal.

Section 2 : **Enforcement**

Article 38

1. A judgment given in a Member State and enforceable in that State shall be enforced in another Member State when, on the application of any interested party, it has been declared enforceable there.
2. However, in the United Kingdom, such a judgment shall be enforced in England and Wales, in Scotland, or in Northern Ireland when, on the application of any interested party, it has been registered for enforcement in that part of the United Kingdom.

Article 39

1. The application shall be submitted to the court or competent authority indicated in the list in Annex II.
2. The local jurisdiction shall be determined by reference to the place of domicile of the party against whom enforcement is sought, or to the place of enforcement.

Article 40

1. The procedure for making the application shall be governed by the law of the Member State in which enforcement is sought.
2. The applicant must give an address for service of process within the area of jurisdiction of the court applied to. However, if the law of the Member State in which enforcement is sought does not provide for the furnishing of such an address, the applicant shall appoint a representative ad litem.
3. The documents referred to in Article 53 shall be attached to the application.

Article 41

The judgment shall be declared enforceable immediately on completion of the formalities in Article 53 without any review under Articles 34 and 35. The party against whom enforcement is sought shall not at this stage of the proceedings be entitled to make any submissions on the application.

Article 42

1. The decision on the application for a declaration of enforceability shall forthwith be brought to the notice of the applicant in accordance with the procedure laid down by the law of the Member State in which enforcement is sought.
2. The declaration of enforceability shall be served on the party against whom enforcement is sought, accompanied by the judgment, if not already served on that party.

Article 43

1. The decision on the application for a declaration of enforceability may be appealed against by either party.
2. The appeal is to be lodged with the court indicated in the list in Annex III.
3. The appeal shall be dealt with in accordance with the rules governing procedure in contradictory matters.
4. If the party against whom enforcement is sought fails to appear before the appellate court in proceedings concerning an appeal brought by the applicant, Article 26(2) to (4) shall apply even where the party against whom enforcement is sought is not domiciled in any of the Member States.
5. An appeal against the declaration of enforceability is to be lodged within one month of service thereof. If the party against whom enforcement is sought is domiciled in a Member State other than that in which the declaration of enforceability was given, the time for appealing shall be two months and shall

run from the date of service, either on him in person or at his residence. No extension of time may be granted on account of distance.

Article 44

The judgment given on the appeal may be contested only by the appeal referred to in Annex IV.

Article 45

1. The court with which an appeal is lodged under Article 43 or Article 44 shall refuse or revoke a declaration of enforceability only on one of the grounds specified in Articles 34 and 35. It shall give its decision without delay.
2. Under no circumstances may the foreign judgment be reviewed as to its substance.

Article 46

1. The court with which an appeal is lodged under Article 43 or Article 44 may, on the application of the party against whom enforcement is sought, stay the proceedings if an ordinary appeal has been lodged against the judgment in the Member State of origin or if the time for such an appeal has not yet expired; in the latter case, the court may specify the time within which such an appeal is to be lodged.
2. Where the judgment was given in Ireland or the United Kingdom, any form of appeal available in the Member State of origin shall be treated as an ordinary appeal for the purposes of paragraph 1.
3. The court may also make enforcement conditional on the provision of such security as it shall determine.

Article 47

1. When a judgment must be recognised in accordance with this Regulation, nothing shall prevent the applicant from availing himself of provisional, including protective, measures in accordance with the law of the Member State requested without a declaration of enforceability under Article 41 being required.
2. The declaration of enforceability shall carry with it the power to proceed to any protective measures.
3. During the time specified for an appeal pursuant to Article 43(5) against the declaration of enforceability and until any such appeal has been determined, no measures of enforcement may be taken other than protective measures against the property of the party against whom enforcement is sought.

Article 48

1. Where a foreign judgment has been given in respect of several matters and the declaration of enforceability cannot be given for all of them, the court or competent authority shall give it for one or more of them.

2. An applicant may request a declaration of enforceability limited to parts of a judgment.

Article 49

A foreign judgment which orders a periodic payment by way of a penalty shall be enforceable in the Member State in which enforcement is sought only if the amount of the payment has been finally determined by the courts of the Member State of origin.

Article 50

An applicant who, in the Member State of origin has benefited from complete or partial legal aid or exemption from costs or expenses, shall be entitled, in the procedure provided for in this Section, to benefit from the most favourable legal aid or the most extensive exemption from costs or expenses provided for by the law of the Member State addressed.

Article 51

No security, bond or deposit, however described, shall be required of a party who in one Member State applies for enforcement of a judgment given in another Member State on the ground that he is a foreign national or that he is not domiciled or resident in the State in which enforcement is sought.

Article 52

In proceedings for the issue of a declaration of enforceability, no charge, duty or fee calculated by reference to the value of the matter at issue may be levied in the Member State in which enforcement is sought.

Section 3 : **Common provisions**

Article 53

1. A party seeking recognition or applying for a declaration of enforceability shall produce a copy of the judgment which satisfies the conditions necessary to establish its authenticity.
2. A party applying for a declaration of enforceability shall also produce the certificate referred to in Article 54, without prejudice to Article 55.

Article 54

The court or competent authority of a Member State where a judgment was given shall issue, at the request of any interested party, a certificate using the standard form in Annex V to this Regulation.

Article 55

1. If the certificate referred to in Article 54 is not produced, the court or competent authority may specify a time for its production or accept an equivalent document

or, if it considers that it has sufficient information before it, dispense with its production.

2. If the court or competent authority so requires, a translation of the documents shall be produced. The translation shall be certified by a person qualified to do so in one of the Member States.

Article 56

No legalisation or other similar formality shall be required in respect of the documents referred to in Article 53 or Article 55(2), or in respect of a document appointing a representative ad litem.

CHAPTER IV : AUTHENTIC INSTRUMENTS AND COURT SETTLEMENTS

Article 57

1. A document which has been formally drawn up or registered as an authentic instrument and is enforceable in one Member State shall, in another Member State, be declared enforceable there, on application made in accordance with the procedures provided for in Articles 38, et seq. The court with which an appeal is lodged under Article 43 or Article 44 shall refuse or revoke a declaration of enforceability only if enforcement of the instrument is manifestly contrary to public policy in the Member State addressed.
2. Arrangements relating to maintenance obligations concluded with administrative authorities or authenticated by them shall also be regarded as authentic instruments within the meaning of paragraph 1.
3. The instrument produced must satisfy the conditions necessary to establish its authenticity in the Member State of origin.
4. Section 3 of Chapter III shall apply as appropriate. The competent authority of a Member State where an authentic instrument was drawn up or registered shall issue, at the request of any interested party, a certificate using the standard form in Annex VI to this Regulation.

Article 58

A settlement which has been approved by a court in the course of proceedings and is enforceable in the Member State in which it was concluded shall be enforceable in the State addressed under the same conditions as authentic instruments. The court or competent authority of a Member State where a court settlement was approved shall issue, at the request of any interested party, a certificate using the standard form in Annex V to this Regulation.

CHAPTER V : GENERAL PROVISIONS

Article 59

1. In order to determine whether a party is domiciled in the Member State whose courts are seised of a matter, the court shall apply its internal law.

2. If a party is not domiciled in the Member State whose courts are seised of the matter, then, in order to determine whether the party is domiciled in another Member State, the court shall apply the law of that Member State.

Article 60

1. For the purposes of this Regulation, a company or other legal person or association of natural or legal persons is domiciled at the place where it has its:
   (a) statutory seat, or
   (b) central administration, or
   (c) principal place of business.
2. For the purposes of the United Kingdom and Ireland "statutory seat" means the registered office or, where there is no such office anywhere, the place of incorporation or, where there is no such place anywhere, the place under the law of which the formation took place.
3. In order to determine whether a trust is domiciled in the Member State whose courts are seised of the matter, the court shall apply its rules of private international law.

Article 61

Without prejudice to any more favourable provisions of national laws, persons domiciled in a Member State who are being prosecuted in the criminal courts of another Member State of which they are not nationals for an offence which was not intentionally committed may be defended by persons qualified to do so, even if they do not appear in person. However, the court seised of the matter may order appearance in person; in the case of failure to appear, a judgment given in the civil action without the person concerned having had the opportunity to arrange for his defence need not be recognised or enforced in the other Member States.

Article 62

In Sweden, in summary proceedings concerning orders to pay (betalningsföreläggande) and assistance (handräckning), the expression "court" includes the "Swedish enforcement service" (kronofogdemyndighet).

Article 63

1. A person domiciled in the territory of the Grand Duchy of Luxembourg and sued in the court of another Member State pursuant to Article 5(1) may refuse to submit to the jurisdiction of that court if the final place of delivery of the goods or provision of the services is in Luxembourg.
2. Where, under paragraph 1, the final place of delivery of the goods or provision of the services is in Luxembourg, any agreement conferring jurisdiction must, in order to be valid, be accepted in writing or evidenced in writing within the meaning of Article 23(1)(a).
3. The provisions of this Article shall not apply to contracts for the provision of financial services.

4. The provisions of this Article shall apply for a period of six years from entry into force of this Regulation.

Article 64

1. In proceedings involving a dispute between the master and a member of the crew of a seagoing ship registered in Greece or in Portugal, concerning remuneration or other conditions of service, a court in a Member State shall establish whether the diplomatic or consular officer responsible for the ship has been notified of the dispute. It may act as soon as that officer has been notified.
2. The provisions of this Article shall apply for a period of six years from entry into force of this Regulation.

Article 65

1. The jurisdiction specified in Article 6(2) and Article 11 in actions on a warranty of guarantee or in any other third party proceedings may not be resorted to Germany, Austria and Hungary. Any person domiciled in another Member State may be sued in the courts:
   (a) of Germany, pursuant to Articles 68 and 72 to 74 of the Code of Civil Procedure (Zivilprozessordnung) concerning third-party notices;
   (b) of Austria, pursuant to Article 21 of the Code of Civil Procedure (Zivilprozessordnung) concerning third-party notices;
   (c) of Hungary, pursuant to Articles 58 to 60 of the Code of Civil Procedure (Polgári perrendtartás) concerning third-party notices.
2. Judgments given in other Member States by virtue of Article 6(2), or Article 11 shall be recognised and enforced in Germany, Austria and Hungary in accordance with Chapter III. Any effects which judgments given in these States may have on third parties by application of the provisions in paragraph 1 shall also be recognised in the other Member States.

CHAPTER VI : TRANSITIONAL PROVISIONS

Article 66

1. This Regulation shall apply only to legal proceedings instituted and to documents formally drawn up or registered as authentic instruments after the entry into force thereof.
2. However, if the proceedings in the Member State of origin were instituted before the entry into force of this Regulation, judgments given after that date shall be recognised and enforced in accordance with Chapter III,
   (a) if the proceedings in the Member State of origin were instituted after the entry into force of the Brussels or the Lugano Convention both in the Member State or origin and in the Member State addressed;
   (b) in all other cases, if jurisdiction was founded upon rules which accorded with those provided for either in Chapter II or in a convention concluded

between the Member State of origin and the Member State addressed which was in force when the proceedings were instituted.

CHAPTER VII : RELATIONS WITH OTHER INSTRUMENTS

Article 67

This Regulation shall not prejudice the application of provisions governing jurisdiction and the recognition and enforcement of judgments in specific matters which are contained in Community instruments or in national legislation harmonised pursuant to such instruments.

Article 68

1. This Regulation shall, as between the Member States, supersede the Brussels Convention, except as regards the territories of the Member States which fall within the territorial scope of that Convention and which are excluded from this Regulation pursuant to Article 299 of the Treaty.
2. In so far as this Regulation replaces the provisions of the Brussels Convention between Member States, any reference to the Convention shall be understood as a reference to this Regulation.

Article 69

Subject to Article 66(2) and Article 70, this Regulation shall, as between Member States, supersede the following conventions and treaty concluded between two or more of them:

- the Convention between Belgium and France on Jurisdiction and the Validity and Enforcement of Judgments, Arbitration Awards and Authentic Instruments, signed at Paris on 8 July 1899,
- the Convention between Belgium and the Netherlands on Jurisdiction, Bankruptcy, and the Validity and Enforcement of Judgments, Arbitration Awards and Authentic Instruments, signed at Brussels on 28 March 1925,
- the Convention between France and Italy on the Enforcement of Judgments in Civil and Commercial Matters, signed at Rome on 3 June 1930,
- the Convention between the United Kingdom and the French Republic providing for the reciprocal enforcement of judgments in civil and commercial matters, with Protocol, signed at Paris on18 January 1934,
- the Convention between the United Kingdom and the Kingdom of Belgium providing for the reciprocal enforcement of judgments in civil and commercial matters, with Protocol, signed at Brussels on 2 May 1934,
- the Convention between Germany and Belgium on the Mutual Recognition and Enforcement of Judgments, Arbitration Awards and Authentic Instruments in Civil and Commercial Matters, signed at Bonn on 30 June 1958,
- the Convention between the Netherlands and Italy on the Recognition and Enforcement of Judgments in Civil and Commercial Matters, signed at Rome on 17 April 1959,

- the Convention between Germany and Austria on the Reciprocal Recognition and Enforcement of Judgments, Settlements and Authentic Instruments in Civil and Commercial Matters, signed at Vienna on 6 June 1959,
- the Convention between Belgium and Austria on the Reciprocal Recognition and Enforcement of Judgments, Arbitral Awards and Authentic Instruments in Civil and Commercial Matters, signed at Vienna on 16 June 1959,
- the Convention between Greece and Germany for the Reciprocal Recognition and Enforcement of Judgments, Settlements and Authentic Instruments in Civil and Commercial Matters, signed in Athens on 4 November 1961,
- the Convention between Belgium and Italy on the Recognition and Enforcement of Judgments and other Enforceable Instruments in Civil and Commercial Matters, signed at Rome on 6 April 1962,
- the Convention between the United Kingdom and the Federal Republic of Germany for the reciprocal recognition and enforcement of judgments in civil and commercial matters, signed at Bonn on 14 July 1960,
- the Convention between the United Kingdom and Austria providing for the reciprocal recognition and enforcement of judgments in civil and commercial matters, signed at Vienna on 14 July 1961, with amending Protocol signed at London on 6 March 1970,
- the Convention between France and Austria on the Recognition and Enforcement of Judgments and Authentic Instruments in Civil and Commercial Matters, signed at Vienna on 15 July 1966,
- the Convention between Spain and France on the Recognition and Enforcement of Judgment Arbitration Awards in Civil and Commercial Matters, signed at Paris on 28 May 1969,
- the Convention between Luxembourg and Austria on the Recognition and Enforcement of Judgments and Authentic Instruments in Civil and Commercial Matters, signed at Luxembourg on 29 July 1971,
- the Convention between Italy and Austria on the Recognition and Enforcement of Judgments in Civil and Commercial Matters, of Judicial Settlements and of Authentic Instruments, signed at Rome on 16 November 1971,
- the Convention between Spain and Italy regarding Legal Aid and the Recognition and Enforcement of Judgments in Civil and Commercial Matters, signed at Madrid on 22 May 1973,
- the Convention between Finland, Iceland, Norway, Sweden and Denmark on the Recognition and Enforcement of Judgments in Civil Matters, signed at Copenhagen on 11 October 1977,
- the Convention between Austria and Sweden on the Recognition and Enforcement of Judgments in Civil Matters, signed at Stockholm on 16 September 1982,
- the Convention between Spain and the Federal Republic of Germany on the Recognition and Enforcement of Judgments, Settlements and Enforceable Authentic Instruments in Civil and Commercial Matters, signed at Bonn on 14 November 1983,

- the Convention between Austria and Spain on the Recognition and Enforcement of Judgments, Settlements and Enforceable Authentic Instruments in Civil and Commercial Matters, signed at Vienna on 17 February 1984,
- the Convention between Finland and Austria on the Recognition and Enforcement of Judgments in Civil Matters, signed at Vienna on 17 November 1986, and
- the Treaty between Belgium, the Netherlands and Luxembourg in Jurisdiction, Bankruptcy, and the Validity and Enforcement of Judgments, Arbitration Awards and Authentic Instruments, signed at Brussels on 24 November 1961, in so far as it is in force.
- the Convention between the Czechoslovak Republic and Portugal on the Recognition and Enforcement of Court Decisions, signed at Lisbon on 23 November 1927, still in force between the Czech Republic and Portugal,
- the Convention between the Federative People's Republic of Yugoslavia and the Republic of Austria on Mutual Judicial Cooperation, signed at Vienna on 16 December 1954,
- the Convention between the Polish People's Republic and the Hungarian People's Republic on the Legal Assistance in Civil, Family and Criminal Matters, signed at Budapest on 6 March 1959,
- the Convention between the Federative People's Republic of Yugoslavia and the Kingdom of Greece on the Mutual Recognition and Enforcement of Judgments, signed at Athens on 18 June 1959,
- the Convention between the Polish People's Republic and the Federative People's Republic of Yugoslavia on the Legal Assistance in Civil and Criminal Matters, signed at Warsaw on 6 February 1960, now in force between Poland and Slovenia,
- the Agreement between the Federative People's Republic of Yugoslavia and the Republic of Austria on the Mutual Recognition and Enforcement of Arbitral Awards and Arbitral Settlements in Commercial Matters, signed at Belgrade on 18 March 1960,
- the Agreement between the Federative People's Republic of Yugoslavia and the Republic of Austria on the Mutual Recognition and Enforcement of Decisions in Alimony Matters, signed at Vienna on 10 October 1961,
- the Convention between Poland and Austria on Mutual Relations in Civil Matters and on Documents, signed at Vienna on 11 December 1963,
- the Treaty between the Czechoslovak Socialist Republic and the Socialist Federative Republic of Yugoslavia on Settlement of Legal Relations in Civil, Family and Criminal Matters, signed at Belgrade on 20 January 1964, still in force between the Czech Republic, Slovakia and Slovenia,
- the Convention between Poland and France on Applicable Law, Jurisdiction and the Enforcement of Judgments in the Field of Personal and Family Law, concluded in Warsaw on 5 April 1967,
- the Convention between the Governments of Yugoslavia and France on the Recognition and Enforcement of Judgments in Civil and Commercial Matters, signed at Paris on 18 May 1971,

- the Convention between the Federative Socialist Republic of Yugoslavia and the Kingdom of Belgium on the Recognition and Enforcement of Court Decisions in Alimony Matters, signed at Belgrade on 12 December 1973,
- the Convention between Hungary and Greece on Legal Assistance in Civil and Criminal Matters, signed at Budapest on 8 October 1979,
- the Convention between Poland and Greece on Legal Assistance in Civil and Criminal Matters, signed at Athens on 24 October 1979,
- the Convention between Hungary and France on Legal Assistance in Civil and Family Law, on the Recognition and Enforcement of Decisions and on Legal Assistance in Criminal Matters and on Extradition, signed at Budapest on 31 July 1980,
- the Treaty between the Czechoslovak Socialist Republic and the Hellenic Republic on Legal Aid in Civil and Criminal Matters, signed at Athens on 22 October 1980, still in force between the Czech Republic, Slovakia and Greece,
- the Convention between the Republic of Cyprus and the Hungarian People's Republic on Legal Assistance in Civil and Criminal Matters, signed at Nicosia on 30 November 1981,
- the Treaty between the Czechoslovak Socialistic Republic and the Republic of Cyprus on Legal Aid in Civil and Criminal Matters, signed at Nicosia on 23 April 1982, still in force between the Czech Republic, Slovakia and Cyprus,
- the Agreement between the Republic of Cyprus and the Republic of Greece on Legal Cooperation in Matters of Civil, Family, Commercial and Criminal Law, signed at Nicosia on 5 March 1984,
- the Treaty between the Government of the Czechoslovak Socialist Republic and the Government of the Republic of France on Legal Aid and the Recognition and Enforcement of Judgments in Civil, Family and Commercial Matters, signed at Paris on 10 May 1984, still in force between the Czech Republic, Slovakia and France,
- the Agreement between the Republic of Cyprus and the Socialist Federal Republic of Yugoslavia on Legal Assistance in Civil and Criminal Matters, signed at Nicosia on 19 September 1984, now in force between Cyprus and Slovenia,
- the Treaty between the Czechoslovak Socialist Republic and the Italian Republic on Legal Aid in Civil and Criminal Matters, signed at Prague on 6 December 1985, still in force between the Czech Republic, Slovakia and Italy,
- the Treaty between the Czechoslovak Socialist Republic and the Kingdom of Spain on Legal Aid, Recognition and Enforcement of Court Decisions in Civil Matters, signed at Madrid on 4 May 1987, still in force between the Czech Republic, Slovakia and Spain,
- the Treaty between the Czechoslovak Socialist Republic and the Polish People's Republic on Legal Aid and Settlement of Legal Relations in Civil, Family, Labour and Criminal Matters, signed at Warsaw on 21 December 1987, still in force between the Czech Republic, Slovakia and Poland,
- the Treaty between the Czechoslovak Socialist Republic and the Hungarian People's Republic on Legal Aid and Settlement of Legal Relations in Civil,

Family and Criminal Matters, signed at Bratislava on 28 March 1989, still in force between the Czech Republic, Slovakia and Hungary,

- the Convention between Poland and Italy on Judicial Assistance and the Recognition and Enforcement of Judgments in Civil Matters, signed at Warsaw on 28 April 1989,
- the Treaty between the Czech Republic and the Slovak Republic on Legal Aid provided by Judicial Bodies and on Settlements of Certain Legal Relations in Civil and Criminal Matters, signed at Prague on 29 October 1992,
- the Agreement between the Republic of Latvia, the Republic of Estonia and the Republic of Lithuania on Legal Assistance and Legal Relationships, signed at Tallinn on 11 November 1992,
- the Agreement between the Republic of Poland and the Republic of Lithuania on Legal Assistance and Legal Relations in Civil, Family, Labour and Criminal Matters, signed in Warsaw on 26 January 1993,
- the Agreement between the Republic of Latvia and the Republic of Poland on Legal Assistance and Legal Relationships in Civil, Family, Labour and Criminal Matters, signed at Riga on 23 February 1994,
- the Agreement between the Republic of Cyprus and the Republic of Poland on Legal Cooperation in Civil and Criminal Matters, signed at Nicosia on 14 November 1996, and
- the Agreement between Estonia and Poland on Granting Legal Assistance and Legal Relations on Civil, Labour and Criminal Matters, signed at Tallinn on 27 November 1998,
- the Convention between Bulgaria and Belgium on certain Judicial Matters, signed at Sofia on 2 July 1930,
- the Agreement between the People's Republic of Bulgaria and the federative People's Republic of Yugoslavia on Mutual Legal ssistance, signed at Sofia on 23 March 1956, still in force between Bulgaria and Slovenia,
- the Treaty between the People's Republic of Romania and the People's Republic of Hungary on Legal Assistance in Civil, Family and Criminal Matters, signed at Bucharest on 7 October 1958,
- the Treaty between the People's Republic of Romania and the Czechoslovak Republic on Legal Assistance in Civil, Family and Criminal Matters, signed at Prague on 25 October 1958, still in force between Romania and Slovakia,
- the Agreement between the People's Republic of Bulgaria and the Romanian People's Republic on Legal Assistance in Civil, Family and Criminal Matters, signed at Sofia on 3 December 1958,
- the Treaty between the People's Republic of Romania and the ederal People's Republic of Yugoslavia on Legal Assistance, signed at Belgrade on 18 October 1960 and its Protocol, still in force between Romania and Slovenia,
- the Agreement between the People's Republic of Bulgaria and the Polish People's Republic on Legal Assistance and Legal Relations in Civil, Family and Criminal Matters, signed at Warsaw on 4 December 1961,

- the Convention between the Socialist Republic of Romania and the Republic of Austria on Legal Assistance in Civil and Family law and the Validity and Service of Documents and its annexed Protocol, signed at Vienna on 17 November 1965,
- the Agreement between the People's Republic of Bulgaria and the Hungarian People's Republic on Legal Assistance in Civil, Family and Criminal Matters, signed at Sofia on 16 May 1966,
- the Convention between the Socialist Republic of Romania and the Hellenic Republic on Legal Assistance in Civil and Criminal Matters and its Protocol, signed at Bucharest on 19 October 1972,
- the Convention between the Socialist Republic of Romania and the Italian Republic on Judicial Assistance in Civil and Criminal Matters, signed at Bucharest on 11 November 1972,
- the Convention between the Socialist Republic of Romania and the French Republic on Legal Assistance in Civil and Commercial Matters, signed at Paris on 5 November 1974,
- the Convention between the Socialist Republic of Romania and the Kingdom of Belgium on Legal Assistance in Civil and Commercial Matters, signed at Bucharest on 30 October 1975,
- the Agreement between the People's Republic of Bulgaria and the Hellenic Republic on Legal Assistance in Civil and Criminal Matters, signed at Athens on 10 April 1976,
- the Agreement between the People's Republic of Bulgaria and the Czechoslovak Socialist Republic on Legal Assistance and Settlement of Relations in Civil, Family and Criminal Matters, signed at Sofia on 25 November 1976,
- the Convention between the Socialist Republic of Romania and the United Kingdom of Great Britain and Northern Ireland on Legal Assistance in Civil and Commercial Matters, signed at London on 15 June 1978,
- the Additional Protocol to the Convention between the Socialist Republic of Romania and the Kingdom of Belgium on Legal Assistance Civil and Commercial Matters, signed at Bucharest on 30 October 1979,
- the Convention between the Socialist Republic of Romania and the Kingdom of Belgium on Recognition and Enforcement of Decisions in Alimony Obligations, signed at Bucharest on 30 October 1979,
- the Convention between the Socialist Republic of Romania and the Kingdom of Belgium on Recognition and Enforcement of Divorce Decisions, signed at Bucharest on 6 November 1980,
- the Agreement between the People's Republic of Bulgaria and the Republic of Cyprus on Legal Assistance in Civil and Criminal Matters, signed at Nicosia on 29 April 1983,
- the Agreement between the Government of the People's Republic of Bulgaria and the Government of the French Republic on Mutual Legal Assistance in Civil Matters, signed at Sofia on 18 January 1989,
- the Agreement between the People's Republic of Bulgaria and the Italian Republic on Legal Assistance and Enforcement of Decisions in Civil Matters, signed at Rome on 18 May 1990,

- the Agreement between the Republic of Bulgaria and the Kingdom of Spain on Mutual Legal Assistance in Civil Matters, signed at Sofia on 23 May 1993,
- the Treaty between Romania and the Czech Republic on Judicial Assistance in Civil Matters, signed at Bucharest on 11 July 1994,
- the Convention between Romania and the Kingdom of Spain on Jurisdiction, Recognition and Enforcement of Decisions in Civil and Commercial Matters, signed at Bucharest on 17 November 1997,
- the Convention between Romania and the Kingdom of Spain — complementary to the Hague Convention relating to civil procedure law (Hague, 1 March 1954), signed at Bucharest on 17 November 1997,
- the Treaty between Romania and the Republic of Poland on Legal Assistance and Legal Relations in Civil Cases, signed at Bucharest on 15 May 1999.

Article 70

1. The Treaty and the Conventions referred to in Article 69 shall continue to have effect in relation to matters to which this Regulation does not apply.
2. They shall continue to have effect in respect of judgments given and documents formally drawn up or registered as authentic instruments before the entry into force of this Regulation.

Article 71

1. This Regulation shall not affect any conventions to which the Member States are parties and which in relation to particular matters, govern jurisdiction or the recognition or enforcement of judgments.
2. With a view to its uniform interpretation, paragraph 1 shall be applied in the following manner:
   (a) this Regulation shall not prevent a court of a Member State, which is a party to a convention on a particular matter, from assuming jurisdiction in accordance with that convention, even where the defendant is domiciled in another Member State which is not a party to that convention. The court hearing the action shall, in any event, apply Article 26 of this Regulation;
   (b) judgments given in a Member State by a court in the exercise of jurisdiction provided for in a convention on a particular matter shall be recognised and enforced in the other Member States in accordance with this Regulation.

   Where a convention on a particular matter to which both the Member State of origin and the Member State addressed are parties lays down conditions for the recognition or enforcement of judgments, those conditions shall apply. In any event, the provisions of this Regulation which concern the procedure for recognition and enforcement of judgments may be applied.

Article 72

This Regulation shall not affect agreements by which Member States undertook, prior to the entry into force of this Regulation pursuant to Article 59 of the Brussels

Convention, not to recognise judgments given, in particular in other Contracting States to that Convention, against defendants domiciled or habitually resident in a third country where, in cases provided for in Article 4 of that Convention, the judgment could only be founded on a ground of jurisdiction specified in the second paragraph of Article 3 of that Convention.

CHAPTER VIII : FINAL PROVISIONS

Article 73

No later than five years after the entry into force of this Regulation, the Commission shall present to the European Parliament, the Council and the Economic and Social Committee a report on the application of this Regulation. The report shall be accompanied, if need be, by proposals for adaptations to this Regulation.

Article 74

1. The Member States shall notify the Commission of the texts amending the lists set out in Annexes I to IV. The Commission shall adapt the Annexes concerned accordingly.
2. The updating or technical adjustments of the forms, specimens of which appear in Annexes V and VI, shall be adopted by the Commission. Those measures, designed to amend non-essential elements of this Regulation, shall be adopted in accordance with the regulatory procedure with scrutiny referred to in Article 75(2).

Article 75

1. The Commission shall be assisted by a committee.
2. Where reference is made to this paragraph, Article 5a(1) to (4) and Article 7 of Decision 1999/468/EC shall apply, having regard to the provisions of Article 8 thereof.

Article 76

This Regulation shall enter into force on 1 March 2002.

This Regulation is binding in its entirety and directly applicable in the Member States in accordance with the Treaty establishing the European Community.

Done at Brussels, 22 December 2000.

For the Council

The President

C. Pierret

ANNEX I

Rules of jurisdiction referred to in Article 3(2) and Article 4(2)

The rules of jurisdiction referred to in Article 3(2) and Article 4(2) are the following:

- in Belgium: Article 15 of the Civil Code (Code civil/Burgerlijk Wetboek) and Article 638 of the Judicial Code (Code judiciaire/Gerechtelijk Wetboek);
- in Germany: Article 23 of the Code of Civil Procedure (Zivilprozessordnung),
- in Greece, Article 40 of the Code of Civil Procedure (Κώδικας Πολιτικής Δικονομίας);
- in France: Articles 14 and 15 of the Civil Code (Code civil),
- in Ireland: the rules which enable jurisdiction to be founded on the document instituting the proceedings having been served on the defendant during his temporary presence in Ireland,
- in Italy: Articles 3 and 4 of Act 218 of 31 May 1995,
- in Luxembourg: Articles 14 and 15 of the Civil Code (Code civil),
- in the Netherlands: Articles 126(3) and 127 of the Code of Civil Procedure (Wetboek van Burgerlijke Rechtsvordering),
- in Austria: Article 99 of the Court Jurisdiction Act (Jurisdiktionsnorm),
- in Portugal: Articles 65 and 65A of the Code of Civil Procedure (Código de Processo Civil) and Article 11 of the Code of Labour Procedure (Código de Processo de Trabalho),
- in Finland: the second, third and fourth sentences of the first paragraph of Section 1 of Chapter 10 of the Code of Judicial Procedure (oikeudenkäymiskaari/rättegångsbalken),
- in Sweden: the first sentence of the first paragraph of Section 3 of Chapter 10 of the Code of Judicial Procedure (rättegångsbalken),
- in the United Kingdom: rules which enable jurisdiction to be founded on:
  (a) the document instituting the proceedings having been served on the defendant during his temporary presence in the United Kingdom; or
  (b) the presence within the United Kingdom of property belonging to the defendant; or
  (c) the seizure by the plaintiff of property situated in the United Kingdom.

ANNEX II

The courts or competent authorities to which the application referred to in Article 39 may be submitted are the following:

- in Belgium, the "tribunal de première instance" or "rechtbank van eerste aanleg" or "erstinstanzliches Gericht",
- in Germany, the presiding judge of a chamber of the "Landgericht",
- in Greece, the "Μονομελές Πρωτοδικείο",
- in Spain, the "Juzgado de Primera Instancia",
- in France, the presiding judge of the "tribunal de grande instance",

- in Ireland, the High Court,
- in Italy, the "Corte d'appello",
- in Luxembourg, the presiding judge of the "tribunal d'arrondissement",
- in the Netherlands, the presiding judge of the "arrondissementsrechtbank";
- in Austria, the "Bezirksgericht",
- in Portugal, the "Tribunal de Comarca",
- in Finland, the "käräjäoikeus/tingsrätt",
- in Sweden, the "Svea hovrätt",
- in the United Kingdom:
  (a) in England and Wales, the High Court of Justice, or in the case of a maintenance judgment, the Magistrate's Court on transmission by the Secretary of State;
  (b) in Scotland, the Court of Session, or in the case of a maintenance judgment, the Sheriff Court on transmission by the Secretary of State;
  (c) in Northern Ireland, the High Court of Justice, or in the case of a maintenance judgment, the Magistrate's Court on transmission by the Secretary of State;
  (d) in Gibraltar, the Supreme Court of Gibraltar, or in the case of a maintenance judgment, the Magistrates' Court on transmission by the Attorney General of Gibraltar.

ANNEX III

The courts with which appeals referred to in Article 43(2) may be lodged are the following:

- in Belgium,
  (a) as regards appeal by the defendant: the "tribunal de première instance" or "rechtbank van eerste aanleg" or "erstinstanzliches Gericht",
  (b) as regards appeal by the applicant: the "Cour d'appel" or "hof van beroep",
- in the Federal Republic of Germany, the "Oberlandesgericht",
- in Greece, the "Εφετείο",
- in Spain, the "Audiencia Provincial",
- in France, the "cour d'appel",
- in Ireland, the High Court,
- in Italy, the "corte d'appello",
- in Luxembourg, the "Cour supérieure de Justice" sitting as a court of civil appeal,
- in the Netherlands:
  (a) for the defendant: the "arrondissementsrechtbank",
  (b) for the applicant: the "gerechtshof",
- in Austria, the "Bezirksgericht",
- in Portugal, the "Tribunal de Relação",
- in Finland, the "hovioikeus/hovrätt",
- in Sweden, the "Svea hovrätt",
- in the United Kingdom:
  (a) in England and Wales, the High Court of Justice, or in the case of a maintenance judgment, the Magistrate's Court;

(b) in Scotland, the Court of Session, or in the case of a maintenance judgment, the Sheriff Court;
(c) in Northern Ireland, the High Court of Justice, or in the case of a maintenance judgment, the Magistrate's Court;
(d) in Gibraltar, the Supreme Court of Gibraltar, or in the case of a maintenance judgment, the Magistrates' Court.

ANNEX IV

The appeals which may be lodged pursuant to Article 44 are the following

- in Belgium, Greece, Spain, France, Italy, Luxembourg and the Netherlands, an appeal in cassation,
- in Germany, a "Rechtsbeschwerde",
- in Ireland, an appeal on a point of law to the Supreme Court,
- in Austria, a "Revisionsrekurs",
- in Portugal, an appeal on a point of law,
- in Finland, an appeal to the "korkein oikeus/högsta domstolen",
- in Sweden, an appeal to the "Högsta domstolen",
- in the United Kingdom, a single further appeal on a point of law.

ANNEX V

Certificate referred to in Articles 54 and 58 of the Regulation on judgments and court settlements

(English, inglés, anglais, inglese, ...)

1. Member State of origin
2. Court or competent authority issuing the certificate
    2.1. Name
    2.2. Address
    2.3. Tel./fax/e-mail
3. Court which delivered the judgment/approved the court settlement[1]
    3.1. Type of court
    3.2. Place of court
4. Judgment/court settlement[2]
    4.1. Date
    4.2. Reference number
    4.3. The parties to the judgment/court settlement[3]
        4.3.1. Name(s) of plaintiff(s)
        4.3.2. Name(s) of defendant(s)

1 Delete as appropriate.
2 Delete as appropriate.
3 Delete as appropriate.

4.3.3. Name(s) of other party(ies), if any

4.4. Date of service of the document instituting the proceedings where judgment was given in default of appearance

4.5. Text of the judgment/court settlement[1] as annexed to this certificate

5. Names of parties to whom legal aid has been granted

The judgment/court settlement[2] is enforceable in the Member State of origin (Articles 38 and 58 of the Regulation) against:

Name:

Done at ... , date ...

Signature and/or stamp ...

ANNEX VI

Certificate referred to in Article 57(4) of the Regulation on authentic instruments

(English, inglés, anglais, inglese ....)

1. Member State of origin
2. Competent authority issuing the certificate
   2.1. Name
   2.2. Address
   2.3. Tel./fax/e-mail
3. Authority which has given authenticity to the instrument
   3.1. Authority involved in the drawing up of the authentic instrument (if applicable)
      3.1.1. Name and designation of authority
      3.1.2. Place of authority
   3.2. Authority which has registered the authentic instrument (if applicable)
      3.2.1. Type of authority
      3.2.2. Place of authority
4. Authentic instrument
   4.1. Description of the instrument
   4.2. Date
      4.2.1. on which the instrument was drawn up
      4.2.2. if different: on which the instrument was registered
   4.3. Reference number
   4.4. Parties to the instrument
      4.4.1. Name of the creditor

[1] Delete as appropriate.

[2] Delete as appropriate.

4.4.2. Name of the debtor

5. Text of the enforceable obligation as annexed to this certificate

The authentic instrument is enforceable against the debtor in the Member State of origin (Article 57(1) of the Regulation)

Done at ..., date ...

Signature and/or stamp ...

30. Regulation (EC) No 593/2008 of the European Parliament and of the Council of 17 June 2008 on the law applicable to contractual obligations (Rome I)

(OJ L 177 , 04/07/2008 p. 6 – 16)

THE EUROPEAN PARLIAMENT AND THE COUNCIL OF THE EUROPEAN UNION,

Having regard to the Treaty establishing the European Community, and in particular Article 61(c) and the second indent of Article 67(5) thereof,

Having regard to the proposal from the Commission,

Having regard to the opinion of the European Economic and Social Committee[1],

Acting in accordance with the procedure laid down in Article 251 of the Treaty[2],

Whereas:

(1) The Community has set itself the objective of maintaining and developing an area of freedom, security and justice. For the progressive establishment of such an area, the Community is to adopt measures relating to judicial cooperation in civil matters with a cross-border impact to the extent necessary for the proper functioning of the internal market.

(2) According to Article 65, point (b) of the Treaty, these measures are to include those promoting the compatibility of the rules applicable in the Member States concerning the conflict of laws and of jurisdiction.

(3) The European Council meeting in Tampere on 15 and 16 October 1999 endorsed the principle of mutual recognition of judgments and other decisions of judicial authorities as the cornerstone of judicial cooperation in civil matters and invited the Council and the Commission to adopt a programme of measures to implement that principle.

(4) On 30 November 2000 the Council adopted a joint Commission and Council programme of measures for implementation of the principle of mutual recognition of decisions in civil and commercial matters[3]. The programme identifies measures relating to the harmonisation of conflict-of-law rules as those facilitating the mutual recognition of judgments.

(5) The Hague Programme[4], adopted by the European Council on 5 November 2004, called for work to be pursued actively on the conflict-of-law rules regarding contractual obligations (Rome I).

(6) The proper functioning of the internal market creates a need, in order to improve the predictability of the outcome of litigation, certainty as to the law

[1] OJ C 318, 23.12.2006, p. 56.

[2] Opinion of the European Parliament of 29 November 2007 (not yet published in the Official Journal) and Council Decision of 5 June 2008.

[3] OJ C 12, 15.1.2001, p. 1.

[4] OJ C 53, 3.3.2005, p. 1.

applicable and the free movement of judgments, for the conflict-of-law rules in the Member States to designate the same national law irrespective of the country of the court in which an action is brought.

(7) The substantive scope and the provisions of this Regulation should be consistent with Council Regulation (EC) No 44/2001 of 22 December 2000 on jurisdiction and the recognition and enforcement of judgments in civil and commercial matters[1] (Brussels I) and Regulation (EC) No 864/2007 of the European Parliament and of the Council of 11 July 2007 on the law applicable to non-contractual obligations (Rome II)[2].

(8) Family relationships should cover parentage, marriage, affinity and collateral relatives. The reference in Article 1(2) to relationships having comparable effects to marriage and other family relationships should be interpreted in accordance with the law of the Member State in which the court is seised.

(9) Obligations under bills of exchange, cheques and promissory notes and other negotiable instruments should also cover bills of lading to the extent that the obligations under the bill of lading arise out of its negotiable character.

(10) Obligations arising out of dealings prior to the conclusion of the contract are covered by Article 12 of Regulation (EC) No 864/2007. Such obligations should therefore be excluded from the scope of this Regulation.

(11) The parties' freedom to choose the applicable law should be one of the cornerstones of the system of conflict-of-law rules in matters of contractual obligations.

(12) An agreement between the parties to confer on one or more courts or tribunals of a Member State exclusive jurisdiction to determine disputes under the contract should be one of the factors to be taken into account in determining whether a choice of law has been clearly demonstrated.

(13) This Regulation does not preclude parties from incorporating by reference into their contract a non-State body of law or an international convention.

(14) Should the Community adopt, in an appropriate legal instrument, rules of substantive contract law, including standard terms and conditions, such instrument may provide that the parties may choose to apply those rules.

(15) Where a choice of law is made and all other elements relevant to the situation are located in a country other than the country whose law has been chosen, the choice of law should not prejudice the application of provisions of the law of that country which cannot be derogated from by agreement. This rule should apply whether or not the choice of law was accompanied by a choice of court or tribunal. Whereas no substantial change is intended as compared with Article 3(3) of the 1980 Convention on the Law Applicable to Contractual Obligations[3]

---

1 OJ L 12, 16.1.2001, p. 1. Regulation as last amended by Regulation (EC) No 1791/2006 (OJ L 363, 20.12.2006, p. 1).

2 OJ L 199, 31.7.2007, p. 40.

3 OJ C 334, 30.12.2005, p. 1.

(the Rome Convention), the wording of this Regulation is aligned as far as possible with Article 14 of Regulation (EC) No 864/2007.

(16) To contribute to the general objective of this Regulation, legal certainty in the European judicial area, the conflict-of-law rules should be highly foreseeable. The courts should, however, retain a degree of discretion to determine the law that is most closely connected to the situation.

(17) As far as the applicable law in the absence of choice is concerned, the concept of "provision of services" and "sale of goods" should be interpreted in the same way as when applying Article 5 of Regulation (EC) No 44/2001 in so far as sale of goods and provision of services are covered by that Regulation. Although franchise and distribution contracts are contracts for services, they are the subject of specific rules.

(18) As far as the applicable law in the absence of choice is concerned, multilateral systems should be those in which trading is conducted, such as regulated markets and multilateral trading facilities as referred to in Article 4 of Directive 2004/39/EC of the European Parliament and of the Council of 21 April 2004 on markets in financial instruments[1], regardless of whether or not they rely on a central counterparty.

(19) Where there has been no choice of law, the applicable law should be determined in accordance with the rule specified for the particular type of contract. Where the contract cannot be categorised as being one of the specified types or where its elements fall within more than one of the specified types, it should be governed by the law of the country where the party required to effect the characteristic performance of the contract has his habitual residence. In the case of a contract consisting of a bundle of rights and obligations capable of being categorised as falling within more than one of the specified types of contract, the characteristic performance of the contract should be determined having regard to its centre of gravity.

(20) Where the contract is manifestly more closely connected with a country other than that indicated in Article 4(1) or (2), an escape clause should provide that the law of that other country is to apply. In order to determine that country, account should be taken, inter alia, of whether the contract in question has a very close relationship with another contract or contracts.

(21) In the absence of choice, where the applicable law cannot be determined either on the basis of the fact that the contract can be categorised as one of the specified types or as being the law of the country of habitual residence of the party required to effect the characteristic performance of the contract, the contract should be governed by the law of the country with which it is most closely connected. In order to determine that country, account should be taken, inter alia, of whether the contract in question has a very close relationship with another contract or contracts.

1 OJ L 145, 30.4.2004, p. 1. Directive as last amended by Directive 2008/10/EC (OJ L 76, 19.3.2008, p. 33).

(22) As regards the interpretation of contracts for the carriage of goods, no change in substance is intended with respect to Article 4(4), third sentence, of the Rome Convention. Consequently, single-voyage charter parties and other contracts the main purpose of which is the carriage of goods should be treated as contracts for the carriage of goods. For the purposes of this Regulation, the term "consignor" should refer to any person who enters into a contract of carriage with the carrier and the term "the carrier" should refer to the party to the contract who undertakes to carry the goods, whether or not he performs the carriage himself.

(23) As regards contracts concluded with parties regarded as being weaker, those parties should be protected by conflict-of-law rules that are more favourable to their interests than the general rules.

(24) With more specific reference to consumer contracts, the conflict-of-law rule should make it possible to cut the cost of settling disputes concerning what are commonly relatively small claims and to take account of the development of distance-selling techniques. Consistency with Regulation (EC) No 44/2001 requires both that there be a reference to the concept of directed activity as a condition for applying the consumer protection rule and that the concept be interpreted harmoniously in Regulation (EC) No 44/2001 and this Regulation, bearing in mind that a joint declaration by the Council and the Commission on Article 15 of Regulation (EC) No 44/2001 states that "for Article 15(1)(c) to be applicable it is not sufficient for an undertaking to target its activities at the Member State of the consumer's residence, or at a number of Member States including that Member State; a contract must also be concluded within the framework of its activities". The declaration also states that "the mere fact that an Internet site is accessible is not sufficient for Article 15 to be applicable, although a factor will be that this Internet site solicits the conclusion of distance contracts and that a contract has actually been concluded at a distance, by whatever means. In this respect, the language or currency which a website uses does not constitute a relevant factor.".

(25) Consumers should be protected by such rules of the country of their habitual residence that cannot be derogated from by agreement, provided that the consumer contract has been concluded as a result of the professional pursuing his commercial or professional activities in that particular country. The same protection should be guaranteed if the professional, while not pursuing his commercial or professional activities in the country where the consumer has his habitual residence, directs his activities by any means to that country or to several countries, including that country, and the contract is concluded as a result of such activities.

(26) For the purposes of this Regulation, financial services such as investment services and activities and ancillary services provided by a professional to a consumer, as referred to in sections A and B of Annex I to Directive 2004/39/EC, and contracts for the sale of units in collective investment undertakings, whether or not covered by Council Directive 85/611/EEC of 20 December 1985 on the coordination of laws, regulations and administrative

provisions relating to undertakings for collective investment in transferable securities (UCITS)[1], should be subject to Article 6 of this Regulation. Consequently, when a reference is made to terms and conditions governing the issuance or offer to the public of transferable securities or to the subscription and redemption of units in collective investment undertakings, that reference should include all aspects binding the issuer or the offeror to the consumer, but should not include those aspects involving the provision of financial services.

(27) Various exceptions should be made to the general conflict-of-law rule for consumer contracts. Under one such exception the general rule should not apply to contracts relating to rights in rem in immovable property or tenancies of such property unless the contract relates to the right to use immovable property on a timeshare basis within the meaning of Directive 94/47/EC of the European Parliament and of the Council of 26 October 1994 on the protection of purchasers in respect of certain aspects of contracts relating to the purchase of the right to use immovable properties on a timeshare basis[2].

(28) It is important to ensure that rights and obligations which constitute a financial instrument are not covered by the general rule applicable to consumer contracts, as that could lead to different laws being applicable to each of the instruments issued, therefore changing their nature and preventing their fungible trading and offering. Likewise, whenever such instruments are issued or offered, the contractual relationship established between the issuer or the offeror and the consumer should not necessarily be subject to the mandatory application of the law of the country of habitual residence of the consumer, as there is a need to ensure uniformity in the terms and conditions of an issuance or an offer. The same rationale should apply with regard to the multilateral systems covered by Article 4(1)(h), in respect of which it should be ensured that the law of the country of habitual residence of the consumer will not interfere with the rules applicable to contracts concluded within those systems or with the operator of such systems.

(29) For the purposes of this Regulation, references to rights and obligations constituting the terms and conditions governing the issuance, offers to the public or public take-over bids of transferable securities and references to the subscription and redemption of units in collective investment undertakings should include the terms governing, inter alia, the allocation of securities or units, rights in the event of over-subscription, withdrawal rights and similar matters in the context of the offer as well as those matters referred to in Articles 10, 11, 12 and 13, thus ensuring that all relevant contractual aspects of an offer binding the issuer or the offeror to the consumer are governed by a single law.

(30) For the purposes of this Regulation, financial instruments and transferable securities are those instruments referred to in Article 4 of Directive 2004/39/EC.

---

1 OJ L 375, 31.12.1985, p. 3. Directive as last amended by Directive 2008/18/EC of the European Parliament and of the Council (OJ L 76, 19.3.2008, p. 42).

2 OJ L 280, 29.10.1994, p. 83.

(31) Nothing in this Regulation should prejudice the operation of a formal arrangement designated as a system under Article 2(a) of Directive 98/26/EC of the European Parliament and of the Council of 19 May 1998 on settlement finality in payment and securities settlement systems[1].

(32) Owing to the particular nature of contracts of carriage and insurance contracts, specific provisions should ensure an adequate level of protection of passengers and policy holders. Therefore, Article 6 should not apply in the context of those particular contracts.

(33) Where an insurance contract not covering a large risk covers more than one risk, at least one of which is situated in a Member State and at least one of which is situated in a third country, the special rules on insurance contracts in this Regulation should apply only to the risk or risks situated in the relevant Member State or Member States.

(34) The rule on individual employment contracts should not prejudice the application of the overriding mandatory provisions of the country to which a worker is posted in accordance with Directive 96/71/EC of the European Parliament and of the Council of 16 December 1996 concerning the posting of workers in the framework of the provision of services[2].

(35) Employees should not be deprived of the protection afforded to them by provisions which cannot be derogated from by agreement or which can only be derogated from to their benefit.

(36) As regards individual employment contracts, work carried out in another country should be regarded as temporary if the employee is expected to resume working in the country of origin after carrying out his tasks abroad. The conclusion of a new contract of employment with the original employer or an employer belonging to the same group of companies as the original employer should not preclude the employee from being regarded as carrying out his work in another country temporarily.

(37) Considerations of public interest justify giving the courts of the Member States the possibility, in exceptional circumstances, of applying exceptions based on public policy and overriding mandatory provisions. The concept of "overriding mandatory provisions" should be distinguished from the expression "provisions which cannot be derogated from by agreement" and should be construed more restrictively.

(38) In the context of voluntary assignment, the term "relationship" should make it clear that Article 14(1) also applies to the property aspects of an assignment, as between assignor and assignee, in legal orders where such aspects are treated separately from the aspects under the law of obligations. However, the term "relationship" should not be understood as relating to any relationship that may exist between assignor and assignee. In particular, it should not cover preliminary questions as regards a voluntary assignment or a contractual

1 OJ L 18, 21.1.1997, p. 1.

2 OJ L 178, 17.7.2000, p. 1.

subrogation. The term should be strictly limited to the aspects which are directly relevant to the voluntary assignment or contractual subrogation in question.

(39) For the sake of legal certainty there should be a clear definition of habitual residence, in particular for companies and other bodies, corporate or unincorporated. Unlike Article 60(1) of Regulation (EC) No 44/2001, which establishes three criteria, the conflict-of-law rule should proceed on the basis of a single criterion; otherwise, the parties would be unable to foresee the law applicable to their situation.

(40) A situation where conflict-of-law rules are dispersed among several instruments and where there are differences between those rules should be avoided. This Regulation, however, should not exclude the possibility of inclusion of conflict-of-law rules relating to contractual obligations in provisions of Community law with regard to particular matters.

This Regulation should not prejudice the application of other instruments laying down provisions designed to contribute to the proper functioning of the internal market in so far as they cannot be applied in conjunction with the law designated by the rules of this Regulation. The application of provisions of the applicable law designated by the rules of this Regulation should not restrict the free movement of goods and services as regulated by Community instruments, such as Directive 2000/31/EC of the European Parliament and of the Council of 8 June 2000 on certain legal aspects of information society services, in particular electronic commerce, in the Internal Market (Directive on electronic commerce)[1].

(41) Respect for international commitments entered into by the Member States means that this Regulation should not affect international conventions to which one or more Member States are parties at the time when this Regulation is adopted. To make the rules more accessible, the Commission should publish the list of the relevant conventions in the Official Journal of the European Union on the basis of information supplied by the Member States.

(42) The Commission will make a proposal to the European Parliament and to the Council concerning the procedures and conditions according to which Member States would be entitled to negotiate and conclude, on their own behalf, agreements with third countries in individual and exceptional cases, concerning sectoral matters and containing provisions on the law applicable to contractual obligations.

(43) Since the objective of this Regulation cannot be sufficiently achieved by the Member States and can therefore, by reason of the scale and effects of this Regulation, be better achieved at Community level, the Community may adopt measures, in accordance with the principle of subsidiarity as set out in Article 5 of the Treaty. In accordance with the principle of proportionality, as set out in

[1] OJ L 345, 19.12.2002, p. 1. Directive as last amended by Directive 2008/19/EC (OJ L 76, 19.3.2008, p. 44).

that Article, this Regulation does not go beyond what is necessary to attain its objective.

(44) In accordance with Article 3 of the Protocol on the position of the United Kingdom and Ireland, annexed to the Treaty on European Union and to the Treaty establishing the European Community, Ireland has notified its wish to take part in the adoption and application of the present Regulation.

(45) In accordance with Articles 1 and 2 of the Protocol on the position of the United Kingdom and Ireland, annexed to the Treaty on European Union and to the Treaty establishing the European Community, and without prejudice to Article 4 of the said Protocol, the United Kingdom is not taking part in the adoption of this Regulation and is not bound by it or subject to its application.

(46) In accordance with Articles 1 and 2 of the Protocol on the position of Denmark, annexed to the Treaty on European Union and to the Treaty establishing the European Community, Denmark is not taking part in the adoption of this Regulation and is not bound by it or subject to its application,

HAVE ADOPTED THIS REGULATION:

CHAPTER I : SCOPE

Article 1 Material scope

1. This Regulation shall apply, in situations involving a conflict of laws, to contractual obligations in civil and commercial matters.

   It shall not apply, in particular, to revenue, customs or administrative matters.

2. The following shall be excluded from the scope of this Regulation:
   (a) questions involving the status or legal capacity of natural persons, without prejudice to Article 13;
   (b) obligations arising out of family relationships and relationships deemed by the law applicable to such relationships to have comparable effects, including maintenance obligations;
   (c) obligations arising out of matrimonial property regimes, property regimes of relationships deemed by the law applicable to such relationships to have comparable effects to marriage, and wills and succession;
   (d) obligations arising under bills of exchange, cheques and promissory notes and other negotiable instruments to the extent that the obligations under such other negotiable instruments arise out of their negotiable character;
   (e) arbitration agreements and agreements on the choice of court;
   (f) questions governed by the law of companies and other bodies, corporate or unincorporated, such as the creation, by registration or otherwise, legal capacity, internal organisation or winding-up of companies and other bodies, corporate or unincorporated, and the personal liability of officers and members as such for the obligations of the company or body;

(g) the question whether an agent is able to bind a principal, or an organ to bind a company or other body corporate or unincorporated, in relation to a third party;
(h) the constitution of trusts and the relationship between settlors, trustees and beneficiaries;
(i) obligations arising out of dealings prior to the conclusion of a contract;
(j) insurance contracts arising out of operations carried out by organisations other than undertakings referred to in Article 2 of Directive 2002/83/EC of the European Parliament and of the Council of 5 November 2002 concerning life assurance the object of which is to provide benefits for employed or self-employed persons belonging to an undertaking or group of undertakings, or to a trade or group of trades, in the event of death or survival or of discontinuance or curtailment of activity, or of sickness related to work or accidents at work.

3. This Regulation shall not apply to evidence and procedure, without prejudice to Article 18.
4. In this Regulation, the term "Member State" shall mean Member States to which this Regulation applies. However, in Article 3(4) and Article 7 the term shall mean all the Member States.

Article 2 Universal application

Any law specified by this Regulation shall be applied whether or not it is the law of a Member State.

CHAPTER II : UNIFORM RULES

Article 3 Freedom of choice

1. A contract shall be governed by the law chosen by the parties. The choice shall be made expressly or clearly demonstrated by the terms of the contract or the circumstances of the case. By their choice the parties can select the law applicable to the whole or to part only of the contract.
2. The parties may at any time agree to subject the contract to a law other than that which previously governed it, whether as a result of an earlier choice made under this Article or of other provisions of this Regulation. Any change in the law to be applied that is made after the conclusion of the contract shall not prejudice its formal validity under Article 11 or adversely affect the rights of third parties.
3. Where all other elements relevant to the situation at the time of the choice are located in a country other than the country whose law has been chosen, the choice of the parties shall not prejudice the application of provisions of the law of that other country which cannot be derogated from by agreement.
4. Where all other elements relevant to the situation at the time of the choice are located in one or more Member States, the parties' choice of applicable law other than that of a Member State shall not prejudice the application of

provisions of Community law, where appropriate as implemented in the Member State of the forum, which cannot be derogated from by agreement.

5. The existence and validity of the consent of the parties as to the choice of the applicable law shall be determined in accordance with the provisions of Articles 10, 11 and 13.

Article 4 Applicable law in the absence of choice

1. To the extent that the law applicable to the contract has not been chosen in accordance with Article 3 and without prejudice to Articles 5 to 8, the law governing the contract shall be determined as follows:
   (a) a contract for the sale of goods shall be governed by the law of the country where the seller has his habitual residence;
   (b) a contract for the provision of services shall be governed by the law of the country where the service provider has his habitual residence;
   (c) a contract relating to a right in rem in immovable property or to a tenancy of immovable property shall be governed by the law of the country where the property is situated;
   (d) notwithstanding point (c), a tenancy of immovable property concluded for temporary private use for a period of no more than six consecutive months shall be governed by the law of the country where the landlord has his habitual residence, provided that the tenant is a natural person and has his habitual residence in the same country;
   (e) a franchise contract shall be governed by the law of the country where the franchisee has his habitual residence;
   (f) a distribution contract shall be governed by the law of the country where the distributor has his habitual residence;
   (g) a contract for the sale of goods by auction shall be governed by the law of the country where the auction takes place, if such a place can be determined;
   (h) a contract concluded within a multilateral system which brings together or facilitates the bringing together of multiple third-party buying and selling interests in financial instruments, as defined by Article 4(1), point (17) of Directive 2004/39/EC, in accordance with non-discretionary rules and governed by a single law, shall be governed by that law.
2. Where the contract is not covered by paragraph 1 or where the elements of the contract would be covered by more than one of points (a) to (h) of paragraph 1, the contract shall be governed by the law of the country where the party required to effect the characteristic performance of the contract has his habitual residence.
3. Where it is clear from all the circumstances of the case that the contract is manifestly more closely connected with a country other than that indicated in paragraphs 1 or 2, the law of that other country shall apply.
4. Where the law applicable cannot be determined pursuant to paragraphs 1 or 2, the contract shall be governed by the law of the country with which it is most closely connected.

Article 5 Contracts of carriage

1. To the extent that the law applicable to a contract for the carriage of goods has not been chosen in accordance with Article 3, the law applicable shall be the law of the country of habitual residence of the carrier, provided that the place of receipt or the place of delivery or the habitual residence of the consignor is also situated in that country. If those requirements are not met, the law of the country where the place of delivery as agreed by the parties is situated shall apply.
2. To the extent that the law applicable to a contract for the carriage of passengers has not been chosen by the parties in accordance with the second subparagraph, the law applicable shall be the law of the country where the passenger has his habitual residence, provided that either the place of departure or the place of destination is situated in that country. If these requirements are not met, the law of the country where the carrier has his habitual residence shall apply.

   The parties may choose as the law applicable to a contract for the carriage of passengers in accordance with Article 3 only the law of the country where:

   (a) the passenger has his habitual residence; or
   (b) the carrier has his habitual residence; or
   (c) the carrier has his place of central administration; or
   (d) the place of departure is situated; or
   (e) the place of destination is situated.
3. Where it is clear from all the circumstances of the case that the contract, in the absence of a choice of law, is manifestly more closely connected with a country other than that indicated in paragraphs 1 or 2, the law of that other country shall apply.

Article 6 Consumer contracts

1. Without prejudice to Articles 5 and 7, a contract concluded by a natural person for a purpose which can be regarded as being outside his trade or profession (the consumer) with another person acting in the exercise of his trade or profession (the professional) shall be governed by the law of the country where the consumer has his habitual residence, provided that the professional:

   (a) pursues his commercial or professional activities in the country where the consumer has his habitual residence, or
   (b) by any means, directs such activities to that country or to several countries including that country,

   and the contract falls within the scope of such activities.
2. Notwithstanding paragraph 1, the parties may choose the law applicable to a contract which fulfils the requirements of paragraph 1, in accordance with Article 3. Such a choice may not, however, have the result of depriving the consumer of the protection afforded to him by provisions that cannot be derogated from by agreement by virtue of the law which, in the absence of choice, would have been applicable on the basis of paragraph 1.

3. If the requirements in points (a) or (b) of paragraph 1 are not fulfilled, the law applicable to a contract between a consumer and a professional shall be determined pursuant to Articles 3 and 4.
4. Paragraphs 1 and 2 shall not apply to:
   (a) a contract for the supply of services where the services are to be supplied to the consumer exclusively in a country other than that in which he has his habitual residence;
   (b) a contract of carriage other than a contract relating to package travel within the meaning of Council Directive 90/314/EEC of 13 June 1990 on package travel, package holidays and package tours[1];
   (c) a contract relating to a right in rem in immovable property or a tenancy of immovable property other than a contract relating to the right to use immovable properties on a timeshare basis within the meaning of Directive 94/47/EC;
   (d) rights and obligations which constitute a financial instrument and rights and obligations constituting the terms and conditions governing the issuance or offer to the public and public take-over bids of transferable securities, and the subscription and redemption of units in collective investment undertakings in so far as these activities do not constitute provision of a financial service;
   (e) a contract concluded within the type of system falling within the scope of Article 4(1)(h).

Article 7 Insurance contracts

1. This Article shall apply to contracts referred to in paragraph 2, whether or not the risk covered is situated in a Member State, and to all other insurance contracts covering risks situated inside the territory of the Member States. It shall not apply to reinsurance contracts.
2. An insurance contract covering a large risk as defined in Article 5(d) of the First Council Directive 73/239/EEC of 24 July 1973 on the coordination of laws, regulations and administrative provisions relating to the taking-up and pursuit of the business of direct insurance other than life assurance[2] shall be governed by the law chosen by the parties in accordance with Article 3 of this Regulation.

   To the extent that the applicable law has not been chosen by the parties, the insurance contract shall be governed by the law of the country where the insurer has his habitual residence. Where it is clear from all the circumstances of the case that the contract is manifestly more closely connected with another country, the law of that other country shall apply.
3. In the case of an insurance contract other than a contract falling within paragraph 2, only the following laws may be chosen by the parties in accordance with Article 3:

1 OJ L 158, 23.6.1990, p. 59.

2 OJ L 228, 16.8.1973, p. 3. Directive as last amended by Directive 2005/68/EC of the European Parliament and of the Council (OJ L 323, 9.12.2005, p. 1).

(a) the law of any Member State where the risk is situated at the time of conclusion of the contract;
(b) the law of the country where the policy holder has his habitual residence;
(c) in the case of life assurance, the law of the Member State of which the policy holder is a national;
(d) for insurance contracts covering risks limited to events occurring in one Member State other than the Member State where the risk is situated, the law of that Member State;
(e) where the policy holder of a contract falling under this paragraph pursues a commercial or industrial activity or a liberal profession and the insurance contract covers two or more risks which relate to those activities and are situated in different Member States, the law of any of the Member States concerned or the law of the country of habitual residence of the policy holder.

Where, in the cases set out in points (a), (b) or (e), the Member States referred to grant greater freedom of choice of the law applicable to the insurance contract, the parties may take advantage of that freedom.

To the extent that the law applicable has not been chosen by the parties in accordance with this paragraph, such a contract shall be governed by the law of the Member State in which the risk is situated at the time of conclusion of the contract.

4. The following additional rules shall apply to insurance contracts covering risks for which a Member State imposes an obligation to take out insurance:
   (a) the insurance contract shall not satisfy the obligation to take out insurance unless it complies with the specific provisions relating to that insurance laid down by the Member State that imposes the obligation. Where the law of the Member State in which the risk is situated and the law of the Member State imposing the obligation to take out insurance contradict each other, the latter shall prevail;
   (b) by way of derogation from paragraphs 2 and 3, a Member State may lay down that the insurance contract shall be governed by the law of the Member State that imposes the obligation to take out insurance.
5. For the purposes of paragraph 3, third subparagraph, and paragraph 4, where the contract covers risks situated in more than one Member State, the contract shall be considered as constituting several contracts each relating to only one Member State.
6. For the purposes of this Article, the country in which the risk is situated shall be determined in accordance with Article 2(d) of the Second Council Directive 88/357/EEC of 22 June 1988 on the coordination of laws, regulations and administrative provisions relating to direct insurance other than life assurance and laying down provisions to facilitate the effective exercise of freedom to

provide services[1] and, in the case of life assurance, the country in which the risk is situated shall be the country of the commitment within the meaning of Article 1(1)(g) of Directive 2002/83/EC.

Article 8 Individual employment contracts

1. An individual employment contract shall be governed by the law chosen by the parties in accordance with Article 3. Such a choice of law may not, however, have the result of depriving the employee of the protection afforded to him by provisions that cannot be derogated from by agreement under the law that, in the absence of choice, would have been applicable pursuant to paragraphs 2, 3 and 4 of this Article.
2. To the extent that the law applicable to the individual employment contract has not been chosen by the parties, the contract shall be governed by the law of the country in which or, failing that, from which the employee habitually carries out his work in performance of the contract. The country where the work is habitually carried out shall not be deemed to have changed if he is temporarily employed in another country.
3. Where the law applicable cannot be determined pursuant to paragraph 2, the contract shall be governed by the law of the country where the place of business through which the employee was engaged is situated.
4. Where it appears from the circumstances as a whole that the contract is more closely connected with a country other than that indicated in paragraphs 2 or 3, the law of that other country shall apply.

Article 9 Overriding mandatory provisions

1. Overriding mandatory provisions are provisions the respect for which is regarded as crucial by a country for safeguarding its public interests, such as its political, social or economic organisation, to such an extent that they are applicable to any situation falling within their scope, irrespective of the law otherwise applicable to the contract under this Regulation.
2. Nothing in this Regulation shall restrict the application of the overriding mandatory provisions of the law of the forum.
3. Effect may be given to the overriding mandatory provisions of the law of the country where the obligations arising out of the contract have to be or have been performed, in so far as those overriding mandatory provisions render the performance of the contract unlawful. In considering whether to give effect to those provisions, regard shall be had to their nature and purpose and to the consequences of their application or non-application.

1 OJ L 172, 4.7.1988, p. 1. Directive as last amended by Directive 2005/14/EC of the European Parliament and of the Council (OJ L 149, 11.6.2005, p. 14).

Article 10 Consent and material validity

1. The existence and validity of a contract, or of any term of a contract, shall be determined by the law which would govern it under this Regulation if the contract or term were valid.
2. Nevertheless, a party, in order to establish that he did not consent, may rely upon the law of the country in which he has his habitual residence if it appears from the circumstances that it would not be reasonable to determine the effect of his conduct in accordance with the law specified in paragraph 1.

Article 11 Formal validity

1. A contract concluded between persons who, or whose agents, are in the same country at the time of its conclusion is formally valid if it satisfies the formal requirements of the law which governs it in substance under this Regulation or of the law of the country where it is concluded.
2. A contract concluded between persons who, or whose agents, are in different countries at the time of its conclusion is formally valid if it satisfies the formal requirements of the law which governs it in substance under this Regulation, or of the law of either of the countries where either of the parties or their agent is present at the time of conclusion, or of the law of the country where either of the parties had his habitual residence at that time.
3. A unilateral act intended to have legal effect relating to an existing or contemplated contract is formally valid if it satisfies the formal requirements of the law which governs or would govern the contract in substance under this Regulation, or of the law of the country where the act was done, or of the law of the country where the person by whom it was done had his habitual residence at that time.
4. Paragraphs 1, 2 and 3 of this Article shall not apply to contracts that fall within the scope of Article 6. The form of such contracts shall be governed by the law of the country where the consumer has his habitual residence.
5. Notwithstanding paragraphs 1 to 4, a contract the subject matter of which is a right in rem in immovable property or a tenancy of immovable property shall be subject to the requirements of form of the law of the country where the property is situated if by that law:
   (a) those requirements are imposed irrespective of the country where the contract is concluded and irrespective of the law governing the contract; and
   (b) those requirements cannot be derogated from by agreement.

Article 12 Scope of the law applicable

1. The law applicable to a contract by virtue of this Regulation shall govern in particular:
   (a) interpretation;
   (b) performance;

(c) within the limits of the powers conferred on the court by its procedural law, the consequences of a total or partial breach of obligations, including the assessment of damages in so far as it is governed by rules of law;
(d) the various ways of extinguishing obligations, and prescription and limitation of actions;
(e) the consequences of nullity of the contract.

2. In relation to the manner of performance and the steps to be taken in the event of defective performance, regard shall be had to the law of the country in which performance takes place.

Article 13 Incapacity

In a contract concluded between persons who are in the same country, a natural person who would have capacity under the law of that country may invoke his incapacity resulting from the law of another country, only if the other party to the contract was aware of that incapacity at the time of the conclusion of the contract or was not aware thereof as a result of negligence.

Article 14 Voluntary assignment and contractual subrogation

1. The relationship between assignor and assignee under a voluntary assignment or contractual subrogation of a claim against another person (the debtor) shall be governed by the law that applies to the contract between the assignor and assignee under this Regulation.
2. The law governing the assigned or subrogated claim shall determine its assignability, the relationship between the assignee and the debtor, the conditions under which the assignment or subrogation can be invoked against the debtor and whether the debtor's obligations have been discharged.
3. The concept of assignment in this Article includes outright transfers of claims, transfers of claims by way of security and pledges or other security rights over claims.

Article 15 Legal subrogation

Where a person (the creditor) has a contractual claim against another (the debtor) and a third person has a duty to satisfy the creditor, or has in fact satisfied the creditor in discharge of that duty, the law which governs the third person's duty to satisfy the creditor shall determine whether and to what extent the third person is entitled to exercise against the debtor the rights which the creditor had against the debtor under the law governing their relationship.

Article 16 Multiple liability

If a creditor has a claim against several debtors who are liable for the same claim, and one of the debtors has already satisfied the claim in whole or in part, the law governing the debtor's obligation towards the creditor also governs the debtor's right to claim recourse from the other debtors. The other debtors may rely on the defences they had against the creditor to the extent allowed by the law governing their obligations towards the creditor.

Article 17 Set-off

Where the right to set-off is not agreed by the parties, set-off shall be governed by the law applicable to the claim against which the right to set-off is asserted.

Article 18 Burden of proof

1. The law governing a contractual obligation under this Regulation shall apply to the extent that, in matters of contractual obligations, it contains rules which raise presumptions of law or determine the burden of proof.
2. A contract or an act intended to have legal effect may be proved by any mode of proof recognised by the law of the forum or by any of the laws referred to in Article 11 under which that contract or act is formally valid, provided that such mode of proof can be administered by the forum.

CHAPTER III : OTHER PROVISIONS

Article 19 Habitual residence

1. For the purposes of this Regulation, the habitual residence of companies and other bodies, corporate or unincorporated, shall be the place of central administration.

   The habitual residence of a natural person acting in the course of his business activity shall be his principal place of business.
2. Where the contract is concluded in the course of the operations of a branch, agency or any other establishment, or if, under the contract, performance is the responsibility of such a branch, agency or establishment, the place where the branch, agency or any other establishment is located shall be treated as the place of habitual residence.
3. For the purposes of determining the habitual residence, the relevant point in time shall be the time of the conclusion of the contract.

Article 20 Exclusion of renvoi

The application of the law of any country specified by this Regulation means the application of the rules of law in force in that country other than its rules of private international law, unless provided otherwise in this Regulation.

Article 21 Public policy of the forum

The application of a provision of the law of any country specified by this Regulation may be refused only if such application is manifestly incompatible with the public policy (ordre public) of the forum.

Article 22 States with more than one legal system

1. Where a State comprises several territorial units, each of which has its own rules of law in respect of contractual obligations, each territorial unit shall be considered as a country for the purposes of identifying the law applicable under this Regulation.
2. A Member State where different territorial units have their own rules of law in respect of contractual obligations shall not be required to apply this Regulation to conflicts solely between the laws of such units.

Article 23 Relationship with other provisions of Community law

With the exception of Article 7, this Regulation shall not prejudice the application of provisions of Community law which, in relation to particular matters, lay down conflict-of-law rules relating to contractual obligations.

Article 24 Relationship with the Rome Convention

1. This Regulation shall replace the Rome Convention in the Member States, except as regards the territories of the Member States which fall within the territorial scope of that Convention and to which this Regulation does not apply pursuant to Article 299 of the Treaty.
2. In so far as this Regulation replaces the provisions of the Rome Convention, any reference to that Convention shall be understood as a reference to this Regulation.

Article 25 Relationship with existing international conventions

1. This Regulation shall not prejudice the application of international conventions to which one or more Member States are parties at the time when this Regulation is adopted and which lay down conflict-of-law rules relating to contractual obligations.
2. However, this Regulation shall, as between Member States, take precedence over conventions concluded exclusively between two or more of them in so far as such conventions concern matters governed by this Regulation.

Article 26 List of Conventions

1. By 17 June 2009, Member States shall notify the Commission of the conventions referred to in Article 25(1). After that date, Member States shall notify the Commission of all denunciations of such conventions.
2. Within six months of receipt of the notifications referred to in paragraph 1, the Commission shall publish in the Official Journal of the European Union:
   (a) a list of the conventions referred to in paragraph 1;
   (b) the denunciations referred to in paragraph 1.

Article 27 Review clause

1. By 17 June 2013, the Commission shall submit to the European Parliament, the Council and the European Economic and Social Committee a report on the application of this Regulation. If appropriate, the report shall be accompanied by proposals to amend this Regulation. The report shall include:
   (a) a study on the law applicable to insurance contracts and an assessment of the impact of the provisions to be introduced, if any; and
   (b) an evaluation on the application of Article 6, in particular as regards the coherence of Community law in the field of consumer protection.
2. By 17 June 2010, the Commission shall submit to the European Parliament, the Council and the European Economic and Social Committee a report on the question of the effectiveness of an assignment or subrogation of a claim against third parties and the priority of the assigned or subrogated claim over a right of another person. The report shall be accompanied, if appropriate, by a proposal to amend this Regulation and an assessment of the impact of the provisions to be introduced.

Article 28 Application in time

This Regulation shall apply to contracts concluded after 17 December 2009.

CHAPTER IV : FINAL PROVISIONS

Article 29 Entry into force and application

This Regulation shall enter into force on the 20th day following its publication in the Official Journal of the European Union.

It shall apply from 17 December 2009 except for Article 26 which shall apply from 17 June 2009.

This Regulation shall be binding in its entirety and directly applicable in the Member States in accordance with the Treaty establishing the European Community.

Done at Strasbourg, 17 June 2008.

For the European Parliament

The President

H.-G. Pöttering

For the Council

The President

J.Lenarčič